MW00915903

WHOLE WORKS

OF

THE RIGHT REV. JEREMY TAYLOR, D.D.

LORD BISHOP OF DOWN, CONNOR, AND DROMORE:

WITH

A LIFE OF THE AUTHOR,

AND

A CRITICAL EXAMINATION OF HIS WRITINGS,

BY

REGINALD HEBER, A.M.

CANON OF ST. ASAPH, RECTOR OF HODNET, AND LATE FELLOW
OF ALL SOULS' COLLEGE, OXFORD.

IN FIFTEEN VOLUMES.

VOL. V.

LONDON:

OGLE, DUNCAN, AND CO. 37, PATERNOSTER ROW, AND 295, HOLBORN;
AND RICHARD PRIESTLEY, 143, HIGH HOLBORN;
J. PARKER, OXFORD; AND DEIGHTON AND SON, CAMBRIDGE.

1822.

CONTENTS

OF

THE FIFTH VOLUME.

───◆───

TITLES OF THE TWENTY-FIVE SERMONS,

THEIR ORDER, NUMBER, AND TEXTS.

───────

SERMON I. II. III.

ADVENT SUNDAY.

PAGE

Dooms-day Book ; or, Christ's Advent to Judgment ········· 1, 16, 34

2 Cor. v. 10.

For we must all appear before the judgment-seat of Christ, that every one may receive the things done in his body, according to that he hath done, whether it be good or bad.

SERMON IV. V. VI.

The Return of Prayers; or, the Conditions of a prevailing Prayer 51, 66, 81

John, ix. 31.

Now we know that God heareth not sinners; but if any man be a worshipper of God, and doth his will, him he heareth.

SERMON VII. VIII. IX.

Of Godly Fear, &c. ························· 98, 112, 126

Heb. xii. part of the 28th and 29th verses.

Let us have grace, whereby we may serve God with reverence and godly fear. For our God is a consuming fire.

SERMON X. XI.

The Flesh and the Spirit ······················ 139, 155

Matth. xxvi. 41; latter part.

The spirit indeed is willing, but the flesh is weak.

iv

SERMON XII. XIII. XIV.

PAGE

Of Lukewarmness and Zeal; or, Spiritual Fervour······ 171, 185, 202

Jerem. xlviii. 10; first part.
Cursed be he that doth the work of the Lord deceitfully.

SERMON XV. XVI.

The House of Feasting; or, the Epicure's Measures·········· 217, 231

1 Cor. xv. 32; last part.
Let us eat and drink, for to-morrow we die.

SERMON XVII. XVIII.

The Marriage-Ring; or, the Mysteriousness and Duties of Marriage·· 248, 263

Ephes. v. 32, 33.

This is a great mystery, but I speak concerning Christ and the church. Nevertheless, let every one of you in particular so love his wife even as himself, and the wife see that she reverence her husband.

SERMON XIX. XX. XXI.

Apples of Sodom; or, the Fruits of Sin················· 279, 296, 311

Rom. vi. 21.
What fruit had ye then in those things whereof ye are now ashamed? For the end of those things is death.

SERMON XXII. XXIII. XXIV. XXV.

The good and evil Tongue.—Of Slander and Flattery.—The Duties of the Tongue·······················(·· 326, 340, 355, 370

Ephes. iv. 29.

Let no corrupt communication proceed out of your mouth, but that which is good to the use of edifying, that it may minister grace unto the hearers.

TITLES OF THIRTEEN SERMONS

(being part of the Twenty-seven Sermons),

THEIR ORDER, NUMBER, AND TEXTS.

SERMON I. II.

WHITSUNDAY.

PAGE

Of the Spirit of Grace ······························· 401, 415

Rom. viii. 9, 10.

But ye are not in the flesh, but in the Spirit, if so be that the Spirit of God dwell in you. Now if any man have not the Spirit of Christ, he is none of his. And if Christ be in you, the body is dead, because of sin; but the Spirit is life, because of righteousness.

SERMON III. IV.

The descending and entailed Curse cut off ················· 432, 447

Exod. xx. 5, 6.

I the Lord thy God am a jealous God, visiting the iniquity of the fathers upon the children unto the third and fourth generation of them that hate me: and shewing mercy unto thousands of them that love me, and keep my commandments.

SERMON V. VI.

The Invalidity of a late or Death-bed Repentance ·········· 462, 478

Jerem. xiii. 16.

Give glory to the Lord your God, before he cause darkness, and before your feet stumble upon the dark mountains, and while ye look for light (or, lest while ye look for light), he shall turn it into the shadow of death, and make it gross darkness.

SERMON VII. VIII.

The Deceitfulness of the Heart ··························· 495, 509

Jerem. xvii. 9.

The heart is deceitful above all things, and desperately wicked; who can know it?

SERMON IX. X. XI.

PAGE

The Faith and Patience of the Saints; or, the righteous Cause
  Oppressed 523, 540, 556

1 Pet. iv. 17, 18.

For the time is come that judgment must begin at the house of God : and if it first begin at us, what shall the end be of them that obey not the Gospel of God ? And if the righteous scarcely be saved, where shall the ungodly and the sinner appear ?

SERMON XII. XIII.

The Mercy of the Divine Judgments; or, God's Method in curing
  Sinners 571, 587

Romans, ii. 4.

Despisest thou the riches of his goodness, and forbearance, and long-suffering, not knowing that the goodness of God leadeth thee to repentance ?

TWENTY-FIVE SERMONS

PREACHED AT

GOLDEN GROVE;

BEING FOR THE

WINTER HALF-YEAR,

BEGINNING ON ADVENT SUNDAY, AND ENDING ON
THE SUNDAY AFTER ASCENSION.

TO

THE RIGHT HONOURABLE

AND TRULY NOBLE

RICHARD LORD VAUGHAN,

EARL OF CARBERY, &c.

———————

MY LORD,

I HAVE now, by the assistance of God, and the advantages of your many favours, finished a year of sermons; which if, like the first year of our Saviour's preaching, it may be ' annus acceptabilis,' ' an acceptable year' to God, and his afflicted handmaid the Church of England, a relief to some of her new necessities, and an institution or assistance to any soul; I shall esteem it among those honours and blessings, with which God uses to reward those good intentions, which himself first puts into our hearts, and then recompenses upon our heads. My Lord, they were first presented to God in the ministries of your family: for this is a blessing, for which your Lordship is to bless God, that your family is, like Gideon's fleece, irriguous with a dew from heaven, when much of the vicinage is dry; for we have cause to remember, that Isaac complained of the

Philistines, who filled up his wells with stones, and rubbish, and left no beverage for the flocks; and therefore they could give no milk to them that waited upon the flocks, and the flocks could not be gathered, nor fed, nor defended.   It was a design of ruin, and had in it the greatest hostility, and so it hath been lately ;

> ————————————— undique totis
> Usque adeò turbatur agris. En ! ipse capellas
> Protinus æger ago; hanc etiam vix, Tityre, duco.

But, my Lord, this is not all : I would fain also complain, that men feel not their greatest evil, and are not sensible of their danger, nor covetous of what they want, nor strive for that which is forbidden them ; but that this complaint would suppose an unnatural evil to rule in the hearts of men ; for who would have in him so little of a man, as not to be greedy of the word of God, and of holy ordinances, even therefore because they are so hard to have ? and this evil, although it can have no excuse, yet it hath a great and a certain cause; for the word of God still creates new appetites, as it satisfies the old ; and enlarges the capacity, as it fills the first propensities of the Spirit.   For all spiritual blessings are seeds of immortality, and of infinite felicities, they swell up to the comprehensions of eternity; and the desires of the soul can never be wearied, but when they are decayed; as the stomach will be craving every day, unless it be sick and abused.   But every man's experience tells him now, that because men have not preaching, they less desire it; their long fasting makes them not to love their meat; and so we have cause to fear, the people will fall to an atrophy, then to a loathing of holy food; and then God's anger will follow the method of our sin, and send a famine of the word and sacraments. This we have the greatest reason to fear, and this fear can be relieved by nothing but by notices and experience of the greatness of the Divine mercies and goodness.

Against this danger in future, and evil in present, as you and all good men interpose their prayers, so have I added this little instance of my care and services; being willing to minister in all offices and varieties of employment, that so I may by all means save some, and confirm others; or at least that myself may be accepted of God in my desiring it. And I think I have some reasons to expect a special mercy in this, because I find, by the constitution of the divine providence, and ecclesiastical affairs, that all the great necessities of the church have been served by the zeal of preaching in public, and other holy ministries in public or private, as they could be had. By this the Apostles planted the church, and the primitive bishops supported the faith of martyrs, and the hardiness of confessors, and the austerity of the retired. By this they confounded heretics, and evil livers, and taught them the ways of the Spirit, and them without pertinacy, or without excuse. It was preaching that restored the splendour of the church, when barbarism, and wars, and ignorance, either sat in, or broke, the doctor's chair in pieces : for then it was that divers orders of Religious, and especially of preachers, were erected ; God inspiring into whole companies of men a zeal of preaching.   And by the same instrument, God restored the beauty of the Church, when it was necessary she should be reformed ; it was the assiduous and learned preaching of those whom God chose for his ministers in that work, that wrought the advantages and persuaded those truths, which are the enamel and beauty of our churches.   And because, by the same means, all things are preserved by which they are produced, it cannot but be certain, that the present state of the church requires a greater care and prudence in this ministry than ever ; especially since, by preaching, some endeavour to supplant preaching, and by intercepting the fruits of the flocks, to dishearten the shepherds from their attendances.

My Lord, your great nobleness and religious charity have taken from me some portions of that glory, which I designed to myself in imitation of St. Paul towards the Corinthian church ; who esteemed it his honour to preach to them without a revenue ; and though also, like him, I have a trade, by which, as I can be more useful to others, and less burdensome to you ; yet to you also, under God, I owe the quiet, and the opportunities, and circumstances of that, as if God had so interweaved the support of my affairs with your charity, that he would have no advantages pass upon me, but by your interest; and that I should expect no reward of the issues of my calling, unless your Lordship have a share in the blessing.

My Lord, I give God thanks that my lot is fallen so fairly, and that I can serve your Lordship in that ministry, by which I am bound to serve God, and that my gratitude and my duty are bound up in the same bundle; but now, that which was yours by a right of propriety, I have made public, that it may still be more yours, and you derive to yourself a comfort, if you shall see the necessity of others served by that which you heard so diligently, and accepted with so much piety, and I am persuaded have entertained with that religion and obedience, which is the duty of all those who know, that sermons are arguments against us, unless they make us better, and that no sermon is received as it ought, unless it makes us quit a vice, or be in love with virtue; unless we suffer it, in some instance or degree, to do the work of God upon our souls.

My Lord, in these sermons I have meddled with no man's interest, that only excepted, which is eternal; but if any man's vice was to be reproved, I have done it with as much severity as I ought. Some cases of conscience I have here determined; but the special design of the whole is, to describe the greater lines of duty, by special arguments: and if any witty censurer shall say, that I tell him nothing but what he knew before; I shall be contented with it, and rejoice that he was so well instructed, and wish also that he needed not a remembrancer: but if, either in the first, or in the second; in the institution of some, or the reminding of others, I can do God any service; no man ought to be offended, that sermons are not like curious inquiries after new nothings, but pursuances of old truths.   However, I have already many fair earnests, that your Lordship will be pleased with this tender of my service, and expression of my great and dearest obligations, which you daily renew or continue upon, my noblest Lord,

Your Lordship's most affectionate

And most obliged Servant,

JEREMY TAYLOR.

PRAYERS.

O LORD God, fountain of life, giver of all good things, who givest to men the blessed hope of eternal life by our Lord Jesus Christ, and hast promised thy Holy Spirit to them that ask him ; be present with us in the dispensation of thy holy word [and sacraments *]: grant that we, being preserved from all evil by thy power, and, among the diversities of opinions and judgments in this world, from all errors and false doctrines, and led into all truth by the conduct of thy Holy Spirit, may for ever obey thy heavenly calling: that we may not be only hearers of the word of life, but doers also of good works, keeping faith and a good conscience, living an unblamable life, usefully and charitably, religiously and prudently, in all godliness and honesty before thee our God, and before all the world, that, at the end of our mortal life, we may enter into the light and life of God, to sing praises and eternal hymns to the glory of thy name in eternal ages, through Jesus Christ our Lord. Amen.

In whose Name, let us pray, in the words which Himself commanded, saying,

OUR Father, which art in heaven, hallowed be thy name; thy kingdom come ; thy will be done in earth, as it is in heaven: give us this day our daily bread ; and forgive us our trespasses, as we forgive them that trespass against us ; and lead us not into temptation, but deliver us from evil : for thine is the kingdom, and the power, and the glory, for ever and ever. Amen.

* This clause is to be omitted, if there be no sacrament that day.

A PRAYER AFTER SERMON.

LORD, pity and pardon, direct and bless, sanctify and save, us all. Give repentance to all that live in sin, and perseverance to all thy sons and servants for his sake, who is thy beloved, and the foundation of all our hopes, our blessed Lord and Saviour Jesus; to whom, with the Father and the Holy Spirit, be all honour and glory, praise and adoration, love and obedience, now and for evermore. Amen.

SERMONS.

SERMON I. ADVENT SUNDAY.

DOOMSDAY BOOK; OR, CHRIST'S ADVENT TO JUDGMENT.

*For we must all appear before the judgment-seat of Christ,
that every one may receive the things done in his body, according to that he hath done, whether it be good or bad.*—2 Cor.
v. 10.

Virtue and vice are so essentially distinguished, and the
distinction is so necessary to be observed in order to the
well-being of men in private and in societies, that to divide
them in themselves, and to separate them by sufficient notices, and to distinguish them by rewards, hath been designed
by all laws, by the sayings of wise men, by the order of
things, by their proportions to good or evil; and the expectations of men have been framed accordingly: that virtue
may have a proper seat in the will and in the affections, and
may become amiable by its own excellences and its appendant blessing; and that vice may be as natural an enemy to a
man as a wolf to a lamb, and as darkness to light; destructive
of its being, and a contradiction of its nature.   But it is not
enough that all the world hath armed itself against vice, and,
by all that is wise and sober amongst men, hath taken the
part of virtue, adorning it with glorious appellatives, encou-
raging it by rewards, entertaining it with sweetness, and
commanding it by edicts, fortifying it with defensatives, and
twining it in all artificial compliances: all this is short of
man's necessity: for this will, in all modest men, secure their
actions in theatres and highways, in markets and churches,
before the eye of judges and in the society of witnesses

but the actions of closets and chambers, the designs and thoughts of men, their discourses in dark places, and the actions of retirements and of the night, are left indifferent to virtue or to vice; and of these, as man can take no cognisance, so he can make no coercitive; and therefore above one half of human actions is, by the laws of man, left unregarded and unprovided for. And, besides this, there are some men who are bigger than laws, and some are bigger than judges, and some judges have lessened themselves by fear and cowardice, by bribery and flattery, by iniquity and compliance; and where they have not, yet they have notices but of few causes; and there are some sins so popular and universal, that to punish them is either impossible or intolerable; and to question such, would betray the weakness of the public rods and axes, and represent the sinner to be stronger than the power that is appointed to be his bridle. And, after all this, we find sinners so prosperous that they escape, so potent that they fear not; and sin is made safe when it grows great;

> ——Facere omnia sævè
> Non impune licet, nisi dum facis——

and innocence is oppressed, and the poor cries, and he hath no helper; and he is oppressed, and he wants a patron. And for these and many other concurrent causes, if you reckon all the causes, that come before all the judicatories of the world, though the litigious are too many, and the matters of instance are intricate and numerous, yet the personal and criminal are so few, that of two thousand sins that cry aloud to God for vengeance, scarce two are noted by the public eye, and chastised by the hand of justice. It must follow from hence, that it is but reasonable, for the interest of virtue and the necessities of the world, that the private should be judged, and virtue should be tied upon the spirit, and the poor should be relieved, and the oppressed should appeal, and the noise of widows should be heard, and the saints should stand upright, and the cause that was ill judged, should be judged over again, and tyrants should be called to account, and our thoughts should be examined, and our secret actions viewed on all sides, and the infinite number of sins which escape here, should not escape finally. And therefore God hath so ordained it, that there shall be a day of doom, wherein all that are let alone by men, shall be questioned by God, and every word and every action shall receive its just recompence of reward. "For we must all appear before the judgment-seat of Christ; that every one may receive the things done in his body, according to that he hath done, whether it be good or bad."

Τὰ ἴδια τοῦ σώματος, so it is in the best copies, not τὰ διὰ, "the things done in the body," so we commonly read it; "the things proper or due to the body;" so the expression is more apt and proper; for not only what is done διὰ σώματος, "by the body," but even the acts of abstracted understanding and violation, the acts of reflection and choice, acts of self-love and admiration, and whatever else can be supposed the proper and peculiar act of the soul or of the spirit, is to be accounted for at the day of judgment: and even these may be called ἴδια τοῦ σώματος, because these are the acts of the man in the state of conjunction with the body. The words have in them no other difficulty or variety, but contain a great truth of the biggest interest, and one of the most material constitutive articles of the whole religion, and the greatest endearment of our duty in the whole world. Things are so ordered by the great Lord of all the creatures, that whatsoever we do or suffer, shall be called to account, and this account shall be exact, and the sentence shall be just, and the reward shall be great; all the evils of the world shall be amended, and the injustices shall be repaid, and the Divine Providence shall be vindicated, and virtue and vice shall for ever be remarked by their separate dwellings and rewards.

This is that which the apostle, in the next verse, calls "the terror of the Lord." It is *his* terror, because himself shall appear in his dress of majesty and robes of justice; and it is *his* terror, because it is, of all the things in the world, the most formidable in itself, and it is most fearful to us: where shall be acted the interest and final sentence of eternity; and because it is so intended, I shall all the way represent it as "the Lord's terror," that we may be afraid of sin, for the destruction of which this terror is intended. 1. Therefore, we will consider the persons that are to be judged, with the circumstances of our advantages or our sorrows; "we must all appear." 2. The Judge and his judgment-seat; "before the judgment-seat of Christ." 3. The sentence that they are to receive; "the things due to the body, good or bad;" according as we now please, but then cannot alter. Every of these is dressed with circumstances of affliction and affrightment to those, to whom such terrors shall appertain as a portion of their inheritance.

1. The persons who are to be judged; even you, and I, and all the world; kings and priests, nobles and learned, the crafty and the easy, the wise and the foolish, the rich and the poor, the prevailing tyrant and the oppressed party, shall all appear to receive their symbol; and this is so far from abating any thing of its terror and our dear concernment, that it much increases it: for, although concerning precepts and discourses, we are apt to neglect in particular, what is recommended in general, and in incidences of mortality and sad events, the singularity of the chance heightens the apprehension of the evil; yet it is so by accident, and only in regard of our imperfection; it being an effect of self-love, or some little creeping envy, which adheres too often to the unfortunate and miserable; or else, because the sorrow is apt to increase by being apprehended to be a rare case, and a singular unworthiness in him who is afflicted, otherwise than is common to the sons of men, companions of his sin, and brethren of his nature, and partners of his usual accidents; yet in final and extreme events, the multitude of sufferers does not lessen but increase the sufferings; and when the first day of judgment happened, that (I mean) of the universal deluge of waters upon the old world, the calamity swelled like the flood, and every man saw his friend perish, and the neighbours of his dwelling, and the relatives of his house, and the sharers of his joys, and yesterday's bride, and the new-born heir, the priest of the family, and the honour of the kindred, all dying or dead, drenched in water and the Divine vengeance; and then they had no place to flee unto, no man cared for their souls; they had none to go unto for counsel, no sanctuary high enough to keep them from the vengeance that rained down from heaven; and so it shall be at the day of judgment, when that world and this, and all that shall be born hereafter, shall pass through the same Red sea, and be all baptized with the same fire, and be involved in the same cloud, in which shall be thunderings and terrors infinite; every man's fear shall be increased by his neighbours' shrieks, and the amazement that

all the world shall be in, shall unite as the sparks of a raging furnace into a globe of fire, and roll upon its own principle, and increase by direct appearances, and intolerable reflections. He that stands in a church-yard in the time of a great plague, and hears the passing-bell perpetually telling the sad stories of death, and sees crowds of infected bodies pressing to their graves, and others sick and tremulous, and death, dressed up in all the images of sorrow, round about him, is not supported in his spirit by the variety of his sorrow : and at doomsday, when the terrors are universal, besides that it is itself so much greater, because it can affright the whole world, it is also made greater by communication and a sorrowful influence; grief being then strongly infectious, when there is no variety of state, but an entire kingdom of fear; and amazement is the king of all our passions, and all the world its subjects : and that shriek must needs be terrible, when millions of men and women, at the same instant, shall fearfully cry out, and the noise shall mingle with the trumpet of the archangel, with the thunders of the dying and groaning heavens, and the crack of the dissolving world, when the whole fabric of nature shall shake into dissolution and eternal ashes. But this general consideration may be heightened with four or five circumstances.

1. Consider what an infinite multitude of angels, and men, and women, shall then appear; it is a huge assembly, when the men of one kingdom, the men of one age in a single province, are gathered together into heaps and confusion of disorder; but then, all kingdoms of all ages, all the armies that ever mustered, all the world that Augustus Cæsar taxed, all those hundreds of millions that were slain in all the Roman wars, from Numa's time till Italy was broken into principalities and small exarchates; all these, and all that can come into numbers, and that did descend from the loins of Adam, shall at once be represented; to which account if we add the armies of heaven, the nine orders of blessed spirits, and the infinite numbers in every order, we may suppose the numbers fit to express the majesty of that God, and the terror of that Judge, who is the Lord and Father of all that unimaginable multitude. "Erit terror ingens tot simul tantorumque populorum."[a]

2. In this great multitude we shall meet all those, who, by their example and their holy precepts, have, like tapers, enkindled with a beam of the Sun of Righteousness, enlightened us, and taught us to walk in the paths of justice. There we shall see all those good men, whom God sent to preach to us, and recal us from human follies and inhuman practices : and when we espy the good man, that chid us for our last drunkenness or adulteries, it shall then also he remembered how we mocked at counsel, and were civilly modest at the reproof, but laughed when the man was gone, and accepted it for a religious compliment, and took our leaves, and went and did the same again. But then, things shall put on another face ; and that we smiled at here and slighted fondly, shall then be the greatest terror in the world ; men shall feel that they once laughed at their own destruction, and rejected health, when it was offered by a man of God upon no other condition, but that they would be wise, and not be in love with death. Then they shall perceive, that if they had obeyed an easy and a sober counsel, they had been partners of the same felicity, which they see so illustrious upon the heads of those preachers, " whose work is with the Lord," and who, by their life and doctrine, endeavoured to snatch the soul of their friend or relatives from an intolerable misery. But he that sees a crown put upon their heads, that give good counsel, and preach holy and severe sermons with designs of charity and piety, will also then perceive that God did not send preachers for nothing, on trifling errands and without regard : but that work, which he crowns in them, he purposed should be effective to us, persuasive to the understanding, and active upon our consciences. Good preachers, by their doctrine, and all good men, by their lives, are the accusers of the disobedient ; and they shall rise up from their seats, and judge and condemn the follies of those who thought their piety to be want of courage, and their discourses pedantical, and their reproofs the priests' trade, but of no signification, because they preferred moments before eternity.

3. There in that great assembly shall be seen all those converts, who upon easier terms, and fewer miracles, and a less experience, and a younger grace, and a seldomer preaching, and more unlikely circumstances, have suffered the work of

God to prosper upon their spirits, and have been obedient to the heavenly calling. There shall stand the men of Nineveh, and they "shall stand upright in judgment," for they, at the preaching of one man, in a less space than forty days, returned unto the Lord their God; but we have heard him call all our lives, and, like the deaf adder, stopped our ears against the voice of God's servants, "charm they never so wisely." There shall appear the men of Capernaum, and the queen of the South, and the men of Berea, and the first-fruits of the Christian church, and the holy martyrs, and shall proclaim to all the world, that it was not impossible to do the work of grace in the midst of all our weaknesses, and accidental disadvantages: and that "the obedience of faith," and "the labour of love," and the contentions of chastity, and the severities of temperance and self-denial, are not such insuperable mountains, but that an honest and sober person may perform them in acceptable degrees, if he have but a ready ear, and a willing mind, and an honest heart: and this scene of honest persons shall make the Divine judgment upon sinners more reasonable, and apparently just, in passing upon them the horrible sentence; for why cannot we as well serve God in peace, as others served him in war? why cannot we love him as well when he treats us sweetly, and gives us health and plenty, honours or fair fortunes, reputation or contentedness, quietness and peace, as others did upon gibbets and under axes, in the hands of tormentors and in hard wildernesses, in nakedness and poverty, in the midst of all evil things, and all sad discomforts? Concerning this no answer can be made.

4. But there is a worse sight than this yet, which, in that great assembly, shall distract our sight, and amaze our spirits. There men shall meet the partners of their sins, and them that drank the round, when they crowned their heads with folly and forgetfulness, and their cups with wine and noises. There shall ye see that poor, perishing soul, whom thou didst tempt to adultery and wantonness, to drunkenness or perjury, to rebellion or an evil interest, by power or craft, by witty discourses or deep dissembling, by scandal or a snare, by evil example or pernicious counsel, by malice or unwariness; and when all this is summed up, and from the variety of its particulars, is drawn into an uneasy load and a formi-

dable sum, possibly we may find sights enough to scare all our confidences, and arguments enough to press our evil souls into the sorrows of a most intolerable death. For, however we make now but light accounts and evil proportions concerning it, yet it will be a fearful circumstance of appearing, to see one, or two, or ten, or twenty accursed souls, despairing, miserable, infinitely miserable, roaring and blaspheming, and fearfully cursing thee as the cause of its eternal sorrows. Thy lust betrayed and rifled her weak, unguarded innocence; thy example made thy servant confident to lie, or to be perjured; thy society brought a third into intemperance and the disguises of a beast: and when thou seest that soul, with whom thou didst sin, dragged into hell, well mayest thou fear to drink the dregs of thy intolerable potion. And most certainly, it is the greatest of evils to destroy a soul, for whom the Lord Jesus died, and to undo that grace which our Lord purchased with so much sweat and blood, pains and a mighty charity. And because very many sins are sins of society and confederation; such are fornication, drunkenness, bribery, simony, rebellion, schism, and many others; it is a hard and a weighty consideration, what shall become of any one of us, who have tempted our brother or sister to sin and death: for though God hath spared our life, and they are dead, and their debt-books are sealed up till the day of account; yet the mischief of our sin is gone before us, and it is like a murder, but more execrable: the soul is dead in trespasses and sins, and sealed up to an eternal sorrow; and thou shalt see, at doomsday, what damnable uncharitableness thou hast done. That soul that cries to those rocks to cover her, if it had not been for thy perpetual temptations, might have followed the Lamb in a white robe; and that poor man, that is clothed with shame and flames of fire, would have shined in glory, but that thou didst force him to be partner of thy baseness. And who shall pay for this loss? a soul is lost by thy means; thou hast defeated the holy purposes of the Lord's bitter passion by thy impurities; and what shall happen to thee, by whom thy brother dies eternally? Of all the considerations that concern this part of the horrors of doomsday, nothing can be more formidable than this, to such whom it does concern: and truly it concerns so many, and amongst so many, perhaps some persons are so tender, that it might affright their hopes, and discompose their industries and spriteful labours of repentance: but that our most merciful Lord hath, in the midst of all the fearful circumstances of his second coming, interwoven this one comfort relating to this, which, to my sense, seems the most fearful and killing circumstance: "Two shall be grinding at one mill; the one shall be taken, and the other left. Two shall be in a bed; the one shall be taken, and the other left;" that is, those who are confederate in the same fortunes, and interests, and actions, may yet have a different sentence: for an early and an active repentance will wash off this account, and put it upon the tables of the cross; and though it ought to make us diligent and careful, charitable and penitent, hugely penitent, even so long as we live, yet when we shall appear together, there is a mercy that shall there separate us, who sometimes had blended each other in a common crime. Blessed be the mercies of God, who hath so carefully provided a fruitful shower of grace, to refresh the miseries and dangers of the greatest part of mankind. Thomas Aquinas was used to beg of God, that he might never be tempted, from his low fortune, to prelacies and dignities ecclesiastical; and that his mind might never be discomposed or polluted with the love of any creature; and that he might, by some instrument or other, understand the state of his deceased brother; and the story says, that he was heard in all. In him it was a great curiosity, or the passion and impertinences of a useless charity, to search after him, unless he had some other personal concernment than his relation of kindred. But truly, it would concern very many to be solicitous concerning the event of those souls, with whom we have mingled death and sin; for many of those sentences, which have passed and decreed concerning our departed relatives, will concern us dearly, and we are bound in the same bundles, and shall be thrown into the same fires, unless we repent for our own sins, and double our sorrows for their damnation.

5. We may consider that this infinite multitude of men, women, angels, and devils, is not ineffective as a number in Pythagoras' tables, but must needs have influence upon every spirit that shall there appear. For the transactions of that court are not like orations spoken by a Grecian orator

in the circles of his people, heard by them that crowd nearest him, or that sound limited by the circles of air, or the enclosure of a wall; but every thing is represented to every person, and then let it be considered, when thy shame and secret turpitude, thy midnight revels and secret hypocrisies, thy lustful thoughts and treacherous designs, thy falsehood to God and startings from thy holy promises, thy follies and impieties shall be laid open before all the world, and that then shall be spoken by the trumpet of an archangel upon the housetop, the highest battlements of heaven, all those filthy words and lewd circumstances, which thou didst act secretly; thou wilt find, that thou wilt have reason strangely to be ashamed. All the wise men in the world shall know how vile thou hast been: and then consider, with what confusion of face wouldest thou stand in the presence of a good man and a severe, if peradventure he should suddenly draw thy curtain, and find thee in the sins of shame and lust; it must be infinitely more, when God and all the angels of heaven and earth, all his holy myriads, and all his redeemed saints, shall stare and wonder at thy impurities and follies. I have read a story, that a young gentleman, being passionately by his mother dissuaded from entering into the severe courses of a religious and single life, broke from her importunity by saying, " Volo servare animam meam;" "I am resolved by all means to save my soul." But when he had undertaken a rule with passion, he performed it carelessly and remissly, and was but lukewarm in his religion, and quickly proceeded to a melancholy and wearied spirit, and from thence to a sickness and the neighbourhood of death: but falling into an agony and a fantastic vision, dreamed that he saw himself summoned before God's angry throne, and from thence hurried into a place of torments, where espying his mother, full of scorn she upbraided him with his former answer, and asked him, why he did not save his soul by all means, according as he undertook. But when the sick man awaked and recovered, he made his words good indeed, and prayed frequently, and fasted severely, and laboured humbly, and conversed charitably, and mortified himself severely, and refused such secular solaces which other good men received to refresh and sustain their infirmities, and gave no other account to them that asked

him but this: If I could not in my ecstasy or dream endure
my mother's upbraiding my follies and weak religion, how
shall I be able to suffer, that God should redargue me at
doomsday, and the angels reproach my lukewarmness, and
the devils aggravate my sins, and all the saints of God deride my follies and hypocrisies? The effect of that man's consideration may serve to actuate a meditation in every one of
us: for we shall all be at that pass, that unless our shame
and sorrows be cleansed by a timely repentance, and covered
by the robe of Christ, we shall suffer the anger of God, the
scorn of saints and angels, and our own shame in the general
assembly of all mankind. This argument is most considerable to them, who are tender of their precious name and sensible of honour; if they rather would choose death than a
disgrace, poverty rather than shame, let them remember that
a sinful life will bring them to an intolerable shame at that
day, when all that is excellent in heaven and earth, shall be
summoned as witnesses and parties in a fearful scrutiny.
The summit is this, all that are born of Adam, shall appear
before God and his Christ, and all the innumerable companies of angels and devils shall be there: and the wicked
shall be affrighted with every thing they see; and there they
shall see those good men, that taught them the ways of life;
and all those evil persons, whom themselves have tempted
into the ways of death; and those who were converted upon
easier terms; and some of these shall shame the wicked,
and some shall curse them, and some shall upbraid them,
and all shall amaze them; and yet this is but the ἀρχὴ
ὠδίνων, the beginning of those evils which shall never end,
till eternity hath a period; but concerning this they must
first be judged; and that is the second general consideration, " we must appear before the judgment-seat of Christ,"
and that is a new state of terrors and affrightments. Christ,
who is our Saviour and is our advocate, shall then be our
judge: and that will strangely change our confidences and
all the face of things.

2. That is then the place and state of our appearance,
" before the judgment-seat of Christ:" for Christ shall rise
from the right hand of his Father; he shall descend towards
us, and ride upon a cloud, and shall make himself illustrious
by a glorious majesty, and an innumerable retinue and cir-

cumstances of terror and a mighty power: and this is that
which Origen affirms to be the sign of the Son of man. Re-
malcus de Vaux, in Harpocrate divino, affirms, that all the
Greek and Latin fathers " consentientibus animis asseve-
rant, hoc signo crucem Christi significari," do unanimously
affirm, that the representment of the cross is the sign of
the Son of man spoken of, Matt. xxiv. 50. And indeed they
affirm it very generally, but Origen after this manner is singular, "hoc signum crucis erit, cum Dominus ad judicandum venerit," so the church used to sing, and so it is in the
Sibyl's verses :

> O lignum felix, in quo Deus ipse pependit ;
> Nec te terra capit, sed cœli tecta videbis,
> Cum renovata Dei facies ignita micabit.

The sign of that cross is the sign of the Son of man, when
the Lord shall come to judgment : and from those words of
Scripture, "they shall look on him whom they have pierced,"
it hath been freely entertained, that at the day of judgment,
Christ shall signify his person by something, that related to
his passion, his cross, or his wounds, or both. I list not to
spin this curious cobweb ; but Origen's opinion seems to me
more reasonable ; and it is more agreeable to the majesty
and power of Christ to signify himself with proportions of
his glory, rather than of his humility ; with effects of his
being exalted into heaven, rather than of his poverty and
sorrows upon earth : and this is countenanced better by
some Greek copies ; τότε φανήσεται σημεῖον τοῦ υἱοῦ τοῦ
ἀνθρώπου ἐν τῷ οὐρανῷ, so it is commonly read, "the sign of
the Son of man in heaven ;" that is (say they), the sign of the
Son of man imprinted upon a cloud ; but it is in others τοῦ
υἱοῦ τοῦ ἀνθρώπου τοῦ ἐν οὐρανοῖς, "the sign of the Son of man
who is in the heavens ;" not that the sign shall be imprinted
on a cloud, or in any part of the heavens, but that he who
is now in the heavens, shall, when he comes down, have a
sign and signification of his own, that is, proper to him, who
is there glorified, and shall return in glory. And he dispa-
rages the beauty of the sun, who inquires for a rule to know,
when the sun shines, or the light breaks forth from its
chambers of the east ; and the Son of man shall need no
other signification, but his infinite retinue, and all the angels

of God worshipping him, and sitting upon a cloud, and leading the heavenly host, and bringing his elect with him, and being clothed with the robes of majesty, and trampling upon devils, and confounding the wicked, and destroying death : but all these great things shall be invested with such strange circumstances, and annexes of mightiness and divinity, that all the world shall confess the glories of the Lord; and this is sufficiently signified by St. Paul, "We shall all be set before the throne or place of Christ's judicature; for it is written, As I live, saith the Lord, every knee shall bow to me, and every tongue shall confess to God :" that is, at the day of judgment, when we are placed ready to receive our sentence, all knees shall bow to the holy Jesus, and confess him to be God the Lord; meaning that our Lord's presence shall be such, as to force obeisance from angels and men and devils; and his address to judgment shall sufficiently declare his person and his office, and his proper glories. This is the greatest scene of majesty that shall be in that day, till the sentence be pronounced; but there goes much before this, which prepares all the world to the expectation and consequent reception of this mighty Judge of men and angels.

The majesty of the Judge, and the terrors of the judgment, shall be spoken aloud by the immediate forerunning accidents, which shall be so great violences to the old constitutions of nature, that it shall break her very bones, and disorder her till she be destroyed. Saint Jerome relates out of the Jews' books, that their doctors used to account fifteen days of prodigy immediately before Christ's coming, and to every day assign a wonder, any one of which if we should chance to see in the days of our flesh, it would affright us into the like thoughts, which the old world had, when they saw the countries round about them covered with water and the Divine vengeance; or as those poor people near Adria, and the Mediterranean sea, when their houses and cities are entering into graves, and the bowels of the earth rent with convulsions and horrid tremblings. The sea (they say) shall rise fifteen cubits above the highest mountains, and thence descend into hollowness and a prodigious drought; and when they are reduced again to their usual proportions, then all the beasts and creeping things, the monsters and the usual inhabitants of the sea, shall be gathered together, and make fearful noises to distract mankind : the birds shall mourn and change their songs into threnes and sad accents: rivers of fire shall rise from the east to west, and the stars shall be rent into threads of light, and scatter like the beards of comets ; then shall be fearful earthquakes, and the rocks shall rend in pieces, the trees shall distil blood, and the mountains and fairest structures shall return unto their primitive dust; the wild beasts shall leave their dens, and come into the companies of men, so that you shall hardly tell how to call them, herds of men, or congregations of beasts ; then shall the graves open and give up their dead, and those which are alive in nature and dead in fear, shall be forced from the rocks whither they went to hide them, and from caverns of the earth, where they would fain have been concealed; because their retirements are dismantled, and their rocks are broken into wider ruptures, and admit a strange light into their secret bowels ; and the men being forced abroad into the theatre of mighty horrors, shall run up and down distracted and at their wits' end; and then some shall die, and some shall be changed, and by this time the elect shall be gathered together from the four quarters of the world, and Christ shall come along with them to judgment.

These signs, although the Jewish doctors reckon them by order and a method, concerning which they had no other revelation (that appears) nor sufficiently credible tradition, yet for the main parts of the things themselves, the Holy Scripture records Christ's own words, and concerning the most terrible of them; the sum of which, as Christ related them and his apostles recorded and explicated, is this, " the earth shall tremble, and the powers of the heavens shall be shaken, the sun shall be turned into darkness, and the moon into blood;" that is : there shall be strange eclipses of the sun, and fearful aspects in the moon, who when she is troubled, looks red like blood ; "the rocks shall rend, and the elements shall melt with fervent heat. The heavens shall be rolled up like a parchment, the earth shall be burned with fire, the hills shall be like wax, for there shall go a fire before him, and a mighty tempest shall be stirred round about him :"

Dies iræ, Dies illa
Solvet seo'lum in favilla;
Teste David, cum Sibyllâ.

The trumpet of God shall sound, and the voice of the archangel, that is, of him who is the prince of all that great army of spirits, which shall then attend their Lord, and wait upon and illustrate his glory; and this also is part of that, which is called the sign of the Son of man; for the fulfilling of all these predictions, and the preaching of the gospel to all nations, and the conversion of the Jews, and these prodigies, and the address of majesty, make up that sign. The notice of which things some way or other came to the very heathen themselves, who were alarmed into caution and sobriety by these dead remembrances:

————Sic cùm, compage solutâ,
Sæocla tot mundi suprema coëgerit hora,
Antiquum repetens iterum chaos, omnia mistis
Sidera sideribus concurrent: ignea pontum
Astra petent, tellus extendere littora nolit,
Excutietque fretum; fratri contraria Phœbe
Ibit, —————————— Totaque discors
Machina divulsi turbabit fœdera mundi. [a]

Which things when they are come to pass, it will be no wonder if men's hearts shall fail them for fear, and their wits be lost with guilt, and their fond hopes destroyed by prodigy and amazement; but it will be an extreme wonder, if the consideration and certain expectation of these things shall not awake our sleeping spirits, and raise us from the death of sin, and the baseness of vice and dishonourable actions, to live soberly and temperately, chastely and justly, humbly and obediently, that is, like persons that believe all this; and such who are not madmen or fools, will order their actions according to these notices. For if they do not believe these things, where is their faith? If they do believe them and sin on, and do as if there were no such thing to come to pass, where is their prudence, and what is their hopes, and where their charity? how do they differ from beasts, save that they are more foolish? for beasts go on and consider not, because they cannot; but we can consider,

[a] Lucan. l. i.

and will not; we know that strange terrors shall affright us all, and strange deaths and torments shall seize upon the wicked, and that we cannot escape, and the rocks themselves will not be able to hide us from the fears of those prodigies, which shall come before the day of judgment : and that the mountains, though, when they are broken in pieces, we call upon them to fall upon us, shall not be able to secure us one minute from the present vengeance ; and yet we proceed with confidence or carelessness, and consider not, that there is no greater folly in the world than for a man to neglect his greatest interest, and to die for trifles and little regards, and to become miserable for such interests, which are not excusable in a child.   He that is youngest, hath not long to live : he that is thirty, forty, or fifty years old, hath spent most of his life, and his dream is almost done, and in a very few months he must be cast into his eternal portion; that is, he must be in an unalterable condition; his final sentence shall pass, according as he shall then be found : and that will be an intolerable condition, when he shall have reason to cry out in the bitterness of his soul, " Eternal woe is to me, who refused to consider, when I might have been saved and secured from this intolerable calamity." But I must descend to consider the particulars and circumstances of the great consideration, " Christ shall be our judge at doomsday."

SERMON II.

PART II.

1. If we consider the person of the Judge, we first perceive, that he is interested in the injury of the crimes he is to sentence.   " Videbunt quem crucifixerunt," " they shall look on him whom they have pierced."   It was for thy sins that the Judge did suffer unspeakable pains, as were enough to reconcile all the world to God : the sum and spirit of which pains could not be better understood than by the consequence of his own words, " My God, my God

why hast thou forsaken me?" meaning that he felt such horrible pure unmingled sorrows, that although his human nature was personally united to the Godhead, yet at that instant he felt no comfortable emanations by sensible perception from the Divinity, but he was so drenched in sorrow, that the Godhead seemed to have forsaken him. Beyond this nothing can be added: but then, that thou hast for thy own particular made all this in vain and ineffective, that Christ thy Lord and Judge should be tormented for nothing, that thou wouldest not accept felicity and pardon, when he purchased them at so dear a price, must needs be an infinite condemnation to such persons. How shalt thou look upon him that fainted and died for love of thee, and thou didst scorn his miraculous mercies? How shall we dare to behold that holy face that brought salvation to us, and we turned away and fell in love with death, and kissed deformity and sins? and yet in the beholding that face consists much of the glories of eternity. All the pains and passions, the sorrows and the groans, the humility and poverty, the labours and the watchings, the prayers and the sermons, the miracles and the prophecies, the whip and the nails, the death and the burial, the shame and the smart, the cross and the grave, of Jesus, shall be laid upon thy score, if thou hast refused the mercies and design of all their holy ends and purposes. And if we remember what a calamity that was, which broke the Jewish nation in pieces, when Christ came to judge them for their murdering him, who was their king and the prince of life ; and consider, that this was but a dark image of the terrors of the day of judgment ; we may then apprehend, that there is some strange unspeakable evil that attends them, that are guilty of this death and of so much evil to their Lord. Now it is certain, if thou wilt not be saved by his death, thou art guilty of his death ; if thou wilt not suffer him to save thee, thou art guilty of destroying him : and then let it be considered, what is to be expected from that Judge, before whom you stand as his murderer and betrayer. But this is but half of that consideration.

2. Christ may be "crucified again," and upon a new account "put to an open shame." For after that Christ had done all this by the direct actions of his priestly office of sacrificing

himself for us, he hath also done very many things for us, which are also the fruits of his first love and prosecution of our redemption. I will not instance in the strange arts of mercy that our Lord uses to bring us to live holy lives; but I consider that things are so ordered, and so great a value set upon our souls, since they are the images of God and redeemed by the blood of the holy Lamb, that the salvation of our souls is reckoned as a part of Christ's reward, a part of the glorification of his humanity. Every sinner that repents, causes joy to Christ, and the joy is so great that it runs over and wets the fair brows and beauteous locks of cherubim and seraphim, and all the angels have a part of that banquet; then it is that our blessed Lord feels the fruits of his holy death, the acceptation of his holy sacrifice, the graciousness of his person, the return of his prayers. For all that Christ did or suffered, and all that he now does as a priest in heaven, is to glorify his Father by bringing souls to God: for this it was that he was born and died, and that he descended from heaven to earth, from life to death, from the cross to the grave; this was the purpose of his resurrection and ascension, of the end and design of all the miracles and graces of God manifested to all the world by him. And now what man is so vile, such a malicious fool, that will refuse to bring joy to his Lord by doing himself the greatest good in the world? They who refuse to do this, are said to " crucify the Lord of life again, and put him to an open shame:" that is, they, as much as in them lies, bring Christ from his glorious joys to the labours of his life, and the shame of his death; they advance his enemies, and refuse to advance the kingdom of their Lord; they put themselves in that state, in which they were when Christ came to die for them; and now that he is in a state that he may rejoice over them (for he hath done all his share towards it), every wicked man takes his head from the blessing, and rather chooses that the devil should rejoice in his destruction, than that his Lord should triumph in his felicity. And now upon the supposition of these premises we may imagine, that it will be an infinite amazement to meet the Lord to be our judge, whose person we have murdered, whose honour we have disparaged, whose purposes we have destroyed, whose joys we have lessened, whose passion we have made ineffectual, and whose love we have trampled under our profane and impious feet.

3. But there is yet a third part of this consideration. As it will be inquired at the day of judgment concerning the dishonours to the person of Christ, so also concerning the profession and institution of Christ, and concerning his poor members; for by these also we make sad reflections upon our Lord. Every man that lives wickedly, disgraces the religion and institution of Jesus, he discourages stran-gers from entering into it, he weakens the hands of them that are in already, and makes that the adversaries speak reproachfully of the name of Christ; but although it is certain our Lord and judge will deeply resent all these things, yet there is one thing which he takes more tenderly, and that is, the uncharitableness of men towards his poor; it shall then be upbraided to them by the Judge, that himself was hungry, and they refused to give meat to him that gave them his body and heart-blood to feed them and quench their thirst; that they denied a robe to cover his nakedness, and yet he would have clothed their souls with the robe of his righteousness, lest their souls should be found naked in the day of the Lord's visitation; and all this unkindness is nothing but that evil men were uncharitable to their brethren, they would not feed the hungry, nor give drink to the thirsty, nor clothe the naked, nor relieve their brother's needs, nor forgive his follies, nor cover their shame, nor turn their eyes from delighting in their affronts and evil accidents; this is it which our Lord will take so tenderly, that his brethren, for whom he died, who sucked the paps of his mother, that fed on his body and are nourished with his blood, whom he hath lodged in his heart and entertains in his bosom, the partners of his spirit and co-heirs of his inhe-ritance, that these should be denied relief and suffered to go away ashamed and unpitied; this our blessed Lord will take so ill, that all those who are guilty of this unkindness, have no reason to expect the favour of the court.

4. To this if we add the almightiness of the Judge, his infinite wisdom and knowledge of all causes and all persons and all circumstances, that he is infinitely just, inflexibly angry, and impartial in his sentence, there can be nothing added either to the greatness or the requisites of a terrible

and an almighty judge. For who can resist him who is almighty? Who can evade his scrutiny that knows all things? Who can hope for pity of him that is inflexible? Who can think to be exempted when the judge is righteous and impartial? But in all these annexes of the great Judge, that which I shall now remark, is that indeed which hath terror in it, and that is the severity of our Lord. For then is the day of vengeance and recompences, and no mercy at all shall be shewed but to them that are the sons of mercy; for the other, their portion is such as can be expected from these premises.

1. If we remember the instances of God's severity in this life, in the days of mercy and repentance, in those days when judgment waits upon mercy and receives laws by the rules and measures of pardon, and that for all the rare streams of loving-kindness issuing out of paradise and refreshing all our fields with a moisture more fruitful than the floods of Nilus, still there are mingled some storms and violences, some fearful instances of the Divine justice; we may more readily expect it will be worse, infinitely worse, at that day when judgment shall ride in triumph, and mercy shall be the accuser of the wicked. But so we read and are commanded to remember, because they are written for our example, that God destroyed at once five cities of the plain and all the country; and Sodom and her sisters are set forth for an example suffering the vengeance of eternal fire. Fearful it was when God destroyed at once twenty-three thousand for fornication, and an exterminating angel in one night killed one hundred and eighty-five thousand of the Assyrians, and the first-born of all the families of Egypt, and for the sin of David in numbering the people, threescore and ten thousand of the people died, and God sent ten tribes into captivity and eternal oblivion and indistinction from a common people for their idolatry. Did not God strike Corah and his company with fire from heaven? and the earth opened and swallowed up the congregation of Abiram? And is not evil come upon all the world for one sin of Adam? Did not the anger of God break the nation of the Jews all in pieces with judgments so great, that no nation ever suffered the like, because none ever sinned so? And at once it was done that God in anger destroyed all the world, and eight persons only

escaped the angry baptism of water, and yet this world is the time of mercy; God hath opened here his magazines, and sent his only Son as the great fountain of it too: here he delights in mercy, and in judgment loves to remember it, and it triumphs over all his works, and God contrives instruments and accidents, chances and designs, occasions and opportunities, for mercy: if therefore now the anger of God make such terrible eruptions upon the wicked people that delight in sin, how great may we suppose that anger to be, how severe that judgment, how terrible that vengeance, how intolerable those inflictions, which God reserves for the full effusion of indignation on the great day of vengeance?

2. We may also guess at it by this; if God upon all single instances, and in the midst of our sins before they are come to the full, and sometimes in the beginning of an evil habit, be so fierce in his anger; what can we imagine it to be in that day, when the wicked are to drink the dregs of that horrid potion, and count over all the particulars of their whole treasure of wrath? "This is the day of wrath, and God shall reveal or bring forth his righteous judgments[c]." The expression is taken from Deut. xxxii. 34. "Is not this laid up in store with me, and sealed up among my treasures? ἐν ἡμέρᾳ ἐκδικήσεως ἀνταποδώσω, I will restore it in the day of vengeance, for the Lord shall judge his people, and repent himself for his servants." For so did the Libyan lion that was brought up under discipline, and taught to endure blows, and eat the meat of order and regular provision, and to suffer gentle usages and the familiarities of societies; but once he brake out into his own wilderness, "Dedidicit pacem subito feritate reversa," and killed two Roman boys; but those that forage in the Libyan mountains, tread down and devour all that they meet or master; and when they have fasted two days, lay up an anger great as is their appetite, and bring certain death to all that can be overcome. God is pleased to compare himself to a lion; and though in this life he hath confined himself with promises and gracious emanations of an infinite goodness, and limits himself by conditions and covenants, and suffers himself to be overcome by prayers, and himself hath invented ways of atonement and

expiation; yet when he is provoked by our unhandsome and unworthy actions, he makes sudden breaches, and tears some of us in pieces; and of others he breaks their bones or affrights their hopes and secular gaieties, and fills their house with mourning and cypress and groans and death : but when this lion of the tribe of Judah shall appear upon his own mountain, the mountain of the Lord, in his natural dress of majesty, and that justice shall have her chain and golden fetters taken off, then justice shall strike, and mercy shall not hold her hands; she shall strike sore strokes, and pity shall not break the blow; and God shall account with us by minutes, and for words, and for thoughts : and then he shall be severe to mark what is done amiss; and that justice may reign entirely, God shall open the wicked man's treasure, and tell the sums and weigh grains and scruples : εἰσὶ γὰρ ὥσπερ ἀγαθῶν, οὕτω κακῶν παρὰ τῷ Θεῷ Θησαυροί· ἐν ἡμέρᾳ γάρ (φησιν) ἐκδικήσεως ἐσφραγίσθαι τοὺς τῶν κακῶν θησαυροὺς, said Philo upon the place of Deuteronomy before-quoted : as there are treasures of good things, and God hath crowns and sceptres in store for his saints and servants, and coronets for martyrs, and rosaries for virgins, and phials full of prayers, and bottles full of tears, and a register of sighs and penitential groans : so God hath a treasure of wrath and fury, and scourges and scorpions, and then shall be produced the shame of lust, and the malice of envy, and the groans of the oppressed, and the persecutions of the saints, and the cares of covetousness, and the troubles of ambition, and the insolences of traitors, and the violences of rebels, and the rage of anger, and the uneasiness of impatience, and the restlessness of unlawful desires; and by this time the monsters and diseases will be numerous and intolerable, when God's heavy hand shall press the *sanies* and the intolerableness, the obliquity and the unreasonableness, the amazement and the disorder, the smart and the sorrow, the guilt and the punishment, out from all our sins, and pour them into one chalice, and mingle them with an infinite wrath, and make the wicked drink off all the vengeance, and force it down their unwilling throats with the violence of devils and accursed spirits,

3. We may guess at the severity of the Judge by the lesser strokes of that judgment, which he is pleased to send upon

sinners in this world to make them afraid of the horrible pains of doomsday : I mean the torments of an unquiet conscience; the amazement and confusions of some sins and some persons. For I have sometimes seen persons surprised in a base action, and taken in the circumstances of crafty theft and secret injustices, before their excuse was ready; they have changed their colour, their speech hath faltered, their tongue stammered, their eyes did wander and fix no where, till shame made them sink into their hollow eye-pits, to retreat from the images and circumstances of discovery; their wits are lost, their reason useless, the whole order of the soul is discomposed, and they neither see, nor feel, nor think, as they use to do, but they are broken into disorder by a stroke of damnation and a lesser stripe of hell; but then if you come to observe a guilty and a base murderer, a condemned traitor, and see him harassed, first by an evil conscience, and then pulled in pieces by the hangman's hooks, or broken upon sorrows and the wheel, we may then guess (as well as we can in this life) what the pains of that day shall be to accursed souls: but those we shall consider afterwards in their proper scene : now only we are to estimate the severity of our Judge by the intolerableness of an evil conscience ; if guilt will make a man despair, and despair will make a man mad, confounded and dissolved in all the regions of his senses and more noble faculties, that he shall neither feel, nor hear, nor see, any thing but spectres and illusions, devils and frightful dreams, and hear noises, and shriek fearfully, and look pale and distracted, like a hopeless man, from the horrors and confusions of a lost battle, upon which all his hopes did stand; then the wicked must at the day of judgment expect strange things and fearful, and such which now no language can express, and then no patience can endure.

Πολλὰς δ' ἐδυμοὺς καὶ γοὺς ἀποφαλαῖς
εὐθηξη. Διὸς γὰρ ἀνυπαρίστατα φρένας.

Then only it can truly be said, that he is inflexible and inexorable. No prayers then can move him, no groans can cause him to pity thee ; therefore pity thyself in time, that when the Judge comes, thou mayest be one of the sons of everlasting mercy, to whom pity belongs as part of thine inheritance ;

for all these shall without any remorse (except his own) be condemned by the horrible sentence.

4. That all may think themselves concerned in this consideration, let us remember that even the righteous and most innocent shall pass through a severe trial. Many of the ancients explicated this severity by the fire of conflagration, which (say they) shall purify those souls at the day of judgment, which in this life have built upon the foundation hay and stubble, works of folly and false opinions, and states of imperfection. So Saint Austin's doctrine was[d], "Hoc agit caminus, alios in sinistra separabit, alios in dextra quodam modo eliquabit: The great fire at doomsday shall throw some into the portion of the left hand, and others shall be purified and represented on the right:" and the same is affirmed by Origen and Lactantius[e]; and St. Hilary thus expostulates, "Since we are to give an account for every idle word, shall we long for the day of judgment," "in quo est nobis indefessus ille ignis obeundus in quo subeunda sunt gravia illa expiandæ a peccatis animæ supplicia: wherein we must every one of us pass that unwearied fire, in which those grievous punishments for expiating the soul from sins must be endured; for to such as have been baptized with the Holy Ghost, it remaineth that they be consummated with the fire of judgment." And St. Ambrose adds, that if any be as Peter or as John, they are baptized with this fire, and he that is purged here, had need to be purged there again: "Illic quoque nos purificet, quando dicat dominus, intrate in requiem meam; Let him also purify us, that every one of us being burned with that flaming sword, not burned up or consumed, we may enter into paradise, and give thanks unto the Lord, who hath brought us into a place of refreshment[f]." This opinion of theirs is in the main of it very uncertain, relying upon the sense of some obscure places of Scripture, is only apt to represent the great severity of the Judge at that day, and it hath in it this only certainty, that even the most innocent person hath great need of mercy, and he that hath the greatest cause of confidence,

[d] In Psalm. ciii.

[e] In Jerem. hom. 13. et in Luc. hom. 14. et Lactantius, lib. vii. Instit. c. xxi. Hilarius in Psal. cxviii. octon iii. et in Mat. can. 2.

[f] In Psalm cxviii. serm. 3.

although he runs to no rocks to hide him, yet he runs to the
protection of the cross, and hides himself under the shadow
of Divine mercies: and he that shall receive the absolution
of the blessed sentence, shall also suffer the terrors of the
day, and the fearful circumstances of Christ's coming. The
effect of this consideration is this, that " if the righteous
scarcely be saved, where shall the wicked and the sinner
appear?" " Quid faciet virgula deserti, ubi concutietur cedrus
paradisi? Quid faciet agnus, cum tremit aries? Si cœlum
fugiat, ubi manebit terra?" said St. Gregory. And if St. Paul,
whose conscience accused him not, yet durst not be too
confident because he was not hereby justified, but might
be found faulty by the severer judgments of his Lord; how
shall we appear with all our crimes and evil habits round
about us? If there be need of much mercy to the servants
and friends of the Judge, then his enemies shall not be able
to stand upright in judgment.

5. But the matter is still of more concernment. The
pharisees believed that they were innocent, if they abstained
from criminal actions, such as were punishable by the judge;
and many Christians think all is well with them, if they abstain from such sins as have a name in the tables of their'
laws : but because some sins are secret and not discernible
to man; others are public but not punished, because they
were frequent and perpetual, and without external mischiefs
in some instances, and only provocations against God; men
think that in their concernments they have no place : and
such are jeering, and many instances of wantonness and
revelling, doing petty spites, and rudeness, and churlishness,
lying and pride : and beyond this, some are very like virtues; as too much gentleness and slackness in government,
or too great severity and rigour of animadversion, bitterness in reproof of sinners, uncivil circumstances, imprudent
handlings of some criminals, and zeal; nay, there are some
vile things, which, through the evil discoursings and worse
manners of men, are passed into an artificial and false reputation, and men are accounted wits for talking atheistically,
and valiant for being murderers, and wise for deceiving and
circumventing our brothers; and many irregularities more,
for all which we are safe enough here. But when the day of
judgment comes, these shall be called to a severe account,
for the Judge is omniscient and knows all things, and his

tribunal takes cognizance of all causes, and hath a coercive
for all, " all things are naked and open to his eyes," saith
St. Paul*; therefore nothing shall escape for being secret:

Ἀπανθ' ὁ μακρὸς κἀναρίθμητος Χρόνος
φύει τ' ἄδηλα———

And all prejudices being laid aside, it shall be considered
concerning our evil rules, and false principles; " cum cepero
tempus, ego justitias judicabo; when I shall receive the
people, I shall judge according unto right[h]:" so we read ;
" when we shall receive time, I will judge justices and judgments:" so the vulgar Latin reads it; that is, in the day of
the Lord, when time is put into his hand and time shall be
no more, he shall judge concerning those judgments which
men here make of things below; and the fighting men shall
perceive the noise of drunkards and fools that cried him up
for daring to kill his brother, to have been evil principles;
and then it will be declared by strange effects, that wealth is
not the greatest fortune; and ambition was but an ill counsellor; and to lie for a good cause was no piety : and to do
evil for the glory of God was but an ill worshipping him;
and that good-nature was not well employed, when it spent
itself in vicious company and evil compliances; and that
piety was not softness and want of courage; and that poverty ought not to have been contemptible; and the cause of
that is unsuccessful, is not therefore evil; and what is folly
here shall be wisdom there ; then shall men curse their evil
guides, and their accursed superinduced necessities and the
evil guises of the world; and then when silence shall be
found innocence, and eloquence in many instances condemned
as criminal ; when the poor shall reign, and generals and tyrants shall lie low in horrible regions ; when he that lost all
shall find a treasure, and he that spoiled him shall be found
naked and spoiled by the destroyer; then we shall find it
true, that we ought here to have done what our Judge, our
blessed Lord, shall do there, that is, take our measures of
good and evil by the severities of the word of God, by the
sermons of Christ, and the four gospels, and by the epistles
of St. Paul, by justice and charity, by the laws of God, and
the laws of wise princes and republics, by the rules of nature,
and the just proportions of reason, by the examples of good

men and the proverbs of wise men, by severity and the rules of discipline: for then it shall be, that truth shall ride in triumph, and the holiness of Christ's sermons shall be manifest to all the world; that the word of God shall be advanced over all the discourses of men, and "wisdom shall be justified by all her children." Then shall be heard those words of an evil and tardy repentance, and the just rewards of folly, "We fools thought their life madness;" but behold they are justified before the throne of God, and we are miserable for ever. Here men think it strange if others will not run into the same excess of riot; but there, they will wonder how themselves should be so mad and infinitely unsafe, by being strangely and inexcusably unreasonable. The sum is this, the Judge shall appear clothed with wisdom, and power, and justice, and knowledge, and an impartial spirit, making no separations by the proportions of this world, but by the measures of God; not giving sentence by the principles of our folly and evil customs, but by the severity of his own laws and measures of the Spirit. "Non est judicium Dei, hominum; God does not judge as man judges."

6. Now that the Judge is come thus arrayed, thus prepared, so instructed, let us next consider the circumstances of our appearing and his sentence; and first consider that men at the day of judgment, that belong not to the portion of life, shall have three sorts of accusers. 1. Christ himself, who is their judge. 2. Their own consciences, whom they have injured and blotted with characters of death and foul dishonour. 3. The devil, their enemy, whom they served.

1. Christ shall be their accuser, not only upon the stock of those direct injuries (which I before reckoned) of crucifying the Lord of life, once and again, &c. but upon the titles of contempt and unworthiness, of unkindness and ingratitude; and the accusation will be nothing else but a plain representation of those artifices and assistances, those bonds and invitations, those constrainings and importunities, which our dear Lord used to us, to make it almost impossible to lie in sin, and necessary to be saved. For it will, it must needs be a fearful exprobration of our unworthiness, when the Judge himself shall bear witness against us, that the wisdom of God himself was strangely employed in bringing us safely to felicity. I shall draw a short scheme, which

although it must needs be infinitely short of what God hath
done for us, yet it will be enough to shame us. 1. God did
not only give his Son for an example, and the Son gave himself for a price for us, but both gave the Holy Spirit to assist
us in mighty graces, for the verifications of faith, and the
entertainments of hope, and the increase and perseverance of
charity. 2. God gave to us a new nature, he put another
principle into us, a third part, a perfective constitution : we
have the Spirit put into us to be a part of us, as properly to
produce actions of holy life, as the soul of man in the body
does produce the natural. 3. God hath exalted human nature, and made it in the person of Jesus Christ to sit above
the highest seat of angels, and the angels are made ministering spirits, ever since their Lord became our brother.
4. Christ hath by a miraculous sacrament given us his body
to eat, and his blood to drink ; he made ways that we may
become all one with him. 5. He hath given us an easy religion, and hath established our future felicity upon natural
and pleasant conditions, and we are to be happy hereafter if
we suffer God to make us happy here ; and things are so
ordered, that a man must take more pains to perish, than to
be happy. 6. God hath found out rare ways to make our
prayers acceptable, our weak petitions, the desires of our
imperfect souls, to prevail mightily with God ; and to lay a
holy violence, and an undeniable necessity upon himself :
and God will deny us nothing but when we ask of him to
do us ill offices, to give us poisons and dangers, and evil
nourishment, and temptations ; and he that hath given such
mighty power to the prayers of his servants, yet will not be
moved by those potent and mighty prayers to do any good
man an evil turn, or to grant him one mischief ; in that only
God can deny us. 7. But in all things else, God hath made
all the excellent things in heaven and earth to join towards
holy and fortunate effects ; for he hath appointed an angel
to present the prayers of saints[i], and Christ makes intercession for us, and the Holy Spirit makes intercession for us
with groans unutterable[k] ; and all the holy men in the world
pray for all and for every one ; and God hath instructed us
with scriptures and precedents, and collateral and direct

assistances to pray; and he encourages us with divers excellent promises, and parables, and examples, and teaches us what to pray and how, and gives one promise to public prayer, and another to private prayer, and to both the blessing of being heard.

8. Add to this account, that God did heap blessings upon us without order, infinitely, perpetually, and in all instances, when we needed, and when we needed not. 9. He heard us when we prayed, giving us all and giving us more than we desired. 10. He desired that we should ask, and yet he hath also prevented our desire. 11. He watched for us, and, at his own charge, sent a whole order of men, whose employment is to minister to our souls: and, if all this had not been enough, he had given us more also. 12. He promised heaven to our obedience, a province for a dish of water, a kingdom for a prayer, satisfaction for desiring it, grace for receiving, and more grace for accepting and using the first. 13. He invited us with gracious words and perfect entertainments. 14. He threatened horrible things to us, if we would not be happy. 15. He hath made strange necessities for us, making our very repentance to be a conjugation of holy actions, and holy times, and a long succession. 16. He hath taken away all excuses from us, he hath called us off from temptation, he bears our charges, he is always beforehand with us in every act of favour, and perpetually slow in striking; and his arrows are unfeathered, and he is so long, first in drawing his sword, and another long while in whetting it, and yet longer in lifting his hand to strike, that, before the blow comes, the man hath repented long, unless he be a fool and impudent; and then God is so glad of an excuse to lay his anger aside, that certainly if, after all this, we refuse life and glory, there is no more to be said; this plain story will condemn us: but the story is very much longer. And as our conscience will represent all our sins to us, so the Judge will represent all his Father's kindnesses, as Nathan did to David, when he was to make the justice of the Divine sentence appear against him. Then it shall be remembered, that the joys of every day's piety would have been a greater pleasure every night, than the remembrance of every night's sin could have been in the morning: 18. That every night, the trouble and labour of the day's virtue would have been

as much passed, and turned to as very a nothing, as the pleasure of that day's sin; but that they would be infinitely distinguished by the remanent effects. Ἄν τι πράξῃς καλὸν μετὰ πόνου, ὁ μὲν πόνος οἴχεται, τὸ δὲ καλὸν μίνει. ἄν τι ποιήσῃς αἰσχρὸν μετὰ ἡδονῆς, τὸ μὲν ἡδὺ οἴχεται, τὸ δὲ αἰσχρὸν μίνει; so Musonius expressed the sense of this inducement; and that this argument would have grown so great by that time we come to die, that the certain pleasures, and rare confidences, and holy hopes, of a death-bed, would be a strange felicity to the man, when he remembers he did obey, if they were compared to the fearful expectations of a dying sinner, who feels, by a formidable and affrighting remembrance, that of all his sins, nothing remains but the gains of a miserable eternity. The offering ourselves to God every morning, and the thanksgiving to God every night, hope and fear, shame and desire, the honour of leaving a fair name behind us, and the shame of dying like a fool, every thing indeed in the world, is made to be an argument and inducement to us to invite us to come to God and be saved; and therefore when this and infinitely more shall, by the Judge, be exhibited in sad remembrances, there needs no other sentence; we shall condemn ourselves with a hasty shame, and a fearful confusion, to see how good God hath been to us, and how base we have been to ourselves. Thus Moses is said to accuse the Jews; and thus also he that does accuse, is said to condemn; as Verres was by Cicero, and Claudia by Domitius, her accuser; and the world of impenitent persons by the men of Nineveh, and all by Christ, their judge. I represent the horror of this circumstance to consist in this : besides the reasonableness of the judgment and the certainty of the condemnation, it cannot but be an argument of an intolerable despair to perishing souls, when he that was our advocate all our life, shall, in the day of that appearing, be our accuser and our judge, a party against us, an injured person, in the day of his power and of his wrath, doing execution upon all his own foolish and malicious enemies.

2. Our conscience shall be our accuser : but this signifies but these two things ; 1. That we shall be condemned for the evils that we have done, and shall then remember; God, by his power, wiping away the dust from the tables of our memory, and taking off the consideration and the voluntary

neglect and rude shufflings of our cases of conscience. For then we shall see things as they are, the evil circumstances and the crooked intentions, the adherent unhandsomeness, and the direct crimes; for all things are laid up safely: and, though we draw a curtain of a cobweb over them, and sew fig-leaves before our shame, yet God shall draw away the curtain, and forgetfulness shall be no more; because with a taper in the hand of God, all the corners of our nastiness shall be discovered. And, 2. It signifies this also; that not only the justice of God shall be confessed by us in our own shame and condemnation, but the evil of the sentence shall be received into us, to melt our bowels and to break our hearts in pieces within us, because we are the authors of our own death, and our own inhuman hands have torn our souls in pieces. Thus far the horrors are great, and when evil men consider it, it is certain they must be afraid to die. Even they that have lived well, have some sad considerations, and the tremblings of humility, and suspicion of themselves. I remember St. Cyprian tells of a good man who, in his agony of death, saw a phantasm of a noble angelical shape, who, frowning and angry, said to him, "Pati timetis, exire non vultis: Quid faciam vobis? Ye cannot endure sickness, ye are troubled at the evils of the world, and yet you are loath to die and be quit of them, what shall I do to you?" Although this is apt to represent every man's condition more or less, yet concerning persons of wicked lives, it hath in it too many sad degrees of truth; they are impatient of sorrow, and justly fearful of death, because they know not how to comfort themselves in the evil accidents of their lives; and their conscience is too polluted to take death for sanctuary, to hope to have amends made to their condition by the sentence of the day of judgment. Evil and sad is their condition, who cannot be contented here, nor blessed hereafter; whose life is their misery, and their conscience is their enemy, whose grave is their prison, and death their undoing, and the sentence of doomsday the beginning of an intolerable condition.

3. The third sort of accusers are the devils; and they will do it with malicious and evil purposes; the prince of the devils hath Διάβολος for one of his chiefest appellatives; " the accuser of the brethren" he is, by his professed malice

and employment; and therefore God, who delights that his
mercy should triumph, and his goodness prevail over all the
malice of men and devils, hath appointed one whose office is
ἐλέγχειν τὸν ἀντιλέγοντα to reprove the accuser, and to resist
the enemy, to be a defender of their cause who belong to
God. The Holy Spirit is Παράκλητος, a defender; the evil
spirit is Διάβολος, the accuser; and they that in this life belong to one or the other, shall, in the same proportion, be
treated at the day of judgment. The devil shall accuse the
brethren, that is, the saints and servants of God, and shall
tell concerning their follies and infirmities, the sins of their
youth, and the weakness of their age, the imperfect grace
and the long schedule of omissions of duty, their scruples
and their fears, their diffidences and pusillanimity, and all
those things which themselves, by strict examination, find
themselves guilty of and have confessed, all their shame and
the matter of their sorrows, their evil intentions and their
little plots, their carnal confidences and too fond adherences
to the things of this world, their indulgence and easiness of
government, their wilder joys and freer meals, their loss of
time and their too forward and apt compliances, their trifling
arrests and little peevishnesses, the mixtures of the world
with the things of the Spirit, and all the incidences of humanity, he will bring forth and aggravate them by the circumstance of ingratitude, and the breach of promise, and the
evacuating of their holy purposes, and breaking their resolutions, and rifling their vows; and all these things being
drawn into an entire representment, and the hills clogged by
numbers, will make the best men in the world seem foul and
unhandsome, and stained with the characters of death and
evil dishonour. But for these there is appointed a defender;
the Holy Spirit, that maketh intercession for us, shall then
also interpose, and against all these things shall oppose the
passion of our blessed Lord, and upon all their defects shall
cast the robe of his righteousness; and the sins of their youth
shall not prevail so much as the repentance of their age;
and their omissions be excused by probable intervening
causes, and their little escapes shall appear single and in
disunion, because they were always kept asunder by penitential prayers and sighings, and their seldom returns of sin by
their daily watchfulness, and their often infirmities by the

sincerity of their souls, and their scruples by their zeal, and their passions by their love, and all by the mercies of God and the sacrifice which their Judge offered, and the Holy Spirit made effective by daily graces and assistances. These, therefore, infallibly go to the portion of the right hand, because the Lord our God shall answer for them. "But as for the wicked, it is not so with them;" for although the plain story of their life be to them a sad condemnation, yet what will be answered when it shall be told concerning them, that they despised God's mercies, and feared not his angry judgments; that they regarded not his word, and loved not his excellences; that they were not persuaded by his promises, nor affrighted by his threatenings; that they neither would accept his government nor his blessings; that all the sad stories that ever happened in both the worlds (in all which himself did escape till the day of his death, and was not concerned in them, save only that he was called upon by every one of them, which he ever heard, or saw, or was told of, to repentance, that all these) were sent to him in vain? But cannot the accuser truly say to the Judge concerning such persons, 'They were thine by creation, but mine by their own choice; thou didst redeem them indeed, but they sold themselves to me for a trifle, or for an unsatisfying interest: thou diedst for them, but they obeyed my commandments: I gave them nothing, I promised them nothing but the filthy pleasure of a night, or the joys of madness, or the delights of a disease: I never hanged upon the cross three long hours for them, nor endured the labours of a poor life thirty-three years together for their interest: only when they were thine by the merit of thy death, they quickly became mine by the demerit of their ingratitude; and when thou hadst clothed their soul with thy robe, and adorned them by thy graces, we stripped them naked as their shame, and only put on a robe of darkness, and they thought themselves secure and went dancing to their grave, like a drunkard to a fight, or a fly unto a candle; and, therefore, they that did partake with us in our faults, must divide with us in our portion and fearful interest?' This is a sad story, because it ends in death, and there is nothing to abate or lessen the calamity. It concerns us, therefore, to consider in time, that he that tempts us, will accuse us, and what he calls plea-

sant now, he shall then say was nothing, and all the gains
that now invite earthly souls and mean persons to vanity,
were nothing but the seeds of folly, and the harvest is pain,
and sorrow, and shame eternal. But then, since this horror
proceeds upon the account of so many accusers, God hath
put it into our power, by a timely accusation of ourselves in
the tribunal of the court Christian, to prevent all the arts of
aggravation, which, at doomsday, shall load foolish and undiscerning souls. He that accuses himself of his crimes
here, means to forsake them, and looks upon them on all
sides, and spies out his deformity, and is taught to hate them,
he is instructed and prayed for, he prevents the anger of
God, and defeats the devil's malice; and, by making shame
the instrument of repentance, he takes away the sting, and
makes that to be his medicine, which otherwise would be his
death. And concerning this exercise, I shall only add what
the patriarch of Alexandria told an old religious person in
his hermitage. Having asked him what he found in that
desert, he was answered only this, " Indesinenter culpare et
judicare meipsum ;—to judge and condemn myself perpetually, that is the employment of my solitude."—The patriarch answered, " Non est alia via; There is no other way."—
By accusing ourselves we shall make the devil's malice useless, and our own consciences clear, and be reconciled to the
Judge by the severities of an early repentance, and then we
need to fear no accusers.

SERMON III.

PART III.

3. IT remains that we consider the sentence itself, " We
must receive according to what we have done in the body,
whether it be good or bad." " Judicaturo Domino lugubre
mundus immugiet, et tribus ad tribum pectora ferient. Po-
tentissimi quondam reges nudo latere palpitabunt :" so St.
Jerome meditates concerning the terror of this consideration;
" The whole world shall groan when the Judge comes to give
his sentence, tribe and tribe shall knock their sides together ;

and through the naked breasts of the most mighty kings, you shall see their hearts beat with fearful tremblings."—"Tunc Aristotelis argumenta parum proderunt, cum venerit filius pauperculæ quæstuariæ judicare orbem terræ." Nothing shall then be worth owning, or the means of obtaining mercy, but a holy conscience; "all the human craft and trifling subtilties shall be useless, when the son of a poor maid shall sit Judge over all the world." When the prophet Joel was describing the formidable accidents in the day of the Lord's judgment, and the fearful sentence of an angry Judge, he was not able to express it, but stammered like a child, or an amazed, imperfect person, "A. A. A. diei, quia prope est dies Domini[k]." It is not sense at first; he was so amazed he knew not what to say; and the Spirit of God was pleased to let that sign remain, like Agamemnon's sorrow for the death of Iphigenia, nothing could describe it but a veil; it must be hidden and supposed; and the stammering tongue, that is full of fear, can best speak that terror, which will make all the world to cry, and shriek, and speak fearful accents, and significations of an infinite sorrow and amazement.

But so it is, there are two great days, in which the fate of all the world is transacted. This life is man's day, in which man does what he please, and God holds his peace. Man destroys his brother, and destroys himself, and confounds governments, and raises armies, and tempts to sin, and delights in it, and drinks drunk, and forgets his sorrow, and heaps up great estates, and raises a family, and a name in the annals, and makes others fear him, and introduces new religions, and confounds the old, and changeth articles as his interest requires, and all this while God is silent, save that he is loud and clamorous with his holy precepts, and overrules the event; but leaves the desires of men to their own choice, and their course of life such as they generally choose. But then God shall have his day too; the day of the Lord shall come, in which he shall speak, and no man shall answer; be shall speak in the voice of thunder and fearful noises, and man shall do no more as he please, but must suffer as he hath deserved. When Zedekiah reigned in Jerusalem, and persecuted the prophets, and destroyed the inte-

[k] Joel i.

rests of religion, and put Jeremy into the dungeon, God held his peace, save only that he warned him of the danger, and told him of the disorder; but it was Zedekiah's day, and he was permitted to his pleasure; but when he was led in chains to Babylon, and his eyes were put out with burning basins and horrible circles of reflected fires, then was God's day, and his voice was the accent of a fearful anger, that broke him all in pieces. It will be all our cases, unless we hear God speak now, and do his work, and serve his interest, and bear ourselves in our just proportions, that is, as such, the very end of whose being and all our faculties is, to serve God, and do justice and charities to our brother. For if we do the work of God in our own day, we shall receive an infinite mercy in the day of the Lord. But what that is, is now to be inquired.

"What we have done in the body." But certainly this is the greatest terror of all. The thunders and the fires, the earthquakes and the trumpets, the brightness of holy angels, and the horror of accursed spirits, the voice of the archangel (who is the prince of the heavenly host) and the majesty of the Judge, in whose service all that army stands girt with holiness and obedience, all those strange circumstances which have been already reckoned, and all those others which we cannot understand, are but little preparatories and umbrages of this fearful circumstance. All this amazing majesty and formidable preparatories, are for the passing of an eternal sentence upon us, according to what we have done in the body. Woe and alas! and God help us all. All mankind is an enemy to God, his nature is accursed, and his manners are depraved. It is with the nature of man, and with all his manners, as Philemon said of the nature of foxes.

Οὐκ ἔστ᾽ ἀλώπηξ, ἡ μὲν εἴρων τῇ φύσει,
Ἡ δ᾽ αὐθέκαστος ἀλλ᾽ ἐὰν τρισμυρίας
Ἀλώπεκας τις συναγάγῃ, μίαν φύσιν
Ἀπεξαπάσαις ὄψεται——

"Every fox is crafty and mischievous, and if you gather a whole herd of them, there is not a good-natured beast amongst them all."—So it is with man; by nature he is the child of wrath, and by his manners he is the child of the devil; we call Christian, and we dishonour our Lord; and we are brethren, but we oppress and murder one another; it is a great degree of sanctity now-a-days, not to be so wicked as the worst of men; and we live at the rate, as if the best of men did design to themselves an easier condemnation; and as if the generality of men considered not concerning the degrees of death, but did believe that in hell no man shall perceive any ease or refreshment in being tormented with a slower fire. For consider what we do in the body; twelve or fourteen years pass, before we choose good or bad; and of that which remains, above half is spent in sleep and the needs of nature; for the other half, it is divided as the stag was when the beasts went a hunting, the lion hath five parts of six. The business of the world takes so much of our remaining portion, that religion and the service of God have not much time left that can be spared; and of that which can, if we consider how much is allowed to crafty arts of cozenage, to oppression and ambition, to greedy desires and avaricious prosecutions, to the vanities of our youth and the proper sins of every age, to the mere idleness of man and doing nothing, to his fantastic imaginations of greatness and pleasures, of great and little devices, of impertinent lawsuits and uncharitable treatings of our brother; it will be intolerable when we consider that we are to stand or fall eternally according to what we have done in the body. Gather it all together, and set it before thine eyes; alms and prayers are the sum of all thy good. Were thy prayers made in fear and holiness, with passion and desire? Were they not made unwillingly, weakly, and wanderingly, and abated with sins in the greatest part of thy life? Didst thou pray with the same affection and labour as thou didst purchase thy estate? Have thine alms been more than thy oppressions, and according to thy power? and by what means didst thou judge concerning it? How much of our time was spent in that? and how much of our estate was spent in this? But let us go one step farther:—How many of us love our enemies? or pray for and do good to them that persecute and affront us? or overcome evil with good, or turn the face again to them that strike us, rather than be revenged? or suffer ourselves to be spoiled or robbed without contention and uncharitable courses? or lose our interest rather than lose our charity? And yet by these precepts we shall be judged. I instance but once more. Our blessed Saviour spake a hard saying:

"Every idle word that men shall speak, they shall give account thereof at the day of judgment. For by thy words thou shalt be justified, and by thy words thou shalt be condemned[1]." And upon this account may every one, weeping and trembling, say with Job, "Quid faciam, cum resurrexerit ad judicandum Deus? What shall I do, when the Lord shall come to judgment[m]?"—Of every idle word—O blessed God! what shall become of them who love to prate continually, to tell tales, to detract, to slander, to backbite, to praise themselves, to undervalue others, to compare, to raise divisions, to boast? Τίς δὲ φρουρήσει πέζαν ὀρθοστάδην, ἄϋπνος, οὐ κάμπτων γόνυ; "Who shall be able to stand upright, not bowing the knee, with the intolerable load of the sins of his tongue?" If of every idle word we must give account, what shall we do for those malicious words, that dishonour God or do despite to our brother? Remember how often we have tempted our brother or a silly woman to sin and death? How often we have pleaded for unjust interests, or by our wit have cozened an easy and a believing person, or given ill sentences, or disputed others into false persuasions? Did we never call good evil, or evil good? Did we never say to others, Thy cause is right, when nothing made it right but favour and money, a false advocate, or a covetous judge? Πᾶν ῥῆμα ἀργὸν, so said Christ, "every idle word," that is, πᾶν ῥῆμα κενὸν, so St. Paul uses it, "every false word[n]," every lie shall be called to judgment; or, as some copies read it, πᾶν ῥῆμα πονηρὸν, "every wicked word," shall be called to judgment. For by ἀργὸν, "idle words," are not meant words that are unprofitable or unwise, for fools and silly persons speak most of those, and have the least accounts to make; but by vain, the Jews usually understood false; and to give their mind to vanity, or to speak vanity, is all one as to mind or speak falsehoods with malicious and evil purposes. But if every idle word, that is, every vain and lying word, shall be called to judgment, what shall become of men that blaspheme God, or their rulers, or princes of the people, or their parents? that dishonour the religion, and disgrace the ministers? that corrupt justice and pervert judgment? that preach evil doctrines, or declare perverse sentences? that take God's holy name in vain, or dishonour the name of God by trifling and frequent swearings; that holy name, by which we hope to be saved, and which all the angels of God fall down to and worship? These things are to be considered, for by our own words we shall stand or fall, that is, as in human judgments the confession of the party, and the contradiction of himself, or the failing in the circumstances of his story, are the confidences or presumptions of law, by which judges give sentence; so shall our words be, not only the means of declaring a secret sentence, but a certain instrument of being absolved or condemned. But upon these premises we see what reason we have to fear the sentence of that day, who have sinned with our tongues. so often, so continually, that if there were no other actions to be accounted for, we have enough in this account to make us die; and yet have committed so many evil actions, that, if our words were wholly forgotten, we have infinite reason to fear concerning the event of that horrible sentence. The effect of which consideration is this, that we set a guard before our lips, and watch over our actions with a care, equal to that fear which shall be at doomsday, when we are to pass our sad accounts. But I have some considerations to interpose.

1. But (that the sadness of this may a little be relieved, and our endeavours be encouraged to a timely care and repentance) consider that this great sentence, although it shall pass concerning little things, yet it shall not pass by little portions, but by general measures; not by the little errors of one day, but by the great proportions of our life; for God takes not notice of the infirmities of honest persons that always endeavour to avoid every sin, but in little intervening instances are surprised; but he judges us by single actions, if they are great, and of evil effects; and by little small instances, if they be habitual. No man can take care concerning every minute; and therefore concerning it Christ will not pass sentence but by the discernible portions of our time, by human actions, by things of choice and deliberation, and by general precepts of care and watchfulness, this sentence shall be exacted. 2. The sentence of that day shall be passed, not by the proportions of an angel, but by the measures of a man; the first follies are not unpardon-

able, but may be recovered; and the second are dangerous, and the third are more fatal : but nothing is unpardonable but perseverance in evil courses. 3. The last judgment shall be transacted by the same principles by which we are guided here: not by strange and secret propositions, or by the fancies of men, or by the subtilties of useless distinctions, or evil persuasions; not by the scruples of the credulous, or the interest of sects, nor the proverbs of prejudice, nor the uncertain definitions of them that give laws to subjects by expounding the decrees of princes; but by the plain rules of justice, by the ten commandments, by the first apprehensions of conscience, by the plain rules of Scripture, and the rules of an honest mind, and a certain justice. So that by this restraint and limit of the final sentence, we are secured we shall not fall by scruple or by ignorance, by interest or by faction, by false persuasions of others, or invincible prejudice of our own, but we shall stand or fall by plain and easy propositions, by chastity or uncleanness, by justice or injustice, by robbery or restitution : and of this we have a great testimony by our judge and Lord himself; " Whatsoever ye shall bind in earth, shall be bound in heaven, and whatsoever ye loose shall be loosed there ;" that is, you shall stand or fall according to the sermons of the gospel ; as the ministers of the word are commanded to preach, so ye must live here, and so ye must be judged hereafter ; ye must not look for that sentence by secret decrees or obscure doctrines, but by plain precepts and certain rules. But there are yet some more degrees of mercy. 4. That sentence shall pass upon us not after the measures of nature, and possibilities, and utmost extents, but by the mercies of the covenant; we shall be judged as Christians rather than as men, that is, as persons to whom much is pardoned, and much is pitied, and many things are (not accidentally, but consequently) indulged, and great helps are ministered, and many remedies supplied, and some mercies extraregularly conveyed, and their hopes enlarged upon the stock of an infinite mercy, that hath no bounds but our needs, our capacities, and our proportions to glory. 5. The sentence is to be given by him that once died for us, and does now pray for us, and perpetually intercedes ; and upon souls that he loves, and in the salvation of which himself hath a great interest and increase of joy. And now upon these premises we may dare to consider what the sentence itself shall be, that shall never be reversed, but shall last for ever and ever.

"Whether it be good or bad." I cannot discourse now the greatness of the good or bad, so far (I mean) as is revealed to us; the considerations are too long to be crowded into the end of a sermon; only in general: 1. If it be good it is greater than all the good of this world, and every man's share then, in every instant of his blessed eternity, is greater than all the pleasures of mankind in one heap.

"Α τοῖς θεοῖς ἀνθρωπος εὔχεται τυχεῖν,
Τῆς ἀθανασίας πρῶτον αὐτὴν εὔχεται·

"A man can never wish for any thing greater than this immortality," said Posidippus. 2. To which I add this one consideration, that the portion of the good at the day of sentence shall be so great, that after all the labours of our life, and suffering persecutions, and enduring affronts, and the labour of love, and the continual fears and cares of the whole duration and abode, it rewards it all, and gives infinitely more; "Non sunt condignæ passiones hujus sæculi;" all the torments and evils of this world are not to be estimated with the joys of the blessed: it is the gift of God; a donative beyond the ὀψώνιον, the military stipend, it is beyond our work and beyond our wages, and beyond the promise and beyond our thoughts, and above our understandings, and above the highest heavens, it is a participation of the joys of God, and of the inheritance of the Judge himself.

Οὐκ ἔστιν πιλάσασθ', οὐδ' ὀφθαλμοῖσιν ἰφανῶν
'Ημετέροις, ἢ χερὶ λαβεῖν, ἥτις τι μεγίστη
Πειθοῖς ἀνθρώποισιν ἁμάξιτος εἰς φρένα πίπτει[o].

It is a day of recompences, in which all our sorrows shall be turned into joys, our persecutions into a crown, the cross into a throne, poverty into the riches of God; loss, and affronts, and inconveniences, and death, into sceptres, and hymns, and rejoicings, and hallelujahs, and such great things which are fit for us to hope, but too great for us to discourse of, while we see as in a glass darkly and imper-

[o] Xenoph.

fectly. And he that chooses to do an evil rather than suffer one, shall find it but an ill exchange that he deferred his little to change for a great one. I remember that a servant in the old comedy, did choose to venture the lash rather than to feel a present inconvenience, " Quia illud aderat malum, istud aberat longius : illud erat præsens, huic erat diecula :" but this will be but an ill account, when the rods shall for the delay be turned into scorpions, and from easy shall become intolerable. Better it is to suffer here, and to stay till the day of restitution for the good and the holy portion; for it will recompense both for the suffering and the stay.

But how if the portion be bad ? It shall be bad to the greatest part of mankind ; that is a fearful consideration ; the greatest part of men and women shall dwell in the portion of devils to eternal ages. So that these portions are like the prophet's figs in the vision; the good are the best that ever were ; and the worst are so bad, that worse cannot be imagined. For though in hell the accursed souls shall have no worse than they have deserved, and there are not there overrunning measures as there are in heaven, and therefore that the joys of heaven are infinitely greater joys than the pains of hell are great pains, yet even these are a full measure to a full iniquity, pain above patience, sorrows without ease, amazement without consideration, despair without the intervals of a little hope, indignation without the possession of any good ; there dwells envy and confusion, disorder and sad remembrances, perpetual woes and continual shriekings, uneasiness and all the evils of the soul. But if we will represent it in some orderly circumstances, we may consider,

1. That here, all the trouble of our spirits are little participations of a disorderly passion ; a man desires earnestly but he hath not, or he envies because another hath something besides him, and he is troubled at the want of one when at the same time he hath a hundred good things ; and yet ambition and envy, impatience and confusion, covetousness and lust, are all of them very great torments ; but there these shall be in essence and abstracted beings ; the spirit of envy, and the spirit of sorrow ; devils, that shall inflict all the whole nature of the evil and pour it into the minds of accursed men, where it shall sit without abatement : for he

that envies there, envies not for the eminence of another that sits a little above him, and excels him in some one good, but he shall envy for all; because the saints have all, and they have none; therefore all their passions are integral, abstracted, perfect passions: and all the sorrow in the world at this time, is but a portion of sorrow; every man hath his share, and yet besides that which all sad men have, there is a great deal of sorrow which they have not, and all the devils' portion besides that; but in hell, they shall have the whole passion of sorrow in every one, just as the whole body of the sun is seen by every one in the same horizon; and he that is in darkness enjoys it not by parts, but the whole darkness is the portion of one as well as of another. If this consideration be not too metaphysical, I am sure it is very sad, and it relies upon this; that as in heaven there are some holy spirits whose crown is all love; and some in which the brightest jewel is understanding; some are purity and some are holiness to the Lord: so in the regions of sorrow, evil and sorrow have an essence and proper being, and are set there to be suffered entirely by every undone man, that dies there for ever.

2. The evils of this world are material and bodily; the pressing of a shoulder, or the straining of a joint; the dislocation of a bone, or the extending of an artery; a bruise in the flesh, or the pinching of the skin; a hot liver, or a sickly stomach; and then the mind is troubled because its instrument is ill at ease: but all the proper troubles of this life are nothing but the effects of an uneasy body, or an abused fancy: and therefore can be no bigger than a blow or a cozenage, than a wound or a dream; only the trouble increases as the soul works it; and if it makes reflex acts, and begins the evil upon its own account, then it multiplies and doubles, because the proper scene of grief is opened, and sorrow peeps through the corners of the soul. But in those regions and days of sorrow, when the soul shall be no more depending upon the body, but the perfect principle of all its actions, the actions are quick and the perceptions brisk; the passions are extreme and the motions are spiritual; the pains are like the horrors of a devil and the groans of an evil spirit; not slow like the motions of a heavy foot, or a loaden arm, but quick as an angel's wing, active

as lightning; and a grief *then*, is nothing like a grief *now;* and the words of a man's tongue which are fitted to the uses of this world, are as unfit to signify the evils of the next, as person, and nature, and hand, and motion, and passion, are to represent the effects of the Divine attributes, actions, and subsistence.

3. The evil portion of the next world is so great, that God did not create or design it in the first intention of things, and production of essences; he made the kingdom of heaven ἀπὸ καταβολῆς κόσμου, from the foundation of the world; for so it is observable that Christ shall say to the sheep at his right hand, " Receive the kingdom prepared for you from the beginning of the world ᵖ;" but to the goats and accursed spirits, he speaks of· no such primitive and original design; it was accidental and a consequent to horrid crimes, that God was forced to invent and to after-create that place of torments.

4. And when God did create and prepare that place, he did not at all intend it for man; it was prepared for the devil and his angels, so saith the Judge himself, " Go ye cursed into everlasting fire, prepared for the devil and his angels ᵠ, ὁ ἡτοίμασεν ὁ πατήρ μου τῷ διαβόλῳ, which my Father prepared for the devil," so some copies read it: God intended it not for man, but man would imitate the devil's pride, and listen to the whispers of an evil spirit, and follow his temptations, and rebel against his maker; and then God also against his first design resolved to throw such persons into that place that was prepared for the devil: for so great was the love of God to mankind, that he prepared joys infinite and never-ceasing for man, before he had created him; but he did not predetermine him to any evil; but when he was forced to it by man's malice, he doing what God forbad him, God cast him thither where he never intended him; but it was not man's portion: he designed it not at first, and at last also he invited him to repentance; and when nothing could do it, he threw man into another's portion, because he would not accept of what was designed to be his own.

5. The evil portion shall be continual without intermission of evil; no days of rest, no nights of sleep, no ease from la-

bour, no periods of the stroke nor taking off the hand, no intervals between blow and blow; but a continued stroke, which neither shortens the life, nor introduces a brawny patience, or the toleration of an ox, but it is the same in every instant, and great as the first stroke of lightning; the smart is as great for ever as at the first change, from the rest of the grave to the flames of that horrible burning. The church of Rome amongst some other strange opinions hath inserted this one into her public offices; that the perishing souls in hell may have sometimes remission and refreshment, like the fits of an intermitting fever: for so it is in the Roman missal printed at Paris, 1626, in the mass for the dead; " Ut quia de ejus vitæ qualitate diffidimus, etsi plenam veniam anima ipsius obtinere non potest, saltem vel inter ipsa tormenta quæ forsan patitur, refrigerium de abundantia miserationum tuarum sentiat :" and something like this is that of Prudentius [r],

> Sunt et spiritibus sæpe nocentibus
> Pœnarum celebres sub Stygo ferim, &c.

The evil spirits have ease of their pain, and he names their holiday, then when the resurrection of our Lord from the grave is celebrated :

> Marcent suppliciis Tartara mitibus,
> Exultatque sui carceris otio
> Umbrarum populus liber ab ignibus :
> Nec fervent solito flumina sulphure.

They then thought, that when the paschal taper burned, the flames of hell could not burn till the holy wax was spent : but because this is a fancy without ground or revelation, and is against the analogy of all those expressions of our Lord, " where the worm dieth not, and the fire is never quenched," and divers others, it is sufficient to have noted it without farther consideration ; the pains of hell have no rest, no drop of water is allowed to cool the tongue, there is no advocate to plead for them, no mercy belongs to their portion, but fearful wrath and continual burnings.

6. And yet this is not the worst of it; for as it is continual during its abode, so its abode is for ever; it is conti-

nual, and eternal. Tertullian speaks something otherwise, "Pro magnitudine cruciatus non diuturni, verum sempiterni;" not continual, or the pains of every day, but such which shall last for ever. But Lactantius is more plain in this affair: "the same Divine fire by the same power and force shall burn the wicked, and shall repair instantly whatsoever of the body it does consume:" "Ac sibi ipsi æternum pabulum subministrabit,—and shall make for itself an eternal fuel."

> Vermibus et flammis et discruciatibus ævum
> Immortale dedit, senio ne pœna periret
> Non pereunte animâ————

So Prudentius, eternal worms, and unextinguished flames, and immortal punishment, are prepared for the ever-never dying souls of wicked men. Origen is charged by the ancient churches for saying, that after a long time the devils and the accursed souls shall be restored to the kingdom of God, and that after a long time again they shall be restored to their state, and so it was from their fall and shall be for ever; and it may be, that might be the meaning of Tertullian's expression, of "cruciatus non diuturni sed sempiterni." Epiphanius charges not the opinion upon Origen, and yet he was free enough in his animadversion and reproof of him; but St. Austin did, and confuted the opinion in his books De Civitate Dei. However, Origen was not the first that said, the pains of the damned should cease; Justin Martyr in his dialogue with Triphon expresses it thus: "Neither do I say that all the souls do die, for that indeed would be to the wicked again unlooked for: what then? The souls of the godly in a better place, of the wicked in a worse, do tarry the time of judgment; then they that are worthy shall never die again, but those that are designed to punishment shall abide so long as God please to have them to live and to be punished." But I observe, that the primitive doctors were very willing to believe, that the mercy of God would find out a period to the torment of accursed souls; but such a period, which should be nothing but eternal destruction, called by the Scripture, "the second death:" only Origen (as I observed) is charged by St. Austin to have said, they shall return into joys, and back again to hell by an eternal revolution. But concerning the death of a wicked soul, and its being broke into pieces with fearful torments, and consumed with the wrath of God, they had entertained some different fancies very early in the church, as their sentences are collected by St. Jerome at the end of his commentaries upon Isaiah. And Irenæus [*] disputes it largely, "that they that are unthankful to God in this short life, and obey him not, shall never have an eternal duration of life in the ages to come," "sed ipse se privat in sæculum sæculi perseverantia,—he deprives his soul of living to eternal ages;" for he supposes an immortal duration not to be natural to the soul, but a gift of God, which he can take away, and did take away from Adam, and restored it again in Christ to them that believe in him and obey him: for the other; they shall be raised again to suffer shame, and fearful torments, and according to the degree of their sins, so shall be continued in their sorrows; and some shall die, and some shall not die: the devil, and the beast, and they that worshipped the beast, and they that were marked with his character, these St. John saith "shall be tormented for ever and ever;" he does not say so of all, but of some certain great criminals; ὅπως ἂν Θεὸς θέλῃ, all so long as God please,—some for ever and ever, and some not so severely; and whereas the general sentence is given to all wicked persons, to all on the left hand, to go into everlasting fire: it is answered, that the fire indeed is everlasting, but not all that enters into it is everlasting, but only the devils for whom it was prepared, and others more mighty criminals (according as St. John intimates): though also *everlasting* signifies only to the end of its proper period.

Concerning this doctrine of theirs so severe, and yet so moderated, there is less to be objected than against the supposed fancy of Origen: for it is a strange consideration to suppose an eternal torment to those to whom it was never threatened, to those who never heard of Christ, to those that lived probably well, to heathens of good lives, to ignorants and untaught people, to people surprised in a single crime, to men that die young in their natural follies and foolish lusts, to them that fall in a sudden gaiety and excessive joy, to all alike; to all infinite and eternal, even to unwarned peo-

[*] Lib. ii. cap. 65.

ple ; and that this should be inflicted by God who infinitely loves his creatures, who died for them, who pardons easily, and pities readily, and excuses much, and delights in our being saved, and would not have us to die, and takes little things in exchange for great : it is certain that God's mercies are infinite, and it is also certain that the matter of eternal torments cannot truly be understood ; and when the schoolmen go about to reconcile the Divine justice to that severity, and consider why God punishes eternally a temporal sin, or a state of evil, they speak variously, and uncertainly, and unsatisfyingly. But, that in this question we may separate the certain from the uncertain ;

1. It is certain that the torments of hell shall certainly last as long as the soul lasts ; for eternal and everlasting can signify no less but to the end of that duration, to the perfect end of the period which it signifies. So Sodom and Gomorrah, when God rained down hell from heaven upon the earth (as Salvian's expression is) they are said " to suffer the vengeance of eternal fire :" that is, of a fire that consumed them finally, and they never were restored : and so the accursed souls shall suffer torments till they be consumed ; who because they are immortal either naturally or by gift, shall be tormented for ever, or till God shall take from them the life that he restored to them on purpose to give them a capacity of being miserable, and the best that they can expect is to despair of all good, to suffer the wrath of God, never to come to any minute of felicity, or of a tolerable state, and to be held in pain till God be weary of striking. This is the gentlest sentence of some of the old doctors.

But, 2. The generality of Christians have been taught to believe worse things yet concerning them ; and the words of our blessed Lord are κόλασις αἰώνιος, eternal affliction or smiting ;

> Nec mortis pœnas mors altera finiet hujus,
> Horaque erit tantis altima nulla malis.

And St. John[a], who well knew the mind of his Lord, saith ; " the smoke of their torment ascendeth up for ever and ever, and they have no rest day nor night:" that is, their torment is continual, and it is eternal. Their second death shall be but a dying to all felicity; for so death is taken in Scripture; Adam died when he ate the forbidden fruit; that is, he was liable to sickness and sorrows, and pain and dissolution of soul and body: and to be miserable, is the worse death of the two; they shall see the eternal felicity of the saints, but they shall never taste of the holy chalice. Those joys shall indeed be for ever and ever; for immortality is part of their reward, and on them the second death shall have no power; but the wicked shall be tormented horribly and insufferably, till "death and hell be thrown into the lake of fire, and shall be no more: which is the second death‡." But that they may not imagine that this second death shall be the end of their pains, St. John speaks expressly what that is, Rev. xxi. 8. "The fearful and unbelieving, the abominable and the murderers, the whoremongers and sorcerers, the idolaters and all liars, shall have their part in the lake which burneth with fire and brimstone: which is the second death;" no dying there, but a being tormented, burning in a lake of fire, that is, the second death. For if life be reckoned a blessing, then to be destitute of all blessing is to have no life; and therefore to be intolerably miserable is this second death, that is, death eternal.

3. And yet if God should deal with man hereafter more mercifully and proportionably to his weak nature, than he does to angels, and as he admits him to repentance here, so in hell also to a period of his smart, even when he keeps the angels in pain for ever; yet he will never admit him to favour, he shall be tormented beyond all the measure of human ages, and be destroyed for ever and ever.

It concerns us all, who hear and believe these things, to do as our blessed Lord will do before the day of his coming; he will call and convert the Jews and strangers: conversion to God is the best preparatory to doomsday: and it concerns all them, who are in the neighbourhood and fringes of the flames of hell, that is, in the state of sin, quickly to arise from the danger, and shake the burning coals off our flesh, lest it consume the marrow and the bones: " Exuenda

‡ Rev. xx. 14.

est velociter de incendio sarcina, priusquam flammis super-
venientibus concremetur. Nemo diu tutus est, periculo
proximus," saith St. Cyprian; "No man is safe long, that is so
near to danger;" for suddenly the change will come, in which
the judge shall be called to judgment, and no man to plead
for him, unless a good conscience be his advocate; and the
rich shall be naked as a condemned criminal to execution;
and there shall be no regard of princes or of nobles, and the
differences of men's account shall be forgotten, and no distinction remaining but of good or bad, sheep and goats, blessed
and accursed souls. Among the wonders of the day of judgment, our blessed Saviour reckons it, that men shall be marrying and giving in marriage, γαμοῦντες καὶ ἐκγαμίζοντες, marrying
and cross-marrying, that is, raising families and lasting greatness and huge estates; when the world is to end so quickly,
and the gains of a rich purchase so very a trifle, but no trifling
danger; a thing that can give no security to our souls, but
much hazards and a great charge. More reasonable it is,
that we despise the world and lay up for heaven, that we
heap up treasures by giving alms, and make friends of unrighteous mammon; but at no hand to enter into a state of
life, that is all the way a hazard to the main interest, and at
the best, an increase of the particular charge. Every degree of riches, every degree of greatness, every ambitious
employment, every great fortune, every eminency above our
brother, is a charge to the accounts of the last day. He
that lives temperately and charitably, whose employment is
religion, whose affections are fear and love, whose desires
are after heaven, and do not dwell below; that man can
long and pray for the hastening of the coming of the day of
the Lord. He that does not really desire and long for that
day, either is in a very ill condition, or does not understand
that he is in a good. I will not be so severe in this meditation as to forbid any man to laugh, that believes himself
shall be called to so severe a judgment; yet St. Jerome said
it, "Coram cœlo et terra rationem reddemus totius nostræ
vitæ; et tu rides? Heaven and earth shall see all the follies
and baseness of thy life: and dost thou laugh?" That we
may, but we have not reason to laugh loudly and frequently
if we consider things wisely, and as we are concerned: but
if we do, yet "præsentis temporis ita est agenda lætitia, ut

sequentis judicii amaritudo nunquam recedat a memoria :—
so laugh here that you may not forget your danger, lest you
weep for ever." He that thinks most seriously and most frequently of this fearful appearance, will find that it is better
staying for his joys till this sentence be past; for then he
shall perceive, whether he hath reason or no. In the mean
time wonder not, that God, who loves mankind so well,
should punish him so severely : for therefore the evil fall
into an accursed portion, because they despised that which
God most loves, his Son and his mercies, his graces and his
Holy Spirit; and they that do all this, have cause to complain
of nothing but their own follies; and they shall feel the accursed consequents then, when they shall see the Judge sit
above them, angry and severe, inexorable and terrible; under
them, an intolerable hell; within them, their consciences clamorous and diseased : without them, all the world on fire;
on the right hand, those men glorified whom they persecuted
or despised : on the left hand, the devils accusing ; for this
is the day of the Lord's terror, and who is able to abide it ?

Seu vigilo intentus studiis, seu dormio, semper
Judicis extremi nostras tuba personet aures.

SERMON IV.

THE RETURN OF PRAYERS; OR, THE CONDITIONS OF A PREVAILING PRAYER.

*Now we know that God heareth not sinners; but if any man be
a worshipper of God, and doth his will, him he heareth.*—
John ix. 31.

I KNOW not which is the greater wonder, either that prayer,
which is a duty so easy and facile, so ready and apted to the
powers, and skill, and opportunities, of every man, should
have so great effects, and be productive of such mighty
blessings; or, that we should be so unwilling to use so easy
an instrument of procuring so much good. The first declares

God's goodness, but this publishes man's folly and weakness,
who finds in himself so much difficulty to perform a condition so easy and full of advantage.   But the order of this
felicity is knotted like the foldings of a serpent; all those
parts of easiness, which invite us to the duty, are become
like the joints of a bulrush, not bendings, but consolidations
and stiffenings: the very facility becomes its objection, and
in every of its stages, we make or find a huge uneasiness.
At first, we do not know what to ask; and when we do, then
we find difficulty to bring our will to desire it; and when
that is instructed and kept in awe, it mingles interest, and
confounds the purposes; and when it is forced to ask
honestly and severely, then it wills so coldly, that God hates
the prayer; and, if it desires fervently, it sometimes turns
that into passion, and that passion breaks into murmurs or
unquietness; or, if that be avoided, the indifference cools
into death, or the fire burns violently and is quickly spent;
our desires are dull as a rock, or fugitive as lightning; either
we ask ill things earnestly, or good things remissly; we
either court our own danger, or are not zealous for our real
safety; or, if we be right in our matter, or earnest in our
affections, and lasting in our abode, yet we miss in the manner; and either we ask for evil ends, or without religious
and awful apprehensions; or we rest in the words and signification of the prayer, and never take care to pass on to
action; or else we sacrifice in the company of Korah, being
partners of a schism, or a rebellion in religion; or we bring
unhallowed censers, our hearts send up to God an unholy
smoke, a cloud from the fires of lust; and either the flames
of lust or rage, of wine or revenge, kindle the beast that is
laid upon the altar; or we bring swine's flesh, or a dog's
neck; whereas God never accepts or delights in a prayer,
unless it be for a holy thing, to a lawful end, presented unto
him upon the wings of zeal and love, or religious sorrow, or
religious joy; by sanctified lips, and pure hands, and a sincere heart.   It must be the prayer of a gracious man; and
he is only gracious before God, and acceptable and effective
in his prayer, whose life is holy, and whose prayer is holy ;
for both these are necessary ingredients to the constitution
of a prevailing prayer; there is a holiness peculiar to the
man, and a holiness peculiar to the prayer, that must adorn

the prayer, before it can be united to the intercession of the holy Jesus, in which union alone our prayers can be prevailing.

"God heareth not sinners."—So the blind man in the text, and confidently, "this we know:" he had reason, indeed, for his confidence; it was a proverbial saying, and every where recorded in their Scriptures, which were read in the synagogues every sabbath-day. "For what is the hope of the hypocrite? (saith Job) Will God hear his cry, when trouble cometh upon him[u]?" No, he will not. "For if I regard iniquity in my heart, the Lord will not hear me[x]," said David; and so said the Spirit of the Lord by the son of David: "When distress and anguish come upon you, then shall they call upon me, but I will not answer; they shall seek me early, but they shall not find me[y]." And Isaiah, "When you spread forth your hands, I will hide mine eyes from you; yea, when you make many prayers, I will not hear; your hands are full of blood[z]." And again, "When they fast, I will not hear their cry; and when they will offer burnt-offerings and oblations, I will not accept them. For they have loved to wander, they have not refrained their feet, therefore the Lord will not accept them; he will now remember their iniquity, and visit their sins[a]." Upon these and many other authorities[b], it grew into a proverb; "Deus non exaudit peccatores." It was a known case, and an established rule in religion; "Wicked persons are neither fit to pray for themselves, nor for others."

Which proposition let us first consider in the sense of that purpose which the blind man spoke it in, and then in the utmost extent of it, as its analogy and equal reason go forth upon us and our necessities. The man was cured of his blindness, and being examined concerning him that did it, named and gloried in his physician: but the spiteful pharisees bid him give glory to God, and defy the minister; for God indeed was good, but he wrought that cure by a wicked hand.—No, says he, this is impossible. If this man were a sinner and a false prophet (for in that instance the accusation was intended), God would not hear his prayer, and work

[u] Job, xxvii. 9.　[x] Psalm, lxvi. 18.　[y] Prov. i. 28.　[z] Isa. i. 15.
[a] Jer. xiv. 12, 10.　[b] Vide etiam. Psalm, xxxiv. 6. Micah, iii. 4. 1 Pet. iii. 12.

miracles by him in verification of a lie.—A false prophet could not work true miracles: this hath received its diminution, when the case was changed; for at that time, when Christ preached, miracles were the only or the great verification of any new revelation; and, therefore, it proceeding from an almighty God, must needs be the testimony of a Divine truth; and if it could have been brought for a lie, there could not then have been sufficient instruction given to mankind, to prevent their belief of false prophets and lying doctrines. But when Christ proved his doctrine by miracles, that no enemy of his did ever do so great before or after him; then he also told, that, after him, his friends should do greater, and his enemies should do some, but they were fewer, and very inconsiderable; and, therefore, could have in them no unavoidable cause of deception, because they were discovered by a propbecy, and caution was given against them by him that did greater miracles, and yet ought to have been believed, if he had done but one; because against him there had been no caution, but many prophecies creating such expectations concerning him, which he verified by his great works. So that, in this sense of working miracles, though it was infinitely true that the blind man said, then when he said it, yet after that the case was altered; and sinners, magicians, astrologers, witches, heretics, simoniacs, and wicked persons of other instances, have done miracles, and God hath heard sinners, and wrougbt his own works by their hands, or suffered the devil to do his works under their pretences; and many, at the day of judgment, shall plead that they have done miracles in Christ's name, and yet they shall be rejected; Christ knows them not, and their portion shall be with dogs, and goats, and unbelievers.

There is, in this case, only this difference; that they who do miracles in opposition to Christ, do them by the power of the devil, to whom it is permitted to do such things, which we think miracles; and that is all one as though they were: but the danger of them is none at all, but to them that will not believe him that did greater miracles, and prophesied of these less, and gave warning of their attending danger, and was confirmed to be a true teacher by voices from heaven, and by the resurrection of his body after a three days' burial: so that to these the proposition still remains

true, "God hears not sinners," God does not work those
miracles; but concerning sinning Christians, God, in this
sense, and towards the purposes of miracles, does hear them,
and hath wrought miracles by them, for they do them " in
the name of Christ," and therefore Christ said, "cannot
easily speak ill of him;" and although they either prevaricate
in their lives, or in superinduced doctrines, yet, because the
miracles are a verification of the religion, not of the opinion,
of the power of truth of Christ, not of the veracity of the
man, God hath heard such persons many times, whom men
have long since, and to this day, called heretics; such were
the Novatians and Arians; for, to the heathens they could
only prove their religion, by which they stood distinguished
from them; but we find not that they wrought miracles
among the Christians, or to verify their superstructures and
private opinions. But, besides this yet, we may also by such
means arrest the forwardness of our judgments and condemnations of persons disagreeing in their opinions from
us; for those persons, whose faith God confirmed by miracles, was an entire faith; and although they might have false
opinions, or mistaken explications of true opinions, either
inartificial or misunderstood, yet we have reason to believe
their faith to be entire; for that which God would have the
heathen to believe, and to that purpose proved it by a
miracle himself intended to accept, first to a holy life, and
then to glory. The false opinion should burn, and themselves escape. One thing more is here very considerable,
that in this very instance of working miracles, God was so
very careful not to hear sinners or permit sinners, till he had
prevented all dangers to good and innocent persons, that the
case of Christ and his apostles working miracles, was so
clearly separated and remarked by the finger of God, and
distinguished from the impostures and pretences of all the
many antichrists that appeared in Palestine, Cyprus, Crete,
Syria, and the vicinage, that there were but very few Christians, that, with hearty persuasions, fell away from Christ,
Θᾶττόν τις τοὺς ἀπὸ Χριστοῦ μεταδιδάξεις, said Galen, " It is not
easy to teach anew him that hath been taught by Christ:"
and St. Austin tells a story of an unbelieving man, that,
being troubled that his wife was a Christian, went to the
oracle to ask by what means he should alter her persuasion;

but he was answered, "it could never be done, he might as well imprint characters upon the face of a torrent, or a rapid river, or himself fly in the air, as alter the persuasion of a hearty and an honest Christian;" I would to God it were so now in all instances, and that it were so hard to draw men from the severities of a holy life, as of old they could be cozened, disputed, or forced out of their faith. Some men are vexed with hypocrisy, and then their hypocrisy was punished with infidelity and a wretchless spirit. Demas, and Simon Magus, and Ecebolius, and the lapsed confessors, are instances of human craft or human weakness; but they are scarce a number that are remarked, in ancient story, to have fallen from Christianity by direct persuasions, or the efficacy of abusing arguments and discourses. The reason of it is the truth in the text: God did so avoid hearing sinners in this affair, that he never permitted them to do any miracles, so as to do any mischief to the souls of good men; and therefore it is said, the enemies of Christ came "in the power of signs and wonders, able to deceive (if it were possible) even the very elect;" but that was not possible; without their faults it could not be; the elect were sufficiently strengthened, and the evidence of Christ's being heard of God, and that none of his enemies were heard of God to any dangerous effect, was so great, that if any Christian had apostatized or fallen away by direct persuasion, it was like the sin of a falling angel, of so direct a malice, that he never could repent, and God never would pardon him, as St. Paul twice remarks in his Epistle to the Hebrews. The result of this discourse is the first sense and explication of the words, "God heareth not sinners," viz. in that in which they are sinners: a sinner in his manners may be heard in his prayer, in order to the confirmation of his faith; but if he be a sinner in his faith, God hears him not at all in that wherein he sins; for God is truth, and cannot confirm a lie, and whenever he permitted the devil to do it, he secured the interest of his elect, that is, of all that believe in him and love him, "lifting up holy hands without wrath and doubting."

2. That which yet concerns us more nearly is, that "God heareth not sinners;" that is, if we be not good men, our prayers will do us no good: we shall be in the condition of them that never pray at all. The prayers of a wicked man

are like the breath of corrupted lungs; God turns away from such unwholesome breathings. But that I may reduce this necessary doctrine to a method, I shall consider that there are some persons whose prayers are sins, and some others whose prayers are ineffectual: some are such who do not pray lawfully; they sin when they pray, while they remain in that state and evil condition; others are such who do not obtain what they pray for, and yet their prayer is not a direct sin: the prayer of the first is a direct abomination, the prayer of the second is hindered; the first is corrupted by a direct state of sin, the latter by some intervening imperfection and unhandsome circumstance of action; and in proportion to these, it is required, 1. that he be in a state and possibility of acceptation; and, 2. that the prayer itself be in a proper disposition. 1. Therefore we shall consider, what are those conditions, which are required in every person that prays, the want of which makes the prayer to be a sin? 2. What are the conditions of a good man's prayer, the absence of which makes that even his prayer return empty? 3. What degrees and circumstances of piety are required to make a man fit to be an intercessor for others, both with holiness in himself and effect to them he prays for? And, 4. as an appendix to these considerations, I shall add the proper indices and signification, by which we may make a judgment whether God hath heard our prayers or no.

1. Whosoever prays to God while he is in a state or in the affection to sin, his prayer is an abomination to God. This was a truth so believed by all nations of the world, that in all religions they ever appointed baptisms and ceremonial expiations, to cleanse the persons, before they presented themselves in their holy offices. "Deorum templa cum adire disponitis, ab omni vos labe puros, lautos, castissimosque præstatis," said Arnobius to the gentiles: "When you address yourselves to the temples of your God, you keep yourselves chaste, and clean, and spotless." They washed their hands and wore white garments, they refused to touch a dead body, they avoided a spot upon their clothes as they avoided a wound upon their head, μὴ καθαρῷ γὰρ καθαροῦ ἐφάπτεσθαι μὴ οὐ θεμιτὸν ᾖ. That was the religious ground they went upon; "an impure thing ought not to touch that

which is holy," much less to approach the prince of purities; and this was the sense of the old world in their lustrations, and of the Jews in their preparatory baptisms; they washed their hands to signify, that they should cleanse them from all iniquity, and keep them pure from blood and rapine; they washed their garments; but that intended, they should not be spotted with the flesh; and their follies consisted in this, that they did not look to the bottom of their lavatories; they did not see through the veil of their ceremonies. "Flagitiis omnibus inquinati veniunt ad precandum, et se pie sacrificasse opinantur, si cutem laverint, tanquam libidines intra pectus inclusas ulla amnis abluat, aut ulla maria purificent," said Lactantius; "They come to their prayers dressed round about with wickedness, *ut quercus hederâ:* and think, God will accept their offering, if their skin be washed; as if a river could purify their lustful souls, or a sea take off their guilt." But David reconciles the ceremony with the mystery, "I will wash my hands, I will wash them in innocency, and so will I go to thine altar." "Hæ sunt veræ munditiæ (saith Tertullian) non quas plerique superstitione curant ad omnem orationem, etiam cum lavacro totius corporis aquam sumentes. This is the true purification, not that which most men do, superstitiously cleansing their hands and washing when they go to prayers, but cleansing the soul from all impiety, and leaving every affection to sin; then they come pure to God:" and this is it which the apostle also signifies, having translated the gentile and Jewish ceremony into the spirituality of the gospel, "I will therefore, that men pray every where, levantes puras manus, lifting up clean hands," so it is in the vulgar Latin; ὁσίους χεῖρας, so it is in the Greek, *holy hands;* that is the purity, that God looks for upon them, that lift up their hands to him in prayer: and this very thing is founded upon the natural constitution of things, and their essential proportion to each other.

1. It is an act of profanation for any unholy person to handle holy things, and holy offices. For if God was ever careful to put all holy things into cancels, and immure them with acts and laws and cautions of separation; and the very sanctification of them was nothing else but the solemn separating them from common usages, that himself might be distinguished from men by actions of propriety; it is na-

turally certain, he that would be differenced from common things, would be infinitely divided from things that are wicked. If things that are lawful may yet be unholy in this sense, much more are unlawful things most unholy in all senses. If God will not admit of that which is beside religion, he will less endure that which is against religion. And therefore if a common man must not serve at the altar, how shall he abide a wicked man to stand there? No: he will not endure him, but he will cast him and his prayer into the separation of an infinite and eternal distance. "Sic profanatis sacris peritura Troja perdidit primum Deos;—So Troy entered into ruin when their prayers became unholy, and they profaned the rites of their religion."

2. A wicked person, while he remains in that condition, is not the natural object of pity: Ἔλεός ἐστι λύπη ὡς ἐπὶ ἀναξίως κακοπαθοῦντι, said Zeno; "Mercy is a sorrow or a trouble at that misery, which falls upon a person which deserved it not." And so Aristotle defines it, it is λύπη τις ἐπὶ τῷ πονηρῷ τοῦ ἀναξίου τυγχάνειν, "when we see the person deserves a better fortune," or is disposed to a fairer entreaty, then we naturally pity him: and Simon pleaded for pity to the Trojans, saying,

————Miserere animi non digna ferentis.

For who pitieth the fears of a base man, who hath treacherously murdered his friend? or who will lend a friendly sigh, when he sees a traitor to his country pass forth through the execrable gates of cities? and when any circumstance of baseness, that is, any thing that takes off the excuse of infirmity, does accompany a sin (such as are ingratitude, perjury, perseverance, delight, malice, treachery), then every man scorns the criminal, and God delights and rejoices in, and laughs at the calamity of such a person. When Vitellius with his hands bound behind him, his imperial robe rent, and with a dejected countenance and an ill name, was led to execution, every man cursed him, but no man wept. "Deformitas exitus misericordiam abstulerat," saith Tacitus, "The filthiness of his life and death took away pity." So it is with us in our prayers; while we love our sin, we must nurse all its children; and when we roar in our lustful beds, and groan with the whips of an exterminating angel, chastising those ὑπογαστρίους ἐπιθυμίας (as Aretas calls them), "the lusts of the lower belly," wantonness, and its mother intemperance, we feel the price of our sin, that which God foretold to be their issues, that which he threatened us withal, and that which is the natural consequence, and its certain expectation, that which we delighted in, and chose, even then when we refused God, and threw away felicity, and hated virtue. For punishment is but the latter part of sin; it is not a new thing and distinct from it: or if we will kiss the hyæna, or clip the lamia about the neck, we have as certainly chosen the tail, and its venomous embraces, as the face and lip. Every man that sins against God and loves it, or, which is all one, continues in it, for by interpretation that is love, hath all the circumstances of unworthiness towards God; he is unthankful, and a breaker of his vows, and a despiser of his mercies, and impudent against his judgments; he is false to his profession, false to his faith; he is an unfriendly person, and useth him barbarously, who hath treated him with an affection not less than infinite; and if any man does half so much evil, and so unhandsomely to a man, we stone him with stones and curses, with reproach, and an unrelenting scorn. And how then shall such a person hope that God should pity him? For God better understands, and deeper resents, and more essentially hates, and more severely exacts, the circumstances and degrees of baseness, than we can do; and therefore proportionably scorns the person and derides the calamity. Is not unthankfulness to God a greater baseness and unworthiness than unthankfulness to our patron? And is not he as sensible of it and more than we? These things are more than words; and therefore if no man pities a base person, let us remember, that no man is so base in any thing as in his unhandsome demeanour towards God. Do we not profess ourselves his servants, and yet serve the devil? Do we not live upon God's provision, and yet stand or work at the command of lust or avarice, human regards and little interests of the world? We call him Father when we desire our portion, and yet spend it in the society of all his enemies. In short, let our actions to God and their circumstances be supposed to be done towards men, and we should scorn ourselves; and how then can we expect God should not scorn us, and reject our prayer, when we have done all the dishonour to him, and with all the unhandsomeness in the world? Take heed lest we fall into a condition of evil, in which it shall be said, you may thank yourselves; and be infinitely afraid lest at the same time we be in a condition of person, in which God will upbraid our unworthiness, and scorn our persons, and rejoice in our calamity. The first is intolerable, the second is irremediable; the first proclaims our folly, and the second declares God's final justice; in the first there is no comfort, in the latter there is no remedy; that therefore makes us miserable, and this renders us desperate.

3. This great truth is farther manifested by the necessary and convenient appendages of prayer required, or advised, or recommended, in Holy Scripture. For why is fasting prescribed together with prayer? For "neither if we eat, are we the better; neither if we eat not, are we the worse;" and God does not delight in that service, the first, second, and third part of which is nothing but pain and self-affliction. But therefore fasting is useful with prayer, because it is a penal duty, and an action of repentance; for then only God hears sinners, when they enter first into the gates of repentance, and proceed in all the regions of sorrow and carefulness; therefore we are commanded to fast, that we may pray with more spirituality, and with repentance; that is, without the loads of meat, and without the loads of sin. Of the same consideration it is that alms are prescribed together with prayer, because it is a part of that charity, without which our souls are enemies to all that, which ought to be equally valued with our own lives. But besides this, we may easily observe what special indecencies there are, which besides the general malignity and demerit, are special deleteries and hinderances to our prayers, by irreconciling the person of him that prays.

1. The first is unmercifulness. Ὄυτε ἐξ ἱεροῦ βωμὸν, οὔτε ἐξ ἀνθρωπίνης φύσεως ἀφαιρετόν τὸν ἔλεον, said one in Stobæus; and they were well joined together: "He that takes mercy from a man, is like him that takes an altar from the temple;" the temple is of no use without an altar, and the man cannot pray without mercy; and there are infinite of prayers sent forth by men which God never attends to, but as to so many sins, because the men live in a course of rapine,

or tyranny, or oppression, or uncharitableness, or something
that is most contrary to God, because it is unmerciful. Remember, that God sometimes puts thee into some images of
his own relation. We beg of God for mercy, and our brother begs of us for pity : and therefore let us deal equally
with God and all the world.   I see myself fall by a too frequent infirmity, and still I beg for pardon, and hope for pity :
thy brother that offends thee, he hopes so too, and would
fain have the same measure, and would be as glad thou
wouldst pardon him, as thou wouldst rejoice in thy own forgiveness.   I am troubled when God rejects my prayer, or,
instead of hearing my petition, sends a judgment : is not
thy tenant, or thy servant, or thy client, so to thee ?   Does
not he tremble at thy frown, and is of an uncertain soul till
thou speakest kindly unto him, and observes thy looks as he
watches the colour of the bean coming from the box of
sentence, life or death depending on it ?   When he begs of
thee for mercy, his passion is greater, his necessities more
pungent, his apprehension more brisk and sensitive, his case
dressed with the circumstance of pity, and thou thyself
canst better feel his condition than thou dost usually perceive the earnestness of thy own prayers to God ; and if
thou regardest not thy brother whom thou seest, whose case
thou feelest, whose circumstances can afflict thee, whose
passion is dressed to thy fancy, and proportioned to thy
capacity,—how shall God regard thy distant prayer, or be
melted with thy cold desire, or softened with thy dry story, or
moved by thy unrepenting soul ? If I be sad, I seek for comfort, and go to God and to the ministry of his creatures for
it ; and is it not just in God to stop his own fountains, and
seal the cisterns and little emanations of the creatures from
thee, who shuttest thy hand, and shuttest thy eye, and
twistest thy bowels against thy brother, who would as fain
be comforted as thou ? It is a strange iliacal passion that so
hardens a man's bowels, that nothing proceeds from him but
the name of his own disease ; a " miserere mei Deus," a
prayer to God for pity upon him, that will not shew pity to
others.   We are troubled when God through severity
breaks our bones, and hardens his face against us ; but we
think our poor brother is made of iron, and not of flesh and
blood, as we are.   God bath bound mercy upon us by the

iron bands of necessity, and though God's mercy is the measure of his justice, yet justice is the measure of our mercy; and as we do to others, it shall be done to us, even in the matter of pardon and of bounty, of gentleness and remission, of bearing each other's burdens, and fair interpretation; " Forgive us our trespasses, as we forgive them that trespass against us," so we pray. The final sentence in this affair is recorded by St. James, " He that shews no mercy, shall have justice without mercy:"[c] as thy poor brother hath groaned under thy cruelty and ungentle nature without remedy, so shalt thou before the throne of God; thou shalt pray, and plead, and call, and cry, and beg again, and in the midst of thy despairing noises be carried into the regions of sorrow, which never did and never shall feel a mercy. " God never can hear the prayers of an unmerciful man."

2. Lust and uncleanness are a direct enemy to the praying man, an obstruction to his prayers; for this is not only a profanation, but a direct sacrilege; it defiles a temple to the ground; it takes from a man all affection to spiritual things, and mingles his very soul with the things of the world; it makes his understanding low, and his reasonings cheap and foolish, and it destroys his confidence, and all his manly hopes; it makes his spirit light, effeminate, and fantastic, and dissolves his attention; and makes his mind so to disaffect all the objects of his desires, that when he prays he is as uneasy as an impaled person, or a condemned criminal upon the hook or wheel; and it hath in it this evil quality, that a lustful person cannot pray heartily against his sin; he cannot desire his cure, for his will is contradictory to his collect, and he would not that God should hear the words of his prayer, which he poor man never intended. For no crime so seizes upon the will as that; some sins steal an affection, or obey a temptation, or secure an interest, or work by the way of understanding, but lust seizes directly upon the will, for the devil knows well that the lusts of the body are soon cured; the uneasiness that dwells there, is a disease very tolerable, and every degree of patience can pass under it. But therefore the devil seizes upon the will, and that is

[c] James, ii. 13.

it that makes adulteries and all the species of uncleanness; and lust grows so hard a cure, because the formality of it is, that it will not be cured; the will loves it, and so long as it does, God cannot love the man; for God is the prince of purities, and the Son of God is the king of virgins, and the Holy Spirit is all love, and that is all purity and all spirituality: and therefore the prayer of an adulterer, or an unclean person, is like the sacrifices to Moloch, or the rites of Flora, "ubi Cato spectator esse non potuit." A good man will not endure them; much less will God entertain such reekings of the Dead Sea and clouds of Sodom. For so an impure vapour,—begotten of the slime of the earth by the fevers and adulterous heats of an intemperate summer-sun, striving by the ladder of a mountain to climb up to heaven, and rolling into various figures by an uneasy, unfixed revolution, and stopped at the middle region of the air, being thrown from his pride and attempt of passing towards the seat of the stars,—turns into an unwholesome flame, and like the breath of hell is confined into a prison of darkness, and a cloud, till it breaks into diseases, plagues, and mildews, stink and blastings: so is the prayer of an unchaste person; it strives to climb the battlements of heaven, but because it is a flame of sulphur, salt, and bitumen, and was kindled in the dishonourable regions below, derived from hell, and contrary to God, it cannot pass forth to the element of love, but ends in barrenness and murmur, fantastic expectations, and trifling imaginative confidences; and they at last end in sorrows and despair. Every state of sin is against the possibility of a man's being accepted; but these have a proper venom against the graciousness of the person, and the power of the prayer. God can never accept an unholy prayer, and a wicked man can never send forth any other; the waters pass through impure aqueducts and channels of brimstone, and therefore may end in brimstone and fire, but never in forgiveness, and the blessings of an eternal charity.

Henceforth, therefore, never any more wonder that men pray so seldom; there are few that feel the relish, and are enticed with the deliciousness, and refreshed with the comforts, and instructed with the sanctity, and acquainted with the secrets of a holy prayer: but cease also to wonder, that of those few that say many prayers, so few find any return of any at all. To make up a good and a lawful prayer, there must be charity, with all its daughters, " alms, forgiveness," not judging uncharitably; there must be purity of spirit, that is, purity of intention; and there must be purity of the body and soul, that is, the cleanness of chastity; and there must be no vice remaining, no affection to sin: for he that brings his body to God, and hath left his will in the power of any sin, offers to God the calves of his lips,. but not a whole burnt-offering; a lame oblation, but not a " reasonable sacrifice;" and therefore their portion shall be amongst them whose prayers were never recorded in the book of life, whose tears God never put into his bottle, whose desires shall remain ineffectual to eternal ages. Take heed you do not lose your prayers; " for by them ye hope to have eternal life;" and let any of you, whose conscience is most religious and tender, consider what condition that man is in, that hath not said his prayers in thirty or forty years together; and that is the true state of him, who hath lived so long in the course of an unsanctified life; in all that while he never said one prayer, that did him any good; but they ought to be reckoned to him upon the account of his sins. He that is in the affection, or in the habit, or in the state, of any one sin whatsoever, is at such distance from and contrariety to God, that he provokes God to anger in every prayer he makes: and then add but this consideration; that prayer is the great sum of our religion, it is the effect, and the exercise, and the beginning, and the promoter, of all graces, and the consummation and perfection of many; and all those persons who pretend towards heaven, and yet are not experienced in the secrets of religion, they reckon their piety, and account their hopes, only upon the stock of a few prayers. It may be they pray twice every day, it may be thrice, and blessed be God for it; so far is very well: but if it shall be remembered and considered, that this course of piety is so far from warranting any one course of sin, that any one habitual and cherished sin destroys the effect of all that piety, we shall see there is reason to account this to be one of those great arguments, with which God hath so bound the duty of holy living upon us, that without a holy life we cannot in any sense be happy, or have the effect of one prayer. But if we be returning and re-

penting sinners, God delights to hear, because he delights
to save us:

——— Si precibus (dixerunt) numina justis
Victa remollescunt———

When a man is holy, then God is gracious, and a holy
life is the best, and it is a continual prayer; and repentance
is the best argument to move God to mercy, because it is
the instrument to unite our prayers to the intercession of the
holy Jesus.

SERMON V.

PART II.

AFTER these evidences of Scripture, and reason derived
from its analogy, there will be less necessity to take any particular notices of those little objections, which are usually
made from the experience of the success and prosperities of
evil persons. For true it is, there is in the world a generation of men that pray long and loud, and ask for vile things,
such which they ought to fear, and pray against, and yet
they are heard; "the fat upon earth eat and worship[d]:" but
if these men ask things hurtful and sinful, it is certain God
hears them not in mercy: they pray to God as despairing
Saul did to his armour-bearer, "Sta super me et interfice
me;" "Stand upon me and kill me;" and he that obeyed his
voice did him dishonour, and sinned against the head of his
king, and his own life. And the vicious persons, of old,
prayed to Laverna,

——— Pulchra Laverna,
Da mihi fallere, da justum sanctumque videri,
Noctem peccatis et fraudibus objice nubem.

' Give me a prosperous robbery, a rich prey, and secret escape,
let me become rich with thieving, and still be accounted
holy :' for every sort of man hath some religion or other, by
the measures of which they proportion their lives and their
prayers; now, as the Holy Spirit of God, teaching us to pray,
makes us like himself, in order to a holy and an effective

[d] Psal. xxii. 29.

prayer; and no man prays well, but he that prays by the Spirit of God, " the Spirit of holiness," and he that prays with the Spirit must be made like to the Spirit; he is first sanctified and made holy, and then made fervent, and then his prayer ascends beyond the clouds: first, he is renewed in the spirit of his mind, and then he is inflamed with holy fires, and guided by a bright star; first purified and then lightened, then burning and shining: so is every man in every of his prayers; he is always like the Spirit by which he prays: if he he a lustful person, he prays with a lustful spirit; if he does not pray for it, he cannot heartily pray against it: if he be a tyrant or a usurper, a robber or a murderer, he hath his Laverna too, by which all his desires are guided, and his prayers directed, and his petitions furnished: he cannot pray against that spirit that possesses him, and hath seized upon his will and affections: if he be filled with a lying spirit, and be conformed to it in the image of his mind, he will be so also in the expressions of his prayer, and the sense of his soul. Since, therefore, no prayer can be good but that which is taught by the Spirit of grace, none holy but the man whom God's Spirit hath sanctified, and therefore none heard to any purposes of blessing, which the Holy Ghost does not make for us (for he makes intercession for the saints; the Spirit of Christ is the precentor or *rector chori*, the master of the choir); it follows that all other prayers, being made with an evil spirit, must have an evil portion; and though the devils by their oracles have given some answers, and by their significations have foretold some future contingencies, and in their government and subordinate rule have assisted some armies, and discovered some treasures, and prevented some snares of chance and accidents of men; yet no man, that reckons by the measures of reason or religion, reckons witches and conjurors amongst blessed and prosperous persons: these and all other evil persons have an evil spirit, by the measures of which their desires begin and proceed on to issue; but this success of theirs neither comes from God, nor brings felicity: but if it comes from God, it is anger; if it descends upon good men, it is a curse; if upon evil men, it is a sin; and then it is a present curse, and leads on to an eternal infelicity. Plutarch reports, that the Tyrians tied their gods with chains, because certain persons did dream, that Apollo said he would leave their city, and go to the party of Alexander, who then besieged the town: and Apollodorus tells of some, that tied the image of Saturn with bands of wool upon his feet. So some Christians; they think God is tied to their sect, and bound to be of their side, and the interest of their opinion; and they think, he can never go to the enemy's party, so long as they charm him with certain forms of words or disguises of their own; and then all the success they have, and all the evils that are prosperous, all the mischiefs they do, and all the ambitious designs that do succeed, they reckon upon the account of their prayers; and well they may: for their prayers are sins, and their desires are evil; they wish mischief, and they act iniquity, and they enjoy their sin: and if this be a blessing or a cursing, themselves shall then judge, and all the world shall perceive, when the accounts of all the world are truly stated; then, when prosperity shall be called to accounts, and adversity shall receive its comforts, when virtue shall have a crown, and the satisfaction of all sinful desires shall be recompensed with an intolerable sorrow, and the despair of a perishing soul. Nero's mother prayed passionately, that her son might be emperor; and many persons, of whom St. James speaks, "pray to spend upon their lusts," and they are heard too: some were not, and very many are: and some, that fight against a just possessor of a country, pray, that their wars may be prosperous; and sometimes they have been heard too: and Julian the apostate prayed, and sacrificed, and inquired of demons, and burned man's flesh, and operated with secret rites, and all that he might craftily and powerfully oppose the religion of Christ; and he was heard too, and did mischief beyond the malice and the effect of his predecessors, that did swim in Christian blood: but when we sum up the accounts at the foot of their lives, or so soon as the thing was understood, and find that the effect of Agrippina's prayer was, that her son murdered her; and of those lustful petitioners, in St. James, that they were given over to the tyranny and possession of their passions, and baser appetites; and the effect of Julian the Apostate's prayer was, that he lived and died a professed enemy of Christ; and the effect of the prayers of usurpers is that they do mischief, and reap curses, and undo mankind, and provoke God, and live hated, and die miserable, and shall possess the fruit of their sin to eternal ages; these will be no objections to the truth of the former discourse; but greater instances, that, if by hearing our prayers, we mean or intend a blessing, we must also, by making prayers, mean, that the man first be holy, and his desires just and charitable, before he can be admitted to the throne of grace, or converse with God by the intercourses of a prosperous prayer.

That is the first general. 2. Many times good men pray, and their prayer is not a sin, but yet it returns empty; because, although the man may be, yet the prayer is not, in proper disposition; and here I am to account to you concerning the collateral and accidental hinderances of the prayers of a good man.

The first thing that hinders the prayer of a good man from obtaining its effects is a violent anger, and a violent storm in the spirit of him that prays. For anger sets the house on fire, and all the spirits are busy upon trouble, and intend propulsion, defence, displeasure, or revenge; it is a short madness, and an eternal enemy to discourse, and sober counsels, and fair conversation; it intends its own object with all the earnestness of perception, or activity of design, and a quicker motion of a too warm and distempered blood; it is a fever in the heart, and a calenture in the head, and a fire in the face, and a sword in the hand, and a fury all over; and therefore can never suffer a man to be in a disposition to pray. For prayer is an action, and a state of intercourse and desire, exactly contrary to this character of anger. Prayer is an action of likeness to the Holy Ghost, the Spirit of gentleness and dove-like simplicity; an imitation of the holy Jesus, whose spirit is meek, up to the greatness of the biggest example, and a conformity to God; whose anger is always just, and marches slowly, and is without transportation, and often hindered, and never hasty, and is full of mercy: prayer is the peace of our spirit, the stillness of our thoughts, the evenness of recollection, the seat of meditation, the rest of our cares, and the calm of our tempest; prayer is the issue of a quiet mind, of untroubled thoughts, it is the daughter of charity, and the sister of meekness; and he that prays to God with an angry, that is, with a troubled and discomposed

spirit, is like him that retires into a barrel to meditate, and
sets up his closet in the out-quarters of an army, and chooses
a frontier-garrison to be wise in. Anger is a perfect aliena-
tion of the mind from prayer, and therefore is contrary to
that attention, which presents our prayers in a right line to
God. For so have I seen a lark rising from his bed of grass,
and soaring upwards, singing as he rises, and hopes to get
to heaven, and climb above the clouds; but the poor bird
was beaten back with the loud sighings of an eastern wind,
and his motion made irregular and inconstant, descending
more at every breath of the tempest, than it could recover by
the libration and frequent weighing of his wings; till the
little creature was forced to sit down and pant, and stay till
the storm was over; and then it made a prosperous flight,
and did rise and sing, as if it had learned music and motion
from an angel, as he passed sometimes through the air, about
his ministries here below: so is the prayer of a good man;
when his affairs have required business, and his business
was matter of discipline, and his discipline was to pass upon
a sinning person, or had a design of charity, his duty met
with infirmities of a man, and anger was its instrument, and
the instrument became stronger than the prime agent, and
raised a tempest, and overruled the man; and then his
prayer was broken, and his thoughts were troubled, and his
words went up towards a cloud, and his thoughts pulled
them back again, and made them without intention; and the
good man sighs for his infirmity, but must be content to lose
the prayer, and be must recover it when his anger is removed,
and his spirit is becalmed, made even as the brow of Jesus,
and smooth like the heart of God; and then it ascends to
heaven upon the wings of the holy dove, and dwells with
God, till it returns, like the useful bee, loaden with a blessing
and the dew of heaven.

But besides this; anger is a combination of many other
things, every one of which is an enemy to prayer; it is λύπη,
and ὄρεξις, and τιμωρία, and it is ζέσις, and it is ἄθροος, and
it is κόλασις, and ἐπιτίμησις; so it is in the several definitions
of it, and in its natural constitution. It hath in it the trouble
of sorrow, and the heats of lust, and the disease of revenge,
and the boilings of a fever, and the rashness of precipitancy,
and the disturbance of persecution; and therefore is a cer-

tain effective enemy against prayer; which ought to be a spiritual joy, and an act of mortification; and to have in it no heats, but of charity and zeal; and they are to be guided by prudence and consideration, and allayed with the deliciousness of mercy, and the serenity of a meek and a quiet spirit; and therefore St. Paul gave caution, that "the sun should not go down upon our anger," meaning, that it should not stay upon us till evening prayer; for it would hinder our evening sacrifice; but the stopping of the first egressions of anger, is a certain artifice of the Spirit of God, to prevent unmercifulness, which turns not only our desires into vanity, but our prayers into sin; and, remember, that Elisha's anger, though it was also zeal, had so discomposed his spirit, when the two kings came to inquire of the Lord, that, though he was a good man and a prophet, yet he could not pray, he could not inquire of the Lord, till by rest and music he had gathered himself into the evenness of a dispassionate and recollected mind; therefore, let your prayers be without wrath. Βούλεται αὐτοὺς ἀναδιδάξαι διὰ συμβόλων, ὁπότε προσέρχοιντο εἰς βωμοὺς εὐξάμενοι ἢ εὐχαριστήσαντες, μηδὲν ἀῤῥώστημα ἢ πάθος ἐπιφέρεσθαι τῇ ψυχῇ; "for God, by many significations, hath taught us, that when men go to the altars to pray or give thanks, they must bring no sin or violent passion along with them to the sacrifice," said Philo.

2. Indifferency and easiness of desire is a great enemy to the good man's prayer. When Plato gave Diogenes a great vessel of wine, who asked but a little, and a few carraways, the Cynic thanked him with his rude expression: "Cum interrogaris, quot sint duo et duo, respondes viginti; ita non secundum ea, quæ rogaris, das; nec ad ea, quæ interrogaris, respondes:" "Thou neither answerest to the question thou art asked, nor givest according as thou art desired; being inquired of, how many are two and two, thou answerest twenty." So it is with God and us in the intercourse of our prayers: we pray for health, and he gives us, it may be, a sickness that carries us into eternal life; we pray for necessary support for our persons and families, and he gives us more than we need; we beg for a removal of a present sadness, and he gives us that which makes us able to bear twenty sadnesses, a cheerful spirit, a peaceful conscience, and a joy in God, as an antepast of eternal rejoicings in the kingdom of God. But,

then, although God doth very frequently give us beyond the
matter of our desires, yet he does not so often give us great
things beyond the spirit of our desires, beyond the quickness,
vivacity, and fervour of our minds : for there is but one thing
in the world that God hates besides sin, that is, indifferency
and lukewarmness[*]; which, although it hath not in it the direct nature of sin, yet it hath this testimony from God, that
it is loathsome and abominable; and, excepting this thing
alone, God never said so of any thing in the New Testament,
but what was a direct breach of a commandment. The reason of it is, because lukewarmness, or an indifferent spirit, is
an undervaluing of God and of religion; it is a separation of
reason from affections, and a perfect conviction of the understanding to the goodness of a duty, but a refusing to follow
what we understand. For he that is lukewarm alway, understands the better way, and seldom pursues it; he hath so
much reason as is sufficient, but he will not obey it; his will
does not follow the dictate of his understanding, and therefore it is unnatural. It is like the fantastic fires of the
night, where there is light and no heat; and therefore may
pass on to the real fires of hell, where there is heat and no
light; and therefore, though an act of lukewarmness is only
an indecency, and no sin; yet a state of lukewarmness is
criminal, and a sinful state of imperfection and indecency;
an act of indifferency hinders a single prayer from being accepted; but a state of it makes the person ungracious and
despised in the court of heaven : and therefore St. James, in
his accounts concerning an effective prayer, not only requires
that he be a just man who prays, but his prayer must be fervent; δέησις δικαίου ἐνεργουμένη, "an effectual fervent prayer,"
so our English reads it; it must be an intent, zealous, busy,
operative prayer; for, consider what a huge indecency it is,
that a man should speak to God for a thing that he values
not; or that he should not value a thing, without which he
cannot be happy; or that he should spend his religion upon
a trifle; and if it be not a trifle, that he should not spend his
affections upon it. If our prayers be for temporal things, I shall
not need stir up your affections to be passionate for their
purchase; we desire them greedily, we run after them intem-

perately, we are kept from them with huge impatience, we are delayed with infinite regrets; we prefer them before our duty, we ask them unseasonably; we receive them with our own prejudice, and we care not; we choose them to our hurt and hinderance, and yet delight in the purchase; and when we do pray for them, we can hardly bring ourselves to it, to submit to God's will, but will have them (if we can) whether he be pleased or no; like the parasite in the comedy, "Qui comedit quod fuit et quod non fuit:" "he ate all, and more than all; what was set before him, and what was kept from him." But, then, for spiritual things, for the interest of our souls, and the affairs of the kingdom, we pray to God with just such a zeal, as a man begs of a chirurgeon to cut him of the stone; or a condemned man desires his executioner quickly to put him out of his pain, by taking away his life; when things are come to that pass, it must be done, but God knows with what little complacency and desire the man makes his request: and yet the things of religion and the Spirit are the only things that ought to be desired vehemently, and pursued passionately, because God hath set such a value upon them, that they are the effects of his greatest loving-kindness; they are the purchases of Christ's blood, and the effect of his continual intercession, the fruits of his bloody sacrifice, and the gifts of his healing and saving mercy, the graces of God's Spirit, and the only instruments of felicity; and if we can have fondnesses for things indifferent or dangerous, our prayers upbraid our spirits, when we beg coldly and tamely for those things, for which we ought to die, which are more precious than the globes of kings, and weightier than imperial sceptres, richer than the spoils of the sea, or the treasures of the Indian hills.

He that is cold and tame in his prayers, hath not tasted of the deliciousness of religion and the goodness of God; he is a stranger to the secrets of the kingdom, and therefore he does not know what it is, either to have hunger or satiety; and therefore, neither are they hungry for God, nor satisfied with the world; but remain stupid and inapprehensive, without resolution and determination, never choosing clearly, nor pursuing earnestly, and therefore never enter into possession; but always stand at the gate of weariness, unnecessary caution, and perpetual irresolution. But so it is too often in our prayers; we come to God because it is civil so to do, and a general custom, but neither drawn thither by love, nor pinched by spiritual necessities, and pungent apprehensions; we say so many prayers, because we are resolved so to do, and we pass through them, sometimes with a little attention, sometimes with none at all; and can we think, that the grace of chastity can be obtained at such a purchase, *that* grace, that hath cost more labours than all the persecutions of faith, and all the disputes of hope, and all the expense of charity besides, amounts to? Can we expect that our sins should be washed by a lazy prayer? Can an indifferent prayer quench the flames of hell, or rescue us from an eternal sorrow? Is lust so soon overcome, that the very naming it can master it? Is the devil so slight and easy an enemy, that he will fly away from us at the first word, spoken without power, and without vehemence? Read, and attend to the accents of the prayers of saints. " I cried day and night before thee, O Lord; my soul refused comfort; my throat is dry with calling upon my God, my knees are weak through fasting;" and, " Let me alone," says God to Moses," and, "I will not let thee go till thou hast blessed me," said Jacob to the angel. And I shall tell you a short character of a fervent prayer out of the practice of St. Jerome, in his epistle 'ad Eustachium de Custodia Virginitatis.' " Being destitute of all help, I threw myself down at the feet of Jesus; I watered his feet with tears, and wiped them with my hair, and mortified the lust of my flesh with the abstinence and hungry diet of many weeks; I remember, that in my crying to God, I did frequently join the night and the day, and never did entertain to call, nor cease for beating my breast, till the mercy of the Lord brought to me peace and freedom from temptation. After many tears, and my eyes fixed in heaven, I thought myself sometimes encircled with troops of angels, and then at last I sang to God, ' We will run after thee into the smell and deliciousness of thy precious ointments;'"—such a prayer as this will never return without its errand. But though your person be as gracious as David or Job, and your desire as holy as the love of angels, and your necessities great as a new penitent, yet it pierces not the clouds, unless it be also as loud as thunder, passionate as the cries of women, and clamorous as necessity. And we may guess at the degrees of importunity by the insinuation of the apostle : " Let the married abstain for a time," *ut vacent orationi et jejunio,* " that they may attend to prayer;" it is a great attendance, and a long diligence, that is promoted by such a separation ; and supposes a devotion, that spends more than many hours : for ordinary prayers, and many hours of every day, might well enough consist with an ordinary cohabitation ; but that which requires such a separation, calls for a longer time and a greater attendance, than we usually consider. For every prayer we make, is considered by God, and recorded in heaven ; but cold prayers are not put into the account, in order to effect and acceptation; but are laid aside like the buds of roses, which a cold wind hath nipped into death, and the discoloured tawny face of an Indian slave : and when in order to your hopes of obtaining a great blessing, you reckon up your prayers, with which you have solicited your suit in the court of heaven, you must reckon, not by the number of the collects, but by your sighs and passions, by the vehemence of your desires, and the fervour of your spirit, the apprehension of your need, and the consequent prosecution of your supply. Christ prayed κραυγαῖς ἰσχυραῖς " with loud cryings," and St. Paul made mention of his scholars in his prayers " night and day." Fall upon your knees and grow there, and let not your desires cool nor your zeal remit, but renew it again and again, and let not your offices and the custom of praying put thee in mind of thy need, but let thy need draw thee to thy holy offices; and remember, how great a God, how glorious a Majesty you speak to ; therefore, let not your devotions and addresses be little. Remember, how great a need thou hast; let not your desires he less. Remember, how great the thing is, you pray for; do not undervalue it with any indifferency. Remember, that prayer is an act of religion ; let it, therefore, be made thy business : and, lastly, Remember, that God hates a cold prayer : and, therefore, will never bless it, but it shall be always ineffectual.

3. Under this title of lukewarmness and tepidity may be comprised also these cautions: that a good man's prayers are sometimes hindered by inadvertency, sometimes by want of perseverance. For inadvertency, or want of attendance to the sense and intention of our prayers, is certainly an

effect of lukewarmness, and a certain companion and appendage to human infirmity; and is only so remedied, as our prayers are made zealous, and our infirmities pass into the strengths of the Spirit. But if we were quick in our perceptions, either concerning our danger, or our need, or the excellency of the object, or the glories of God, or the niceties and perfections of religion, we should not dare to throw away our prayers so like fools, or come to God and say a prayer with our mind standing at distance, trifling like untaught boys at their books, with a truantly spirit. I shall say no more to this, but that, in reason, we can never hope, that God in heaven will hear our prayers, which we ourselves speak, and yet hear not at the same time, when we ourselves speak them with instruments joined to our ears; even with those organs, which are parts of our hearing faculties. If they be not worth our own attending to, they are not worth God's hearing; if they are worth God's attending to, we must make them so by our own zeal, and passion, and industry, and observation, and a present and a holy spirit.

But concerning perseverance, the consideration is something distinct. For when our prayer is for a great matter, and a great necessity, strictly attended to, yet we pursue it only by chance or humour, by the strengths of fancy, and natural disposition; or else our choice is cool as soon as hot, like the emissions of lightning, or like a sunbeam often interrupted with a cloud, or cooled with intervening showers : and our prayer is without fruit, because the desire lasts not, and the prayer lives like the repentance of Simon Magus, or the trembling of Felix, or the Jews' devotion for seven days of unleavened bread, during the Passover, or the feast of tabernacles : but if we would secure the blessing of our prayers, and the effect of our prayers, we must never leave till we have obtained what we need.

There are many that pray against a temptation for a month together, and so long as the prayer is fervent, so long the man hath a nolition, and a direct enmity against the lust; he consents not all that while; but when the month is gone, and the prayer is removed, or become less active, then the temptation returns, and forages, and prevails, and seizes upon all our unguarded strengths. There are some desires which have a period, and God's visitations expire in mercy at the revolution of a certain number of days; and our prayer must dwell so long, as God's anger abides; and in all the storm we must outcry the noise of the tempest, and the voices of that thunder. But if we become hardened, and by custom and cohabitation with the danger lose our fears, and abate of our desires and devotions, many times we shall find, that God, by a sudden breach upon us, will chastise us for letting our hands go down. Israel prevailed no longer than Moses held up his hands in prayer; and he was forced to continue his prayer, till the going down of the sun; that is, till the danger was over, till the battle was done. But when our desires, and prayers, are in the matter of spiritual danger, they must never be remitted, because danger continues for ever, and, therefore, so must our watchfulness, and our guards. "Vult enim Deus rogari, vult cogi, vult quadam importunitate vinci," says St. Gregory; "God loves to be invited, entreated, importuned, with an unquiet restless desire and a persevering prayer." Χρὴ ἀδιαλείπτως εὔχεσθαι τῆς περὶ τὸ θεῖον θρησκείας, said Proclus. That is a holy and a religious prayer, that never gives over, but renews the prayer, and dwells upon the desire; for this only is effectual. Δηθύνοντι βροτῷ κρατεροὶ μάκαρες τελέθουσι, "God hears the persevering man, and the unwearied prayer." For it is very considerable, that we be very curious to observe; that many times a lust is sopita, non mortua, 'it is asleep;' the enemy is at truce, and at quiet for a while, but not conquered, 'not dead;' and if we put off our armour too soon, we lose all the benefit of our former war, and are surprised by indiligence and a careless guard. For God sometimes binds the devil in a short chain, and gives his servants respite, that they may feel the short pleasures of a peace, and the rest of innocence; and perceive, what are the eternal felicities of heaven, where it shall be so for ever; but then we must return to our warfare again; and every second assault is more troublesome, because it finds our spirits at ease, and without watchfulness, and delighted with a spiritual rest, and keeping holyday. But let us take heed; for whatsoever temptation we can be troubled withal by our natural temper, or by the condition of our life, or the evil circumstances of our condition, so long as we have capacity to feel it, so long we are in danger, and must "watch thereunto with prayer" and continual diligence. And when your temptations let you alone, let not your God alone; but lay up prayers and the blessings of a constant devotion against the day of trial. Well may your temptation sleep, but if your prayers do so, you may chance to be awakened with an assault that may ruin you. However, the rule is easy: Whatsoever you need, ask it of God so long as you want it, even till you have it. For God, therefore, many times defers to grant, that thou mayest persevere to ask; and because every holy prayer is a glorification of God by the confessing many of his attributes, a lasting and a persevering prayer is a little image of the hallelujahs and services of eternity; it is a continuation to do that, according to our measures, which we shall be doing to eternal ages: therefore, think not, that five or six hearty prayers can secure to thee a great blessing, and a supply of a mighty necessity. He that prays so, and then leaves off, hath said some prayers, and done the ordinary offices of his religion; but hath not secured the blessing, nor used means reasonably proportionable to a mighty interest.

4. The prayers of a good man are oftentimes hindered, and destitute of their effect, for want of praying in good company; for sometimes an evil or an obnoxious person hath so secured and ascertained a mischief to himself, that he that stays in his company or his traffic, must also share in his punishment: and the Tyrian sailors with all their vows and prayers could not obtain a prosperous voyage, so long as Jonas was within the bark; for in this case the interest is divided, and the public sin prevails above the private piety. When the philosopher asked a penny of Antigonus, he told him 'it was too little for a king to give;' when he asked a talent, he told him 'it was too much for a philosopher to receive;' for he did purpose to cozen his own charity, and elude the other's necessity, upon pretence of a double inequality. So it is in the case of a good man mingled in evil company; if a curse be too severe for a good man, a mercy is not to be expected by evil company; and his prayer, when it is made in common, must partake of that event of things which is appropriate to that society. The purpose of this caution is, that every good man be careful, that he do not mingle his devotion in the communions of heretical persons, and in schismatical conventicles; for al-

though he be like them that follow Absalom in the simplicity
of their heart, yet his intermedial fortune, and the event of
his present affairs, may be the same with Absalom's; and it
is not a light thing, that we curiously choose the parties of
our communion. I do not say it is necessary to avoid all
the society of evil persons; "for then we must go out of the
world;" and when we have thrown out a drunkard, possibly we have entertained a hypocrite; or when a swearer is
gone, an oppressor may stay still; or if that be remedied,
yet pride is soon discernible, but not easily judicable: but
that which is of caution in this question, is, that we never
mingle with those, whose very combination is a sin; such
as were Corah and his company that rebelled against Moses
their prince; and Dathan and Abiram that made a schism
in religion against Aaron the priest: for so said the Spirit
of the Lord, " Come out from the congregation of these
men, lest ye perish in their company;" and all those that
were abused in their communion, did perish in the gainsaying of Corah. It is a sad thing to see a good man
cozened by fair pretences, and allured into an evil snare;
for besides, that he dwells in danger, and cohabits with a
dragon, and his virtue may change by evil persuasion, into
an evil disposition, from sweetness to bitterness, from thence
to evil speaking, from thence to believe a lie, and from
believing to practise it;—besides this, it is a very great sadness, that such a man should lose all his prayers to very
many purposes. God will not respect the offering of those
men, who assemble by a peevish spirit; and therefore, although God in pity regards the desires of a good man, if
innocently abused, yet as it unites in that assembly, God
will not hear it to any purposes of blessing, and holiness:
unless " we keep the unity of the Spirit in the bond of peace,"
we cannot have the blessing of the Spirit in the returns of a
holy prayer; and all those assemblies, which meet together
against God or God's ordinance, may pray and call, and cry
loudly, and frequently, and still they provoke God to anger;
and many times he will not have so much mercy for them,
as to deny them; but lets them prosper in their sin, till it
swells to intolerable and unpardonable. But when good
men pray with one heart, and in a holy assembly, that is,
holy in their desires, lawful in their authority, though the

persons be of different complexions, then the prayer flies up
to God like the hymns of a choir of angels; for God,—that
made body and soul to be one man, and God and man to be
one Christ; and three persons are one God, and his praises
are sung to him by choirs, and the persons are joined in
orders, and the orders into hierarchies, and all, that God
might be served by unions and communities;—loves that his
church should imitate the concords of heaven, and the unions
of God, and that every good man should promote the interests
of his prayers by joining in the communion of saints in the
unions of obedience and charity, with the powers that God
and the laws have ordained.

The sum is this: If the man that makes the prayer, be an
unholy person, his prayer is not the instrument of a blessing, but a curse; but when the sinner begins to repent truly,
then his desires begin to be holy. But if they be holy, and
just, and good, yet they are without profit and effect, if the
prayer be made in schism, or an evil communion, or if it be
made without attention, or if the man soon gives over, or if
the prayer be not zealous, or if the man be angry. There
are very many ways for a good man to become unblessed,
and unthriving in his prayers, and he cannot be secure unless he be in the state of grace, and his spirit be quiet, and
his mind be attentive, and his society be lawful, and his
desires earnest and passionate, and his devotions persevering, lasting till his needs be served or exchanged for another
blessing: so that, what Lælius (apud Cicer. de senectute) said
concerning old age, "neque in summa inopia levis esse se-
nectus potest, ne sapienti quidem, nec insipienti etiam in
summa copia non gravis;" "that a wise man could not hear
old age, if it were extremely poor; and yet if it were very rich,
it were intolerable to a fool;" we may say concerning our
prayers; they are sins and unholy, if a wicked man makes
them; and yet if they be made by a good man, they are ineffective, unless they be improved by their proper dispositions. A good man cannot prevail in his prayers, if his
desires be cold, and his affections trifling, and his industry
soon weary, and his society criminal; and if all these appendages of prayer be observed, yet they will do no good
to an evil man; for his prayer that begins in sin, shall end
in sorrow.

SERMON VI.

PART III.

3. NEXT I am to inquire and consider, What degrees and circumstances of piety are required to make us fit to be intercessors for others, and to pray for them with probable effect? I say ' with probable effect;' for when the event principally depends upon that which is not within our own election, such as are the lives and actions of others, all that we can consider in this affair is, whether we be persons fit to pray in the behalf of others, that hinder not, but are persons within the limit and possibilities of the present mercy. When the emperor Maximinus was smitten with the wrath of God, and a sore disease, for his cruel persecuting the Christian cause, and putting so many thousand innocent and holy persons to death, and he understood the voice of God and the accents of thunder, and discerned that cruelty was the cause,—he revoked their decrees made against the Christians, recalled them from their caves and deserts, their sanctuaries, and retirements, and enjoined them to pray for the life and health of their prince. They did so; and they who could command mountains to remove and were obeyed, they who could do miracles, they who with the key of prayer could open God's four closets, of the *womb* and the *grave*, of *providence* and *rain*,—could not obtain for their bloody emperor one drop of mercy, but he must die miserable for ever. God would not be entreated for him; and though he loved the prayer because he loved the advocates, yet Maximinus was not worthy to receive the blessing. And it was threatened to the rebellious people of Israel, and by them to all people that should sin grievously against the Lord, God " would break their staff of bread," and even the righteous should not be prevailing intercessors; " Though Noah, Job, or Daniel, were there, they should deliver but their own souls by their righteousness, saith the Lord God[a]:" and when Abraham prevailed very far with God in the behalf

---

[a] Ezek. xiv. 14

of Sodom, and the five cities of the plain, it had its period: if there had been ten righteous in Sodom, it should have been spared for their sakes; but four only were found, and they only delivered their own souls too; but neither their righteousness, nor Abraham's prayer, prevailed any farther. And we have this case also mentioned in the New Testament: " If any man see his brother sin a sin which is not unto death, he shall ask, and he shall give him life for them that sin not unto death[b]." At his prayer the sinner shall receive pardon; God shall " give him life for them," to him that prays in their behalf that sin, provided it be " not a sin unto death;" for " there is a sin unto death, but I do not say that he shall pray for it:" there his commission expires, and his power is confined. For there are some sins of that state and greatness that God will not pardon. St. Austin in his books ' de Sermone Domini in Monte' affirms it, concerning some one single sin of a perfect malice. It was also the opinion of Origen and Athanasius, and is followed by Venerable Bede; and whether the Apostle means a peculiar state of sin, or some one single great crime which also supposes a precedent and a present state of criminal condition; it is such a thing as will hinder our prayers from prevailing in their behalf: we are therefore not encouraged to pray, because they cannot receive the benefit of Christ's intercession, and therefore much less of our advocation, which only can prevail by virtue and participation of his mediation. For whomsoever Christ prays, for them we pray; that is, for all them that are within the covenant of repentance, for all whose actions have not destroyed the very being of religion, who have not renounced their faith, nor voluntarily quit their hopes, nor openly opposed the Spirit of grace, nor grown by a long progress to a resolute and final impiety, nor done injustices greater than sorrow, or restitution, or recompence, or acknowledgment. However, though it may be uncertain and disputed concerning the number of " sins unto death," and therefore to pray, or not to pray, is not matter of duty;—yet it is all one as to the effect, whether we know them or no; for though we intend charity, when we pray for the worst of men,—yet concerning the event God will take care, and will certainly return thy prayer upon thy own head, though thou didst desire it should water and refresh thy neighbour's dryness; and St. John so expresses it, as if he had left the matter of duty undetermined; because the instances are uncertain; yet the event is certainly none at all, therefore because we are not encouraged to pray, and because it is a " sin unto death;" that is, such a sin that hath no portion in the promises of life, and the state of repentance. But now, suppose the man, for whom we pray, to be capable of mercy, within the covenant of repentance, and not far from the kingdom of heaven; yet,

1. No prayers of others can farther prevail, than to remove this person to the next stage in order to felicity. When St. Monica prayed for her son, she did not pray to God to save him, but to convert him; and when God intended to reward the prayers and alms of Cornelius, he did not do it by giving him a crown, but by sending an apostle to him to make him a Christian; the meaning of which observation is, that we may understand, that as, in the person prayed for, there ought to be the great disposition of being in a savable condition; so there ought also to be all the intermedial aptnesses: for just as he is disposed, so can we prevail; and the prayers of a good man first prevail in behalf of a sinner, that he shall be invited, that he shall be reproved,—and then that he shall attend to it, then that he shall have his heart opened, and then that he shall repent: and still a good man's prayers follow him through the several stages of pardon, of sanctification, of restraining graces, of a mighty Providence, of great assistance, of perseverance, and a holy death. No prayers can prevail upon an indisposed person. For the sun himself cannot enlighten a blind eye, nor the soul move a body whose silver cord is loosed, and whose joints are untied by the rudeness and dissolutions of a pertinacious sickness. But then, suppose an eye quick and healthful, or apt to be refreshed with light and a friendly prospect; yet a glow-worm or a diamond, the shells of pearl, or a dead man's candle, are not enough to make him discern the beauties of the world, and to admire the glories of creation. Therefore,

2. As the persons must be capable for whom we pray, so they that pray for others, must be persons extraordinary

in something. 1. If persons be of an extraordinary piety,
they are apt to be intercessors for others. This appears in
the case of Job: when the wrath of God was kindled
against Eliphaz and his two friends, God commanded them
to offer a sacrifice, but " my servant Job shall pray for you,
for him will I accept[c]:" and it was so in the case of the
prevaricating Israelites ; God was full of indignation against
them, and smote them ; " then stood up Phinehas and prayed,
and the plague ceased." For this man was a good man,
and the spirit of an extraordinary zeal filled him, and he did
glory to God in the execution upon Zimri and his fair
Midianite. And it was a huge blessing, that was entailed
upon the posterity of Abraham, Isaac, and Jacob ; because
they had a great religion, a great power with God, and
their extraordinary did consist especially in the matter of
prayers and devotion ; for that was eminent in them, besides
their obedience : for so Maimonides tells concerning them,
that Abraham first instituted morning-prayer. The affairs of
religion had not the same constitution then as now. They
worshipped God never but at their memorials, and in places,
and seldom times of separation. They bowed their head
when they came to a hallowed stone, and upon the top of
their staff, and worshipped when they came to a consecrated
pillar, but this was seldom ; and they knew not the secrets
and the privileges of a frequent prayer, of intercourses with
God by ejaculations, and the advantages of importunity :
and the doctors of the Jews,—that record the prayer of Noah,
who in all reason knew the secret best, because he was to
teach it to all the world,—yet have transmitted to us but a
short prayer of some seven lines long ; and this he only said
within the ark, in that great danger, once on a day, provoked by his fear, and stirred up by a religion then made
actual, in those days of sorrow and penance. But in the
descending ages, when God began to reckon a church in
Abraham's family ; there began to be a new institution of
offices, and Abraham appointed that God should be prayed
to every morning. Isaac being taught by Abraham, made a
law, or at least commended the practice, and adopted it into
the religion, that God should be worshipped by decimation
or tithing of our goods ; and he added an order of prayer to

[c] Chap. xlii. 7, 8.

be said in the afternoon; and Jacob, to make up the office complete, added evening-prayer; and God was their God, and they became fit persons to bless, that is, of procuring blessings to their relatives; as appears in the instances of their own families; of the king of Egypt, and the cities of the plain. For a man of an ordinary piety is like Gideon's fleece, wet in its own locks; but it could not water a poor man's garden; but so does a thirsty land drink all the dew of heaven that wets its face, and a greater shower makes no torrent, nor digs so much as a little furrow, that the drills of the water might pass into rivers, or refresh their neighbour's weariness; but when the earth is full, and hath no strange consumptive needs, then at the next time, when God blesses it with a gracious shower, it divides into portions, and sends it abroad in free and equal communications, that all that stand round about, may feel the shower. So is a good man's prayer; his own cup is full, it is crowned with health, and overflows with blessings, and all, that drink of his cup and eat at his table, are refreshed with his joys, and divide with him in his holy portions. And indeed he hath need of a great stock of piety, who is first to provide for his own necessities, and then to give portions to a numerous relation. It is a great matter, that every man needs for himself,—the daily expenses of his own infirmities, the unthriving state of his omission of duties, and recessions from perfection,—and sometimes the great losses and shipwrecks, the plunderings and burning of his house by a fall into a deadly sin; and most good men are in this condition, that they have enough to do to live, and keep themselves above water; but how few men are able to pay their own debts, and lend great portions to others? The number of those who can effectually intercede for others to great purposes of grace and pardon, are as soon told as the number of wise men, as the gates of a city, or the entries of the river Nilus.

But then do but consider, what a great engagement this is to a very strict and holy life. If we chance to live in times of an extraordinary trouble, or if our relatives can be capable of great dangers or great sorrows, or if we ourselves would do the noblest friendship in the world, and oblige others by acts of greatest benefit; if we would assist their

souls and work towards their salvation; if we would be
public ministers of the greatest usefulness to our country;
if we would support kings, and relieve the great necessities
of kingdoms; if we would be effective in the stopping of a
plague, or in the success of armies;—a great and an exemplar
piety, and a zealous and holy prayer, can do all this. " Semper tu hoc facito, ut cogites, id optimum esse, tute ut sis
optimus; si id nequeas, saltem ut optimis sis proximus:"
' He that is the best man towards God, is certainly the best
minister to his prince or country, and therefore do thou endeavour to be so, and if thou canst not be so, be at least next
to the best.' For in that degree in which our religion is
great, and our piety exemplar, in the same we can contribute
towards the fortune of a kingdom: and when Elijah was
taken into heaven, Elisha mourned for him, because it was
a loss to Israel: " My father, my father, the chariots of
Israel and horsemen thereof." But consider how useless
thou art, when thou canst not by thy prayers obtain so much
mercy, as to prevail for the life of a single trooper, or in a
plague beg of God for the life of a poor maidservant; but
the ordinary emanations of Providence shall proceed to issue
without any arrest, and the sword of the angel shall not be
turned aside in one single infliction. Remember, although
he is a great and excellent person, that can prevail with God
for the interest of others; yet thou, that hast no stock of
grace and favour, no interest in the court of Heaven, art but
a mean person, extraordinary in nothing; thou art unregarded by God, cheap in the sight of angels, useless to thy
prince or country; thou mayest hold thy peace in a time of
public danger. For kings never pardon murderers at the
intercession of thieves; and if a mean mechanic should beg
a reprieve for a condemned traitor, he is ridiculous and impudent: so is a vicious advocate, or an ordinary person
with God. It is well if God will hear him begging for his
own pardon, he is not yet disposed to plead for others.

And yet every man that is in the state of grace, every
man that can pray without a sinful prayer, may also intercede for others; and it is a duty for all men to do it; all
men, I say, who can pray at all acceptably: " I will, therefore, that prayers, and supplications, and intercessions, and
giving of thanks, be made for all men;" and this is a duty

that is prescribed to all them, that are concerned in the duty and in the blessings of prayer; but this is it which I say— if their piety be but ordinary, their prayer can be effectual but in easy purposes, and to smaller degrees; but he,—that would work effectually towards a great deliverance, or in great degrees towards the benefit or ease of any of his relatives,—can be confident of his success but in the same degree in which his person is gracious. "There are strange things in heaven;" judgments there are made of things and persons by the measures of religion, and a plain promise produces effects of wonder and miracle; and the changes that are there made, are not effected by passions, and interests, and corporal changes; and the love that is there, is not the same thing that is here; it is more beneficial, more reasonable, more holy, of other designs, and strange productions; and upon that stock it is, that a holy poor man,—that possesses no more (it may be) than a ewe-lamb, that eats of his bread, and drinks of his cup, and is a daughter to him, and is all his temporal portion,—this poor man is ministered to by angels, and attended to by God, and the Holy Spirit makes intercession for him, and Christ joins the man's prayer to his own advocation, and the man by prayer shall save the city, and destroy the fortune of a tyrant-army, even then when God sees it good it should be so : for he will no longer deny him any thing, but when it is no blessing; and when it is otherwise, his prayer is most heard when it is most denied.

2. That we should prevail in intercessions for others, we are to regard and to take care, that as our piety, so also must our offices be extraordinary. He that prays to recover a family from an hereditary curse, or to reverse a sentence of God, to cancel a decree of Heaven gone out against his friend; he that would heal the sick with his prayer, or with his devotion prevail against an army, must not expect such great effects upon a morning or evening collect, or an honest wish put into the recollections of a prayer, or a period put in on purpose. Mamercus, bishop of Vienna, seeing his city and all the diocess in great danger of perishing by an earthquake, instituted great litanies, and solemn supplications, besides the ordinary devotions of his usual hours of prayer; and the church from his example took up the practice, and

translated it into an anniversary solemnity, and upon St.
Mark's day did solemnly intercede with God to divert or
prevent his judgments falling upon the people, " majoribus
litaniis," so they are called; with the more solemn supplications they did pray unto God in behalf of their people.
And this hath in it the same consideration, that is in every
great necessity ; for it is a great thing for a man to be so
gracious with God as to be able to prevail for himself and
his friend, for himself and his relatives; and therefore in
these cases, as in all great needs, it is the way of prudence
and security, that we use all those greater offices, which God
hath appointed as instruments of importunity, and arguments
of hope, and acts of prevailing, and means of great effect and
advocation : such as are, separating days for solemn prayer,
all the degrees of violence and earnest address, fasting and
prayer, alms and prayer, acts of repentance and prayer,
praying together in public with united hearts, and, above
all, praying in the susception and communication of the
holy sacrament; the effects and admirable issues of which
we know not, and perceive not; we lose because we desire
not, and choose to lose many great blessings rather than
purchase them with the frequent commemoration of that
sacrifice, which was offered up for all the needs of mankind,
and for obtaining all favours and graces to the catholic
church. Εὐχῆς δικαίας οὐκ ἀνήκοος Θεὸς, " God never refuses to bear a holy prayer ;" and our prayers can never be
so holy, as when they are offered up in the union of Christ's
sacrifice : for Christ, by that sacrifice, reconciled God and
the world ; and because our needs continue, therefore we are
commanded to continue the memory, and to represent to
God that which was done to satisfy all our needs : then we
receive Christ; we are, after a secret and mysterious, but
most real and admirable manner, made all one with Christ ;
and if God giving us his Son could not but ' with him give us
all things else,' how shall he refuse our persons, when we are
united to his person, when our souls are joined to his soul,
our body nourished by his body, and our souls sanctified by
his blood, and clothed with his robes, and marked with his
character, and sealed with his Spirit, and renewed with holy
vows, and consigned to all his glories, and adopted to his
inheritance? when we represent his death, and pray in virtue

of his passion, and imitate his intercession, and do that which God commands, and offer him in our manner that which he essentially loves; can it be that either any thing should be more prevalent, or that God can possibly deny such addresses and such importunities? Try it often, and let all things else be answerable, and you cannot have greater reason for your confidence. Do not all the Christians in the world, that understand religion, desire to have the holy sacrament when they die; when they are to make their great appearance before God, and to receive their great consignation to their eternal sentence, good or bad? And if then be their greatest needs, that is their greatest advantage, and instrument of acceptation. Therefore if you have a great need to be served, or a great charity to serve, and a great pity to minister, and a dear friend in a sorrow, take Christ along in thy prayers: in all thy ways thou canst, take him; take him in affection, and take him in a solemnity; take him by obedience, and receive him in the sacrament; and if thou then offerest up thy prayers, and makest thy needs known; if thou nor thy friend be not relieved; if thy party be not prevalent, and the war be not appeased, or the plague be not cured, or the enemy taken off, there is something else in it: but thy prayer is good and pleasing to God, and dressed with circumstances of advantage, and thy person is apt to be an intercessor, and thou hast done all that thou canst; the event must be left to God; and the secret reasons of the denial, either thou shalt find in time, or thou mayest trust with God, who certainly does it with the greatest wisdom and the greatest charity. I have in this thing only one caution to insert; viz.

That in our importunity and extraordinary offices for others, we must not make our accounts by multitude of words, and long prayers, but by the measures of the spirit, by the holiness of the soul, and the justness of the desire, and the usefulness of the request, and its order to God's glory, and its place in the order of providence, and the sincerity of our heart, and the charity of our wishes, and the perseverance of our advocation. There are some (as Tertullian observes), "Qui loquacitatem facundiam existimant, et impudentiam constantiam deputant;" " they are praters and they are impudent, and they call that constancy and impor-

tunity :" concerning which, the advice is easy : many words
or few are extrinsical to the nature, and not at all considered
in the effects of prayer; but much desire, and much holiness,
are essential to its constitution; but we must be very curious, that our importunity do not degenerate into impudence
and rude boldness. Capitolinus said of Antonius the emperor and philosopher, " Sane quamvis esset constans, erat
etiam verecundus ;" " he was modest even when he was most
pertinacious in his desires." So must we; though we must
not be ashamed to ask for whatsoever we need, " Rebus
semper pudor absit in arctis :" and in this sense it is true,
that Stasimus in the comedy said concerning meat, " Vere-
cundari neminem apud mensam decet, Nam ibi de divinis et
humanis cernitur :" " men must not be bashful so as to lose
their meat; for that is a necessary that cannot be dispensed
withal :" so it is in our prayers; whatsoever our necessity
calls to us for, we must call to God for; and he is not pleased
with that rusticity or fond modesty of being ashamed to ask
of God any thing, that is honest and necessary; yet our
importunity hath also bounds of modesty, but such as are
to be expressed with other significations; and he is rightly
modest towards God, who, without confidence in himself,
but not without confidence in God's mercy, or without great
humility of person, and reverence of address, presents his
prayers to God as earnestly as he can; provided always,
that in the greatest of our desires, and holy violence, we
submit to God's will, and desire him to choose for us. Our
modesty to God in prayers hath no other measures but these:
1. Distrust of ourselves: 2. Confidence in God: 3. Humility
of person: 4. Reverence of address: and, 5. Submission to
God's will. These are all, unless you also will add that of
Solomon, " Be not rash with thy mouth, and let not thy
heart be hasty to utter a thing before God; for God is in
heaven, and thou upon earth; therefore let thy words be few."
These things being observed, let your importunity be as
great as it can; it is still the more likely to prevail, by how
much it is the more earnest, and signified and represented
by the most offices extraordinary.

3. The last great advantage towards a prevailing intercession for others, is, that the person, that prays for his
relatives, be a person of an extraordinary dignity, employ-

ment, or designation. For God hath appointed some persons and callings of men to pray for others, such are fathers for their children, bishops for their dioceses, kings for their subjects, and the whole order ecclesiastical for all the men and women in the Christian church. And it is well it is so; for, as things are now, and have been too long, how few are there that understand it to be their duty, or part of their necessary employment, that some of their time, and much of their prayers, and an equal portion of their desires, be spent upon the necessities of others. All men do not think it necessary, and fewer practise it frequently, and they but coldly, without interest and deep resentment: it is like the compassion we have in other men's miseries, we are not concerned in it, and it is not our case, and our hearts ache not when another man's children are made fatherless, or his wife a sad widow: and just so are our prayers for their relief: if we thought their evils to be ours,—if we and they, as members of the same body, had sensible and real communications of good and evil,—if we understood what is really meant by being " members one of another," or if we did not think it a spiritual word of art, instrumental only to a science, but no part of duty, or real relation,—surely we should pray more earnestly one for another than we usually do. How few of us are troubled, when he sees his brother wicked, or dishonourably vicious? Who is sad and melancholy, when his neighbour is almost in hell? when he sees him grow old in iniquity? How many days have we set apart for the public relief and interests of the kingdom? How earnestly have we fasted, if our prince be sick or afflicted? What alms have we given for our brother's conversion? Or if this be great, how importunate and passionate have we been with God by prayer in his behalf, by prayer and secret petition? But, however, though it were well, very well, that all of us would think of this duty a little more; because, besides the excellency of the duty itself, it would have this blessed consequent, that for whose necessities we pray, if we do desire earnestly they should be relieved, we would, whenever we can and in all we can, set our hands to it; and if we pity the orphan-children, and pray for them heartily, we would also, when we could, relieve them charitably: but though it were therefore very well, that things were thus

with all men, yet God, who takes care of us all, makes provision for us in special manner; and the whole order of the
clergy are appointed by God to pray for others, to be ministers of Christ's priesthood, to be followers of his advocation, to stand between God and the people, and to present
to God all their needs, and all their desires. That this God
hath ordained and appointed, and that this rather he will
bless and accept, appears by the testimony of God himself,
for he only can be witness in this particular, for it depends
wholly upon his gracious favour and acceptation. It was
the case of Abraham and Abimelech: " Now, therefore,
restore the man his wife, for he is a prophet, and he will
pray for thee, and thou shalt live[d];" and this caused confidence in Micah: " Now know I that the Lord will do me
good, seeing I have a Levite to my priest[e]:" meaning that
in his ministry, in the ministry of priests, God hath established the alternate returns of blessing and prayers, the intercourses between God and his people; and through the
descending ages of the synagogue it came to be transmitted
also to the Christian church, that the ministers of religion
are advocates for us under Christ, by " the ministry of reconciliation," by their dispensing the holy sacraments, by
" the keys of the kingdom of heaven," by baptism and the
Lord's supper, by " binding and loosing," by " the word of
God and prayer;" and, therefore, saith St. James, " If any
man be sick among you, let him send for the elders of the
church, and let them pray over him[f]:" meaning that God
hath appointed them especially, and will accept them in
ordinary and extraordinary; and this is that which is meant
by blessing. A father blesses his child, and Solomon blessed
his people, and Melchisedec the priest blessed Abraham,
and Moses blessed the sons of Israel, and God appointed
the Levitical priests to " bless the congregation;" and this
is more than can be done by the people; for though they
can say the same prayer, and the people pray for their kings,
and children for their parents, and the flock for the pastor,
yet they cannot bless him as he blesseth them; " for the
less is blessed of the greater, and not the greater of the
less;" and this is " without all contradiction," said St.
Paul[g]: the meaning of the mystery is this, That God hath

appointed the priest to pray for the people, and because he hath made it to be his ordinary office and employment, he also intends to be seen in that way, which he hath appointed, and chalked out for us; his prayer, if it be "found in the way of righteousness," is the surer way to prevail in his intercessions for the people.

But upon this stock comes in the greatest difficulty of the text: for if "God heareth not sinners," there is an infinite necessity, that the ministers of religion should be very holy: for all their ministries consist in preaching and praying; to these two are reducible all the ministries ecclesiastical, which are of Divine institution: so the apostles summed up their employment: " But we will give ourselves continually to prayer, and to the ministry of the word[b]:" to exhort, to reprove, to comfort, to cast down, to determine cases of conscience, and to rule in the church by " the word of their proper ministry;" and the very making laws ecclesiastical, is the ministry of the word; for so their dictates pass into laws by being duties enjoined by God, or the acts, or exercises, or instruments of some enjoined graces. To prayer is reduced " administration of the sacraments;" but " binding and loosing," and " visitation of the sick," are mixed offices, partly relating to one, partly to the other. Now although the word of God preached will have a great effect, even though it be preached by an evil minister, a vicious person; yet it is not so well there, as from a pious man, because by prayer also his preaching is made effectual, and by his good example his homilies and sermons are made active; and therefore it is very necessary in respect of this half of the minister's office, ' the preaching of the word,' he be a good man; unless he be, much perishes to the people, most of the advantages are lost. But then for the other half, all those ministries which are by way of prayer, are rendered extremely invalid, and ineffectual, if they be ministered by an evil person. For upon this very stock it was that St. Cyprian affirmed, that none were to be chosen to the ministry but " immaculati et integri antistites, ' holy and upright men,' who, offering their sacrifices worthily to God and holily, may be heard in their prayers, which they make for the safety of the Lord's people[i]." But he presses this caution to

[b] Acts, vi. 4.   [i] Lib. i. Ep. 4.

a farther issue: that it is not only necessary to choose holy persons to these holy ministries for fear of losing the advantages of a sanctified ministry, but also that the people may not be guilty of an evil communion, and a criminal state of society. " Nec enim sibi plebs blandiatur, quasi immunis a contagione delicti esse possit, cum sacerdote peccatore communicans; ' The people cannot be innocent if they communicate with a vicious priest:' for so said the Lord by the prophet Hosea, Sacrificia eorum panis luctûs; for ' their sacrifices are like bread of sorrow,' whosoever eats thereof shall be defiled." The same also he says often and more vehemently, *ibid. et lib.* 4. *ep.* 2. But there is yet a farther degree of this evil. It is not only a loss, and also criminal to the people to communicate with a minister of a notorious evil life and scandalous, but it is affirmed by the doctors of the church to be wholly without effect; and their prayers are sins, their sacraments are null and ineffective, their communions are without consecration, their hand is χεὶρ ἄκυρος, " a dead hand," the blessings vain, their sacrifices rejected, their ordinations imperfect, their order is vanished, their character is extinguished, and the Holy Ghost will not descend upon the mysteries, when he is invocated by unholy hands, and unsanctified lips. This is a sad story, but it is expressly affirmed by Dionysius, by St. Jerome upon the second chapter of Zephaniah[k], affirming that they do wickedly, who affirm " Eucharistiam imprecantis facere verba, non vitam; et necessariam esse tantum solennem orationem et non sacerdotum merita:" " that the eucharist is consecrated by the word and solemn prayer, and not by the life and holiness of the priest;" and by St. Gelasius[l], by the author of the imperfect work attributed to St. Chrysostom[m], who quotes the eighth book of the Apostolical Constitutions for the same doctrine; the words of which in the first chapter are so plain, that Bovius[n] and Sixtus Senensis[o] accuse both the author of the Apostolical Constitutions, and St. Jerome, and the author of these homilies, to be guilty of the doctrine of John Huss, who for the crude delivery of this truth was sentenced by the council of Constance. To the same sense

[k] Ad Demo.   [l] 1. q. 1. c. sacro sancta.   [m] Homil. 53.
[n] In Scholiis ad hunc locum.   [o] Lib. vi. A. D. 108. Biblioth.

and signification of doctrine is that, which is generally agreed upon by almost all persons; that he that enters into his ministry by simony, receives nothing but a curse, which is expressly affirmed by Petrus Damiani[p], and Tarasius[q] the patriarch of Constantinople, by St. Gregory[r], and St. Ambrose[s].

For if the Holy Ghost leaves polluted temples and unchaste bodies, if he takes away his grace from them that abuse it, if the Holy Ghost would not have descended upon Simon Magus at the prayer of St. Peter, if St. Peter had taken money for him; it is but reasonable to believe, the Holy Ghost will not descend upon the simoniacal, unchaste concubinaries, schismatics, and scandalous priests, and excommunicate. And beside the reasonableness of the doctrine, it is also farther affirmed by the council of Neocæsarea, by St. Chrysostom[t], Innocentius[u], Nicholaus the first[v], and by the Master of the Sentences upon the saying of God by the prophet Malachi, i. " Maledicam benedictionibus vestris," " I will curse your blessings :" upon the stock of these scriptures, reasons, and authorities, we may see how we are to understand this advantage of intercession. The prayer and offices of the holy ministers are of great advantages for the interest of the people; but if they be ministered to by evil men, by vicious and scandalous ministers, this extraordinary advantage is lost, they are left to stand alone or to fall by their own crimes ; so much as is the action of God, and so much as is the piety of the man that attends and prays in the holy place with the priest, so far he shall prevail, but no farther ; and, therefore, the church hath taught her ministers to pray thus in their preparatory prayer to consecration; " Quoniam me peccatorem inter te et eundem populum medium esse voluisti, licèt in me boni operis testimonium non agnoscas, officium dispensationis creditæ non recuses, nec per me, indignum famulum tuum, eorum salutis pereat pretium, pro quibus victima factus salutaris, dignatus es fieri redemptio." For we must know, that God hath not put the salvation of any man into the power of another. And although the church of Rome, by calling the priest's actual intention

p Ep. 16. Biblioth. pp. tom. 3. n. 19.   q Decret. 1. q. 1. ad. c. eos qui.
r Lib. vi. regist. 5. in decretis et l. vii. c. 120.   s De dignit. sacerd. c. 5.
t Cap. 9. orat. 4. de sacerd.   u 1. in ep. 20. hom. 1. part. 2. ep. 27.
v Ep. 9. tom. 3. ad Micael. imperator. d. in 4. dist. 13.

simply necessary, and the sacraments also indispensably
necessary, hath left it in the power of every curate to damn
very many of his parish; yet it is otherwise with the accounts of truth, and the Divine mercy; and, therefore, he
will never exact the sacraments of us by the measures and
proportions of an evil priest, but by the piety of the com-
municant, by the prayers of Christ, and the mercies of God.
But although the greatest interest of salvation depends not
upon this ministry; yet, as by this we receive many advantages, if the minister be holy: so, if he be vicious, we lose all
that which could be conveyed to us by his part of the holy
ministration; every man and woman in the assembly prays
and joins in the effect, and for the obtaining the blessing;
but the more vain persons are assembled, the less benefits
are received, even by good men there present: and, therefore, much is the loss, if a wicked priest ministers, though
the sum of affairs is not entirely turned upon his office or
default; yet many advantages are. For we must not think,
that the effect of the sacraments is indivisibly done at once,
or by one ministry; but they operate by parts, and by moral
operation, by the length of time, and whole order of piety,
and holy ministries; every man is συνεργὸς τοῦ Θεοῦ, " a
fellow-worker with God," in the work of his salvation; and
as in our devotion, no one prayer of our own alone prevails
upon God for grace and salvation, but all the devotions of
our life are upon God's account for them; so is the blessing
of God brought upon the people by all the parts of their
religion, and by all the assistances of holy people, and by
the ministries, not of one, but of all God's ministers, and
relies finally upon our own faith, and obedience, and the
mercies of God in Jesus Christ; but yet, for want of holy
persons to minister, much diminution of blessing, and a loss
of advantage is unavoidable; therefore, if they have great
necessities, they can best hope, that God will be moved to
mercy on their behalf, if their necessities be recommended
to God by persons of a great piety, of a holy calling, and by
the most solemn offices.

Lastly, I promised to consider concerning the signs of
having our prayers heard: concerning which, there is not
much of particular observation; but if our prayers be according to the warrant of God's word, if we ask according

to God's will things honest and profitable, we are to rely upon the promises ; and we are sure that they are heard; and, besides this, we can have no sign but " the thing signified;" when we feel the effect, then we are sure God hath heard us ; but till then we are to leave it with God, and not to ask a sign of that, for which he hath made us a promise. And yet Cassian hath named one sign, which, if you give me leave, I will name unto you. " It is a sign we shall prevail in our prayers, when the Spirit of God moves us to pray,— ' cum fiducia et quasi securitate impetrandi,' ' with a confidence and a holy security of receiving what we ask*'." But this is no otherwise a sign, but because it is a part of the duty; and trusting in God is an endearing him, and doubting is a dishonour to him; and he that doubts, hath no faith ; for all good prayers rely upon God's word, and we must judge of the effect by providence : for he that asks what is "not lawful," hath made an unholy prayer; if it be lawful and " not profitable," we are then heard, when God denies us ; and if both these be in the prayer, " he that doubts, is a sinner," and then God will not hear him; but beyond this I know no confidence is warrantable; and if this be a sign of prevailing, then all the prudent prayers of all holy men shall certainly be heard ; and because that is certain, we need no farther inquiry into signs.

I sum up all in the words of God by the prophet; " Run to and fro through the streets of Jerusalem, and see, and know, and seek in the broad places thereof, if you can find a man; if there be any that executeth judgment, that seeketh truth, ' virum quærentem fidem,' ' a man that seeketh for faith ;' ' et propitius ero ei,' ' and I will pardon it*'." God would pardon all Jerusalem for one good man's sake; there are such days and opportunities of mercy, when God, at the prayer of one holy person, will save a people; and Ruffinus spake a great thing, but it was hugely true; " Quis dubitet mundum stare precibus sanctorum ?" " the world itself is established and kept from dissolution by the prayers of saints ;" and the prayers of saints shall hasten the day of judgment; and we cannot easily find two effects greater. But there are many other very great ones; for the prayers of holy men appease God's wrath, drive away temptations, and resist and over-

* Collat. ix. c. 23.　　　　　　　　　　x Jer. v. 1.

come the devil: holy prayer procures the ministry and service of angels, it rescinds the decrees of God, it cures sicknesses and obtains pardon, it arrests the sun in its course,
and stays the wheels of the chariot of the moon; it rules
over all God's creatures, and opens and shuts the storehouses
of rain; it unlocks the cabinet of the womb, and quenches
the violence of fire; it stops the mouths of lions, and reconciles our sufferance and weak faculties, with the violence of
torment and sharpness of persecution; it pleases God and
supplies all our needs. But prayer that can do thus much
for us, can do nothing at all without holiness; for " God
heareth not sinners, but if any man be a worshipper of God,
and doth his will, him he heareth."

SERMON VII.

OF GODLY FEAR, &c.

PART I.

*Let us have grace, whereby we may serve God with reverence
and godly fear. For our God is a consuming fire.*—Heb. xii.
part of the 28th and 29th verses.

EXΩMEN τὴν χάριν, so our Testaments usually read it, from
the authority of Theophylact; " Let us have grace," but
some copies read in the indicative mood ἔχομεν, " We have
grace, by which we do serve;" and it is something better
consonant to the discourse of the Apostle. For having enu-
merated the great advantages, which the Gospel hath above
those of the law, he makes an argument ' a majori;' and answers a tacit objection. The law was delivered by angels,
but the Gospel by the Son of God: the law was delivered
from Mount Sinai, the Gospel from Mount Sion, from " the
heavenly Jerusalem:" the law was given with terrors and
noises, with amazements of the standers-by, and Moses
himself, " the minister, did exceedingly quake and fear," and
gave demonstration how infinitely dangerous it was by

breaking that law to provoke so mighty a God, who with his voice did shake the earth; but the Gospel was given by a meek Prince, a gentle Saviour, with a still voice, scarce heard in the streets. But that this may be no objection, he proceeds and declares the terror of the Lord : 'Deceive not yourselves, our Lawgiver appeared so upon earth, and was so truly, but now he is ascended into heaven, and from thence he speaks to us.' " See that ye refuse not him that speaketh; for if they escaped not, who refused him that spake on earth, much more shall not we escape, if we turn away from him that speaketh from heaven[y];" for as God once shook the earth, and that was full of terror, so our Lawgiver shall do, and much more, and be far more terrible, Ἔτι ἅπαξ ἐγὼ σείσω τὸν οὐρανὸν καὶ τὴν γῆν καὶ τὴν θάλασσαν καὶ τὴν ξηράν, said the prophet Haggai, which the Apostle quotes here, he once shook the earth. But "once more I shake;" σείσω, it is in the prophecy, " I *will* shake, not the earth only, but also heaven[z]," with a greater terror than was upon Mount Sinai, with the voice of an archangel, with the trump of God, with a concussion so great, that heaven and earth shall be shaken in pieces, and new ones come in their room. This is an unspeakable and an unimaginable terror: Mount Sinai was shaken, but it stands to this day; but when that shaking shall be, " the things that are shaken, shall be no more; that those things that cannot be shaken, may remain:" that is, not only that the celestial Jerusalem may remain for ever, but that you, who do not turn away from the faith and obedience of the Lord Jesus, you, who cannot be shaken nor removed from your duty, you may remain for ever; that when the rocks rend, and the mountains fly in pieces like the drops of a broken cloud, and the heavens shall melt, and the sun shall be a globe of consuming fire, and the moon shall be dark like an extinguished candle, then you poor men, who could be made to tremble with an ague, or shake by the violence of a northern wind, or be removed from your dwellings by the unjust decree of a persecutor, or be thrown from your estates by the violence of an unjust man, yet could not be removed from your duty, and though you went trembling, yet would go to death for the testimony of a holy cause, and you that would die for your faith, would also live

[y] Heb. xii. 25. [z] ii. 6.

according to it; you shall be established by the power of
God, and supported by the arm of your Lord, and shall in
all this great shaking be unmovable; as the corner-stone of
the gates of the New Jerusalem, you shall remain and abide
for ever. This is your case. And, to sum up the whole
force of the argument, the Apostle adds the words of Moses:
as it was then, so it is true now, " Our God is a consuming
fire*:" he was so to them that brake the law, but he will be
much more to them that disobey his Son; he made great
changes then, but those which remain, are far greater, and
his terrors are infinitely more intolerable; and therefore, although he came not in the spirit of Elias, but with meekness
and gentle insinuations, soft as the breath of heaven, not
willing to disturb the softest stalk of a violet, yet his second
coming shall be with terrors such as shall amaze all the world,
and dissolve it into ruin and à chaos. This truth is of so
great efficacy to make us do our duty, that now we are sufficiently enabled with this consideration. This is the grace
which we have to enable us, this terror will produce fear, and
fear will produce obedience, and " we therefore have grace,"
that is, we have such a motive to make us reverence God and
fear to offend him, that he that dares continue in sin, and refuses to hear him that speaks to us from heaven, and from
thence shall come with terrors, this man despises the grace
of God, he is a graceless, fearless, impudent man, and he
shall find that true in ' hypothesi,' and in his own ruin, which
the Apostle declares in ' thesi,' and by way of caution, and
provisionary terror, " Our God is a consuming fire;" this is
the sense and design of the text.

Reverence and godly fear, they are the effects of this
consideration, they are the duties of every Christian, they
are the graces of God. I shall not press them only to purposes of awfulness and modesty of opinion, and prayers,
against those strange doctrines, which some have introduced
into religion, to the destruction of all manners and prudent
apprehensions of the distances of God and man; such as are
the doctrine of necessity of familiarity with God, and a civil
friendship, and a parity of estate, and an evenness of adoption; from whence proceed rudeness in prayer, flat and

* Deut. iv. 24.

indecent expressions, affected rudeness, superstitious sitting
at the holy sacrament, making it to be a part of religion to
be without fear and reverence; the stating of the question is
a sufficient reproof of this folly; whatsoever actions are
brought into religion without " reverence and godly fear,"
are therefore to be avoided, because they are condemned in
this advice of the Apostle, and are destructive of those effects
which are to be imprinted upon our spirits by the terrors of
the day of judgment. But this fear and reverence, the
Apostle intends, should be a deletery to all sin whatsoever:
φοβερὸν, δηλητήριον· φόβος, φυγή· says the Etymologicum:
" Whatsoever is terrible, is destructive of that thing for
which it is so;" and if we fear the evil effects of sin, let us
fly from it, we ought to fear its alluring face too; let us be
so afraid, that we may not dare to refuse to hear him whose
throne is heaven, whose voice is thunder, whose tribunal is
clouds, whose seat is the right hand of God, whose word is
with power; whose law is given with mighty demonstration
of the Spirit, who shall reward with heaven and joys eternal,
and who punishes his rebels, that will not have him to reign
over them, with brimstone and fire, with a worm that never
dies, and a fire that never is quenched; let us fear him who
is terrible in his judgments, just in his dispensation, secret
in his providence, severe in his demands, gracious in his
assistances, bountiful in his gifts, and is never wanting to us
in what we need; and if all this be not argument strong
enough to produce fear, and that fear great enough to secure
obedience, all arguments are useless, all discourses are vain,
the grace of God is ineffective, and we are dull as the dead
sea; inactive as a rock, and we shall never dwell with God
in any sense, but as " he is a consuming fire," that is, dwell
in everlasting burnings.

Αἰδὼς καὶ εὐλάβεια, Reverence and caution, modesty and fear,
μετὰ εὐλαβείας καὶ δέους, so it is in some copies, with caution
and fear; or if we render εὐλάβεια to be ' fear of punishment,'
as it is generally understood by interpreters of this place,
and is in Hesychius εὐλαβεῖσθαι, φυλάττεσθαι, φοβεῖσθαι, then
the expression is the same in both words, and it is all one
with the other places of Scripture, " Work out your salvation with fear and trembling," degrees of the same duty; and
they signify all those actions and graces, which are the

proper effluxes of fear; such as are reverence, prudence, caution, and diligence, chastity and a sober spirit: εὐλάβεια, σεμνότης, so also say the grammarians; and it means plainly this; since our God will appear so terrible at his second coming, " let us pass the time of our sojourning here in fear[b]," that is, modestly, without too great confidence of our-selves: soberly, without bold crimes, which when a man acts, he must put on shamelessness; reverently towards God, as fearing to offend him; diligently observing his command-ments, inquiring after his will, trembling at his voice, at-tending to his word, reverencing his judgments, fearing to provoke him to anger; for " it is a fearful thing to fall into the hands of the living God." Thus far it is a duty.

Concerning which, that I may proceed orderly, I shall first consider how far fear is a duty of Christian religion. 2. Who and what states of men ought to fear, and upon what reasons. 3. What is the excess of fear, or the obliquity and irregularity whereby it becomes dangerous, penal, and crimi-nal; a state of evil, and not a state of duty.

1. Fear is taken sometimes in Holy Scripture for the whole duty of man, for his whole religion towards God. " And now, Israel, what doth the Lord thy God require of thee, but to fear the Lord thy God[c]," &c. *fear* is *obedience*, and *fear* is *love*, and *fear* is *humility*, because it is the parent of all these, and is taken for the whole duty to which it is an introduction. " The fear of the Lord is the beginning of wisdom, and a good understanding have all they that do thereafter; the praise of it endureth for ever[d];" and " Fear God and keep his commandments, for this is the whole duty of man[e]:" and thus it is also used in the New Testament: " Let us cleanse ourselves from all filthiness of the flesh and spirit, perfecting holiness in the fear of God[f]."

2. *Fear* is sometimes taken for *worship*: for so our blessed Saviour expounds the words of Moses in Matt. iv. 10. taken from Deut. x. 20. " Thou shalt fear the Lord thy God," so Moses; " Thou shalt worship the Lord thy God, and him only shalt thou serve," said our blessed Saviour; and so it was used by the prophet Jonah; " I am a Hebrew, and I fear the Lord the God of heaven[g]," that is, I worship him;

b 1 Pet. i. 17.   c Deut. x. 12.   d Psal. cxi. 10.
e Eccles. xii. 13.   f 2 Cor. vii. 1.   g Jonah, i. 9.

he is the Deity that I adore, that is, my worship and my religion; and because the new colony of Assyrians did not do so, at the beginning of their dwelling there, " they feared not the Lord," that is, they worshipped other gods, and not the God of Israel, therefore God sent lions among them, which slew many of them[b]. Thus far fear is not a distinct duty, but a word signifying something besides itself; and therefore cannot come into the consideration of this text. Therefore, 3. *Fear*, as it is a religious passion, is divided as the two Testaments are; and relates to the old and new covenant, and accordingly hath its distinction. In the law, God used his people like servants; in the Gospel, he hath made us to be sons. In the law, he enjoined many things, hard, intricate, various, painful, and expensive; in the Gospel, he gave commandments, not hard, but full of pleasure, necessary and profitable to our life, and well-being of single persons and communities of men. In the law, he hath exacted those many precepts by the covenant of exact measures, grains and scruples; in the Gospel, he makes abatement for human infirmities, temptations, moral necessities, mistakes, errors, for every thing that is pitiable, for every thing that is not malicious and voluntary. In the law, there are many threatenings, and but few promises, the promise of temporal prosperities branched into single instances; in the Gospel, there are but few threatenings, and many promises: and when God by Moses gave the ten commandments, only one of them was sent out with a promise, the precept of obedience to all our parents and superiors; but when Christ in his first sermon recommended eight duties[i], Christian duties to the college of disciples, every one of them begins with a blessing and ends with a promise, and therefore *grace* is opposed to the *law*[k]. So that, upon these differing interests, the world put on the affections of servants, and sons: they of old feared God as a severe Lord, much in his commands, abundant in threatenings, angry in his executions, terrible in his name, in his majesty and appearance, dreadful unto death; and this the Apostle calls πνεῦμα δουλείας, " the spirit of bondage," or of a servant. But we have not received that Spirit, εἰς φόβον, " unto fear," not a servile fear,

[b] 2 Kings, xvii. 25.   [i] Matt. v. ad v. 10.   [k] John, i. 17. Rom. vi. 14, 15.

" but the Spirit of adoption" and filial fear we must have[1];
God treats like sons, he keeps us under discipline, but designs us to the inheritance: and his government is paternal,
his disciplines are merciful, his conduct gentle, his Son is
our Brother, and our Brother is our Lord, and our Judge is
our Advocate, and our Priest hath felt our infirmities, and
therefore knows how to pity them, and he is our Lord, and
therefore he can relieve them: and from hence we have affections of sons; so that a fear we must not have, and yet a
fear we must have; and by these proportions we understand
the difference: " Malo vereri quàm timeri me à meis," said
one in the comedy, " I had rather be reverenced than feared
by my children." The English doth not well express the
difference, but the Apostle doth it rarely well. For that
which he calls πνεῦμα δουλείας in Rom. viii. 15. he calls
πνεῦμα δειλίας, 2 Tim. i. 7. The spirit of bondage is the
spirit of *timorousness*, or *fearfulness*, rather than *fear;* when
we are fearful that God will use us harshly: or when we
think of the accidents that happen, worse than the things
are, when they are proportioned by measures of eternity:
and from this opinion conceive forced resolutions and unwilling obedience. Χείρους δὲ ὅσοι οὐ δι' αἰδῶ, ἀλλὰ διὰ φόβον
αὐτὸ δρῶσι, καὶ φεύγοντες οὐ τὸ αἰσχρόν, ἀλλὰ τὸ λυπηρὸν, said
Aristotle ; " Good men are guided by reverence, not by fear,
and they avoid not that which is afflictive, but that which is
dishonest;" they are not so good whose rule is otherwise.
But that we may take more exact measures, I shall describe
the proportions of Christian or godly fear by the following
propositions.

1. Godly fear is ever without despair;—because Christian fear is an instrument of duty, and that duty without hope
can never go forward. For what should that man do, who,
like Nausiclides, οὔτε ἔαρ, οὔτε φίλους ἔχει, ' hath neither
spring nor harvest,' friends nor children, rewards nor hopes ?
A man will very hardly be brought to deny his own pleasing
appetite, when for so doing he cannot hope to have recompence; when the mind of a man is between hope and fear, it
is intent upon its work; " At postquam adempta spes est,
lassus, curâ confectus, stupet," " If you take away the hope,

the mind is weary, spent with care, hindered by amazements:" "Aut aliquem sumpserimus temeraria in Deos desperatione," saith Arnobius; "A despair of mercy makes men to despise God:" and the damned in hell, when they shall for ever be without hope, are also without fear; their hope is turned into despair, and their fear into blasphemy, and they curse the fountain of blessing, and revile God to eternal ages. When Dionysius the tyrant imposed intolerable tributes upon his Sicilian subjects, it amazed them, and they petitioned and cried for help and flattered him, and feared and obeyed him carefully; but he imposed still new ones, and greater, and at last left them poor as the valleys of Vesuvius, or the top of Ætna; but then, all being gone, the people grew idle and careless, and walked in the markets and public places, cursing the tyrant, and bitterly scoffing his person and vices; which when Dionysius heard, he caused his publicans and committees to withdraw their impost: for 'now (says he) they are dangerous, because they are desperate,' νῦν γὰρ, ὅτε οὐδὲν ἔχουσιν, καταφρονοῦσιν ἡμῶν. When men have nothing left, they will despise their rulers: and so it is in religion; "Audaces cogimur esse metu." If our fears be unreasonable, our diligence is none at all; and from whom we hope for nothing, neither benefit nor indemnity; we despise his command, and break his yoke, and trample it under our most miserable feet: and therefore, Æschylus calls these people Θερμοὺς, 'hot,' mad, and furious, careless of what they do, and he opposes them to pious and holy people. Let your confidence be allayed with fear, and your fear be sharpened with the intertextures of a holy hope, and the active powers of our souls are furnished with feet and wings, with eyes and hands, with consideration and diligence, with reason and encouragements: but despair is part of the punishment that is in hell, and the devils still do evil things, because they never hope to receive a good, nor find a pardon.

2. Godly fear must always be with honourable opinion of God,—without disparagements of his mercies, without quarrellings at the intrigues of his providence, or the rough ways of his justice; and therefore it must be ever relative to ourselves and our own failings and imperfections.

Θαρσεῖτ'· νύσσα Ζεὺς αὐχένα λαβὼν ἔχει.

' God never walks perversely towards us, unless we walk
crookedly towards him:' and therefore persons,—that only consider the greatness and power of God, and dwell for ever in the
meditation of those severe executions, which are transmitted
to us by story, or we observe by accident and conversation,
—are apt to be jealous concerning God, and fear him as an
enemy, or as children fear fire, or women thunder, only because it can hurt them; " Sæpius illud cogitant, quid possit
is, cujus in ditione sunt, quam quid debeat facere" (*Cicero
pro Quinctio*): ' They remember oftener what God can do,
than what he will;' being more affrighted at his judgments,
than delighted with his mercy. Such as were the Lacedæ-
monians, whenever they saw a man grow popular, or wise, or
beloved, and by consequence powerful, they turned him out
of the country: and because they were afraid of the power
of Ismenias, and knew that Pelopidas and Pherenicius and
Androclydes could hurt them, if they listed, they banished
them from Sparta, but they let Epaminondas alone, ὡς διὰ
μὲν φιλοσοφίαν ἀπράγμονα, διὰ δὲ πενίαν ἀδύνατον, ' as being
studious and inactive, and poor, and therefore harmless:' it
is harder when men use God thus, and fear him as the great
justiciary of the world; who sits in heaven, and observes all
we do, and cannot want excuse to punish all mankind.
But this caution I have now inserted for their sakes, whose
schools and pulpits raise doctrinal fears concerning God;
which, if they were true, the greatest part of mankind would
be tempted to think, they have reason not to love God; and
all the other part, that have not apprehended a reason to
hate him, would have very much reason to suspect his severity, and their own condition. Such are they, which say,
That God hath decreed the greatest part of mankind to eternal damnation; and that only to declare his severity, and to
manifest his glory by a triumph in our torments, and rejoicings in the gnashing of our teeth. And they also fear
God unreasonably, and speak no good things concerning
his name, who say, That God commands us to observe laws
which are impossible; that think he will condemn innocent
persons for errors of judgment, which they cannot avoid;
that condemn whole nations for different opinions, which
they are pleased to call heresy; that think God will exact
the duties of a man by the measures of an angel, or will not

make abatement for all our pitiable infirmities. The precepts of this caution are, that we remember God's mercies to be over all his works, that is, that he shews mercy to all his creatures that need it; that God delights to have his mercy magnified in all things, and by all persons, and at all times, and will not suffer his greatest honour to be most of all undervalued; and therefore as he, that would accuse God of injustice, were a blasphemer, so he that suspects his mercy, dishonours God as much, and produces in himself that fear, which is the parent of trouble, but no instrument of duty.

3. Godly fear is operative, diligent, and instrumental, to caution and strict walking:—for so fear is the mother of holy living; and the Apostle urges it by way of upbraiding: "What! do we provoke God to anger? Are we stronger than he[m]?" meaning, 'that if we be not strong enough to struggle with a fever, if our voices cannot outroar thunder, if we cannot check the ebbing and flowing of the sea, if we cannot add one cubit to our stature, how shall we escape the mighty hand of God?' And here, heighten our apprehensions of the Divine power, of his justice and severity, of the fierceness of his anger and the sharpness of his sword, the heaviness of his hand and the swiftness of his arrows, as much as ever you can;' provided the effect pass on no farther, but to make us reverent and obedient: but that fear is unreasonable, servile, and unchristian, that ends in bondage and servile affections, scruple and trouble, vanity and incredulity, superstition and desperation : its proper bounds are "humble and devout prayers," and "a strict and a holy piety" according to his laws, and "glorifications of God," or speaking good things of his holy name; and then it cannot be amiss: we must be full of confidence towards God, we must with cheerfulness rely upon God's goodness for the issue of our souls, and our final interests; but this expectation of the Divine mercy must be in the ways of piety : "Commit yourselves to God in well-doing as unto a faithful Creator[o]." Alcibiades was too timorous; who being called from banishment refused to return, and being asked, If he durst not trust his country, answered, Τὰ μὲν ἄλλα πάντα, περὶ δὲ ψυχῆς τῆς ἐμῆς οὐδὲ τῇ μητρί· μήπως ἀγνοήσασα, τὴν

μέλαιναν ἀντὶ τῆς λευκῆς ἐπενέγκη ψῆφον, "In every thing else, but in the question of his life he would not trust his mother, lest ignorantly she should mistake the black bean for the white, and intending a favour should do him a mischief." We must, we may most safely, trust God with our souls ; the stake is great, but the venture is none at all : for he is our Creator, and he is faithful ; he is our Redeemer, and he bought them at a dear rate ; he is our Lord, and they are his own ; he prays for them to his heavenly Father, and therefore he is an interested person. So that he is a party, and an advocate, and a judge too ; and therefore, there can be no greater security in the world on God's part : and this is our hope, and our confidence : but because we are but earthen vessels under a law, and assaulted by enemies, and endangered by temptations ; therefore it concerns us to fear, lest we make God our enemy, and a party against us. And this brings me to the next part of the consideration ; Who and what states of men ought to fear, and for what reasons? For, as the former cautions did limit, so this will encourage ; those did direct, but this will exercise, our godly fear.

I. I shall not here insist upon the general reasons of fear, which concern every man, though it be most certain, that every one hath cause to fear, even the most confident and holy, because his way is dangerous and narrow, troublesome and uneven, full of ambushes and pitfalls ; and I remember what Polynices said in the tragedy, when he was unjustly thrown from his father's kingdom, and refused to treat of peace but with a sword in his hand, Ἅπαντα γὰρ τολμῶσι δεινὰ φαίνεται, Ὅταν δι' ἐχθρᾶς ποὺς ἀμείβηται χθονός·[a] "Every step is a danger for a valiant man, when he walks in his enemy's country ;" and so it is with us : we are espied by God and observed by angels ; we are betrayed within, and assaulted without ; the devil is our enemy, and we are fond of his mischiefs ; he is crafty, and we love to be abused ; he is malicious, and we are credulous ; he is powerful, and we are weak ; he is too ready of himself, and yet we desire to be tempted ; the world is alluring, and we consider not its vanity ; sin puts on all pleasures, and yet we take it, though it puts us to pain : in short, we are vain, and credulous, and sensual, and trifling ; we are tempted, and tempt ourselves,

[a] Apud Eurip. in Phœnissis.

and we sin frequently, and contract evil habits, and they become second natures, and bring in a second death miserable and eternal: every man hath need to fear, because every man hath weakness, and enemies, and temptations, and dangers, and causes, of his own. But I shall only instance in some peculiar sorts of men, who, it may be, least think of it, and, therefore, have most cause to fear.

1. Are those of whom the Apostle speaks, " Let him that thinketh he standeth, take heed lest he fall[p]." Ἐν ξυνῷ ἰχθύι ἄκανθαι οὐκ ἔνεισιν (ὥς φησιν ὁ Δημόκριτος), said the Greek proverb; " In ordinary fish we shall never meet with thorns, and spiny prickles:" and in persons of ordinary even course of life, we find in it too often, that they have no checks of conscience, or sharp reflections upon their condition; they fall into no horrid crimes, and they think all is peace round about them. But you must know, that as grace is the improvement and bettering of nature, and Christian graces are the perfections of moral habits, and are but new circumstances, formalities, and degrees; so it grows in natural measures by supernatural aids, and it hath its degrees, its strengths and weaknesses, its promotions and arrests, its stations and declensions, its direct sicknesses and indispositions: and there is a state of grace that is next to sin; it inclines to evil and dwells with a temptation; its acts are imperfect, and the man is within the kingdom, but he lives in its borders, and is ' dubiæ jurisdictionis.' These men have cause to fear; these men seem to stand, but they reel indeed, and decline towards danger and death. " Let these men (saith the Apostle) take heed lest they fall," for they shake already; such are persons, whom the Scriptures call " weak in faith." I do not mean new beginners in religion, but such, who have dwelt long in its confines, and yet never enter into the heart of the country; such whose faith is tempted, whose piety does not grow; such who yield a little; people that do all that they can lawfully do, and study how much is lawful, that they may lose nothing of a temporal interest; people that will not be martyrs in any degree, and yet have good affections; and love the cause of religion, and yet will suffer nothing for it: these are such which the Apostle speaks, δοκοῦσιν ἱστάναι, " they think they stand," and

[p] 1 Cor. x. 12.

so they do upon one leg, that is, so long as they are un-tempted; but when the tempter comes, then they fall and bemoan themselves, that by losing peace they lost their in-heritance. There are a great many sorts of such persons: some, when they are full, are content and rejoice in God's providence; but murmur and are amazed, when they fall into poverty. They are chaste, so long as they are within the protection of marriage, but when they return to liberty, they fall into bondage, and complain they cannot help it. They are temperate and sober, if you let them alone at home: but call them abroad, and they will lose their sober thoughts, as Dinah did her honour, by going into new company. These men in these estates think they stand, but God knows they are soon weary, and stand stiff as a cane, which the heat of the Syrian star, or the flames of the sun cannot bend; but one sigh of a northern wind shakes them into the tremblings of a palsy: in this the best advice is, that such persons should watch their own infirmities, and see on which side they are most open, and by what enemies they use to fall, and to fly from such parties, as they would avoid death. But certainly they have great cause to fear, who are sure to be sick when the weather changes; or can no longer retain their possession, but till an enemy please to take it away; or will preserve their honour, but till some smiling temptation ask them to forego it.

2. They also have great reason to fear, whose repentance is broke into fragments, and is never a whole or entire change of life: I mean those, that resolve against a sin, and pray against it, and hate it in all the resolutions of their un-derstanding, till that unlucky period comes, in which they use to act it; but then they sin as certainly, as they will in-fallibly repent it, when they have done: there are a very great many Christians, who are esteemed of the better sort of penitents, yet feel this feverish repentance to be their best state of health; they fall certainly in the returns of the same circumstances, or at a certain distance of time; but, God knows, they do not get the victory over their sin, but are within its power. For this is certain, they who sin and re-pent, and sin again in the same or like circumstances, are in some degree under the power and dominion of sin; when their action can be reduced to an order or a method, to a

rule or a certainty, that oftener hits than fails, that sin is
habitual; though it be the least habit, yet a habit it is;
every course, or order, or method of sin, every constant or
periodical return, every return that can be regularly observed,
or which a man can foresee, or probably foretell, even then
when he does not intend it, but prays against it, every such
sin is to be reckoned, not for a single action, or upon the
accounts of a pardonable infirmity, but it is a combination,
an evil state, such a thing as the man ought to fear concerning himself, lest he be surprised and called from this world,
before this evil state be altered: for if he be, his securities
are but slender, and his hopes will deceive him. It was a
severe doctrine that was maintained by some great clerks
and holy men in the primitive church, " That repentance
was to be but once after baptism:" " One faith, one Lord,
one baptism, one repentance⁹;" all these the Scripture
saith; and it is true, if by repentance we mean the entire
change of our condition; for he that returns willingly to the
state of an unbelieving, or heathen, profane person, entirely
and choosingly, in defiance of, and apostacy from, his religion, cannot be renewed again; as the Apostle twice affirms
in his Epistle to the Hebrews. But then, concerning this
state of apostacy, when it happened in the case, not of faith,
but of charity and obedience, there were many fears and jealousies: they were, therefore, very severe in their doctrines,
lest men should fall into so evil a condition, they enlarged
their fear, that they might be stricter in their duty; and generally this they did believe, that every second repentance
was worse than the first, and the third worse than the second,
and still as the sin returned, the Spirit of God did the less
love to inhabit; and if he were provoked too often, would
so withdraw his aids and comfortable cohabitation, that the
church had little comfort in such children; so said Clemens
Alexandr. Stromat. 2. Αἱ δὲ συνεχεῖς καὶ ἐπάλληλαι ἐπὶ τοῖς
ἁμαρτήμασι μετάνοιαι, οὐδὲν τῶν καθάπαξ μὴ πεπιστευκότων δια-
φέρουσιν· " Those frequent and alternate repentances, that
is, repentances and sinnings interchangeably, differ not from
the conditions of men that are not within the covenant of
grace, from them that are not believers," ἢ μόνῳ τῷ συναισ-
θέσθαι ὅτι ἁμαρτάνουσι, "save only (says he) that these men

perceive, that they sin ;" they do it, more against their conscience than infidels and unbelievers ; and therefore, they
do it with less honesty and excuse, καὶ οὐκ οἶδ᾽ ὁπότερον αὐτοῖς χεῖρον, ἢ τὸ εἰδότα ἁμαρτάνειν, ἢ μετανοήσαντα, ἐφ᾽ οἷς ἥμαρ-
τον, πλημμελεῖν αὖϑις· "I know not which is worse, either to
sin knowingly or willingly ; or to repent of our sin, and sin
it over again." And the same severe doctrine is delivered
by Theodoret in his twelfth book against the Greeks, and is
hugely agreeable to the discipline of the primitive church :
and it is a truth of so great severity, that it ought to quicken
the repentance, and sour the gaieties, of easy people, and
make them fear : whose repentance is, therefore, ineffectual,
because it is not integral or united, but broken in pieces by
the intervention of new crimes ; so that the repentance is
every time to begin anew ; and then let it be considered,
what growth that repentance can make, that is never above
a week old, that is for ever in its infancy, that is still in its
birth, that never gets the dominion over sin. These men, 1
say, ought to fear, lest God reject their persons, and deride
the folly of their new-begun repentances, and at last be
weary of giving them more opportunities, since they approve
all, and make use of none ; their understanding is right, and
their will a slave, their reason is for God, and their affections
for sin ; these men (as the Apostle's expression is) "walk
not as wise, but as fools :" for we deride the folly of those
men, that resolve upon the same thing a thousand times,
and never keep one of those resolutions. These men are
vain and light, easy and effeminate, childish and abused ;
these are they of whom our blessed Saviour said those sad
decretory words, "Many shall seek to enter in, and shall
not be able."

SERMON VIII.

PART II.

THEY have great reason to fear, whose sins are not yet remitted ; for they are within the dominion of sin, within the
kingdom of darkness, and the regions of fear : light makes

us confident; and sin checks the spirit of a man into pusillanimity and cowardice of a girl or a conscious boy: and
they do their work in the days of peace and wealthy fortune,
and come to pay their symbol in a war or in a plague; then
they spend of their treasure of wrath, which they laid up in
their vessels of dishonour: and, indeed, want of fear brought
them to it; for if they had known how to have accounted concerning the changes of mortality, if they could have reckoned right concerning God's judgments falling upon sinners,
and remembered, that themselves are no more to God than
that brother of theirs that died in a drunken surfeit, or was
killed in a rebel war, or was, before his grave, corrupted by
the shames of lust; if they could have told the minutes of
their life, and passed on towards their grave at least in religious and sober thoughts, and considered that there must
come a time for them to die, and "after death comes judgment," a fearful and intolerable judgment,—it would not have
come to this pass, in which their present condition of affairs
does amaze them, and their sin hath made them liable unto
death, and that death is the beginning of an eternal evil. In
this case it is natural to fear; and if men consider their condition, and know that all the felicity, and all the security,
they can have, depends upon God's mercy pardoning their
sins,—they cannot choose but fear infinitely, if they have not
reason to hope that their sins are pardoned. Now concerning this, men indeed have generally taken a course to put
this affair to a very speedy issue. " God is merciful," and
" God forgive me," and all is done: it may be a few sighs,
like the deep sobbings of a man that is almost dead with
laughter, that is, a trifling sorrow, returning upon a man
after he is full of sin, and hath pleased himself with violence,
and revolving only by a natural change from sin to sorrow,
from laughter to a groan, from sunshine to a cloudy day; or,
it may be, the good man hath left some one sin quite, or
some degrees of all sin, and then the conclusion is firm,
he is 'rectus in curia,' his sins are pardoned, he was indeed in
an evil condition, but " now he is purged," he " is sanctified" and clean. These things are very bad: but it is much
worse that men should continue in their sin, and grow old in
it, and arrive at confirmation, and the strength of habitual
wickedness, and grow fond of it; and yet think if they die,

their account stands as fair in the eyes of God's mercy, as St. Peter's, after his tears and sorrow. Our sins are not pardoned easily and quickly ; and the longer and the greater hath been the iniquity, the harder and more difficult and uncertain is the pardon; it is a great progress to return from all the degrees of death to life, to motion, to quickness, to purity, to acceptation, to grace, to contention, and growth in grace, to perseverance, and so to pardon : for pardon stands no where, but at the gates of heaven. It is a great mercy, that signifies a final and universal acquittance. God sends it out in little scrolls, and excuses you from falling by the sword of an enemy, or the secret stroke of an angel in the days of the plague; but these are but little entertainments and enticings of our hopes to work on towards the great pardon, which is registered in the leaves of the book of life. And it is a mighty folly to think, that every little line of mercy signifies glory and absolution from the eternal wrath of God; and therefore, it is not to be wondered at, that wicked men are unwilling to die; it is a greater wonder, that many of them die with so little resentment of their danger and their evil. There is reason for them to tremble, when the judge summons them to appear. When his messenger is clothed with horror, and speaks in thunder; when their conscience is their accuser, and their accusation is great, and their bills uncancelled, and they have no title to the cross of Christ, no advocate, no excuse ; when God is their enemy, and Christ is the injured person, and the Spirit is grieved, and sickness and death come to plead God's cause against the man ; then there is reason, that the natural fears of death should be high and pungent, and those natural fears increased by the reasonable and certain expectations of that anger, which God hath laid up in heaven for ever, to consume and destroy his enemies.

And, indeed, if we consider upon how trifling and inconsiderable grounds most men hope for pardon (if at least that may be called hope, which is nothing but a careless boldness, and an unreasonable wilful confidence), we shall see much cause to pity very many, who are going merrily to a sad and intolerable death. Pardon of sins is a mercy, which Christ purchased with his dearest blood, which he ministers to us upon conditions of an infinite kindness, but yet of great holiness and obedience, and an active living faith; it is a grace, that the most holy persons beg of God with mighty passion, and labour for with a great diligence, and expect with trembling fears, and concerning it many times suffer sadnesses with uncertain souls, and receive it by degrees, and it enters upon them by little portions, and it is broken as their sighs and sleeps. But so have I seen the returning sea enter upon the strand; and the waters, rolling towards the shore, throw up little portions of the tide, and retire as if nature meant to play, and not to change the abode of waters; but still the flood crept by little steppings, and invaded more by his progressions than he lost by his retreat; and having told the number of its steps, it possesses its new portion till the angel calls it back, that it may leave its unfaithful dwelling of the sand: so is the pardon of our sins; it comes by slow motions, and first quits a present death, and turns, it may be, into a sharp sickness; and if that sickness prove not health to the soul, it washes off, and it may be, will dash against the rock again, and proceed to take off the several instances of anger and the periods of wrath, but all this while it is uncertain concerning our final interest, whether it be ebb or flood; and every hearty prayer, and every bountiful alms still enlarges the pardon, or adds a degree of probability and hope; and then a drunken meeting, or a covetous desire, or an act of lust, or looser swearing, idle talk, or neglect of religion, makes the pardon retire; and while it is disputed between Christ and Christ's enemy, who shall be Lord, the pardon fluctuates like the wave, striving to climb the rock, and is washed off like its own retinue, and it gets possession by time and uncertainty, by difficulty and the degrees of a hard progression. When David had sinned but in one instance, interrupting the course of a holy life by one sad calamity, it pleased God to pardon him; but see upon what hard terms: he prayed long and violently, he wept sore, he was humbled in sackcloth and ashes, he ate the bread of affliction and drank his bottle of tears; he lost his princely spirit, and had an amazed conscience; he suffered the wrath of God, and the sword never did depart from his house: his son rebelled, and his kingdom revolted; he fled on foot, and maintained spies against his child; he was forced to send an army against him that was dearer than his own eyes, and to fight against him whom he would not hurt for all the riches of Syria and Egypt; his concubines were defiled by an incestuous mixture, in the face of the sun, before all Israel; and his child, that was the fruit of sin, after a seven days' fever, died, and left him nothing of his sin to shew, but sorrow, and the scourges of the Divine vengeance; and, after all this, God pardoned him finally, because he was for ever sorrowful, and never did the sin again. He that hath sinned a thousand times for David's once, is too confident, if he thinks that all his shall be pardoned at a less rate than was used to expiate that one mischief of the religious king: " the Son of David" died for his father David, as well as he did for us; he was " the Lamb slain from the beginning of the world;" and yet that death, and that relation, and all the heap of the Divine favours, which crowned David with a circle richer than the royal diadem, could not exempt him from the portion of sinners, when he descended into their pollutions. I pray God we may find the " sure mercies of David," and may have our portion in the redemption wrought by the " Son of David;" but we are to expect it upon such terms as are revealed, such which include time, and labour, and uncertainty, and watchfulness, and fear, and holy living. But it is a sad observation, that the case of pardon of sins is so administered, that they, that are most sure of it, have the greatest fears concerning it; and they, to whom it doth not belong at all, are as confident as children and fools, who believe every thing they have a mind to, not because they have reason so to do, but because without it they are presently miserable. The godly and holy persons of the church " work out their salvation with fear and trembling;" and the wicked go to destruction with gaiety and confidence: these men think all is well, while they are " in the gall of bitterness;" and good men are tossed in a tempest, crying and praying for a safe conduct; and the sighs of their fears, and the wind of their prayers, waft them safely to their port. Pardon of sins is not easily obtained; because they who only certainly can receive it, find difficulty, and danger, and fears, in the obtaining it; and therefore, their case is pitiable and deplorable, who, when they have least reason to expect pardon, yet are most confident and careless.

But because there are sorrows on one side, and dangers on the other, and temptations on both sides, it will concern all sorts of men to know, when their sins are pardoned. For then, when they can perceive their signs certain and evident, they may rest in their expectations of the Divine mercies; when they cannot see the signs, they may leave their confidence, and change it into repentance, and watchfulness, and stricter observation; and, in order to this, I shall tell you that which shall never fail you; a certain sign, that you may know whether or no, and when, and in what degree, your persons are pardoned.

1. I shall not consider the evils of sin by any metaphysical and abstracted effects, but by sensible, real, and material. He that revenges himself of another, does something that will make his enemy grieve, something that shall displease the offender as much as sin did the offended; and therefore, all the evils of sin are such as relate to us, and are to be estimated by our apprehensions. Sin makes God angry; and God's anger, if it be not turned aside, will make us miserable and accursed; and therefore, in proportion to this we are to reckon the proportion of God's mercy in forgiveness, or his anger in retaining.

2. Sin hath obliged us to suffer many evils, even whatsoever the anger of God is pleased to inflict; sickness and dishonour, poverty and shame, a caitiff spirit and a guilty conscience, famine and war, plague and pestilence, sudden death and a short life, temporal death or death eternal, according as God in the several covenants of the law and gospel hath expressed.

3. For in the law of Moses, sin bound them to nothing but temporal evils, but they were sore, and heavy, and many; but these only there were threatened: in the Gospel, Christ added the menaces of evils spiritual and eternal.

4. The great evil of the Jews was their abscission and cutting off from being God's people, to which eternal damnation answers amongst us; and as sickness, and war, and other intermedial evils, were lesser strokes, in order to the final anger of God against their nation; so are these and spiritual evils intermedial, in order to the eternal destruction of sinning and unrepenting Christians.

5. When God had visited any of the sinners of Israel

with a grievous sickness, then they lay under the evil of
their sin, and were not pardoned till God took away the
sickness; but the taking the evil away, the evil of the punishment, was the pardon of the sin; " to pardon the sin is
to spare the sinner:" and this appears; for when Christ had
said to the man sick of the palsy, " Son, thy sins are forgiven
thee^r," the pharisees accused him of blasphemy, because
none had power to forgive sins but God only; Christ, to
vindicate himself, gives them an ocular demonstration, and
proves his words: " That ye may know, the Son of Man
hath power on earth to forgive sins, he saith to the man sick
of the palsy, Arise, and walk;" then he pardoned the sin,
when he took away the sickness, and proved the power by
reducing it to act: for if pardon of sins be any thing else, it
must be easier or harder: if it be easier, then sin hath not
so much evil in it as a sickness, which no religion as yet
ever taught: if it be harder, then Christ's power to do that,
which was harder, could not be proved by doing that which
was easier. It remains, therefore, that it is the same thing
to take the punishment away, as to procure or give the pardon; because, as the retaining the sin was an obligation to
the evil of punishment, so the remitting the sin is the dis-
obliging to its penalty. So far then the case is manifest.

6. The next step is this; that, although in the Gospel
God punishes sinners with temporal judgments, and sicknesses, and deaths, with sad accidents, and evil angels, and
messengers of wrath; yet, besides these lesser strokes, he
hath scorpions to chastise, and loads of worse evils to oppress the disobedient: he punishes one sin with another,
vile acts with evil habits, these with a hard heart, and this
with obstinacy, and obstinacy with impenitence, and impenitence with damnation. Now, because the worst of evils,
which are threatened to us, are such which consign to hell
by persevering in sin, as God takes off our love and our
affections, our relations and bondage under sin, just in the
same degree he pardons us; because the punishment of sin
being taken off and pardoned, there can remain no guilt.
Guiltiness is an insignificant word, if there be no obligation
to punishment. Since therefore spiritual evils, and progressions in sin, and the spirit of reprobation, and impenitence,

and accursed habits, and perseverance in iniquity, are the worst of evils ; when these are taken off, the sin hath lost its venom, and appendant curse : for sin passes on to eternal death only by the line of impenitence, and it can never carry us to hell, if we repent timely and effectually ; in the same degree, therefore, that any man leaves his sin, just in the same degree he is pardoned, and he is sure of it : for although curing the temporal evil was the pardon of sins among the Jews, yet we must reckon our pardon by curing the spiritual. If I have sinned against God in the shameful crime of lust, then God hath pardoned my sins, when, upon my repentance and prayers, he hath given me the grace of chastity. My drunkenness is forgiven, when I have acquired the grace of temperance, and a sober spirit. My covetousness shall no more be a damning sin, when I have a loving and charitable spirit ; loving to do good, and despising the world : for every farther degree of sin being a nearer step to hell, and by consequence the worst punishment of sin, it follows inevitably, that according as we are put into a contrary state, so are our degrees of pardon, and the worst punishment is already taken off. And therefore, we shall find, that the great blessing, and pardon, and redemption, which Christ wrought for us, is called " sanctification, holiness," and " turning us away from our sins :" so St. Peter ; " Ye know that you were not redeemed with corruptible things, as silver and gold, from your vain conversation[1];" that is your redemption, that is your deliverance : you were taken from your sinful state ; that was the state of death, this of life and pardon ; and therefore they are made *synonyma* by the same Apostle ; " According as his Divine power hath given us all things that pertain to life and godliness[2]:" ' to live' and 'to be godly,' is all one ; to remain in sin and abide in death, is all one ; to redeem us from sin, is to snatch us from hell ; he that gives us godliness, gives us life, and that supposes the pardon, or the abolition of the rites of eternal death : and this was the conclusion of St. Peter's sermon, and the sum total of our redemption and of our pardon ; " God having raised up his Son, sent him to bless you, in turning away every one of you from your iniquity[3]:" this is the end of Christ's passion and bitter death, the purpose of all his and all our

* 1 Pet. i. 18.　　　† 2 Pet. i. 3.　　　* Acts iii. 26.

preaching, the effect of baptism, purging, washing, sanctifying; the work of the sacrament of the Lord's supper; and the same body that was broken, and the same blood that was shed for our redemption, is to conform us into his image and likeness of living and dying, of doing and suffering. The case is plain: just as we leave our sins, so God's wrath shall be taken from us; as we get the graces contrary to our former vices, so infallibly we are consigned to pardon. If therefore you are in contestation against sin, while you dwell in difficulty, and sometimes yield to sin, and sometimes overcome it, your pardon is uncertain, and is not discernible in its progress; but when sin is mortified, and your lusts are dead, and under the power of grace, and you are " led by the Spirit," all your fears concerning your state of pardon are causeless, and afflictive without reason; but so long as you live at the old rate of lust or intemperance, of covetousness or vanity, of tyranny or oppression, of carelessness or irreligion, flatter not yourselves; you have no more reason to hope for pardon than a beggar for a crown, or a condemned criminal to be made heir-apparent to that prince, whom he would traitorously have slain.

4. They have great reason to fear concerning their condition, who having been in the state of grace, who having begun to lead a good life, and given their names to God by solemn deliberate acts of will and understanding, and made some progress in the way of godliness, if they shall retire to folly, and unravel all their holy vows, and commit those evils, from which they formerly ran as from a fire or inundation; their case hath in it so many evils, that they have great reason to fear the anger of God, and concerning the final issue of their souls. For, return to folly hath in it many evils beyond the common state of sin and death; and such evils, which are most contrary to the hopes of pardon. 1. He that falls back into those sins he hath repented of, does " grieve the Holy Spirit of God, by which he was sealed to the day of redemption." For so the antithesis is plain and obvious: if " at the conversion of a sinner there is joy before the beatified spirits, the angels of God," and that is the consummation of our pardon and our consignation to felicity, then we may imagine how great an evil it is to " grieve the Spirit of God," who is greater than the angels. The children of

Israel were carefully warned, that they should not offend the angel : " Behold, I send an angel before thee, beware of him, and obey his voice; provoke him not, for he will not pardon your transgressions[x]," that is, he will not spare to punish you if you grieve him : much greater is the evil, if we grieve him, who sits upon the throne of God, who is the Prince of all the spirits : and besides, grieving the Spirit of God is an affection, that is as contrary to his felicity, as lust is to his holiness; both which are essential to him. " Tristitia enim omnium spirituum nequissima est, et pessima servis Dei, et omnium spiritus exterminat, et cruciat Spiritum sanctum," said Hennas : "Sadness is the greatest enemy to God's servants; if you grieve God's Spirit, you cast him out;" for he cannot dwell with sorrow and grieving; unless it be such a sorrow, which by the way of virtue passes on to joy and never-ceasing felicity. Now by grieving the Holy Spirit, is meant those things which displease him, doing unkindness to him; and then the grief, which cannot in proper sense seize upon him, will in certain effects return upon us : " Ita enim dico (said Seneca); sacer intra nos Spiritus sedet, bonorum malorumque nostrorum observator et custos; hic prout à nobis tractatus est, ita nos ipse tractat :" " There is a Holy Spirit dwells in every good man, who is the observer and guardian of all our actions; and as we treat him, so will he treat us." " Now we ought to treat him sweetly and tenderly, thankfully and with observation :" " Deus præcepit, Spiritum Sanctum, utpote pro naturæ suæ bono tenerum et delicatum, tranquillitate, et lenitate, et quiete, et pace tractare," said Tertullian de ' Spectaculis.' The Spirit of God is a loving and kind Spirit, gentle and easy, chaste and pure, righteous and peaceable; and when he hath done so much for us as to wash us from our impurities, and to cleanse us from our stains, and straighten our obliquities, and to instruct our ignorances, and to snatch us from an intolerable death, and to consign us to the day of redemption, that is, to the resurrection of our bodies from death, corruption, and the dishonours of the grave, and to appease all the storms and uneasiness, and to " make us free as the sons of God," and furnished with the riches of the kingdom; and all this with

innumerable arts, with difficulty, and in despite of our lusts
and reluctances, with parts and interrupted steps, with wait-
ings and expectations, with watchfulness and stratagems,
with inspirations and collateral assistances; after all this
grace, and bounty, and diligence, that we should despite this
grace, and trample upon the blessings, and scorn to receive
life at so great an expense, and love of God; this is so great
a baseness and unworthiness, that by troubling the tenderest
passions, it turns into the most bitter hostilities; by abusing
God's love it turns into jealousy, and rage, and indignation.
" Go and sin no more, lest a worse thing happen to thee."

2. Falling away after we have begun to live well, is a great
cause of fear; because there is added to it the circumstance
of inexcusableness.   The man hath been taught the secrets
of the kingdom, and therefore his understanding hath been
instructed; he hath tasted the pleasures of the kingdom, and
therefore his will hath been sufficiently entertained.   He was
entered into the state of life, and renounced the ways of
death; his sin began to be pardoned, and his lusts to be
crucified; he felt the pleasures of victory, and the blessings
of peace, and therefore fell away, not only against his reason,
but also against his interest; and to such a person the questions of his soul have been so perfectly stated, and his prejudices and inevitable abuses so clearly taken off, and he was
so made to view the paths of life and death, that if he chooses
the way of sin again, it must be, not by weakness, or the infelicity of his breeding, or the weakness of his understanding, but a direct preference or prelation, a preferring sin
before grace, the spirit of lust before the purities of the soul,
the madness of drunkenness before the fulness of the Spirit,
money before our friend, and above our religion, and heaven,
and God himself.   This man is not to be pitied upon pretence that he is betrayed; or to be relieved, because he is
oppressed with potent enemies; or to be pardoned, because
he could not help it: for he once did help it, he did overcome his temptation, and choose God, and delight in virtue,
and was an heir of heaven, and was a conqueror over sin,
and delivered from death; and he may do so still, and God's
grace is upon him more plentifully, and the lust does not
tempt so strongly; and, if it did, he hath more power to resist it; and therefore, if this man falls, it is because he wil-

fully chooses death, it is the portion that he loves and descends into with willing and unpitied steps. " Quam vilis facta es, nimis iterans vias tuas !" said God to Judah[y].

3. He that returns from virtue to his old vices, is forced to do violence to his own reason, to make his conscience quiet: he does it so unreasonably, so against all his fair inducements, so against his reputation, and the principles of his society, so against his honour, and his promises, and his former discourses and his doctrines, his censuring of men for the same crimes, and the bitter invectives and reproofs which in the days of his health and reason he used against his erring brethren, that he is now constrained to answer his own arguments, he is entangled in his own discourses, he is ashamed with his former conversation; and it will be remembered against him, how severely he reproved, and how reasonably he chastised the lust, which now he runs to in despite of himself and all his friends. And because this is his condition, he hath no way left him, but either to be impudent, which is hard for him at first; it being too big a natural change to pass suddenly from grace to immodest circumstances and hardnesses of face and heart: or else, therefore, he must entertain new principles, and apply his mind to believe a lie; and then begins to argue, 'There is no necessity of being so severe in my life; greater sinners than I have been saved; God's mercies are greater than all the sins of man; Christ died for us, and if I may not be allowed to sin this sin, what ease have I by his death? or, This sin is necessary, and I cannot avoid it; or, It is questionable, whether this sin be of so deep a die as is pretended; or, flesh and blood is always with me, and I cannot shake it off; or, there are some sects of Christians that do allow it, or, if they do not, yet they declare it easily pardonable, upon no hard terms, and very reconcilable with the hopes of heaven; or, the Scriptures are not rightly understood in their pretended condemnations; or else, other men do as bad as this, and there is not one in ten thousand but hath his private retirements from virtue; or else, when I am old, this sin will leave me, and God is very pitiful to mankind.'—But while the man, like an entangled bird, flutters in the net, and wildly discomposes

that which should support him, and that which holds him,
the net and his own wings, that is, the laws of God and his
own conscience and persuasion, he is resolved to do the
thing, and seeks excuses afterward; and when he hath
found out a fig-leaved apron that he could put on, or a cover
for his eyes, that he may not see his own deformity, then he
fortifies his error with irresolution and inconsideration; and
he believes it, because he will; and he will, because it serves
his turn: then he is entered upon his state of fear; and if he
does not fear concerning himself, yet his condition is fearful,
and the man hath νοῦν ἀδόκιμον, " a reprobate mind," that
is, a judgment corrupted by lust: vice hath abused his reasoning, and if God proceeds in the man's method, and lets
him alone in his course, and gives him over to believe a lie,
so that he shall call good evil, and evil good, and come to
be heartily persuaded that his excuses are reasonable, and
his pretences fair,—then the man is desperately undone
" through the ignorance that is in him," as St. Paul describes his condition; " his heart is blind, he is past feeling,
his understanding is darkened," then he may " walk in the
vanity of his mind," and " give himself over to lascivious-
ness," and shall " work all uncleanness with greediness*;"
then he needs no greater misery: this is the state of evil,
which his fear ought to have prevented, but now it is past
fear, and is to be recovered with sorrow, or else to be run
through, till death and hell are become his portion; " fiunt
novissima illius pejora prioribus;" " His latter end is worse
than his beginning*."

4. Besides all this, it might easily be added, that he that
falls from virtue to vice again, adds the circumstance of
ingratitude to his load of sins; he sins against God's mercy,
and puts out his own eyes, he strives to unlearn what with
labour he hath purchased, and despises the trouble of his
holy days, and throws away the reward of virtue for an interest, which himself despised the first day in which he began
to take sober counsels; he throws himself back in the accounts
of eternity, and slides to the bottom of the hill, from whence
with sweat and labour of his hands and knees he had long
been creeping; he descends from the spirit to the flesh, from

<hr>

* Ephes. iv. 17, 18.   * Matt. xii. 45. Vide 2 Pet. ii. 20.

honour to dishonour, from wise principles to unthrifty practices; like one of " the vainer fellows," who grows a fool, and a prodigal, and a beggar, because he delights in inconsideration, in the madness of drunkenness, and the quiet of a lazy and unprofitable life. So that this man hath great cause to fear; and, if he does, his fear is as the fear of enemies and not sons: I do not say, that it is a fear that is displeasing to God; but it is such a one, as may arrive at goodness, and the fear of sons, if it be rightly managed.

For we must know, that no fear is displeasing to God; no fear of itself, whether it be fear of punishment, or fear to offend; the " fear of servants," or the " fear of sons:" but the effects of fear do distinguish the man, and are to be entertained or rejected accordingly. If a servile fear makes us to remove our sins, and so passes us towards our pardon, and the receiving such graces which may endear our duty and oblige our affection; that fear is imperfect, but not criminal; it is " the beginning of wisdom," and the first introduction to it; but if that fear sits still, or rests in a servile mind, or a hatred of God, or speaking evil things concerning him, or unwillingness to do our duty, that which at first was indifferent, or at the worst imperfect, proves miserable and malicious; so we do our duty, it is no matter upon what principles we do it; it is no matter where we begin, so from that beginning we pass on to duties and perfection. If we fear God as an enemy, an enemy of our sins, and of our persons for their sakes, as yet this fear is but a servile fear; it cannot be a filial fear, since we ourselves are not sons; but if this servile fear makes us to desire to be reconciled to God, that he may no longer stay at enmity with us, from this fear we shall soon pass to carefulness, from carefulness to love, from love to diligence, from diligence to perfection; and the enemies shall become servants, and the servants shall become adopted sons, and pass into the society and the participation of the inheritance of Jesus: for this fear is also reverence, and then our God, instead of being " a consuming fire," shall become to us the circle of a glorious crown, and a globe of eternal light.

SERMON IX.

PART III.

I AM now to give account concerning the excess of fear, not directly and abstractedly, as it is a passion, but as it is subjected in religion, and degenerates into superstition : for so among the Greeks, fear is the ingredient and half of the constitution of that folly ; Δεισιδαιμονία, φοβήθεια, said Hesychius, " it is a fear of God." Δεισιδαίμων, δειλὸς, that is more; it is a timorousness : " the superstitious man is afraid of the gods," (said the etymologist) δεδιὼς τοὺς θεοὺς ὥσπερ τοὺς τυράννους, " fearing of God, as if he were a tyrant," and an unreasonable exacter of duty upon unequal terms, and disproportionable, impossible degrees, and unreasonable, and great and little instances.

1. But this fear some of the old philosophers thought unreasonable in all cases, even towards God himself; and it was a branch of the Epicurean doctrine, that God meddled not with any thing below, and was to be loved and admired, but not feared at all; and therefore they taught men neither to fear death, nor to fear punishment after death, nor any displeasure of God : " His terroribus ab Epicuro soluti non metuimus Deos," said Cicero[b]; and thence came this acceptation of the word, that superstition should signify ' an unreasonable fear of God :' it is true, he and all his scholars extended the case beyond the measure, and made all fear unreasonable; but then if we, upon grounds of reason and Divine revelation, shall better discern the measure of the fear of God; whatsoever fear we find to be unreasonable, we may by the same reason call it superstition, and reckon it criminal, as they did all fear; that it may be called superstition, their authority is sufficient warrant for the grammar of the appellative; and that it is criminal, we shall derive from better principles.

But, besides this, there was another part of its definition, Δεισιδαίμων, ὁ τὰ εἴδωλα σίβων· εἰδωλολάτρης, " The superstitious man is also an idolater," δειλὸς παρὰ Θεοὺς, " one that is afraid of something besides God." The Latins, according to their custom, imitating the Greeks in all their learned notices of things, had also the same conception of this, and by their word *superstitio* understood ' the worship of demons,' or separate spirits ; by which they meant, either their *minores Deos*, or else their ἥρωας ἀποθεωθέντας, ' their braver personages, whose souls were supposed to live after death ;' the fault of this was the object of their religion : they gave a worship or a fear, to whom it was not due ; for whenever they worshipped the great God of heaven and earth, they never called that superstition in an evil sense, except the Ἄθεοι, ' they that believed there was no God at all.' Hence came the etymology of superstition : it was a worshipping or fearing the spirits of their dead heroes, " quos superstites credebant," " whom they thought to be alive" after their ἀποθέωσις, or deification, " quos superstantes credebant," " standing in places and thrones above us ;" and it alludes to that admirable description of old age, which Solomon made beyond all the rhetoric of the Greeks and Romans ; " Also they shall be afraid of that which is high, and fears shall be in the way[c];" intimating the weakness of old persons, who, if ever they have been religious, are apt to be abused into superstition; they are " afraid of that which is high ;" that is, of spirits, and separate souls of those excellent beings, which dwell in the regions above ; meaning, that then they are superstitious. However, fear is most commonly its principle, always its ingredient. For if it enter first by credulity and a weak persuasion, yet it becomes incorporated into the spirit of the man, and thought necessary, and the action it persuades to, dares not be omitted, for fear of evil themselves dream of : upon this account the sin is reducible to two heads : the 1. is superstition of an undue object; 2. superstition of an undue expression to a right object.

1. Superstition of an undue object, is that which the etymologist calls τῶν εἰδώλων σέβασμα, " the worshipping of idols ;" the Scripture adds Θύειν δαιμονίοις, " a sacrificing to demons[d]" in St. Paul, and in Baruch; where, although we usually read it " sacrificing to devils," yet it was but

accidental that they were such; for those indeed were evil
spirits who had seduced them, and tempted them to such
ungodly rites (and yet they who were of the Pythagorean
sect, pretended a more holy worship, and did their devotion
to angels); but whosoever shall worship angels, do the same
thing; they worshipped them because they are good and
powerful, as the Gentiles did the devils, whom they thought
so; and the error which the Apostle reproves, was not in
matter of judgment, in mistaking bad angels for good, but
in matter of manners and choice; they mistook the creature
for the Creator; and therefore, it is more fully expressed
by St. Paul, in a general signification, " they worshipped
the creature," παρὰ τὸν κτίσαντα, " besides the Creator[f];" so it
should be read; if we worship any creature besides God,
worshipping so as the worship of him becomes a part of religion, it is also a direct superstition; but, concerning this
part of superstition, I shall not trouble this discourse, because I know no Christians blamable in this particular but
the church of Rome, and they that communicate with her in
the worshipping of images, of angels, and saints, burning
lights and perfumes to them, making offerings, confidences,
advocations and vows to them; and direct and solemn Divine worshipping the symbols of bread and wine, when they
are consecrated in the holy sacrament. These are direct
superstition, as the word is used by all authors, profane and
sacred, and are of such evil report, that wherever the word
superstition does signify any thing criminal, these instances
must come under the definition of it. They are λατρεία
τῆς κτίσεως, λατρεία παρὰ τὸν κτίσαντα, " cultus supersti-
tum" " cultus dæmonum;" and therefore, besides that they
have ἴδιον ἔλεγχον, ' a proper reproof' in Christian religion, are condemned by all wise men which call superstition
criminal.

But as it is superstition to worship any thing παρὰ τὸν
κτίσαντα, " besides the Creator:" so it is superstition to
worship God παρὰ τὸ εὔσχημον, παρὰ τὸ πρέπον, παρ' ὃ δεῖ,
" otherwise than is decent, proportionable, or described."
Every inordination of religion, that is not in defect, is properly called superstition: ὁ μὲν εὐσεβὴς φίλος θεῷ, ὁ δὲ δεισιδαίμων κόλαξ θεοῦ, said Maximus Tyrius; "The true wor-

[f] Rom. i. 25.

shipper is a lover of God, the superstitious man loves him not, but flatters." To which if we add, that fear, unreasonable fear, is also superstition, and an ingredient in its definition, we are taught by this word to signify all irregularity and inordination in actions of religion. The sum is this: the atheist called all worship of God superstition; the Epicurean called all fear of God superstition, but did not condemn his worship; the other part of wise men called all unreasonable fear and inordinate worship superstition, but did not condemn all fear: but the Christian, besides this, calls every error in worship, in the manner, or excess, by this name, and condemns it.

Now because the three great actions of religion are, ' to worship God,' 'to fear God,' and 'to trust in him,' by the inordination of these three actions, we may reckon three sorts of this crime; 'the excess of fear,' and 'the obliquity in trust,' and 'the errors in worship,' are the three sorts of superstition: the first of which is only pertinent to our present consideration.

1. Fear is the duty we owe to God, as being the God of power and justice, the great Judge of heaven and earth, the avenger of the cause of widows, the patron of the poor, and the advocate of the oppressed, a mighty God and terrible: and so essential an enemy to sin, that he spared not his own Son, but gave him over to death, and to become a sacrifice, when he took upon him our nature, and became a person obliged for our guilt. Fear is the great bridle of intemperance, the modesty of the spirit, and the restraint of gaieties and dissolutions; it is the girdle to the soul, and the handmaid to repentance; the arrest of sin, and the cure or antidote to the spirit of reprobation; it preserves our apprehensions of the Divine Majesty, and hinders our single actions from combining to sinful habits; it is the mother of consideration, and the nurse of sober counsels; and it puts the soul to fermentation and activity, making it to pass from trembling to caution, from caution to carefulness, and carefulness to watchfulness, from thence to prudence; and, by the gates and progresses of repentance, it leads the soul on to love, and to felicity, and to joys in God, that shall never cease again. Fear is the guard of a man in the day's prosperity, and it stands upon the watch-towers and spies the approaching danger, and gives warning to them that laugh loud, and

feast in the chambers of rejoicing, where a man cannot consider by reason of the noises of wine, and jest, and music: and if prudence takes it by the hand, and leads it on to duty, it is a state of grace, and a universal instrument to infant religion, and the only security of the less perfect persons ; and, in all senses, is that homage we owe to God, who sends often to demand it, even then, when he speaks in thunder, or smites by a plague, or awakens us by threatenings, or discomposes our easiness by sad thoughts, and tender eyes, and fearful hearts, and trembling considerations.

But this so excellent grace is soon abused in the best and most tender spirits ; in those who are softened by nature and by religion, by infelicities or cares, by sudden accidents or a sad soul ; and the devil observing, that fear, like spare diet, starves the fevers of lust, and quenches the flames of hell, endeavours to heighten this abstinence so much as to starve the man, and break the spirit into timorousness and scruple, sadness and unreasonable tremblings, credulity and trifling observation, suspicion and false accusations of God ; and then vice, being turned out at the gate, returns in at the postern, and does the work of hell and death by running too inconsiderately in the paths, which seem to lead to heaven. But so have I seen a harmless dove, made dark with an artificial night, and her eyes sealed and locked up with a little quill, soaring upward and flying with amazement, fear, and an undiscerning wing ; she made towards heaven, but knew not, that she was made a train and an instrument, to teach her enemy to prevail upon her and all her defenceless kindred : so is a superstitious man, zealous and blind, forward and mistaken, he runs towards heaven as he thinks, but he chooses foolish paths ; and out of fear takes any thing that he is told ; or fancies and guesses concerning God by measures taken from his own diseases and imperfections.   But fear, when it is inordinate, is never a good counsellor, nor makes a good friend ; and he that fears God as his enemy, is the most completely miserable person in the world.   For if he with reason believes God to be his enemy, then the man needs no other argument to prove that he is undone than this, that the fountain of blessing (in this state in which the man is) will never issue any thing upon him but cursings.   But if he fears this without reason, he makes his fears true by the very suspicion of God, doing him dishonour, and then doing those fond and trifling acts of jealousy, which will make God to be what the man feared he already was. We do not know God, if we can think any hard thing concerning him. If God be merciful, let us only fear to offend him ; but then let us never be fearful, that he will destroy us, when we are careful not to displease him. There are some persons so miserable and scrupulous, such perpetual tormentors of themselves with unnecessary fears, that their meat and drink is a snare to their consciences ; if they eat, they fear they are gluttons ; if they fast, they fear they are hypocrites ; and if they would watch, they complain of sleep as of a deadly sin ; and every temptation, though resisted, makes them cry for pardon ; and every return of such an accident makes them think God is angry ; and every anger of God will break them in pieces.

These persons do not believe noble things concerning God ; they do not think, that he is as ready to pardon them, as they are to pardon a sinning servant ; they do not believe how much God delights in mercy, nor how wise he is to consider and to make abatement for our unavoidable infirmities ; they make judgment of themselves by the measures of an angel, and take the account of God by the proportions of a tyrant. The best that can be said concerning such persons is, that they are hugely tempted, or hugely ignorant. For although 'ignorance' is by some persons named the 'mother of devotion ;' yet, if it falls in a hard ground, it is the 'mother of atheism ;' if in a soft ground, it is the 'parent of superstition ;' but if it proceeds from evil or mean opinions of God (as such scruples and unreasonable fears do many times), it is an evil of a great impiety, and, in some sense, if it were in equal degrees, is as bad as atheism : for so he that says, There was no such man as Julius Cæsar, does him less displeasure, than he that says, There was, but that he was a tyrant, and a bloody parricide. And the Cimmerians were not esteemed impious for saying, that there was no sun in the heavens ; but Anaxagoras was esteemed irreligious for saying, the sun was a very stone : and though to deny there is a God is a high impiety and intolerable, yet he says worse, who, believing there is a God, says, He delights in human sacrifices, in miseries, and death, in tormenting his servants, and punishing their very infelicities and unavoidable mischances. To be God, and to be essentially and infinitely good, is the same thing; and therefore, to deny either is to be reckoned among the greatest crimes in the world.

Add to this, that he that is afraid of God, cannot in that disposition love him at all ; for what delight is there in that religion, which draws me to the altar as if I were going to be sacrificed, or to the temple as to the dens of bears ? " Oderunt quos metuunt, sed colunt tamen:" "Whom men fear, they hate certainly, and flatter readily, and worship timorously ;" and he that saw Hermolaus converse with Alexander, and Pausanias follow Philip the Macedonian, or Chæreas kissing the feet of Caius Caligula, would have observed how sordid men are made with fear, and how unhappy and how hated tyrants are in the midst of those acclamations, which are loud, and forced, and unnatural, and without love or fair opinion. And therefore, although the atheist says, " There is no God," the scrupulous, fearful, and superstitious man, does heartily wish what the other does believe.

But that the evil may be proportionable to the folly, and the punishment to the crime, there is no man more miserable in the world than the man who fears God as his enemy, and religion as a snare, and duty intolerable, and the commandments as impossible, and his Judge as implacable, and his anger as certain, insufferable, and unavoidable: whither shall this man go? where shall he lay his burden? where shall he take sanctuary? for he fears the altars as the 'places where his soul bleeds and dies; and God, who is his saviour, he looks upon as his enemy; and, because he is Lord of all, the miserable man cannot change his service, unless it be apparently for a worse. And therefore, of all the evils of the mind, fear is certainly the worst and the most intolerable : levity and rashness have in them some spritefulness, and greatness of action ; anger is valiant; desire is busy and apt to hope; crudelity is oftentimes entertained and pleased with images and appearances : but fear is dull, and sluggish, and treacherous, and flattering, and dissembling, and miserable, and foolish. Every false opinion concerning God is pernicious and dangerous ; but if it be joined with trouble of spirit, as fear, scruple, and superstition are,—it is like a wound with an inflammation, or a strain of a sinew with a contusion or contrition of the part, painful and unsafe; it puts on two actions when itself is driven; it urges reason and circumscribes it, and makes it pitiable and ridiculous in its consequent follies; which, if we consider it, will sufficiently reprove the folly, and declare the danger.

Almost all ages of the world have observed many instances of fond persuasions and foolish practices proceeding from violent fears and scruples in matter of religion. Diomedon and many other captains were condemned to die, because after a great naval victory they pursued the flying enemies, and did not first bury their dead. But Chabrias, in the same case, first buried the dead, and by that time the enemy rallied, and returned, and his navy, and made his masters pay the price of their importune superstition: they feared where they should not, and where they did not, they should. From hence proceeds observation of signs and unlucky days; and the people did so, when the Gregorian account began, continuing to call those unlucky days which were so signified in their tradition or *erra pater*, although the day upon this account fell ten days sooner; and men were transported with many other trifling contingencies and little accidents; which, when they are once entertained by weakness, prevail upon their own strength, and in sad natures and weak spirits have produced effects of great danger and sorrow. Aristodemus, king of the Messenians, in his war against the Spartans, prevented the sword of the enemy by a violence done upon himself, only because his dogs howled like wolves; and the soothsayers were afraid, because the briony grew up by the walls of his father's house: and Nicias, general of the Athenian forces, sat with his arms in his bosom, and suffered himself and forty thousand men tamely to fall by the insolent enemy, only because he was afraid of the labouring and eclipsed moon. When the marble statues in Rome did sweat (as naturally they did against all rainy weather), the augurs gave an alarm to the city; but if lightning struck the spire of the Capitol, they thought the sum of affairs, and the commonwealth itself, was endangered. And this heathen folly hath stuck so close to the Christians, that all the sermons of the church for sixteen hundred years have not cured them all: but the practices of weaker people, and the artifice of ruling priests, have superinduced many new ones. When Pope Eugenius sang mass at Rheims, and some few drops from the chalice were spilt upon the pavement, it was thought to foretell mischief, wars and bloodshed to all Christendom, though it was nothing but carelessness and mischance of the priest : and because Thomas Becket, archbishop of Canterbury, sang the mass of requiem upon the day he was reconciled to his prince, it was thought to foretell his own death by that religious office : and if men can listen to such whispers, and have not reason and observation enough to confute such trifles, they shall still be affrighted with the noise of birds, and every night-raven shall foretell evil as Micaiah to the king of Israel, and every old woman shall be a prophetess, and the events of human affairs, which should be managed by the conduct of counsel, of reason, and religion, shall succeed by chance, by the flight of birds, and the meeting with an evil eye, by the falling of the salt, or the decay of reason, of wisdom, and the just religion of a man.

To this may be reduced the observation of dreams, and fears commenced from the fancies of the night. For the superstitious man does not rest, even when he sleeps ; neither is he safe, because dreams usually are false, but he is afflicted for fear they should tell true. Living and waking men have one world in common, they use the same air and fire, and discourse by the same principles of logic and reason ; but men that are asleep, have every one a world to himself, and strange perceptions ; and the superstitious hath none at all : his reason sleeps, and his fears are waking ; and all his rest, and his very securities, to the fearful man turn into affrights and insecure expectation of evils, that never shall happen ; they make their rest uneasy and chargeable, and they still vex their weary soul, not considering there is no other sleep, for sleep to rest in : and therefore, if the sleep be troublesome, the man's cares be without remedy, till they be quite destroyed. Dreams follow the temper of the body, and commonly proceed from trouble or disease, business or care, an active head and a restless mind, from fear or hope, from wine or passion, from fulness or emptiness, from fantastic remembrances, or from some demon, good or bad : they are without rule and without reason, they are as contingent, as if a man should study to make a prophecy, and by saying ten thousand things may hit upon one true, which was therefore not foreknown, though it was forespoken ; and they have

no certainty, because they have no natural causality nor
proportion to those effects, which many times they are said
to foresignify. The dream of the yolk of an egg importeth
gold (saith Artemidorus); and they that use to remember
such fantastic idols, are afraid to lose a friend when they
dream their teeth shake, when naturally it will rather signify a scurvy; for a natural indisposition and an imperfect
sense of the beginning of a disease, may vex the fancy into
a symbolical representation; for so the man that dreamed
he swam against the stream of blood, had a pleurisy beginning in his side; and he that dreamt he dipped his foot
into water, and that it was turned to a marble, was enticed
into the fancy by a beginning dropsy; and if the events do
answer in one instance, we become credulous in twenty.
For want of reason we discourse ourselves into folly and
weak observation, and give the devil power over us in those
circumstances, in which we can least resist him. Ἐν ὄρφνῃ
δραπέτης μέγα σθένει, "A thief is confident in the twilight[s];" if
you suffer impressions to be made upon you by dreams, the
devil hath the reins in his own hands, and can tempt you by
that, which will abuse you, when you can make no resistance.
Dominica, the wife of Valens the emperor, dreamed, that God
threatened to take away her only son for her despiteful usage
of St. Basil: the fear proceeding from this instance was safe
and fortunate; but if she had dreamed in the behalf of a
heretic, she might have been cozened into a false proposition
upon a ground weaker than the discourse of a waking child.
Let the grounds of our actions be noble, beginning upon
reason, proceeding with prudence, measured by the common
lines o fmen, and confident upon the expectation of a usual
providence. Let us proceed from causes to effects, from
natural means to ordinary events, and believe felicity not to
be a chance but a choice; and evil to be the daughter of sin
and the Divine anger, not of fortune and fancy; let us fear
God, when we have made him angry, and not be afraid of
him, when we heartily and laboriously do our duty; our fears
are to be measured by open revelation and certain experience,
by the threatenings of God and the sayings of wise men,
and their limit is reverence, and godliness is their end; and
then fear shall be a duty, and a rare instrument of many: in

s Eurip. Rhes. 69.

all other cases it is superstition or folly, it is sin or punishment, the ivy of religion, and the misery of an honest and a weak heart; and is to be cured only by reason and good company, a wise guide and a plain rule, a cheerful spirit and a contented mind, by joy in God according to the commandments, that is, " a rejoicing evermore."

2. But, besides this superstitious fear, there is another fear directly criminal, and it is called " worldly fear," of which the Spirit of God hath said, " But the fearful and incredulous shall have their part in the lake that burneth with fire and brimstone, which is the second death[h];" that is, such fears, which make men to fall in the time of persecution, those that dare not own their faith in the face of a tyrant, or in despite of an accursed law. For though it be lawful to be afraid in a storm, yet it is not lawful to leap into the sea; though we may be more careful for our fears, yet we must be faithful too; and we may fly from the persecution till it overtakes us; but when it does, we must not change our religion for our safety, or leave the robe of baptism in the hand of the tempter, and run away by all means. St. Athanasius for forty-six years did run and fight, he disputed with the Arians and fled from their officers; and he that flies, may be a man worth preserving, if he hears his faith along with him, and leaves nothing of his duty behind. But when duty and life cannot stand together, he that then flies a persecution by delivering up his soul, is one that hath no charity, no love to God, no trust in promises, no just estimation of the rewards of a noble contention. " Perfect love casts out fear" (saith the Apostle); that is, he that loves God, will not fear to die for him, or for his sake to be poor. In this sense, no man can fear man and love God at the same time; and when St. Lawrence triumphed over Valerianus, St. Sebastian over Dioclesian, St. Vincentius over Dacianus, and the armies of martyrs over the proconsuls, accusers, and executioners, they shewed their love to God by triumphing over fear, and "leading captivity captive," by the strength of their Captain, whose "garments were red from Bozrah."

3. But this fear is also tremulous and criminal, if it be a trouble from the apprehension of the mountains and difficulties of duty, and is called pusillanimity. For some see themselves

[h] Rev. xxi. 8.

encompassed with temptations, they observe their frequent falls, their perpetual returns from good purposes to weak performances, the daily mortifications that are necessary, the resisting natural appetites, and the laying violent hands upon the desires of flesh and blood, the uneasiness of their spirits, and their hard labours, and therefore this makes them afraid ; and because they despair to run through the whole duty, in all its parts and periods, they think it as good not to begin at all, as after labour and expense to lose the jewel and the charges of their venture. St. Augustine compares such men to children and fantastic persons, affrighted with phantasms and spectres ; " terribiles visu formæ," the sight seems full of horror ; but touch them, and they are very nothing, the mere daughters of a sick brain and a weak heart, an infant experience and a trifling judgment : so are the illusions of a weak piety, or an unskilful confident soul : they fancy to see mountains of difficulty ; but touch them, and they seem like clouds riding upon the wings of the wind, and put on shapes as we please to dream. He that denies to give alms for fear of being poor, or to entertain a disciple for fear of being suspected of the party, or to own a duty for fear of being put to venture for a crown ; he that takes part of the intemperance, because he dares not displease the company, or in any sense fears the fears of the world, and not the fear of God,—this man enters into his portion of fear betimes, but it will not be finished to eternal ages. To fear the censures of men, when God is your judge ; to fear their evil, when God is your defence ; to fear death, when he is the entrance to life and felicity, is unreasonable and pernicious ; but if you will turn your passion into duty, and joy, and security, fear to offend God, to enter voluntarily into temptation ; fear the alluring face of lust, and the smooth entertainments of intemperance ; fear the anger of God, when you have deserved it ; and, when you have recovered from the snare, then infinitely fear to return into that condition, in which whosoever dwells, is the heir of fear and eternal sorrow.

Thus far I have discoursed concerning good fear and bad, that is, filial and servile : they are both good, if by servile we intend initial, or the new beginning fear of penitents ; a fear to offend God upon less perfect considerations : but servile fear is vicious, when it still retains the affection of slaves, and

when its effects are hatred, weariness, displeasure, and want
of charity : and of the same cognations are those fears, which
are superstitious, and worldly.

But to the former sort of virtuous fear, some also add
another, which they call angelical, that is, such a fear as the
blessed angels have, who before God hide their faces, and
tremble at his presence, and "fall down before his footstool,"
and are ministers of his anger and messengers of his mercy,
and night and day worship him with the profoundest adoration.   This is the same that is spoken of in the text: " Let
us serve God with reverence and godly fear;" all holy fear
partakes of the nature of this which divines call angelical,
and it is expressed in acts of adoration, of vows and holy
prayers, in hymns and psalms, in the eucharist and reveren-
tial addresses; and, while it proceeds in the usual measures
of common duty, it is but human ; but as it rises to great
degrees, and to profection, it is angelical and Divine; and
then it appertains to mystic theology, and therefore is to
be considered in another place; but, for the present, that
which will regularly concern all our duty, is this, that when
the fear of God is the instrument of our duty, or God's worship, the greater it is, it is so much the better.   It is an old
proverbial saying among the Romans, " Religentem esse,
oportet; religiosum, nefas;" " Every excess in the actions of
religion is criminal;" they supposing, that, in the services of
their gods, there might be too much.   True it is, there may
be too much of their undecent expressions; and in things indifferent, the very multitude is too much, and becomes an
undecency : and if it be in its own nature undecent or disproportionable to the end, or the rules, or the analogy, of the
religion, it will not stay for numbers to make it intolerable ;
but in the direct actions of glorifying God, in doing any
thing of his commandments, or any thing which he commands, or counsels, or promises to reward, there can never
be excess or superfluity : and therefore, in these cases, do
as much as you can ; take care that your expressions be
prudent and safe, consisting with thy other duties ; and for
the passions or virtues themselves, let them pass from beginning to great progresses, from man to angel, from the
imperfection of man to the perfections of the sons of God ;
and, whenever we go beyond the bounds of nature, and grow

up with all the extension, and in the very commensuration of a full grace, we shall never go beyond the excellences of God: for ornament may be too much, and turn to curiosity; cleanness may be changed into niceness; and civil compliance may become flattery; and mobility of tongue may rise into garrulity; and fame and honour may be great unto envy; and health itself, if it be athletic, may by its very excess become dangerous: but wisdom, and duty, and comeliness, and discipline, a good mind, and the fear of God, and doing honour to his holy name, can never exceed: but if they swell to great proportions, they pass through the measures of grace, and are united to felicity in the comprehensions of God, in the joys of an eternal glory.

SERMON X.

THE FLESH AND THE SPIRIT.

PART I.

The spirit indeed is willing, but the flesh is weak.—Matt. xxvi. 41; latter part.

FROM the beginning of days, man hath been so cross to the Divine commandments, that in many cases there can be no reason given, why a man should choose some ways, or do some actions, but only because they are forbidden. When God bade the Israelites rise and go up against the Canaanites and possess the land, they would not stir; the men were Anakims, and the cities were impregnable; and there was a lion in the way: but, presently after, when God forbade them to go, they would and did go, though they died for it. I shall not need to instance in particulars, when the whole life of man is a perpetual contradiction; and the state of disobedience is called the "contradictions of sinners;" even the man in the Gospel, that had two sons, they both crossed him, even he that obeyed him, and he that obeyed him not: for the one said he would, and did not; the other said he would

not, and did; and so do we: we promise fair, and do nothing;
and they that do best, are such as come out of darkness into
light, such as said "they would not," and at last have better
bethought themselves.   And who can guess at any other
reason, why men should refuse to be temperate? For he that
refuseth the commandment, first does violence to the commandment, and puts on a preternatural appetite; he spoils
his health and he spoils his understanding; he brings to
himself a world of diseases and a healthless constitution;
smart and sickly nights; a loathing stomach and a staring
eye, a giddy brain and a swelled belly, gouts and dropsies;
catarrhs and oppilations.   If God should enjoin men to
suffer all this, heaven and earth should have heard our complaints against unjust laws, and impossible commandments:
for we complain already, even when God commands us to
drink so long as it is good for us; this is one of the impossible laws: it is impossible for us to know when we are dry, or
when we need drink; for if we do know, I am sure it is possible enough, not to lift up the wine to our heads. And when our
blessed Saviour hath commanded us to love our enemies, we
think we have so much reason against it, that God will easily
excuse our disobedience in this case; and yet there are some
enemies, whom God hath commanded us not to love, and those
we dote on, we cherish and feast them, and as St. Paul in another case, "upon our uncomely parts we bestow more abundant comeliness."   For whereas our body itself is a servant
to our soul, we make it an heir of all things, and treat it here
already, as if it were in majority; and make that, which at
the best was but a weak friend, to become a strong enemy;
and hence proceed the vices of the worst, and the follies and
imperfections of the best: the spirit is either in slavery or
in weakness, and when the flesh is not strong to mischief, it
is weak to goodness; and even to the apostles our blessed
Lord said, " The spirit is willing, but the flesh is weak."

"The spirit," that is, ὁ ἔσω ἄνθρωπος, "the inward man,"
or the reasonable part of man, especially as helped by the Spirit
of grace, *that* is willing; for it is the principle of all good
actions, the ἐνεργητικὸν, ' the power of working' is from the
spirit; but the flesh is but a dull instrument, and a broken
arm, in which there is a principle of life, but it moves uneasily; and the flesh is so weak, that in Scripture to be " in

the flesh" signifies a state of weakness and infirmity ; so the humiliation of Christ is expressed by being " in the flesh," Θεὸς φανερωθεὶς ἐν σαρκὶ, " God manifested in the flesh ;" and what St. Peter calls " put to death in the flesh," St. Paul calls " crucified through weakness ;" and " ye know that through the infirmity of the flesh I preached unto you," said St. Paul : but here, flesh is not opposed to the spirit as a direct enemy, but as a weak servant : for if the flesh be powerful and opposite, the spirit stays not there :

———— veniunt ad candida tecta columbæ : (Ovid.)

The old man and the new cannot dwell together; and therefore here, where the spirit inclining to good, well disposed, and apt to holy counsels, does inhabit in society with the flesh, it means only a weak and unapt nature, or a state of infant grace ; for in both these, and in these only, the text is verified.

1. Therefore we are to consider the infirmities of the flesh naturally. 2. Its weakness in the first beginnings of the state of grace, its daily pretensions and temptations, its excuses and lessenings of duty. 3. What remedies there are in the spirit to cure the evils of nature. 4. How far the weakness of the flesh can consist with the Spirit of grace in well-grown Christians. This is the sum of what I intend upon these words.

1. Our nature is too weak, in order to our duty and final interest, that at first it cannot move one step towards God, unless God, by his preventing grace, puts into it a new possibility.

Οὐδὲν ἀκιδνότερον γαῖα τρέφει ἀνθρώποιο,
Πάντων, ὅσσά τι γαῖαν ἐπὶ πνείει τι καὶ ἕρπει. Od. σ. 130.

" There is nothing that creeps upon the earth, nothing that ever God made, weaker than man;" for God fitted horses and mules with strength, bees and pismires with sagacity, harts and hares with swiftness, birds with feathers and a light airy body ; and they all know their times, and are fitted for their work, and regularly acquire the proper end of their creation; but man, that was designed to an immortal duration, and the fruition of God for ever, knows not how to obtain it ; he is made upright to look up to heaven, but he knows no more how to purchase it than to climb it. Once, man went to

make an ambitious tower to outreach the clouds, or the preternatural risings of the water, but could not do it; he cannot
promise himself the daily bread of his necessity upon the
stock of his own wit or industry; and for going to heaven,
he was so far from doing that naturally, that as soon as ever
he was made, he became the son of death, and he knew not
how to get a pardon for eating of an apple against the Divine
commandment: Καὶ ἦμεν φύσει τέκνα ὀργῆς, said the Apostle[1]:
" By nature we are the sons of wrath," that is, we were born
heirs of death, which death came upon us from God's anger
for the sin of our first parents; or by nature, that is, ὄντως,
ἀληθῶς, "really," not by the help of fancy, and fiction of
law, for so Œcumenius and Theophylact expound it[1]; but
because it does not relate to the sin of Adam in its first intention, but to the evil state of sin, in which the Ephesians
walked before their conversion; it signifies, that our nature
of itself is a state of opposition to the Spirit of grace; it is
privatively opposed, that is, that there is nothing in it that
can bring us to felicity; nothing but an obediential capacity;
our flesh can become sanctified, as " the stones can become
children unto Abraham," or as dead seed can become living
corn; and so it is with us, that it is necessary God should
make us a new creation, if he means to save us; he must
take our hearts of stone away, and give us hearts of flesh; he
must purge the old leaven, and make us a new conspersion;
he must destroy the flesh, and must breathe into us 'spiritum vitæ,' the celestial breath of life, without which we can
neither live, nor move, nor have our being. " No man can
come unto me (said Christ), unless my Father draw him:"
ὑπ᾽ ἔρωτος ἁρπασθέντες οὐρανίου, καθάπερ οἱ βακχευόμενοι καὶ
κορυβαντιῶντες ἐνθουσιάζουσι, μέχρις ἂν τὸ ποθούμενον ἴδωσι.
'The Divine love must come upon us and snatch us' from our
imperfection, enlighten our understanding, move and stir our
affections, open the gates of heaven, turn our nature into
grace, entirely forgive our former prevarications, take us by
the hand, and lead us all along; and we only contribute our
assent unto it; just as a child when he is tempted to learn
to go, and called upon, and guided, and upheld, and constrained to put his feet to the ground, lest he feel the danger
by the smart of a fall; just so is our nature, and our state of

[1] Ephes. ii. 3.

flesh. God teaches us and invites us, he makes us willing, and then makes us able, he lends us helps, and guides our hands and feet; and all the way constrains us, but yet so as a reasonable creature can be constrained; that is, made willing with arguments, and new inducements, by a state of circumstances and conditional necessities: and as this is a great glorification of the free grace of God, and declares our manner of co-operation, so it represents our nature to be weak as a child, ignorant as infancy, helpless as an orphan, averse as an uninstructed person, in so great degrees that God is forced to bring us to a holy life, by arts great and many as the power and principles of the creation; with this only difference, that the subject matter and object of this new creation is a free agent: in the first it was purely obediential and passive; and as the passion of the first was an effect of the same power that reduced it to act, so the freedom of the second is given us in our nature by Him, that only can reduce it to act; for it is a freedom that cannot therefore choose, because it does not understand, nor taste, nor perceive, the things of God; and therefore, must by God's grace be reduced to action, as at first the whole matter of the world was by God's almightiness; for so God "worketh in us to will and to do of his own good pleasure." But that I may instance in particulars: Our natural weakness appears best in two things, even in the two great instances of temptations, pleasure, and pain; in both which the flesh is destroyed, if it be not helped by a mighty grace, as certainly as the canes do bow their heads before the breath of a mighty wind.

1. In pleasure we see it by the public miseries and follies of the world. An old Greek said well, Οὐδὲν ἀτεχνῶς ὑγιές ἐστιν, ἀλλά εἰσι τοῦ κέρδους ἅπαντες ἥττονες· "There is amongst men nothing perfect, because men carry themselves as persons that are less than money," servants of gain and interest; we are like the foolish poet that Horace tells of:

> Gestit enim nummum in loculos demittere ; post hoc
> Securus, cadat, an recto stet fabula talo. Ep. 2. 1. 175.

Let him but have money for rehearsing his comedy, he cares not whether you like it or no; and if a temptation of money comes strong and violent, you may as well tie a wild dog to quietness with the guts of a tender kid, as suppose that most

men can do virtuously, when they may sin at a great price.
Men avoid poverty, not only because it hath some inconveniences, for they are few and little; but because it is the
nurse of virtue; they run from it as children from strict parents and tutors, from those that would confine them to reason, and sober counsels, that would make them labour, that
they may become pale and lean, that they may become wise:
but because riches is attended by pride and lust, tyranny and
oppression, and hath in its hand all that it hath in its heart,
and sin waits upon wealth ready dressed and fit for action;
therefore, in some temptations they confess, how little their
souls are, they cannot stand that assault; but because this
passion is the daughter of voluptuousness, and very often
is but a servant-sin, ministering to sensual pleasures, the
great weakness of the flesh is more seen in the matter of
carnal crimes, lust and drunkenness. "Nemo enim se adsuefa-
cit ad vitandum et ex animo evellendum ea, quæ molesta ei
non sunt:" "Men are so in love with pleasure, that they cannot think of mortifying or crucifying their lust; we do violence to what we hate, not to what we love." But the weakness of the flesh, and the empire of lust, are visible in nothing
so much, as in the captivity and folly of wise men. For you
shall see some men fit to govern a province, sober in their
counsels, wise in the conduct of their affairs, men of discourse and reason, fit to sit with princes, or to treat concerning peace and war, the fate of empires and the changes
of the world; yet these men shall fall at the beauty of a
woman, as a man dies at the blow of an angel, or gives up
his breath at the sentence and decree of God. Was not Solomon glorious in all things, but when he bowed to Pharaoh's
daughter, and then to devils? And is it not published by
the sentence and observation of all the world, that the
bravest men have been softened into effeminacy by the
lisping charms and childish noises of women and imperfect
persons? A fair slave bowed the neck of stout Polydamas,
which was stiff and inflexible to the contentions of an enemy:
and suppose a man set, like the brave boy of the king of Ni-
comedia, in the midst of temptation by a witty beauty, tied
upon a bed with silk and pretty violences, courted with
music and perfumes, with promises and easy postures, invited by opportunity and importunity, by rewards and im-

punity, by privacy and a guard; what would his nature do in this throng of evils and vile circumstances? The grace of God secured the young gentleman, and the spirit rode in triumph; but what can flesh do in such a day of danger? Is it not necessary, that we take in auxiliaries from reason and religion, from heaven and earth, from observation and experience, from hope and fear, and cease to be what we are, lest we become what we ought not? It is certain that in the cases of temptations to voluptuousness, a man is naturally, as the prophet said of Ephraim, ' like a pigeon that hath no heart,' no courage, no conduct, no resolution, no discourse, but falls as the water of Nilus when it comes to its cataracts,—it falls infinitely and without restraint: and if we consider, how many drunken meetings the sun sees every day, how many markets, and fairs, and clubs, that is, so many solemnities of drunkenness are at this instant under the eye of heaven, that many nations are marked for intemperance, and that it is less noted because it is so popular, and universal, and that even in the midst of the glories of Christianity there are so many many persons drunk, or too full with meat, or greedy of lust; even now that the Spirit of God is given to us to make us sober, and temperate, and chaste,—we may well imagine, since all men have flesh, and all men have not the Spirit, the flesh is the parent of sin and death, and it can be nothing else.

2. And it is no otherwise, when we are tempted with pain. We are so impatient of pain, that nothing can reconcile us to it; not the laws of God, not the necessities of nature, not the society of all our kindred, and of all the world, not the interest of virtue, not the hopes of heaven; we will submit to pain upon no terms, but the basest and most dishonourable; for if sin bring us to pain, or affront, or sickness, we choose that, so it be in the retinue of a lust, and a base desire; but we accuse nature, and blaspheme God, we murmur and are impatient, when pain is sent to us, from him, that ought to send it, and intends it as a mercy, when it comes. But in the matter of afflictions and bodily sickness, we are so weak and broken, so uneasy and unapt to sufferance, that this alone is beyond the cure of the old philosophy. Many can endure poverty, and many can retire from shame and laugh at home, and very many can endure to be slaves; but when pain and sharpness are to be endured

for the interests of virtue, we find but few martyrs; and they
that are, suffer more within themselves by their fears and
their temptations, by their uncertain purposes and violence
to nature, than the hangman's sword; the martyrdom is
within; and then he hath won his crown, not when he hath
suffered the blow, but when he hath overcome his fears, and
made his spirit conqueror. It was a sad instance of our
infirmity, when of the forty martyrs of Cappadocia, set in a
freezing lake, almost consummate, and an angel was reaching the crown, and placing it upon their brows, the flesh
failed one of them, and drew the spirit after it; and the man
was called off from his scene of noble contention, and died
in warm water:

> ———— Odi artus, fragilemque hunc corporis usum
> Desertorem animi ————

We carry about us the body of death, and we bring evils
upon ourselves by our follies, and then know not how to
bear them; and the flesh forsakes the spirit. And, indeed, in
sickness the infirmity is so very great, that God in a manner
at that time hath reduced all religion into one virtue; patience
with its appendages is the sum total of almost all our duty,
that is proper to the days of sorrow: and we shall find it
enough to entertain all our powers, and to employ all our
aids; the counsels of wise men and the comforts of our
friends, the advices of Scripture and the results of experience, the graces of God, and the strength of our own resolutions, are all then full of employments, and find it work
enough to secure that one grace. For then it is, that a
cloud is wrapped about our heads, and our reason stoops
under sorrow; the soul is sad, and its instrument is out of
tune; the auxiliaries are disordered, and every thought sits
heavily; then a comfort cannot make the body feel it, and
the soul is not so abstracted to rejoice much without its
partner; so that the proper joys of the soul,—such as are
hope, and wise discourses, and satisfactions of reason, and
the offices of religion,—are felt, just as we now perceive the
joys of heaven, with so little relish, that it comes as news of
a victory to a man upon the rack, or the birth of an heir to
one condemned to die; he hears a story, which was made to
delight him, but it came when he was dead to joy, and all

its capacities; and, therefore, sickness, though it be a good monitor, yet it is an ill stage to act some virtues in; and a good man cannot then do much; and therefore, he that is in a state of flesh and blood, can do nothing at all.

But in these considerations we find our nature in disadvantages; and a strong man may be overcome, when a stronger comes to disarm him; and pleasure and pain are the violences of choice and chance; but it is no better in any thing else: for nature is weak in all its strengths, and in its fights, at home and abroad, in its actions and passions; we love some things violently, and hate others unreasonably; any thing can fright us, when we would be confident, and nothing can scare us when we ought to fear; the breaking of a glass puts us into a supreme anger, and we are dull and indifferent as a stoic when we see God dishonoured; we passionately desire our preservation, and yet we violently destroy ourselves, and will not be hindered; we cannot deny a friend, when he tempts us to sin and death, and yet we daily deny God, when he passionately invites us to life and health; we are greedy after money, and yet spend it vainly upon our lusts; we hate to see any man flattered but ourselves, and we can endure folly, if it be on our side, and a sin for our interest; we desire health, and yet we exchange it for wine and madness; we sink when a persecution comes, and yet cease not daily to persecute ourselves, doing mischiefs worse than the sword of tyrants, and great as the malice of a devil.

But to sum up all the evils that can be spoken of the infirmities of the flesh; the proper nature and habitudes of men are so foolish and impotent, so averse and peevish to all good, that a man's will is of itself only free to choose evils. Neither is it a contradiction to say liberty, and yet suppose it determined to one object only; because that one object is the thing we choose. For although God hath set life and death before us, fire and water, good and evil, and hath primarily put man into the hands of his own counsel, that he might have chosen good as well as evil; yet because he did not, bnt fell into an evil condition and corrupted manners, and grew in love with it, and infected all his children with vicious examples; and all nations of the world have contracted some universal stains, and " the thoughts of men's hearts are only evil, and that continually," and " there is not one that doth

good, no, not one that sinneth not:" since (I say) all the
world have sinned, we cannot suppose a liberty of indifferency to good and bad; it is impossible in such a liberty,
that there should be no variety, that all should choose the
same thing; but a liberty of complacency or delight we may
suppose; that is so, that though naturally he might choose
good, yet morally he is so determined with his love to evil,
that good seldom comes into dispute; and a man runs to
evil as he runs to meat or sleep; for why else should it be,
that every one can teach a child to be proud, or to swear, to
lie, or to do little spites to his playfellow, and can train him
up to infant-follies? But the severity of tutors, and the care
of parents, discipline and watchfulness, arts and diligence,
all is too little to make him love but to say his prayers, or
to do that, which becomes persons designed for honest purposes, and his malice shall outrun his years; he shall be a
man in villany, before he is by law capable of choice or inheritance; and this indisposition lasts upon us for ever; even
as long as we live, just in the same degrees as flesh and
blood do rule us: Σώματος μὲν γὰρ ἀῤῥωστίαν ἰᾶται τέχνη,
ψυχῆς δὲ νόσημα ἰατρὸς ἰᾶται Θάνατος· " Art of physicians
can cure the evils of the body, but this strange propensity to
evil nothing can cure but death;" the grace of God eases the
malignity here, but it cannot be cured but by glory: that is,
this freedom of delight, or perfect unabated election of evil,
which is consequent to the evil manners of the world, although it be lessened by the intermedial state of grace, yet
it is not cured until it be changed into its quite contrary;
but as it is in heaven, all that is happy, and glorious, and
free, yet can choose nothing but the love of God, and excellent things, because God fills all the capacities of saints, and
there is nothing without him that hath any degrees of amiability: so in the state of nature, of flesh and blood; there is
so much ignorance of spiritual excellences, and so much
proportion to sensual objects, which in most instances and
in many degrees are prohibited, that, as men naturally know
no good, but to please a wild, undetermined, infinite appetite, so they will nothing else but what is good in their limit
and proportion; and it is with us as it was with the she-
goat that suckled the wolf's whelp; he grew up by his
nurse's milk, and at last having forgot his foster-mother's

kindness, ate that udder which gave him drink and nourishment:

Improbitas nullo flectitur obsequio;

For no kindness will cure an ill-nature and a base disposition: so are we in the first constitution of our nature; so perfectly given to natural vices, that by degrees we degenerate into unnatural, and no education or power of art can make us choose wisely or honestly: Ἐγὼ δὲ μίαν εὐγένειαν οἶδα τὴν ἀρετήν, said Phalaris; "There is no good nature but only virtue:" till we are new created, we are wolves and serpents, free and delighted in the choice of evil, but stones and iron to all excellent things and purposes.

2. Next I am to consider the weakness of the flesh, even when the state is changed, in the beginning of the state of grace: for many persons, as soon as the grace of God rises in their hearts, are all on fire, and inflamed; it is with them as Homer said of the Sirian star.

Λαμπρότατος μὲν ὅγ' ἐστί, κακὸν δέ τι σῆμα τέτυκται,
Καί τε φέρει πολλὸν πυρετὸν δειλοῖσι βροτοῖσιν.   Il. χ. 30.

'It shines finely, and brings fevers;' splendour and zeal are the effects of the first grace, and sometimes the first turns into pride, and the second into uncharitableness; and either by too dull and slow motions, or by too violent and unequal, the flesh will make pretences, and too often prevail upon the spirit, even after the grace of God hath set up its banners in our hearts.

1. In some dispositions that are forward and apt, busy and unquiet, when the grace of God hath taken possession, and begins to give laws, it seems so pleasant and gay to their undiscerning spirits to be delivered from the sottishness of lust, and the follies of drunkenness, that, reflecting upon the change, they begin to love themselves too well, and take delight in the wisdom of the change, and the reasonableness of the new life; and then they, hating their own follies, begin to despise them that dwell below; it was the trick of the old philosophers whom Aristophanes (Nub. 103.) thus describes, τοὺς ἀλαζόνας, Τοὺς ὠχριῶντας, τοὺς ἀνυποδήτους λέγεις· "pale, and barefoot, and proud;" that is, persons singular in their habit, eminent in their institution, proud and pleased in their persons, and despisers of them that are less glorious

in their virtue than themselves; and for this very thing our blessed Saviour remarks the pharisees, they were severe and fantastical advancers of themselves, and judges of their neighbours; and here, when they have mortified corporal vices, such which are scandalous and punishable by men, they keep the spiritual, and those that are only discernible by God: these men do but change their sin from scandal to danger, and that they may sin more safely, they sin more spiritually.

2. Sometimes the passions of the flesh spoil the changes of the spirit, by natural excesses, and disproportion of degrees; it mingles violence with industry, and fury with zeal, and uncharitableness with reproof, and censuring with discipline, and violence with desires, and immortifications in all the appetites and prosecutions of the soul. Some think it is enough in all instances, if they pray hugely and fervently; and that it is religion, impatiently to desire a victory over our enemies, or the life of a child, or an heir to be born; they call it holy, so they desire it in prayer; that if they reprove a vicious person, they may say what they list, and be as angry as they please; that when they demand but reason, they may enforce it by all means; that when they exact duty of their children, they may be imperious and without limit; that if they design a good end, they may prosecute it by all instruments; that when they give God thanks for blessings, they may value the things as high as they list, though their persons come into a share of the honour; here the spirit is willing and holy, but the flesh creeps too busily, and insinuates into the substance of good actions, and spoils them by unhandsome circumstances; and then the prayer is spoiled for want of prudence or conformity to God's will, and discipline and government are embittered by an angry spirit; and the father's authority turns into an uneasy load; by being thrust like an unequal burden to one side, without allowing equal measures to the other: and if we consider it wisely, we shall find, that in many good actions the flesh is the bigger ingredient, and we betray our weak constitutions, even when we do justice, or charity; and many men pray in the flesh, when they pretend they pray by the Spirit.

3. In the first changes and weak progresses of our spiritual life, we find a long weakness upon us, because we are

long before we begin, and the flesh was powerful, and its habits strong, and it will mingle indirect pretences with all the actions of the spirit; if we mean to pray, the flesh thrusts in thoughts of the world; and our tongue speaks one thing, and our hearts mean another; and we are hardly brought to say our prayers, or to undertake a fasting-day, or to celebrate a communion: and if we remember that all these holy actions should be done, and that we have many opportunities of doing them all, and yet do them very seldom, and then very coldly, it will be found at the foot of the account, that our flesh and our natural weakness prevail oftener than our spiritual strengths: οἱ πολὺν χρόνον δεθέντες, κἂν λυθεῖεν, οὐ δυνάμενοι βαδίζειν, ὑποσκελίζονται· 'they that are bound long in chains, feel such a lameness in the first restitutions of their liberty,' ὑπὸ τῆς πολυχρονίου τῶν δεσμῶν συνηθείας, 'by reason of the long-accustomed chain and pressure,' that they may stay till nature hath set them free, and the disease be taken off as well as the chain; and when the soul is got free from her actual pressure of sins, still the wound remains, and a long habitude, and longing after it, a looking back; and upon the presenting the old object, the same company, or the remembrance of the delight, the fancy strikes, and the heart fails, and the temptations return and stand dressed in form and circumstances, and ten to one but the man dies again.

4. Some men are wise and know their weaknesses, and to prevent their startings back, will make fierce and strong resolutions, and bind up their gaps with thorns, and make a new hedge about their spirits; and what then? This shews, indeed, that "the spirit is willing;" but the storm arises, and winds blow, and rain descends, and presently the earth trembles, and the whole fabric falls into ruin and disorder. A resolution (such as we usually make) is nothing but a little trench, which every child can step over; and there is no civil man that commits a willing sin, but he does it against his resolution; and what Christian lives, that will not say and think that he hath repented in some degree; and yet still they commit sin, that is, they break all their holy purposes as readily as they lose a dream; and so great is our weakness, that to most men the strength of a resolution is just such a restraint as he suffers, who is imprisoned in a curtain, and secured with doors and bars of the finest linen:'

for though " the spirit be strong" to resolve, " the flesh is weak" to keep it.

5. But when they have felt their follies, and see the linen-veil rent, some, that are desirous to please God, back their resolutions with vows, and then the spirit is fortified, and the flesh may tempt and call, but the soul cannot come forth, and therefore it triumphs, and acts its interest easily and certainly; and then the flesh is mortified: it may be so. But do not many of us inquire after a vow? And if we consider, it may be it was rash, or it was an impossible matter, or without just consideration, and weighing of circumstances, or the case is altered, and there is a new emergent necessity, or a vow is no more than a resolution made in matter of duty; both are made for God, and in his eye and witness; or if nothing will do it, men grow sad and weary, and despair, and are impatient, and bite the knot in pieces with their teeth, which they cannot by disputing, and the arts of the tongue. A vow will not secure our duty, because it is not stronger than our appetite; and the spirit of man is weaker than the habits and superinduced nature of the flesh; but by little and little it falls off, like the finest thread twisted upon the traces of a chariot, it cannot hold long.

6. Beyond all this, some choose excellent guides, and stand within the restraints of modesty, and a severe monitor; and the Spirit of God hath put a veil upon our spirits; and by modesty in women and young persons, by reputation in the more aged, and by honour in the more noble, and by conscience in all, hath fortified the spirit of man, that men dare not prevaricate their duty, though they be tempted strongly, and invited perpetually; and this is a partition-wall, that separates the spirit from the flesh, and keeps it in its proper strength and retirements. But here the spirit of man, for all that it is assisted, strongly breaks from the en-closure, and runs into societies of flesh, and sometimes despises reputation, and sometimes supplies it with little arts of flattery, and self-love; and is modest as long as it can be secret; and when it is discovered, it grows impudent; and a man shelters himself in crowds and heaps of sinners, and believes that it is no worse with him than with other mighty criminals, and public persons, who bring sin into credit among fools and vicious persons; or else men take

false measures of fame or public honesty, and the world being broken into so many parts of disunion, and agreeing in nothing but in confederate vice, and grown so remiss in governments, and severe accounts, every thing is left so loose, that honour and public fame, modesty and shame, are now so slender guards to the spirit, that the flesh breaks in, and makes most men more bold against God than against men, and against the laws of religion than of the commonwealth.

7. When the spirit is made willing by the grace of God, the flesh interposes in deceptions and false principles. If you tempt some man to a notorious sin, as to rebellion, to deceive his trust, or to be drunk, he will answer, he had rather die than do it: but put the sin civilly to him, and let it be disguised with little excuses, such things which indeed are trifles, but yet they are colours fair enough to make a weak pretence, and the spirit yields instantly. Most men choose the sin, if it be once disputable whether it be a sin or no? If they can but make an excuse, or a colour, so that it shall not rudely dash against the conscience with an open professed name of sin, they suffer the temptation to do its worst. If you tempt a man, you must tell him it is no sin, or it is excusable: this is not rebellion, but necessity, and self-defence; it is not against my allegiance, but is a performing of my trust; I do it for my friend, not against my superior; I do it for a good end, and for his advantage: this is not drunkenness, but free mirth, and fair society; it is refreshment, and entertainment of some supernumerary hours, but it is not a throwing away my time, or neglecting a day of salvation; and if there be any thing more to say for it, though it be no more than Adam's fig-leaves, or the excuses of children and truants, it shall be enough to make the flesh prevail, and the spirit not to be troubled: for so great is our folly, that the flesh always carries the cause, if the spirit can be cozened.

8. The flesh is so mingled with the spirit, that we are forced to make distinctions in our appetite, to reconcile our affections to God and religion, lest it be impossible to do our duty; we weep for our sins, but we weep more for the death of our dearest friends, or other temporal sadnesses; we say we had rather die than lose our faith, and yet we do not

live according to it; we lose our estates, and are impatient; we lose our virtue, and bear it well enough; and what virtue is so great, as more to be troubled for having sinned, than for being ashamed, and beggared, and condemned to die? Here we are forced to a distinction: there is a valuation of price, and a valuation of sense: or the spirit hath one rate of things, and the flesh hath another; and what we believe the greatest evil, does not always cause to us the greatest trouble; which shews plainly, that we are imperfect carnal persons, and the flesh will in some measure prevail over the spirit; because we will suffer it in too many instances, and cannot help it in all.

9. The spirit is abated and interrupted by the flesh, because the flesh pretends it is not able to do those ministries which are appointed in order to religion; we are not able to fast; or, if we watch, it breeds gouts and catarrhs; or, charity is a grace too expensive, our necessities are too big to do it; or, we cannot suffer pain; and sorrow breeds death, and therefore our repentances must be more gentle, and we must support ourselves in all our calamities: for we cannot bear our crosses without a freer refreshment, and this freedom passes on to licence; and many melancholy persons drown their sorrows in sin and forgetfulness, as if sin were more tolerable than sorrow, and the anger of God an easier load than a temporal care: here the flesh betrays its weakness and its follies: for the flesh complains too soon, and the spirit of some men, like Adam being too fond of his Eve, attends to all its murmurs and temptations; and yet the flesh is able to bear far more than is required of it in usual duties. Custom of suffering will make us endure much, and fear will make us suffer more, and necessity makes us suffer any thing; and lust and desire make us to endure more than God is willing we should; and yet we are nice, and tender, and indulgent to our weaknesses, till our weaknesses grow too strong for us. And what shall we do to secure our duty, and to be delivered of ourselves, that the body of death, which we bear about us, may not destroy the life of the spirit?

I have all this while complained, and you see not without cause; I shall afterward tell you the remedies for all this evil. In the meantime, let us have but mean opinions of

ourselves; let us watch every thing of ourselves as of suspected persons, and magnify the grace of God, and be humbled for our stock and spring of follies, and let us look up
to him, who is the Fountain of grace and spiritual strengths:

Ζεῦ βασιλεῦ, τὰ μὲν ἐσθλὰ καὶ εὐχομένοις καὶ ἀνεύκτοις
Ἄμμι δίδου· τὰ δὲ λυγρὰ καὶ εὐχομένων ἀπερύκοις·

Br. An. T. 3. p. 250.

and pray that God would give us what we ask, and what we
ask not; for we want more helps than we understand, and
we are nearer to evil than we perceive, and we bear sin and
death about us, and are in love with it; and nothing comes
from us but false principles, and silly propositions, and weak
discourses, and startings from our holy purposes, and care
of our bodies, and of our palates, and the lust of the lower
belly; these are the employment of our lives; but if we design to live happily, and in a better place, it must be otherwise with us; we must become new creatures; and have another definition, and have new strengths, which we can only
derive from God, whose " grace is sufficient for us," and
strong enough to prevail over all our follies and infirmities.

SERMON XI.

PART II.

3. If it be possible to cure an evil nature, we must inquire
after remedies for all this mischief. In order to which I shall
consider; 1. That since it is our flesh and blood that is the
principle of mischief, we must not think to have it cured by
washings and light medicaments; the physician that went to
cure the hectic with quicksilver and fasting-spittle, did his
patient no good, but himself became a proverb; and he that
by easy prayers and a seldom fast, by the scattering of a
little alms, and the issues of some more natural virtue, thinks
to cure his evil nature, does fortify his indisposition, as a
stick is hardened by a little fire, which by a great one is
devoured. " Quanto satius est mentem eluere, quæ malis
cupiditatibus sordidatur, et, uno virtutis ac fidei lavacro,

universa vitia depellere[k]?" "Better it is by an entire body of
virtue, by a living and active faith, to cleanse the mind from
every vice, and to take off all superinduced habits of sin;"
" Quod qui fecerit, quamlibet inquinatum ac sordidum cor-
pus gerat, satis purus est." If we take this course, although
our body is foul, and our affections unquiet, and our rest
discomposed, yet we shall be masters of our resolution, and
clean from habitual sins, and so cure our evil nature. For
our nature was not made evil but by ourselves; but yet we
are naturally evil, that is, by a superinduced nature; just as
drunkards and intemperate persons have made it necessary
to drink extremely, and their nature requires it, and it is
health to them; they die without it, because they have made
themselves a new constitution, and another nature, but much
worse than that which God made; their sin made this new
nature; and this new nature makes sin necessary and unavoidable: so it is in all other instances; our nature is evil,
because we have spoiled it; and, therefore, the removing the
sin which we have brought in, is the way to cure our nature:
for this evil nature is not a thing which we cannot avoid;
we made it, and, therefore, we must help it; but as in the
superinducing this evil nature, we were thrust forward by the
world and the devil, by all objects from without, and weakness from within; so in the curing it, we are to be helped by
God and his most holy Spirit.

Βαθεῖαν ἄλοκα διὰ φρενὸς καρπούμενος,
Ἐξ ἧς τὰ κεδνὰ βλαστάνει βουλεύματα.

Æsch. Sept. Blomf. 590.

We must have a new nature put into us, which must be the
principle of new counsels, and better purposes, of holy actions and great devotion; and this nature is derived from
God, and is a grace and a favour of heaven. The same Spirit, that caused the holy Jesus to be born after a new and
strange manner, must also descend upon us, and cause us to
be born again, and to begin a new life upon the stock of a
new nature. 'Απ' ἐκείνου ἤρξατο θεία καὶ ἀνθρωπίνη συνυφαί-
νεσθαι φύσις, ἵν' ἡ ἀνθρωπίνη τῇ πρὸς τὸ θειότερον κοινωνίᾳ γέ-
νηται θεία, said Origen; " From him it first began that a
Divine and human nature were weaved together, that the
human nature by communication with the celestial may also

[k] Lactantius.

become Divine;" οὐκ ἐν μόνῳ τῷ Ἰησοῦ, ἀλλὰ ἐν πᾶσι τοῖς μετὰ τὸ πιστεύειν ἀναλαμβάνουσι βίον, ὃν Ἰησοῦς ἐδίδαξεν; " not only in Jesus, but in all that first believe in him, and then obey him, living such a life as Jesus taught:" and this is the sum total of the whole design; as we have lived to the flesh, so we must hereafter live to the Spirit: as our nature hath been flesh, not only in its original, but in habits and affection; so our nature must be spirit in habit and choice, in design and effectual prosecutions; for nothing can cure our old death, but this new birth: and this is the recovery of our nature, and the restitution of our hopes, and, therefore, the greatest joy of mankind.

——— φίλον μὲν φέγγος ἡλίου τόδε,
Καλὸ δὲ πόντου χεῦμα ἰδεῖν εὐήνεμον,
Γῆ τ᾽ ἠρινὸ θάλλουσα, πλούτιο δ᾽ ὕδωρ,

" It is a fine thing to see the light of the sun, and it is pleasant to see the storm allayed and turned into a smooth sea and a fresh gale; our eyes are pleased to see the earth begin to live, and to produce her little issues with particoloured coats:"

Ἀλλ᾽ οὐδὲν οὕτω λαμπρὸν, εὐ᾽ ἰδεῖν καλὸν,
Ὡς τοῖς ἀπαισι καὶ πόθῳ δεδηγμένοις
Παίδων νεογνὼ ἐν δόμοις ἰδεῖν φάος.

" Nothing is so beauteous as to see a new birth in a childless family;" and it is excellent to hear a man discourse the hidden things of nature, and unriddle the perplexities of human notices and mistakes; it is comely to see a wise man sit in the gates of the city, and give right judgment in difficult causes: but all this is nothing to the excellences of a new birth; to see the old man carried forth to funeral with the solemn tears of repentance, and buried in the grave of Jesus, and in his place a new creation to arise, a new heart and a new understanding, and new affections, and excellent appetites: for nothing less than this can cure all the old distempers.

2. Our life, and all our discourses, and every observation, and a state of reason, and a union of sober counsels, are too little to cure a peevish spirit, and a weak reasoning, and silly principles, and accursed habits, and evil examples, and per-

[1] Euripides. Dan.

verse affections, and a whole body of sin and death.   It was
well said in the comedy : *(Adelph.* 857.)

> Nunquam ita quisquam bene subducta ratione ad vitam fuit,
> Quin res, ætas, usus semper aliquid apportet novi,
> Aliquid moneat ; ut illa, quæ te scire credas, nescias,
> Et quæ tibi putaris prima, in experiundo ut repudies.

Men at first think themselves wise, and are always most confident, when they have the least reason ; and to-morrow they
begin to perceive yesterday's folly, and yet they are not
wise ; but as the little embryo, in the natural sheet and lap
of its mother, first distinguishes into a little knot, and that
in time will be the heart, and then into a bigger bundle,
which after some days' abode grows into two little spots, and
they, if cherished by nature, will become eyes, and each part
by order commences into weak principles, and is preserved
with nature's great curiosity ; that it may assist first to distinction, then to order, next to usefulness, and from thence to
strength, till it arrive at beauty, and a perfect creature ; so
are the necessities, and so are the discourses of men ; we
first learn the principles of reason, which break obscurely
through a cloud, and bring a little light, and then we discern a folly, and by little and little leave it, till that enlight-
ens the next corner of the soul : and then there is a new discovery ; but the soul is still in infancy and childish follies ;
and every day does but the work of one day ; but therefore
art and use, experience and reason, although they do something, yet they cannot do enough, there must be something
else : but this is to be wrought by a new principle, that is,
by the Spirit of grace : nature and reason alone cannot do
it, and therefore the proper cure is to be wrought by those
general means of inviting and cherishing, of getting and entertaining God's Spirit, which when we have observed, we
may account ourselves sufficiently instructed towards the
repair of our breaches, and reformation of our evil nature.

1. The first great instrument of changing our whole nature into the state of grace, flesh into the spirit, is a firm belief, and a perfect assent to, and hearty entertainment of, the
promises of the gospel ; for Holy Scripture speaks great words
concerning faith.   " It quenches the fiery darts of the devil,"
saith St. Paul[m]; " it overcomes the world," saith St. John[n]; it is

---

■ Ephes. iv. 4. 16.   ■ John, iv. 5.

the fruit of the Spirit, and the parent of love; it is obedience, and it is humility, and it is a shield, and it is a breastplate, and a work, and a mystery, it is a fight, and it is a victory, it is pleasing God, and it is that " whereby the just do live ;" by " faith we are purified," and by " faith we are sanctified," and by " faith we are justified," and by " faith we are saved :" by this " we have access to the throne of grace," and by it our prayers shall prevail " for the sick," by it we stand, and by it we walk, and by this " Christ dwells in our hearts," and by it all the miracles of the church have been done : it gives great patience to suffer, and great confidence to hope, and great strength to do, and infallible certainty to enjoy the end of all our faith, and satisfaction of all our hopes, and the reward of all our labours, even " the most mighty prize of our high calling :" and if faith be such a magazine of spiritual excellences, of such universal efficacy, nothing can be a greater antidote against the venom of a corrupted nature. But then this is not a grace seated finally in the understanding, but the principle that is designed to, and actually productive of, a holy life ; it is not only a believing the propositions of Scripture as we believe a proposition in the metaphysics, concerning which a man is never the honester whether it be true or false; but it is a belief of things that concern us infinitely, things so great that if they be so true as great, no man that hath his reason and can discourse, that can think and choose, that can desire and work towards an end, can possibly neglect. The great object of our faith, to which all other articles do minister, is resurrection of our bodies and souls to eternal life, and glories infinite. Now is it possible that a man that believes this, and that he may obtain it for himself, and that it was prepared for him, and that God desires to give it him,—that he can neglect and despise it, and not work for it, and perform such easy conditions upon which it may be obtained ? Are not most men of the world made miserable at a less price than a thousand pounds a year? Do not all the usurers and merchants, all tradesmen and labourers, under the sun toil and care, labour and contrive, venture and plot, for a little money; and no man gets, and scarce any man desires, so much of it as he can lay upon three acres of ground ; not so much as will fill a great house. And is this sum, that is such a trifle, such a poor limited heap of dirt, the reward of all the labour and the end of all the care, and the design of all the malice, and the recompence of all the wars, of the world; and can it be imaginable, that life itself, and a long life, an eternal and happy life, a kingdom, a perfect kingdom and glorious, that shall never have ending, nor ever shall be abated with rebellion, or fears, or sorrow, or care; that such a kingdom should not be worth the praying for, and quitting of an idle company, and a foolish humour, or a little drink, or a vicious silly woman, for it? Surely men believe no such thing: they do not rely upon those fine stories that are read in books, and published by preachers, and allowed by the laws of all the world.   If they did, why do they choose intemperance and a fever, lust and shame, rebellion and danger, pride and a fall, sacrilege and a curse, gain and passion, before humility and safety, religion and a constant joy, devotion and peace of conscience, justice and a quiet dwelling, charity and a blessing ; and, at the end of all this, a kingdom more glorious than all the beauties of the sun did ever see.   " Fides est velut quoddam æternitatis exemplar, præterita simul et præsentia et futura sinu quodam vastissimo comprehendit, ut nihil ei prætereat, nil pereat, præeat nihil;" now, " Faith is a certain image of eternity, all things are present to it, things past and things to come," are all so before the eyes of faith, that he in whose eye that candle is enkindled, beholds heaven as present, and sees how blessed a thing it is to die in God's favour, and to be chimed to our grave with the music of a good conscience.   Faith converses with the angels, and antedates the hymns of glory: every man that hath this grace, is as certain that there are glories for him, if he perseveres in duty, as if he had heard and sung the thanksgiving-song for the blessed sentence of doomsday.   And therefore it is no matter, if these things are separate and distant objects ; none but children and fools are taken with the present trifle, and neglect a distant blessing, of which they have credible and believed notices.   Did the merchant see the pearls and the wealth he designed to get in the trade of twenty years ? And is it possible that a child should, when he learns the first rudiments of grammar, know, what excellent things there are in learning, whither he designs his labour, and his hopes? We labour for that which is uncertain, and distant, and believed, and hoped for with many allays, and seen with diminution, and a troubled ray; and what excuse can there be that we do not labour for that, which is told us by God, and preached by his only Son, and confirmed by miracles, and which Christ himself died to purchase, and millions of martyrs died to witness, and which we see good men and wise believe with an assent stronger than their evidence, and which they do believe because they do love, and love because they do believe? There is nothing to be said, but that faith which did enlighten the blind, and cleanse the lepers, and washed the soul of the Æthiopian; that faith that cures the sick, and strengthens the paralytic, and baptizes the catechumens, and justifies the faithful, and repairs the penitent, and confirms the just, and crowns the martyrs; that faith, if it be true and proper, Christian and alive, active and effective in us, is sufficient to appease the storm of our passions, and to instruct all our ignorances, and to make us wise unto salvation; it will, if we let it do its first intention, chastise our errors, and discover our follies; it will make us ashamed of trifling interests and violent prosecutions, of false principles and the evil disguises of the world; and then our nature will return to the innocence and excellency in which God first estated it; that is, our flesh will be a servant of the soul, and the soul a servant to the spirit; and then, because faith makes heaven to be the end of our desires, and God the object of our love and worshippings, and the Scripture the rule of our actions, and Christ our lord and master, and the Holy Spirit our mighty assistant and our counsellor, all the little uglinesses of the world, and the follies of the flesh, will be uneasy and unsavoury, unreasonable, and a load; and then that grace, the grace of faith, that lays hold upon the holy Trinity, although it cannot understand it, and beholds heaven before it can possess it, shall also correct our weaknesses, and master all our adversations: and though we cannot in this world be perfect masters, and triumphant persons, yet we be conquerors and more; that is, conquerors of the direct hostility, and sure of a crown to be revealed in its due time.

2. The second great remedy of our evil nature, and of the loads of the flesh, is devotion, or a state of prayer and intercourse with God. For the gift of the Spirit of God, which is the great antidote of our evil natures, is properly and expressly promised to prayer: "If you, who are evil, give good things

to your children that ask you, how much more shall your
Father from heaven give his Holy Spirit to them that ask it ?"
That which in St. Luke ° is called ἅγιον πνεῦμα, ' the Holy
Spirit,' is called in St. Matthew, τὰ ἀγαθὰ, ᴾ ' good things ;'
that is, the Holy Spirit is all that good that we shall need towards our pardon, and our sanctification, and our glory, and
this is promised to prayer; to this purpose Christ taught us
the Lord's Prayer, by which we are sufficiently instructed in
obtaining this magazine of holy and useful things. But
prayer is but one part of devotion, and though of admirable
efficacy towards the obtaining this excellent promise, yet it
is to be assisted by the other parts of devotion, to make it a
perfect remedy to our great evil. He that would secure his
evil nature, must be a devout person; and he that is devout,
besides that he prays frequently, he delights in it as it is a
conversation with God; he rejoices in God, and esteems him
the light of his eyes, and the support of his confidence, the
object of his love, and the desire of his heart; the man is
uneasy, but when he does God service; and his soul is at
peace and rest, when he does what may be accepted: and
this is that which the Apostle counsels, and gives in precept;
" Rejoice in the Lord always, and again I say rejoice ۹;" that
is, as the Levites were appointed to rejoice, because God
was their portion in tithes and offerings, so now that in the
spiritual sense God is our portion, we should rejoice in him,
and make him our inheritance, and his service our employment, and the peace of conscience to be our rest, and then it
is impossible we should be any longer slaves to sin, and afflicted by the baser employments of the flesh, or carry burdens for the devil; and therefore the scholiast upon Juvenal
observed well, " Nullum malum gaudium est," " No true joy
can be evil;" and therefore it was improperly said of Virgil,
" Mala gaudia mentis," calling lust and wild desires, "the evil
joys of the mind ;" " Gaudium enim nisi sapienti non contin-
gere," said Seneca ; " None but a wise and a good man can
truly rejoice ;" the evil laugh loud, and sigh deeply, they
drink drunk, and forget their sorrows, and all the joys of
evil men are only arts of forgetfulness, devices to cover their
sorrow, and make them not see their death, and its affrighting circumstances ; but the heart never can rejoice and be

° Luke, xi. 13.　　　ᴾ Matt. vii. 11.　　　۹ Phil. iv. 4.

secure, he pleased and be at rest, but when it dwells with holiness : the joys that come from thence, are safe and great, unchangeable and unabated, healthful and holy ; and this is true joy : and this is that which can cure all the little images of pleasure and temptation, which debauch our nature, and make it dwell with hospitals, in the region of diseases and evil sorrows. St. Gregory well observed the difference, saying that "Corporeal pleasures, when we have them not, enkindle a flame and a burning desire in the heart, and make a man very miserable before he tastes them ; the appetite to them is like the thirst and the desires of a fever;" the pleasure of drinking will not pay for the pain of the desire ; and "when they are enjoyed, they instantly breed satiety and loathing. But spiritual rejoicings and delights are loathed by them that have them not, and despised by them that never felt them ;" but when they are once tasted, they increase the appetite and swell into bigger capacities; and the more they are eaten, the more they are desired ; and cannot become a weariness, because they satisfy all the way, and only increase the desire, because themselves grow bigger and more amiable. And therefore when this new and stranger appetite, and consequent joy arises in the heart of man, it so fills all the faculties, that there is no gust, no desire left for toads and vipers, for hemlock and the deadly nightshade.

> Sirenas, hilarem navigantium poenam,
> Blandasque mortes, gaudiumque crudele,
> Quas nemo quondam deserebat auditas,
> Pallax Ulysses dicitur reliquisse. *Mart.* 3. 64.

Then a man can hear the music of songs and dances, and think them to be heathenish noises; and if he be engaged in the society of a woman-singer, he can be as unconcerned as a marble statue ; he can be at a feast and not be defiled, he can pass through theatres as through a street: then he can look on money as his servant, " nec distant æra lupinis ;" he can use it as the Greeks did their sharp coins, to cast accounts withal, and not from thence take the accounts of his wealth or his felicity. If you can once obtain but to delight in prayer, and to long for the day of a communion, and to be pleased with holy meditation, and to desire God's grace with great passion, and an appetite keen as a wolf upon the void plains of the north; if you can delight in God's love, and consider concerning his providence, and busy yourselves in the pursuit of the affairs of his kingdom, then you have the grace of devotion, and your evil nature shall be cured.

3. Because this great cure is to be wrought by the Spirit of God, which is a new nature in us, we must endeavour to abstain from those things; which by a special malignity are directly opposite to the spirit of reason, and the Spirit of grace; and those are drunkenness and lust. He that is full of wine, cannot be full of the Spirit of God: St. Paul noteth the hostility; " Be not drunk with wine, but be filled with the Spirit *:" a man that is a drunkard, does *perire cito*, ' he perishes quickly,' his temptations that come to him, make but short work with him; a drunkard is ἄσωτος; our English well expresses it, it is 'a sottishness,' and the man is ἀκόλαστος, ἄχρειος, ἄχρηστος, 'a useless, senseless person:' εἶτ᾽ οὐχ᾽ ἁπάντων ἐστὶ τὸ μεθύειν κακὸν μέγιστον ἀνθρώποισι καὶ βλαβερώτατον; " Of all the evils of the world, nothing is worse to a man's self, nothing is more harmful than this;" ἀποστεροῦντα ἑαυτὸν τοῦ φρονεῖν, ὃ μέγιστον ἡμῖν ἀγαθὸν ἔχει ἡ φύσις, said Crobylus; 'it deprives a wise man of his counsel and his understanding.' Now, because it is the greatest good that nature hath, that which takes it away, must needs be our greatest enemy. Nature is weak enough of itself, but drunkenness takes from it all the little strengths that are left to it, and destroys the Spirit; and the man can neither have the strengths of nature, nor the strengths of grace; and how then can the man do wisely or virtuously? " Spiritus sanctus amat sicca corda," " The Spirit of God loves dry hearts," said the Christian proverb; and Josephus said of Samson, Δῆλον ἦν προφητεύσων ἀπὸ τῆς περὶ τὴν δίαιταν σωφροσύνης, "It appears he was a prophet, or a man full of the Spirit, by the temperance of his diet;" and now that all the people are holy unto the Lord, they must ἀοίνους ἁγνείας ἔχειν, as Plutarch said of their consecrated persons; they must have " dry and sober purities :" for by this means their reason is useful, and their passions not violent, and their discourse united, and the precious things of their memory at hand, and they can pray and read, and they can meditate and practise, and then they can learn where their natural weaknesses are most urgent, and how

* Ephes. v. 18.

they can be tempted, and can secure their aids accordingly; but how is it possible, that such a man should cure all the evils of his nature, and repair the breaches of Adam's sin, and stop all the effect which is upon him from all the evils of the world, if he delights in seas of drink, and is pleased with the follies of distempered persons, and laughs loud at the childish humours and weak discourses of the man, that can do nothing but that for which Dionysius slew Antiphon, and Timagenes did fall from Cæsar's friendship; that is, play the fool and abuse his friend; he cannot give good counsel or spend an hour in wise sayings; but half a day they can talk " ut foret, unde corona cachinnum tollere posait," to make the crowd laugh, and consider not.

And the same is the case of lust; because it is exactly contrary to Christ the king of virgins, and his Holy Spirit, who is the prince of purities and holy thoughts; it is a captivity of the reason, and an enraging of the passions, it wakens every night, and rages every day, it desires passionately, and prosecutes violently, it hinders business and distracts counsel, it brings jealousies and enkindles wars, it sins against the body, and weakens the soul, it defiles a temple, and drives the Holy Spirit forth, and it is so entire a prosecution of the follies and weaknesses of nature; such a snare and a bait to weak and easy fools, that it prevails infinitely, and rages horribly, and rules tyrannically; it is a very fever in the reason, and a calenture in the passions; and therefore either it must be quenched, or it will be impossible to cure our evil natures: the curing of this is not the remedy of a single evil, but it is a doing violence to our whole nature; and therefore hath in it the greatest courage and an equal conduct, and supposes spiritual strengths great enough to contest against every enemy.

4. Hitherto is to be reduced, that we avoid all flatterers and evil company; for it was impossible that Alexander should be wise and cure his pride and his drunkenness, so long as he entertained Agesius and Agnon, Bagoas and Demetrius, and slew Parmenio and Philotas, and murdered wise Callisthenes; for he that loves to be flattered, loves not to change his pleasure; but had rather to hear himself called wise, than to be so. Flattery does bribe an evil nature, and corrupt a good one; and make it love to give wrong judg-

ment, and evil sentences: he that loves to be flattered, can never want some to abuse him, but he shall always want one to counsel him, and then he can never be wise.

5. But I must put these advices into a heap; he therefore that will cure his evil nature, must set himself against his chiefest lust, which when he hath overcome, the lesser enemies will come in of themselves. He must endeavour to reduce his affections to an indifferency; for all violence is an enemy to reason and counsel, and is that state of disease for which he is to inquire remedies.

6. It is necessary that in all actions of choice he deliberate and consider, that he may never do that for which he must ask a pardon, and he must suffer shame and smart: and therefore Cato did well reprove Aulus Albinus for writing the Roman story in the Greek tongue, of which he had but imperfect knowledge; and himself was put to make his apology for so doing: Cato told him that he was mightily in love with a fault, that he had rather beg a pardon than be innocent; Who forced him to need the pardon? And when beforehand we know we must change from what we are or do worse, it is a better compendium not to enter in from whence we must uneasily retire.

7. In all the contingencies of chance and variety of action, remember that thou art the maker of thy own fortune, and of thy own sin; charge not God with it either before or after; the violence of thy own passion is no superinduced necessity from him, and the events of providence in all its strange variety can give no authority or patronage to a foul forbidden action, though the next chance of war or fortune be prosperous and rich. An Egyptian robber, sleeping under a rotten wall, was awakened by Serapis, and sent away from the ruin; but being quit from the danger, and seeing the wall to slide, he thought that the demon loved his crime, because he had so strangely preserved him from a sudden and a violent death. But Serapis told him, Θάνατον μὲν ἄλυπον Νῦν ἔφυγες, σταυρῷ δ' ἴσθι φυλαττόμενος, "I saved you from the wall, to reserve you for the wheel;" from a short and private death, to a painful and disgraceful; and so it is very frequently in the event of human affairs: men are saved from one death, and reserved for another; or are preserved here, to be destroyed hereafter; and they that would judge

of actions by events, must stay till all events are passed, that is, till all their posterity be dead, and the sentence is given at doom's-day; in the mean time the evils of our nature are to be looked upon without all accidental appendages; as they are in themselves, as they have an irregularity and disorder, an unreasonableness and a sting; and be sure to rely upon nothing, but the truth of laws and promises; and take severe accounts by those lines, which God gave us on purpose to reprove our evil habits and filthy inclinations. Men that are not willing to be cured, are glad of any thing to cozen them; but the body of death cannot be taken off from us, unless we be honest in our purposes, and severe in our counsels, and take just measures, and glorify God, and set ourselves against ourselves, that we may be changed into the likeness of the sons of God.

8. Avoid all delay in the counsels of religion. Because the aversation and perverseness of a child's nature may be corrected easily; but every day of indulgence and excuse increases the evil, and makes it still more natural, and still more necessary.

9. Learn to despise the world; or, which is a better compendium in the duty, learn but truly to understand it; for it is a cozenage all the way; the head of it is a rainbow, and the face of it is flattery; its words are charms, and all its stories are false; its body is a shadow, and its hands do knit spiders' webs; it is an image and a noise, with an hyena's lip and a serpent's tail; it was given to serve the needs of our nature; and instead of doing it, it creates strange appetites, and nourishes thirsts and fevers; it brings care, and debauches our nature, and brings shame and death as the reward of all our cares. Our nature is a disease, and the world does nourish it; but if you leave to feed upon such unwholesome diet, your nature reverts to its first purities, and to the entertainments of the grace of God.

4. I am now to consider, how far the infirmities of the flesh can be innocent, and consist with the Spirit of grace. For all these counsels are to be entertained into a willing spirit, and not only so, but into an active: and so long as the spirit is only willing, the weakness of the flesh will in many instances become stronger than the strengths of the spirit. For he that hath a good will, and does not do good

actions, which are required of him, is hindered, but not by
God that requires them, and therefore by himself, or his worst
enemy. But the measures of this question are these:

1. If the flesh hinders us of our duty, it is our enemy;
and then our misery is not, that the flesh is weak, but that
it is too strong; but, 2. when it abates the degrees of duty
and stops its growth, or its passing on to action and effect,
then it is weak, but not directly nor always criminal. But
to speak particularly.

1. If our flesh hinders us of any thing that is a direct
duty, and prevails upon the spirit to make it do an evil action, or contract an evil habit, the man is in a state of bondage
and sin: his flesh is the mother of corruption and an enemy
to God. It is not enough to say, I desire to serve God, and
cannot as I would: I would fain love God above all things
in the world, but the flesh hath appetites of its own that must
be observed: I pray to be forgiven as I forgive others; but
flesh and blood cannot put up such an injury: for know that
no infirmity, no unavoidable accident, no necessity, no poverty, no business, can hinder us from the love of God, or
forgiving injuries, or being of a religious and a devout spirit:
poverty and the intrigues of the world are things, that can
no more hinder the spirit in these duties, than a strong
enemy can hinder the sun to shine, or the clouds to drop
rain. These things which God requires of us, and exacts
from us with mighty penalties, these he hath made us able
to perform; for he knows that we have no strength but
what he gives us; and therefore, as he binds burdens upon
our shoulders, so he gives us strength to bear them: and
therefore, he that says he cannot forgive, says only that his
lust is stronger than his religion; his flesh prevails upon his
spirit. For what necessity can a man have to curse him,
whom he calls enemy? or to sue him, or kill him, or do
him any spite? A man may serve all his needs of nature,
though he does nothing of all this; and if he be willing,
what hinders him to love, to pardon, to wish well, to desire?
The willing is the doing in this case; and he that says he is
willing to do his duty, but he cannot, does not understand
what he says. For all the duty of the inner man consists in
the actions of the will, and there they are seated, and to it all
the inferior faculties obey in those things which are direct

emanations and effects of will. He that desires to love God, does love him; indeed men are often cozened with pretences, and in some good mood, or warmed with a holy passion, but it signifies nothing; because they will not quit the love of God's enemies; and therefore, they do not desire what they say they do: but if the will and heart be right, and not false and dissembling, this duty is or will be done infallibly.

2. If the spirit and the heart be willing, it will pass on to outward actions in all things, where it ought, or can. He that hath a charitable soul, will have a charitable hand; and will give his money to the poor, as he hath given his heart to God. For these things which are in our hand, are under the power of the will, and therefore are to be commanded by it. He that says to the naked, "Be warm and clothed," and gives him not the garment that lies by him, or money to buy one, mocks God, and the poor, and himself. "Nequam illud verbum est, ' Bene vult,' nisi qui bene facit," said the comedy; "It is an evil saying, ' He wishes well,' unless he do well *."

3. Those things which are not in our power, that is, such things in which the flesh is inculpably weak, or naturally or politically disabled, the will does the work of the outward and of the inward man; we cannot clothe Christ's body, he needs it not, and we cannot approach so sacred and separate a presence; but if we desire to do it, it is accounted as if we had. The ignorant man cannot discourse wisely and promote the interest of souls, but he can love souls, and desire their felicity: though I cannot build hospitals and colleges, or pour great sums of money into the lap of the poor, yet if I encourage others and exhort them, if I commend and promote the work, I have done the work of a holy religion. For in these and the like cases, the outward work is not always set in our power, and therefore, without our fault, is omitted, and can be supplied by that which is in our power.

4. For that is the last caution concerning this question. No man is to be esteemed of a willing spirit, but he that endeavours to do the outward work, or to make all the supplies that he can; not only by the forwardness of his spirit, but by the compensation of some other charities, or devotion,

* Trinummus. 2. 6. 38.

or religion. "Silver and gold have I none," and therefore I
can give you none : but I wish you well ; how will that appear? Why thus, "Such as I have, I will give you; rise
up and walk." I cannot give you God, but I can give you
counsel; I cannot relieve your need, but I can relieve your
sadness; I cannot cure you, but I can comfort you; I cannot
take away your poverty, but I can ease your spirit; and
"God accepts us" (saith the Apostle) "according to what a
man hath, and not according to what he hath not." Only
as our desires are great, and our spirits are willing, so we
shall find ways to make supply of our want of ability and
expressed liberality.

> Et labor ingenium misero dedit, et sua quemque
> Advigilare sibi jussit fortuna premendo.

What the poor man's need will make him do, that also the
good man's charity will ; it will find out ways and artificers
of relief, in kind or in value ; in comfort or in prayers ; in
doing it himself or procuring others.

> Πάντα δὲ ταῦτ' ἐδίδαξε πυρὶ πάντολμος ἀνάγκη.

The necessity of our fortune, and the willingness of our spirits will do all this ; all that it can, and something that it
cannot; "You have relieved the saints" (saith St. Paul)
"according to your power, yea, and beyond your power;"
only let us be careful in all instances, that we yield not to
the weakness of the flesh, nor listen to its fair pretences ; for
the flesh can do more than it says, we can do more than we
think we can; and if we do some violence to the flesh, to
our affairs, and to the circumstances of our fortune, for the
interest of our spirit, we shall make our flesh useful, and the
spirit strong ; the flesh and its weakness shall no more be an
objection, but shall comply, and co-operate, and serve all the
necessities of the spirit.

SERMON XII.

OF LUKEWARMNESS AND ZEAL; OR, SPIRITUAL FERVOUR.

PART I.

Cursed be he that doth the work of the Lord deceitfully.
Jer. xlviii. 10. ver. first part.

CHRIST's kingdom,—being in order to the kingdom of his Father, which shall be manifest at the day of judgment,—must therefore be spiritual; because then it is, that all things must become spiritual, not only by way of eminency, but by entire constitution and perfect change of natures. Men shall be like angels, and angels shall be comprehended in the lap of spiritual and eternal felicities; the soul shall not understand by material phantasms, neither be served by the provisions of the body, but the body itself shall become spiritual, and the eye shall see intellectual objects, and the mouth shall feed upon hymns and glorifications of God ; the belly shall be then made satisfied by the fulness of righteousness, and the tongue shall speak nothing but praises, and the propositions of a celestial wisdom ; the motion shall be the swiftness of an angel, and it shall be clothed with white as with a garment: holiness is the sun, and righteousness is the moon in that region; our society shall be choirs of singers, and our conversation wonder; contemplation shall be our food, and love shall be ' the wine of elect souls.' And as to every natural appetite there is now proportioned an object, crass, material, unsatisfying, and allayed with sorrow and uneasiness: so there be new capacities and equal objects; the desires shall be fruition, and the appetite shall not suppose want, but a faculty of delight, and an immeasurable complacency: the will and the understanding, love and wonder, joys every day and the same for ever : this shall be their state who shall be accounted worthy of the resurrection to this life; where the body shall be a partner, but no servant; where it shall have no work of its own, but it shall rejoice with the soul; where the soul shall rule without resistance or an enemy ; and we shall be fitted to enjoy God,

who is the Lord and Father of spirits. In this world, we see
it is quite contrary: we long for perishing meat, and fill our
stomachs with corruption; we look after white and red, and
the weaker beauties of the night; we are passionate after
rings and seals, and enraged at the breaking of a crystal;
we delight in the society of fools and weak persons; we
laugh at sin and contrive mischiefs; and the body rebels
against the soul and carries the cause against all its just pretences; and our soul itself is, above half of it, earth and
stone, in its affections and distempers; our hearts are hard
and inflexible to the softer whispers of mercy and compassion, having no loves for any thing but strange flesh, and
heaps of money, and popular noises, for misery and folly;
and therefore we are a huge way off from the kingdom of
God, whose excellences, whose designs, whose ends, whose
constitution, is spiritual and holy, and separate and sublime
and perfect.   Now between these two states of natural flesh,
and heavenly spirit, that is, the powers of darkness, and the
regions of light, the miseries of man, and the perfections of
God; the imperfection of nature where we stand by our
creation, and supervening follies, and that state of felicities,
whither we are designed by the mercies of God,—there is a
middle state, ‘ the kingdom of grace,’ wrought for us by our
Mediator, the man Christ Jesus, who came to perfect the
virtue of religion, and the designs of God, and to reform our
nature, and to make it possible for us to come to that spiritual state, where all felicity does dwell.   The religion that
Christ taught, is a spiritual religion; it designs (so far as
this state can permit) to make us spiritual; that is, so as the
Spirit be the prevailing ingredient.   God must now be worshipped in spirit, and not only so, but with a fervent spirit;
and though God in all religions did seize upon the spirit, and
even under Moses' law did, by the shadow of the ceremony,
require the substantial worship, and, by cutting off the flesh,
intended the circumcision of the heart; yet because they were
to mind the outward action, it took off much from the intention and activity of the spirit; man could not do both ba-
sily.   And then they failed also in the other part of a spiritual
religion; for the nature of a spiritual religion is, that in it
we serve God with our hearts and affections; and because
while the spirit prevails, we do not to evil purposes of abate-

ment converse with flesh and blood, this service is also fervent, intense, active, wise, and busy, according to the nature of things spiritual. Now, because God always perfectly intended it, yet because he less perfectly required it in the law of Moses, I say they fell short in both.

For, 1. They so rested in the outward action, that they thought themselves chaste, if they were no adulterers, though their eyes were wanton as kids, and their thoughts polluted as the springs of the wilderness, when a panther and a lioness descend to drink and lust; and if they did not rob the temple, they accounted it no sin if they murmured at the riches of religion; and Josephus reproves Polybius, for saying that Antiochus was punished for having a design of sacrilege; and therefore Tertullian says of them, they were " nec plenæ, nec adeo timendæ disciplinæ ad innocentiæ veritatem;" this was "their righteousness" which Christ said unless we will " exceed, we shall not enter into the kingdom of heaven," where all spiritual perfections are in state and excellency.

2. The other part of a spiritual worship is a fervour and a holy zeal of God's glory, greatness of desire, and quickness of action : of all this the Jews were not careful at all, excepting the zealots amongst them, and they were not only fervent but inflamed; and they had the earnestness of passion for the holy warmth of religion, and instead of an earnest charity they had a cruel discipline, and for fraternal correction they did destroy a sinning Israelite : and by both these evil states of religion they did " the work of the Lord deceitfully;" they either gave him the action without the heart, or zeal without charity, or religion without zeal, or ceremony without religion, or indifferency without desires; and then God is served by the outward man and not the inward; or by part of the inward and not all; by the understanding and not by the will; or by the will, when the affections are cold and the body unapt, and the lower faculties in rebellion, and the superior in disorder, and the work of God is left imperfect, and our persons ungracious, and our ends unacquired, and the state of a spiritual kingdom not at all set forward towards any hope or possibility of being obtained. All this Christ came to mend; and by his laws did make provision that God should be served entirely, according as

God always designed, and accordingly required by his prophets, and particularly in my text, that his work be done sincerely, and our duty with great affection; and by these two provisions; both the intention and the extension are secured; our duty shall be entire, and it shall be perfect, we shall be neither lame nor cold, without a limb, nor without natural heat, and then "the work of the Lord will prosper in our hands:" but if we fail in either, we do "the Lord's work deceitfully," and then we are accursed. For so saith the Spirit of God, "Cursed be he, that doth the work of the Lord deceitfully."

1. Here then is the duty of us all: 1. God requires of us to serve him with an integral, entire, or a whole worship and religion. 2. God requires of us to serve him with earnest and intense affections; the entire purpose of both which, I shall represent in its several parts by so many propositions. 3. I shall consider concerning the measures of zeal and its inordinations.

1. He that serves God with the body without the soul, serves God deceitfully. "My son, give me thy heart;" and though I cannot think that nature was so sacramental, as to point out the holy and mysterious Trinity by the triangle of the heart, yet it is certain that the heart of man is God's special portion, and every angle ought to point out towards him directly; that is, the soul of man ought to be presented to God, and given him as an oblation to the interest of his service.

1. For, to worship God with our souls confesses one of his glorious attributes; it declares him to be the searcher of hearts, and that he reads the secret purposes, and beholds the smallest arrests of fancy, and bends in all the flexures and intrigues of crafty people; and searches out every plot and trifling conspiracy against him, and against ourselves, and against our brethren.

2. It advances the powers and concernments of his providence, and confesses all the affairs of men, all their cabinets and their nightly counsels, their snares and two-edged mischiefs to be overruled by him; for what he sees he judges, and what he judges he rules, and what he rules must turn to his glory; and of this glory he reflects rays and influences upon his servants, and it shall also turn to their good.

3. This service distinguishes our duty towards God from all our conversation with man, and separates the Divine commandments from the imperfect decrees of princes and republics: for these are satisfied by the outward work, and cannot take any other cognizance of the heart, and the will of man, but as himself is pleased to signify. He that wishes the 'fiscus' empty, and that all the revenues of the crown were in his counting-house, cannot be punished by the laws, unless himself become his own traitor and accuser; and therefore what man cannot discern, he must not judge, and must not require. But God sees it, and judges it, and requires it, and therefore reserves this as his own portion, and the chiefest feudal right of his crown.

4. He that secures the heart, secures all the rest; because this is the principle of all the moral actions of the whole man, and the hand obeys this, and the feet walk by its prescriptions; we eat and drink by measures which the soul desires and limits; and though the natural actions of men are not subject to choice and rule, yet the animal actions are under discipline; and although it cannot be helped that we shall desire, yet our desires can receive measures, and the laws of circumstances, and be reduced to order, and nature be changed into grace, and the actions animal (such as are, eating, drinking, laughing, weeping, &c.) shall become actions of religion; and those that are simply natural (such as, being hungry and thirsty) shall be adopted into the retinue of religion, and become religious by being ordered or chastised, or suffered, or directed; and therefore God requires the heart, because he requires all; and all cannot be secured, without the principle be enclosed. But he that seals up a fountain, may drink up all the waters alone, and may best appoint the channel where it shall run, and what grounds it shall refresh.

5. That I may sum up many reasons in one; God by requiring the heart secures the perpetuity and perseverance of our duty, and its sincerity, and its integrity, and its perfection: for so also God takes account of little things; it being all one in the heart of man, whether maliciously it omits a duty in a small instance or in a great; for although the expression hath variety and degrees in it, in relation to those purposes of usefulness and charity whither God designs it,

yet the obedience and disobedience are all one, and shall be
equally accounted for; and therefore the Jew Tryphon disputed against Justin, that the precepts of the Gospel were
impossible to be kept, because it also requiring the heart of
man, did stop every egression of disorders: for making the
root holy and healthful, as the balsam of Judea, or the drops
of manna in the evening of the sabbath; it also causes that
nothing spring thence but gums fit for incense, and oblations
for the altar of proposition, and a cloud of perfume fit to
make atonement for our sins; and being united to the great
sacrifice of the world, to reconcile God and man together.
Upon these reasons you see it is highly fit that God should
require it, and that we should pay the sacrifice of our hearts;
and not at all think that God is satisfied with the work of
the hands, when the affections of the heart are absent. He
that prays because he would be quiet, and would fain be quit
of it, and communicates for fear of the laws, and comes to
church to avoid shame, and gives alms to be eased of an importunate beggar, or relieves his old parents because they
will not die in their time, and provides for his children lest
he be compelled by laws and shame, but yet complains of
the charge of God's blessings; this man is a servant of the
eyes of men, and offers parchment or a white skin in sacrifice, but the flesh and the inwards he leaves to be consumed
by a stranger fire. And therefore, this is a deceit that robs
God of the best, and leaves that for religion which men pare
off: it is sacrilege, and brings a double curse.

2. He that serves God with the soul without the body,
when both can be conjoined, "doth the work of the Lord deceitfully."—Paphnutius, whose knees were cut for the testimony of Jesus, was not obliged to worship with the humble
flexures of the bending penitents: and blind Bartimeus could
not read the holy lines of the law, and therefore that part of
the work was not his duty; and God shall not call Lazarus
to account for not giving alms, nor St. Peter and St. John
for not giving silver and gold to the lame man, nor Epaphro-
ditus for not keeping his fasting-days when he had his sickness. But when God hath made the body an apt minister to
the soul, and hath given money for alms, and power to protect the oppressed, and knees to serve in prayer, and hands
to serve our needs, then the soul alone is not to work; but

as Rachel gave her maid to Jacob, and she bore children to
her lord upon her mistress's knees; and the children were
reckoned to them both, because the one had fruitful desires,
and the other a fruitful womb: so must the body serve the
needs of the spirit; that what the one desires the other may
effect, and the conceptions of the soul may be the productions of the body, and the body must bow when the soul wor-
ships, and the hand must help when the soul pities, and both
together do the work of a holy religion; the body alone can
never serve God without the conjunction and preceding act
of the soul; and sometimes the soul without the body is imperfect and vain; for in some actions there is a body and a
spirit, a material and a spiritual part: and when the action
hath the same constitution that a man hath, without the act
of both, it is as imperfect as a dead man; the soul cannot
produce the body of some actions any more than the body
can put life into it; and therefore an ineffective pity and a
lazy counsel, an empty blessing and gay words, are but deceitful charity.

Quod peto, da, Cai; non peto consilium. *Mart.* 2. 30.

He that gave his friend counsel to study the law, when he
desired to borrow twenty pounds, was not so friendly in his
counsel as he was useless in his charity; spiritual acts can
cure a spiritual malady, but if my body needs relief, because
you cannot feed me with diagrams, or clothe me with Euclid's
Elements, you must minister a real supply by a corporal charity to my corporal necessity. This proposition is not only
useful in the doctrine of charity, and the virtue of religion,
but in the professions of faith, and requires that it be public,
open, and ingenuous. In matters of necessary duty it is not
sufficient to have it to ourselves, but we must also have it to
God, and all the world; and as in the heart we believe, so
by the mouth we confess unto salvation: he is an ill man
that is only a Christian in his heart, and is not so in his profession and publications; and as your heart must not be
wanting in any good professions and pretences, so neither
must public profession be wanting in every good and necessary persuasion. The faith and the cause of God must be
owned publicly; for if it be the cause of God, it will never
bring us to shame. I do not say, whatever we think we must

tell it to all the world, much less at all times, and in all circumstances; but we must never deny that, which we believe
to be the cause of God, in such circumstances, in which we
can and ought to glorify him. But this extends also to other
instances. He that swears a false oath with his lips, and
unswears it with his heart, hath deceived one more than he
thinks for; himself is the most abused person: and when
my action is contrary to men, they will reprove me; but when
it is against my own persuasion, I cannot but reprove myself;
and am witness, and accuser, and party, and guilty, and then
God is the judge, and his anger will be a fierce executioner,
because we do the Lord's work deceitfully.

3. They are "deceitful in the Lord's work," that reserve
one faculty for sin, or one sin for themselves; or one action
to please their appetite, and many for religion.—Rabbi Kim-
chi taught his scholars, "Cogitationem pravam Deus non
habet vice facti, nisi concepta fuerit in Dei fidem et religio-
nem;" "That God is never angry with an evil thought,
unless it be a thought of apostacy from the Jews' religion;"
and therefore, provided that men be severe and close in their
sect and party, they might roll in lustful thoughts; and the
torches they light up in the temple, might smoke with anger
at one end, and lust at the other, so they did not flame out
in egressions of violence and injustice, in adulteries and
fouler complications: nay, they would give leave to some degrees of evil actions; for R. Moses and Selomoh taught,
that if the most part of the man's actions were holy and just,
though in one he sinned often, yet the greater ingredient
should prevail, and the number of good works should outweigh the lesser account of evil things; and this pharisaical
righteousness is too frequent even among Christians. For
who almost is there that does not count fairly concerning
himself, if he reckons many virtues upon the stock of his religion, and but one vice upon the stock of his infirmity; half
a dozen to God, and one for his company, or his friend; his
education or his appetite? And if he hath parted from his
folly, yet he will remember the flesh-pots, and please himself
with a fantastic sin, and call it home through the gates of
his memory, and place it at the door of fancy, that there he
may behold it, and consider concerning what he hath parted
withal, out of the fears and terrors of religion, and a neces-

sary unavoidable conscience. Do not many men go from
sin to sin, even in their repentance? they go backward from
sin to sin, and change their crime as a man changes his uneasy load, and shakes it off from one shoulder to support it
with the other. How many severe persons, virgins, and widows are so pleased with their chastity, and their abstinence
even from lawful mixtures, that by this means they fall into
a worse pride? Insomuch that I remember St. Augustine
said, "Audeo dicere superbis continentibus expedit cadere,"
"They that are chaste and proud, it is sometimes a remedy
for them to fall into sin," and by the shame of lust to cure
the devil of pride, and by the sin of the body to cure the
worser evils of the spirit; and therefore he adds, that he did
believe, God in a severe mercy did permit the barbarous nations, breaking in upon the Roman empire, to violate many
virgins professed in cloisters and religious families to be as a
mortification of their pride, lest the accidental advantages of
a continent life should bring them into the certain miseries
of a spiritual death, by taking away their humility, which
was more necessary than their virgin-state; it is not a cure
that men may use, but God permits it sometimes with greater
safety through his wise conduct and overruling providence;
St. Peter was safer by his fall (as it fell out in the event of
things) than by his former confidence. Man must never
cure a sin by a sin; but he that brings good out of our evil
he can when he please. But I speak it, to represent how
deceitfully many times we do the work of the Lord. We
reprove a sinning brother, but do it with a pompous spirit;
we separate from scandal, and do it with glory, and a gaudy
heart; we are charitable to the poor, but will not forgive our
unkind enemies; or, we pour relief into their bags, but we
please ourselves and drink drunk, and hope to commute with
God, giving the fruit of our labours or effluxes of money
for the sin of our souls: and upon this account it is, that
two of the noblest graces of a Christian are to very many
persons made a savour of death, though they were intended
for the beginning and the promotion of an eternal life; and
those are faith and charity; some men think if they have
faith, it is enough to answer all the accusations of sin, which
our consciences or the devils make against us: if I be a wanton person, yet my faith shall hide it, and faith shall cover

the follies of drunkenness, and I may all my life rely upon
faith, at last to quit my scores.   For he that is most careful
is not innocent, but must be saved by faith; and he that is
least careful may have faith, and that will save him.   But
because these men mistake concerning faith, and consider
not, that charity or a good life is a part of that faith that
saves us, they hope to be saved by the word, they fill their
bellies with the story of Trimalcion's banquet, and drink
drunk with the news of wine; they eat shadows, and when
they are drowning, catch at the image of the trees, which
hang over the water, and are reflected from the bottom.

But thus many men do with charity; "Give alms and all
things shall be clean unto you," said our blessed Saviour:
and therefore, many keep a sin alive, and make account to
pay for it, and God shall be put to relieve his own poor at
the price of the sin of another of his servants; charity shall
take lust or intemperance into protection, and men will
not be kind to their brethren, unless they will be also at
the same time unkind to God.   I have understood concerning divers vicious persons, that none have been so free in
their donatives and offerings to religion and the priest as they:
and the hospitals that have been built, and the highways
mended at the price of souls, are too many for Christendom
to boast of in behalf of charity.   But as others mistake concerning faith, so these do concerning its twin-sister.   The
first bad faith without charity, and these have charity without hope; " For every one that hath this hope," that is, the
hope of receiving the glorious things of God promised in the
Gospel, "purifies himself even as God is pure;" faith and
charity too, must both suppose repentance; and repentance
is the abolition of the whole body of sin, the purification of
the whole man.   But the sum of the doctrine and case of conscience in this particular is this.

1. Charity is a certain cure of sins that are past, not that
are present.—He that repents and leaves his sin, and then
relieves the poor, and pays for his folly by a diminution of
his own estate, and the supplies of the poor, and his ministering to Christ's poor members, turns all his former crimes
into holiness; he purges the stains and makes amends for
his folly, and commutes for the baser pleasure with a more
noble usage: so said Daniel to Nebuchadnezzar, " Break off

thy sins by righteousness, and thine iniquities by shewing mercy to the poor[t]:" first be just, and then be charitable; for it is pity, alms,—which is one of the noblest services of God, and the greatest mercy to thy brother,—should be spent upon sin, and thrown away upon folly.

' 2. Faith is the remedy of all our evils; but then, it is never of force, but when we either have endeavoured or undertaken to do all good; this in baptism, that after: faith and repentance at first; and faith and charity at last; and, because we fail often by infirmity, and sometimes by inadvertency; sometimes by a surprise and often by omission; and all this even in the midst of a sincere endeavour to live justly, and perfectly; therefore the passion of our Lord pays for this, and faith lays hold upon that. But without a hearty and sincere intent, and vigorous prosecution of all the parts of our duty, faith is but a word, not so much as a cover to a naked bosom, nor a pretence big enough to deceive persons, that are not willing to be cozened.

3. The bigger ingredient of virtue and evil actions will prevail, but it is only when virtue is habitual, and sins are single, interrupted, casual, and seldom, without choice and without affection; that is, when our repentance is so timely, that it can work for God more than we served under the tyranny of sin; so that if you will account the whole life of man, the rule is good, and the greater ingredient shall prevail; and he shall certainly be pardoned and excepted, whose life is so reformed, whose repentance is so active, whose return is so early, that he hath given bigger portions to God, than to God's enemy. But if we account so, as to divide the measures in present possession, the bigger part cannot prevail; a small or a seldom sin spoils not the sea of piety; but when the affection is divided, a little ill destroys the whole body of good; the cup in a man's right hand must be ἄκρατος κεκερασμένος, it must be "pure, although it be mingled;" that is, the whole affection must be for God, that must be pure and unmingled; if sin mingles in seldom and unapproved instances, the drops of water are swallowed up with a whole vintage of piety, and the bigger ingredient is the prevailing; in all other cases it is not so: for one sin that we choose and love and delight in, will not be excused

[t] Dan. iv. 27.

by twenty virtues: and as one broken link dissolves the union
of the whole chain, and one jarring untuned string spoils the
whole music; so is every sin that seizes upon a portion of
our affections; if we love one, that one destroys the acceptation of all the rest: and as it is in faith, so it is in charity.
He that is a heretic in one article, hath no saving faith in
the whole; and so does every vicious habit, or unreformed
sin, destroy the excellency of the grace of charity; a wilful
error in one article is heresy, and every vice in one instance
is malice, and they are perfectly contrary, and a direct darkness to the two eyes of the soul, faith and charity.

4. There is one deceit more yet, in the matter of the extension of our duty, destroying the integrity of its constitution: for they do the work of God deceitfully, who think God
sufficiently served with abstinence from evil, and converse
not in the acquisition and pursuit of holy charity and religion.   This Clemens Alexandrinus affirms of the pharisees;
they were μετὰ ἀποχὴν κακῶν δικαιούμενοι, they hoped to be
"justified by abstinence from things forbidden;" but if we
will be βασιλικοὶ, "sons of the kingdom," we must μετὰ τῆς ἐν
τούτοις τελειώσεως καὶ τὸν πλησίον ἀγαπᾶν, καὶ εὐεργετεῖν; besides this, and 'supposing a proportionable perfection in such
an innocence, we must love our brother and do good to him,'
and glorify God by a holy religion, in the communion of
saints, in faith and sacraments, in alms and counsel, in for-
givenesses and assistances.   " Flee from evil, and do the
thing that is good, and dwell for evermore," said the Spirit
of God in the Psalms: and St. Peter, "Having escaped the
corruption that is in the world through lust, give all diligence
to add to your faith virtue, to virtue patience, to patience
godliness, and brotherly-kindness, and charity:" many persons think themselves fairly assoiled, because they are no
adulterers, no rebels, no drunkards, not of scandalous lives;
in the meantime, like the Laodiceans, they are "naked and
poor;" they have no catalogue of good things registered in
heaven, no treasures in the repositories of the poor, neither
have the poor often prayed concerning them, "Lord, remember thy servants for this thing, at the day of judgment."   A
negative religion is in many things the effects of laws, and
the appendage of sexes, the product of education, the issues
of company and of the public, or the daughter of fear and

natural modesty, or their temper and constitution, and civil
relations, common fame, or necessary interest. Few women
swear and do the debaucheries of drunkards; and they are
guarded from adulterous complications by spies and shame,
by fear and jealousy, by the concernment of families, and
reputation of their kindred, and therefore they are to account
with God beyond this civil and necessary innocence, for humility and patience, for religious fancies and tender consciences, for tending the sick and dressing the poor, for
governing their house and nursing their children; and so it
is in every state of life. When a prince or prelate, a noble
and a rich person, hath reckoned all his immunities and degrees of innocence from those evils that are incident to inferior persons, or the worse sort of their own order, they do
" the work of the Lord," and their own too, very " deceitfully,"
unless they account correspondences of piety to all their
powers and possibilities: they are to reckon and consider concerning what oppressions they have relieved, what causes and
what fatherless they have defended, how the work of God and
of religion, of justice and charity, hath thrived in their hands.
If they have made peace, and encouraged religion by their example and by their laws, by rewards and collateral encouragements, if they have been zealous for God and for religion, if
they have employed ten talents to the improvement of God's
bank, then they have done God's work faithfully; if they account otherwise, and account only by ciphers and negatives,
they can expect only the rewards of innocent slaves; they shall
escape the 'furca' and the wheel, the torments of lustful persons, and the crown of flames, that is reserved for the ambitious;
or they shall be not gnawn with the vipers of the envious, or
the shame of the ungrateful; but they can never upon this account hope for the crowns of martyrs, or the honourable rewards of saints, the coronets of virgins, and chaplets of doctors and confessors: and though murderers and lustful persons, the proud and the covetous, the heretic and schismatic,
are to expect flames and scorpions, pains and smart (' pœnam
sensus,' the schools call it); yet the lazy and the imperfect,
the harmless sleeper and the idle worker, shall have ' pœnam
damni,' the loss of all his hopes, and the dishonours of the
loss; and in the sum of affairs it will be no great difference whether we have loss or pain, because there can be no

greater pain imaginable than to lose the sight of God to
eternal ages.

5. Hither are to be reduced as deceitful workers, those
that promise to God, but mean not to pay what they once intended; people that are confident in the day of ease, and fail
in the danger; they that pray passionately for a grace, and if
it be not obtained at that price go no farther, and never contend in action for what they seem to contend in prayer; such
as delight in forms and outsides, and regard not the substance
and design of every institution; that think it a great sin to
taste bread before the receiving the holy sacrament, and yet
come to communicate with an ambitious and revengeful soul;
that make a conscience of eating flesh, but not of drunkenness; that keep old customs and old sins together; that pretend one duty to excuse another; religion against charity,
or piety to parents against duty to God, private promises
against public duty, the keeping of an oath against breaking
of a commandment, honour against modesty, reputation
against piety, the love of the world in civil instances to countenance enmity against God; these are the deceitful workers
of God's work; they make a schism in the duties of religion,
and a war in heaven worse than that between Michael and
the dragon; for they divide the Spirit of God, and distinguish his commandments into parties and factions; by seeking an excuse, sometimes they destroy the integrity and perfect constitution of duty, or they do something whereby the
effect and usefulness of the duty is hindered: concerning all
which this only can be said, they who serve God with a lame
sacrifice and an imperfect duty defective in its constituent
parts, can never enjoy God; because he can never be divided:
and though it be better to enter into heaven with one foot,
and one eye, than that both should be cast into hell, because
heaven can make recompense for this loss; yet nothing can
repair his loss who for being lame in his duty shall enter into
hell, where nothing is perfect, but the measures and duration
of torment, and they both are next to infinite.

SERMON XIII.

PART II.

2. THE next inquiry, is into the intention of our duty: and here it will not be amiss to change the word ' fraudulenter,' or ' dolose,' into that which some of the Latin copies do use, " Maledictus, qui facit opus Dei *negligenter:*" " Cursed is he, that doth the work of the Lord *negligently*, or remissly: and it implies, that as our duty must be whole, so it must be fervent; for a languishing body may have all its parts, and yet be useless to many purposes of nature: and you may reckon all the joints of a dead man, but the heart is cold, and the joints are stiff and fit for nothing but for the little people that creep in graves: and so are very many men; if you sum up the accounts of their religion, they can reckon days and months of religion, various offices, charity and prayers, reading and meditation, faith and knowledge, catechism and sacraments, duty to God, and duty to princes, paying debts and provision for children, confessions and tears, discipline in families, and love of good people; and, it may be, you shall not reprove their numbers, or find any lines unfilled in their tables of accounts; but when you have handled all this and considered, you will find at last you have taken a dead man by the hand, there is not a finger wanting, but they are stiff as icicles, and without flexure as the legs of elephants: such are they whom St. Bernard describes, " Whose spiritual joy is allayed with tediousness, whose compunction for sins is short and seldom, whose thoughts are animal and their designs secular, whose religion is lukewarm; their obedience is without devotion, their discourse without profit, their prayer without intention of heart, their reading without instruction, their meditation is without spiritual advantages, and is not the commencement and strengthening of holy purposes; and they are such whom modesty will not restrain, nor reason bridle, nor discipline correct, nor the fear of death and hell can keep from yielding to the imperiousness of a foolish lust, that dishonours a man's understanding, and makes his reason, in which he most glories, to be weaker than the discourse of a girl,

and the dreams of the night. In every action of religion
God expects such a warmth and a holy fire to go along,
that it may be able to enkindle the wood upon the altar, and
consume the sacrifice; but God hates an indifferent spirit.
Earnestness and vivacity, quickness and delight, perfect
choice of the service, and a delight in the prosecution, is all
that the spirit of a man can yield towards his religion : the
outward work is the effect of the body; but if a man does
it heartily and with all his mind, then religion hath wings
and moves upon wheels of fire; and therefore, when our
blessed Saviour made those capitulars and canons of religion,
to ' love God,' and to ' love our neighbour ;' besides, that
the material part of the duty, ' love,' is founded in the spirit,
as its natural seat, he also gives three words to involve the
spirit in the action, and but one for the body : " Thou shalt
love the Lord thy God with all thine heart, and with all thy
soul, and with all thy mind;" and, lastly, " with all thy
strength ;" this brings in the body too ; because it hath some
strength; and some significations of its own ; but heart and
soul and mind mean all the same thing in a stronger and
more earnest expression ; that is, that we do it hugely, as
much as we can, with a clear choice, with a resolute understanding, with strong affections, with great diligence :
" Enerves animos odisse virtus solet," " Virtue hates weak
and ineffective minds," and tame easy prosecutions ; Lori-
pedes, people whose arm is all flesh, ' whose foot is all leather,'
and an unsupporting skin; they creep like snakes, and pursue the noblest mysteries of religion, as Naaman did the
mysteries of Rimmon, only in a compliment, or for secular
regards; but without the mind, and therefore without zeal :
" I would thou wert either hot or cold," said the Spirit of
God to the Angel or Bishop of Laodicea. In feasts or sacrifices the ancients did use ' apponere frigidam,' or ' calidam;'
sometimes they drank hot drink, sometimes they poured
cold upon their graves or in their wines, but no services of
tables or altars were ever with lukewarm. God hates it
worse than stark cold; which expression is the more considerable, because in natural and superinduced progressions,
from extreme to extreme, we must necessarily pass through
the midst ; and therefore, it is certain, a lukewarm religion
is better than none at all, as being the doing some parts of

the work designed, and nearer to perfection than the utmost
distance could be; and yet that God hates it more, must
mean, that there is some appendant evil in this state which
is not in the other, and that accidentally it is much worse:
and so it is, if we rightly understand it; that is, if we consider it, not as a being in, or passing through the middle
way, but as a state and a period of religion. If it be in
motion, a lukewarm religion is pleasing to God; for God
hates it not for its imperfection, and its natural measures of
proceeding; but if it stands still and rests there, it is a state
against the designs, and against the perfection of God: and
it hath in it these evils:

1. It is a state of the greatest imprudence in the world;
for it makes a man to spend his labour for that which profits
not, and to deny his appetite for an unsatisfying interest;
he puts his monies in a napkin, and he that does so, puts
them into a broken bag; he loses the principal for not increasing the interest. He that dwells in a state of life that
is unacceptable, loses the money of his alms, and the rewards
of his charity, his hours of prayer, and his parts of justice,
he confesses his sins and is not pardoned, he is patient but
hath no hope, and he that is gone so far out of his country,
and stands in the middle way, hath gone so far out of his
way; he had better have stayed under a dry roof, in the
house of banishment, than to have left his Gyarus, the island
of his sorrow, and to dwell upon the Adriatic: so is he that
begins a state of religion, and does not finish it; he abides
in the highway, and though he be nearer the place, yet is as
far from the rest of his country as ever; and therefore, all
that beginning of labour was in the prejudice of his rest,
but nothing to the advantages of his hopes. He that hath
never begun, hath lost no labour; 'Jactura præteritorum,'
'the loss of all that he hath done,' is the first evil of the
negligent and lukewarm Christian; according to the saying
of Solomon: " He that is remiss or idle in his labour, is the
brother of him that scattereth his goods[a]."

2. The second appendant evil is, that lukewarmness is
the occasion of greater evil;—because the remiss easy Christian shuts the gate against the heavenly breathings of God's
Holy Spirit; he thinks every breath, that is fanned by the

[a] Prov. xviii. 9.

wings of the holy Dove, is not intended to encourage his fires, which burn and smoke, and peep through the cloud already; it tempts him to security; and, if an evil life be a certain in-let to a second death, despair on one side, and security on the other, are the bars and locks to that door, he can never pass forth again while that state remains; whoever slips in his spiritual walking does not presently fall; but if that slip does not awaken his diligence, and his caution, then his ruin begins, "vel pravæ institutionis deceptus exordio, aut per longam mentis incuriam, et virtute animi decidente," as St. Austin observes; "either upon the pursuit of his first error, or by a careless spirit, or a decaying slackened resolution;" all which are the direct effects of lukewarmness. But so have I seen a fair structure begun with art and care, and raised to half its stature, and then it stood still by the misfortune or negligence of the owner, and the rain descended, and dwelt in its joints, and supplanted the contexture of his pillars, and having stood awhile, like the antiquated temple of a deceased oracle, it fell into a hasty age, and sunk upon its own knees, and so descended into ruin: so is the imperfect, unfinished spirit of a man; it lays the foundation of a holy resolution, and strengthens it with vows and arts of prosecution, it raises up the walls, sacraments, and prayers, reading, and holy ordinances; and holy actions begin with a slow motion, and the building stays, and the spirit is weary, and the soul is naked, and exposed to temptation, and in the days of storm take in every thing that can do it mischief; and it is faint and sick, listless and tired, and it stands till its own weight wearies the foundation, and then declines to death and sad disorder, being so much the worse, because it hath not only returned to its first follies, but hath superadded unthankfulness and carelessness, a positive neglect and a despite of holy things, a setting a low price to the things of God, laziness and wretchlessness: all which are evils superadded to the first state of coldness, whither he is with all these loads and circumstances of death easily revolved.

3. A state of lukewarmness is more incorrigible than a state of coldness; while men flatter themselves, that their state is good, that they are rich and need nothing, that their lamps are dressed, and full of ornament. There are many, that think they are in their country as soon as ever they are

weary, and measure not the end of their hopes by the possession of them, but by their precedent labour; which they overvalue, because they have easy and effeminate souls. St. Bernard complains of some that say, "Sufficit nobis, nolumus esse meliores quam patres nostri:" "It is enough for us to be as our forefathers," who were honest and useful in their generations, but be not over-righteous. These men are such as think, they have knowledge enough to need no teacher, devotion enough to need no new fires, perfection enough to need no new progress, justice enough to need no repentance; and then because the spirit of a man and all the things of this world are in perpetual variety and change, these men decline, when they have gone their period; they stand still, and then revert; like a stone returning from the bosom of a cloud, where it rested as long as the thought of a child, and fell to its natural bed of earth, and dwelt below for ever. He that says, he will take care he be no worse, and that he desires to be no better, stops his journey into heaven, but cannot be secure against his descending into hell: and Cassian spake a hard saying: "Frequenter vidimus de frigidis et carnalibus ad spiritualem venisse fervorem, de tepidis et animalibus omnino non vidimus:" ' Many persons from vicious, and dead, and cold, have passed into life and an excellent grace, and a spiritual warmth, and holy fires; but from lukewarm and indifferent never any body came to an excellent condition, and state of holiness:' ' rarissime,' St. Bernard says, ' very extremely seldom;' and our blessed Saviour said something of this. "The publicans and the harlots go before you into the kingdom of heaven;" they are moved by shame, and punished by disgrace, and remarked by punishments, and frighted by the circumstances and notices of all the world, and separated from sober persons by laws and an intolerable character, and the sense of honour, and the care of their persons, and their love of civil society, and every thing in the world can invite them towards virtues. But the man that is accounted honest, and does justice, and some things of religion, unless he finds himself but upon his way, and feels his wants, and groans under the sense of his infirmities, and sighs under his imperfections, and accounts himself " not to have comprehended," but " still presses towards the mark of his calling," unless (I say) he still increases in his appetites of religion, as he does in his progression, he will think he needs no counsellor, and the Spirit of God whispers to an ear, that is already filled with noises, and cannot attend to the heavenly calling. The stomach, that is already full, is next to loathing; and that's the prologue to sickness, and a rejecting the first wholesome nutriment, which was entertained to relieve the first natural necessities: "Qui non proficit, vult deficere," said St. Bernard: ' He that goes not forward in the love of God, and of religion, does not stand still, but goes for all that;' but whither such a motion will lead him, himself without a timely care shall feel by an intolerable experiment.

In this sense and for these reasons it is, that although a lukewarm Christian hath gone forward some steps towards a state of holiness, and is advanced beyond him that is cold, and dead and unconcerned; and therefore, speaking absolutely and naturally, is nearer the kingdom of God than he that is not yet set out; yet accidentally, and by reason of these ill appendages, he is worse, in greater danger, in a state equally unacceptable, and therefore must either go forward, and still do the work of God carefully, and diligently, with a fervent spirit, and an active hand, with a willing heart, and a cheerful eye, or it had been better he had never begun.

2. It concerns us next to inquire concerning the duty in its proper instances, that we may perceive to what parts and degrees of duty it amounts; we shall find it especially in the duties of faith, of prayer, and of charity.

1. Our faith must be strong, vigorous, active, confident, and patient, reasonable, and unalterable, without doubting, and fear, and partiality. For the faith of very many men seems a duty so weak and indifferent, is so often untwisted by violence, or ravelled and entangled in weak discourses, or so false and fallacious by its mixture of interest, that though men usually put most confidences in the pretences of faith, yet no pretences are more unreasonable.

1. Our faith and persuasions in religion is most commonly imprinted in us by our country, and we are Christians at the same rate as we are English or Spaniards, or of such a family; our reason is first stained and spotted with the die of our kindred, and country, and our education puts it in grain, and whatsoever is against this we are taught to call a temp-

tation: in the meantime, we call these accidental and artificial persuasions by the name of faith, which is only the air of the country, or an heir-loom of the family, or the daughter of a present interest. Whatever it was that brought us in, we are to take care, that when we are in, our faith be noble, and stand upon its most proper and most reasonable foundation; it concerns us better to understand that religion, which we call faith, and that faith whereby we hope to be saved.

2. The faith and the whole religion of many men is the production of fear. Men are threatened into their persuasions, and the iron rod of a tyrant converts whole nations to his principles, when the wise discourses of the religion seems dull as sleep, and unprevailing as the talk of childhood. That is but a deceitful faith, which our timorousness begot, and our weakness nurses, and brings up. The religion of a Christian is immortal, and certain, and persuasive, and infallible, and unalterable, and therefore, needs not be received by human and weak convoys, like worldly and mortal religions: that faith is lukewarm, and easy, and trifling, which is only a belief of that, which a man wants courage to disbelieve.

3. The faith of many men is such, that they dare not trust it: they will talk of it, and serve vanity, or their lust, or their company, or their interest by it, but when the matter comes to a pinch, they dare not trust it; when Antisthenes was initiated into the mysteries of Orpheus, the priest told him, that all that were of that religion, immediately after death should be perfectly happy[x]; the philosopher asked him, Why he did not die, if he believed what he said? Such a faith as that was fine to talk of at table, or eating the sacrifices of the religion, when the mystic man was ἔνθεος, full of wine and flesh, of confidence and religion; but to die, is a more material consideration, and to be chosen upon no grounds, but such a faith, which really comes from God, and can secure our reason, and our choice, and perfect our interest and designs. And it hath been long observed concerning those bold people, that use their reason against God that gave it, they have one persuasion in their health, and

---

[x] His qui sacris visis abeunt ad Inferos,
Homines beati sunt, solis quia vivere
Contingit illic istis; turba cætera
Omnium malorum generi incidit.

another in their sickness and fears; when they are well, they
blaspheme; when they die, they are superstitious. It was
Bias's case, when he was poisoned by the atheisms of Theo-
dorus, no man died more like a coward and a fool; " as if
the gods were to come and go as Bias pleased to think and
talk :" so one said of his folly. If God be to be feared when
we die, he is also to be feared in all our life, for he can for
ever make us die; he that will do it once, and that when he
please, can always. And therefore, all those persuasions
against God, and against religion, are only the production
of vicious passions, of drink or fancy, of confidence and ignorance, of boldness or vile appetites, of vanity or fierceness,
of pride or flatteries; and atheism is a proportion so unnatural and monstrous, that it can never dwell in a man's heart
as faith does, in health and sickness, in peace and war, in
company and alone, at the beginning and at the end of a
design; but comes from weak principles, and leaves shallow
and superficial impressions; but when men endeavour to
strengthen and confirm it, they only strive to make themselves worse than they can. Naturally a man cannot be an
atheist: for he that is so, must have something within him
that is worse either than man or devil.

4. Some measure their faith by shows and appearances,
by ceremonies and names, by professions and little institutions. Diogenes was angry at the silly priest, that thought
he should be immortal because he was a priest, and would
not promise so concerning Agesilaus, and Epaminondas,
two noble Greeks, that had preserved their country, and
lived virtuously. The faith of a Christian hath no signification at all but obedience and charity; if men be just, and
charitable, and good, and live according to their faith, then
only they are Christians; whatsoever else is pretended is but
a shadow, and the image of a grace; for since in all the sects
and institutions of the world, the professors did, in some
reasonable sort, conform to the rules of the profession (as
appears in all the schools of philosophers, and religions of the
world, and the practices of the Jews, and the usages and the
country-customs of the Turks), it is a strange dishonour to
Christianity, that in it alone men should pretend to the faith
of it, and do nothing of what it persuades, and commands
upon the account of those promises, which it makes us to

believe. He that means to please God by his faith, must
have his faith begotten in him by the Spirit of God, and proper arguments of religion; he must profess it without fear,
he must dare to die for it, and resolve to live according to
its institution; he must grow more confident and more holy,
have fewer doubtings and more virtues, he must be resolute
and constant, far from indifferency, and above secular regards; he must by it regulate his life, and value it above his
life; he must ' contend earnestly for the faith,' by the most
prevailing arguments, by the arguments of holy living and
ready dying, by zeal and patience, by conformity and humility, by reducing words to actions, fair discourses to perfect
persuasions, by loving the article, and increasing in the
knowledge and love of God, and his son Jesus Christ; and
then his faith is not negligent, deceitful, artificial, and improper; but true, and holy, and reasonable, and useful, zealous
and sufficient; and therefore, can never be reproved.

2. Our prayers[j] and devotions must be fervent and zealous, not cold, patient, easy, and soon rejected; but supported by a patient spirit, set forwards by importunity, continued by perseverance, waited on by attention and a present
mind, carried along with holy, but strong desires; and bal-
lasted with resignation, and conformity to the Divine will;
and then it is, as God likes it, and does the work to God's
glory and our interest effectively.   He that asks with a
doubting mind, and a lazy desire, begs for nothing but to be
denied; we must in our prayers be earnest and fervent, or
else we shall have but a cold answer; for God gives his
grace according as we can receive it; and whatsoever evil
returns we meet in our prayers, when we ask for good things,
is wholly by reason of our wandering spirits and cold desires;
we have reason to complain that our minds wander in our
prayers, and our diversions are more prevailing than all our
arts of application, and detention; and we wander sometimes
even when we pray against wandering: and it is in some
degrees natural and inevitable: but although the evil is not
wholly to be cured, yet the symptoms are to be eased; and
if our desires were strong, and fervent, our minds would in
the same proportion be present: we see it by a certain and
regular experience; what we love passionately, we perpetu-

ally think on, and it returns upon us whether we will or no;
and in a great fear, the apprehension cannot be shaken off;
and therefore, if our desires of holy things were strong and
earnest, we should most certainly attend our prayers : it is a
more violent affection to other things, that carries us off
from this ; and therefore, if we loved passionately, what we
ask for daily, we should ask with hearty desires, and an
earnest appetite, and a present spirit ; and however it be
very easy to have our thoughts wander, yet it is our indifferency and lukewarmness that make it so natural : and you
may observe it, that so long as the light shines bright, and
the fires of devotion, and desires flame out, so long the mind
of a man stands close to the altar, and waits upon the sacrifice ; but as the fires die, and desires decay, so the mind
steals away, and walks abroad to see the little images of
beauty and pleasure, which it beholds in the falling stars
and little glow-worms of the world. The river that runs slow
and creeps by the banks, and begs leave of every turf to let
it pass, is drawn into little hollownesses, and spends itself in
smaller portions, and dies with diversion ; but when it runs
with vigorousness and a full stream, and breaks down every
obstacle, making it even as its own brow, it stays not to be
tempted by little avocations, and to creep into holes, but
runs into the sea through full and useful channels: so is a
man's prayer, if it moves upon the feet of an abated appetite;
it wanders into the society of every trifling accident, and
stays at the corners of the fancy, and talks with every object
it meets, and cannot arrive at heaven, but when it is carried
upon the wings of passion and strong desires, a swift motion
and a hungry appetite, it passes on through all the intermedial regions of clouds, and stays not till it dwells at the foot
of the throne, where mercy sits, and thence sends holy
showers of refreshment. I deny not but some little drops
will turn aside, and fall from the full channel by the weakness of the banks, and hollowness of the passage ; but the
main course is still continued : and although the most earnest
and devout persons feel and complain of some looseness of
spirit, and unfixed attentions, yet their love and their desire
secure the main portions, and make the prayer to be strong,
fervent, and effectual. Any thing can be done by him, that
earnestly desires what he ought ; secure but your affections

and passions, and then no temptation will be too strong;
' A wise man, and a full resolution, and an earnest spirit, can
do any thing of duty;' but every temptation prevails, when
we are willing to die ; and we usually lend nothing to devotion but the offices that flatter our passions ; we can desire
and pray for any thing, that may serve our lust, or promote
those ends which we covet, but ought to fear and flee from:
but the same earnestness, if it were transplanted into religion
and our prayers, would serve all the needs of the spirit, but
for want of it we do " the Lord's work deceitfully."

3. Our charity also must be fervent: " Malus est miles
qui ducem suum gemens sequitur;" " He that follows his
general with a heavy march, and a heavy heart, is but an ill
soldier;" but our duty to God should be hugely pleasing,
and we should rejoice in it: it must pass on to action, and
do the action vigorously ; it is called in Scripture κόπος
ἀγάπης, ' the labour' and travail ' of love.' ' A friend at a
sneeze and an alms-basket full of prayers,' a love that is lazy,
and a service that is useless, and a pity without support, are
the images and colours of that grace, whose very constitution and design is, beneficence and well-doing. He that
loves passionately, will not only do all that his friend needs,
but all that himself can; for although the law of charity is
fulfilled by acts of profit, and bounty, and obedience, and
labour, yet it hath no other measures but the proportions
and abundance of a good mind ; and according to this, God
requires that we be περισσεύοντες ἐν τῷ ἔργῳ τοῦ Κυρίου,
" abounding," and that " always in the work of the Lord;"
if we love passionately, we shall do all this ; for love endures
labour and calls it pleasure, it spends all and counts it a
gain, it suffers inconveniences and is quickly reconciled to
them ; if dishonours and affronts be to be endured, love
smiles and calls them favours, and wears them willingly.

> ——————— Alii jacuere ligati
> Turpiter, atque aliquis de Diis non tristibus optat
> Sic fieri turpis,———————

" It is the Lord," said David, and " I will yet be more vile,
and it shall be honour unto me;" thus did the disciples of
our Lord go " from tribunals, rejoicing, that they were
accounted worthy to suffer stripes for that beloved name;"

o 2

and we are commanded " to rejoice in persecutions, to resist
unto blood, to strive to enter in at the strait gate, not to be
weary of well-doing;" do it hugely, and do it always. " Non
enim votis neque suppliciis mulieribus auxilia Deorum pa-
rantur; sed vigilando, agendo, bene consulendo, omnia pros-
pere cedunt." No man can obtain the favour of God by
words and imperfect resolutions, by lazy actions and a remiss piety; but by severe counsels and sober actions, by
watchfulness and prudence, by doing excellent things with
holy intentions and vigorous prosecutions. " Ubi socordiæ
et ignaviæ te tradideris, nequicquam Deos implorabis :" if
your virtues be lazy, your vices will be bold and active : and
therefore Democritus said well, that the painful and the soft-
handed people in religion differ just as good men and bad ;
" nimirum, spe bona," the labouring charity hath ' a good
hope,' but a cool religion hath none at all ; and the distinction will have a sad effect to eternal ages.

These are the great scenes of duty, in which we are to be
fervent and zealous; but because earnestness and zeal are
circumstances of a great latitude, and the zeal of the present
age is stark cold, if compared to the fervours of the apostles,
and other holy primitives ; and in every age a good man's
care may turn into scruple, if he sees that he is not the best
man, because he may reckon his own estate to stand in the
confines of darkness, because his spark is not so great as his
neighbour's fires, therefore it is fit that we consider concerning the degrees of the intention and forward heats ; for when
we have found out the lowest degrees of zeal, and a holy
fervour, we know that duty dwells there, and whatsoever is
above it, is a degree of excellence ; but all that is less than
it, is lukewarmness, and the state of an ungracious and an
unaccepted person.

1. No man is fervent and zealous as he ought, but he
that prefers religion before business, charity before his own
ease, the relief of his brother before money, heaven before
secular regards, and God before his friend or interest. Which
rule is not to be understood absolutely, and in particular
instances, but always generally ; and when it descends to
particulars, it must be in proportion to circumstances, and
by their proper measures : for,

1. In the whole course of life it is necessary, that we pre-

fer religion before any state that is either contrary to it, or
a lessening of its duties.—He that hath a state of life, in
which he cannot at all, in fair proportions, tend to religion,
must quit great proportions of that, that he may enjoy more
of this ; this is that which our blessed Saviour calls " pulling
out the right eye, if it offend thee."

2. In particular actions, when the necessity is equal, he,
that does not prefer religion, is not at all zealous;—for
although all natural necessities are to be served before the
circumstances and order of religion, yet our belly and our
back, our liberty and our life, our health and a friend, are to
be neglected rather than a duty, when it stands in its proper
place, and is required.

3. Although the things of God are by a necessary zeal
to be preferred before the things of the world, yet we must
take heed, that we do not reckon religion, and orders of
worshipping, only to be " the things of God," and all other
duties to be " the things of the world;" for it was a pharisaical device to cry *Corban*, and to refuse to relieve their aged
parents : it is good to give to a church, but it is better to give
to the poor; and though they must be both provided for, yet
in cases of dispute mercy carries the cause against religion
and the temple.   And although Mary was commended for
choosing the better part, yet Mary had done worse, if she
had been at the foot of her Master, when she should have
relieved a perishing brother.   Martha was troubled with
much serving; that was " more than need," and therefore
she was to blame ; and sometimes hearing in some circumstances may be " more than needs;" and some women are
" troubled with over-much hearing," and then they had better
have been serving the necessities of their house.

4. This rule is not to be extended to the relatives of
religion; for although the things of the Spirit are better
than the things of the world, yet a spiritual man is not in
human regards to be preferred before princes and noble
personages.   Because a man is called spiritual in several
regards, and for various measures and manners of partaking
of the Spirit of grace, or co-operating towards the works of
the Spirit.   A king and a bishop both have callings in order
to godliness, and honesty, and spiritual effects, towards the
advancement of Christ's kingdom, whose representatives

severally they are. But whether of these two works more immediately, or more effectively, cannot at all times be known; and therefore from hence no argument can be drawn concerning doing them civil regards; and possibly, ' the partaking the Spirit' is a nearer relation to him, than doing his ministries, and serving his ends upon others; and if relations to God and God's Spirit could bring an obligation of giving proportionable civil honour, every holy man might put in some pretence for dignities above some kings and some bishops. But as the things of the Spirit are in order to the affairs of another world, so they naturally can infer only such a relative dignity, as can be expressed in spiritual manners. But because such relations are subjected in men of this life, and we now converse especially in material and secular significations, therefore we are to express our regards to men of such relations by proportionable expressions : but because civil excellences are the proper ground of receiving and exacting civil honours, and spiritual excellences do only claim them accidentally, and indirectly; therefore, in titles of honour and human regards, the civil pre-eminence is the appendix of the greatest civil power and employment, and is to descend in proper measures; and for a spiritual relation to challenge a temporal dignity, is as if the best music should challenge the best clothes, or a lutestring should contend with a rose for the honour of the greatest sweetness. Add to this, that although temporal things are in order to spiritual, and therefore are less perfect, yet this is not so naturally; for temporal things are properly in order to the felicity of man in his proper and present constitution; and it is by a supernatural grace, that now they are thrust forward to a higher end of grace and glory; and therefore temporal things, and persons, and callings, have properly the chiefest temporal regard; and Christ took nothing of this away from them, but put them higher, by sanctifying and ennobling them. But then the higher calling can no more suppose the higher man, than the richest trade can suppose the richest man. From callings to men, the argument is fallacious; and a smith is a more useful man than he that teaches logic, but not always to be more esteemed, and called to stand at the chairs of princes and nobles. Holy persons and holy things, and all great relations, are to be valued by general proportions to their correlatives; but if we descend to make minute and exact proportions, and proportion an inch of temporal to a minute of spiritual, we must needs be hugely deceived, unless we could measure the motion of an angel by a string, or the progressions of the Spirit by weight and measure of the staple. And yet if these measures were taken, it would be unreasonable that the lower of the higher kind should be preferred before the most perfect and excellent in a lower order of things. A man generally is to be esteemed above a woman, but not the meanest of her subjects before the most excellent queen; not always this man before this woman. Now kings and princes are the best in all temporal dignities; and therefore if they had in them no spiritual relations and consequent excellences (as they have very many), yet are not to be undervalued to spiritual relations, which in this world are very imperfect, weak, partial; and must stay till the next world before they are in a state of excellency, propriety, and perfection; and then also all shall have them, according to the worth of their persons, not of their calling.

But, lastly, what men may not challenge, is not their just and proper due; but spiritual persons and the nearest relatives to God stand by him, but so long as they dwell low and safe in humility, and rise high in nothing but in labours, and zeal of souls, and devotion. In proportion to this rule, a church may be pulled down to save a town, and the vessels of the church may be sold to redeem captives, when there is a great calamity imminent, and prepared for relief, and no other way to succour it.

But in the whole, the duty of zeal requires, that we neglect an ordinary visit rather than an ordinary prayer, and a great profit rather than omit a required duty. No excuse can legitimate a sin; and he that goes about to distinguish between his duty and his profit, and if he cannot reconcile them, will yet tie them together like a hyena and a dog, this man pretends to religion but secures the world, and is indifferent and lukewarm towards that, so he may be warm and safe in the possession of this.

2. To that fervour and zeal that is necessary and a duty, it is required that we be constant and persevering. "Esto fidelis ad mortem," said the Spirit of God to the angel of the

church of Smyrna, " Be faithful unto death, and I will give
thee a crown of life." For he that is warm to day and cold
to-morrow, zealous in his resolution and weary in his practices, fierce in the beginning and slack and easy in his progress, hath not yet well chosen what side he will be of; he
sees not reason enough for religion, and he hath not confidence enough for its contrary ; and therefore he is " duplicis
animi," as St. James calls him ; " of a doubtful mind." For
religion is worth as much to-day as it was yesterday, and
that cannot change though we do; and if we do, we have
left God, and whither be can go that goes from God, his own
sorrows will soon enough instruct him. This fire must never
go out, but it must be like the fire of heaven, it must shine
like the stars, though sometimes covered with a cloud, or
obscured by a greater light ; yet they dwell for ever in their
orbs, and walk in their circles, and observe their circumstances, but go not out by day nor night, and set not when
kings die, nor are extinguished when nations change their
government : so must the zeal of a Christian be, a constant
incentive of his duty; and though sometimes his hand is
drawn back by violence or need, and his prayers shortened
by the importunity of business, and some parts omitted by
necessities, and just compliances, yet still the fire is kept
alive ; it burns within when the light breaks not forth, and
is eternal as the orb of fire, or the embers of the altar of
incense.

3. No man is zealous as he ought, but he that delights in
the service of God :—without this no man can persevere, but
must faint under the continual pressure of an uneasy load.
If a man goes to his prayers as children go to school, or give
alms as those that pay contribution, and meditate with the
same willingness, with which young men die, this man does
' personam sustinere,' ' he acts a part' which he cannot long
personate, but will find so many excuses and silly devices to
omit his duty, such tricks to run from that, which will make
him happy; he will so watch the eyes of men, and be so sure
to do nothing in private ; he will so often distinguish and
mince the duty into minutes and little particles, he will so tie
himself to the letter of the law, and be so careless of the intention and spiritual design, be will be so punctual in the ceremony and trifling in the secret, and he will be so well pleased

when he is hindered by an accident not of his own procuring, and will have so many devices to defeat his duty, and to cozen himself, that he will certainly manifest, that he is afraid of religion, and secretly hates it; he counts it a burden, and an objection, and then the man is sure to leave it, when his circumstances are so fitted. But if we delight in it, we enter into a portion of the reward, as soon as we begin the work, and the very grace shall be stronger than the temptation in its very pretence of pleasure; and therefore it must needs be pleasing to God, because it confesses God to be the best master, religion the best work, and it serves God with choice, and will, and reconciles our nature to it, and entertains our appetite; and then there is no 'ansa' or 'handle' left, whereby we can easily be drawn from duty, when all parties are pleased with the employment. But this delight is not to be understood as if it were always required, that we should feel an actual cheerfulness, and sensible joy; such as was that of Jonathan,' when he had newly tasted honey, and the light came into his eyes, and he was refreshed and pleasant. This happens sometimes, when God pleases to entice, or reward a man's spirit, with little antepasts of heaven; but such a delight only is necessary, and a duty, that we always choose our duty regularly, and undervalue the pleasures of temptation, and proceed in the work of grace with a firm choice and unabated election; our joy must be a joy of hope, a joy at the least of confident sufferers, the joys of faith and expectation; "rejoicing in hope," so the Apostle calls it; that is, a going forward upon such a persuasion as sees the joys of God laid up for the children of men: and so the sun may shine under a cloud; and a man may rejoice in persecution, and delight in losses; that is, though his outward man groans and faints, and dies, yet his spirit, ὁ ἔσω ἄνθρωπος, 'the inner man,' is confident and industrious, and hath a hope by which it lives and works unto the end: it was the case of our blessed Saviour in his agony; his " soul was exceeding sorrowful unto death," and the load of his Father's anger crushed his shoulder, and bowed his knees to the ground; and yet he chose it, and still went forward, and resolved to die, and did so; and what we choose we delight in; and we think it to be eligible, and therefore amiable, and fit by its proper excellences and appendages to be delighted in; it is not pleasant to the flesh at all times, for its dignity is spiritual and heavenly; but therefore it is proportioned to the spirit, which is as heavenly as the reward, and therefore can feel the joys of it, when the body hangs the head, and is uneasy and troubled.

These are the necessary parts of zeal; of which if any man fails, he is in a state of lukewarmness: and that is a spiritual death. As a banished man or a condemned person is dead civilly; he is 'diminutus capite,' he is not reckoned in the 'census,' nor partakes of the privileges, nor goes for a person, but is reckoned among things in the possession of others: so is a lukewarm person; he is 'corde diminutus,' he is spiritually dead, his heart is estranged from God, his affections are lessened, his hope diminished, and his title cancelled; and he remains so, unless, 1. He prefers religion before the world, and, 2. Spiritually rejoices in doing his duty, and, 3. Does it constantly, and with perseverance. These are the heats and warmth of life; whatsoever is less than this, is a disease, and leads to the coldness and dishonours of the grave.

SERMON XIV.

PART III.

So long as our zeal and forwardness in religion hath only these constituted parts, it hath no more than can keep the duty alive: but beyond this, there are many degrees of earnestness and vehemence, which are progressions towards the state of perfection, which every man ought to design and desire to be added to his portion: of this sort I reckon frequency in prayer, and alms above our estate. Concerning which two instances, I have these two cautions to insert.

1. Concerning frequency in prayer, it is an act of zeal so ready and prepared for the spirit of a man, so easy and useful, so without objection, and so fitted for every man's affairs, his necessities and possibilities, that he that prays but seldom, cannot in any sense pretend to be a religious person. For in Scripture there is no other rule for the frequency of

prayer given us, but by such words which signify we should
do it 'always,' 'pray continually:' and, "Men ought always
to pray and not to faint." And then, men have so many necessities, that if we should esteem our needs to be the circumstances and positive determination of our times of prayer,
we should be very far from admitting limitation of the former
words, but they must mean, that we ought to pray frequently
every day. For in danger and trouble, natural religion
teaches us to pray; in a festival fortune our prudence and
our needs enforce us equally. For though we feel not a present smart, yet we are certain then is our biggest danger:
and if we observe how the world treats her darlings, men of
riches and honour, of prosperity and great success, we cannot but confess them to be the most miserable of all men, as
being in the greatest danger of losing their biggest interest.
For they are bigger than the iron hand of law, and they
cannot be restrained with fear: the hand grasps a power of
doing all that, which their evil heart can desire, and they
cannot be restrained with disability to sin; they are flattered
by all mean, and base, and undiligent persons, which are the
greatest part of mankind; but few men dare reprove a potent
sinner; he shall every day be flattered and seldom counselled:
and his great reflections and opinions of his condition make
him impatient of reproof, and so he cannot be restrained with
modesty: and therefore as the needs of the poor man, his
rent-day, and the cries of his children, and the oppression
he groans under, and his δυσκολόκοιτος μέριμνα, his uneasy,
'ill-sleeping care,'—will make him run to his prayers, that in
heaven a new decree may be passed every day for the provisions of his daily bread: so the greater needs of the rich,
their temptations, and their dangers, the flattery and the vanity, the power and the pride, their business and evil estate
of the whole world upon them, call upon them to be zealous
in this instance, that they 'pray often,' that they 'pray
without ceasing;' for there is great reason they should
do so, and great security and advantage, if they do; for he
that prays well and prays often, must needs be a good and a
blessed man; and truly he that does not, deserves no pity
for his misery. For when all the troubles and dangers of his
condition may turn into his good, if he will but desire they
should; when upon such easy terms he may be happy, for

there is no more trouble in it than this, "Ask and ye shall
receive;" that is all that is required: no more turnings and
variety in their road; when (I say) at so cheap a rate, a poor
man may be provided for, and a rich man may escape damnation, be that refuses to apply himself to this remedy, quickly,
earnestly, zealously, and constantly, deserves the smart of
his poverty, and the care of it, and the scorn, if he be poor;
and if he be rich, it is fit he should (because be desires it)
die by the evils of his proper danger. It was observed by
Cassian, "Orationibus maxime insidiantur Dæmones;" "The
devil is more busy to disturb our prayers, than to hinder any
thing else." For else it cannot be imagined, why we should
be brought to pray so seldom; and to be so listless to them,
and so trifling at them. No, the devil knows, upon what
hard terms he stands with the praying man; he also knows,
that it is a mighty emanation of God's infinite goodness and
a strange desire of saving mankind, that he hath to so easy
a duty promised such mighty blessings. For God knowing,
that upon hard terms we would not accept of heaven itself,
and yet hell was so intolerable a state, that God who loved
us, would affix heaven to a state of prayer and devotion;
this, because the devil knows to be one of the greatest arts
of the Divine mercy, he labours infinitely to supplant; and if
he can but make men unwilling to pray, or to pray coldly,
or to pray seldom, he secures his interest, and destroys the
man's; and it is infinitely strange, that he can and doth prevail so much in this so unreasonable temptation. "Oppo-
suisti nubem, ne transiret oratio," the mourning prophet complained[a]; " there was a cloud passed between heaven and the
prayer of Judah;" a little thing God knows; it was a wall,
which might have been blown down with a few hearty sighs,
and a few penitential tears; or if the prayers had ascended
in a full and numerous body, themselves would have broken
through that little partition; but so the devil prevails often;
" opponit nubem," "he claps a cloud between:" some little
objection; 'a stranger is come;' or 'my head aches;' or 'the
church is too cold;' or 'I have letters to write;' or, 'I am
not disposed;' or, 'it is not yet time;' or, 'the time is past:'
these, and such as these are the clouds the devil claps between heaven and us; but these are such impotent objections,

[a] Lam. iii. 44.

that they were as soon confuted as pretended, by all men that are not fools, or professed enemies of religion, but that they are clouds, which sometimes look like lions and bears, castles and walls of fire, armies and horses; and indeed are any thing that a man will fancy; and the smallest article of objection managed and conducted by the devil's arts, and meeting with a wretchless, careless, undevout spirit, is a lion in the way, and a deep river; it is impassable, and it is impregnable. Γίγνονται πάνθ' ὅ, τι βούλονται νεφέλαι· λύκοι ἐὰν Σίμωνα κατίδωσι, ἔλαφοι τῷ Κλεωνύμῳ*; as the sophister said in the Greek comedy, " Clouds become any thing as they are represented; wolves to Simon, harts to Cleonymus;" for the devil fits us with clouds, according as we can be abused; and if we love affairs of the world, he can contrive its circumstances so, that they shall cross our prayers; and so it is in every instance: and the best way to cure this evil is prayer; pray often, and pray zealously, and the Sun of Righteousness will scatter these clouds, and warm our hearts with his holy fires: but it is in this as in all acquired habits; the habit makes the action easy and pleasant; but this habit cannot be gotten without frequent actions: habits are the daughters of action; but then they nurse their mother, and produce daughters after her image, but far more beautiful and prosperous. For in frequent prayer there is so much rest and pleasure, that as soon as ever it is perceived, the contrary temptation appears unreasonable; none are so unwilling to pray, as they that pray seldom; for they that do pray often, and with zeal, and passion, and desire, feel no trouble so great, as when they are forced to omit their holy offices and hours of prayers. It concerns the devil's interest to keep us from all the experience of the rewards of a frequent and holy prayer; and so long as you will not try and " taste how good and gracious the Lord is" to the praying man, so long you cannot see the evil of your coldness and lukewarm state; but if you would but try, though it be but for curiosity's sake, and inform yourselves in the vanity of things, and the truth of pretences, and the certainty of theological propositions, you should find yourselves taken in a golden snare, which will tie you to nothing but felicity, and safety, and holiness, and pleasure. But then the caution,

* Arist. Nιφέλαι. 348.

which I intended to insert, is this ; that frequency in prayers, and that part of zeal which relates to it, is to be upon no account but of a holy spirit, a wise heart, and reasonable persuasion; for if it begin upon passion or fear, in imitation of others, or desires of reputation, honour and fantastic principles, it will be unblessed and weary, unprosperous and without return of satisfaction : therefore if it happen to begin upon a weak principle, be very curious to change the motive, and with all speed let it be turned into religion and the love of holy things : then, let it be as frequent as it can prudently, it cannot be amiss.

When you are entered into a state of zealous prayer, and a regular devotion, whatever interruption you can meet with, observe their causes, and be sure to make them irregular, seldom, and contingent, that your omissions may be seldom and casual, as a bare accident ; for which no provisions can be made : for if ever it come, that you take any thing habitually and constantly from your prayers, or that you distract from them very frequently, it cannot be but you will become troublesome to yourself; your prayers will be uneasy, they will seem hinderances to your more necessary affairs of passion and interest, and the things of the world : and it will not stand still, till it comes to apostacy, and a direct dispute and contempt of holy things.   For it was an old rule, and of a sad experience, " Tepiditas, si callum obduxerit, fiet apostasia :" ' If your lukewarmness be habitual and a state of life, if it once be hardened by the usages of many days, it changes the whole state of the man, it makes him an apostate to devotion.' Therefore be infinitely careful in this particular, always remembering the saying of St. Chrysostom ; " Docendi, prædicandi officia et alia cessant suo tempore, precandi autem nunquam;" ' There are seasons for teaching, and preaching, and other outward offices : but prayer is the duty of all times, and of all persons, and in all contingencies : from other things, in many cases, we may be excused, but from prayer never.' In this, therefore, καλὸν ζηλοῦσθαι, " it is good to be zealous."

2. Concerning the second instance I named, viz. To give alms above our estate, it is an excellent act of zeal, and needs no other caution to make it secure from illusion and danger, but that our egressions of charity do not prejudice justice.

See that your alms do not other men wrong; and let them do what they can to thyself, they will never prejudice thee by their abundance; but then be also careful, that the pretences of justice do not cozen thyself of thy charity, and the poor of thine alms, and thy soul of the reward. He that is in debt, is not excused from giving alms, till his debts are paid; but only from giving away such portions which should and would pay them, and such which he intended should do it: there are 'lacernæ divitiarum,' and crumbs from the table, and the gleanings of the harvest, and the scatterings of the vintage, which in all estates are the portions of the poor, which being collected by the hand of Providence, and united wisely, may become considerable to the poor, and are the necessary duties of charity; but beyond this also, every considerable relief to the poor is not a considerable diminution to the estate; and yet if it be, it is not always considerable in the accounts of justice; for nothing ought to be pretended against the zeal of alms, but the certain omissions, or the very probable retarding the doing that, to which we are otherwise obliged. He that is going to pay a debt, and in the way meets an indigent person that needs it all, may not give it to him, unless he knows by other means to pay the debt; but if he can do both, he hath his liberty to lay out his money for a crown. But then in the case of provision for children, our restraint is not so easy, or discernible; 1. Because we are not bound to provide for them in a certain portion, but may do it by the analogies and measures of prudence, in which there is a great latitude. 2. Because our zeal of charity is a good portion for them, and lays up a blessing for inheritance. 3. Because the fairest portions of charity are usually short of such sums, which can be considerable in the duty of provision for our children. 4. If we for them could be content to take any measure less than all, any thing under every thing that we can, we should find the portions of the poor made ready to our hands sufficiently to minister to zeal, and yet not to intrench upon this case of conscience; but the truth is, we are so careless, so unskilled, so unstudied, in religion,—that we are only glad to make an excuse, and to defeat our souls of the reward of the noblest grace: we are contented, if we can but make a pretence; for we are highly pleased if our conscience be quiet, and care not so much that our duty be performed, much less that our eternal interest be advanced in bigger portions. We care not, we strive not, we think not, of getting the greater rewards of heaven; and he whose desires are so indifferent for the greater, will not take pains to secure the smallest portion; and it is observable, that ἐλάχιστος ἐν τῇ βασιλείᾳ, "the least in the kingdom of heaven [a]," is as much as οὐδεὶς, "as good as none;" if a man will be content with his hopes of the lowest place there, and will not labour for something beyond it, he does not value it at all; and it is ten to one, but he will lose that for which he takes so little pains, and is content with so easy a security. He,—that does his alms, and resolves that in no case he will suffer inconvenience for his brother, whose case it may be is intolerable, —should do well to remember, that God, in some cases, requires a greater charity; and it may be, we shall be called to die for the good of our brother: and that although it always supposes a zeal, and a holy fervour, yet sometimes it is also a duty, and we lose our lives if we go to save them; and so we do with our estates, when we are such good husbands in our religion, that we will serve all our own conveniences before the great needs of a hungry and afflicted brother, God oftentimes takes from us that which with so much curiosity we would preserve, and then we lose our money, and our reward too.

3. Hither is to be reduced the accepting and choosing the counsels evangelical: the virgin or widow estate in order to religion: selling all, and giving it to the poor: making ourselves eunuchs for the kingdom of heaven: offering ourselves to death voluntarily, in exchange or redemption of the life of a most useful person, as "Aquila and Priscilla, who ventured their lives for St. Paul:" the zeal of souls: St. Paul's preaching to the Corinthian church without wages: remitting of rights and forgiving of debts, when the obliged person could pay, but not without much trouble: protection of calamitous persons with hazard of our own interest and a certain trouble; concerning which and all other acts of zeal, we are to observe the following measures, by which our zeal will become safe and holy, and by them also we shall per-

ceive the excesses of zeal, and its inordinations: which is the next thing I am to consider.

1. The first measure, by which our zeal may comply with our duty, and its actions become laudable, is charity to our neighbour. For since God receives all that glorification of himself, whereby we can serve and minister to his glory, reflected upon the foundation of his own goodness, and bounty, and mercy, and all the hallelujahs that are or ever shall be sung in heaven, are praises and thanksgivings; and that God himself does not receive glory from the acts of his justice, but then when his creatures will not rejoice in his goodness and mercy: it follows that we imitate this original excellency, and pursue God's own method; that is, glorify him ' in via misericordiæ,' ' in the way of mercy' and bounty, charity and forgiveness, love and fair compliances: there is no greater charity in the world than to save a soul, nothing that pleases God better, nothing that can be in our hands greater or more noble, nothing that can be a more lasting and delightful honour, than that a perishing soul,—snatched from the flames of an intolerable hell, and borne to heaven upon the wings of piety and mercy by the ministry of angels, and the graces of the Holy Spirit,—shall to eternal ages bless God and bless thee; Him, for the author and finisher of salvation, and thee for the minister and charitable instrument: that bright star must needs look pleasantly upon thy face for ever, which was by thy hand placed there, and, had it not been for thy ministry, might have been a sooty coal, in the regions of sorrow. Now, in order to this, God hath given us all some powers and ministries, by which we may by our charity promote this religion, and the great interest of souls: counsels and prayers, preaching and writing, passionate desires and fair examples going before others in the way of godliness, and bearing the torch before them, that they may see the way and walk in it. This is a charity, that is prepared more or less for every one; and, by the way, we should do well to consider, what we have done towards it. For as it will be a strange arrest at the day of judgment to Dives, that he fed high and suffered Lazarus to starve, and every garment,—that lies by thee and perishes, while thy naked brother does so too for want of it,—shall be a bill of indictment against thy unmerciful soul; so it will

be in every instance: in what thou couldest profit thy brother and didst not, thou art accountable; and then tell over the times, in which thou hast prayed for the conversion of thy sinning brother; and compare the times together, and observe, whether thou hast not tempted him or betrayed him to sin, or encouraged him in it; or didst not hinder him, when thou mightest, more frequently than thou hast, humbly, and passionately, and charitably, and zealously, bowed thy head, and thy heart, and knees, to God to redeem that poor soul from hell, whither thou seest him descending with as much indifferency as a stone into the bottom of the well. In this thing καλὸν ζηλοῦσθαι, " it is a good thing to be zealous," and put forth all your strength, for you can never go too far. But then be careful, that this zeal of thy neighbour's amendment be only expressed in ways of charity, not of cruelty, or importune justice. " He that strikes the prince for justice," as Solomon's expression is, " is a companion of murderers;" and he that out of zeal of religion, shall go to convert nations to his opinion by destroying Christians, whose faith is entire and summed up by the apostles: this man breaks the ground with a sword, and sows tares, and waters the ground with blood, and ministers to envy and cruelty, to errors and mistake, and there comes up nothing but poppies to please the eye and fancy, disputes and hypocrisy, new summaries of religion estimated by measures of anger, and accursed principles; and so much of the religion as is necessary to salvation, is laid aside, and that brought forth that serves an interest, not holiness; that fills the schools of a proud man, but not that which will fill heaven. Any zeal is proper for religion, but the zeal of the sword and the zeal of anger; this is πικρία ζήλου, " the bitterness of zeal[a];" and it is a certain temptation to every man against his duty: for if the sword turns preacher, and dictates propositions by empire instead of arguments, and engraves them in men's hearts with a poniard, that it shall be death to believe what I innocently and ignorantly am persuaded of, it must needs be unsafe to " try the spirits, to try all things," to make inquiry; and yet without this liberty, no man can justify himself before God and man, nor confidently say that his religion is best; since he cannot without a final danger

[a] James, iii. 14.

make himself able to give a right sentence, and to follow
that which he finds to be the best; this may ruin souls by
making hypocrites, or careless and compliant against conscience or without it; but it does not save souls, though
peradventure it should force them to a good opinion: this is
inordination of zeal; for Christ,—by reproving St. Peter, drawing his sword, even in the cause of Christ, for his sacred,
and yet injured person, διδάσκει μὴ χρῆσθαι μαχαίρᾳ, κἂν τὸν
θεὸν δοκεῖ τις ἐκδικεῖν (saith Theophylact),—" teaches us not
to use the sword though in the cause of God, or for God
himself;" because he will secure his own interest, only let
him be served as himself is pleased to command: and it is
like Moses's passion, it throws the tables of the law out of
our hands, and breaks them in pieces out of indignation to
see them broken. This is zeal, that is now in fashion, and
hath almost spoiled religion; men, like the zealots of the
Jews, cry up their sect, and in it their interest; ζηλοῦσι μα-
θητὰς, καὶ μαχαίρας ἀνασύρονται; " they affect disciples and
fight against the opponents;" and we shall find in Scripture,
that when the apostles began to preach the meekness of the
Christian institution, salvations and promises, charity and
humility, there was a zeal set up against them; the apostles
were zealous for the Gospel, the Jews were zealous for the
law: and see what different effects these two zeals did produce; the zeal of the law came to this, ἐθορύβουν τὴν πόλιν,
and ἐδίωξαν μέχρι θανάτου, and ἀνασύρονται, and ὀχλοποιή-
σαντες, " they stirred up the city, they made tumults, they
persecuted this way unto the death, they got letters from the
high-priest, they kept Damascus with a garrison," they sent
parties of soldiers to silence and to imprison the preachers,
and thought they did God service, when they put the apostles
to death, and they swore " neither to eat nor to drink, till
they had killed Paul." It was an old trick of the Jewish
zeal,

Non monstrare vias, eadem nisi sacra colenti :
Quæsitum ad fontem solos deducere verpos. *Juv.* 14. 104.

They would not shew the way to a Samaritan, nor give a
cup of cold water but to a circumcised brother; that was their
zeal. But the zeal of the apostles was this, they preached
publicly and privately, they prayed for all men, they wept to

God for the hardness of men's hearts, they "became all things to all men, that they might gain some," they travelled through deeps and deserts, they endured the heat of the Sirian star, and the violence of Euroclydon, winds and tempests, seas and prisons, mockings and scourgings, fastings and poverty, labour and watching, they endured every man and wronged no man, they would do any good thing and suffer any evil, if they had but hopes to prevail upon a soul; they persuaded men meekly, they entreated them humbly, they convinced them powerfully, they watched for their good, but meddled not with their interest; and this is the Christian zeal, the zeal of meekness, the zeal of charity, the zeal of patience, ἐν τούτοις καλὸν ζηλοῦσθαι, "In these it is good to be zealous," for you can never go far enough.

2. The next measure of zeal is prudence. For, as charity is the matter of zeal; so is discretion the manner. It must always be for good to our neighbour, and there need no rules for the conducting of that, provided the end be consonant to the design, that is, that charity be intended, and charity be done. But there is a zeal also of religion or worshipping, and this hath more need of measures and proper cautions. For religion can turn into a snare; it may be abused into superstition, it may become weariness in the spirit, and tempt to tediousness, to hatred, and despair : and many persons, through their indiscreet conduct, and furious marches, and great loads taken upon tender shoulders and inexperienced, have come to be perfect haters of their joy, and despisers of all their hopes; being like dark lanterns, in which a candle burns bright, but the body is encompassed with a crust and a dark cloud of iron; and these men keep the fires and light of holy propositions within them, but the darkness of hell, the hardness of a vexed heart, hath shaded all the light, and makes it neither apt to warm nor to enlighten others, but it turns to fire within, a fever and a distemper dwell there, and religion is become their torment.

1. Therefore our zeal must never carry us beyond that which is profitable. There are many institutions, customs, and usages, introduced into religion upon very fair motives, and apted to great necessities; but to imitate those things, when they are disrobed of their proper ends is an importune zeal, and signifies nothing but a forward mind, and an easy

heart, and an imprudent head; unless these actions can be invested with other ends and useful purposes. The primitive church were strangely inspired with a zeal of virginity, in order to the necessities of preaching and travelling, and easing the troubles and temptations of persecution; but when the necessity went on, and drove the holy men into deserts, that made colleges of religious, and their manner of life was such, so united, so poor, so dressed, that they must love 'more non seculari,' 'after the manner of men divorced from the usual intercourses of the world :' still their desire of single life increased, because the old necessity lasted, and a new one did supervene. Afterward, the case was altered, and then the single life was not to be chosen for itself, nor yet imitation of the first precedents ; for it could not be taken out from their circumstances and be used alone. He therefore that thinks he is a more holy person for being a virgin or a widower, or that is bound to be so, because they were so ; or that he cannot be a religious person, because he is not so;—hath zeal indeed, but not according to knowledge. But now if the single state can be taken out and put to new appendages, and fitted to the end of another grace or essential duty of religion, it will well become a Christian zeal to choose it so long, as it can serve the end with advantage and security. Thus also a zealous person is to choose his fastings ; while they are necessary to him, and are acts of proper mortification, while he is tempted, or while he is under discipline, while he repents, or while he obeys; but some persons fast in zeal, but for nothing else ; fast when they have no need, when there is need they should not; but call it religion to be miserable or sick ; here their zeal is folly, for it is neither an act of religion nor of prudence, to fast when fasting probably serves no end of the spirit; and therefore in the fasting-days of the church, although it is warrant enough to us to fast, if we had no end to serve in it but the mere obedience, yet it is necessary that the superiors should not think the law obeyed, unless the end of the first institution be observed : a fasting-day is a day of humiliation, and prayer ; and fasting being nothing itself, but wholly the handmaid of a farther grace, ought not to be divested of its holiness and sanctification, and left like the walls of a ruinous church where there is no duty performed to God, but there remains

something of that, which used to minister to religion. The
want of this consideration hath caused so much scandal and
dispute, so many snares and schisms, concerning ecclesiastical fasts. For when it was undressed and stripped of all the
ornaments and useful appendages, when from a solemn day it
grew to be common; from thence to be less devout by being
less seldom and less useful; and then it passed from a day of
religion to be a day of order, and from fasting till night, to fasting till evening-song, and evening-song to be sung about twelve
o'clock; and from fasting it was changed to a choice of food,
from eating nothing to eating fish, and that the letter began
to be stood upon, and no usefulness remained but what every
of his own piety should put into it, but nothing was enjoined
by the law, nothing of that exacted by the superiors, then
the law fell into disgrace, and the design became suspected,
and men were first ensnared and then scandalized, and then
began to complain without remedy, and at last took remedy
themselves without authority; the whole affair fell into a disorder and mischief; and zeal was busy on both sides, and on
both sides was mistaken, because they fell not upon the proper remedy, which was to reduce the law to the usefulness
and advantages of its first intention. But this I intended
not to have spoken.

2. Our zeal must never carry us beyond that which is safe.
Some there are, who in their first attempts and entries upon
religion, while the passion, that brought them in, remains,
undertake things as great as their highest thoughts; no repentance is sharp enough, no charities expensive enough,
no fastings afflictive enough, then 'totis quinquatribus orant;'
and finding some deliciousness at the first contest, and in
that activity of their passion, they make vows to bind themselves for ever to this state of delicacies. The onset is fair:
but the event is this. The age of a passion is not long, and
the flatulent spirit being breathed out, the man begins to
abate of his first heats, and is ashamed: but then he considers that all was not necessary, and therefore he will
abate something more; and from something to something,
at last it will come to just nothing, and the proper effect
of this is, indignation, and hatred of holy things, an impudent spirit, carelessness or despair. Zeal sometimes carries a man into temptation: and he that never thinks he loves

God dutifully or acceptably, because he is not imprisoned
for him or undone, or designed to martyrdom, may desire a
trial that will undo him. It is like fighting of a duel to shew
our valour. Stay till the king commands you to fight and
die, and then let zeal do its noblest offices. This irregularity
and mistake was too frequent in the primitive church, when
men and women would strive for death, and be ambitious to
feel the hangman's sword; some miscarried in the attempt,
and became sad examples of the unequal yoking a frail spirit
with a zealous driver.

3. Let zeal never transport us to attempt any thing but
what is possible. M. Teresa made a vow, that she would
do always that, which was absolutely the best. But neither
could her understanding always tell her which was so, nor
her will always have the same fervours: and it must often
breed scruples, and sometimes tediousness, and wishes that
the vow were unmade. He that vows never to have an ill
thought, never to commit an error, hath taken a course, that
his little infirmities shall become crimes, and certainly be imputed by changing his unavoidable infirmity into vow-breach.
Zeal is a violence to a man's spirit, and unless the spirit be
secured by the proper nature of the duty, and the circumstances of the action, and the possibilities of the man; it is
like a great fortune in the meanest person, it bears him beyond his limit, and breaks him into dangers and passions,
transportations and all the furies of disorder, that can happen
to an abused person.

4. Zeal is not safe, unless it be 'in re probabili' too, it
must be 'in a likely matter.' For we that find so many excuses to untie all our just obligations, and distinguish our
duty into so much fineness, that it becomes like leaf-gold
apt to be gone at every breath; it cannot be prudent that we
zealously undertake, what is not probable to be effected: if
we do, the event can be nothing but portions of the former
evil, scruple and snares, shameful retreats and new fantastic
principles. In all our undertakings we must consider what
is our state of life, what our natural inclinations, what is our
society, and what are our dependences; by what necessities
we are borne down, by what hopes we are biassed; and by
these let us measure our heats and their proper business. A
zealous man runs up a sandy hill; the violence of motion is
his greatest hinderance: and a passion in religion destroys as

much of our evenness of spirit, as it sets forward any outward work; and therefore although it be a good circumstance and degree of a spiritual duty, so long as it is within, and relative to God and ourselves, so long it is a holy flame; but if it be in an outward duty, or relative to our neighbours, or in an instance not necessary, it sometimes spoils the action, and always endangers it. But I must remember, we live in an age in which men have more need of new fires to be kindled within them, and round about them, than of any thing to allay their forwardness: there is little or no zeal now but the zeal of envy, and killing as many as they can, and damning more than they can; πύρωσις and καπνὸς πυρώσεως 'smoke and lurking fires' do corrode and secretly consume: therefore this discourse is less necessary. A physician would have but small employment near the Riphæan mountains, if he could cure nothing but calentures; catarrhs, and dead palsies, colds and consumptions, are their evils, and so is lukewarmness and deadness of spirit, the proper maladies of our age: for though some are hot, when they are mistaken, yet men are cold in a righteous cause; and the nature of this evil is to be insensible; and the men are farther from a cure, because they neither feel their evil, nor perceive their danger. But of this I have already given account: and to it, I shall only add what an old spiritual person told a novice in religion, asking him the cause why he so frequently suffered tediousness in his religious offices; "Nondum vidisti requiem quam speramus, nec tormenta quæ timemus;"— "Young man, thou hast not seen the glories which are laid up for the zealous and devout, nor yet beheld the flames which are prepared for the lukewarm, and the haters of strict devotion." But the Jews tell, that Adam having seen the beauties and tasted the delicacies of paradise, repented and mourned upon the Indian mountains for three hundred years together: and we who have a great share in the cause of his sorrows, can by nothing be invited to a persevering, a great, a passionate religion, more than by remembering what he lost, and what is laid up for them whose hearts are burning lamps, and are all on fire with Divine love, whose flames are fanned with the wings of the Holy Dove, and whose spirits shine and burn with that fire, which the Holy Jesus came to enkindle upon the earth.

SERMON XV.

THE HOUSE OF FEASTING; OR THE EPICURE'S
MEASURES.

PART I.

Let us eat and drink, for to-morrow we die.—1 Cor. xv. 32.
last part.

THIS is the epicure's proverb, begun upon a weak mistake, started by chance from the discourses of drink, and thought witty by the undiscerning company, and prevailed infinitely, because it struck their fancy luckily, and maintained the merry-meeting; but as it happens commonly to such discourses, so this also, when it comes to be examined by the consultations of the morning, and the sober hours of the day, it seems the most witless, and the most unreasonable in the world. When Seneca (ep. 18.) describes the spare diet of Epicurus and Metrodorus, he uses this expression : " Liberaliora sunt alimenta carceris : sepositos ad capitale supplicium, non tam anguste, qui occisurus est, pascit :" " The prison keeps a better table ; and he that is to kill the criminal to-morrow morning, gives him a better supper overnight." By this he intended to represent his meal to be very short ; for as dying persons have but little stomach to feast high, so they that mean to cut their throat, will think it a vain expense to please it with delicacies, which, after the first alteration, must be poured upon the ground, and looked upon as the worst part of the accursed thing. And there is also the same proportion of unreasonableness, that because men shall " die to-morrow," and by the sentence and unalterable decree of God they are now descending to their graves, that therefore they should first destroy their reason, and then force dull time to run faster, that they may die sottish as beasts, and speedily as a fly : but they thought there was no life after this ; or if there were, it was without pleasure, and every soul thrust into a hole, and a dorter of a span's length allowed for his rest, and for his walk ; and in the shades below no numbering of healths by the numeral letters of Philenium's name, no fat mullets, no oysters of Lucrinus, no Lesbian or Chian wines. Τοῦτο σαφῶς, ἄνθρωπε, μαθὼν εὔφραινε σεαυτόν. Therefore now enjoy the delicacies of nature, and feel the descending wines distilled through the limbeck of thy tongue, and larynx, and suck the delicious juices of fishes, the marrow of the laborious ox, and the tender lard of Apulian swine, and the condited bellies of the scarus; but lose no time, for the sun drives hard, and the shadow is long, and " the days of mourning are at hand," but the number of the days of darkness and the grave cannot be told.

Thus they thought they discoursed wisely, and their wisdom was turned into folly; for all their arts of providence, and witty securities of pleasure, were nothing but unmanly prologues to death, fear, and folly, sensuality and beastly pleasures. But they are to be excused rather than we. They placed themselves in the order of beasts and birds, and esteemed their bodies nothing but receptacles of flesh and wine, larders and pantries; and their soul the fine instrument of pleasure and brisk perception of relishes and gusts, reflections and duplications of delight; and therefore they treated themselves accordingly. But then, why we should do the same things, who are led by other principles, and a more severe institution, and better notices of immortality, who understand what shall happen to a soul hereafter, and know that this time is but a passage to eternity, this body but a servant to the soul, this soul a minister to the Spirit, and the whole man in order to God and to felicity; this, I say, is more unreasonable than to eat *aconita* to preserve our health, and to enter into the flood that we may die a dry death; this is a perfect contradiction to the state of good things, whither we are designed, and to all the principles of a wise philosophy, whereby we are instructed that we may become " wise unto salvation." That I may therefore do some assistances towards the curing the miseries of mankind, and reprove the follies and improper motions towards felicity, I shall endeavour to represent to you,

1. That plenty and the pleasures of the world are no proper instruments of felicity.

2. That intemperance is a certain enemy to it; making life unpleasant, and death troublesome and intolerable.

3. I shall add the rules and measures of temperance in eating and drinking, that nature and grace may join to the constitution of man's felicity.

1. Plenty and the pleasures of the world are no proper instruments of felicity. It is necessary that a man have some violence done to himself, before he can receive them: for nature's bounds are; "non esurire, non sitire, non algere," "to be quit from hunger, and thirst, and cold," that is, to have nothing upon us that puts us to pain; against which she hath made provisions by the fleece of the sheep, and the skins of the beasts, by the waters of the fountain, and the herbs of the field, and of these no good man is destitute, for that share that he can need to fill those appetites and necessities, he cannot otherwise avoid: τῶν ἁρπούντων οὐδεὶς πένης ἐστί. For it is unimaginable that nature should be a mother, natural and indulgent to the beasts of the forest, and the spawn of fishes, to every plant and fungus, to cats and owls, to moles and bats, making her storehouses always to stand open to them; and that, for the Lord of all these, even to the noblest of her productions, she should have made no provisions, and only produced in us appetites sharp as the stomach of wolves, troublesome as the tyger's hunger, and then run away, leaving art and chance, violence and study, to feed us and to clothe us. This is so far from truth, that we are certainly more provided for by nature than all the world besides; for every thing can minister to us; and we can pass into none of nature's cabinets, but we can find our table spread: so that what David said to God, " Whither shall I go from thy presence? If I go to heaven, thou art there; if I descend to the deep, thou art there also; if I take the wings of the morning, and flee into the uttermost parts of the wilderness, even there thou wilt find me out, and thy right hand shall uphold me," we may say it concerning our table, and our wardrobe; if we go into the fields, we find them tilled by the mercies of heaven, and watered with showers from God to feed us, and to clothe us; if we go down into the deep, there God hath multiplied our stores, and filled a magazine which no hunger can exhaust; the air drops down delicacies, and the wilderness can sustain us, and all that is in nature, that which feeds lions, and that which the ox eats, that which the fishes live upon, and that

which is the provision for the birds, all that can keep us
alive; and if we consider that of the beasts and birds, for
whom nature hath provided but one dish, it may be flesh or
fish, or herbs or flies, and these also we secure with guards
from them, and drive away birds and beasts from that provision which nature made for them, yet seldom can we find
that any of these perish with hunger : much rather shall we
find that we are secured by the securities proper for the more
noble creatures by that Providence that disposes all things,
by that mercy that gives us all things, which to other creatures are ministered singly ; by that labour, that can procure
what we need; by that wisdom, that can consider concerning
future necessities; by that power, that can force it from inferior creatures; and by that temperance, which can fit our
meat to our necessities.   For if we go beyond what is needful, as we find sometimes more than was promised, and very
often more than we need, so we disorder the certainty of our
felicity, by putting that to hazard which nature hath secured.
For it is not certain, that if we desire to have the wealth of
Susa, or garments stained with the blood of the Tyrian fish,
that if we desire to feed like Philoxenus, or to have tables
loaden like the boards of Vitellius, that we shall never want.
It is not nature that desires these things, but lust and violence;
and by a disease we entered into the passion and the necessity, and in that state of trouble it is likely we may dwell for
ever, unless we reduce our appetites to nature's measures.

> Si ventri bene, si lateri est pedibusque tuis, nil
> Divitiæ poterant regales addere majus*.

And therefore it is, that plenty and pleasures are not the
proper instruments of felicity.   Because felicity is not a
jewel that can be locked in one man's cabinet.   God intended
that all men should be made happy, and he, that gave to all
men the same natural desires, and to all men provision of
satisfactions by the same meats and drinks, intended, that it
should not go beyond that measure of good things, which
corresponds to those desires, which all men naturally have.

He that cannot be satisfied with common provision, hath
a bigger need than he that can; it is harder, and more contingent, and more difficult, and more troublesome, for him
to be satisfied; βρυάζω τῷ κατὰ τὸ σωμάτιον ἡδεῖ, ὕδατι καὶ

* Horace. Ep. 1. 12. 5.

ἄρτῳ χρώμενος, προσπτύω ταῖς ἐκ πολυτελείας ἡδοναῖς, said Epicurus; "I feed sweetly upon bread and water, those sweet and easy provisions of the body, and I defy the pleasures of costly provisions;" and the man was so confident that he had the advantage over wealthy tables, that he thought himself happy as the immortal gods, ἑτοῖμος ἔρχεσθαι τῷ Διὶ ὑπὲρ εὐδαιμονίας διαγωνίζεσθαι, μάζαν ἔχων καὶ ὕδωρ: for these provisions are easy, they are to be gotten without amazing cares; no man needs to flatter if he can live as nature did intend: " Magna pars libertatis est bene moratus venter*:" he need not swell his accounts, and intricate his spirit with arts of subtilty and contrivance; he can be free from fears, and the chances of the world cannot concern him. And this is true, not only in those severe and anchoretical and philosophical persons, who lived meanly as a sheep, and without variety as the Baptist, but in the same proportion it is also true in every man, that can be contented with that which is honestly sufficient. Maximus Tyrius considers concerning the felicity of Diogenes, a poor Sinopean, having not so much nobility as to be born in the better parts of Greece: but he saw that he was compelled by no tyrant to speak or do ignobly; he had no fields to till, and therefore took no care to buy cattle, and to hire servants; he was not distracted when a rent-day came, and feared not when the wise Greeks played the fool and fought who should be lord of that field that lay between Thebes and Athens; he laughed to see men scramble for dirty silver, and spend ten thousand Attick talents for the getting the revenues of two hundred philippicks; he went with his staff and bag into the camp of the Phocenses, and the soldiers reverenced his person and despised his poverty, and it was truce with him whosoever had wars; and the diadem of kings, and the purple of the emperors, the mitre of high-priests, and the divining-staff of soothsayers, were things of envy and ambition, the purchase of danger, and the rewards of a mighty passion; and men entered into them by trouble and extreme difficulty, and dwelt under them as a man under a falling roof, or as Damocles under the tyrant's sword,

Nunc lateri incumbens—mox deinde supinus,
Nunc cubat in faciem, nunc recto pectore surgens,

Senec.

sleeping like a condemned man; and let there be what pleasure men can dream of in such broken slumbers, yet the fear
of waking from this illusion, and parting from this fantastic
pleasure, is a pain and torment which the imaginary felicity
cannot pay for. " Cui cum paupertate bene convenit, dives
est: non qui parum habet, sed qui plus cupit, pauper est."
All our trouble is from within us; and if a dish of lettuce
and a clear fountain can cool all my heats, so that I shall
have neither thirst nor pride, lust nor revenge, envy nor ambition, I am lodged in the bosom of felicity; and, indeed, no
men sleep so soundly, as they that lay their head upon nature's lap. For a single dish, and a clear chalice lifted from
the springs, can cure my hunger and thirst: but the meat of
Ahasuerus's feast cannot satisfy my ambition and my pride.
" Nulla re egere, Dei proprium; quàm paucissimis autem,
Deo proximum," said Socrates. He, therefore, that hath
the fewest desires and the most quiet passions, whose wants
are soon provided for, and whose possessions cannot be disturbed with violent fears, he that dwells next door to satisfaction, and can carry his needs and lay them down where
he please,—this man is the happy man; and this is not to be
done in great designs, and swelling fortunes. " Dives jam
factus desiit gaudere lente; cariùs edit et bibit, et lætatur
dives, quàm pauper, qui in quolibet, in parato, inempto
gaudet, et facile epulari potest; dives nunquam." For as it
is in plants which nature thrusts forth from her navel, she
makes regular provisions, and dresses them with strength and
ornament, with easiness and full stature; but if you thrust
a jessamine there where she would have had a daisy grow,
or bring the tall fir from dwelling in his own country, and
transport the orange or the almond-tree near the fringes of
the north-star, nature is displeased, and becomes unnatural,
and starves her sucklings, and renders you a return less than
your charge and expectation: so it is in all our appetites;
when they are natural and proper, nature feeds them and
makes them healthful and lusty, as the coarse issue of the
Scythian clown; she feeds them and makes them easy without cares and costly passion; but if you thrust an appetite
into her, which she intended not, she gives you sickly and
uneasy banquets, you must struggle with her for every drop
of milk she gives beyond her own needs; you may get gold

from her entrails, and at a great charge provide ornaments for
your queens and princely women : but our lives are spent in
the purchase; and when you have got them, you must have
more : for these cannot content you, nor nourish the spirit.
' Ad supervacua sudatur;' ' A man must labour infinitely to
get more than he needs;' but to drive away thirst and hunger, a man needs not sit in the fields of the oppressed poor,
nor lead armies, nor break his sleep, ' et contumeliosam hu-
manitatem pati,' ' and to suffer shame,' and danger, and envy,
and affront, and all the retinue of infelicity.

———————— Quis non Epicurum
Suspicit, exigui letum plantaribus horti ? *Juv. 13. 122.*

If men did but know, what felicity dwells in the cottage
of a virtuous poor man, how sound his sleeps, how quiet his
breast, how composed his mind, how free from care, how
easy his provision, how healthful his morning, how sober his
night, how moist his mouth, how joyful his heart, they would
never admire the noises, and the diseases, the throng of passions, and the violence of unnatural appetites, that fill the
houses of the luxurious and the heart of the ambitious.

Nam neque divitibus contingunt gaudia solis. *Hor. Ep. 1. 17. 9.*

These which you call pleasures, are but the imagery and fantastic appearances, and such appearances even poor men may
have.   It is like felicity, that the king of Persia should come
to Babylon in the winter, and to Susa in the summer ; and
be attended with all the servants of one hundred and twenty-
seven provinces, and with all the princes of Asia.   It is like
this, that Diogenes went to Corinth in the time of vintage,
and to Athens when winter came ; and instead of courts, visited the temples and the schools, and was pleased in the
society of scholars and learned men, and conversed with the
students of all Asia and Europe. If a man loves privacy, the
poor fortune can have that when princes cannot; if he loves
noises, he can go to markets and to courts, and may glut
himself with strange faces, and strange voices, and stranger
manners, and the wild designs of all the world: and when
that day comes in which we shall die, nothing of the eating
and drinking remains, nothing of the pomp and luxury, but
the sorrow to part with it, and shame to have dwelt there
where wisdom and virtue seldom come, unless it be to call

men to sober counsels, to a plain, and a severe, and a more
natural way of living; and when Lucian derides the dead
princes and generals, and says that in hell they go up and
down selling salt meats and crying muscles, or begging; and he
brings in Philip of Macedon, ἐν γωνιδίῳ τινὶ μισθοῦ ἀκούμενον
τὰ σαθρὰ τῶν ὑποδημάτων, ' mending of shoes in a little stall;'
he intended to represent, that in the shades below, and in the
state of the grave, the princes and voluptuous have a being
different from their present plenty; but that their condition
is made contemptible and miserable by its disproportion to
their lost and perishing voluptuousness. The result is this,
that Tiresias (Nɛĸ. 21.) told the ghost of Menippus, inquiring
what state of life was nearest to felicity, Ὁ τῶν ἰδιωτῶν ἄριστος
βίος, καὶ σωφρονέστερος, 'The private life, that which is freest
from tumult and vanity,' noise and luxury, business and ambition, nearest to nature and a just entertainment to our necessities; that life is nearest to felicity. Τοιαῦτα λῆρον ἡγη-
σάμενος, τοῦτο μόνον ἐξ ἅπαντος θηράσῃ, ὅπως, τὸ παρὸν εὖ Ͽέμι-
νος, παραδράμῃς γελῶν τὰ πολλὰ καὶ περὶ μηδὲν ἐσπουδακώς·
therefore despise the swellings and the diseases of a disordered life, and a proud vanity; be troubled for no outward
thing beyond its merit, enjoy the present temperately, and
you cannot choose but be pleased to see, that you have so
little share in the follies and miseries of the intemperate
world.

2. Intemperance in eating and drinking is the most contrary course to the Epicure's design in the world; and the
voluptuous man hath the least of pleasure; and upon this
proposition, the consideration is more material and more
immediately reducible to practice, because in eating and
drinking, men please themselves so much, and have the necessities of nature to usher in the inordination of gluttony
and drunkenness, and our need leads in vice by the hand,
that we know not how to distinguish our friend from our
enemy; and St. Austin is sad upon this point; " Thou,
O Lord, hast taught me that I should take my meat as I take
my physic; but while I pass from the trouble of hunger to
the quietness of satisfaction, in the very passage I am ensnared by the cords of my own concupiscence. Necessity
bids me pass, but I have no way to pass from hunger to fulness, but over the bridge of pleasure; and although health

and life be the cause of eating and drinking, yet pleasure, a dangerous pleasure, thrusts herself into attendance, and sometimes endeavours to be the principal; and I do that for pleasure's sake which I would only do for health; and yet they have distinct measures, whereby they can be separated, and that which is enough for health, is too little for delight, and that which is for my delight, destroys my health, and still it is uncertain for what end I do indeed desire; and the worst of the evil is this, that the soul is glad because it is uncertain, and that an excuse is ready, that under the pretence of health, " obumbret negotium voluptatis," " the design of pleasure may be advanced and protected." How far the ends of natural pleasure may lawfully be enjoyed, I shall afterward consider: in the meantime, if we remember that the epicure's design is pleasure principally, we may the better reprove his folly by considering, that intemperance is a plain destruction to all that, which can give real and true pleasure.

2. It is an enemy to health, without which it is impossible to feel any thing of corporal pleasure. 2. A constant full table hath in it less pleasure than the temperate provisions of the hermit, or the labourer, or the philosophical table of scholars, and the just pleasures of the virtuous. 3. Intemperance is an impure fountain of vice, and a direct nurse of uncleanness. 4. It is a destruction of wisdom. 5. It is a dishonour and disreputation to the person and the nature of the man.

1. It is an enemy to health: which is, as one calls it, " ansa voluptatum et condimentum vitæ;" it is ' that handle by which we can apprehend, and perceive pleasures, and that sauce that only makes life delicate;' for what content can a full table administer to a man in a fever? And he that hath a sickly stomach, admires at *his* happiness, that can feast with cheese and garlic, unctuous beverages, and the low-tasted spinach: health is the opportunity of wisdom, the fairest scene of religion, the advantages of the glorifications of God, the charitable ministries to men; it is a state of joy and thanksgiving, and in every of its period feels a pleasure from the blessed emanations of a merciful Providence. The world does not minister, does not feel, a greater pleasure, than to be newly delivered from the racks or the gratings of the

stone, and the torments and convulsions of a sharp cholic:
and no organs, no harp, no lute, can sound out the praises
of the Almighty Father so spritefully, as the man that rises
from his bed of sorrows, and considers what an excellent
difference he feels from the groans and intolerable accents
of yesterday.   Health carries us to church, and makes us rejoice in the communion of saints; and an intemperate table
makes us to lose all this.   For this is one of those sins,
which St. Paul affirms to be πρόδηλοι, προάγουσαι εἰς κρίσιν,
" manifest, leading before unto judgment."   It bears part of
its punishment in this life, and hath this appendage, like the
sin against the Holy Ghost, that it is not remitted in this
world, nor in the world to come: that is, if it be not repented
of, it is punished here and hereafter, which the Scripture does
not affirm concerning all sins, and all cases.

   But in this the sinner gives sentence with his mouth, and
brings it to execution with his hands;

> Pœna tamen præsens, cum tu deponis amictum
> Turgidus, et crudum pavonem in balnea portas.

The old gluttons among the Romans, Heliogabalus, Tigel-
lius, Crispus, Montanus, " notæque per oppida buccæ[b],"
famous epicures, mingled their meats with vomitings; so
did Vitellius, and entered into their baths to digest their
pheasants, that they might speedily return to the mullet and
the eels of Syëne, and then they went home and drew their
breath short till the morning, and it may be not at all before
night:

> Hinc subitæ mortes, atque intestata senectus[i].

Their age is surprised at a feast, and gives them not time to
make their will, but either they are choked with a large
morsel, and there is no room for the breath of the lungs, and
the motions of the heart; or a fever burns their eyes out, or
a quinsey punishes that intemperate throat that had no religion, but the eating of the fat sacrifices, the portions of the
poor and of the priest; or else they are condemned to a lethargy if their constitutions be dull; and, if active, it may be
they are wild with watching.

g Juv. 1. 143.   b Ib. 3. 35.   i Ib. 1. 144.

Plurimos hic ægr moritur vigilando : sed illum
Languorem peperit cibus imperfectus, et hærens
Ardenti stomacho.ᵏ————— ——

So that the epicure's genial proverb may be a little altered,
and say, " Let us eat and drink, for by this means to-morrow
we shall die ;" but that is not all, for these men lead a healthless life; that is, are long, are every day dying, and at last
die with torment. Menander was too short in his expression,
μόνος οὗτος φαίνεται εὐθάνατος; that it is indeed death, but
gluttony is ' a pleasant death.'

————— Ἔχοντα πολλὴν τὴν χολάδα παχὺν,
Καὶ μόλις λαλοῦντα, καὶ τὸ πνεῦμ' ἔχοντα πᾶν ἄπω,
Ἐσθίοντα καὶ λέγοντα, Σήπωμ' ὑπὸ τῆς ἡδονῆς.

For this is the glutton's pleasure, "To breathe short and dif-
ficultly, scarce to be able to speak, and when he does, he
cries out, I die and rot with pleasure." But the folly is as
much to be derided as the men to be pitied, that we daily
see men afraid of death with a most intolerable apprehension,
and yet increase the evil of it, the pain, and the trouble, and
the suddenness of its coming, and the appendage of an insufferable eternity.

Rem struere exoptas cæso bove, Mercuriumque
Arcessis fibrâˡ ————— ————

They pray for herds of cattle, and spend the breeders upon
feasts and sacrifices. For why do men go to temples and
churches, and make vows to God and daily prayers, that
God would give them a healthful body, and take away their
gout, and their palsies, their fevers and apoplexies, the pains
of the head and the gripings of the belly, and arise from
their prayers, and pour in loads of flesh and seas of wine, lest
there should not be matter enough for a lusty disease ?

Poscis opem nervis, corpusque fidele senectæ :
Esto age : sed grandes patinæ tucetaque crassa
Annuere his superos vetuere, Jovemque morantur.ᵐ

But this is enough that the rich glutton shall have his
dead body condited and embalmed ; he may be allowed to
stink and suffer corruption while he is alive ; these men are
for the present living sinners and walking rottenness, and
hereafter will be dying penitents and perfumed carcasses, and

ᵏ Juv. 3. 232.   ˡ Pers. 2. 44.   ᵐ Pers. sat. 2.

Q 2

their whole felicity is lost in the confusions of their unnatural disorder. When Cyrus had espied Astyages and his fellows coming drunk from a banquet loaden with variety of follies and filthiness, their legs failing them, their eyes red and staring, cozened with a moist cloud and abused by a doubled object, their tongues full of sponges, and their heads no wiser, he thought they were poisoned, and he had reason: for what malignant quality can be more venomous and hurtful to a man than the effect of an intemperate goblet, and a full stomach? It poisons both the soul and body. All poisons do not kill presently, and this will in process of time, and hath formidable effects at present.

But therefore methinks the temptations, which men meet withal from without, are in themselves most unreasonable and soonest confuted by us. He that tempts me to drink beyond my measure, civilly invites me to a fever; and to lay aside my reason as the Persian women did their garments and their modesty at the end of feasts : and all the question then will be, Which is the worse evil, to refuse your uncivil kindness, or to suffer a violent head-ache, or to lay up heaps big enough for an English surfeit? Creon in the tragedy said well ;

Κρεῖσσον δέ μαι νῦν πρός σ' ἀπίχθισθαι, γύναι,
'Η μαλθακισθένθ' ὕστερον μέγα στίνειν·,

" It is better for me to grieve thee, O stranger, or to be affronted by thee, than to be tormented by thy kindness the next day and the morrow after;" and the freedman of Domitius, the father of Nero, suffered himself to be killed by his lord : and the son of Praxaspes by Cambyses, rather than they would exceed their own measures up to a full intemperance, and a certain sickness and dishonour. For, as Plutarch said well, to avoid the opinion of an uncivil man, or being clownish, to run into a pain of thy sides or belly, into madness or a head-ache, is the part of a fool and a coward, and of one that knows not how to converse with men, 'citra pocula et nidorem,' in any thing but in the famelic smells of meat and vertiginous drinkings.

Ebrius et petolans, qui nullum forte occidit,
Dat pœnas, noctem patitur, lugentis amicum,
Pelidæ ――――――― °

"A drunkard and a glutton feels the torments of a restless night, although he hath not killed a man;" that is, just like murderers and persons of an affrighting conscience; so wakes the glutton, so broken, and sick, and disorderly are the slumbers of the drunkard. Now let the epicure boast his pleasures, and tell how he hath swallowed the price of provinces, and gobbets of delicious flesh, purchased with the reward of souls; let him brag "furorem illum conviviorum, et fœdissimum patrimoniorum exitium culinam," "of the madness of delicious feasts, and that his kitchen hath destroyed his patrimony;" let him tell that he takes in every day,[p]

Quantum Sasseia bibebat,

As much wine as would refresh the sorrows of forty languishing prisoners; or let him set up his vainglorious triumph,

Ut quod ' multi Damalin meri
' Bassum Threicia' vicit ' amystide' ;

That he hath knocked down Damalis with the twenty-fifth bottle, and hath outfeasted Anthony or Cleopatra's luxury; it is a goodly pleasure and himself shall bear the honour.

——————— Rarum ac memorabile magni
Gutturis exemplum, conducendusque magister[r].

But for the honour of his banquet he hath some ministers attending that he did not dream of, and in the midst of his loud laughter, the gripes of his belly, and the fevers of the brain, "Pallor et genæ pendulæ, oculorum ulcera, tremulæ manus, furiales somni, inquies nocturna," as Pliny reckons them, "paleness and hanging cheeks, ulcers of the eyes, and trembling hands, dead or distracted sleeps," these speak aloud, that to-day you 'eat and drink, that to-morrow you die,' and die for ever.

It is reported concerning Socrates, that when Athens was destroyed by the plague, he in the midst of all the danger escaped untouched by sickness, because by a spare and severe diet, he had within him no tumult of disorderly humours, no factions in his blood, no loads of moisture prepared for charnel-houses, or the sickly hospitals; but a vigorous heat, and a well-proportioned radical moisture; he had enough for health and study, philosophy and religion, for the tem-

ples and the academy, but no superfluities to be spent in
groans and sickly nights: and all the world of gluttons is
hugely convinced of the excellency of temperance in order
to our moral felicity and health, because when themselves
have left virtue, and sober diet, and counsels, and first lost
their temperance, and then lost their health, they are forced
to go to temperance and abstinence, for their cure. "Vilis
enim tenuisque mensa (ut loquuntur pueri) sanitatis mater
est*," then a thin diet and an humble body, fasting and
emptiness, and arts of scattering their sin and sickness,
is in season; but by the same means they might preserve
their health, by which they do restore it; but when they
are well, if they return to their full tables and oppressing
meals, their sickness was but like Vitellius' vomiting, that
they might eat again; but so they may entail a fit of sickness
upon every full moon, till both their virtue and themselves
decrease into the corruptions and rottenness of the grave.
But if they delight in sharp fevers and horrid potions, in
sour palates and heaps of that which must be carried forth,
they may reckon their wealthy pleasures to be very great and
many, if they will but tell them one by one with their sicknesses and the multitude of those evils they shall certainly
feel, before they have thrown their sorrows forth. "These
men (as St. Paul's expression is) heap up wrath against the
day of wrath, and the revelation of the day of God's most
righteous judgments." Strange therefore it is, that for the
stomach, which is scarce a span long, there should be provided so many furnaces and ovens, huge fires and an army
of cooks, cellars swimming with wine, and granaries sweat-
ing with corn; and that into one belly should enter the vintage of many nations, the spoils of distant provinces, and the
shell-fishes of several seas. When the heathens feasted their
gods, they gave nothing but a fat ox, a ram, or a kid; they
poured a little wine upon the altar, and burned a handful of
gum: but when they feasted themselves, they had many vessels filled with Campanian wine, turtles of Liguria, Sicilian
beeves, and wheat from Egypt, wild boars from Illyrium, and
Grecian sheep, variety, and load, and cost, and curiosity:
and so do we. It is so little we spend in religion, and so
very much upon ourselves, so little to the poor, and so with-

* Chrysost.

out measure to make ourselves sick, that we seem to be in love with our own mischief, and so passionate for necessity and want, that we strive all the ways we can to make ourselves need more than nature intended. I end this consideration with the saying of the cynic; It is to be wondered at, that men eat so much for pleasure's sake : and yet for the same pleasure should not give over eating, and betake themselves to the delights of temperance, since to be healthful and holy is so great a pleasure. However, certain it is, that no man ever repented, that he arose from the table sober, healthful, and with his wits about him; but very many have repented, that they sat so long, till their bellies swelled, and their health, and their virtue, and their God, is departed from them.

SERMON XVI.

PART II.

2. A CONSTANT full table is less pleasant than the temperate provisions of the virtuous, or the natural banquets of the poor. Χάρις τῇ μακαρίᾳ φύσει, ὅτι τὰ ἀναγκαῖα ἐποίησεν εὐπόριστα, τὰ δὲ δυσπόριστα οὐκ ἀναγκαῖα, said Epicurus ; " Thanks be to the God of nature, that he hath made that which is necessary, to be ready at hand, and easy to be had ; and that which cannot easily be obtained, is not necessary it should be at all ;" which in effect is to say, It cannot be constantly pleasant : for necessity and want make the appetite, and the appetite makes the pleasure ; and men are infinitely mistaken when they despise the poor man's table, and wonder how he can endure that life, that is maintained without the exercise of pleasure, and that he can suffer his day's labour, and recompense it with unsavoury herbs, and potent garlic, with watercresses, and bread coloured like the ashes that gave it hardness : he hath a hunger that gives it deliciousness ; and we may as well wonder that a lion eats raw flesh, or that a wolf feeds upon the turf ; they have an appetite proportionable to this meat ; and their necessity, and their hunger, and their use, and their nature, are the cooks that dress their provisions, and make them delicate :

and yet if water and pulse, natural provisions, and the simple diet, were not pleasant, as indeed they are not to them who have been nursed up and accustomed to the more delicious, ἔπειτα πλουτῶν οὐκ ἔθ᾽ ἥδεται φακῶν, yet it is a very great pleasure to reduce our appetites to nature, and to make our reason rule our stomach, and our desires comply with our fortunes, and our fortunes be proportionable to our persons. " Non est voluptas aqua et polenta (said a philosopher); sed summa voluptas est, posse ex his capere voluptatem." ' It is an excellent pleasure to be able to take pleasure in worts and water,' in bread and onions ; for then a man can never want pleasure when it is so ready for him, that nature hath spread it over all its provisions. Fortune and art give delicacies ; nature gives meat and drink ; and what nature gives, fortune cannot take away ; but every change can take away what only is given by the bounty of a full fortune ; and if in satisfaction and freedom from care, and security and proportions to our own natural appetite, there can be pleasure, then we may know how to value the sober and natural tables of the virtuous and wise, before that state of feastings which a war can lessen, and a tyrant can take away, or the pirates may intercept, or a blast may spoil, and is always contingent, and is so far from satisfying, that either it destroys the appetite, and capacity of pleasure, or increases it beyond all the measures of good things.

He that feasts every day, feasts no day ; ἐτρύφησεν, ὥστε μὴ πολὺν τρυφᾷν χρόνον. And however you treat yourselves, sometimes you will need to be refreshed beyond it ; but what will you have for a festival, if you wear crowns every day ? even a perpetual fulness will make you glad to beg pleasure from emptiness, and variety from poverty or an humble table.

> Plerumque gratæ principibus vices.
> Mundæque parvo sub lare pauperum
> Cœnæ, sine aulæis, et ostro,
> Sollicitam explicuere frontem[1].

But, however, of all things in the world a man may best and most easily want pleasure, which if you have enjoyed, it passes away at the present, and leaves nothing at all behind it, but sorrow and sour remembrance. No man felt a greater pleasure in a goblet of wine than Lysimachus, when he

[1] Hor. Od. 3. 29. 16.

fought against the Getæ, and himself and his whole army were compelled by thirst to yield themselves to bondage; but when the wine was sunk as far as his navel, the pleasure was gone, and so was his kingdom and his liberty: for though the sorrow dwells with a man pertinaciously, yet the pleasure is swift as lightning, and more pernicious; but the pleasures of a sober and a temperate table are pleasures till the next day, καὶ τῇ ὑστεραίᾳ ἡδέως γίνονται, as Timotheus said of Plato's scholars; they converse sweetly, and ʻ are of perfect temper and delicacy of spirit even the next morning:' whereas the intemperate man is forced to lie long in bed, and forget that there is a sun in the sky; he must not be called till he hath concocted, and slept his surfeit into a truce and a quiet respite; but whatsoever this man hath suffered, certain it is that the poor man's head did not ache, neither did he need the juice of poppies, or costly cordials, physicians or nurses, to bring him to his right shape again, like Apuleius's ass, with eating roses: and let him turn his hour-glass, he will find his head aches longer than his throat was pleased; and, which is worst, his glass runs out with joggings and violence, and every such concussion with a surfeit makes his life look nearer its end, and ten to one but it will, before its natural period, be broken in pieces. If these be the pleasures of an epicure's table, I shall pray that my friends may never feel them; but he that sinneth against his Maker, shall fall into the calamities of intemperance.

3. Intemperance is the nurse of vice; Ἀφροδίτης γάλα, ʻ Venus-milk,' so Aristophanes calls wine; πάντων δεινῶν μητρόπολις, ʻ the mother of all grievous things;' so Pontianus. For by the experience of all the world, it is the bawd to lust: and no man must ever dare to pray to God for a pure soul in a chaste body, if himself does not live temperately, if himself " make provisions for the flesh, to fulfil the lusts of it;" for in this case he shall find " that which enters into him, shall defile him" more than he can be cleansed by those vain prayers, that come from his tongue, and not from his heart. Intemperance makes rage and choler, pride and fantastic principles; it makes the body a sea of humours, and those humours the seat of violence: by faring deliciously every day, men become senseless of the

evils of mankind, inapprehensive of the troubles of their
brethren, unconcerned in the changes of the world, and the
cries of the poor, the hunger of the fatherless, and the thirst
of widows: οὐκ ἐκ τῶν μαζοφάγων οἱ τύραννοι, ἀλλ᾽ ἐκ τῶν
τρυφωμένων, said Diogenes; " Tyrants never come from the
cottages of them that eat pulse and coarse fare, but from the
delicious beds and banquets of the effeminate and rich
feeders." For, to maintain plenty and luxury, sometimes
wars are necessary, and oppressions and violence: but no
landlord did ever grind the face of his tenants, no prince
ever sucked blood from his subjects for the maintenance of
a sober and a moderate proportion of good things. And
this was intimated by St. James, " Do not rich men oppress
you, and draw you before the judgment-seat[u]?" For all men
are passionate to live according to that state in which they
were born, or to which they are devolved, or which they have
framed to themselves; those therefore that love to live high
and deliciously,

Et quibus in solo vivendi causa palato[x],

who live not to God but to their belly, not to sober counsels
but to an intemperate table, have framed to themselves a
manner of living, which oftentimes cannot be maintained
but by injustice and violence, which coming from a man
whose passions are made big with sensuality and an habitual
folly, by pride and forgetfulness of the condition and miseries of mankind, are always unreasonable, and sometimes
intolerable.

——— regustatum digito terebrare salinum
Contentus perages, si vivere cum Jove tendis[y].

Formidable is the state of an intemperate man, whose sin begins with sensuality, and grows up in folly and weak discourses, and is fed by violence, and applauded by fools and
parasites, full bellies and empty heads, servants and flatterers, whose hands are full of flesh and blood, and their hearts
empty of pity and natural compassion; where religion cannot inhabit, and the love of God must needs be a stranger;
whose talk is loud and trifling, injurious and impertinent;

[u] Jam. ii. 6.   [x] Juv. 11. 11.   [y] Pers. 5. 138.

and whose employment is the same with the work of the sheep or the calf, always to eat; their loves are the lusts of the lower belly; and their portion is in the lower regions to eternal ages, where their thirst, and their hunger, and their torment, shall be infinite.

4. Intemperance is a perfect destruction of wisdom. Παχεῖα γαστὴρ λεπτὸν οὐ τίκτει νόον, "A full-gorged belly never produced a sprightly mind:" and therefore these kind of men are called γαστέρες ἀργαί, "slow bellies," so St. Paul concerning the intemperate Cretans out of their own poet: they are like the tigers of Brazil, which when they are empty, are bold, and swift, and full of sagacity ; but being full, sneak away from the barking of a village-dog. So are these men, wise in the morning, quick and fit for business ; but when the sun gives the sign to spread the tables, and intemperance brings in the messes, and drunkenness fills the bowls, then the man falls away, and leaves a beast in his room; nay, worse, νεκύας μεσαύχενας, they are dead all but their throat and belly, so Aristophanes hath fitted them with a character, "Carcasses above half way." Plotinus descends one step lower yet; affirming such persons, ἀποδενδρωθῆναι, "to be made trees," whose whole employment and life is nothing but to feed and suck juices from the bowels of their nurse and mother; and indeed commonly they talk as trees in a wind and tempest, the noise is great and querulous, but it signifies nothing but trouble and disturbance. A full meal is like Sisera's banquet, at the end of which there is a nail struck into a man's head : ὡς συγκολλῶσα καὶ οἷον καθηλοῦσα τὴν ψυχὴν πρὸς τὴν τοῦ σώματος ἀπόλαυσιν, so Porphyry; "it knocks a man down, and nails his soul to the sensual mixtures of the body." For what wisdom can be expected from them, whose soul dwells in clouds of meat, and floats up and down in wine, like the spilled cups which fell from their hands, when they could lift them to their heads no longer? πολλάκις γὰρ ἐν οἴνου κύμασί τις ναυαγεῖ : it is a perfect shipwreck of a man, the pilot is drunk, and the helm dashed in pieces, and the ship first reels, and by swallowing too much is itself swallowed up at last. And therefore the Navis Agrigentina, the madness of the young fellows of Agrigentum, who being drunk, fancied themselves in a storm, and the house the ship, was more than the wild fancy of their cups ;

it was really so, they were all cast away, they were broken
in pieces by the foul disorder of the storm.

> *Hinc Vini atque somni degener socordia,*
> *Libido sordens, inverecundus lepos,*
> *Variæque pestes languidorum sensuum.*
> *Hinc et frequenti marcida oblectamine*
> *Scintilla mentis intorpescit nobilis,*
> *Animosque pigris steriit in præcordiis* [1].

' The senses languish, the spark of Divinity that dwells within
is quenched; and the mind snorts, dead with sleep and fulness in the fouler regions of the belly.'

So have I seen the eye of the world looking upon a fen-
ny bottom, and drinking up too free draughts of moisture,
gathered them into cloud, and that cloud crept about his
face, and made him first look red, and then covered him with
darkness and an artificial night : so is our reason at a feast,

> *Potrem resudans crapulam*
> *Obstrangulatæ mentis ingenium premit.*

The clouds gather about the head, and according to the method and period of the children, and productions of darkness,
it first grows red, and that redness turns into an obscurity,
and a thick mist, and reason is lost to all use and profitable-
ness of wise and sober discourses ; ἀναθυμίασις θολωδεστέρα
οὖσα ἐπισκοτεῖ τῇ ψυχῇ, " a cloud of folly and distraction
darkens the soul," and makes it crass and material, polluted
and heavy, clogged and laden like the body : ψυχὴ κάθυδρος
ταῖς ἐκ τοῦ οἴνου ἀναθυμιάσεσι καὶ νεφέλαις δίκην σώματος ποιου-
μένη. ' And there cannot be any thing said worse, reason
turns into folly, wine and flesh into a knot of clouds, the soul
itself into a body,' and the spirit into corrupted meat; there
is nothing left but the rewards and portions of a fool to be
reaped and enjoyed there, where flesh and corruption shall
dwell to eternal ages; and therefore in Scripture such men
are called βαρυκάρδιοι. " Hesternis vitiis animum quoque
prægravant:" Their heads are gross, their souls are emerged
in matter, and drowned in the moistures of an unwholesome
cloud; they are dull of hearing, slow in apprehension, and
to action they are as unable as the hands of a child, who too
hastily hath broken the enclosures of his first dwelling.

[1] Prudent. hym. de Jejun.   [a] Clem. Alexand.

But temperance is reason's girdle, and passion's bridle; σῶα φρόνησις, so Homer in Stobæus; that is σωφροσύνη; "prudence is safe," while the man is temperate; and therefore σώφρον is opposed τῷ χαλίφρονι, " A temperate man is no fool;" for temperance is the σωφρονιστήριον, such as Plato appointed to night-walkers, a prison to restrain their inordinations; it is ῥώμη ψυχῆς, as Pythagoras calls it; κρηπὶς ἀρετῆς, so Socrates; κόσμος ἀγαθῶν πάντων, so Plato; ἀσφάλεια τῶν καλλίστων ἕξεων, so Jamblichus; it is " the strength of the soul, the foundation of virtue, the ornament of all good things, and the corroborative of all excellent habits."

5. After all this, I shall the less need to add, that intemperance is a dishonour, and disreputation to the nature, and the person, and the manners of a man. But naturally men are ashamed of it, and the needs of nature shall be the veil for their gluttony, and the night shall cover their drunkenness : τέγγε πνεύμονα οἴνῳ, τὸ γὰρ ἄστρον περιστέλλεται[b], which the Apostle rightly renders, " They that are drunk, are drunk in the night ;" but the priests of Heliopolis never did sacrifice to the sun with wine; meaning, that this is so great a dishonour, that the sun ought not to see it; and they that think there is no other eye but the sun that sees them, may cover their shame by choosing their time; just as children do their danger by winking hard, and not looking on. Σκυθίζειν, καὶ ζωρότερον πιεῖν, καὶ δεινῶς φαγεῖν, " To drink sweet drinks and hot, to quaff great draughts, and to eat greedily ;" Theoprastus makes them characters of a clown[c].

3. And now that I have told you the foulness of the epicure's feasts and principles, it will be fit that I describe the measures of our eating and drinking, that the needs of nature may neither become the cover to an intemperate dish, nor the freer refreshment of our persons be changed into scruples, that neither our virtue nor our conscience fall into an evil snare.

1. The first measure of our eating and drinking, is our " natural needs," μήτε ἀλγεῖν κατὰ σῶμα, μήτε ταράττεσθαι κατὰ ψυχήν; these are the measures of nature, ' that the body be free from pain, and the soul from violence.' Hunger, and thirst, and cold, are the natural diseases of the body; and

food and raiment are their remedies, and therefore are the
measures.

In quantum sitis atque fames et frigora poscunt,
Quantum, Epicure, tibi parvis suffecit in hortis[d].

But in this there are two cautions. 1. Hunger and thirst
are only to be extinguished while they are violent and troublesome, and are not to be provided for to the utmost extent
and possibilities of nature; a man is not hungry so long till
he can eat no more, but till its sharpness and trouble is over,
and he that does not leave some reserves for temperance,
gives all that he can to nature, and nothing at all to grace;
for God hath given a latitude in desires and degrees of appetite; and when he hath done, he laid restraint upon it in some
whole instances, and of some parts in every instance; that
man might have something to serve God of his own, and
something to distinguish him from a beast in the use of their
common faculties. Beasts cannot refrain, but fill all the
capacity when they can; and if a man does so, he does what
becomes a beast, and not a man. And therefore there are
some little symptoms of this inordination, by which a man
may perceive himself to have transgressed his measures;
" ructation, uneasy loads, singing, looser pratings, importune
drowsiness, provocation of others to equal and full chalices;"
and though in every accident of this signification it is hard
for another to pronounce that the man hath sinned, yet by
these he may suspect himself, and learn the next time to
hold the bridle harder.

2. " This hunger must be natural," not artificial and provoked; for many men make necessities to themselves, and
then think they are bound to provide for them. It is necessary to some men to have garments made of the Calabrian
fleece, stained with the blood of the *murex*, and to get money
to buy pearls round and orient; ' scelerata hoc fecit culpa;'
but it is the man's luxury that made it so; and by the same
principle it is, that in meats, what is abundant to nature is
defective and beggarly to art; and when nature willingly
rises from table, when the first course of flesh plain and
natural is done, then art, and sophistry, and adulterate
dishes, invite him to taste and die, μέχρί τινος ἐσμὲν σάρκες,
μέχρί τινος τῆς γῆς κύπτομεν[e]; well may a sober man wonder

[d] Juv. xiv. 319.   [e] Chrysost.

that men should be so much in love with earth and corruption, the parent of rottenness and a disease, that even then, when by all laws witches and enchanters, murderers and man-stealers, are chastised and restrained with the iron hands of death; yet that men should at great charges give pensions to an order of men, whose trade it is to rob them of their temperance, and wittily to destroy their health; κατωφερεῖς καὶ χαμαιζήλους καὶ τοὺς ἐκ τῆς γῆς κεπολογοῦντας, the Greek fathers call such persons ;

—— curvæ in terris animæ et cœlestiom inanes ;

people bowed down to the earth; " lovers of pleasures more than lovers of God :" ' Aretinas mentes,' so Antidamus calls them, men framed in the furnaces of Etruria, " Aretine spirits[f]," beginning and ending in flesh and filthiness; dirt and clay all over. But go to the crib, thou glutton, and there it will be found that when the charger is clean, yet nature's rules were not prevaricated; the beast eats up all his provisions because they are natural and simple; or if he leaves any, it is because he desires no more than till his needs be served; and neither can a man (unless he be diseased in body or in spirit, in affection or in habit) eat more of natural and simple food than to the satisfaction of his natural necessities. He that drinks a draught or two of water and cools his thirst, drinks no more till his thirst returns; but he that drinks wine, drinks again longer than it is needful, even so long as it is pleasant. Nature best provides for herself when she spreads her own table; but when men have gotten super-induced habits, and new necessities, art that brought them in, must maintain them, but " wantonness and folly wait at the table, and sickness and death take away."

2. Reason is the second measure, or rather the rule whereby we judge of intemperance; for whatsoever loads of meat and drink make the reason useless or troubled, are effects of this deformity; not that reason is the adequate measure; for a man may be intemperate upon other causes, though he do not force his understanding, and trouble his head. Some are strong to drink, and can eat like a wolf, and love to do so, as fire to destroy the stubble; such were those harlots in the comedy, " Quæ cum amatore suo cum cœnant, liguriunt :"[g] These persons are to take their accounts from

[f] Viz. ab Areto, onde sicut ex aliis Etruriæ figulinis, testacea vasa Romam deferebant.　　　　　[g] Eunuch. 5. 4. 14.

the measures of religion, and the Spirit: though they can talk
still or transact the affairs of the world, yet if they be not fitted for the things of the spirit, they are too full of flesh or
wine, and cannot, or care not to attend to the things of God.
But reason is the limit, beyond which temperance never wanders; and in every degree in which our discourse is troubled,
and our soul is lifted from its wheels, in the same degree the
sin prevails. "Dum sumus in quadam delinquendi libidine,
nebulis quibusdam insipientiæ mens obducitur," saith St.
Ambrose; when the flesh-pots reek, and the uncovered dishes
send forth a nidor and hungry smells, that cloud hides the face,
and puts out the eye of reason; and then tell them, ' Mors in
olla,' that ' Death is in the pot,' and folly is in the chalice;
that those smells are fumes of brimstone, and vapours of
Egypt; that they will make their heart easy, and their head
sottish, and their colour pale, and their hands trembling, and
their feet tormented.

> Mullorum, leporumque et suminis exitus hic est,
> Sulphureusque color, carnificesque pedes [b].

For that is the end of delicacies, δυσωδία, λευκὸς ἰδεῖν, ἐντρυ-
φερὸς, αἰθρίας καὶ πόνων ἄπειρος, as Dio Chrysostom, "paleness, and effeminacy, and laziness, and folly;" yet under the
dominion of the pleasures of sensuality, men are so stripped
of the use of reason, that they are not only useless in wise
counsels and assistances, but they have not reason enough
to avoid the evils of their own throat and belly; when once
their reason fails, we must know, that their temperance and
their religion went before.

3. Though reason be so strictly to be preserved at our
tables as well as at our prayers, and we can never have leave
to do any violence to it; yet the measures of nature may be
enlarged beyond the bounds of prime and common necessity.
For besides hunger and thirst, there are some labours of the
body, and others of the mind, and there are sorrows and
loads upon the spirit by its communications with the indispositions of the body; and as the labouring man may be
supplied with bigger quantities, so the student and contem-
plative man with more delicious and sprightful nutriment: for
as the tender and more delicate easily-digested meats will

not help to carry burdens upon the neck, and hold the plough
in society and yokes of the laborious oxen; so neither will
the pulse and the leeks, Lavinian sausages, and the Cisalpine
suckets or gobbets of condited bull's-flesh, minister such
delicate spirits to the thinking man; but his notion will be
flat as the noise of the Arcadian porter, and thick as the first
juice of his country lard, unless he makes his body a fit servant to the soul, and both fitted for the employment.

But in these cases necessity, and prudence, and experience, are to make the measures and the rule; and so long as
the just end is fairly designed, and aptly ministered to, there
ought to be no scruple concerning the quantity or quality of
the provision: and he that would stint a swain by the com-
mons of a student, and give Philotas the Candian the leavings of Plato, does but ill serve the ends of temperance, but
worse of prudence and necessity.

4. Sorrow and a wounded spirit may as well be provided
for in the quantity and quality of meat and drink, as any
other disease; and this disease by this remedy as well as
by any other. For, great sorrow and importune melancholy
may be as great a sin as a great anger; and if it be a sin in its
nature, it is more malignant and dangerous in its quality; as
naturally tending to murmur and despair, weariness of religion, and hatred of God, timorousness and jealousies, fantastic images of things, and superstition; and therefore, as it
is necessary to restrain the fevers of anger, so also to warm
the freezings and dulness of melancholy by prudent and temperate, but proper and apportioned diets; and if some meats
and drinks make men lustful, or sleepy, or dull, or lazy, or
sprightly, or merry; so far as meats and drinks can minister
to the passion, and the passion minister to virtue, so far by
this means they may be provided for. " Give strong drink
to him that is ready to perish, and wine to those that be of
heavy hearts; let him drink and forget his poverty, and remember his misery no more[i]," said King Lemuel's mother.
But this is not intended to be an habitual cure, but single
and occasional; for he that hath a pertinacious sorrow, is
beyond the cure of meat and drink, and if this becomes every
day's physic, it will quickly become every day's sin. Then,
it must always keep within the bounds of reason, and never

[i] Prov. xxxi. 6.

seize upon any portions of affection : the Germans use to mingle music with their bowls, and drink by the measures of the six notes of music;

Ut relevet miserum fatum, solitosque labores:

But they sing so long, that they forget not their sorrow only, but their virtue also, and their religion : and there are some men that fall into drunkenness, because they would forget a lighter calamity, running into the fire to cure a calenture, and beating their brains out to be quit of the aching of their heads. A man's heaviness is refreshed long before he comes to drunkenness ; for when he arrives thither, he hath but changed his heaviness, and taken a crime to boot.

5. Even when a man hath no necessity upon him, no pungent sorrow, or natural or artificial necessity, it is lawful in some cases of eating and drinking to receive pleasure and intend it. For whatsoever is natural and necessary, is therefore not criminal, because it is of God's procuring ; and since we eat for need, and the satisfaction of our need is a removing of a pain, and that in nature is the greatest pleasure, it is impossible that in its own nature it should be a sin. But in this case of conscience, these cautions are to be observed:

1. So long as nature ministers the pleasure and not art, it is materially innocent. " Si tuo veniat jure, luxuria est[k]:" but it is safe while it enters upon nature's stock ; for it is impossible that the proper effect of health, and temperance, and prudent abstinence, should be vicious ; and yet these are the parents of the greatest pleasure, in eating and drinking. "Malum panem expecta, bonus fiet; etiam illum tenerum tibi et siligineum fames reddet :" ' If you abstain and be hungry, you shall turn the meanest provision into delicate, and desirable.'

2. Let all the pleasure of meat and drink be such as can minister to health, and be within the former bounds. For since pleasure in eating and drinking is its natural appendage, and like a shadow follows the substance, as the meat is to be accounted, so is the pleasure : and if these be observed, there is no difference whether nature or art be the cook. For some constitutions, and some men's customs, and some men's educations, and necessities, and weaknesses, are such, that

[k] Seneca.

their appetite is to be invited, and their digestion helped, but all this while we are within the bounds of nature and need.

3. It is lawful, when a man needs meat to choose the pleasanter, even merely for their pleasures ; that is, because they are pleasant, besides that they are useful ; this is as lawful as to smell of a rose, or to lie in feathers, or change the posture of our body in bed for ease, or to hear music, or to walk in gardens rather than the highways ; and God hath given us leave to be delighted in those things, which he made to that purpose, that we may also be delighted in him that gives them. For so as the more pleasant may better serve for health, and directly to refreshment, so collaterally to religion : always provided, that it be in its degree moderate, and we temperate in our desires, without transportation and violence, without unhandsome usages of ourselves, or taking from God and from religion any minutes and portions of our affections. When Eicadastes, the epicure, saw a goodly dish of hot meat served up, he sung the verse of Homer,

Τῶ δ᾽ ἐγὼ ἀντίος εἶμι, καὶ ἐν πυρὶ χεῖρας ἔχοιτο,

and swallowed some of it greedily, till by its bands of fire it curled his stomach, like parchment in the flame, and he was carried from his banquet to his grave.

Non potuit fato nobiliore mori[1]:

It was fit he should die such a death, but that death bids us beware of that folly.

4. Let the pleasure as it came with meat, so also pass away with it. Philoxenus was a beast; ηὔξατό ποτε τὴν γεράνου αὐχένα ἔχειν, 'he wished his throat as long as a crane's,' that he might be long in swallowing his pleasant morsels ; " Mœret quod magna pars felicitatis exclusa esset corporis angustiis;" 'he mourned because the pleasure of eating was not spread over all his body,' that he might have been an epicure in his hands : and indeed, if we consider it rightly, great eating and drinking is not the greatest pleasure of the taste, but of the touch ; and Philoxenus might feel the unctuous juice slide softly down his throat, but he could not taste it in the middle of the long neck ; and we see that they who mean to feast exactly, or delight the palate, do ' libare,' or

[1] Mart. xi. 70.

'pitissare,' take up little proportions and spread them upon
the tongue or palate; but full morsels and great draughts are
easy and soft to the touch; but so is the feeling of silk, or
handling of a melon, or a mole's skin, and as delicious too
as eating when it goes beyond the appetites of nature, and
the proper pleasures of taste, which cannot be perceived but
by a temperate man. And therefore let not the pleasure be
intended beyond the taste; that is, beyond those little natural measures in which God intended that pleasure should accompany your tables. Do not run to it beforehand, nor chew
the cud when the meal is done; delight not in fancies, and
expectations, and remembrances of a pleasant meal; but let
it descend ' in latrinam,' together with the meals whose at-
tendant pleasure is.

5. Let pleasure be the less principal, and used as a servant : it may be modest and prudent to strew the dish with
sugar, or to dip thy bread in vinegar; but to make thy meal
of sauces, and to make the accessory become the principal,
and pleasure to rule the table, and all the regions of thy soul,
is to make a man less and lower than an oglio, of a cheaper
value than a turbot; a servant and a worshipper of sauces,
and cooks, and pleasure, and folly.

6. Let pleasure, as it is used in the regions and limits of
nature and prudence, so also be changed into religion and
thankfulness. "Turtures cum bibunt, non resupinant colla,"
say naturalists ; " Turtles when they drink, lift not up their
bills ;" and if we swallow our pleasures without returning the
honour and the acknowledgment to God that gave them, we
may " large bibere, jumentorum modo," " drink draughts as
large as an ox," but we shall die like an ox, and change our
meats and drinks into eternal rottenness. In all religions it
hath been permitted to enlarge our tables in the days of sacrifices and religious festivity.

> Qui Veicntanum festis potare diebus
> Campana solitus trulla, vappamque profestis [m].

For then the body may rejoice in fellowship with the soul,
and then a pleasant meal is religious, if it be not inordinate.
But if our festival-days, like the Gentile sacrifices, end in
drunkenness[n], and our joys in religion pass into sensuality
and beastly crimes, we change the holy-day into a day of

[m] Hor. Serm. ii. 3. 143.   [n] Μεθύειν, μετὰ τὸ θύειν.

death, and ourselves become a sacrifice as in the day of slaughter.

To sum up this particular; there are, as you perceive, many cautions to make our pleasure safe, but any thing can make it inordinate, and then scarce any thing can keep it from becoming dangerous.

> Habet omnis hoc voluptas :
> Stimulis agit furentes.
> Apiumque par volantum,
> Ubi grata mella fudit,
> Fugit, et nimis tenaci
> Ferit icta corda morsu[o].

And the pleasure of the honey will not pay for the smart of the sting. " Amores enim et deliciæ maturè et celeriter deflorescunt, et in omnibus rebus, voluptatibus maximis fastidium finitimum est:" " Nothing is so soon ripe and rotten as pleasure: and upon all possessions and states of things, loathing looks as being not far off; but it sits upon the skirts of pleasure."

> Ὅς δὲ τρικτίζας
> Ἐπηρξάμενος μελιχρῶν ἴθιγεν,
> Ἢ μέγα κλαίστι τικρὰν μερίδα,
> Τῶν ἀντίων συνοφελκομένων.

" He that greedily puts his hand to a delicious table, shall weep bitterly when he suffers the convulsions and violence by the divided interests of such contrary juices:"

> Ὅδι γὰρ χθονίας θέσμος ἀνάγκας
> Διχίθεν θάνατος βίον ἀνυχαῖ.

" For this is the law of our nature and fatal necessity; life is always poured forth from two goblets."

And now, after all this, I pray consider, what a strange madness and prodigious folly possess many men, that they love to swallow death and diseases and dishonour, with an appetite which no reason can restrain. We expect our servants should not dare to touch what we have forbidden to them; we are watchful that our children should not swallow poisons, and filthiness, and unwholesome nourishment; we take care that they should be well-mannered and civil and of fair demeanour; and we ourselves desire to be, or at least to be accounted, wise, and would infinitely scorn to be called

[o] Boetius, l. 3. Metr. 7.

fools; and we are so great lovers of health, that we will buy
it at any rate of money or observance; and then for honour,
it is that which the children of men pursue with passion, it
is one of the noblest rewards of virtue, and the proper ornament of the wise and valiant, and yet all these things are not
valued or considered, when a merry meeting, or a looser
feast, calls upon the man to act a scene of folly and madness,
and healthlessness and dishonour. We do to God what we
severely punish in our servants; we correct our children for
their meddling with dangers, which themselves prefer before
immortality; and though no man think himself fit to be despised,
yet he is willing to make himself a beast, a sot, and a ridiculous monkey, with the follies and vapours of wine; and when
he is high in drink or fancy, proud as a Grecian orator in the
midst of his popular noises, at the same time he shall talk
such dirty language, such mean low things, as may well become a changeling and a fool, for whom the stocks are prepared by the laws, and the just scorn of men. Every drunkard clothes his head with a mighty scorn; and makes himself
lower at that time than the meanest of his servants; the boys
can laugh at him when he is led like a cripple, directed like
a blind man, and speaks like an infant imperfect noises, lisping with a full and spongy tongue, and an empty head, and
a vain and foolish heart: so cheaply does he part with his
honour for drink or loads of meat; for which honour he is
ready to die, rather than bear it to be disparaged by another;
when himself destroys it, as bubbles perish with the breath
of children. Do not the laws of all wise nations mark the
drunkard for a fool, with the meanest and most scornful punishment? and is there any thing in the world so foolish as a
man that is drunk? But, good God! what an intolerable sorrow hath seized upon great portions of mankind, that this
folly and madness should possess the greatest spirits, and
the wittiest men, the best company, the most sensible of the
word honour, and the most jealous of losing the shadow, and
the most careless of the thing? Is it not a horrid thing, that
a wise or a crafty, a learned or a noble person, should dishonour himself as a fool, destroy his body as a murderer,
lessen his estate as a prodigal, disgrace every good cause that
he can pretend to by his relation, and become an appellative
of scorn, a scene of laughter or derision, and all, for the

reward of forgetfulness and madness? for there are in immoderate drinking no other pleasures.

Why do valiant men and brave personages fight and die rather than break the laws of men, or start from their duty to their prince, and will suffer themselves to be cut in pieces rather than deserve the name of a traitor, or perjured? and yet these very men, to avoid the hated name of glutton or drunkard, and to preserve their temperance, shall not deny themselves one luscious morsel, or pour a cup of wine on the ground, when they are invited to drink by the laws of the circle or wilder company.

Methinks it were but reason, that if to give life to uphold a cause be not too much, they should not think it too much to be hungry and suffer thirst for the reputation of that cause; and therefore much rather that they would think it but duty to be temperate for its honour, and eat and drink in civil and fair measures, that themselves might not lose the reward of so much suffering, and of so good a relation, nor that which they value most be destroyed by drink.

There are in the world a generation of men that are engaged in a cause which they glory in, and pride themselves in its relation and appellative: but yet for that cause they will do nothing but talk and drink; they are valiant in wine, and witty in healths, and full of stratagem to promote debauchery; but such persons are not considerable in wise accounts; that which I deplore is, that some men prefer a cause before their life, and yet prefer wine before that cause, and by one drunken meeting set it more backward in its hopes and blessings, than it can be set forward by the counsels and arms of a whole year. God hath ways enough to reward a truth without crowning it with success in the hands of such men. In the meantime they dishonour religion, and make truth be evil spoken of, and innocent persons to suffer by their very relation, and the cause of God to be reproached in the sentences of erring and abusing people; and themselves lose their health and their reason, their honour and their peace, the rewards of sober counsels, and the wholesome effects of wisdom.

Arcanum neque tu scrutaberis illius unquam;
Commissumque teges, et vino tortus et ira P.

P Hor. Ep. 1. 18. 37.

Wine discovers more than the rack, and he that will be drunk is not a person fit to be trusted : and though it cannot be expected men should be kinder to their friend, or their prince, or their honour, than to God, and to their own souls, and to their own bodies ; yet when men are not moved by what is sensible and material, by that which smarts and shames presently, they are beyond the cure of religion, and the hopes of reason; and therefore they must " lie in hell like sheep, death gnawing upon them, and the righteous shall have dominion over them in the morning" of the resurrection.

> Seras tutior ibis ad lucernas :
> Hæc hora est tua, cum furit Lyæus,
> Cum regnat rosa, cum madent capilli ⁹.

Much safer it is to go to the severities of a watchful and a sober life ; for all that time of life is lost, when wine, and rage, and pleasure, and folly, steal away the heart of a man, and make him go singing to his grave.

I end with the saying of a wise man: He is fit to sit at the table of the Lord, and to feast with saints, who moderately uses the creatures which God hath given him : but he that despises even lawful pleasures, οὐ μόνον συμπότης τῶν θεῶν ἀλλὰ καὶ συνάρχων, ' shall not only sit and feast with God, but reign together with him,' and partake of his glorious kingdom.

SERMON XVII.

THE MARRIAGE RING; OR, THE MYSTERIOUSNESS AND DUTIES OF MARRIAGE.

PART I.

This is a great mystery, but I speak concerning Christ and the church. Nevertheless, let every one of you in particular so love his wife even as himself, and the wife see that she reverence her husband.—Ephes. v. 32, 33.

THE first blessing God gave to man, was society : and that society was a marriage, and that marriage was confederate

⁹ Mart. 10. 19. 18.

by God himself, and hallowed by a blessing: and at the same time, and for very many descending ages, not only by the instinct of nature, but by a superadded forwardness (God himself inspiring the desire), the world was most desirous of children, impatient of barrenness, accounting single life a curse, and a childless person hated by God[r]. The world was rich and empty, and able to provide for a more numerous posterity than it had.

———'Εξις, Νουμὴνω, τὴνα,
Χίλλαν ἐχων στοχὸς ἢ οἰδὶ τὰ τὴνα φιλῖ'.

You that are rich, Numenius, you may multiply your family; poor men are not so fond of children, but when a family could drive their herds, and set their children upon camels, and lead them till they saw a fat soil watered with rivers, and there sit down without paying rent, they thought of nothing but to have great families, that their own relations might swell up to a patriarchate, and their children be enough to possess all the regions that they saw, and their grandchildren become princes, and themselves build cities and call them by the name of a child, and become the fountain of a nation. This was the consequent of the first blessing, 'increase and multiply.' The next blessing was, 'the promise of the Messias,' and that also increased in men and women a wonderful desire of marriage : for as soon as God had chosen the family of Abraham to be the blessed line, from whence the world's Redeemer should descend according to the flesh, every of his daughters hoped to have the honour to be his mother, or his grandmother, or something of his kindred: and to be childless in Israel was a sorrow to the Hebrew women great as the slavery of Egypt, or their dishonours in the land of their captivity[t].

But when the Messias was come, and the doctrine was published, and his ministers but few, and his disciples were to suffer persecution, and to be of an unsettled dwelling, and the nation of the Jews, in the bosom and society of

---

[r] Quæmlibet hominem cui non est uxor, minimè esse hominem; cum etiam in scriptura dicatur, "Masculum et fœminam creavit eos, et vocavit nomen eorum Adam seu hominem." R. Eliezer dixit in Gen. Bab. Quicunque negligit præceptum de multiplicatione humani generis, habendum esse veluti homicidam.

[s] Brunck. Anal. ii. 348.

[t] Christiani et apud Athenas, τὰς τοῦ ἀγαμίου καὶ ὀλιγαμίου Ναας refert Julius Pollux l. 3. περὶ ἀγάμων. Idem etiam Lacedæmone et Romæ, vide Festum verb. Uxorium atque ibi Jos. Scal.

which the church especially did dwell, were to be scattered
and broken all in pieces with fierce calamities, and the
world was apt to calumniate and to suspect and dishonour
Christians upon pretences and unreasonable jealousies, and
that to all these purposes the state of marriage brought
many inconveniences ; it pleased God in this new creation
to inspire into the hearts of his servants a disposition and
strong desires to live a single life, lest the state of marriage
should in that conjunction of things become an accidental
impediment to the dissemination of the Gospel, which called
men from a confinement in their domestic charges to travel,
and flight, and poverty, and difficulty, and martyrdom :
upon this necessity the Apostles and apostolical men published doctrines, declaring the advantages of single life,
not by any commandment of the Lord, but by the spirit of
prudence, διὰ τὴν ἐνεστῶσαν ἀνάγκην, ' for the present and
then incumbent necessities,' and in order to the advantages
which did accrue to the public ministries and private piety[u].
" There are some (said our blessed Lord) who make themselves eunuchs for the kingdom of heaven," that is, for the
advantages and the ministry of the Gospel, " non ad vitæ
bonæ meritum" (as St. Austin in the like case); not that it is
a better service of God in itself[x], but that it is useful to the
first circumstances of the Gospel and the infancy of the
kingdom, because the unmarried person does μεριμνᾷν τὰ τοῦ
κυρίου, ' is apt to spiritual and ecclesiastical employments' :
first ἅγιος, and then ἁγιαζόμενος, ' holy in his own person,
and then sanctified to public ministries ;' and it was also of
ease to the Christians themselves, because, as then it was,
when they were to flee, and to flee for aught they knew in
winter, and they were persecuted to the four winds of heaven ;
and the nurses and the women with child were to suffer a
heavier load of sorrow because of the imminent persecutions ; and above all, because of the great fatality of ruin
upon the whole nation of the Jews, well it might be said by
St. Paul, θλίψιν τῇ σαρκὶ ἕξουσιν οἱ τοιοῦτοι, " Such shall have

* Etiam Judæi, qui præceptum esse viris παιδοποιεῖν aiunt, uno ore concedunt,
tamen dispensatum esse eum in qui assiduo legis studio vacare volunt, alias etiam
immunibus ab acriori carnis stimulo. *Maimon.* 15. Haleoh. Ishoth.

    ᵡ Οὐ ψέγω δὲ τοὺς λοιποὺς μακαρίους, ὅτι γάμοις προσωμίλησαν ὧν ἱμνήσθαι ἀρτι-
εὔχομαι γὰρ ἄξιος Θεοῦ εὑρεθεὶς πρὸς τοῖς ἴχνεσιν αὐτῶν εὑρεθῆναι ἐν τῇ βασιλείᾳ εἰς Ἀ-
βραάμ, καὶ Ἰσαὰκ, καὶ Ἰακώβ, εἰς Ἰώσηφ, καὶ Ἡσαΐαν καὶ τῶν ἄλλων προφητῶν, εἰς Πέτρου
καὶ Παύλου, καὶ τῶν ἄλλων ἀποστόλων, &c. Epist. ad Philadelph.

trouble in the flesh," that is, they that are married shall, and
so at that time they had: and therefore it was an act of
charity to the Christians to give that counsel, ἐγὼ δὲ ὑμῖν
φείδομαι, 'I do this to spare you,' and θέλω ὑμᾶς ἀμερίμνους εἶναι: for when the case was altered, and that storm was over,
and the first necessities of the Gospel served, and 'the sound
was gone out into all nations;' in very many persons it was
wholly changed, and not the married but the unmarried had
θλίψιν ἐν σαρκὶ, " trouble in the flesh;" and the state of
marriage returned to its first blessing, " et non erat bonum
homini esse solitarium," " and it was not good for man to be
alone."

But in this first interval, the public necessity and the private zeal mingling together did sometimes overact their love
of single life, even to the disparagement of marriage, and to
the scandal of religion; which was increased by the occasion
of some pious persons renouncing their contract of marriage,
not consummate, with believers. For when Flavia Domitilla
being converted by Nereus and Achilleus the eunuchs, refused to marry Aurelianus, to whom she was contracted; if
there were not some little envy and too sharp hostility in the
eunuchs to a married state, yet Aurelianus thought himself
an injured person, and caused St. Clemens, who veiled her,
and his spouse hoth, to die in the quarrel. St. Thecla being
converted by St. Paul, grew so in love with virginity, that
she leaped back from the marriage of Tamyris, where she was
lately engaged. St. Iphigenia denied to marry king Hyrta-
cus, and it is said to be done by the advice of St. Matthew.
And Susanna the niece of Dioclesian refused the love of
Maximianus the emperor; and these all had been betrothed;
and so did St. Agnes, and St. Felicula, and divers others
then and afterward: insomuch, that it was reported among
the Gentiles, that the Christians did not only hate all that
were not of their persuasion, but were enemies of the chaste
laws of marriage; and indeed some that were called Christians were so; " forbidding to marry, and commanding to abstain from meats." Upon this occasion it grew necessary
for the Apostle to state the question right, and to do honour
to the holy rite of marriage, and to snatch the mystery from
the hands of zeal and folly, and to place it in Christ's right
hand, that all its beauties might appear, and a present con-

venience might not bring in a false doctrine, and a perpetual sin, and an intolerable mischief. The Apostle, therefore, who himself[y] had been a married man, but was now a widower, does explicate the mysteriousness of it, and describes its honours, and adorns it with rules and provisions of religion, that, as it begins with honour, so it may proceed with piety, and end with glory.

For although single life hath in it privacy and simplicity of affairs, such solitariness and sorrow, such leisure and inactive circumstances of living, that there are more spaces for religion if men would use them to these purposes; and because it may have in it much religion and prayers, and must have in it a perfect mortification of our strongest appetites, it is therefore a state of great excellency; yet concerning the state of marriage, we are taught from Scripture and the sayings of wise men, great things are honourable. "Marriage is honourable in all men;" so is not single life; for in some it is a snare and a πόρωσις, 'a trouble in the flesh,' a prison of unruly desires, which is attempted daily to be broken. Celibate or single life is never commanded; but in some cases marriage is; and he that burns, sins often if he marries not; he that cannot contain must marry, and he that can contain is not tied to a single life, but may marry and not sin. Marriage was ordained by God, instituted in Paradise, was the relief of a natural necessity, and the first blessing from the Lord; he gave to man not a friend, but a wife, that is, a friend and a wife too (for a good woman is in her soul the same that a man is, and she is a woman only in her body; that she may have the excellency of the one, and the usefulness of the other, and become amiable in both): it is the seminary of the church, and daily brings forth sons and daughters unto God; it was ministered to by angels, and Raphael waited upon a young man that he might have a blessed marriage, and that that marriage might repair two sad families, and bless all their relatives. Our blessed Lord, though he was born of a maiden, yet she was veiled under the cover of marriage, and she was married to a widower; for Joseph the supposed father of our Lord had children by a former wife.

---

[y] Ὡς Πέτρου καὶ Παύλου καὶ τῶν Ἀποστόλων τῶν γάμοις προσημιλησάντων οὐκ ἐπὶ ἐπιθυμίας τῆς περὶ τὸ πράγμα, ἀλλ' ἐπ' ἐννοίας ἑαυτῶν τῶν γόνους ἰσχεν ἑκάστους. Ignatius epistol. ad Philadelph. Et Clemens idem ait apud Eusebium Hist. Eccles. lib. 3. sed tamen eam non circumduxit sicut Petrus : probat autem ex Philip. 4.

The first miracle that ever Jesus did, was to do honour to a wedding; marriage was in the world before sin, and is in all ages of the world the greatest and most effective antidote against sin, in which all the world had perished, if God had not made a remedy: and although sin hath soured marriage, and stuck the man's head with cares, and the woman's bed with sorrows in the production of children; yet these are but throes of life and glory, and "she shall be saved in child-bearing, if she be found in faith and righteousness." Marriage is a school and exercise of virtue; and though marriage hath cares, yet the single life hath desires, which are more troublesome and more dangerous, and often end in sin, while the cares are but instances of duty and exercises of piety: and therefore, if single life hath more privacy of devotion, yet marriage hath more necessities and more variety of it, and is an exercise of more graces. In two virtues, celibate or single life may have the advantage of degrees ordinarily and commonly,—that is, in chastity and devotion: but as in some persons this may fail, and it does in very many, and a married man may spend as much time in devotion as any virgins or widows do; yet as in marriage even those virtues of chastity and devotion are exercised; so in other instances, this state hath proper exercises and trials for those graces, for which single life can never be crowned; here is the proper scene of piety and patience, of the duty of parents and the charity of relatives'; here kindness is spread abroad, and love is united and made firm as a centre: marriage is the nursery of heaven; the virgin sends prayers to God, but she carries but one soul to him; but the state of marriage fills up the numbers of the elect, and hath in it the labour of love, and the delicacies of friendship, the blessing of society, and the union of hands and hearts; it hath in it less of beauty, but more of safety, than the single life; it hath more care, but less danger; it is more merry, and more sad; is fuller of sorrows, and fuller of joys; it lies under more burdens, but is supported by all the

ʸ Χρὴ τὰς διηγήσεις φύσεως ἀντίχεσθαι τῷ παῖδας παῖδον καταλείπειν διὰ τῷ θεῷ ἐπορίζας ἀπ' αὐτοῦ παραδιδόναι. Plato.

Adde, quod Eunuchus nulla pietate movetur,
Nec generi natisve cavet: clementia cunctis
In similes, animosque ligant consortia damni.
                              Claudian. In Eutrop. i. 187.

strengths of love and charity, and those burdens are delightful. Marriage is the mother of the world*, and preserves kingdoms, and fills cities, and churches, and heaven itself. Celibate, like the fly in the heart of an apple, dwells in a perpetual sweetness, but sits alone, and is confined and dies in singularity; but marriage, like the useful bee, builds a house
and gathers sweetness from every flower, and labours and
unites into societies and republics, and sends out colonies,
and feeds the world with delicacies, and obeys their king,
and keeps order, and exercises many virtues, and promotes
the interest of mankind, and is that state of good things to
which God hath designed the present constitution of the
world.

> Τοῦτων ἱνδύσμως ἄλοχου λαθὶ, καί τινα κύσμω
> Δὲς βροτὼ ἀντὶ σίθου. φαῦγα δὶ μαχλοσύνω.   *Br. An. 3. 93.*

Single life makes men in one instance to be like angels,
but marriage in very many things makes the chaste pair to
be like to Christ. "This is a great mystery," but it is the
symbolical and sacramental representation of the greatest
mysteries of our religion. Christ descended from his Father's
bosom, and contracted his divinity with flesh and blood,
and married our nature, and we became a church, the spouse
of the Bridegroom, which he cleansed with his blood, and
gave her his Holy Spirit for a dowry, and heaven for a join-
ture; begetting children unto God by the Gospel. This
spouse he hath joined to himself by an excellent charity, he
feeds her at his own table, and lodges her nigh his own heart,
provides for all her necessities, relieves her sorrows, determines her doubts, guides her wanderings, he is become her
head, and she as a signet upon his right hand; be first indeed
was betrothed to the synagogue and had many children by
her, but she forsook her love, and then he married the church
of the Gentiles, and by her as by a second venter had a more
numerous issue, "atque una domus est omnium filiorum ejus,"
"all the children dwell in the same house," and are heirs
of the same promises, entitled to the same inheritance. Here
is the eternal conjunction, the indissoluble knot, the exceed-

---

> * Καλὰ τὰ φαρθνίως κεμμέλιο· φαρθνία δὶ
> Τὼ βίω ἔλαστω ἀν, πᾶστ φυλαττομένω.   *Brunck. An. 3. 93.*

Siquis patriam majorem parentum extinguit, in eo culpa est, quod facit pro sua parte
qui se eunuchat aut aliqua liberos producit, i. e. differt eorum procreationem.
Varro in ' lege Mænia.'

ing love of Christ, the obedience of the spouse, the communicating of goods, the uniting of interests, the fruit of marriage, a celestial generation, a new creature; "Sacramentum hoc magnum est;" "This is the sacramental mystery," represented by the holy rite of marriage; so that marriage is divine in its institution, sacred in its union, holy in the mystery, sacramental in its signification, honourable in its appellative, religious in its employments: it is advantage to the societies of men, and it is 'holiness to the Lord.' "Dico autem in Christo et ecclesia," "It must be in Christ and the church."

If this be not observed, marriage loses its mysteriousness: but because it is to effect much of that which it signifies, it concerns all that enter into those golden fetters to see that Christ and his church be in at every of its periods, and that it be entirely conducted and overruled by religion; for so the Apostle passes from the sacramental rite to the real duty; "Nevertheless," that is, although the former discourse were wholly to explicate the conjunction of Christ and his church by this similitude, yet it hath in it this real duty, "that the man love his wife, and the wife reverence her husband:" and this is the use we shall now make of it, the particulars of which precept I shall thus dispose:

1. I shall propound the duty as it generally relates to man and wife in conjunction. 2. The duty and power of the man. 3. The rights and privileges and the duty of the wife.

1. "In Christo et ecclesia;" that begins all, and there is great need it should be so: for they that enter into a state of marriage, cast a die of the greatest contingency, and yet of the greatest interest in the world, next to the last throw for eternity.

Νῦν γὰρ δὴ πάντεσσιν ἐπὶ ξυροῦ ἵσταται ἀκμῆς,
Ἢ μάλα λυγρὸς ὄλεθρος Ἀχαιοῖς, ἢ βιῶναι [b].

Life or death, felicity or a lasting sorrow, are in the power of marriage. A woman indeed ventures most, for she hath no sanctuary to retire to from an evil husband; she must dwell upon her sorrow, and hatch the eggs which her own folly or infelicity hath produced; and she is more under it, because her tormentor hath a warrant of prerogative, and the woman may complain to God as subjects do of tyrant princes, but otherwise she hath no appeal in the causes of unkindness.

[b] Il. x. 173.

And though the man can run from many hours of his sadness, yet he must return to it again, and when he sits among his neighbours, he remembers the objection that lies in his bosom, and he sighs deeply.

Ah tum te miseram, malique fati,
Quem, attraotis pedibus, patente porta,
Percurrent mugilesque raphanique[c].

The boys, and the pedlars, and the fruiterers, shall tell of this man, when he is carried to his grave, that he lived and died a poor wretched person. The stags in the Greek epigram, whose knees were clogged with frozen snow upon the mountains, came down to the brooks of the valleys, χλιῆναι νοτεροῖς νάμασιν ὠκὺ γόνυ, " hoping to thaw their joints with the waters of the stream[d];" but there the frost overtook them, and bound them fast in ice, till the young herdsmen took them in their stranger snare. It is the unhappy chance of many men, finding many inconveniences upon the mountains of single life, they descend into the valleys of[e] marriage to refresh their troubles, and there they enter into fetters, and are bound to sorrow by the cords of a man's or woman's peevishness : and the worst of the evil is, they are to thank their own follies ; for they fell into the snare by entering an improper way : Christ and the church were no ingredients in their choice : but as the Indian women enter into folly for the price of an elephant, and think their crime warrantable ; so do men and women change their liberty for a rich fortune (like Eriphyle the Argive, Ἡ χρυσὸν φίλου ἀνδρὸς ἐδέξατο τιμήεντα, 'she preferred gold before a good man'), and shew themselves to be less than money, by overvaluing that to all the content and wise felicity of their lives : and when they have counted the money and their sorrows together, how willingly would they[f] buy, with the loss of all that money, modesty, or sweet nature, to their relative ! the odd thousand pounds would gladly be allowed in good nature and fair

[c] Catull. 15. 19.   [d] Brun. An. 2. 135.
[e] Ἄχρι ἂν ᾖς ἄγαμος, Νευμήνιε, πάντα δοκεῖ σοι
    Ἐν τῷ ζῆν εἶναι τἀγαθὰ τῶν ἀγαθῶν.
  Εἶθ' ὅταν εἰσίλθῃ γαμετὴ, πάλιν εὐθὺ δοκεῖ σοι
    Ἐν τῷ ζῆν εἶναι πάντα κακὸν τὰ κακά.
  Ἀλλὰ χάριν τίκτων, &c.
[f] Non ego illam mihi dotem duco esse, quæ dos dicitur ;
  Sed pudicitiam, et pudorem, et sedatum cupidinem,
  Deum metum, parentum amorem, et cognatûm concordiam.
                              Plaut. in Amphit. 2. 2. 209.

manners. As very a fool is he that chooses for beauty[f] principally; "cui sunt eruditi oculi, et stulta mens" (as one said), "whose eyes are witty, and their souls sensual;" it is an ill band of affections to tie two hearts together by a little thread of red and white.

Οὐδεμίαν (φησὶν ἡ τραγῳδία)
Ὥρας κάλλος εἰς πόσιν ξυνάορον.

And they can love no longer but until the next ague comes; and they are fond of each other but at the chance of fancy, or the smallpox, or childbearing, or care, or time, or any thing that can destroy a pretty flower[g]. But it is the basest of all, when lust is the paranymph, and solicits the suit, and makes the contract, and joins the hands; for this is commonly the effect of the former, according to the Greek proverb;

Ἀλλ᾽ ἦτοι πρώτιστα λέων γένετ᾽ ἠΰγένειος,
Αὐτὰρ ἔπειτα δράκων, καὶ πάρδαλις, ἠδὲ μέγας σῦς[h].

At first for his fair cheeks and comely beard, 'the beast is taken for a lion, but at last he is turned to a dragon, or a leopard, or a swine.' That which is at first beauty on the face, may prove lust in the manners.

Αὐτοῖς δὲ τοῖς θεοῖσι τὸ αἰσχρὸν μόνον
Καὶ μηρὸν, ὥσπερ παιδημασταῖς, δίότε.

So Eubulus wittily reprehended such impure contracts: they offer in their marital sacrifices nothing but the thigh, and that which the priests cut from the goats, when they were laid to bleed upon the altars. Ἐὰν εἰς κάλλος σώματος βλέψῃ τις (ὁ λόγος φησὶ), καὶ αὐτῷ ἡ σὰρξ εἶναι κατ᾽ ἐπιθυμίαν δόξῃ καλὴ, σαρκικῶς ἰδὼν, καὶ ἁμαρτηκὼς δι᾽ οὗ τεθαύμακε, κρίνεται, said St. Clement: "He or she that looks too curiously upon the beauty of the body, looks too low, and hath flesh and corruption in his heart, and is judged sensual and earthly in his affections and desires." Begin therefore with God, Christ is the president of marriage, and the Holy Ghost is the fountain of purities and chaste loves, and he joins the hearts; and therefore, let our first suit be in the court of heaven, and

---

[f] Facies, non uxor amatur.
[g] Tres rugæ subeant, et se cutis arida laxet,
Fiant obscuri dentes, oculique minores,
'Collige sarcinulas (dicet libertus) et exi.' *Juven*. Sat. 6.
[h] Od. δ. 456.

with designs of piety, or safety, or charity; let no impure spirit defile the virgin purities and 'castifications of the soul' (as St. Peter's phrase is); let all such contracts begin with religious affections.

Conjugium petimus, partumque uxoris; at illis
Notum, qui pueri, qualisve futura sit uxor[i].

"We sometimes beg of God, for a wife or a child; and he alone knows what the wife shall prove, and by what dispositions and manners, and into what fortune that child shall enter:" but we shall not need to fear concerning the event of it, if religion, and fair intentions, and prudence manage, and conduct it all the way. The preservation of a family, the production of children, the avoiding fornication, the refreshment of our sorrows by the comforts of society; all these are fair ends of marriage and hallow the entrance: but in these there is a special order; society was the first designed, "It is not good for man to be alone;"—children was the next, "Increase and multiply;"—but the avoiding fornication came in by the superfœtation of the evil accidents of the world. The first makes marriage delectable, the second necessary to the public, the third necessary to the particular; this is for safety, for life, and heaven itself;

Nam simulac venas inflavit tetra libido,
Huc juvenes æquum est descendere;————[k]

The other have in them joy and a portion of immortality: the first makes the man's heart glad; the second is the friend of kingdoms, and cities, and families; and the third is the enemy to hell, and an antidote of the chiefest inlet to damnation: but of all these the noblest end is the multiplying of children. "Mundus cum patet, Deorum tristium atque inferûm quasi patet janua; propterea uxorem, liberorum quærendorum causa, ducere religiosum est," said Varro; "it is religion to marry for children[l];" and Quintilian put it into the definition of a wife, "est enim uxor quam jungit, quam diducit utilitas; cujus hæc reverentia est, quod videtur inventa in causa liberorum;" and therefore St. Ignatius, when he had spoken of Elias, and Titus, and Clement, with an honourable mention of their virgin-state, lest he might seem to

[i] Juv. 10. 352.   [k] Hor. S. 1. 2. 33.   [l] Macrobius ex Varrone.

have lessened the married Apostles, at whose feet in Christ's kingdom he thought himself unworthy to sit, he gives this testimony,—they were τοῖς γάμοις προσομιλήσαντες οὐχ ὑπὸ προθυμίας τῆς περὶ τὸ πρᾶγμα, ἀλλ' ὑπ' εὐνοίας ἑαυτῶν τοῦ γένους ἔσχον ἐκείνους, "that they might not be disparaged in their great names of holiness and severity, they were secured by not marrying to satisfy their lower appetites, but out of desire of children[m]." Other considerations, if they be incident and by way of appendage, are also considerable in the accounts of prudence: but when they become principals, they defile the mystery, and make the blessing doubtful : " Amabit sapiens, cupient cæteri," said Afranius; " Love is a fair inducement, but desire and appetite are rude, and the characterisms of a sensual person:"—"Amare justi et boni est, cupere impotentis ;" " To love, belongs to a just and a good man ; but to lust, or furiously and passionately to desire, is the sign of impotency and an unruly mind."

2. Man and wife are equally concerned to avoid all offences of each other in the beginning of their conversation : every little thing can blast an infant blossom ; and the breath of the south can shake the little rings of the vine, when first they begin to curl like the locks of a new-weaned boy ; but when by age and consolidation they stiffen into the hardness of a stem, and have, by the warm embraces of the sun and the kisses of heaven, brought forth their clusters, they can endure the storms of the north, and the loud noises of a tempest, and yet never be broken : so are the early unions of an unfixed marriage ; watchful and observant, jealous and busy, inquisitive and careful, and apt to take alarm at every unkind word. For infirmities do not manifest themselves in the first scenes, but in the succession of a long society ; and it is not chance or weakness when it appears at first, but it is want of love or prudence, or it will be so expounded; and that which appears ill at first, usually affrights the inexperienced man or woman, who makes unequal conjectures, and fancies mighty sorrows by the proportions of the new and early unkindness. It is a very great passion, or a huge folly, or a certain want of love, that cannot preserve the colours and beauties of kindness, so long as public honesty requires a man to wear their sorrows for the death

[m] Epist. ad Philadelph.

of a friend. Plutarch compares a new marriage to a vessel before the hoops are on; μετὰ ἀρχὰς μὲν ὑπὸ τῆς τυχούσης ῥαδίως διασπᾶται προφάσεως, "every thing dissolves their tender compaginations ;" χρόνῳ τῶν ἁρμῶν σύμπηξιν λαβόντων, μόγις ὑπὸ πυρὸς καὶ σιδήρου διαλύεται, "but when the joints are stiffened and are tied by a firm compliance and proportioned bending, scarcely can it be dissolved without fire or the violence of iron." After the hearts of the man and the wife are endeared and hardened by a mutual confidence, and experience longer than artifice and pretence can last, there are a great many remembrances, and some things present, that dash all little unkindnesses in pieces. The little boy in the Greek epigram[a], that was creeping down a precipice, was invited to his safety by the sight of his mother's pap, when nothing else could entice him to return: and the bond of common children, and the sight of her that nurses what is most dear to him, and the endearments of each other in the course of a long society, and the same relation, is an excellent security to redintegrate and to call that love back, which folly and trifling accidents would disturb.

> ——— Tormentum ingens nubentibus hæret,
> Quas nequeunt parere, et partu retinere maritos[o].

When it is come thus far, it is hard untwisting the knot ; but be careful in its first coalition, that there be no rudeness done ; for, if there be, it will for ever after be apt to start and to be diseased.

3. Let man and wife be careful to stifle little things[p], that, as fast as they spring, they be cut down and trod upon; for if they be suffered to grow by numbers, they make the spirit peevish, and the society troublesome, and the affections loose and easy by an habitual aversation. Some men are more vexed with a fly than with a wound ; and when the gnats disturb our sleep, and the reason is disquieted but not perfectly awakened, it is often seen that he is fuller of trouble than if, in the daylight of his reason, he were to contest with a potent enemy. In the frequent little accidents of a family, a man's reason cannot always be awake; and when his discourses are imperfect, and a trifling trouble makes him yet

[a] Μαζὸν τῶ λαμῶ λύτρα καὶ θανάτου.   Brunck. An. 2. 196.

[o] Juv. 2. 137.

[p] Quædam parva quidem, sed non tolerando maritis.   Juv. 6. 184.

more restless, he is soon betrayed to the violence of passion.
It is certain that the man or woman are in a state of weakness
and folly then, when they can be troubled with a trifling accident; and therefore, it is not good to tempt their affections,
when they are in that state of danger. In this case the caution is, to subtract fuel from the sudden flame; for stubble,
though it be quickly kindled, yet it is as soon extinguished,
if it be not blown by a pertinacious breath, or fed with new
materials. Add no new provocations to the accident, and
do not inflame this, and peace will soon return, and the dis-
content will pass away soon, as the sparks from the collision
of a flint : ever remembering, that discontents proceeding
from daily little things, do breed a secret undiscernible disease, which is more dangerous than a fever proceeding from
a discerned notorious surfeit.

4. Let them be sure to abstain from all those things,
which by experience and observation they find to be contrary to each other. They that govern elephants, never appear
before them in white; and the masters of bulls keep from
them all garments of blood and scarlet, as knowing that they
will be impatient of civil usages and discipline, when their
natures are provoked by their proper antipathies. The ancients in their martial hieroglyphics used to depict Mercury
standing by Venus, to signify, that by fair language and
sweet entreaties, the minds of each other should be united ;
and hard by them, " Suadam et Gratias descripserunt," they
would have all deliciousness of manners, compliance and
mutual observance to abide⁹.

5. Let the husband and wife infinitely avoid a curious distinction of mine and thine ; for this hath caused all the laws,
and all the suits, and all the wars, in the world ; let them,
who have but one person, have also but one interest. The
husband and wife are heirs to each other (as Dionysius Hali-
carnasseus relates from Romulus) if they die without children; but if there be children, the wife is τοῖς παισὶν ἰσόμοιρος,
'a partner in the inheritance.' But during their life, the use
and employment is common to both their necessities, and in

¶ ——Hujus enim rari summique voluptas
Nulla boni, quoties animo corrupta superbo
Plus aloes quàm mellis habet —
Juven. Sat. 6. 180.

this there is no other difference of right, but that the man hath
the dispensation of all, and may keep it from his wife, just as
the governor of a town may keep it from the right owner; he
hath the power, but no right, to do so. And when either of
them begins to impropriate, it is like a tumour in the flesh,
it draws more than its share; but what it feeds on, turns to
a bile; and therefore, the Romans forbade any donations to
be made between man and wife, because neither of them
could transfer a new right of those things, which already they
had in common; but this is to be understood only concerning the uses of necessity and personal conveniences; for so
all may be the woman's, and all may be the man's, in several
regards. Corvinus dwells in a farm and receives all its profits, and reaps and sows as he please, and eats of the corn
and drinks of the wine—it is his own: but all that also is his
lord's, and for it Corvinus pays acknowledgment; and his
patron hath such powers and uses of it as are proper to the
lord's; and yet, for all this, it may be the king's too, to all the
purposes that be can need, and is all to be accounted in the
census and for certain services and times of danger : so are
the riches of a family; they are a woman's as well as a man's:
they are hers for need, and hers for ornament, and hers for
modest delight, and for the uses of religion and prudent charity; but the disposing them into portions of inheritance,
the assignation of charges and governments, stipends and rewards, annuities and greater donatives, are the reserves of the
superior right, and not to be invaded by the under-possessors.
But in those things, where they ought to be common, if the
spleen or the belly swells and draws into its capacity much
of that which should be spent upon those parts, which have
an equal right to be maintained,—it is a dropsy or a consumption of the whole, something that is evil because it is unnatural and monstrous. Macarius, in his thirty-second Homily,
speaks fully in this particular ; a woman betrothed to a man
bears all her portion, and with a mighty love pours it into
the hands of her husband, and says, ἐμὸν οὐδὲν ἔχω, " I have
nothing of my own;" my goods, my portion, my body, and
my mind, are yours. Νόμῳ γὰρ ἅπαντα γίγνεται τοῦ γεγαμη-
κότος, τὴν πλοῦτον, τὴν δόξαν, τοὺς ἐπαίνους, "All that a woman
hath, is reckoned to the right of her husband; not her wealth
and her person only, but her reputation and her praise ;" so

Lucian[r]. But as the earth, the mother of all creatures here below, sends up all its vapours and proper emissions at the command of the sun, and yet requires them again to refresh her own needs, and they are deposited between them both in the bosom of a cloud, as a common receptacle, that they may cool his flames, and yet descend to make her fruitful: so are the proprieties of a wife to be disposed of by her lord; and yet all are for her provisions, it being a part of his need to refresh and supply her, and it serves the interest of both while it serves the necessities of either.

These are the duties of them both, which have common regards and equal necessities and obligations; and, indeed, there is scarce any matter of duty, but it concerns them both alike, and is only distinguished by names, and hath its variety by circumstances and little accidents: and what in one is called 'love,' in the other is called 'reverence;' and what in the wife is 'obedience,' the same in the man is 'duty.' He provides, and she dispenses; he gives commandments, and she rules by them; he rules her by authority, and she rules him by love; she ought by all means to please him, and he must by no means displease her. For as the heart is set in the midst of the body, and though it strikes to one side by the prerogative of nature, yet those throbs and constant motions are felt on the other side also, and the influence is equal to both: so it is in conjugal duties; some motions are to the one side more than to the other, but the interest is on both, and the duty is equal in the several instances. If it be otherwise, the man enjoys a wife as Periander did his dead Melissa, by an unnatural union, neither pleasing nor holy, useless to all the purposes of society, and dead to content.

SERMON XVIII.

PART II.

The next inquiry is more particular, and considers the power and duty of the man; " Let every one of you so love his wife even as himself;" she is as himself, the man hath power over her as over himself, and must love her equally.

r 'Περίφον διδύσαλος.

A husband's power over his wife is paternal and friendly, not magisterial and despotic. The wife is in 'perpetua tutela,' under conduct and counsel; for the power a man hath, is founded in the understanding, not in the will or force; it is not a power of coercion, but a power of advice, and that government that wise men have over those, who are fit to be conducted by them: "Et vos in manu et in tutela non in servitio debetis habere eas; et malle patres vos, et viros, quam dominos dici," said Valerius in Livy; 'husbands should rather be fathers than lords.' Homer adds more soft appellatives to the character of a husband's duty; πατὴρ μὲν γάρ ἐστι αὐτῇ καὶ πότνια μητὴρ, ἠδὲ κασίγνητος, 'Thou art to be a father and a mother to her, and a brother:' and great reason, unless the state of marriage should be no better than the condition of an orphan. For she that is bound to leave father, and mother, and brother for thee, either is miserable like a poor fatherless child, or else ought to find all these, and more, in thee. Medea in Euripides had cause to complain when she found it otherwise.

> Πάντων δ᾽, ὅσ᾽ ἐστ᾽ ἔμψυχα, καὶ γνώμην ἔχει,
> Γυναῖκές ἐσμεν ἀθλιώτατον φυτόν,
> Ἃς πρῶτα μὲν δεῖ χρημάτων ὑπερβολῇ
> Πόσιν πρίασθαι, δεσπότην τε σώματος
> Λαβεῖν[*].

Which St. Ambrose[t] well translates: 'It is sad, when virgins are with their own money sold to slavery; and that services are in better state than marriages; for they receive wages, but these buy their fetters, and pay dear for their loss of liberty;' And therefore, the Romans expressed the man's power over his wife but by a gentle word; "Nec vero mulieribus præfectus reponatur, qui apud Græcos creari solet, sed sit censor qui viros doceat moderari uxoribus;" said Cicero; "Let there be no governor of the woman appointed, but a censor of manners, one to teach the men to moderate their wives," that is, fairly to induce them to the measures of their own proportions. It was rarely observed of Philo, Εὖ τὸ μὴ φάναι, ἡ γυνὴ ἥν ἔδωκας ἐμοὶ, ἀλλὰ, μετ᾽ ἐμοῦ· οὐ γὰρ ἐμοὶ ὡς κτῆμα τὴν αἴσθησιν ἔδωκας, ἀλλὰ καὶ αὐτὴν ἀφῆκας ἄνετον καὶ ἐλεύθερον· "When Adam made that fond excuse for his folly in eating the forbidden fruit, he said 'The

* Med. 232. Porson.   t Exhor. ad virg.

woman thou gavest to be *with* me, she gave me.' He says
not ' The woman which thou gavest *to* me,' no such thing;
she is none of his goods, none of his possessions, not to be
reckoned amongst his servants; God did not give her to him
so; but ' The woman thou gavest to be with me,' that is, to be
my partner, the companion of my joys and sorrows, thou
gavest her for use, not for dominion.'' The dominion of a
man over his wife is no other than as the soul rules the body;
for which it takes a mighty care, and uses it with a delicate
tenderness, and cares for it in all contingencies, and watches
to keep it from all evils, and studies to make for it fair provisions, and very often is led by its inclinations and desires,
and does never contradict its appetites, but when they are
evil, and then also not without some trouble and sorrow; and
its government comes only to this, it furnishes the body with
light and understanding, and the body furnishes the soul
with hands and feet; the soul governs, because the body
cannot else be happy, but the government is no other than
provision; as a nurse governs a child, when she causes him
to eat, and to be warm, and dry, and quiet: and yet even the
very government itself is divided; for man and wife in the
family, are as the sun and moon in the firmament of heaven;
he rules by day, and she by night, that is, in the lesser and
more proper circles of her affairs, in the conduct of domestic
provisions and necessary offices, and shines only by his light,
and rules by his authority; and as the moon in opposition
to the sun shines brightest, that is, then, when she is in her
own circles and separate regions; so is the authority of the
wife then most conspicuous, when she is separate and in her
proper sphere; in ' gynæceo,' in the nursery and offices of
domestic employment: but when she is in conjunction with
the sun her brother, that is, in that place and employment
in which his care and proper offices are employed, her light
is not seen, her authority hath no proper business; but else
there is no difference: for they were barbarous people, among
whom wives were instead of servants, said Spartianus in Caracalla; and it is a sign of impotency and weakness, to force
the camels to kneel for their load, because thou hast not
spirit and strength enough to climb; to make the affections
and evenness of a wife bend by the flexures of a servant, is a
sign the man is not wise enough to govern, when another

stands by. So many differences as can be in the appellatives
of 'dominus' and 'domina,' governor and governess, lord
and lady, master and mistress, the same difference there is
in the authority of man and woman, and no more; 'Si tu
Caius, ego Caia,' was publicly proclaimed upon the threshold
of the young man's house, when the bride entered into his
hands and power; and the title of 'domina' in the sense of
the civil law, was among the Romans given to wives.

Hi Dominam Ditis thalamo dedocere adorti [t],

said Virgil: where, though Servius says it was spoken after
the manner of the Greeks, who called the wife Δέσποιναν,
'lady' or 'mistress,' yet it was so amongst both the nations.

'Ac domus Dominam voca,' says Catullus [u];
'Hærebit Dominæ vir comes ipse suæ,' so Martial;

And, therefore, although there is just measure of subjection
and obedience due from the wife to the husband (as I shall
after explain), yet nothing of this expressed is in the man's
character, or in his duty; he is not commanded to rule, nor
instructed how, nor bidden to exact obedience, or to defend
his privilege; all his duty is signified by love, 'by nourishing
and cherishing [x],' by being joined with her in all the unions
of charity, by 'not being bitter to her [y],' by 'dwelling with
her according to knowledge, giving honour to her [z]:' so that
it seems to be with husbands, as it is with bishops and priests,
to whom much honour is due, but yet so that if they stand
upon it, and challenge it, they become less honourable: and
as amongst men and women humility is the way to be preferred; so it is in husbands, they shall prevail by cession, by
sweetness and counsel, and charity and compliance. So that
we cannot discourse of the man's right, without describing
the measures of his duty; that therefore follows next.

"Let him love his wife even as himself:"—that is his
duty, and the measure of it too; which is so plain, that if he
understands how he treats himself, there needs nothing be
added concerning his demeanour towards her, save only that
we add the particulars, in which Holy Scripture instances
this general commandment.

[t] Æneid. 6. 397.   [u] Epithal. Julia. 61.   [x] Ephes. v. 25.
[y] Col. iii. 19.   [z] 1 Pet. iii. 7.

Mὴ πικραίνετε. That is the first. " Be not bitter against her;" and this is the least index and signification of love; a civil man is never bitter against a friend or a stranger, much less to him that enters under his roof, and is secured by the laws of hospitality. But a wife does all that and more; she quits all her interest for his love, she gives him all that she can give, she is as much the same person as another can be the same, who is conjoined by love, and mystery, and religion, and all that is sacred and profane.

> Non equidem hoc dubites, amborum fœdere certo
> Consentire dies, et ab uno sidere duoi [a];

They have the same fortune, the same family, the same children, the same religion, the same interest, ' the same flesh,' ' erunt duo in carnem unam;' and therefore this the Apostle urges for his *μὴ πικραίνετε*, " no man hateth his own flesh, but nourisheth and cherisheth it;" and he certainly is strangely sacrilegious and a violater of the rights of hospitality and sanctuary, who uses her rudely, who is fled for protection, not only to his house, but also to his heart and bosom. A wise man will not wrangle with any one, much less with his dearest relative; and if it is accounted indecent to embrace in public, it is extremely shameful to brawl in public: for the other is in itself lawful; but this never, though it were assisted with the best circumstances of which it is capable. Marcus Aurelius said, that ' a wise man ought often to admonish his wife, to reprove her seldom, but never to lay his hands upon her [b];' " neque verberibus neque maledictis exasperandam uxorem," said the doctors of the Jews; and Homer brings in Jupiter sometimes speaking sharply to Juno (according to the Greek liberty and empire), but made a pause at striking her,

> Οὐ μὲν ἀλλ', εἰ αὖτε κακοφραδίης ἀλεγεινὴς
> Πρώτα ἐπαύρεαι, καὶ σε πληγῇσιν ἱμάσσω [c].

And the ancients use to sacrifice to Juno *γαμήλιος*, or ' the

---

[a] Pers. 5. 45.
[b] Ah lapis est ferrumque, suam quicumque puellam
  Verberat: e cœlo deripit ille Deos.
  Sit satis e membris tenuem præscindere vestem:
  Sit satis ornatos dissoluisse comæ:
  Sit lacrymas movisse satis; quater ille beatus,
  Quo tenera irato flere puella potest.
  Sed manibus qui sævus erit, scutumque sudemque
  Is gerat, et miti sit procul a Venere. *Tibull.* 1. 10. 60
[c] Iliad. O. 16.

president of marriage,' without gall; and St. Basil observes
and urges it, by way of upbraiding quarrelling husbands;
"Etiam vipera virus ob nuptiarum venerationem evomit,"
"The viper casts all his poison, when he marries his female;"
"Tu duritiam animi, tu feritatem, tu crudelitatem ob unionis
reverentiam non deponis[d]?" He is worse than a viper, who
for the reverence of this sacred union will not abstain from
such a poisonous bitterness; and how shall he embrace that
person whom he hath smitten reproachfully; for those kindnesses are indecent which the fighting-man pays unto his
wife. St. Chrysostom preaching earnestly against this barbarous inhumanity of striking the wife, or reviling her with
evil language, says, it is as if a king should beat his viceroy
and use him like a dog; from whom most of that reverence
and majesty must needs depart, which he first put upon him,
and the subjects shall pay him less duty, how much his
prince hath treated him with less civility; but the loss re-
dounds to himself; and the government of the whole family
shall be disordered, if blows be laid upon that shoulder
which together with the other ought to bear nothing but the
cares and the issues of a prudent government. And it is observable, that no man ever did this rudeness for a virtuous
end; it is an incompetent instrument, and may proceed from
wrath and folly, but can never end in virtue and the unions
of a prudent and fair society. "Quod si verberaveris, exas-
perabis morbum" (saith St. Chrysostom): "asperitas enim
mansuetudine, non alia asperitate, dissolvitur;" "If you
strike, you exasperate the wound," and (like Cato at Utica
in his despair) tear the wounds in pieces; and yet he that
did so ill to himself whom he loved well, he loved not women
tenderly, and yet would never strike; and if the man cannot
endure her talking, how can she endure his striking? But
this caution contains a duty in it which none prevaricates,
but the meanest of the people, fools and bedlams, whose
kindness is a curse, whose government is by chance and violence, and their families are herds of talking cattle.

> Sic alternos reficit cursus
> Alternus Amor, sic astrigeris
> Bellum discors exulat oris.
> Hæc concordia temperat æquis
> Elementa modis, ut pugnantia
> Vicibus cedant humida siccis,
> Jungantque fidem frigora flammis.

[d] Homil. 7. Hexam.

The marital love is infinitely removed from all possibility of such rudenesses : it is a thing pure as light, sacred as a temple, lasting as the world ; "Amicitia, quæ desinere potuit, nunquam vera fuit," said one ; "That love, that can cease, was never true :" it is ὁμιλία, so Moses called it ; it is εὔνοια, so St. Paul ; it is φιλότης, so Homer ; it is φιλοφροσύνη, so Plutarch ; that is, it contains in it all 'sweetness,' and all 'society,' and 'felicity,' and all 'prudence,' and all 'wisdom.' For there is nothing can please a man without love ; and if a man be weary of the wise discourses of the Apostles, and of the innocency of an even and a private fortune, or hates peace or a fruitful year, he hath reaped thorns and thistles from the choicest flowers of paradise ; 'for nothing can sweeten felicity itself, but love;' *but when a man dwells in love, then the breasts of his wife are pleasant as the droppings upon the hill of Hermon, her eyes are fair as the light of heaven, she is a fountain sealed, and he can quench his thirst, and ease his cares, and lay his sorrow down upon her lap, and can retire home to his sanctuary and refectory, and his gardens of sweetness and chaste refreshments. No man can tell but he that loves his children, how many delicious accents make a man's heart dance in the pretty conversation of those dear pledges ; their childishness, their stammering, their little angers, their innocence, their imperfections, their necessities, are so many little emanations of joy and comfort to him that delights in their persons and society ; but he that loves not his wife and children, feeds a lioness at home, and broods a nest of sorrows ; and blessing itself cannot make him happy ; so that all the commandments of God enjoining a man to 'love his wife,' are nothing but so many necessities and capacities of joy. 'She that is loved, is safe ; and he that loves is joyful.' Love is a union of all things excellent ; it contains in it, proportion and satisfaction, and rest and confidence ; and I wish that this were so much proceeded in, that the heathens themselves could not go beyond us in this virtue, and its proper, and its appendant happiness. Tiberius Gracchus chose to die for the safety of his wife ; and yet me-

* Felices ter et amplius,
Quos irrupta tenet copula, nec malis
Divulsos querimoniis,
Supremâ citius solvet amor die.
Horat. Od. 1. 13. 18.

thinks to a Christian to do so, should be no hard thing; for many servants will die for their masters, and many gentlemen will die for their friend; but the examples are not so many of those, that are ready to do it for their dearest relatives, and yet some there have been. Baptista Fregosa tells of a Neapolitan, that gave himself a slave to the Moors, that he might follow his wife; and Dominicus Catalusius, the prince of Lesbos, kept company with his lady, when she was a leper; and these are greater things than to die.

But the cases in which this can be required, are so rare and contingent, that Holy Scripture instances not the duty in this particular; but it contains in it, that the husband should nourish and cherish her, that he should refresh her sorrows and entice her fears into confidence and pretty arts of rest; for even the fig-trees that grew in paradise, had sharp-pointed leaves, and harshnesses fit to mortify the too-forward lusting after the sweetness of the fruit. But it will concern the prudence of the husband's love to make the cares and evils as simple and easy as he can, by doubling the joys and acts of a careful friendship, by tolerating her infirmities[f] (because by so doing, he either cures her, or makes himself better), by fairly expounding all the little traverses of society and communication, 'by taking every thing by the right handle,' as Plutarch's expression is; for there is nothing but may be misinterpreted, and yet if it be capable of a fair construction, it is the office of love to make it.

Εὖ λέγεις ὅ, ὅτ' ἂν τι λέξῃ, χρὴ δοκεῖν, κἂν μὴ λέγῃ.
Κρίνεσθαι, ἃ 'ν τῷ ξυνόντι πρὸς χάριν μᾶλλον λέγειν ἔ.

Love will account that to be well said, which, it may be, was not so intended; and then it may cause it to be so, another time.

3. Hither also is to be referred that he secure the interest of her virtue and felicity by a fair example; for a wife to a husband is a line or superficies, it hath dimensions of its own, but no motion or proper affections; but commonly puts on such images of virtues or vices as are presented to her by her husband's idea: and if thou beest vicious, com-

[f] Uxoris vitium tollas opus est, aut feras:
Qui tollit vitium, uxorem commodiusculam sibi præstat;
Qui fert, sese meliorem facit.   Varro.
[g] Eurip. Book. t. 2. p. 490.

plain not that she is infected that lies in thy bosom; the interest of whose loves ties her to transcribe thy copy, and write after the characters of thy manners. Paris was a man of pleasure, and Helena was an adulteress, and she added covetousness upon her own account. But Ulysses was a prudent man, and a wary counsellor, sober and severe; and he efformed his wife into such imagery as he desired; and she was chaste as the snows upon the mountains, diligent as the fatal sisters, always busy, and always faithful; γλῶσσαν μὲν ἀργὴν, χεῖρα δ'εἶχεν ἐργάτην· ' she had a lazy tongue, and a busy hand.'

4. Above all the instances of love let him preserve towards her an inviolable faith, and an unspotted chastity [b]; for this is the marriage-ring, it ties two hearts by an eternal hand; it is like the cherubim's flaming sword, set for the guard of paradise; he that passes into that garden, now that it is immured by Christ and the church, enters into the shades of death. No man must touch the forbidden tree, that in the midst of the garden, which is the tree of knowledge and life. Chastity is the security of love, and preserves all the mysteriousness like the secrets of a temple. Under this lock is deposited security of families, the union of affections, the repairer of accidental breaches.

——— Καὶ σφ' ἄχρντα πάντα λύσαν·
Εἰς οἴσιν ἀνέσαιμι ἡμαθῶσαι φιλότητι [i].

This is a grace that is shut up and secured by all arts of heaven, and the defence of laws, the locks and bars of modesty, by honour and reputation, by fear and shame, by interest and high regards; and that contract that is intended to be for ever, is yet dissolved, and broken by the violation of this; nothing but death can do so much evil to the holy rites of marriage, as unchastity and breach of faith can. The shepherd Cratis falling in love with a she-goat, had his brains beaten out with a buck as he lay asleep; and by the laws of the Romans, a man might kill his daughter or his wife, if he surprised her in the breach of her holy vows, which are as sacred as the threads of life, secret as the privacies of the sanctuary, and holy as the society of angels. "Nullæ sunt inimicitiæ nisi amoris acerbæ;" and God that commanded us

[b] Καὶ ἀνόθευτον παρῶσι τὸ γάμον.

[i] Il. ξ. 205.

to forgive our enemies, left it in our choice, and hath not commanded us to forgive an adulterous husband or a wife; but the offended party's displeasure may pass into an eternal separation of society and friendship. Now in this grace it is fit that the wisdom and severity of the man should hold forth a pure taper, that his wife may, by seeing the beauties and transparencies of that crystal, dress her mind and her body by the light of so pure reflections; it is certain he will expect it from the modesty and retirement, from the passive nature and colder temper, from the humility and fear, from the honour and love, of his wife, that she be pure as the eye of heaven: and therefore it is but reason that the wisdom and nobleness, the love and confidence, the strength and severity, of the man, should be as holy and certain in this grace, as he is a severe exactor of it at her hands, who can more easily be tempted by another, and less by herself.

These are the little lines of a man's duty, which, like threads of light from the body of the sun, do clearly describe all the regions of his proper obligations. Now concerning the woman's duty, although it consists in doing whatsoever her husband commands, and so receives measures from the rules of his government, yet there are also some lines of life depicted upon her hands, by which she may read and know how to proportion out her duty to her husband.

1. The first is obedience; which because it is no where enjoined that the man should exact of her, but often commanded to her to pay, gives demonstration that it is a voluntary cession that is required; such a cession as must be without coercion and violence on his part, but upon fair inducements, and reasonableness in the thing, and out of love and honour on her part. When God commands us to love him, he means we should obey him; " This is love, that ye keep my commandments ;" and " if ye love me" (said our Lord), " keep my commandments :" now as Christ is to the church, so is man to the wife: and therefore obedience is the best instance of her love; for it proclaims her submission, her humility, her opinion of his wisdom, his pre-eminence in the family, the right of his privilege, and the injunction imposed by God upon her sex, that although in sorrow she bring forth children, yet with love and choice she should obey. The man's authority is love, and the woman's love is obedience;

and it was not rightly observed of him that said, when the
woman fell, 'God made her timorous, that she might be ruled,'
apt and easy to obey; for this obedience is no way founded
in fear, but in love and reverence. "Receptæ reverentiæ est,
si mulier viro subsit," said the law[k]; unless also that we
will add, that it is an effect of that modesty which like ru-
bies adorns the necks and cheeks of women. "Pudicitia est,
pater, Eos magnificare, qui nos socias sumpserunt sibi[l]," said
the maiden in the comedy: " it is modesty to advance and
highly to honour them, who have honoured us by making us
to be the companions" of their dearest excellences; for the woman that went before the man in the way of death, is commanded to follow him in the way of love; and that makes
the society to be perfect, and the union profitable, and the
harmony complete.

> Inferior matrona suo sit, Prisce, marito ;
> Non aliter fuerint fœmina virque pares [m].

For then the soul and body make a perfect man, when the
soul commands wisely, or rules lovingly, and cares profitably,
and provides plentifully, and conducts charitably that body
which is its partner, and yet the inferior. But if the body
shall give laws, and, by the violence of the appetite, first
abuse the understanding, and then possess the superior portion of the will and choice, the body and the soul are not apt
company, and the man is a fool, and miserable. If the soul
rules not, it cannot be a companion ; either it must govern,
or be a slave ; never was king deposed and suffered to live
in the state of peerage and equal honour, but made a prisoner,
or put to death ; and those women, that had rather lead the
blind than follow prudent guides, rule fools and easy men
than obey the powerful and wise, never made a good society in
a house : a wife never can become equal but by obeying ; but
so her power, while it is in minority, makes up the authority of
the man integral, and becomes one government, as themselves
are one man. " Male and female created he them, and called
their name Adam," saith the Holy Scripture[n]; they are but
one : and therefore, the several parts of this one man must
stand in the place where God appointed, that the lower parts

[k] C. alis D. se. lut. Matrim.   [l] Plautus in Sticho. 1. 2. 43.
[m] Mart. 8. 12.   [n] Gen. v. 2.

may do their offices in their own station, and promote the common interest of the whole. A ruling woman is intolerable.

> ————Faciunt graviora coactæ
> Imperio sexus °.

But that is not all; for she is miserable too: for,

> Τὰ δευτερεῖα τὴν γυναῖκα δεῖ λέγειν,
> Τὴν δ' ἡγεμονίαν τῶν ὅλων τὸν ἄνδρ' ἔχειν ᵖ.

It is a sad calamity for a woman to be joined to a fool or a weak person; it is like a guard of geese to keep the capitol; or as if a flock of sheep should read grave lectures to their shepherd, and give him orders where he shall conduct them to pasture. " O vere Phrygiæ, neque enim Phryges :" it is a curse that God threatened sinning persons; " Devoratum est robur eorum, facti sunt quasi mulieres. Effœminati dominabuntur eis ᑫ ;" " to be ruled by weaker people ;" δοῦλον γενέσθαι παραφρονοῦντος δεσπότου ʳ, "to have a fool to one's master," is the fate of miserable and unblessed people: and the wife can be no ways happy, unless she be governed by a prudent lord, whose commands are sober counsels, whose authority is paternal, whose orders are provisions, and whose sentences are charity.

But now concerning the measures and limits of this obedience, we can best take accounts from Scripture: ἐν παντὶ, saith the Apostle, " in all things ˢ ;" " ut Domino," " as to the Lord ;" and that is large enough; ' as unto a lord,' ' ut ancilla domino ;' so St. Jerome understands it, who neither was a friend to the sex, nor to marriage; but his mistake is soon confuted by the text; it is not " ut dominis," be subject to your husbands " as unto lords," but ὡς τῷ Κυρίῳ, that is, ' in all religion,' in reverence and in love, in duty and zeal, in faith and knowledge; or else ὡς τῷ Κυρίῳ may signify, ' wives be subject to your husbands ; but yet so, that at the same time ye be subject to the Lord.' For that is the measure of ἐν παντὶ, " in all things ;" and it is more plain in the parallel place, ὡς ἀνῆκεν ἐν Κυρίῳ, " as it is fit in the Lord ᵗ :" religion must be the measure of your obedience and subjection: "intra limites disciplinæ;" so Tertullian expresses it. Πάντα μὲν τῷ ἀνδρὶ πειθομένῃ, ὡς μηδὲν, ἄκοντος ἐκείνου, πράξαι ποτὲ, πλὴν ὅσα εἰς ἀρετὴν καὶ σοφίαν διαφέρειν νομίζεται· so Clemens Alex[u]: " In all things let the wife be subject to the husband, so as to do nothing against his will; those only things excepted, in which he is impious or refractory in things pertaining to wisdom and piety."

But in this also there is some peculiar caution. For although in those things which are of the necessary parts of faith and holy life, the woman is only subject to Christ, who only is and can be Lord of consciences, and commands alone where the conscience is instructed and convinced: yet as it is part of the man's office to be a teacher, and a prophet, and a guide, and a master; so also it will relate very much to the demonstration of their affections to obey his counsels, to imitate his virtues, to be directed by his wisdom, to have her persuasion measured by the lines of his excellent religion: οὐχ ἧττον δὲ σεμνὸν ἀκοῦσαι γαμετῆς λεγούσης, ἀνὴρ σύ μοι ἐσσὶ καθηγητὴς καὶ φιλόσοφος καὶ διδάσκαλος τῶν καλλίστων καὶ θειοτάτων· " It were hugely decent," saith Plutarch, " that the wife should acknowledge her husband for her teacher and her guide;" for then when she is what he please to efform her, he hath no cause to complain if she be no better: τὰ δὲ τοιαῦτα μαθήματα πρῶτον ἀφίστησι τῶν ἀτόπων τὰς γυναῖκας; " his precept and wise counsels can draw her off from vanities;" and, as he said of geometry, that, if she be skilled in that, she will not easily be a gamester or a dancer, may perfectly be said of religion. If she suffers herself to be guided by his counsel, and efformed by his religion; either he is an ill master in his religion, or he may secure in her and for his advantage an excellent virtue. And although in matters of religion the husband hath no empire and command, yet if there be a place left to persuade, and entreat, and induce by arguments, there is not in a family a greater endearment of affections than the unity of religion: and anciently ' it was not permitted to a woman to have a religion by herself:' " Eosdem quos maritus, nosse Deos et colere solos uxor debet," said Plutarch. And the rites which a woman performs severally from her husband, are not pleasing to God; and therefore Pomponia Græcina, because she entertained a

stranger religion, was permitted to the judgment of her husband Plantius : and this whole affair is no stranger to Christianity, for the Christian woman was not suffered to marry
an unbelieving man ; and although this is not to be extended
to different opinions within the limits of the common faith :
yet thus much advantage is won or lost by it ; that the compliance of the wife, and submission of her understanding to
the better rule of her husband in matters of religion, will
help very much to warrant her, though she should be misper-
suaded in a matter less necessary ; yet nothing can warrant
her in her separate rites and manners of worshippings, but
an invincible necessity of conscience, and a curious infallible
truth ; and if she be deceived alone, she hath no excuse ; if
with him, she hath much pity, and some degrees of warranty
under the protection of humility, and duty, and dear affections ; and she will find that it is part of her privilege and
right to partake of the mysteries and blessings of her husband's religion. Γυναῖκα γαμετὴν μετὰ νόμους ἱεροὺς συνελ-
θοῦσαν ἀνδρὶ κοινωνὸν ἁπάντων εἶναι, χρημάτων τε καὶ ἱερῶν,
said Romulus : "A woman by the holy laws hath right to
partake of her husband's goods, and her husband's sacrifices,
and holy things." Where there is a schism in one bed, there
is a nursery of temptations, and love is persecuted and in
perpetual danger to be destroyed ; there dwell jealousies,
and divided interests, and differing opinions, and continual
disputes[y], and we cannot love them so well, whom we believe
to be less beloved of God ; and it is ill uniting with a person,
concerning whom my persuasion tells me, that he is like to
live in hell to eternal ages.

2. The next line of the woman's duty is compliance, which
St. Peter calls, " the bidden man of the heart, the ornament
of a meek and a quiet spirit[z]," and to it he opposes ' the outward and pompous ornament of the body ;' concerning which,
as there can be no particular measure set down to all persons, but the proportions were to be measured by the customs of wise people, the quality of the woman, and the desires of the man ; yet it is to be limited by Christian modes-

[y] ———— Quis deditus autem
Usque adeò est, ut non illam, quam laudibus effert,
Horreat, inque diem septenis oderit horis?
                                        Juven. Sat. 6. 181.
[z] 1 Pet. iii. 4.

ty, and the usages of the more excellent and severe matrons. Menander in the comedy brings in a man turning his wife from his house, because she stained her hair yellow, which was then the beauty.

Κἂν ᾖ ἔρα' ἀπ' οἴκων τόνδε τὴν γυναῖκα γὰρ Τὴν σώφρον' οὐ δεῖ τὰς τρίχας ξανθὰς ποιεῖν. Cleric. p. 258.

A wise woman should not paint. A studious gallantry in clothes cannot make a wise man love his wife the better[a]. Εἰς τοὺς τραγῳδοὺς χρήσιμ', οὐκ εἰς τὸν βίον, said the comedy; "Such gaieties are fit for tragedies, but not for the uses of life:" "Decor occultus, et tecta venustas," that is the Christian woman's fineness; ' the hidden man of the heart,' sweetness of manners, humble comportment, fair interpretation of all addresses, ready compliance, high opinion of him and mean of herself[b].

Ἐν κοινῷ λύπης ἡδονῆς τ' ἔχειν μέρος, ' To partake secretly, and in her heart, of all his joys and sorrows,' to believe him comely and fair[c], though the sun hath drawn a cyprus over him; for as marriages are not to be contracted by the hands and eye, but with reason and the hearts; so are these judgments to be made by the mind, not by the sight: and diamonds cannot make the woman virtuous, nor him to value her who sees her put them off then, when charity and modesty are her brightest ornaments.

Οὐ κόσμος, οἶα, ὦ τλῆμον, ἀλλ' ἀκοσμία Φαίνοιτ' ἂν εἶναι σῶν μαργαρίτης φρενῶν, &c.

And, indeed, those husbands that are pleased with indecent gaieties of their wives, are like fishes taken with ointments and intoxicating baits, apt and easy for sport and mockery, but useless for food ; and when Circe had turned Ulysses's companions into hogs and monkeys, by pleasures

[a] Quid juvat ornato procedere, vita, capillo,
Teque peregrinis vendere muneribus,
Naturæque decus mercato perdere cultu,
Nec sinere in propriis membra nitere bonis ?
Propert. l. 1. el. 1.

[b] Malo Venusinam, quàm te, Cornelia mater
Graechorum, si cum magnis virtutibus affers
Grande supercilium, et numeras in dote triumphos.
Juven. Sat. 6. 167.

[c] Πρῶτα μὲν γε ταῦθ' ὑπάρχειν· κἂν ἄμορφος ᾖ πόσις, χρὴ δοκεῖν εὔμορφον εἶναι τῇ γυναῖ κεκτημένῃ· οὐ γὰρ ὀφθαλμὸς τὸ κρίνον ἐστὶν ἀλλὰ νοῦς.

and the enchantments of her bravery and luxury, they were
no longer useful to her, she knew not what to do with them;
but on wise Ulysses she was continually enamoured. Indeed, the outward ornament is fit to take fools, but they are
not worth the taking; but she that hath a wise husband,
must entice him to an eternal dearness by the veil of modesty and the grave robes of chastity, the ornament of meekness and the jewels of faith and charity; she must have no
fucus but blushings, her brightness must be purity, and she
must shine round about with sweetnesses and friendship,
and she shall be pleasant while she lives, and desired when
she dies. If not,

> ――――――― Κατθανοῦσα δὲ κείσεαι,
> Οὐδὲ τις μνημοσύνα σέθεν ἔσσεται,
> Οὐ γὰρ μετέχεις ῥόδων τῶν ἐκ Πιερίας.

Her grave shall be full of rottenness and dishonour, and her
memory shall be worse after she is dead : ' after she is dead;'
for that will be the end of all merry meetings; and I choose
this to be the last advice to both.

3. " Remember the days of darkness, for they are many;"
the joys of the bridal-chambers are quickly past, and the remaining portion of the state is a dull progress, without variety
of joys, but not without the change of sorrows; but that
portion that shall enter into the grave, must be eternal. It
is fit that I should infuse a bunch of myrrh into the festival
goblet, and, after the Egyptian manner, serve up a dead man's
bones at a feast : I will only shew it, and take it away again;
it will make the wine bitter, but wholesome. But those
married pairs that live, as remembering that they must part
again, and give an account how they treat themselves and
each other, shall, at that day of their death, be admitted to
glorious espousals; and when they shall live again, be married to their Lord, and partake of his glories, with Abraham
and Joseph, St. Peter and St. Paul, and all the married
saints.

> Θνητὰ τὰ τῶν θνητῶν, καὶ πάντα παρέρχεται ἡμᾶς·
> Ἢν δὲ μὴ, ἀλλ' ἡμεῖς αὐτὰ παρερχόμεθα [d].

'All those things that now please us shall pass from us, or we
from them;' but those things that concern the other life, are

---

permanent as the numbers of eternity : and although at the resurrection there shall be no relation of husband and wife, and no marriage shall be celebrated but the marriage of the Lamb ; yet then shall be remembered how men and women passed through this state which is a type of that, and from this sacramental union all holy pairs shall pass to the spiritual and eternal, where love shall be their portion, and joys shall crown their heads, and they shall lie in the bosom of Jesus, and in the heart of God to eternal ages.   Amen.

SERMON XIX.

APPLES OF SODOM; OR, THE FRUITS OF SIN.

PART I.

What fruit had ye then in those things whereof ye are now ashamed? For the end of those things is death.—Romans vi. 21.

THE son of Sirach did prudently advise concerning making judgments of the felicity or infelicity of men ; " Judge none blessed before his death ; for a man shall be known in his children*." Some men raise their fortunes from a cottage to the chairs of princes, from a sheep-cote to a throne, and dwell in the circles of the sun, and in the lap of prosperity ; their wishes and success dwell under the same roof, and Providence brings all events into their design, and ties both ends together with prosperous successes ; and even the little conspersions and intertextures of evil accidents in their lives, are but like a feigned note of music, by an artificial discord making the ear covetous, and then pleased with the harmony into which the appetite was enticed by passion, and a pretty restraint ; and variety does but adorn prosperity, and make it of a sweeter relish, and of more advantages ; and some of these men descend into their graves without a change of fortune.

Eripitur persona, manet res.

* Ecclus. xi. 28.

Indeed, they cannot longer dwell upon the estate, but that remains unrifled, and descends upon their heir, and all is well till the next generation: but if the evil of his death, and the change of his present prosperity, for an intolerable danger of an uncertain eternity, does not sour his full chalice; yet if his children prove vicious or degenerous, cursed or unprosperous, we account the man miserable, and his grave to be strewed with sorrows and dishonours. The wise and valiant Chabrias grew miserable by the folly of his son Ctesippus; and the reputation of brave Germanicus began to be ashamed, when the base Caligula entered upon his scene of dishonourable crime. Commodus, the wanton and feminine son of wise Antoninus, gave a check to the great name of his father; and when the son of Hortensius Corbio was prostitute, and the heir of Q. Fabius Maximus was disinherited by the sentence of the city prætor, as being unworthy to enter into the fields of his glorious father, and young Scipio the son of Africanus was a fool and a prodigal; posterity did weep afresh over the monuments of their brave progenitors, and found that infelicity can pursue a man, and overtake him in his grave.

This is a great calamity when it falls upon innocent persons: and that Moses died upon Mount Nebo, in the sight of Canaan, was not so great an evil, as that his sons Eliezer and Gerson were unworthy to succeed him; but that priesthood was devolved to his brother, and the principality to his servant: and to Samuel, that his sons proved corrupt, and were exauthorated for their unworthiness, was an allay to his honour and his joys, and such as proclaims to all the world, that the measures of our felicity are not to be taken by the lines of our own person, but of our relations too; and he that is cursed in his children, cannot be reckoned among the fortunate.

This which I have discoursed concerning families in general, is most remarkable in the retinue and family of sin; for it keeps a good house, and is full of company and servants, it is served by the possessions of the world, it is courted by the unhappy, flattered by fools, taken into the bosom by the effeminate, made the end of human designs, and feasted all the way of its progress: wars are made for its interest, and men give or venture their lives that their sin may be prosperous; all the outward senses are its handmaids, and the inward senses are of its privy-chamber; the understanding is its counsellor, the will its friend, riches are its ministers, nature holds up its train, and art is its emissary to promote its interest and affairs abroad: and, upon this account, all the world is enrolled in its taxing-tables, and are subjects or friends of its kingdom, or are so kind to it as to make too often visits, and to lodge in its borders; because all men stare upon its pleasures, and are enticed to taste of its wanton delicacies. But then if we look what are the children of this splendid family, and see what issue sin produces, ἐστὶ γὰρ τέκνα καὶ τῷδε,—it may help to untie the charm. Sin and concupiscence marry together, and riot and feast it high, but their fruits, the children and production of their filthy union, are ugly and deformed, foolish and ill-natured; and the Apostle calls them by their name, 'shame' and 'death.' These are the fruits of sin, 'the apples of Sodom,' fair outsides, but if you touch them, they turn to ashes and a stink; and if you will nurse these children, and give them whatsoever is dear to you, then you may be admitted into the house of feasting, and chambers of riot where sin dwells; but if you will have the mother, you must have the daughters; the tree and the fruits go together; and there is none of you all that ever entered into this house of pleasure, but he left the skirts of his garment in the hands of shame, and had his name rolled in the chambers of death. "What fruit had ye then ?" That is the question.

In answer to which question we are to consider, 1. What is the sum total of the pleasure of sin? 2. What fruits and relishes it leaves behind by its natural efficiency? 3. What are its consequents by its demerit, and the infliction of the superadded wrath of God, which it hath deserved? Of the first St. Paul gives no account; but by way of upbraiding asks, 'what they had?' that is, nothing that they dare own, nothing that remains: and where is it? shew it; what is become of it? Of the second he gives the sum total: all its natural effects are 'shame' and its appendages. The third, or the superinduced evils by the just wrath of God, he calls 'death,' the worst name in itself, and the greatest of evils that can happen.

1. Let us consider what pleasures there are in sin; most

of them are very punishments. I will not reckon or consider concerning envy, which one in Stobæus[f] calls κάκιστον καδικώτατον Θεὸν, "the basest spirit, and yet very just;" because it punishes the delinquent in the very act of sin, doing as Ælian says of the polypus, εἴτις αὐτῷ γίνοιται ἀθηρία, τῶν ἑαυ τοῦ πλοκάμων παρέτραγε, "when he wants his prey, he devours his own arms; (i. 27.)" and the leanness, and the secret pangs, and the perpetual restlessness of an envious man, feed upon his own heart, and drink down his spirits, unless he can ruin or observe the fall of the fairest fortunes of his neighbour. The fruits of this tree are mingled and sour, and not to be endured in the very eating. Neither will I reckon the horrid affrightments and amazements of murder, nor the uneasiness of impatience, which doubles every evil that it feels, and makes it a sin, and makes it intolerable; nor the secret grievings, and continual troubles of peevishness, which makes a man incapable of receiving good, or delighting in beauties and fair entreaties in the mercies of God and charities of men.

It were easy to make a catalogue of sins, every one of which is a disease, a trouble in its very constitution and its nature: such are loathing of spiritual things, bitterness of spirit, rage, greediness, confusion of mind, and irresolution, cruelty and despite, slothfulness and distrust, unquietness and anger, effeminacy and niceness, prating and sloth, ignorance and inconstancy, incogitancy and cursing, malignity and fear, forgetfulness and rashness, pusillanimity and despair, rancour and superstition: if a man were to curse his enemy, he could not wish him a greater evil than these: and yet these are several kinds of sin which men choose, and give all their hopes of heaven in exchange for one of these diseases. Is it not a fearful consideration, that a man should rather choose eternally to perish than to say his prayers heartily, and affectionately? but so it is with very many men; they are driven to their devotions by custom, and shame, and reputation, and civil compliances; they sigh and look sour when they are called to it, and abide there as a man under the chirurgeon's hands, smarting and fretting all the while; or else he passes the time with incogitancy, and hates the employment, and suffers the torment of prayers which he loves not; and all this, although for so doing it is certain

f Florileg. tit. 38.

he may perish : what fruit, what deliciousness, can he fancy in being weary of his prayers ? there is no pretence or colour for these things. Can any man imagine a greater evil to the body and soul of a man than madness, and furious eyes, and a distracted look, paleness with passion, and trembling hands and knees, and furiousness, and folly in the heart and head ? and yet this is the pleasure of anger, and for this pleasure men choose damnation. But it is a great truth, that there are but very few sins that pretend to pleasure : although a man be weak and soon deceived, and the devil is crafty, and sin is false and impudent, and pretences are too many,—yet most kinds of sins are real and prime troubles to the very body, without all manner of deliciousness, even to the sensual, natural, and carnal part ; and a man must put on something of a devil before he can choose such sins, and he must love mischief because it is a sin ; for in most instances there is no other reason in the world. Nothing pretends to pleasure but the lust of the lower belly, ambition, and revenge ; and although the catalogue of sins is numerous as the production of fishes, yet these three only can be apt to cozen us with a fair outside ; and yet upon the survey of what fruits they bring, and what taste they have in the manducation, besides the filthy relish they leave behind, we shall see how miserably they are abused and fooled, that expend any thing upon such purchases.

2. For a man cannot take pleasure in lusts of the flesh, in gluttony, or drunkenness, unless he be helped forward with inconsideration and folly. For we see it evidently that grave and wise persons, men of experience and consideration, are extremely less affected with lust and loves than the harebrained boy ; the young gentleman that thinks nothing in the world greater than to be free from a tutor, he indeed courts his folly, and enters into the possession of lust without abatement ; consideration dwells not there : but when a sober man meets with a temptation, and is helped by his natural temper, or invited by his course of life ; if he can consider, he hath so many objections and fears, so many difficulties and impediments, such sharp reasonings and sharper jealousies concerning its event, that if he does at all enter into folly, it pleases him so little, that he is forced to do it in despite of himself ; and the pleasure is so allayed, that he

knows not whether it be wine or vinegar ; his very apprehension and instruments of relish are filled with fear and contradicting principles, and the deliciousness does but 'affricare
cutem,' it went ' but to the skin ;' but the allay went farther ;
it kept a guard within, and suffered the pleasure to pass no
farther. A man must resolve to be a fool, a rash inconsiderate person, or he will feel but little satisfaction in the enjoyment of his sin: indeed, he that stops his nose, may drink
down such corrupted waters ; and he understood it well who
chose rather to be a fool,

> Dum mea delectent mala me, vel denique fallant,
> Quàm sapere et ringi.   *Hor.* Ep. 2. 2. 127.

' so that his sins might delight him, or deceive him, than to
be wise and without pleasure in the enjoyment.' So that in
effect a man must lose his discerning faculties before he dis-
cerns the little fantastic joys of his concupiscence ; which de-
monstrates how vain, how empty of pleasure that is, that is
beholden to folly and illusion, to a juggling and a plain cozenage, before it can be fancied to be pleasant. For it is a
strange beauty that he that hath the best eyes, cannot perceive, and none but the blind or blear-eyed people can see ;
and such is the pleasure of lust, which, by every degree of
wisdom that a man hath, is lessened and undervalued.

3. For the pleasures of intemperance, they are nothing
but the relics and images of pleasure, after that nature hath
been feasted ; for so long as she needs, that is, so long as
temperance waits, so long pleasure also stands there ; but as
temperance begins to go away, having done the ministries
of nature, every morsel, and every new goblet, is still less delicious, and cannot be endured but as men force nature by
violence to stay longer than she would : how have some men
rejoiced when they have escaped a cup ! and when they cannot escape, they pour it in, and receive it with as much pleasure as the old women have in the Lapland dances ; they
dance the round, but there is a horror and a harshness in the
music ; and they call it pleasure, because men bid them do
so : but there is a devil in the company, and such as is his
pleasure, such is theirs : he rejoices in the thriving sin, and
the swelling fortune of his darling drunkenness, but his joys
are the joys of him that knows and always remembers, that

he shall infallibly have the biggest damnation; and then let it be considered how forced a joy that is, that is at the end of an intemperate feast.

Nec bene mendaci risus componitur ore,
Nec bene sollicitis ebria verba sonant ꞇ.

Certain it is, intemperance takes but nature's leavings; when the belly is full, and nature calls to take away, the pleasure that comes in afterward, is next to loathing : it is like the relish and taste of meats at the end of the third course, or sweetness of honey to him that hath eaten till he can endure to take no more; and in this, there is no other difference of these men from them that die upon another cause, than was observed among the Phalangia of old, τὰ μὲν ποιεῖ γελῶντας ἀποθνήσκειν, τὰ δὲ κλαίοντας, "some of these make men die laughing, and some to die weeping:" so does the intemperate, and so does his brother that languishes of a consumption; this man dies weeping, and the other dies laughing; but they both die infallibly, and all his pleasure is nothing but the sting of a serpent,' immixto liventia mella veneno,' it wounds the heart, and he dies with a tarantula, dancing and singing till he bows his neck, and kisses his bosom with the fatal noddings and declensions of death.

4. In these pretenders to pleasure (which you see are but few, and they not very prosperous in their pretences), there is mingled so much trouble to bring them to act an enjoyment, that the appetite is above half tired before it comes ; it is necessary a man should be hugely patient that is ambitious, ' ambulare per Britannos, Scythicas pati pruinas :' no man buys death and damnation at so dear a rate, as he that fights for it, and endures cold and hunger,——— ' Patiens liminis et solis,' ' the heat of the sun, and the cold of the threshold;' the dangers of war, and the snares of a crafty enemy; he lies upon the ground with a severity greater than the penances of a hermit, and fasts beyond the austerity of a rare penitent; with this only difference, that the one does it for heaven, and the other for an uncertain honour, and an eternity of flames. But, however, by this time that he hath won something, he hath spent some years,

ꞇ Tibullus. 3. 6. 35. Heyne. p. 219.

and he hath not much time left him to rest in his new purchase, and he hath worn out his body, and lessened his capacity of feeling it; and although it is ten to one he cannot escape all the dangers he must venture at, that he may come near his trifle, yet, when he is arrived thither, he can never long enjoy, nor well perceive or taste it; and therefore, there are more sorrows at the gate, than there can dwell comforts in all the rooms of the houses of pride and great designs. And thus it is in revenge, which is pleasant only to a devil, or a man of the same cursed temper. He does a thing which ought to trouble him, and will move him to pity, what his own vile hands have acted; but if he does not pity, that is, be troubled with himself, and wish the things undone, he hath those affections by which the devil doth rejoice in destroying souls; which affections a man cannot have, unless he be perfectly miserable, by being contrary to God, to mercy, and to felicity; and, after all, the pleasure is false, fantastic, and violent, it can do him no good, it can do him hurt, it is odds but it will, and on him that takes revenge, revenge shall be taken, and by a real evil he shall dearly pay for the goods that are but airy and fantastical; it is like a rolling stone, which, when a man hath forced up a hill, will return upon him with a greater violence, and break those bones whose sinews gave it motion. The pleasure of revenge is like the pleasure of eating chalk and coals; a foolish disease made the appetite, and it is entertained with an evil reward; it is like the feeding of a cancer or a wolf; the man is restless till it be done, and when it is, every man sees how infinitely he is removed from satisfaction or felicity.

5. These sins when they are entertained with the greatest fondness from without, it must have an extreme little pleasure, because there is a strong faction, and the better party against them: something that is within contests against the entertainment, and they sit uneasily upon the spirit when the man is vexed, that they are not lawful. The Persian king gave Themistocles a goodly pension, assigning Magnesia with the revenue of fifty talents for his bread, Lampsacum for his wine, and Myos for his meat; but all the while he fed high and drunk deep, he was infinitely afflicted that every thing went cross to his undertaking, and he could not bring his ends about to betray his country; and at last he

mingled poison with his wine and drank it off, having first
entreated his friends to steal for him a private grave in his
own country. Such are the pleasures of the most pompous
and flattering sins : their meat and drink are good and pleasant at first, and it is plenteous and criminal ; but its employment is base, it is so against a man's interest, and against
what is, and ought to be, dearest to him, that he cannot persuade his better parts to consent, but must fight against them
and all their arguments. These things are against a man's
conscience, that is, against his reason and his rest : and something within makes his pleasure sit uneasily. But so do violent perfumes make the head ache, and therefore wise persons reject them ; and the eye refuses to stare upon the beauties of the sun, because it makes it weep itself blind ; and if
a luscious dish please my palate, and turns to loathing in the
stomach, I will lay aside that evil, and consider the danger
and the bigger pain, not that little pleasure. So it is in sin ;
it pleases the senses, but diseases the spirit, and wounds
that : and that it is apt to smart as the skin, and is as considerable in the provisions of pleasure and pain respectively :
and the pleasure of sin to a contradicting reason, are like the
joys of wine to a condemned man,

> ———Difficile est imitari gaudia falsa ;
> Difficile est tristi fingere mente jocum. (*Tibull.*)

It will be very hard to delight freely in that which so vexes
the more tender and most sensible part ; so that, what Pliny
said of the poppies growing in the river Caicus, ἔχει ἀντὶ καρ-
ποῦ λίθον, 'it brings a stone instead of a flower or fruit :' so
are the pleasures of these pretending sins ; the flower at the
best is stinking, but there is a stone in the bottom ; it is gra-
vel in the teeth, and a man must drink the blood of his own
gums when he manducates such unwholesome, such unpleasant fruit.

> ———Vitiorum gaudia vulnus habent.

They make a wound, and therefore are not very pleasant.
Τὸ γὰρ ζῆν μὴ καλῶς, μέγας πόνος, ' It is a great labour and
travail, to live a vicious life.'

6. The pleasure in the acts of these few sins that do pretend to it, is a little limited nothing, confined to a single faculty, to one sense, having nothing but the skin for its organ

or instrument, an artery, or something not more considerable than a lutestring; and at the best, it is but the satisfaction of an appetite which reason can cure, which time can appease, which every diversion can take off; such as is not perfective of his nature, nor of advantage to his person; it is a desire to no purpose, and as it comes with no just cause, so can be satisfied with no just measures; it is satisfied before it comes to a vice, and when it is come thither, all the world cannot satisfy it: a little thing will weary it, but nothing can content it. For all these sensual desires are nothing but an impatience of being well and wise, of being in health, and being in our wits; which two things if a man could endure, (and it is but reasonable, a man would think, that we should) he would never lust to drown his heart in seas of wine, or oppress his belly with loads of undigested meat, or make himself base by the mixtures of a harlot, by breaking the sweetest limits and holy festivities of marriage. " Malum impatientia est boni," said Tertullian, it is nothing else; to please the sense is but to do a man's self mischief; and all those lusts tend to some direct dissolution of a man's health or his felicity, his reason or his religion; it is an enemy that a man carries about him: and as the Spirit of God said concerning Babylon, " Quantum in deliciis fuit, tantum date illi tormentum et luctum," " Let her have torment and sorrow according to the measure of her delights," is most eminently true in the pleasing of our senses; the lust and desire is a torment, the remembrance and the absence is a torment, and the enjoyment does not satisfy, but disables the instrument, and tires the faculty; and when a man hath but a little of what his sense covets, he is not contented, but impatient for more; and when he hath loads of it, he does not feel it. For he that swallows a full goblet does not taste his wine: and this is the pleasure of the sense; nothing contents it but that which he cannot perceive, and it is always restless, till it be weary; and all the way unpleased, till it can feel no pleasure; and that which is the instrument of sense, is the means of its torment; by the faculty by which it tastes, by the same it is afflicted; for so long as it can taste, it is tormented with desire, and when it can desire no longer, it cannot feel pleasure.

7. Sin hath little or no pleasure in its very enjoyment;

because its very manner of entry and production is by a curse
and a contradiction; it comes into the world like a viper
through the sides of its mother, by means unnatural, violent,
and monstrous. Men love sin only because it is forbidden;
"Sin took occasion by the law," saith St. Paul; it could not
come in upon its own pretences, but men rather suspect secret pleasure in it because there are guards kept upon it.

Sed quia cæcus inest vitiis amor, omne futurum
Despicitur, suadentque brevem præsentia fructum,
Et ruit in vetitam damni secura libido.

Men run into sin with blind affections and against all reason despise the future, hoping for some little pleasure for
the present; and all this is only because they are forbidden:
do not many men sin out of spite? Some out of the spirit of
disobedience, some by wildness and indetermination, some
by imprudence, and because they are taken in a fault;

————— Frontemque à crimine sumunt;

some because they are reproved; many by custom, others by
importunity:

Ordo fuit crevisse malis ————

It grows upon crab-stocks, and the lust itself is sour and unwholesome: and since it is evident, that very many sins come
in wholly upon these accounts, such persons and such sins
cannot pretend pleasure; but as naturalists say of pulse,
"Cum maledictis et probris serendum præcipiunt, ut lætius
proveniat;" "the country-people were used to curse it and rail
upon it all the while that it was sowing, that it might thrive
the better;" it is true with sins, they grow up with curses,
with spite and contradiction, peevishness and indignation,
pride and cursed principles; and therefore, pleasure ought
not to be the inscription of the box; for that is the least
part of its ingredient and constitution.

8. The pleasures in the very enjoying of sin are infinitely trifling and inconsiderable, because they pass away so
quickly; if they be in themselves little, they are made less
by their volatile and fugitive nature; but if they were great,
then their being so transient does not only lessen the delight, but changes it into a torment, and loads the spirit of
the sinner with impatience and indignation Is it not a high

upbraiding to the watchful adulterer, that after he hath con-
trived the stages of his sin, and tied many circumstances together with arts and labour, and these join and stand knit
and solid only by contingency, and are very often borne away
with the impetuous torrent of an inevitable accident, like
Xerxes' bridge over the Hellespont; and then he is to begin
again, and sets new wheels a-going; and by the arts, and the
labour, and the watchings, and the importunity, and the violence, and the unwearied study, and indefatigable diligence,
of many months, he enters upon possession, and finds them
not of so long abode as one of his cares, which in so vast
numbers made so great a portion of his life afflicted. Πρόσ-
καιρον ἁμαρτίας ἀπόλαυσιν, " the enjoying of sin for a season,"
St. Paul [a] calls it; he names no pleasures; our English translation uses the word of *enjoying pleasures:* but if there were
any, they were but for that season, that instant, that very
transition of the act, which dies in its very birth, and of
which we can only say as the minstrel sung of Pacuvius,
when he was carried dead from his supper to his bed, βεβίωκε,
βεβίωκε. A man can scarce have time enough to say it is
alive, but that it was: "nullo non se die extulit," it died
every day, it lived never unto life, but lived and died unto
death, being its mother and its daughter: the man died before the sin did live; and when it had lived, it consigned him
to die eternally.

Add to this, that it so passes away, that nothing at all
remains behind it that is pleasant: it is like the path of an
arrow in the air; the next morning no man can tell what is
become of the pleasures of the last night's sin: they are no
where but in God's books, deposited in the conscience,
and sealed up against the day of dreadful accounts; but
as to the man, they are as if they never had been; and
then, let it be considered, what a horrible aggravation it will
be to the miseries of damnation, that a man shall for ever
perish for that, which if he looks round about he cannot see, nor tell where it is. " He that dies, dies for that
which is not;" and in the very little present he finds it an
unrewarding interest, to walk seven days together over sharp
stones only to see a place from whence he must come back
in an hour. If it goes off presently, it is not worth the la-

[a] Heb. xi. 25.

bour; if it stays long, it grows tedious; so that it cannot be pleasant, if it stays; and if it does stay, it is not to be valued: "Hæc mala mentis gaudia." It abides too little a while to be felt, or called pleasure; and if it should abide longer, it would be troublesome as pain, and loathed like the tedious speech of an orator pleading against the life of the innocent.

9. Sin hath in its best advantages but a trifling, inconsiderable pleasure: because not only God and reason, conscience and honour, interest and laws, do sour it in the sense and gust of pleasure, but even the devil himself either being overruled by God, or by a strange insignificant malice, makes it troublesome and intricate, entangled and involved; and one sin contradicts another, and vexes the man with so great variety of evils, that if in the course of God's service he should meet with half the difficulty, he would certainly give over the whole employment. Those that St. James speaks of, who "prayed that they might spend it upon their lusts," were covetous and prodigal, and therefore must endure the torments of one to have the pleasure of another; and which is greater, the pleasure of spending, or the displeasure that it is spent and does not still remain after its consumption, is easy to tell: certain it is, that this lasts much longer. Does not the devil often tempt men to despair, and by that torment put bars and locks upon them, that they may never return to God? Which what else is it but a plain indication that it is intended, the man should feel the images and dreams of pleasure, no longer but till he be without remedy? Pleasure is but like sentries or wooden frames, set under arches, till they be strong by their own weight and consolidation to stand alone; and when by any means the devil hath a man sure, he takes no longer care to cozen him with pleasures, but is pleased that men should begin an early hell, and be tormented before the time. Does not envy punish or destroy flattery; and self-love sometimes torment the drunkard; and intemperance abate the powers of lust, and make the man impotent; and laziness become a hinderance to ambition; and the desires of man wax impatient upon contradicting interests, and by crossing each other's design on all hands lessen the pleasure, and leave the man tormented?

10. Sin is of so little relish and gust, so trifling a pleasure, that it is always greater in expectation than it is in the

possession. But if men did beforehand see, what the utmost is, which sin ministers to please the beastly part of man, it were impossible it should be pursued with so much earnestness and disadvantages. It is necessary it should promise more than it can give; men could not otherwise be cozened. And if it be inquired, why men should sin again, after they had experience of the little and great deception? it is to be confessed, it is a wonder they should: but then we may remember, that men sin again, though their sin did afflict them; they will be drunk again, though they were sick ; they will again commit folly, though they be surprised in their shame, though they have needed an hospital; and therefore, there is something else that moves them, and not the pleasure; for they do it without and against its interest; but either they still proceed, hoping to supply by numbers what they find not in proper measures; or God permits them to proceed as an instrument of punishment; or their understandings and reasonings grow cheaper; or they grow in love with it, and take it upon any terms ; or contract new appetites, and are pleased with the baser and the lower reward of sin: but whatsoever can be the cause of it, it is certain, by the experience of all the world, that the fancy is higher, the desires more sharp, and the reflection more brisk, at the door and entrance of the entertainment, than in all the little and shorter periods of its possession: for then it is but limited by the natural measures, and abated by distemper, and loathed by enjoying, and disturbed by partners, and dishonoured by shame and evil accidents; so that as men coming to the river Lucius, ἔχει μὲν λευκύτατον ὑδάτων καὶ ῥεῖ διειδέστατα, and seeing ' waters pure' as the tears of the spring, or the pearls of the morning, expect that in such a fair promising bosom, the inmates should be fair and pleasant; τίκτει δὲ ἰχθῦς μελάνας ἰσχυρῶς, but find ' the fishes black,' filthy, and unwholesome; so it is in sin; its face is fair and beauteous,

Ἡ πικεραῖς λεύσσουσα κόραις μαλακώτερτν ὕπνου,
Αύσιδος ἀλκυὼν, τιρεντὸ ἄθυρμα μίθυς.

Softer than sleep, or the dreams of wine, tenderer than the curds of milk ; ' Et Euganea quantumvis mollior agna;' but when you come to handle it, it is filthy, rough as the porcupine, black as the shadows of the night, and having promised a fish it gives a scorpion, and a stone instead of bread.

11. The fruits of its present possession, the pleasures of its taste, are less pleasant, because no sober person, no man that can discourse, does like it long.

———— Breve sit quod turpiter audes. *Juv.* 8. 165.

But he approves it in the height of passion, and in the disguises of a temptation; but at all other times he finds it ugly and unreasonable; and the very remembrances must at all times abate its pleasures, and sour its delicacies. In the most parts of a man's life he wonders at his own folly, and prodigious madness, that it should be ever possible for him to be deluded by such trifles; and he sighs next morning, and knows it over-night; and is it not therefore certain, that he leans upon a thorn, which he knows will smart, and he dreads the event of to-morrow? But so have I known a bold trooper fight in the confusion of a battle, and being warm with heat and rage, received, from the swords of his enemy, wounds open like a grave; but he felt them not, and when, by the streams of blood, he found himself marked for pain, he refused to consider then what he was to feel to-morrow: but when his rage had cooled into the temper of a man, and clammy moisture had checked the fiery emission of spirits, he wonders at his own boldness, and blames his fate, and needs a mighty patience to bear his great calamity. So is the bold and merry sinner, when he is warm with wine and lust, wounded and bleeding with the strokes of hell, he twists with the fatal arm that strikes him, and cares not; but yet it must abate his gaiety, because he remembers that when his wounds are cold and considered, he must roar or perish, repent or do worse, that is, be miserable or undone. The Greeks call this τῶν σάκκων εὐδαιμονίαν, 'the felicity of condemned slaves feasted high in sport.' Dion Prusias reports, that when the Persians had got the victory, they would pick out the noblest slave, καὶ καθίζουσιν εἰς τὸν θρόνον τοῦ βασιλέως, καὶ τὴν ἐσθῆτα δίδωσιν τὴν αὐτὴν καὶ τρυφᾷν, καὶ παλλακαῖς χρῆσθαι, 'they make him a king for three days, and clothe him with royal robes, and minister to him all the pleasure he can choose, and all the while he knows he is to die a sacrifice to mirth and folly.' But then, let it be remembered,

what checks and allays of mirth the poor man starts at, when
he remembers the axe and the altar where he must shortly
bleed; and by this we may understand what that pleasure
is, in the midst of which the man sighs deeply, when he
considers what opinion he had of this sin, in the days of
counsel and sober thoughts; and what reason against it, he
shall feel to-morrow when he must weep or die. Thus it
happens to sinners according to the saying of the prophet,
" Qui sacrificant hominem, osculabuntur Vitulum," " He that
gives a man in sacrifice shall kiss the calf[1];" that is, shall be
admitted to the seventh chapel of Moloch to kiss the idol:
a goodly reward for so great a price, for so great an inquiry.

After all this I do not doubt but these considerations
will meet with some persons that think them to be ' protes-
tatio contra factum,' and fine pretences against all experience; and that, for all these severe sayings, sin is still so
pleasant as to tempt the wisest resolution. Such men are in
a very evil condition: and in their case only I come to understand the meaning of those words of Seneca; " Malorum ultimum est mala sua amare, ubi turpia non solum de-
lectant, sed etiam placent:" " It is the worst of evils when
men are so in love with sin that they are not only delighted with them, but pleased also;" not only feel the relish with too quick a sense, but also feel none of the objections, nothing of the pungency, the sting, or the lessening
circumstances. However, to these men I say this only, that
if by experience they feel sin pleasant, it is as certain also
by experience, that most sins are in their own nature sharpnesses and diseases; and that very few do pretend to pleasure: that a man cannot feel any deliciousness in them, but
when he is helped by folly and inconsideration; that is, a
wise man cannot, though a boy or a fool can, be pleased
with them: that they are but relics and images of pleasure
left upon nature's stock, and therefore, much less than the
pleasures of natural virtues: that a man must run through
much trouble before he brings them to act and enjoyment:
that he must take them in despite of himself, against reason
and his conscience, the tenderest parts of man and the most
sensible of affliction: they are at the best so little, that they
are limited to one sense, not spread upon all the faculties

[1] Hosea, xiii. 2.

like the pleasures of virtue, which make the bones fat by
an intellectual rectitude, and the eyes sprightly by a wise
proposition, and pain itself to become easy by hope and a
present rest within : it is certain (I say) by a great experience, that the pleasures of sin enter by cursings and a contradictory interest, and become pleasant not by their own relish, but by the viciousness of the palate, by spite and peevishness, by being forbidden and unlawful : and that which
is its sting is, at some times, the cause of all its sweetness
it can have: they are gone sooner than a dream : they are
crossed by one another, and their parent is their tormentor ;
and when sins are tied in a chain, with that chain they dash
one another's brains out, or make their lodging restless : it
is never liked long; and promises much and performs little ;
it is great at distance, and little at hand, against the nature
of all substantial things; and, after all this, how little pleasure is left, themselves have reason with scorn and indignation to resent. So that, if experience can be pretended
against experience, there is nothing to be said to it but the
words which Phryne desired to be written on the gates of
Thebes, Ἀλέξανδρος κατέσκαψεν, ἀνέστησε δὲ Φρύνη ἡ ἑταίρα,
" Phryne the harlot built it up, but Alexander dug it down :"
the pleasure is supported by little things, by the experience
of fools and them that observed nothing, and the relishes
tasted by artificial appetites, by art and cost, by violence
and preternatural desires, by the advantage of deception
and evil habits, by expectation and delays, by dreams and
inconsiderations : these are the harlot's hands that build the
fairy castle, but the bands of reason and religion, sober
counsels and the voice of God, experience of wise men and
the sighings and intolerable accents of perishing or returning sinners, dig it down, and sow salt in the foundations, that
they may never spring up in the accounts of men that delight not in the portion of fools and forgetfulness. " Neque
enim Deus ita viventibus quicquam promisit boni, neque ipsa per se mens humana, talium sibi conscia, quicquam boni
sperare audet :" "To men that live in sin, God hath promised no good, and the conscience itself dares not expect it[k]."

[k] Plat. de Rep.

SERMON XX.

PART II.

WE have already opened this dunghill, covered with snow, which was indeed on the outside white as the spots of leprosy, but it was no better; and if the very colours and instruments of deception, if the fucus and ceruse be so spotted and sullied, what can we suppose to be under the wrinkled skin, what in the corrupted liver, and in the sinks of the body of sin? That we are next to consider: but if we open the body, and see what a confusion of all its parts, what a rebellion and tuumlt of the humours, what a disorder of the members, what a monstrosity or deformity is all over, we shall be infinitely convinced, that no man can choose a sin, but upon the same ground on which he may choose a fever, or long for madness or the gout. Sin, in its natural efficiency, hath in it so many evils, as must needs affright a man, and scare the confidence of every one that can consider.

When our blessed Saviour shall conduct his church to the mountains of glory, he shall " present it to God without spot or wrinkle[1]," that is, pure and vigorous, entirely freed from the power and the infection of sin. Upon occasion of which expression it hath been spoken, that sin leaves in the soul a stain or spot, permanent upon the spirit, discomposing the order of its beauty, and making it appear to God ' in sordibus,' ' in such filthiness,' that he who ' is of pure eyes cannot behold.' But, concerning the nature or proper effects of this spot or stain, they have not been agreed: some call it an obligation or a guilt of punishment; so Scotus. Some fancy it to be an elongation from God, by a dissimilitude of conditions; so Peter Lombard. Alexander of Ales says it is a privation of the proper beauty and splendour of the soul, with which God adorned it in the creation and superaddition of grace; and upon this expression they most agree, but seem not to understand what they mean by it; and it signifies no more, but as you, describing sickness, call it a want of health, and folly, a want of wisdom; which is indeed to say, what a thing is not, but not to tell what it

[1] Eph. v.

is: but that I may not be hindered by this consideration, we may observe, that the spots and stains of sin are metaphorical significations of the disorder and evil consequents of sin; which it leaves partly upon the soul, partly upon the state and condition of man, as meekness is called an ornament, and faith a shield, and salvation a helmet, and sin itself a wrinkle, corruption, rottenness, a burden[m], a wound, death, filthiness: so it is a defiling of a man; that is, as the body contracts nastiness and dishonour by impure contacts, and adherences; so does the soul receive such a change, as must be taken away before it can enter into the eternal regions, and house of purity. But it is not a distinct thing, not an inherent quality, which can be separated from other evil effects of sin, which I shall now reckon by their more proper names; and St. Paul comprises under the scornful appellative of ' shame.'

1. The first natural fruit of sin is ignorance. Man was first tempted by the promise of knowledge; he fell into darkness by believing the devil holding forth to him a new light. It was not likely good should come of so foul a beginning; that the woman should believe the devil putting on no brighter shape than a snake's skin, she neither being afraid of sin, nor affrighted to hear a beast speak, and he pretending so weakly in the temptation, that he promised only that they should know evil; for they knew good before; and all that was offered to them was the experience of evil: and it was no wonder that the devil promised no more, for sin never could perform any thing but an experience of evil, no other knowledge can come upon that account; but the wonder was, why the woman should sin for no other reward, but for that which she ought to have feared infinitely; for nothing could have continued her happiness, but not to have known evil. Now this knowledge was the introduction of ignorance. For when the understanding suffered itself to be so baffled as to study evil, the will was as foolish to fall in love with it, and they conspired to undo each other. For when the will began to love it, then the understanding was set on work to commend, to advance, to conduct and to approve, to believe it, and to be factious in behalf of the

[m] Κατὰ δ' αἰθάλου
Κιλῶ' ἐκτρέπεται αἰχμεραι, &c. *Hecub.* 905. Porson.

new purchase. I do not believe, the understanding part of man received any natural decrement or diminution. For if to the devils their naturals remain entire, it is not likely that the lesser sin of man should suffer a more violent and effective mischief. Neither can it be understood how the reasonable soul, being immortal both in itself and its essential faculties, can lose or be lessened in them, any more than it can die. But it received impediment, by new propositions: it lost and willingly forgot what God had taught, and went away from the fountain of truth, and gave trust to the father of lies, and it must without remedy grow foolish; and so a man came to know evil, just as a man is said to taste of death: for, in proper speaking, as death is not to be felt, because it takes away all sense; so neither can evil be known, because whatsoever is truly cognoscible, is good and true; and therefore all the knowledge a man gets by sin is to feel evil: he knows it not by discourse, but by sense; not by proposition, but by smart; the devil doing to man as Æsculapius did to Neoclides, ὄξει διέμενος σφηττίῳ, Κατέπλασεν αὐτοῦ τὰ βλέφαρα, ἵνα 'Ὀδυνῷτο μᾶλλον· ' he gave him a formidable collyrium to torment him more:' the effect of which was, ὅτι βλέπειν τὸν Πλοῦτον ταχὺ ἐποίησεν, Τὸν δὲ Νεοκλείδη μᾶλλον ἐποίησεν τυφλόν: (Arist. Pl. 720.) ' the devil himself grew more quicksighted to abuse us,' but we became more blind by that opening of our eyes. I shall not need to discourse of the philosophy of this mischief, and by the connexion of what causes ignorance doth follow sin: but it is certain, whether a man would fain be pleased with sin, or be quiet or fearless when he hath sinned, or continue in it, or persuade others to it, he must do it by false propositions, by lyings, and such weak discourses as none can believe but such as are born fools, or such as have made themselves so, or are made so by others. Who in the world is a verier fool, a more ignorant, wretched person, than he that is an atheist? A man may better believe there is no such man as himself, and that he is not in being, than that there is no God: for himself can cease to be, and once was not, and shall be changed from what he is, and in very many periods of his life knows not that he is; and so it is every night with him when he sleeps: but none of these can happen to God; and if he knows it not, he is a fool. Can any thing in this world be more foolish than to think that all this rare fabric of heaven and earth can come by chance, when all the skill of art is not able to make an oyster? To see rare effects, and no cause; an excellent government and no prince; a motion without an immoveable; a circle without a centre; a time without eternity; a second without a first; a thing that begins not from itself, and therefore not to perceive there is something from whence it does begin, which must be without beginning; these things are so against philosophy and natural reason, that he must needs be a beast in his understanding that does not assent to them; this is the atheist: " The fool hath said in his heart, There is no God." That is his character: the thing framed, says that nothing framed it; the tongue never made itself to speak, and yet talks against him that did; saying, that which is made, is, and that which made it, is not. But this folly is as infinite as hell, as much without light or bound, as the chaos or the primitive nothing. But in this, the devil never prevailed very far; his schools were always thin at these lectures: some few people have been witty against God, that taught them to speak before they knew to spell a syllable; but either they are monsters in their manners, or mad in their understandings, or ever find themselves confuted by a thunder or a plague, by danger or death.

But the devil hath infinitely prevailed in a thing that is almost as senseless and ignorant as atheism, and that is idolatry; not only making God after man's image, but in the likeness of a calf, of a cat, of a serpent; making men such fools as to worship a quartan ague, fire and water, onions and sheep. This is the skill man learned, and the philosophy that he is taught, by believing the devil. What wisdom can there be in any man, that calls good evil, and evil good; to say fire is cold, and the sun black; that fornication can make a man happy, or drunkenness can make him wise? And this is the state of a sinner, of every one that delights in iniquity; he cannot be pleased with it if he thinks it evil; he cannot endure it, without believing this proposition, That there is in drunkenness or lust pleasure enough, good enough, to make him amends for the intolerable pains of damnation. But then if we consider upon what nonsense principles the state of an evil life relies, we must in reason

be impatient, and with scorn and indignation drive away the
fool; such as are—sense is to be preferred before reason, interest before religion, a lust before heaven, moments before
eternity, money above God himself; that, a man's felicity
consists in that which a beast enjoys; that, a little in present,
uncertain, fallible possession, is better than the certain state
of infinite glories hereafter: what child, what fool, can think
things more weak, and more unreasonable? And yet if men
do not go upon these grounds, upon what account do they
sin? Sin hath no wiser reasons for itself than these: μῶρος
ἔχει πυραύστου μόρον: the same argument that a fly hath to
enter into a candle, the same argument a fool hath that enters into sin; it looks prettily, but rewards the eye, as burning basons do, with intolerable circles of reflected fire. Such
are the principles of a sinner's philosophy. And no wiser
are his hopes; all his hopes that he hath are, that he shall
have time to repent of that which he chooses greedily; that
he whom he every day provokes will save him, whether he
will or no; that he can, in an instant, or in a day, make
amends for all the evils of forty years; or else, that he shall
be saved whether he does or no; that heaven is to be had
for a sigh, or a short prayer, and yet hell shall not be consequent to the affections, and labours, and hellish services,
of a whole life; he goes on and cares not, he hopes without
a promise, and refuses to believe all the threatenings of God;
but believes he shall have a mercy for which he never had a
revelation. If this be knowledge or wisdom, then there is
no such thing as folly, no such disease as madness.

But then consider, that there are some sins whose very
formality is a lie. Superstition could not be in the world, if
men did believe God to be good and wise, free and merciful,
not a tyrant, not an unreasonable exactor: no man would
dare do in private, what he fears to do in public, if he did
know that God sees him there, and will bring that work of
darkness into light. But he is so foolish as to think, that if
he sees nothing, nothing sees him; for if men did perceive
God to be present, and yet do wickedly, it is worse with them
than I have yet spoke of; and they believe another lie, that
to be seen by man will bring more shame, than to be discerned
by God; or that the shame of a few men's talk is more
intolerable than to be confounded before Christ, and his army

of angels, and saints, and all the world. He that excuses a fault by telling a lie, believes it better to be guilty of two faults, than to be thought guilty of one; and every hypocrite thinks it not good to be holy, but to be accounted so, is a fine thing; that is, that opinion is better than reality, and that there is in virtue nothing good but the fame of it. And the man that takes revenge, relies upon this foolish proposition; that his evil that he hath already suffered grows less if another suffers the like; that his wound cannot smart, if by my hand he dies that gave it; ἥξει τι μέλος γοερὸν γοεραῖς, the sad accents and doleful tunes are increased by the number of mourners, but the sorrow is not lessened.

I shall not need to thrust into this account the other evils of mankind that are the events of ignorance, but introduced by sin; such as are, our being moved by what we see strongly, and weakly by what we understand; that men are moved rather by a fable than by a syllogism, by parables than by demonstrations, by examples than by precepts, by seeming things than by real, by shadows than by substances; that men judge of things by their first events, and measure the events by their own short lives, or shorter observations; that they are credulous to believe what they wish, and incredulous of what makes against them, measuring truth or falsehood by measures that cannot fit them, as foolishly as if they should judge of a colour by the dimensions of a body, or feel music with the hand; they make general conclusions from particular instances, and take account of God's actions by the measures of a man. Men call that justice that is on their side, and all their own causes are right, and they are so always; they are so when they affirm them in their youth, and they are so when they deny them in their old age; and they are confident in all their changes; and their first error, which they now see, does not make them modest in the proposition which they now maintain; for they do not understand that what was, may be so again: "So foolish and ignorant was I (said David), and as it were a beast before thee." Ambition is folly, and temerity is ignorance, and confidence never goes without it, and impudence is worse, and zeal or contention is madness, and prating is want of wisdom, and lust destroys it, and makes a man of a weak spirit, and a cheap reasoning; and there are in the catalogue of sins very many, which are directly kinds, and parts, and appendages, of ignorance; such as are, blindness of mind, affected ignorance, and wilful; neglect of hearing the word of God, resolved incredulity, forgetfulness of holy things, lying and believing a lie; this is the fruit of sin, this is the knowledge that the devil promised to our first parents as the rewards of disobedience; and although they sinned as weakly and fondly, φρονήματος τό-πριν στερηθέντες, upon as slight grounds, and trifling a temptation, and as easy a deception, as many of us since, yet the causes of our ignorance are increased by the multiplication of our sins; and if it was so bad in the green tree, it is much worse in the dry; and no man is so very a fool as the sinner, and none are wise but the servants of God,

Μοῦνα Χαλδαῖοι σοφίαν λάχον, ἠδ᾽ ἄρ᾽ Ἑβραῖοι,
Αὐτογένεθλον ἄνακτα σεβαζόμενοι θεὸν ἁγνῶς.

"The wise Chaldees and the wiser Hebrews, which worship God chastely and purely, they only have a right to be called wise;" all that do not so are fools and ignorants, neither knowing what it is to be happy, nor how to purchase it; ignorant of the noblest end, and of the competent means towards it: they neither know God nor themselves, and no ignorance is greater than this, or more pernicious. What man is there in the world that thinks himself covetous or proud? and yet millions there are who, like Harpaste, think that the house is dark, but not themselves. Virtue makes our desires temperate and regular, it observes our actions, condemns our faults, mortifies our lusts, watches all our dangers and temptations: but sin makes our desires infinite, and we would have we cannot tell what; we strive that we may forget our faults; we labour that we may neither remember nor consider; we justify our errors, and call them innocent, and that which is our shame we miscall honour; and our whole life hath in it so many weak discourses and trifling propositions, that the whole world of sinners is like the hospital of the 'insensati,' madness and folly possess the greater part of mankind. What greater madness is there than to spend the price of a whole farm in contention for three sheaves of corn? and yet 'tantum pectora cæcæ Noctis habent,' this is the wisdom of such as are contentious, and love their own will

more than their happiness, their humour more than their
peace.

—— Furor est post omnia perdere animum [a].

Men lose their reason, and their religion, and themselves at
last, for want of understanding; and all the wit and discourses
by which sin creeps in, are but φροντίδων βουλεύματα, γλώσσης τι κόμποι, " frauds of the tongue, and consultations of
care [b]:" but in the whole circle of sins there is not one wise
proposition, by which a man may conduct his affairs, or himself become instructed to felicity. This is the first natural
fruit of sin : it makes a man a fool, and this hurt sin does to
the understanding, and this is shame enough to that in which
men are most apt to glory.

Sin naturally makes a man weak; that is, unapt to do
noble things : by which I do not understand a natural disability : for it is equally ready for a man to will good as evil,
and as much in the power of his hands to be lifted up in
prayer to God as against his brother in a quarrel ; and between a virtuous object and his faculties there is a more apt
proportion, than between his spirit and a vice; and every act
of grace does more please the mind, than an act of sin does
delight the sense ; and every crime does greater violence to
the better part of man, than mortification does to the lower;
and oftentimes a duty consists in a negative, as, not to be
drunk, not to swear, and it is not to be understood that a
man hath naturally no power not to do; if there be a natural
disability, it is to action, not to rest or ceasing ; and therefore in this case, we cannot reasonably nor justly accuse our
nature, but we have reason to blame our manners, which have
introduced upon us a moral disability ; that is, not that the
faculty is impotent and disabled, but that the whole man is;
for the will in many cases desires to do good, and the understanding is convinced and consents, and the hand can obey,
and the passions can he directed, and be instrumental to
God's service : but because they are not used to it, the will
finds a difficulty to do them so much violence, and the understanding consents to their lower reasonings, and the desires of the lower man do will stronger; and then the whole
man cannot do the duty that is expected. There is a law in

[a] Juv. 8. 97.   [b] Hecub. 630.

the members, and he that gave that law is a tyrant, and the subjects of that law are slaves, and oftentimes their ear is bored; and they love their fetters, and desire to continue that bondage for ever; the law is the law of sin, the devil is the tyrant, custom is the sanction or the firmament of the law ; and every vicious man is a slave, and chooses the vilest master, and the basest of services, and the most contemptible rewards. " Lex enim peccati est violentia consuetudinis, qua trahitur et tenetur animus etiam invitus, eo merito quo in eam volens illabitur," said St. Austin ; " The law of sin is the violence of custom, which keeps a man's mind against his mind, because he entered willingly," and gave up his own interest; which he ought to have secured for his own felicity, and for his service who gave for it an invaluable price: and indeed in questions of virtue and vice there is no such thing as nature; or it is so inconsiderable, that it hath in it nothing beyond an inclination which may be reverted ; and very often not so much : nothing but a perfect indifferency, we may if we will, or we may choose ; but custom brings in a new nature, and makes a bias in every faculty. To a vicious man some sins become necessary ; temperance makes him sick ; severity is death to him, it destroys his cheerfulness and activity, it is as his nature, and the desire dwells for ever with him, and his reasonings are framed for it and his fancy, and in all he is helped by example, by company, by folly, and inconsideration ; and all these are a faction and a confederacy against the honour and service of God. And in this, philosophy is at a stand, nothing can give an account of it but experience and sorrowful instances ; for it is infinitely unreasonable, that when you have discoursed wisely against unchastity, and told, that we are separated from it by a circumvallation of laws of God and man, that it dishonours the body, and makes the spirit captive, that it is fought against by arguments sent from all the corners of reason and religion, and the man knows all this, and believes it, and prays against his sin, and hates himself for it, and curses the actions of it; yet oppose against all this but a fable or a merry story, a proverb or a silly saying, the sight of his mistress, or any thing but to lessen any one of the arguments brought against it, and that man shall as certainly and clearly be determined to that sin, as if he had on his side all the reason of the world.

Δεινὸν γὰρ ἦθος καὶ ἐξομοιῶσαι καὶ βιάσασθαι πρὸς φύσιν[p],Custom does as much as nature can do; it does sometimes more, and superinduces a disposition contrary to our natural temper. Eudemus had so used his stomach to so unnatural drinks, that, as himself tells the story, he took in one day two-and-twenty potions in which hellebore was infused, and rose at noon, and supped at night, and felt no change: so are those that are corrupted with evil customs, nothing will purge them; if you discourse wittily, they hear youn ot; or, if they do, they have twenty ways to answer, and twice twenty to neglect it: if you persuade them to promise to leave their sin, they do but shew their folly at the next temptation, and tell you that they did not mean it: and if you take them at an advantage when their hearts are softened with a judgment or a fear, with a shame or an indignation, and then put the bars and locks of vows upon them, it is all one; one vow shall hinder but one action, and the appetite shall be doubled by the restraint, and the next opportunity shall make an amends for the first omission: or else the sin shall enter by parts: the vow shall only put the understanding to make a distinction, or to change the circumstance, and under that colour the crime shall be admitted, because the man is resolved to suppose the matter so dressed was not vowed against. But then, when that is done, the understanding shall open that eye that did but wink before, and see that it was the same thing, and secretly rejoice that it was so cozened: for now the lock is opened, and the vow was broken against his will, and the man is at liberty again, because be did the thing at unawares, οὐ θέλων τε καὶ θέλων, still he is willing to believe the sin was not formal vow-breach, but now he sees he broke it materially, and because the hand is broken, the yoke is in pieces; therefore the next action shall go on upon the same stock of a single iniquity, without being affrighted in his conscience at the noise of perjury. I wish we were all so innocent as not to understand the discourse; but it uses to be otherwise.

> Nam si discedas, laqueo tenet ambitiosi
> Consuetudo mali:———et ægro in corde senescit [q].

' Custom hath waxen old in his deceived heart, and made snares for him that he cannot disentangle himself;' so true is that saying of God by the prophet, " Can an Ethiopian change his skin ? then may ye learn to do well, when ye are accustomed to do evil." But I instance in two things, which, to my sense, seem great aggravations of the slavery and weakness of a customary sinner.

The first is, that men sin against their interest. They know they shall be ruined by it ; it will undo their estates, lose their friends, ruin their fortunes, destroy their body, empoverish the spirit, load the conscience, discompose his rest, confound his reason, amaze him in all his faculties, destroy his hopes, and mischief enough besides; and when he considers this, he declares against it ; but, " cum bona verba erumpant, affectus tamen ad consuetudinem relabuntur," " the man gives good words, but the evil custom prevails ;" and it happens as in the case of the Tirynthians, who, to free their nation from a great plague, were bidden only to abstain from laughter, while they offered their sacrifice : but they had been so used to a ridiculous effeminacy, and vain course of conversation, that they could not, though the honour and splendour of the nation did depend upon it. God of his mercy keep all Christian people from a custom in sinning ! for if they be once fallen thither, nothing can recover them but a miraculous grace.

2. The second aggravation of it is, that custom prevails against experience. Though the man hath already smarted, though he hath been disgraced and undone, though he lost his relation and his friends, he is turned out of service, and disemployed, he begs with a load of his old sins upon his shoulders,—yet this will not cure an evil custom : do we not daily see how miserable some men make themselves with drunkenness and folly ? Have not we seen them that have been sick with intemperance, deadly sick, enduring for one drunken meeting more pain than is in all the fasting-days of the whole year? and yet, do they not the very next day go to it again ? Indeed, some few are smitten into the beginning of repentance, and they stay a fortnight, or a month, and, it may be, resist two or three invitations ; but yet the custom is not gone,

Nec tu, cùm obstiteris semel, instantique negaris
Parere imperio, ' Rupi jam vincula,' dicas :

'Think not the chain is off, when thou hast once or twice re-

sisted ; or if the chain be broke, part remains on thee, like a
cord upon a dog's neck,'

Nam et luctata canis nodum abripit ; attamen illi,
Cum fugit, a collo trahitur pars longa catenæ [r].

He is not free that draws his chain after him ; and he that
breaks off from his sins with greatest passion, stands in need
of prosperous circumstances, and a strange freedom from
temptation, and accidental hardness, and superinduced confidence, and a preternatural severity ; " Opus est aliqua for-
tunæ indulgentia adhuc inter humana luctanti, dum nodum
illum exsolvit et omne vinculum mortale [s]," for the knot can
hardly be untied which a course of evil manners hath bound
upon the soul ; and every contingency in the world can entangle him, that wears upon his neck the links of a broken
chain. " Nam qui ab eo quod amat, quam extemplo sua-
viis sagittatis percussus est, ilico res foras labitur, liquitur ;"
if he sees his temptation again he is ἐπικλώμενος ὑπ᾽ εὐνοίας,
his kindness to it, and conversation with his lust, undoes
him, and breaks his purposes, and then he dies again, or
falls upon that stone, that with so much pains he removed a
little out of his way ; and he would lose the spent wealth, or
the health, and the reputation, over again, if it were in his
power. Philomusus was a wild young fellow in Domitian's
time, and he was hard put to it to make a large pension to
maintain his lust and luxury, and he was every month put to
beggarly arts to feed his crime. But when his father died
and left him all, he disinherited himself ; he spent it all,
though he knew he was to suffer that trouble always, which
vexed his lustful soul in the frequent periods of his violent
want [t].

Now, this is such a state of slavery, that persons that are
sensible ought to complain, δουλείαν δουλεύειν πάνυ ἰσχυράν·
that they serve worse lords than Egyptian task-masters,
there is a lord within that rules and rages," Intus et in
jecore ægro pascuntur domini ;" sin dwells there, and makes
a man a miserable servant : and this is not only a metaphorical expression, under which some spiritual and metaphysical truth is represented, but it is a physical, material truth ;
and a man endures hardship, he cannot move but at this
command; and not his outward actions only, but his will and

[r] Pers. v. 157.   [s] Seneca de vitâ beatâ.   [t] Martial. lib. 3. 10.

his understanding too, are kept in fetters and foolish bondage: μίμνησο, ὅτι νευροσπαστοῦν ἐστὶν ἐκεῖνο, τὸ ἔνδον ἐγκεκρυμ-
μένον· ἐκεῖνο ῥητορεία, ἐκεῖνο ζωὴ, ἐκεῖνο ἄνθρωπος, said Marcus
Antoninus (11.38.); 'The two parts of a man are rent in sunder,
and that that prevails, is the life, it is the man, it is the eloquence, persuading every thing to its own interest.' And now
consider what is the effect of this evil. A man by sin is made
a slave, he loses that liberty that is dearer to him than life itself; and, like the dog in the fable, we suffer chains and ropes
only for a piece of bread, when the lion thought liberty a
sufficient reward and price for hunger, and all the hardnesses
of the wilderness. Do not all the world fight for liberty,
and at no terms will lay down arms, till at least they be cozened with the image and colour of it? οὐ θνήσκει ζῆλος
ἐλευθερίας; and yet for the pleasure of a few minutes we
give ourselves into bondage; and all the world does it, more
or less.

> Θεῦ. οὐκ ἔστι θνητῶν, ὅστις ἐστ' ἐλεύθερος.
> Ἢ χρημάτων γὰρ δοῦλός ἐστιν, ἢ τύχης,
> Ἢ πλῆθος αὐτὸν πόλεος, ἢ νόμων γραφαὶ
> Εἴργουσι χρῆσθαι μὴ κατὰ γνώμην τρόποις[a].

Either men are slaves to fortune, or to lust; to covetousness,
or tyranny; something or other compels him to usages
against his will and reason; and when the laws cannot rule
him, money can; " Divitiæ enim apud sapientem virum in
servitute sunt, apud stultum in imperio :" for " Money is the
wise man's servant, and the fool's master ;" but the bondage
of a vicious person, is such a bondage as the child hath in
the womb, or rather as a sick man in his bed; we are bound
fast by our disease, and a consequent weakness; we cannot
go forth though the doors be open, and the fetters knocked
off, and virtue and reason, like St. Peter's angel, call us,
and beat us upon the sides, and offer to go before us, yet we
cannot come forth from prison ; for we have by our evil customs given hostages to the devil, never to stir from the enemy's quarter; and this is the greatest bondage that is imaginable, the bondage of conquered, wounded, unresisting
people : ἀδέσποτος ἡ ἀρετὴ, 'virtue only is the truest liberty :'
" and if the Son of God make us free, then are we free
indeed."

[a] Euripid. Hecuba. Purson. 858.

3. Sin does naturally introduce a great baseness upon the spirit, expressed in Scripture, in some cases, by the devil's entering into a man, as it was in the case of Judas, 'after he had taken the sop, Satan entered into him [x];' and St. Cyprian, speaking of them that after baptism lapsed into foul crimes, affirms, that " spiritu immundo quasi redeunte quatiuntur, ut manifestum sit diabolum in baptismo fide credentis excludi, si fides postmodum defecerit regredi [y];" " faith, and the grace of baptism, turn the devil out of possession ; but when faith fails, and we lose the bands of religion, then the devil returns ;" that is, the man is devolved into such sins, of which there can be no reason given, which no excuse can lessen, which are set off with no pleasure, advanced by no temptations, which deceive by no allurements and flattering pretences; such things which have a proper and direct contrariety to the good spirit, and such as are not restrained by human laws ; because they are states of evil rather than evil actions, principles of mischief rather than direct emanations ; such as are unthankfulness, impiety, giving a secret blow, fawning hypocrisy, detraction, impudence, forgetfulness of the dead, and forgetting to do that in their absence which we promised to them in presence;

Οὐκοῦν τῷ αἰσχρὸν, εἰ βλέποντι μὲν φίλῳ
Χρώμεσθ', ἐπεὶ δ' ὄλωλι, μὴ χρώμισθ' ἔτι [x] ;

concerning which sorts of unworthiness, it is certain they argue a most degenerous spirit, and they are the effect, the natural effect, of malice and despair, an unwholesome ill-natured soul, a soul corrupted in its whole constitution. I remember that in the apologues of Phædrus, it is told concerning an ill-natured fellow, that he refused to pay his symbol, which himself and all the company had agreed should be given for every disease that each man had; he denying his itch to be a disease : but the company taking off the refuser's hat for a pledge, found that he had a scald head, and so demanded the money double; which he pertinaciously resisting, they threw him down, and then discovered he was broken-bellied, and justly condemned him to pay three philippics :

—— Quæ fuerat fabula, pœna fuit.

One disease discovers itself by the hiding of another; and

that being opened discovers a third; he that is almost taken
in a fault, tells a lie to escape; and to protect that lie, he
forswears himself; and that he may not be suspected of
perjury, he grows impudent; and that sin may not shame
him, he will glory in it, like the slave in the comedy, who,
being torn with whips, grinned, and forced an ugly smile that
it might not seem to smart. There are some sins which a
man that is newly fallen, cannot entertain. There is no crime
made ready for a young sinner, but that which nature prompts
him to. Natural inclination is the first tempter, then compliance, then custom, but this being helped by a consequent
folly, dismantles the soul, making it to hate God, to despise
religion, to laugh at severity, to deride sober counsels, to
flee from repentance, to resolve against it, to delight in sin
without abatement of spirit or purposes: for it is an intolerable thing for a man to be tormented in his conscience for
every sin he acts; that must not be; he must have his sin
and his peace too, or else he can have neither long: and because true peace cannot come, for "There is no peace, saith
my God, to the wicked," therefore they must make a fantastic peace by a studied cozening of themselves, by false
propositions, by carelessness, by stupidity, by impudence,
by sufferance, and habit, by conversation, and daily acquaint-
ances, by doing some things, as Absalom did when he lay
with his father's concubines, to make it impossible for him
to repent, or to be forgiven, something to secure him in the
possession of hell; "Tute hoc intristi, quod tibi exedendum
est," the man must through it now; and this is it that makes
men fall into all baseness of spiritual sins, [Ἀσεβὴς ἐλθὼν εἰς
βάϑος κακῶν καταφρονεῖ, 'When a man is come to the bottom
of his wickedness, he despises all'] such as malice and despite, rancour and impudence, malicious, studied ignorance,
voluntary contempt of all religion, hating of good men and
good counsels, and taking every wise man and wise action to
be his enemy; οὐδὲν οὕτως ἀναίσχυντον ποιεῖ ὡς πονηρὸν
συνειδός. And this is that baseness of sin which Plato so
much detested, that he said "he should blush to be guilty
of, though he knew God would pardon him, and that men
should never know it, 'propter solam peccati turpitudi-
nem,' for the very baseness that is in it." A man that is
false to his God, will also, if an evil temptation overtakes

him, betray his friend ; and it is notorious in the covetous
and ambitious:

> Ἀχάριστον ὑμῶν σπέρμα, ὅσοι δημηγόρους
> Ζηλοῦτε τιμάς· μηδὲ γεγνώσκοισθ᾽ ἐμοί,
> Οἳ τοὺς φίλους βλάπτοντες οὐ φροντίζετε,
> Ἣν τοῖσι πολλοῖς πρὸς χάριν λέγητέ τι ª.

They are an unthankful generation, and, to please the people,
or to serve their interest, will hurt their friends. That man
hath so lost himself to all sweetness and excellency of spirit,
that is gone thus far in sin, that he looks like a condemned man, or is like the accursed spirits, preserved in
chains of darkness and impieties unto the judgment of the
great day, ἄνθρωπος δ᾽ ἀεὶ ὁ μὲν πονηρὸς οὐδὲν ἄλλο πλὴν
κακός· 'this man can be nothing but evil ;' for these inclinations and evil forwardnesses, this dyscrasy and gangrened
disposition, do always suppose a long or a base sin for their
parent; and the product of these is a wretchless spirit ; that
is, an aptness to any unworthiness, and an unwillingness to
resist any temptation ; a perseverance in baseness, and a consignation to all damnation: Δράσαντι δ᾽ αἰσχρὰ δεινά τ᾽ ἀποτίμια
Δαίμων δίδωκεν, ' If men do evil things, evil things shall be
their reward.' If they obey the evil spirit, an evil spirit shall
be their portion ; and the devil shall enter into them as he
entered into Judas, and fill them full of iniquity.

SERMON XXI.

PART III.

ALTHOUGH these are shameful effects of sin, and a man
need no greater dishonour than to be a fool and a slave, and
a base person, all which sin infallibly makes him; yet there
are some sins, which are directly shameful in their nature, and
proper disreputation; and a very great many sins are the
worst and basest in several respects; that is, every of them
hath a venomous quality of its own, whereby it is marked
and appropriated to a peculiar evil spirit. The devil's sin
was the worst, because it came from the greatest malice :
Adam's was the worst, because it was of most universal

ª Eur. Hecub. Parson. 258.

efficacy and dissemination : Judas's sin the worst, because against the most excellent person; and the relapses of the godly are the worst, by reason they were the most obliged persons. But the ignorance of the law is the greatest of evils, if we consider its danger; but covetousness is worse than it, if we regard its incurable and growing nature; luxury is most alien from spiritual things, and is the worst of all in its temptation and our proneness; but pride grows most venomous by its unreasonableness and importunity, arising even from the good things a man hath; even from graces, and endearments, and from being more in debt to God. Sins of malice, and against the Holy Ghost, oppugn the greatest grace with the greatest spite ; but idolatry is perfectly hated by God by a direct enmity. Some sins are therefore most heinous, because to resist them is most easy, and to act them there is the least temptation : such as are, severally, lying and swearing. There is a strange poison in the nature of sins, that, of so many sorts, every one of them should be the worst. Every sin hath an evil spirit, a devil of its own, to manage, to conduct, and to imbitter it : and although all these are God's enemies, and have an appendant shame in their retinue, yet to some sins shame is more appropriate, and a proper ingredient in their constitutions : such as are lying, and lust, and vow-breach, and inconstancy. God sometimes cures the pride of a man's spirit by suffering his evil manners, and filthy inclination, to be determined upon lust ; lust makes a man afraid of public eyes, and common voices; it is (as all sins else are, but this especially) a work of darkness ; it does debauch the spirit, and make it to decay and fall off from courage and resolution, constancy and severity, the spirit of government and a noble freedom; and those punishments, which the nations of the world have inflicted upon it, are not smart so much as shame : lustful souls are cheap and easy, trifling and despised, in all wise accounts; they are so far from being fit to sit with princes, that they dare not chastise a sinning servant that is private to their secret follies ; it is strange to consider what laborious arts of concealment, what excuses and lessenings, what pretences and fig-leaves, men will put before their nakedness and crimes; shame was the first thing that entered upon the sin of Adam : and when the second world began, there was a strange scene of shame acted by Noah and his sons, and it ended in slavery and baseness to all descending generations.

We see the event of this by too sad an experience. What arguments, what hardness, what preaching, what necessity, can persuade men to confess their sins? They are so ashamed of them, that to be concealed they prefer before their remedy; and yet in penitential confession the shame is going off, it is like Cato's coming out of the theatre, or the philosopher from the tavern; it might have been shame to have entered, but glory to have departed for ever; and yet ever to have relation to sin is so shameful a thing, that a man's spirit is amazed, and his face is confounded, when he is dressed of so shameful a disease. And there are but few men that will endure it, but rather choose to involve it in excuses and denial, in the clouds of lying, and the white linen of hypocrisy: and yet, when they make a veil for their shame, such is the fate of sin, the shame grows the bigger and the thicker; we lie to men, and we excuse it to God; either some parts of lying or many parts of impudence, darkness or forgetfulness, running away or running farther in, these are the covers of our shame, like menstruous rags upon a skin of leprosy: but so sometimes we see a decayed beauty besmeared with a lying fucus, and the chinks filled with ceruse; besides that it makes no real beauty, it spoils the face, and betrays evil manners: it does not hide old age, or the change of years, but it discovers pride or lust; it was not shame to be old, or wearied and worn out with age, but it is a shame to dissemble nature by a wanton vizor. So sin retires from blushing into shame; if it be discovered, it is not to be endured, and if we go to hide it, we make it worse. But then if we remember how ambitious we are for fame and reputation, for honour and a fair opinion, for a good name all our days, and when our days are done; and that no ingenuous man can enjoy any thing he hath, if he lives in disgrace; and that nothing so breaks a man's spirit as dishonour, and the meanest person alive does not think himself fit to be despised; we are to consider into what an evil condition sin puts us, for which we are not only disgraced and disparaged here, marked with disgraceful punishments, despised by good men, our follies derided, our company avoided, and hooted at by boys, talked of in fairs and markets, pointed at and described by appel-

latives of scorn, and every body can chide us, and we die
unpitied, and lie in our graves eaten up by worms, and a foul
dishonour; but after all this, at the day of judgment, we shall
be called from our charnel-houses, where our disgrace could
not sleep, and shall, in the face of God, in the presence of
angels and devils, before all good men and all the evil, see
and feel the shame of all our sins written upon our foreheads:
here in this state of misery and folly we make nothing of it;
and though we dread to be discovered to men, yet to God
we confess our sins without a trouble or a blush; but tell an
even story, because we find some forms of confession prescribed in our prayer-books; and, that it may appear how indifferent and unconcerned we seem to be, we read and say
all, and confess the sins we never did, with as much sorrow
and regret, as those that we have acted a thousand times.
But in that strange day of recompenses, we shall find the
devil to upbraid the criminal, Christ to disown them, the
angels to drive them from the seat of mercy, and shame to be
their smart, the consigning them to damnation; they shall
then find, that they cannot dwell where virtue is rewarded,
and where honour and glory have a throne; there is no veil
but what is rent, no excuse to any but to them that are declared as innocent: no circumstances concerning the wicked
to be considered, but them that aggravate; then the disgrace
is not confined to the talk of a village, or a province, but is
scattered to all the world: not only in one age shall the shame
abide, but the men of all generations shall see and wonder
at the vastness of that evil that is spread upon the souls of
sinners for ever and ever; ἀγὼν μέγας, Πλήρης στεναγμῶν,
οὐδὲ δακρύων κενός. (Hec. 234.) No night shall then hide it;
for in those regions of darkness where the dishonoured man
shall dwell for ever, there is nothing visible but the shame;
there is light enough for that, but darkness for all things
else: and then he shall reap the full harvest of his shame;
all that for which wise men scorned him, and all that for
which God hated him; all that in which he was a fool, and
all that in which he was malicious; that which was public,
and that which was private; that which fools applauded, and
that which himself durst not own; the secrets of his lust,
and the criminal contrivances of his thoughts; the base and
odious circumstances, and the frequency of the action, and

the partner of his sin; all that which troubles his conscience, and all that he willingly forgets,—shall be proclaimed by the trumpet of God, by the voice of an archangel, in the great congregation of spirits and just men.

There is one great circumstance more of the shame of sin, which extremely enlarges the evil of a sinful state, but that is not consequent to sin by a natural emanation, but is super-induced by the just wrath of God: and therefore is to be considered in the third part, which is next to be handled.

3. When the Bœotians asked the oracle, by what they should become happy ? the answer was made, Ἀσεβήσαντας εὐπράξειν· ' Wicked and irreligious persons are prosperous :' and they taking the devil at his word, threw the inspired Pythian, the ministering witch, into the sea, hoping so to become mighty in peace and war. The effect of which was this, the devil was found a liar, and they fools at first, and at last felt the reward of irreligion. For there are to some crimes such events, which are not to be expected from the connexion of natural causes, but from secret influences and undiscernible conveyances ; that a man should be made sick for receiving the holy sacrament unworthily, and blind for resisting the words of an apostle, a preacher of the laws of Jesus, and die suddenly for breaking of his vow, and com-mitting sacrilege, and be under the power and scourge of an exterminating angel for climbing his father's bed,—these are things beyond the world's philosophy ; but as in nature, so in divinity too, there are sympathies and antipathies, effects which we feel by experience, and are forewarned of by reve-lation, which no natural reason can judge, nor any providence can prevent, but by living innocently, and complying with the commandments of God. The rod of God, which 'cometh not into the lot of the righteous,' strikes the sinning man with sore strokes of vengeance.

1. The first that I shall note is, that which I called the ag-gravation of the shame of sin ; and that is, an impossibility of being concealed in most cases of heinous crimes, Μηδέποτε μηδὲν αἰσχρὸν ποιήσας ἔλπιζε λήσειν, ' Let no man suppose that he shall for ever hide his sin :' a single action may be conveyed away under the covert of an excuse or a privacy, escaping as Ulysses did the search of Polyphemus, and it

shall in time be known that it did escape, and shall be discovered that it was private; that is, that it is so no longer. But
no wicked man that dwelt and delighted in sin, did ever go
off from his scene of unworthiness without a filthy character;
the black veil is thrown over him before his death, and by
some contingency or other he enters into his cloud, because
few sins determine finally in the thoughts; but if they dwell
there, they will also enter into action, and then the sin discovers itself; or else the injured person will proclaim it, or
the jealous man will talk of it before it is done, or curious people will inquire and discover, or the spirit of detraction shall
be let loose upon him, and in spite shall declare more than
he knows, not more than is true. The ancients, especially
the scholars of Epicurus, believed that no man could be secured or quiet in his spirit from being discovered. " Scelus
aliqua tutum, nulla securum tulit;" " They are not secure,
even when they are safe;" but are afflicted with perpetual
jealousies; and every whisper is concerning them, and all
new noises are arrests to their spirits; and the day is too
light, and the night is too horrid, and both are the most op-
portune for their discovery; and besides the undiscernible
connexion of the contingencies of Providence, many secret
crimes have been published by dreams, and talkings in their
sleep. It is the observation of Lucretius[b],

> Multi de magnis per somnum rebu' loquuntur
> Indicioque sui facti persæpe fuere [b].

And what their understanding kept a guard upon, their fancy let loose; fear was the bars and locks, but sleep became
the key to open, even then when all the senses were shut,
and God ruled alone without the choice and discourse of man.
And though no man regards the wilder talkings of a distracted man, yet it hath sometimes happened, that a delirium and
a fever, fear of death, and the intolerable apprehensions of
damnation, have opened the cabinet of sin, and brought to
light all that was acted in the curtains of night;

> Quippe ubi se multi, per somnia sæpe loquentes,
> Aut morbo delirantes, protraxe ferantur,
> Et, celata diu, in medium peccata dedisse[c].

But there are so many ways of discovery, and amongst so

[b] IV. 1016.   [c] Lucr. V. 1157.

many, some one does so certainly happen, that they are well
summed up by Sophocles,[d] by saying, that "Time hears
all, and tells all;"

Πρὸς ταῦτα κρύπτε μηδὲν, ὡς ὁ πάνθ' ὁρῶν
Καὶ πάντ' ἀκούων, πάντ' ἀναπτύσσει χρόνος.

A cloud may be its roof and cover till it passes over, but
when it is driven by a fierce wind, or runs fondly after the
sun, it lays open a deformity, which like an ulcer had a skin
over it, and pain within, and drew to it a heap of sorrows
big enough to run over all its enclosures. Many persons
have betrayed themselves by their own fears, and knowing
themselves never to be secure enough, have gone to purge
themselves of what nobody suspected them; offered an apology, when they had no accuser, but one within; which, like
a thorn in the flesh, or like 'a word in a fool's heart,' was
uneasy till it came out. "Non amo se nimium purgitantes,"
when men are "over-busy in justifying themselves," it is a
sign themselves think they need it. Plutarch tells of a
young gentleman that destroyed a swallow's nest, pretending to them that reproved him for doing the thing, which in
their superstition the Greeks esteemed so ominous, that the
little bird accused him for killing his father. And to this
purpose it was that Solomon gave counsel: " Curse not the
king, no, not in thy thought, nor the rich in thy bedchamber; for a bird of the air shall carry the voice, and that
that hath wings, shall tell the matter[e]:" murder and treason
have by such strange ways been revealed, as if God had appointed an angel president of the revelation, and had kept
this in secret and sure ministry to be as an argument to destroy atheism from the face of the earth, by opening the secrets of men with this key of providence. Intercepting of
letters, mistaking names, false inscriptions, errors of messengers, faction of the parties, fear in the actors, horror in the
action, the majesty of the person, the restlessness of the
mind, distracted looks, weariness of the spirit, and all under
the conduct of the divine wisdom, and the divine vengeance,
make the covers of the most secret sin transparent as a net,
and visible as the Chian wines in the purest crystal.

For besides that God takes care of kings, and of the lives
of men,—

[d] ΗΙΠΠΟΝ. frag.   [e] Eo. x. 20.

Ἡ δὲ πάσσω μὲν ἴεργει ἀπὸ χροὸς, ὡς ὅτε μήτηρ
Παιδὸς ἐέργει μυῖαν, ὅθ' ἡδεῖ λέξατο ὕπνῳ,

driving away evil from their persons, and " watching as a mother to keep gnats and flies from her dear boy sleeping in
the cradle ;" there are, in the machinations of a mighty mischief, so many motions to be concentred, so many wheels
to move regularly, and the hand that turns them does so
tremble, and there is so universal a confusion in the conduct,
that unless it passes suddenly into act, it will be prevented
by discovery, and if it be acted it enters into such a mighty
horror, that the face of a man will tell what his heart did
think, and his hands have done. And, after all, it was seen
and observed by him that stood behind the cloud, who shall
also bring every work of darkness into light in the day of
strange discoveries and fearful recompenses: and in the
meantime certain it is, that no man can long put on a person
and act a part, but his evil manner will peep through the
corners of the white robe, and God will bring a hypocrite
to shame even in the eyes of men.

2. A second superinduced consequent of sin brought
upon it by the wrath of God, is sin; when God punishes sin
with sin he is extremely angry; for then the punishment is
not medicinal, but final and exterminating; God in that
case takes no care concerning him, though he dies, and dies
eternally. I do not here speak of those sins which are naturally consequent to each other, as evil words to evil
thoughts, evil actions to evil words, rage to drunkenness,
lust to gluttony, pride to ambition; but such which God
suffers the man's evil nature to be tempted to by evil opportunities : Θεῶν ἀναγκαῖον τόδε, 'This is the wrath of God,'
and the man is without remedy. It was a sad calamity,
when God punished David's adultery by permitting him to
fall to murder,—and Solomon's wanton and inordinate love,
with the crime of idolatry,—and Ananias's sacrilege with
lying against the Holy Ghost,—and Judas's covetousness
with betraying his Lord, and that betraying with despair,
and that despair with self-murder.

——— Παρακαλεῖ δ' ἐπεῖθεν αὖ
Λύπη τις ἄλλη, διάδοχος κακῶν κακοῖς.

" One evil invites another ;" and when God is angry and

‡ Homer. Il. θ. 130.   § Eur. Hecub. Porson. 591.

withdraws his grace, and the Holy Spirit is grieved and departs from his dwelling, the man is left at the mercy of the merciless enemy, and he shall receive him only with variety of mischiefs; like Hercules when he had broken the horn of Achelous, he was almost drowned with the flood that sprung from it; and the evil man, when he hath passed the first scene of his sorrows, shall be enticed or left to fall into another. For it is a certain truth, that he who resists, or that neglects to use, God's grace, shall fall into that evil condition, that when he wants it most, he shall have least. It is so with every man; he that hath the greatest want of the grace of God, shall want it more, if this great want proceeded once from his own sin. "Habenti dahitur," said our blessed Lord, "To him that hath, shall he given, and he shall have more abundantly; from him that hath not, shall be taken, even that which he hath." It is a remarkable saying of David's; "I have thought upon thy name, O Lord, in the night-season, and have kept thy law; this I had because I kept thy commandments[b]:" keeping God's commandments, was rewarded with keeping God's commandments. And in this world God hath not a greater reward to give; for so the soul is nourished unto life, so it grows up with the increase of God, so it passes on to a perfect man in Christ, so it is consigned for heaven, and so it enters into glory; for glory is the perfection of grace, and when our love to God is come to its state and perfection, then we are within the circles of a diadem, and then we are within the regions of felicity. And there is the same reason in the contrary instance.

The wicked person falls into sin, and this he had, because he sinned against his Maker. "Tradidit Deus eos in desideria cordis eorum:" and it concerns all to observe it; and if ever we find that a sin succeeds a sin in the same instance, it is because we refuse to repent; but if a sin succeeds a sin in another instance, as, if lust follows pride, or murder drunkenness; it is a sign that God will not give us the grace of repentance: he is angry at us with a destructive fury, he hath dipped his arrows in the venom of the serpent, and whets his sword in the forges of hell; then it is time that a man withdraw his foot, and that he start back from the preparations of an intolerable ruin: for though men in this

case grow insensible, and that is part of the disease, διὰ τοῦτο
μέγα ἐστὶ κακὸν, ὅτι οὐδὲν εἶναι δοκεῖ, saith Chrysostom; ' It is the
biggest part of the evil that the man feels it not ;' yet the very
antiperistasis, or the contrariety, the very horror and bigness
of the danger, may possibly make a man to contend to leap out
of the fire; and sometimes God works a miracle, and besides
his own rule delights to reform a dissolute person, to force a
man from the grave, to draw him against the bent of his evil
habits; yet it is so seldom, that we are left to consider, that
such persons are in a desperate condition, who cannot be
saved unless God is pleased to work a miracle.

3. Sin brings in its retinue, fearful plagues and evil angels, messengers of the displeasure of God, concerning which,
τῶν τεθνηκότων ἅλις (Hec. 282.), ' there are enough of dead ;'
I mean, the experience is so great, and the notion so common,
and the examples so frequent, and the instances so sad, that
there is scarce any thing new in this particular to be noted ;
but something is remarkable, and that is this,—that God, even
when he forgives the sin, does reserve such ὑστερήματα τῆς
θλίψεως, ' remains of punishment,' and those not only to
the less perfect, but to the best persons, that it makes demonstration, that every sinner is in a worse condition than
he dreams of. For consider; can it be imagined that any
one of us should escape better than David did? We have
reason to tremble when we remember what he suffered, even
when God had sealed his pardon. Did not God punish Zedekiah with suffering his eyes to be put out in the house of
bondage? Was not God so angry with Valentinian, that he
gave him into his enemy's hand to be flayed alive? Have
not many persons been struck suddenly in the very act of
sin, and some been seized upon by the devil and carried away
alive? These are fearful contingencies : but God hath been
more angry yet; rebellion was punished in Korah and his
company, by the gaping of the earth, and the men were
buried alive; and Dathan and Abiram were consumed with
fire for usurping the priests' office : but God hath struck
severely since that time; and for the prostitution of a lady
by the Spanish king, the Moors were brought in upon his
kingdom, and ruled there for seven hundred years. And
have none of us known an excellent and good man to have
descended, or rather to have been thrust, into a sin, for which

he hath repented, which he hath confessed, which he hath rescinded, and which he hath made amends for as he could, and yet God was so severely angry, that this man was suffered to fall in so big a calamity, that he died by the hands of violence, in a manner so seemingly impossible to his condition, that it looked like the biggest sorrow that hath happened to the sons of men? But then, let us consider, how many and how great crimes we have done; and tremble to think, that God hath exacted so fearful pains and mighty punishments for one such sin, which we, it may be, have committed frequently. Our sin deserves as bad as theirs: and God is impartial, and we have no privilege, no promise of exemption, no reason to hope it; what then do we think shall become of this affair? Where must we suffer this vengeance? For that it is due, that it is just we suffer it, these sad examples are a perfect demonstration. We have done that, for which God thought flaying alive not to be too big a punishment: that for which God hath smitten kings with formidable plagues; that for which governments have been changed, and nations enslaved, and churches destroyed, and the candlestick removed, and famines and pestilences have been sent upon a whole kingdom; and what shall become of us? Why do we vainly hope, it shall not be so with us? If it was just for these men to suffer what they did, then we are at least to expect so much; and then, let us consider, into what a fearful condition sin hath put us, upon whom a sentence is read, that we shall be plagued like Zedekiah, or Korah, or Dathan, or the king of Spain, or any other king, who were, for aught we know, infinitely more innocent and more excellent persons than any of us. What will become of us? For God is as just to us as to them; and Christ died for them as well as for us; and they have repented more than we have done; and what mercy can we expect, that they might not hope for, upon at least as good ground as we? God's ways are secret, and his mercies and justice dwell in a great abyss; but we are to measure our expectations by revelation and experience. But then what would become of us, if God should be as angry at our sin as at Zedekiah's, or king David's? Where have we in our body room enough for so many stripes, as our sin ought justly to

be punished withal; or what security or probability have we
that he will not so punish us?

For I did not represent this sad story, as a matter of possibility only, that we may fear such fearful strokes as we see
God lay upon sinners; but we ought to look upon it as a
thing that will come some way or other, and, for aught we
know, we cannot escape it. So much, and more, is due for
the sin; and though Christ hath redeemed our souls, and
if we repent we shall not die eternally, yet he hath no where
promised we shall not be smitten. It was an odd saying of
the devil to a sinner whom he would fain have had to despair;
" Me è cœlo ad Barathrum demisit peccatum, et vos ullum in
terra locum tutum existimabitis ?" " Sin thrust me from
heaven to hell, and do you think on earth to have security?"—
Men use to presume that they shall go unpunished; but we
see what little reason we have to flatter and undo ourselves,
πᾶσι γὰρ κοινὸν τόδε, τὸν μὲν κακὸν κακόν τι πάσχειν, ' He that hath
sinned must look for a judgment,' and how great that is, we
are to take our measures by those sad instances of vengeance
by which God hath chastised the best of men, when they have
committed but a single sin, ὀλέθριον, ὀλέθριον κακὸν, ' sin is'
damnable and ' destructive:' and therefore, as the ass refused the barley which the fatted swine left, perceiving by it
he was fatted for the slaughter,

> Tuum libenter prorsus appeterem cibum,
> Nisi, qui nutritus illo est, jugulatus foret[1];

we may learn to avoid these vain pleasures which cut the
throat after they are swallowed, and leave us in that condition
that we may every day fear, lest that evil happen unto us,
which we see fall upon the great examples of God's anger;
and our fears cannot, ought not, at all to be taken off, but by
an effective, busy, pungent, hasty, and a permanent repentance; and then also but in some proportions, for we cannot
be secured from temporal plagues, if we have sinned; no repentance can secure us from all that; nay, God's pardon, or
remitting his final anger, and forgiving the pains of hell,
does not secure us here: ἡ νέμεσις παρὰ πόδας βαίνει; but sin
lies at the door ready to enter in, and rifle all our fortunes.

　　1. But this hath two appendages, which are very consi-

[1] Phædrus. 5. 4.

derable; and the first is, that there are some mischiefs which are the proper and appointed scourges of certain sins, and a man need not ask; " Cujus vulturis hoc erit cadaver (Mart. 6. 62.)?" ' what vulture,' what death, what affliction, ' shall destroy this sinner?' The sin hath a punishment of his own, which usually attends it, as giddiness does a drunkard. He that commits sacrilege, is marked for a vertiginous and changeable fortune; " Make them, O my God, like unto a wheel[k]," of an inconstant state : and we and our fathers have seen it, in the change of so many families, which have been undone by being made rich: they took the lands from the church, and the curse went along with it, and the misery and the affliction lasted longer than the sin. Telling lies frequently hath for its punishment to be ' given over to believe a lie,' and, at last, that nobody shall believe it but himself; and then the mischief is full, he becomes a dishonoured and a baffled person. The consequent of lust is properly shame; and witchcraft is still punished with baseness and beggary; and oppression of widows hath a sting; for the tears of the oppressed are, to the oppressor, like the waters of jealousy, making the belly to swell, and the thigh to rot; the oppressor seldom dies in a tolerable condition; but is remarked towards his end with some horrible affliction. The sting of oppression is darted as a man goes to his grave. In these, and the like, God keeps a rule of striking, ' In quo quis peccat, in eo punitur.' The divine judgment did point at the sin, lest that be concealed by excuses, and protected by affection, and increased by passion, and destroy the man by its abode. For some sins are so agreeable to the spirit of a fool and an abused person, because he hath framed his affections to them and they comply with his unworthy interest, that when God, out of an angry kindness, smites the man and punishes the sin, the man does carefully defend his beloved sin, as the serpent does his head, which he would most tenderly preserve. But therefore God, that knows all our tricks and devices, our stratagems, to be undone, hath therefore apportioned out his punishments by analogies, by proportions, and entail: so that when every sin enters into its proper portion, we may discern why God is angry, and labour to appease him speedily.

2. The second appendage to this consideration is this,

[k] Psal. lxxxiii.

that there are some states of sin, which expose a man to
all mischief, as it can happen, by taking off from him all
his guards and defences; by driving the good spirit from him,
by stripping him of the guards of angels. But this is the effect of an habitual sin, a course of an evil life, and it is called
in Scripture, "a grieving the good Spirit of God." But
the guard of angels is, in Scripture, only promised to them
that live godly; "The angels of the Lord pitch their tents
round about them that fear him, and deliver them," said
David[1].

> Τῇ δὲ θρήνω πυρόεντι παρεστᾶσιν συλόμαχθαι
> Ἄγγελαι, οἵτι μίμηλι βροτοῖς ἐν πάντα τελεῖται.

And the Hellenists use to call the angels ἐγρηγόρους, 'watchmen;' which custody is at first designed and appointed for
all, when by baptism they give up their names to Christ, and
enter into the covenant of religion. And of this the heathen
have been taught something by conversation with the Hebrews and Christians; "unicuique nostrûm dare pædagogum
Deum," said Seneca to Lucilius, "non primarium, sed ex
eorum numero, quos Ovidius vocat ex plebe deos :" "There
is a guardian god assigned to every one of us, of the number
of those which are of the second order ;" such are those of
whom David speaks, "Before the gods will I sing praise unto
thee ;" and it was the doctrine of the stoics, that to every
one there was assigned a genius, and a Juno : "Quamobrem
major cœlitum populus etiam quàm hominum intelligi potest,
quum singuli ex semetipsis totidem Deos faciant, Junones
geniosque adoptando sibi," said Pliny : "Every one does
adopt gods into his family, and get a genius and a Juno of
their own." "Junonem meam iratam habeam ;" it was the oath
of Quartilla in Petronius (25. 4.); and Socrates in Plato is said
to 'swear by his Juno ;' though afterward, among the Romans, it became the woman's oath, and a note of effeminacy ;
but the thing they aimed at was this, that God took a care
of us below, and sent a ministering spirit for our defence;
but, that this is only upon the accounts of piety, they
knew not. But we are taught it by the Spirit of God in
Scripture. For, "the angels are ministering spirits, sent
forth to minister to the good of them who shall be heirs of
salvation[m];" and concerning St. Peter, the faithful had an

[1] Psal. xxxiii. 4. 7.   [m] Heb. i. 14.

opinion, that it might be 'his angel;' agreeing to the doctrine of our blessed Lord, who spake of angels appropriate to his little ones, to infants, to those that belong to him. Now what God said to the sons of Israel, is also true to us Christians; " Behold, I send an angel before thee: beware of him, and obey his voice, provoke him not; for he will not pardon your transgressions[n]." So that if we provoke the Spirit of the Lord to anger by a course of evil living, either the angel will depart from us, or, if he stays, he will strike us. The best of these is bad enough, and he is highly miserable,

—— Qui non sit tanto hoc Custode securus,

whom an angel cannot defend from mischief, nor any thing secure him from the wrath of God. It was the description and character which the Erythrean sibyl gave to God,

Ἄφθαρτος, ἀτιστὴς αἰώνιος, αἰθέρα ναίων,
Τοῖς τ' ἀκάκοις ἄκακον προφέρων πολὺ μεῖζονα μισθὸν,
Τοῖς δὲ κακοῖς ἀδίκοις τι χόλον καὶ θυμὸν ἐγείρων.

It is God's appellative to be 'a giver of excellent rewards to just and innocent persons : but to assign to evil men fury, wrath, and sorrow, for their portion.' If I should launch farther into this dead sea, I should find nothing but horrid shriekings, and the skulls of dead men utterly undone. Fearful it is to consider, that sin does not only drive us into calamity, but it makes us also impatient, and imbitters our spirit in the sufferance : it cries aloud for vengeance, and so torments men before the time even with such fearful outcries, and horrid alarms, that their hell begins before the fire is kindled. It hinders our prayers, and consequently makes us hopeless and helpless. It perpetually affrights the conscience, unless by its frequent stripes it brings a callousness and an insensible damnation upon it. It makes us to lose all that which Christ purchased for us, all the blessings of his providence, the comforts of his Spirit, the aids of his grace, the light of his countenance, the hopes of his glory; it makes us enemies to God, and to he hated by him more than he hates a dog : and with a dog shall be his portion to eternal ages; with this only difference, that they shall both he equally excluded from heaven, but the dog shall not, and the sinner shall, descend into hell; and, which is the confirmation of all evil, for a transient sin God shall inflict an eternal death. Well might it be said in the words of God by the prophet, "Ponam Babylonem in possessionem erinacei," "Babylon shall be the possession of a hedgehog:" that is, a sinner's dwelling, encompassed round with thorns and sharp prickles, afflictions and uneasiness all over. So that he that wishes his sin big and prosperous, wishes his bee as big as a bull, and his hedgehog like an elephant; the pleasure of the honey would not cure the mighty sting; and nothing make recompense, or be a good, equal to the evil of an eternal ruin. But of this there is no end. I sum up all with the saying of Publius Mimus; "Tolerabilior est qui mori jubet, quàm qui male vivere," 'He is more to be endured that puts a man to death, than he that betrays him into sin:'—for the end of this is 'death eternal.'

SERMON XXII.

THE GOOD AND EVIL TONGUE.

PART I.

Let no corrupt communication proceed out of your mouth, but that which is good to the use of edifying, that it may minister grace unto the hearers.—Ephes. iv. 29.

He that had an ill memory, did wisely comfort himself by reckoning the advantages he had by his forgetfulness. For by this means he was hugely secured against malice and ambition; for his anger went off with the short notice and observation of the injury; and he saw himself unfit for the businesses of other men, or to make records in his head, and undertake to conduct the intrigues of affairs of a multitude, who was apt to forget the little accounts of his own seldom reading. He also remembered this, that his pleasures in reading books were more frequent, while he remembered but little of yesterday's study, and to-morrow the book is news, and, with its novelties, gives him fresh entertainment, while the retaining brain lays the book aside, and is full already. Every book is new to an ill memory, and one long book is a library, and its parts return fresh as the morning, which becomes a new day, though by the revolution of the same sun. Besides these, it brought him to tell truth for fear of shame, and in mere necessity made his speech little, and his discoursings short; because the web drawn from his brain was soon spun out, and his fountain grew quickly dry, and left running through forgetfulness. He that is not eloquent and fair-spoken, hath some of these comforts to plead in excuse of his ill fortune, or defective nature. For if he can but hold his peace, he shall be sure not to be troublesome to his company, nor marked for lying, nor become tedious with multiplicity of idle talk; he shall be presumed wise, and oftentimes is so; he shall not feel the wounds of contention, nor be put to excuse an ill-taken saying, nor sigh for the folly of an irrecoverable word; if his fault be that he hath not spoken, that can at any time be mended, but if he sinned in speaking, it cannot be unspoken again. Thus he escapes the dishonour of not being believed, and the trouble of being suspected; be shall never fear the sentence of judges, nor the decrees of courts, high reproaches, or the angry words of the proud, the contradiction of the disputing man, or the thirst of talkers. By these, and many other advantages, he that holds his peace, and he that cannot speak, may please themselves; and he may at least have the rewards and effects of solitariness, if he misses some of the pleasures of society. But by the use of the tongue, God hath distinguished us from beasts, and by the well or ill using it, we are distinguished from one another; and therefore, though silence be innocent as death, harmless as a rose's breath to a distant passenger, yet it is rather the state of death than life; and therefore, when the Egyptians sacrificed to Harpocrates, their god of silence, in the midst of their rites they cried out, γλῶσσα δαίμων, ' the tongue is an angel,' good or bad, that is as it happens; silence was to them a god, but the tongue is greater; it is the band of human intercourse, and makes men apt to unite in societies and republics; and I remember what one of the ancients said, that we are better in the company of a known dog, than of a man whose speech is not known, " ut externus

alieno non sit hominis vice ;" " a stranger to a stranger in his
language, is not as a man to a man ;" for by voices and homilies, by questions and answers, by narratives and invectives, by counsel and reproof, by praises and hymns, by
prayers and glorifications, we serve God's glory, and the
necessities of men ; and by the tongue our tables are made
to differ from mangers, our cities from deserts, our churches
from herds of beasts, and flocks of sheep. " Faith comes
by hearing, and hearing by the word of God," spoken by the
tongues of men and angels ; and the blessed spirits in heaven cease not from saying, night and day, their Τρισάγιον,
' their song of glory' to him that sitteth on the throne, and
to the Lamb, for ever and ever ; and then our employment
shall be glorious as our state, when our tongues shall to
eternal ages sing hallelujahs to their Maker and Redeemer ;
and therefore, since nature hath taught us to speak, and God
requires it, and our thankfulness obliges us, and our necessities engage us, and charity sometimes calls for it, and innocence is to be defended, and we are to speak in the cause
of the oppressed, and open our mouths in the cause of God,
and it is always a seasonable prayer, that God would open
our lips, that our mouth may do the work of heaven, and
declare his praises, and shew forth his glory ; it concerns us
to take care that nature be changed into grace, necessity
into choice, that, while we speak the greatness of God, and
minister to the needs of our neighbour, and do the works of
life and religion, of society and prudence, we may be fitted to
bear a part in the songs of angels, when they shall rejoice
at the feast of the marriage-supper of the Lamb. But the
tongue is a fountain both of bitter waters and of pleasant ; it
sends forth blessing, and cursing ; it praises God, and rails
at men ; it is sometimes set on fire, and then it puts whole
cities in combustion ; it is unruly, and no more to be restrained than the breath of a tempest ; it is volatile and fugitive : reason should go before it, and when it does not, repentance comes after it ; it was intended for an organ of the
divine praises, but the devil often plays upon it, and then it
sounds like the screech-owl, or the groans of death ; sorrow
and shame, folly and repentance, are the notes and formidable
accents of that discord. We all are naturally λογόφιλοι,
' lovers of speech,' more or less ; and God reproves it not,

provided that we be also φιλόλογοι, ' wise and material, useful and prudent, in our discourses.' For since speech is for
conversation, let it be also charitable and profitable, let it
be without sin, but not without profit and grace to the hearers, and then it is as God would have it; and this is the precept of the text, first telling us what we should avoid, and
then telling us what we should pursue; what our discourse
ought not to be, and, secondly, what it ought to be ; there
being no more variety in the structure of the words, I shall,
1. discourse of the vices of the tongue ; 2. of its duty and
proper employment.

I. " Let no corrupt communication proceed out of your
mouth ;" πᾶς ὁ σαπρὸς λόγος, corrupt or ' filthy' communication; so we read it: and it seems properly to note such
communication as ministers to wantonness ; such as are the
Fescennines of Ausonius, the excrement and spume of Martial's verse, and the Ephesiaca of Xenophon ; indeed, this is
such a rudeness as is not to be admitted into civil conversation ; and is wittily noted by the Apostle, charging that " fornication should not be once named among them, as becometh
saints ;" not meaning that the vice should not have its name
and filthy character, but that nothing of it he named, in
which it can be tempting or offensive ; nothing tending to
it, or teaching of it, should be named : we must not have
πόρνον λόγον, ' fornication in our talk ;' that is, such a baseness, that it not only grieves the Divine Spirit, but dishonours all its channels and conveyances : the proper language
of the sin is not fit to be used so much as in reproof; and
therefore, I have sometimes wondered, how it came to pass,
that some of the ancients, men wise and modest, chaste and
of sober spirits, have fallen into a fond liberty of declamation against uncleanness, using such words which bring that
sin upon the stage of fancy, and offend ' auriculas non ca-
lentes,' ' sober and chaste ears.' For who can, without
blushing, read Seneca describing the looking-glass of Ho-
stius, or the severe but looser words of Persius, or the reproofs of St. Jerome himself, that great patron of virginity,
and exacter of chastity? yet more than once he reproves
filthy things with unhandsome language : St. Chrysostom
makes an apology for them that do so ; ἐὰν μὲν γὰρ σεμνῶς
εἴπῃς, οὐ δυνήσῃ καθικέσθαι τοῦ ἀκούοντος· ἐὰν δὲ βουληθῇς κα-

θάψασθαι, σφοδρῶς ἀνάγκην ἔχεις ἀπογυμνῶσαι σαφέστερον τὰ λεγόμενα°, " you cannot profit the hearers unless you discover the filthiness," for the withdrawing the curtain is shame and confutation enough for so great a baseness ; and chirurgeons care not how they defile their hand, so they may do profit to the patient.   And, indeed, there is a material difference in the design of him that speaks ; if he speaks ἐξ οἰκείου πάθους, ' according to his secret affection' and private folly, it is certainly intolerable : but yet if he speaks ἀπὸ κηδεμονίας, ' out of a desire to profit' the hearer, and cure the criminal, though it be in the whole kind of it honest, and well meant ; yet, that it is imprudent,

(Irritamentum Veneris languentis, et acres
Divitis urticæ P.)

and not wholly to be excused by the fair meaning, will soon be granted by all who know what danger and infection it leaves upon the fancy, even by those words by which the spirit is instructed. ' Ab hâc scabie teneamus ungues ;' it is not good to come near the leprosy, though to cleanse the leper's skin.

But the word which the Apostle uses, σαπρὸς λόγος, means more than this.   Σαπρὸν οὐ τὸ μοχθηρὸν φαῦλον, ἀλλὰ τὸ παλαιὸν, said Eupolis ; and so it signifies 'musty, rotten, and outworn with age;' εἰρήνης σαπρᾶς, 'rusty peace,' so Aristophanes (Pax. 554.): and, according to this acception of the word, we are forbidden to use all language that is in any sense corrupted, unreasonable, or useless; language proceeding from an old iniquity, evil habits, or unworthy customs, called, in the style of Scripture, ' the remains of the old man,' and by the Greeks, ' doting' or ' talking fondly ;' τὸ παιδαρίον εἶ, καὶ φρονεῖς ἀρχαῖά ; ' the boy talks like an old dotard.' 2. Σαπρὸς signifies ' wicked, filthy, or reproachful ;' σαπρὸν, αἰσχρὸν, ἀκάθαρτον, ' any thing that is in its own nature criminal and disgraceful, any language that ministers to mischief.' But it is worse than all this : σαπρὸς ὁ ἀφανισμὸς, ' it is a deletery, an extinction of all good ;' for ἀφανίζομαι is φθείρω, λυμαίνομαι, καταλύω, it is ' a destruction, an entire corruption,' of all morality ; and to this sense is that of Menander, quoted by St. Paul, φθείρουσιν ἤδη χρησθ' ὁμιλίαι κακαί· " Evil words corrupt good manners." And therefore, under this word is comprised all the evil of the tongue, that wicked instrument of the unclean spirit, in the capacity of all the appellatives. 1. Here is forbidden the useless, vain, and trifling conversation, the Βεελζεβοὺλ, ' the god of flies,' so is the devil's name ; he rules by these little things, by trifles and vanity, by idle and useless words, by the intercourses of a vain conversation. 2. The devil is Διάβολος, 'an accuser' of the brethren, and the calumniating, slandering, and under-valuing, detracting tongue does his work ; that is, λόγος αἰσχρός, the second that I named ; for αἰσχρότης is λοιδορία, μῖσος, so Hesychius ; it is ' slander, hatred, and calumny.' 3. But the third is Ἀπολλύων, the devil's worst appellative, ' the destroyer,' the dissolute, wanton, tempting, destroying conversation ; and its worst instance of all is flattery, that malicious, cozening devil, that strengthens our friend in sin, and ruins him from whom we have received, and from whom we expect, good. Of these in order : and first, of the trifling, vain, useless, and impertinent conversation, σαπρὸς λόγος, " Let no *vain* communication proceed out of your mouth."

1. The first part of this inordination is ' Multiloquium,' ' talking too much ;' concerning which, because there is no rule or just measure for the quantity, and it is as lawful, and sometimes as prudent, to tell a long story as a short, and two as well as one, and sometimes ten as well as two : all such discourses are to take their estimate by the matter and the end, and can only be altered by their circumstances and ap-pendages. Much speaking is sometimes necessary, some-times useful, sometimes pleasant ; and when it is none of all these, though it be tedious and imprudent, yet it is not always criminal. Such was the humour of the gentleman Martial speaks of : he was a good man, and full of sweetness and justice and nobleness, but he would read his nonsense-verses to all companies ; at the public games, and in private feasts, in the baths, and on the beds, in public and in private, to sleeping and waking people.

> Vis, quantum facias mali, videre?
> Vir justus, probus, innocens timeris [q].

Every one was afraid of him, and though he was good, yet he was not to be endured. The evil of this is very considerable

[q] 3. 44. 17.

in the accounts of prudence, and the effects and plaisance of conversation : and the ancients described its evil well by a proverbial expression ; for when a sudden silence arose, they said that Mercury was entered upon, meaning, that he being their 'loquax numen,' their 'prating god,' yet that quitted him not, but all men stood upon their guard, and called for aid and rescue, when they were seized upon so tedious an impertinence. And, indeed, there are some persons so full of nothings, that, like the straight sea of Pontus, they perpetually empty themselves by their mouth, making every company or single person they fasten on to be their Propontis ; such a one as was Anaximenes, λέξεων ποταμὸς, νοῦ δὲ σταλαγμός· 'He was an ocean of words, but a drop of understanding.' And if there were no more in this than the matter of prudence, and the proper measures of civil conversation, it would yet highly concern old men[r], and young men and women[s], to separate from their persons the reproach of their sex and age, that modesty of speech be the ornament of the youthful, and a reserved discourse be the testimony of the old man's prudence. 'Adolescens' from Ἀδολίσχης, said one : 'a young man is a talker for want of wit,' and an old man for want of memory ; for while he remembers the things of his youth, and not how often he hath told them in his old age, he grows in love with the trifles of his youthful days, and thinks the company must do so to : but he canonizes his folly, and, by striving to bring reputation to his first days, he loses the honour of his last.   But this thing is considerable to farther issues ; for though no man can say, that much speaking is a sin, yet the Scripture says, " In multiloquio peccatum non deerit ;" 'Sin goes along with it, and is an ingredient in the whole composition.' For it is impossible but a long and frequent discourse must be served with many passions, and they are not always innocent ; for he that loves to talk much, must 'rem corradere,' 'scrape materials together' to furnish out the scenes and long orations ; and some talk themselves into anger, and some furnish out their dialogues with the lives of others ; either they detract, or censure, or they flatter themselves, and tell their own stories with

---

[r] Supellex ejus garrulitas. Comœd.

[s] Muliebre ingenium proluvium. Accius in Andromedà.—Sola laboranti potuit succurrere lunæ. Juv. 6. 443.

friendly circumstances, and pride creeps up the sides of the discourse; and the man entertains his friend with his own panegyric; or the discourse looks one way and rows another, and more minds the design than its own truth; and most commonly will be so ordered, that it shall please the company (and that truth or honest plainness seldom does); or there is a bias in it, which the more of weight and transportation it hath, the less it hath of ingenuity. "Non credo auguribus qui aureis rebus divinant;" like soothsayers, men speak fine words to serve ends, and then they are not believed, or at last are found liars, and such discourses are built up to serve the ministries or pleasures of the company, but nothing else. Pride and flattery, malice and spite, self-love and vanity, these usually wait upon much speaking; and the reward of it is, that the persons grow contemptible and troublesome, they engage in quarrels, and are troubled to answer exceptions; some will mistake them, and some will not believe them, and it will be impossible that the mind should be perpetually present to a perpetual talker, but they will forget truth and themselves, and their own relations. And upon this account it is, that the doctors of the primitive church do literally expound those minatory words of our blessed Saviour; "Verily I say unto you, of every idle word that men shall speak, they shall give account at the day of judgment[1]." And by 'idle words,' they understand, such as are not useful to edification and instruction. So St. Basil: "So great is the danger of an idle word, that though a word be in its own kind good, yet, unless it be directed to the edification of faith, he is not free from danger that speaks it[a]:" to this purpose are the words of St. Gregory; "While the tongue is not restrained from idle words," "ad temeritatem stultæ increpationis efferatur," "it is made wild, or may be brought forth to rashness and folly:" and therein lies the secret of the reproof: "A periculo liber non est, et ad temeritatem efferatur," "the man is not free from danger, and he may grow rash[x]," and foolish, and run into crimes, whilst he gives his tongue the reins, and lets it wander, and so it may be fit to be reproved, though in its nature it were innocent. I deny not, but sometimes they are more severe. St. Gregory calls every word 'vain' or 'idle,' "quod aut ratione justæ necessitatis, aut intentione piæ utilitatis caret⁷:" and St. Jerome calls it 'vain,' "quod sine utilitate et loquentis dicitur et audientis," "which profits neither the speaker nor the hearer⁸." The same is affirmed by St. Chrysostom⁸ and Gregory Nyssen⁶ upon Ecclesiastes; and the same seems intimated in the word κενὸν ῥῆμα, or ῥῆμα ἀργὸν, as it is in some copies, ' every word that is idle, or *empty* of business.' But, for the stating of the case of conscience, I have these things to say.

1. That the words of our blessed Saviour, being spoken to the Jews, were so certainly intended as they best and most commonly understood, and by 'vain' they understood 'false' or 'lying,' not 'useless' or 'imprudent;' and yet so, though our blessed Saviour hath not so severely forbidden every empty, insignificant discourse; and yet he hath forbidden every lie, though it be 'in genere bonorum,' as St. Basil's expression is; that is, 'though it be in the intention charitable, or in the matter innocent.'

2. "Of every idle word we shall give account;" but yet so, that sometimes the κρίμα, ' the judgment,' shall fall upon the words, not upon the persons; they be hay and stubble, useless and impertinent, light and easy, the fire shall consume them, and himself shall escape with that loss; he shall then have no honour, no fair return for such discourses, but they shall with loss and prejudice be rejected and cast away.

3. If all unprofitable discourses be reckoned for idle words, and put upon the account, yet even the capacities of profit are so large and numerous, that no man hath cause to complain that his tongue is too much restrained by this severity. For in all the ways in which he can do himself good or his neighbour, he hath his liberty; he is only to secure the words from being directly criminal, and himself from being arrested with a passion, and then he may reckon it lawful, even upon the severest account, to discourse freely, while he can instruct, or while he can please, his neighbour;

Aut prodesse volunt, aut delectare ⁶————

while himself gets a fair opinion and a good name, apt

⁷ C. 17. ubi sup.   ⁸ Matt. xii.   ⁸ In Ps. cxviii.
       ⁶ Cap. 1.   ⁶ Hor. A. P. 333.

to serve honest and fair purposes; he may discourse himself into a friendship, or help to preserve it; he may serve the works of art or nature, of business public or private, the needs of his house, or the uses of mankind; he may increase learning, or confirm his notices, cast in his symbol of experience and observation, till the particulars may become a proverbial sentence and a rule; he may serve the ends of civility and popular addresses, or may instruct his brother or himself, by something, which, at that time, shall not be reduced to a precept by way of meditation, but is of itself apt at another time to do it; he may speak the praises of the Lord by discoursing of any of the works of creation, and himself or his brother may afterward remember it to that purpose; he may counsel or teach, reprove or admonish, call to mind a precept, or disgrace a vice, reprove it by a parable or a story, by way of idea or witty representment; and he that can find talk beyond all this, discourse that cannot become useful in any one of these purposes, may well be called a prating man, and expect to give account of his folly, in the days of recompense.

4. Although, in this latitude, a man's discourses may be free and safe from judgment, yet the man is not, unless himself design it to good and wise purposes; not always actually, but by an habitual and general purpose. Concerning which he may, by these measures, best take his accounts.

1. That he be sure to speak nothing that may minister to a vice, willingly and by observation.

2. If any thing be of a suspicious and dubious nature, that he decline to publish it.

3. That, by a prudent moral care, he watch over his words, that he do none of this injury and unworthiness.

4. That he offer up to God in his prayers all his words, and then look to it, that he speak nothing unworthy to be offered.

5. That he often interweave discourses of religion, and glorifications of God, instructions to his brother, and ejaculations of his own, something or other not only to sanctify the order of his discourses, but to call him back into retirement and sober thoughts, lest he wander and be carried off too far into the wild regions of impertinence; and this

Zeno calls γλῶσσαν εἰς νοῦν ὑποβρέξαι, " to dip our tongues
in understanding." In all other cases the rule is good, Ἢ
λέγε τι σιγῆς κρεῖττον, ἢ σιγὴν ἔχε, "Either keep silence, or speak
something that is better than it ᵈ;" ἢ σιγὴν καίριον, ἢ λόγον
ὠφέλιμον, so Isocrates, consonantly enough to this evangelical precept; " a seasonable silence, or a profitable discourse," choose you whether; for whatsoever cometh of
more, is sin, or else is folly at hand, and will be sin at a
distance.

5. This account is not to be taken by little traverses and
intercourses of speech, but by greater measures, and more
discernible portions, such as are commensurate to valuable
portions of time; for however we are pleased to throw away
our time, and are weary of many parts of it, yet are impatiently troubled when all is gone; yet we are as sure to account for every considerable portion of our time, as for every
sum of money we receive; and in this it was, that St. Bernard gave caution, " Nemo parvi æstimet tempus, quod in
verbis consumitur otiosis," " Let no man think it a light
matter, that he spend his precious time in idle words ᵉ;" let
no man be so weary of what flies away too fast, and cannot
be recalled, as to use arts and devices to pass the time away
in vanity, which might be rarely spent in the interests of
eternity. Time is given us to repent in, to appease the divine anger, to prepare for and hasten to the society of angels,
to stir up our slackened wills. and enkindle our cold devotions, to weep for our daily iniquities, and to sigh after, and
work for, the restitution of our lost inheritance ; and the reward is very inconsiderable, that exchanges all this for the
pleasure of a voluble tongue : and indeed this is an evil, that
cannot be avoided by any excuse that can be made for
words, that are, in any sense, idle,—though, in all senses of
their own nature and proper relations, they be innocent.
They are a throwing away something of that, which is to be
expended for eternity, and put on degrees of folly, according as they are tedious and expensive of time to no good
purposes. I shall not after all this need to reckon more of
the evil consequent to the vain and great talker; but if these
already reckoned were not a heap big enough, I could easily

add this great evil : that the talking-man makes himself arti-
ficially deaf, being like a man in the steeple when the bells
ring, you talk to a deaf man, though you speak wisely ;

Οἶα ἂν δυναίμην μὴ στήσαντα πιμπλάναι
Σοφοὺς ἐναντίον ἀνὴρ μὴ σοφῷ λόγοις [f].

Good counsel is lost upon him, and he hath served all his
ends when he pours out whatsoever he took in; for he therefore loaded his vessel, that he might pour it forth into the
sea.

These and many more evils, and the perpetual unavoidable necessity of sinning by much talking, hath given great
advantages to silence, and made it to be esteemed an act
of discipline and great religion. St. Romualdus, upon the
Syrian mountain, severely kept a seven years' silence : and
Thomas Cantipratensis tells of a religious person, in a mo-
nastery in Brabant, that spake not one word in sixteen years.
But they are greater examples which Palladius tells of;
Ammona, who lived with three thousand brethren in so
great silence, as if he were an anchoret; but Theona was
silent for thirty years together ; and Johannes, surnamed Si-
lentiarius, was silent for forty-seven years. But this morosity and sullenness are so far from being imitable and laudable, that if there were no direct prevarication of any commands expressed or intimated in Scripture, yet it must certainly either draw with it, or be itself, an infinite omission of
duty; especially in the external glorifications of God, in the
institution or advantages of others, in thanksgiving and public offices, and in all the effects and emanations of spiritual
mercy. This was to make amends for committing many
sins by omitting many duties; and, instead of digging out
the offending eye, to pluck out both, that they might neither see the scandal nor the duty ; for fear of seeing what
they should not, to shut their eyes against all light. It was
more prudent which was reported of St. Gregory Nazianzen,
who made silence an act of discipline, and kept it a whole
Lent in his religious retirements. " Cujus facti mei si cau-
sam quæris" (said he in his account he gives of it), " idcirco
à sermone prorsus abstinui, ut sermonibus meis moderari
discam;" " I then abstained wholly, that all the year after I

[f] Eurip. Beck. T. t. p. 480.

might be more temperate in my talk." This was in him an
act of caution; but how apt it was to minister to his purpose
of a moderated speech for the future, is not certain; nor the
philosophy of it, and natural efficacy, easy to be apprehended.
It was also practised by way of penance, with indignation
against the follies of the tongue, and the itch of prating; so to
chastise that petulant member, as if there were a great pleasure in prating, which when it grew inordinate, it was to be
restrained and punished like other lusts. I remember it
was reported of St. Paul the hermit, scholar of St. Anthony,
that, having once asked whether Christ or the old prophets
were first, he grew so ashamed of his foolish question, that
he spake not a word for three years following: and Sulpi-
tius, as St. Jerome reports of him, being deceived by the Pe-
lagians, spoke some fond things, and, repenting of it, held his
tongue to his dying day, " ut peccatum quod loquendo con-
traxerat, tacendo penitus emendaret." Though the pious
mind is in such actions highly to be regarded, yet I am no
way persuaded of the prudence of such a deadness and Libi-
tinarian religion;

Murmura cum secum et rabiosa silentia rodunt,

so such importune silence was called, and understood to be
a degree of stupidity and madness; for so physicians, among
the signs of that disease in dogs, place their not barking;
and yet, although the excess and unreasonableness of this may
be well chastised by such a severe reproof, yet it is certain,
in silence there is wisdom, and there may be deep religion.
So Aretæus, describing the life of a studious man, among
others, he inserts this, they are ἄχροοι, καὶ ἐν νεότητι γηραλέοι,
καὶ ὑπ' ἐννοίας κωφοί· "without colour, pale and wise when they
are young, and, by reason of their knowledge, silent" as mutes,
and dumb as the Seriphian frogs. And indeed it is certain,
great knowledge, if it be without vanity, is the most severe
bridle of the tongue. For so have I heard, that all the noises
and prating of the pool, the croaking of frogs and toads, is
hushed and appeased upon the instant of bringing upon them
the light of a candle or torch. Every beam of reason and
ray of knowledge checks the dissolutions of the tongue. But,
" Ut quisque contemptissimus et maximè ludibrio est, ita so-
lutissimæ linguæ est," said Seneca; " Every man, as he is a

fool and contemptible, so his tongue is hanged loose;" being like a bell, in which there is nothing but tongue and noise.

Silence therefore is the cover of folly, or the effect of wisdom; it is also religious; and the greatest mystic rites of any institution are ever the most solemn and the most silent; the words in use are almost made synonymous : " There was silence made in heaven for awhile," said St. John, who noted it upon occasion of a great solemnity, and mysterious worshippings or revelations to be made there. Ἦ μάλα τις θεὸς ἔνδον, " One of the gods is within," said Telemachus; upon occasion of which his father reproved his talking.

Σίγα, καὶ κατὰ σὸν νόον ἴσχανε, μηδ᾿ ἐρέεινε·
Αὕτη τοι δίκη ἐστὶ θεῶν, οἳ Ὄλυμπον ἔχουσι f.

" Be thou also silent and say little ; let thy soul be in thy hand, and under command ; for this is the rite of the gods above." And I remember, that when Aristophanes ʰ describes the religion in the temple of Æsculapius, ὁ πρόσπολος, εἰπὼν, ἥν τις αἰσθῆται ψόφου, Σιγᾷν: " The priest commanded great silence when the mysteriousness was nigh ;" and so among the Romans :

Ite igitur, pueri, linguis animisque faventes,
Sertaque delubris et farra imponite cultris.

But now, although silence is become religious, and is wise, and reverend, and severe, and safe, and quiet, ἄδαλος, καὶ ἄλυπος, καὶ ἀνώδυνος, as Hippocrates affirms of it, " without thirst, and trouble, and anguish ;" yet it must be καίριος, it must be 'seasonable,' and just, not commenced upon chance or humour, not sullen and ill-natured, not proud and full of fancy, not pertinacious and dead, not mad and uncharitable, ' nam sic etiam tacuisse nocet.' He that is silent in a public joy hath no portion in the festivity, or no thankfulness to him that gave the cause of it. And though, of all things in the world, a prating religion, and much talk in holy things, does most profane the mysteriousness of it, and dismantles its regards, and makes cheap its reverence, and takes off fear and awfulness, and makes it loose and garish, like the laughters of drunkenness, yet even in religion there are seasons to speak; and it was sometimes ' pain and grief' to David to be silent ; but yet, although tedious and dead silence hath not a just

f Od. τ. 40.　　　　　　ʰ Plutus. Brunck. 670.

z 2

measure of praise and wisdom ; yet the worst silence of a religious person is more tolerable and innocent, than the usual pratings of the looser and foolish men. "Pone, Domine, custodiam ori meo et ostium circumstantiæ labiis meis," said David ; " Put a guard, O Lord, unto my mouth, and a door unto my lips ;" upon which St. Gregory said well, " Non parietem, sed ostium petit, quod viz. aperitur etclauditur;" "He did not ask for a wall, but for a door; a door that might open and shut :" and it were well it were so indeed : " Labia tua sicut vitta coccinea ;" so Christ commends his spouse in the Canticles; " Thy lips are like a scarlet hair-lace," that is, tied up with modesty from folly and dissolution. For however that few people offend in silence and keeping the door shut too much, yet, in opening it too hastily, and speaking too much and too foolishly, no man is without a load of guiltiness; and some mouths, like the gates of death,

Noctes atque dies patent :

" are open night and day ;" and he who is so, cannot be innocent. It is said of Cicero, he never spake a word which himself would fain have recalled, he spake nothing that repented him. St. Austin, in his seventh epistle to Marcellinus, says, it was the saying of a fool and a sot, not of a wise man ; and yet I have read the same thing to have been spoken by the famous abbot Pambo, in the primitive church; and if it could be well said of this man, who was sparing and severe in talk, it is certain, it could not be said of the other, who was a talking, bragging person.

SERMON XXIII.

PART II.

THE consideration hitherto hath been of the immoderation and general excess in speaking, without descending to particular cases : but because it is a principle and parent of much evil, it is with great caution to be cured, and the evil consequents will quickly disband. But when we draw near to give counsel, we shall find, that upon a talking person scarce any medicine will stick.

1. Plutarch advises, that ' such men should give them-selves to writing,' that, making an issue in the arm, it should drain the floods of the head ; supposing, that if the humour were any way vented, the tongue might be brought to reason. But the experience of the world hath confuted this; and when Ligurinus had writ a poem, he talked of it to all com-panies he came in[i]; but, however, it can be no hurt to try ; for some have been cured of bleeding at the nose, by opening a vein in the arm.

2. Some advise, that such persons should keep company with their betters, with grave, and wise, and great persons, before whom men do not usually bring forth all, hut the bet-ter parts, of their discourse: and this is apt to give assistance by the help of modesty ; and might do well, if men were not apt to learn to talk more in the society of the aged, and, out of a desire to seem wise and knowing, be apt to speak before their opportunity.

3. Consideration of the dangers and consequent evils hath some efficacy in nature to restrain our looser talkings, by the help of fear and prudent apprehensions. Ælian tells of the geese flying over the mountain Taurus[k]; that, for fear of eagles, nature hath taught them to carry stones in their mouths, till they be past their danger ; care of ourselves, de-sire of reputation, appetite of being believed, love of socie-ties and fair compliances, fear of quarrels and misinterpreta-tion, of law-suits and affronts, of scorn and contempt, of in-finite sins, and consequently the intolerable wrath of God ; these are the great endearments of prudent and temperate speech.

Some advise, that such persons should change their speech into business and action : and it were well if they changed it into any good thing, for then the evil were cured ; but ac-tion and business are not the cure alone, unless we add soli-tariness ; for the experience of this last age hath made us to feel, that companies of working people have nursed up a strange religion ; the first, second, and third part of which, is talking and folly, save only that mischief, and pride, and fighting, came in the retinue. But he that works, and works

---

[i] Mart. 3. 44.

[k] Ἕκαστος λίθον ἐνδακόντες, ὥσπερῶν ἐμβαλόντες σφίσι στόμια, διαπέτονται, κ. τ. λ. (V. c. 29. Schneid. p. 157.)

alone, he hath employment, and no opportunity. But this is but a cure of the symptom and temporary effect; but the disease may remain yet. Therefore,

5. Some advise, that the business and employment of the tongue be changed into religion; and if there be a ' pruritus,' or ' itch' of talking, let it be in matters of religion, in prayers and pious discourses, in glorifications of God, and the wise sayings of Scripture and holy men; this indeed will secure the material part, and make that the discourses in their nature shall be innocent. But I fear this cure will either be improper, or insufficient. For in prayers, multitude of words is sometime foolish, very often dangerous; and, of all things in the world, we must be careful we bring not to God ' the sacrifice of fools;' and the talking much of the things of Scripture hath ministered often to vanity, and divisions. But therefore, whoever will use this remedy must never dwell long upon any one instance, but by variety of holy duties entertain himself; for he may easily exceed his rule in any thing, but in speaking honourably of God, and in that let him enlarge himself as he can; he shall never come to equal, much less to exceed, that which is infinite.

6. But some men will never be cured without a cancer or a quinsy; and such persons are taught by all men what to do; for if they would avoid all company, as willingly as company avoids them, they might quickly have a silence great as midnight, and prudent as the Spartan brevity. But God's grace is sufficient to all that will make use of it; and there is no way for the cure of this evil, but the direct obeying of a counsel, and submitting to the precept, and fearing the divine threatening: always remembering, that " of every word a man speaks, he shall give account at the day of judgment:" I pray God shew us all a mercy in that day, and forgive us the sins of the tongue. Amen.

" Cito lutum colligit amnis exundans," said St. Ambrose; let your language be restrained within its proper channels, and measures; for," if the river swells over the banks, it leaves nothing but dirt and filthiness behind;" and, besides the great evils and mischiefs of a wicked tongue,—the vain tongue, and the trifling conversation, hath some proper evils; 1. ' Stulti-loquium,' or ' speaking like a fool:' 2. ' Scurrilitas,' or ' immoderate and absurd jesting:' and, 3. Revealing secrets.

1. Concerning stultiloquy, it is to be observed, that the masters of spiritual life mean not, the talk and useless babble of weak and ignorant persons; because in their proportions they may serve their little mistaken ends of civility and humanity, as seemingly to them, as the strictest and most observed words of the wiser; if it be their best, their folly may be pitied, but not reproved; and to them there is no caution to be added, but that it were well if they would put the bridle into the hands of another, who may give them check when themselves cannot; and no wisdom can be required or useful to them, but to suspect themselves and choose to be conducted by another. For so the little birds and laborious bees,—who, having no art and power of contrivance, no distinction of time, or foresight of new necessities, yet, being guided by the hand, and counselled by the wisdom, of the Supreme Power, their Lord, and ours,—do things with greater niceness and exactness of art, and regularity of time, and certainty of effect, than the wise counsellor, who, standing at the back of the prince's chair, guesses imperfectly, and counsels timorously, and thinks by interest, and determines extrinsical events by inward and unconcerning principles; because these have understanding, but it is less than the infinity of accidents and contingencies without; but the other having none, are wholly guided by him, that knows and determines all things: so it is in the imperfect designs and actions and discourses of weaker people; if they can be ruled by an understanding without, when they have none within, they shall receive this advantage, that their own passions shall not transport their minds, and the divisions and weakness of their own sense and notices shall not make them uncertain and indeterminate; and the measures they shall walk by, shall be disinterest, and even, and dispassionate, and full of observation.

But that which is here meant by stultiloquy, or foolish speaking, is the 'lubricum verbi,' as St. Ambrose calls it, 'the slipping with the tongue;' which prating people often suffer, whose discourses betray the vanity of their spirit, and discover 'the hidden man of the heart.' For no prudence is a sufficient guard, or can always stand 'in excubiis,' 'still watching,' when a man is in perpetual floods of talk: for prudence attends after the manner of an angel's ministry;

it is dispatched on messages from God, and drives away enemies, and places guards, and calls upon the man to awake,
and bids him send out spies and observers, and then goes
about his own ministries above : but an angel does not sit
by a man, as a nurse by the baby's cradle, watching every
motion, and the lighting of a fly upon the child's lip: and so
is prudence : it gives rules, and proportions out our measures,
and prescribes us cautions, and, by general influences, orders
our particulars ; but he that is given to talk, cannot be secured by all this ; the emissions of his tongue are beyond
the general figures and lines of rule ; and he can no more be
wise in every period of a long and running talk, than a lute-
nist can deliberate and make every motion of his hand by
the division of his notes, to be chosen and distinctly voluntary. And hence it comes, that at every corner of the mouth
a folly peeps out, or a mischief creeps in. A little pride and
a great deal of vanity will soon escape, while the man minds
the sequel of his talk, and not that ugliness of humour,
which the severe man, that stood by, did observe, and was
ashamed of. Do not many men talk themselves into anger,
screwing up themselves with dialogues of fancy, till they
forget the company and themselves ? And some men hate to
be contradicted, or interrupted, or to be discovered in their
folly ; and some men being a little conscious, and not striving to amend by silence, they make it worse by discourse ;
a long story of themselves,—a tedious praise of another collaterally to do themselves advantage,—a declamation against
a sin to undo the person, or oppress the reputation, of their
neighbour,—unseasonable repetition of that which neither
profits nor delights,—trifling contentions about a goat's
beard, or the blood of an oyster,—anger and animosity, spite
and rage,—scorn and reproach begun upon questions which
concern neither of the litigants,—fierce disputations,—strivings for what is past, and for what shall never be : these are
the events of the loose and unwary tongue ; which are like
flies and gnats upon the margin of a pool ; they do not sting
like an asp, or bite deep as a bear ; yet they can vex a man
ainto a fever and impatience, and make him incapable of rest
an d counsel.

2. The second is scurrility, or foolish jesting. This the
Apostle so joins with the former μωρολογία, " foolish speak-

ing, and jestings which are not convenient[1]," that some think this to be explicative of the other, and that St. Paul, using the word εὐτραπελία (which all men before his time used in a good sense), means not that which indeed is witty and innocent, pleasant and apt for institution, but that which fools and parasites call εὐτραπελία, but indeed is μωρολογία ; what they call facetiousness and pleasant wit, is indeed to all wise persons a mere stultiloquy, or talking like a fool ; and that kind of jesting is forbidden. And indeed I am induced fully to this understanding of St. Paul's words, by the conjunctive particle ἤ, which he uses, καὶ αἰσχρότης καὶ μωρολογία, ἢ εὐτραπελία, " and filthiness and foolish talking, or jesting;" just as in the succeeding verse, he joins ἀκαθαρσία ἢ πλεονεξία, " uncleanness (so we read it) or covetousness;" one explicates the other ; for by ' covetousness' is meant any ' defraudation ;' πλεονέκτης, ' fraudator,' so St. Cyprian renders it: and πλεονεκτεῖν St. Jerome derives from πλέον ἔχειν, ' to take more than a man should ;' and therefore, when St. Paul said, " Let no man circumvent his brother in any matter," he expounds it of ' adultery;' and in this very place he renders πλεονεξίαν, 'stuprum,' ' lust ;' and, indeed, it is usual in Scripture, that covetousness,—being so universal, so original a crime, such a prolific sin,—be called by all the names of those sins by which it is either punished, or to which it tempts, or whereby it is nourished ; and as here it is called ' uncleanness,' or ' corruption ;' so, in another place, it is called ' idolatry.' But to return; this jesting, which St. Paul reproves, is a direct μωρολογία, or the jesting of mimics and players, that of the fool in the play, which, in those times and long before, and long after, were of that licentiousness, that they would abuse Socrates or Aristides : and because the rabble were the laughers, they knew how to make them roar aloud with a slovenly and wanton word, when they understood not the salt and ingenuity of a witty and useful answer, or reply ; as is to be seen in the intertextures of Aristophanes's comedies. But in pursuance of this of St. Paul, the fathers of the church have been very severe in the censures of this liberty. St. Ambrose forbids all : " Non solum profusos, sed etiam omnes jocos declinandos arbitror ;" " Not only the looser jestings, but even all, are to be avoided[m]:" nay, "licet inter-

[1] Ephes. v. 4.   [m] Lib. de Offic.

dum joca honesta et suavia sint, tamen ab ecclesiæ horrent regula," "the church allows them not, though they be otherwise honest and pleasant; for how can we use those things we find not in Holy Scriptures?" St. Basil gives reason for this severity: "Jocus facit animam remissam et erga præcepta Dei negligentem;" and, indeed, that cannot be denied; those persons whose souls are dispersed and ungathered by reason of a wanton humour to intemperate jesting, are apt to be trifling in their religion. St. Jerome is of the same opinion, and adds a commandment of a full authority, if at least the record was right; for he quotes a saying of our blessed Saviour out of the Gospel of the Nazarenes; "Nunquam læti sitis, nisi cum fratrem vestrum in charitate videritis;" "Never be merry, but when you see your brother in charity[b]:" and when you are merry, St. James hath appointed a proper expression of it, and a fair entertainment to the passion; "If any man be merry, let him sing psalms." But St. Bernard, who is also strict in this particular, yet he adds the temper. Though jestings be not fit for a Christian, "Interdum tamen si incidant, ferendæ fortassis, referendæ nunquam: magis interveniendum caute et prudenter nugacitati:" "If they seldom happen, they are to be borne, but never to be returned and made a business of; but we must rather interpose warily and prudently to hinder the growth and progress of the trifle."

But concerning this case of conscience, we are to remember, these holy persons found jesting to be a trade[c]; such were the 'ridicularii' among the Romans, and the γελωτοποιοί among the Greeks; and this trade, besides its own unworthiness, was mingled with infinite impieties; and in the institution, and in all the circumstances of its practice, was not only against all prudent severity, but against modesty and chastity, and was a license in disparagement of virtue; and the most excellent things and persons were by it undervalued; so that in this throng of evil circumstances finding a humour placed, which, without infinite wariness, could never pretend to innocence, it is no wonder they forbade all; and so also did St. Paul upon the same account. And in the same state of reproof to this day, are all that do as they did: such as are professed jesters, people that play the fool for money, whose employment and study is to unclothe them-

[b] In ep. ad Ephes.   [c] Vide S. Chrysost. Homil. 6. in Matth.

selves of the covers of reason or modesty, that they may be laughed at. And let it be considered, how miserable every sinner is, if he does not deeply and truly repent; and when the man is wet with tears, and covered with sorrow, crying out mightily against his sins, how ugly will it look when this is remembered, the next day, that he plays the fool, and raises his laughter louder than his prayers and yesterday's groans, for no interest but that he may eat! A penitent and a jester is like a Grecian piece of money, on which were stamped a Helena on one side, and a Hecuba on the other, a rose and a deadly aconite, a Paris and an Æsop,—nothing was more contrary; and upon this account this folly was reproved by St. Jerome; "Verum et hæc à sanctis viris penitus propellenda, quibus magis convenit stere atque lugere;" "Weeping, and penitential sorrow, and the sweet troubles of pity and compassion, become a holy person P," much better than a scurrilous tongue.   But the whole state of this question is briefly this.

1. If jesting be unseasonable, it is also intolerable; Γέλως ἄκαιρος ἐν βροτοῖς δεινὸν κακόν q.

2. If it be immoderate, it is criminal, and a little thing here makes the excess; it is so in the confines of folly, that, as soon as it is out of doors, it is in the regions of sin.

3. If it be in an ordinary person, it is dangerous; but if in an eminent, a consecrated, a wise, and extraordinary person, it is scandalous. "Inter sæculares nngæ sunt, in ore Sacerdotis blasphemiæ," so St. Bernard.

4. If the matter be not of an indifferent nature, it becomes sinful by giving countenance to a vice, or making virtue to become ridiculous.

5. If it be not watched that it complies with all that hear, it becomes offensive and injurious.

6. If it be not intended to fair and lawful purposes, it is sour in the using.

7. If it be frequent, it combines and clusters into a formal sin.

8. If it mingles with any sin, it puts on the nature of that new unworthiness, beside the proper ugliness of the thing itself; and, after all these, when can it be lawful or apt for Christian entertainment?

The Ecclesiastical History reports, that many jests pass-

ed between St. Anthony, the father of the hermits, and his
scholar St. Paul; and St. Hilarion is reported to have been
very pleasant, and of facete, sweet, and more lively conversation; and, indeed, plaisance, and joy, and a lively spirit,
and a pleasant conversation, and the innocent caresses of a
charitable humanity, is not forbidden; "Plenum tamen sua-
vitatis et gratiæ sermonem non esse indecorum," St. Ambrose affirmed; and here in my text our conversation is commanded to be such, ἵνα δῷ χάριν, "that it may minister
grace," that is, favour, complaisance, cheerfulness; and be
acceptable and pleasant to the bearer: and so must be our
conversation; it must be as far from sullenness as it ought
to be from lightness, and a cheerful spirit is the best convoy
for religion; and though sadness does in some cases become
a Christian, as being an index of a pious mind, of compassion, and a wise, proper resentment of things, yet it serves
but one end, being useful in the only instance of repentance;
and hath done its greatest works, not when it weeps and
sighs, but when it hates and grows careful against sin. But
cheerfulness and a festival spirit fill the soul full of harmony, it composes music for churches and hearts, it makes and
publishes glorifications of God, it produces thankfulness, and
serves the end of charity: and when the oil of gladness runs
over, it makes bright and tall emissions of light and holy
fires, reaching up to a cloud, and making joy round about:
and therefore, since it is so innocent, and may be so pious
and full of holy advantage, whatsoever can innocently minister to this holy joy, does set forward the work of religion
and charity. And, indeed, charity itself, which is the vertical
top of all religion, is nothing else but a union of joys, concentred in the heart, and reflected from all the angles of
our life and intercourse. It is a rejoicing in God, a gladness in our neighbour's good, a pleasure in doing good, a rejoicing with him; and without love we cannot have any joy
at all. It is this that makes children to be a pleasure, and
friendship to be so noble and divine a thing; and upon this
account it is certain, that all that which can innocently
make a man cheerful, does also make him charitable; for
grief, and age, and sickness, and weariness, these are peevish and troublesome; but mirth and cheerfulness are content,
and civil, and compliant, and communicative, and love to

do good, and swell up to felicity only upon the wings of charity. Upon this account, here is pleasure enough for a Christian at present; and if a facete discourse, and an amicable friendly mirth, can refresh the spirit, and take it off from the vile temptation of peevish, despairing, uncomplying melancholy, it must needs be innocent and commendable. And we may as well be refreshed by a clean and a brisk discourse, as by the air of Campanian wines; and our faces and our heads may as well be anointed and look pleasant with wit and friendly intercourse, as with the fat of the balsam-tree; and such a conversation no wise man ever did, or ought to reprove. But when the jest hath teeth and nails, biting or scratching our brother,—when it is loose and wanton,—when it is unseasonable,—and much, or many,—when it serves ill purposes, or spends better time,—then it is the drunkenness of the soul, and makes the spirit fly away, seeking for a temple where the mirth and the music are solemn and religious.

But, above all the abuses which ever dishonoured the tongues of men, nothing more deserves the whip of an exterminating angel, or the stings of scorpions, than profane jesting: which is a bringing of the Spirit of God to partake of the follies of a man; as if it were not enough for a man to be a fool, but the wisdom of God must be brought into those horrible scenes: he that makes a jest of the words of Scripture, or of holy things, plays with thunder, and kisses the mouth of a cannon just as it belches fire and death; he stakes heaven at spurn-point, and trips cross and pile whether ever he shall see the face of God or no; he laughs at damnation, while he had rather lose God, than lose his jest; nay (which is the horror of all), he makes a jest of God himself, and the Spirit of the Father and the Son to become ridiculous. Some men use to read Scripture on their knees, and many with their heads uncovered, and all good men with fear and trembling, with reverence and grave attention. "Search the Scriptures, for therein ye hope to have life eternal;" and, "All Scripture is written by inspiration of God, and is fit for instruction, for reproof, for exhortation, for doctrine," not for jesting; but he that makes that use of it, had better part with his eyes in jest, and give his heart to make a tennis-ball; and, that I may speak the worst thing in the

world of it, it is as like the material part of the sin against the
Holy Ghost, as jeering of a man is to abusing him; and no
man can use it but he, that wants wit and manners, as well
as he wants religion.

3. The third instance of the vain, trifling conversation and
immoderate talking, is, revealing secrets; which is a dis-
mantling and renting of the robe from the privacies of human
intercourse; and it is worse than denying to restore that
which was entrusted to our charge; for this not only injures
his neighbour's right, but throws it away, and exposes it to
his enemy; it is a denying to give a man his own arms, and
delivering them to another, by whom he shall suffer mischief. · He that entrusts a secret to his friend, goes thither
as to a sanctuary, and to violate the rites of that is sacrilege, and profanation of friendship, which is the sister of religion, and the mother of secular blessing; a thing so sacred,
that it changes a kingdom into a church, and makes interest
to be piety, and justice to become religion. But this mischief grows according to the subject-matter and its effect;
and the tongue of a babbler may crush a man's bones, or
break his fortune upon her own wheel; and whatever the effect be, yet of itself it is the betraying of a trust, and, by reproach, oftentimes passes on to intolerable calamities, like
a criminal to his scaffold through the execrable gates of cities; and, though it is infinitely worse that the secret is laid
open out of spite or treachery, yet it is more foolish when it
is discovered for no other end but to serve the itch of talking,
or to seem to know, or to be accounted worthy of a trust;
for so some men open their cabinets, to shew only that a treasure is laid up, and that themselves were valued by their
friend, when they were thought capable of a secret; but they
shall be so no more, for he that by that means goes in pursuit of reputation, loses the substance by snatching at the
shadow, and, by desiring to be thought worthy of a secret,
proves himself unworthy of friendship or society. Davila
tells of a French Marquis, young and fond, to whom the
Duke of Guise had conveyed notice of the intended mas-
sacre; which when he had whispered into the king's ear,
where there was no danger of publication, but only would
seem a person worthy of such a trust, he was instantly murdered, lest a vanity like that might unlock so horrid a mystery.

I have nothing more to add concerning this, but that if this vanity happens in the matters of religion, it puts on some new circumstances of deformity : and if he, that ministers to the souls of men, and is appointed to "restore him that is overtaken in a fault," shall publish the secrets of a conscience, he prevaricates the bands of nature and religion ; instead of a father, he turns ' an accuser,' a Διάβολος, he weakens the hearts of the penitent, and drives the repenting man from his remedy by making it to be intolerable ; and so religion becomes a scandal, and his duty is made his disgrace, and Christ's yoke does bow his head unto the ground, and the secrets of the Spirit pass into the flames of the world, and all the sweetnesses by which the severity of the duty are alleviated and made easy, are imbittered and become venomous by the tongue of a talking fool.   Valerius Soranus was put to death by the old and braver Romans, "ob meritum profanæ vocis, quòd, contra interdictum, Romæ nomen eloqui fuit ausus ;" "because by prating he profaned the secret of their religion, and told abroad that name of the city" which the Tuscan rites had commanded to be concealed, lest the enemies of the people should call from them their tutelar gods, which they could not do but by telling the proper relation.   And in Christianity, all nations have consented to disgrace that priest, who loves the pleasure of a fool's tongue before the charity of souls, and the arts of the Spirit, and the nobleness of the religion ; and they have inflicted upon him all the censures of the church, which in the capacity of an ecclesiastical person he can suffer.

These I reckon as the proper evils of the vain and trifling tongue ; for though the effect passes into farther mischief, yet the original is weakness and folly, and all that unworthiness which is not yet arrived at malice.   But hither also, upon the same account, some other irregularities of speech are reducible, which, although they are of a mixed nature, yet are properly acted by a vain and loose tongue ; and therefore here may be considered not improperly.

1. The first is common swearing, against which St. Chrysostom spends twenty homilies : and by the number and weight of arguments hath left this testimony, that it is a foolish vice, but hard to be cured ; infinitely unreasonable, but strangely prevailing ; almost as much without remedy, as it

is without pleasure; for it enters first by folly, and grows by custom, and dwells with carelessness, and is nursed by irreligion, and want of the fear of God; it profanes the most holy things, and mingles dirt with the beams of the sun, follies and trifling talk interweaved and knit together with the sacred name of God; it placeth the most excellent of things in the meanest and basest circumstances, it brings the secrets of heaven into the streets, dead men's bones into the temple; nothing is a greater sacrilege than to prostitute the great name of God to the petulancy of an idle tongue, and blend it as an expletive to fill up the emptiness of a weak discourse. The name of God is so sacred, so mighty, that it rends mountains, it opens the bowels of the deepest rocks, it casts out devils, and makes hell to tremble, and fills all the regions of heaven with joy; the name of God is our strength and confidence, the object of our worshippings, and the security of all our hopes; and when God had given himself a name, and immured it with dread and reverence, like the garden of Eden with the swords of cherubim, and none durst speak it but he whose lips were hallowed, and that at holy and solemn times, in a most holy and solemn place; I mean the high-priest of the Jews at the solemnities when he entered into the sanctuary,—then he taught all the world the majesty and veneration of his name; and therefore it was that God made restraints upon our conceptions and expressions of him: and, as he was infinitely curious, that, from all the appearances he made to them, they should not depict or engrave any image of him; so he took care that even the tongue should be restrained, and not be too free in forming images and representments of his name; and therefore, as God drew their eyes from vanity, by putting his name amongst them, and representing no shape; so even when he had put his name amongst them, he took it off from the tongue and placed it before the eye; for Jehovah was so written on the priest's mitre, that all might see and read, but none speak it but the priest. But, besides all this, there is one great thing concerning the name of God, beyond all that can be spoken or imagined else; and that is, that when God the Father was pleased to pour forth all his glories, and imprint them upon his holy Son in his exaltation, it was by giving him his holy name, the Tetragrammaton, or Jehovah made articulate; to signify 'God manifested in the flesh;' and so he wore the character of God, and became the bright image of his person.

Now all these great things concerning the name of God, are infinite reproofs of common and vain swearing by it; God's name is left us here to pray by, to hope in, to be the instrument and conveyance of our worshippings, to be the witness of truth and the judge of secrets, the end of strife and the avenger of perjury, the discerner of right and the severe exacter of all wrongs; and shall all this be unhallowed by impudent talking of God without sense, or fear, or notices, or reverence, or observation?

One thing more I have to add against this vice of a foolish tongue, and that is, that, as much prating fills the discourse with lying, so this trifling swearing changes every trifling lie into a horrid perjury; and this was noted by St. James; "But, above all things, swear not at all," ἵνα μὴ ὑπὸ κρίσιν πίσητε, "that ye may not fall into condemnation⁹;" so we read it, following the Arabian, Syrian, and Latin books, and some Greek copies; and it signifies, that all such swearing, and putting fierce appendages to every word, like great iron bars to a straw basket or the curtains of a tent, is a direct condemnation of ourselves: for while we by much talking regard truth too little, and yet bind up our trifles with so severe a band, we are condemned by our own words; for men are made to expect, what you bound upon them by an oath, and account your trifle to be serious; of which when you fail, you have given sentence against yourself: and this is agreeable to those words of our blessed Saviour, "Of every idle word you shall give account ʳ;"—" for by thy words thou shalt be condemned, and by thy words thou shalt be justified." But there is another reading of these words, which hath great emphasis and power, in this article, "Swear not at all," ἵνα μὴ εἰς ὑπόκρισιν πίσητε, "that you may not fall into hypocrisy," that is, into the disreputation of a lying, deceiving, cozening person; for he that will put his oath to every common word, makes no great matter of an oath; for in swearing commonly, he must needs sometimes swear without consideration, and therefore without truth; and he that

⁹ Chap. v. 12.　　　　ʳ Matt. xii.

does so, in any company, tells the world he makes no great matter of being perjured.

All these things put together may take off our wonder at St. James's expression, of πρὸ πάντων, " *above all things* swear not;" it is a thing so highly to be regarded, and yet is so little considered, that it is hard to say, whether there be in the world any instance, in which men are so careless of their danger and damnation, as in this.

2. The next appendage of vain and trifling speech is contention, wrangling and perpetual talk, proceeding from the spirit of contradiction : " Profert enim mores plerumque oratio, et animi secreta detegit. Nec sine causa Græci prodiderunt, ' ut vivat, quemque etiam dicere,' " said Quintilian[*]: " For the most part, a man's words betray his manners, and unlock the secrets of the mind : and it was not without cause that the Greeks said, ' As a man lives, so he speaks;' " for so indeed Menander, ἀνδρὸς χαρακτὴρ ἐκ λόγου γνωρίζεται '; and Aristides, οἷος ὁ τρόπος, τοιοῦτος καὶ ὁ λόγος: so that it is a sign of a peevish, an angry, and quarrelling disposition, to be disputative, and busy in questions, and impertinent oppositions.

You shall meet with some man (such were the sceptics, and such were the Academics, of old) who will not endure any man shall be of their opinion, and will not suffer men to speak truth, or to consent to their own propositions, but will put every man to fight for his own possessions, disturbing the rest of truth, and all the dwellings of unity and consent: ' clamosum altercatorem,' Quintilian[*] calls such a one.   This is περίσσευμα καρδίας, 'an overflowing of the heart,' and of the gall ; and it makes men troublesome, and intricates all wise discourses, and throws a cloud upon the face of truth ; and while men contend for truth, error, dressed in the same habit, slips into her chair, and all the litigants court her for the divine sister of wisdom.   ' Nimium altercando veritas amittitur:' There is noise but no harmony, fighting but no victory, talking but no learning; all are teachers, and are wilful, every man is angry, and without reason and without charity.

Ἔγχος ἔχων στόμα Σπῶρα, ἔσχε ξίφος, ἀσπίδα φωνὴν,

"Their mouth is a spear, their language is a two-edged sword, their throat is a shield," as Nonnus's expression is;

    * 11. 1. 30. Gesner.   † Winterton. Min. P. γνῶμαι Α. β.   * 6. 4. 15.

and the clamours and noises of this folly is that which St.
Paul reproves in this chapter; "Let all bitterness and cla-
mour be put away." People that contend earnestly, talk
loud; "Clamor equus est iræ; cum prostraveris, equitem de-
jeceris," saith St. Chrysostom; "Anger rides upon noise as
upon a horse; still the noise, and the rider is in the dirt;"
and, indeed, so to do is an act of fine strength, and the clean-
est spiritual force that can be exercised in this instance; and
though it be hard, in the midst of a violent motion, instantly
to stop, yet by strength and good conduct it may be done.
But he whose tongue rides upon passion, and is spurred by
violence and contention, is like a horse or mule without a
bridle, and without understanding, τῶν δὲ κεκραγότων οὐδεὶς
σώφρων ἐστί: "No person, that is clamorous, can be wise."

These are the vanities and evil fruits of the easy talker;
the instances of a trifling impertinent conversation; and yet,
it is observable, that although the instances in the beginning
be only vain, yet in the issue and effects they are troublesome
and full of mischief: and, that we may perceive, that even
all effusion and multitude of language and vainer talk cannot be innocent, we may observe that there are many good
things which are wholly spoiled, if they do but touch the
tongue; they are spoiled with speaking: such as is, the
sweetest of all Christian graces, humility,—and the noblest
actions of humanity, the doing favours, and acts of kindness.
If you speak of them, you pay yourself, and lose your kindness;
humility is by talking changed into pride and hypocrisy, and
patience passes into peevishness, and secret trust into perfi-
diousness, and modesty into dissolution, and judgment into
censure; but by silence, and a restrained tongue, all the first
mischiefs are avoided, and all these graces preserved.

SERMON XXIV.

PART III.

OF SLANDER AND FLATTERY.

HE that is twice asked a question, and then answers, is to
be excused if he answers weakly: but he that speaks before

he be asked, had need take care he speak wisely ; for if he
does not, he hath no excuse ; and, if he does, yet it loses half
its beauty; and therefore, the old man gave good counsel in
the comedy to the boy, ὦ παῖ, σιώπα, πόλλ' ἔχει σιγὴ καλά[x] :
the profits of a restrained modest tongue cannot easily be
numbered, any more than the evils of an unbridled and dissolute. But they were but infant-mischiefs, which, for the most
part, we have already observed, as the issues of vain and idle
talking; but there are two spirits worse than these ; 1. the
spirit of detraction ; and, 2. the spirit of flattery. The first
is Διαβολὴ, from whence the devil hath his name; he is ' an
accuser' of the brethren.   But the second is worse; it is
θανατηφόρος or θανάσιμος, 'damnable' and ' deadly ;' it is
the nurse of vice, and the poison of the soul.   These are
σαπροὶ λόγοι, ' sour' and ' filthy communications ;' the first
is rude, but the latter is most mischievous; and both of them
to be avoided like death, or the despairing murmurs of the
damned.

1. Let no calumny, no slandering, detracting communication proceed out of your mouth; the first sort of this is that
which the Apostle calls *whispering*, which signifies to abuse
our neighbour secretly, by telling a private story of him :

————— linguàque refert audita susurra[y] ;

for here the man plays a sure game, as he supposes, a mischief
without a witness,

Φιλολοιδόροιο γλώσσης
Φεύγω βέλεμνα κοῦφα,

as Anacreon[z] calls them ; " the light, swift arrows of a calumniating tongue ;" they pierce into the heart and bowels of
the man speedily. These are those which the Holy Scripture
notes by the disgraceful name of ' talebearers ;' " Thou shalt
not go up and down as a talebearer among the people[a] ;" for
" there are six things which God hates" (saith Solomon),
" yea, the seventh is an abomination unto him[b];" it is βδέλυγμα,
as bad, and as much hated by God, as an idol, and that is, ' a
whisperer,' or ' talebearer, that soweth contention amongst
brethren[c]."   This kind of communication was called συκο-
φαντία among the Greeks, and was as much hated as the pub-

[x] Menander Clerc. p. 220.   [y] Ovid. M. 7. 825.   [z] Od. 43. 11.
[a] Levit. xix. 6.   [b] Prov. vi. 17.   [c] Prov. xxvi. 20.

licans among the Jews: πονηρὸν, ὦ ἄνδρες Ἀθηναῖοι, πονηρὸν συκοφάντης, " It is a vile thing, O ye Athenians, it is a vile thing, for a man to be a sycophant, or a talebearer:" and the dearest friendships in the world cannot be secure, where such whisperers are attended to.

> Te fingente nefas, Pyladen odisset Orestes,
> Theseu Pirithoi destituisset amor.
> Tu Siculos fratres, et majus nomen Atridas,
> Et Ledæ poteras dissociare genus [d].

But this crime is a conjugation of evils, and is productive of infinite mischiefs ; it undermines peace, and saps the foundation of friendship ; it destroys families, and rends in pieces the very heart and vital parts of charity ; it makes an evil man, party, and witness, and judge, and executioner of the innocent, who is hurt though he deserved it not;

> Et, si non aliquà nocuisses, mortuus esses [e].

and no man's interest or reputation, no man's peace or safety, can abide, where this nurse of jealousy, and parent of contention, like the earwig, creeps in at the ear, and makes a diseased noise, and a scandalous murmur.

2. But such tongues as these, where they dare, and where they can safely, love to speak louder, and then it is *detraction;* when men, under the colour of friendship, will certainly wound the reputation of a man, while, by speaking some things of him fairly, he shall without suspicion be believed when he speaks evil of him ; such was he that Horace speaks of, " Me Capitolinus convictore usus amicoque," &c. " Capitolinus is my friend, and we have long lived together, and obliged each other by mutual endearments, and I am glad he is acquitted by the criminal judges ;"

> Sed tamen admiror, quo pacto judicium illud
> Fugerit :

" Yet I confess, I wonder how he should escape; but will say no more, because he is my friend [f]." Καινὸς γὰρ ἔτι τις οὗτος εὕρηται τρόπος διαβολῆς, τὸ μὴ ψέγοντας ἀλλ' ἐπαινοῦντας λυμαίνεσθαι, says Polybius ; " This is a new way of accusation, to destroy a man by praises." These men strike obliquely, like a wild swine, or the οἱ ἐν νεύροις βόες, ἐπὶ τῶν ὤμων ἔχουσι τὰ κέρατα, " like bulls in a yoke, they have horns

---

[d] Martial. 7. 24.   [e] Virg. Buc. 3. 15.   [f] Hor. S. 1. 4. 100.

upon their necks," and do you a mischief when they plough your ground; and, as Joab slew Abner, he took him by the beard and kissed him, and smote him under the fifth rib, that he died; so doth the detracting tongue, like the smooth-tongued lightning, it will break your bones when it kisses the flesh; so Syphax did secretly wound Masinissa, and made Scipio watchful and implacable against Sophonisba, only by commending her beauty and her wit, her constancy and unalterable love to her country, and by telling how much himself was forced to break his faith by the tyranny of her prevailing charms. This is that which the apostle calls πονη-ρίαν, ' a crafty and deceitful way of hurting,' and renders a man's tongue venomous as the tongue of a serpent, that bites even though he be charmed.

3. But the next is more violent, and that is, *railing* or reviling; which Aristotle, in his Rhetorics, says, is very often the vice of boys and of rich men, who,—out of folly or pride, want of manners, or want of the measures of a man, wisdom, and the just proportions of his brethren,—do use those that err before them, most scornfully and unworthily; and Tacitus noted it of the Claudian family in Rome, an old and inbred pride and scornfulness made them apt to abuse all, that fell under their power and displeasure; " Quorum superbiam frustra per obsequium et modestiam effugeres[a]." No observance, or prudence, no modesty, can escape the reproaches of such insolent and high talkers. A. Gellius tells of a boy that would give every one that he met, a box on the ear; and some men will give foul words, having a tongue rough as a cat, and biting like an adder; and all their reproofs are direct scoldings, their common intercourse is open contumely. There have been, in these last ages, examples of judges, who would reproach the condemned and miserable criminal, deriding his calamity, and reviling his person. Nero did so to Thraseas; and the old heathens to the primitive martyrs; " pereuntibus addita ludibria," said Tacitus of them[b]; they crucified them again, by putting them to suffer the shame of their fouler language; they railed at them, when they bowed their heads upon the cross, and groaned forth the saddest accents of approaching death. This is that evil that possessed those, of whom the Psalmist speaks : " Our tongues are our

r Agric. c. 30.   h Ann. 15. 44.

own; we are they that ought to speak; who is Lord over
us?" that is, our tongues cannot be restrained; and St.
James said something of this, "The tongue is an unruly member, which no man can tame[i];" that is, no private person, but
a public way; for he that can rule the tongue, is fit also to
rule the whole body, that is, the church or congregation;
magistrates and the governors of souls, they are by severity
to restrain this inordination, which indeed is a foul one;

'Ὅς ἄρα ἀὶθι τι διαβόλου γλώττης χρίψαι ἐν ἀνθρώποις ἔτερον κακὸν

' No evil is worse, or of more open violence to the rest and
reputation of men, than a reproachful tongue.' And it were
well if we considered this evil, to avoid it in those instances,
by which our conversation is daily stained. Are we not often too imperious against our servants? Do we not entertain
and feed our own anger with vile and basest language? Do not
we chastise a servant's folly or mistake, his error or his
chance, with language fit to be used by none but vile persons, and towards none but dogs? Our blessed Saviour, restraining the hostility and murder of the tongue, threatens hell-fire to them that call their brother ' fool;' meaning,
that all language, which does really, and by intention, disgrace him in the greater instances, is as directly against the
charity of the Gospel, as killing a man was against the severity and justice of the law. And although the word itself
may be used to reprove the indiscretions, and careless follies,
of an idle person; yet it must be used only in order to his
amendment,—by an authorized person,—in the limits of a just
reproof,—upon just occasion,—and so as may not do him mischief in the event of things. For so we find that our blessed
Saviour called his disciples, ἀνοήτους, ' foolish[k];' and St.
James used ἄνθρωπε κενὲ, 'vain man,' signifying the same
with the forbidden ' raca,' κενὸν, ' vain, useless, or empty;'
and St. Paul calls the Galatians, ' mad, and foolish, and be-
witched;' and Christ called Herod, ' fox;' and St. John
called the Pharisees, ' the generation of vipers;' and all this
matter is wholly determined by the manner, and with what
mind, it is done: if it be for correction and reproof towards
persons that deserve it, and by persons whose authority can
warrant a just and severe reproof, and this also be done pru-

dently, safely, and usefully,—it is not contumely; but when men, upon all occasions, revile an offending person, lessening his value, souring his spirit, and his life, despising his infirmities, tragically expressing his lightest misdemeanour, οἱ ὑπὸ μικρῶν ἁμαρτημάτων ἀνυπερβλήτως ὀργιζόμενοι, ' being tyrannically declamatory, and intolerably angry for a trifle;'—these are such, who, as Apollonius the philosopher said, will not suffer the offending person to know when his fault is great, and when it is little. For they, who always put on a supreme anger, or express the less anger with the highest reproaches, can do no more to him that steals, than to him that breaks a crystal; ' non plus æquo, non diutius æquo,' was a good rule for reprehension of offending servants; but no more anger, no more severe language, than the thing deserves; if you chide too long, your reproof is changed into reproach; if too bitterly, it becomes railing; if too loud, it is immodest; if too public, it is like a dog.

Τὸ δ' ἐπιδιώκειν, εἰς τι τὴν ἰδὼν τρέχειν
Ἔτι λαιδορουμένα, κυνός ἐστ' ἔργα, 'Ρόδη. *Menand. Cler.* p. 90.

So the man told his wife in the Greek comedy; ' To follow me in the streets with thy clamorous tongue, is to do as dogs do,' not as persons civil or religious.

4. The fourth instance of the calumniating, filthy communication, is that which we properly call *slander*, or the inventing evil things, falsely imputing crimes to our neighbour: " Falsum crimen quasi venenatum telum," said Cicero[1]; " A false tongue or a foul lie against a man's reputation, is like a poisoned arrow," it makes the wound deadly, and every scratch to be incurable. " Promptissima vindicta contumelia," said one; to reproach and rail, is a revenge that every girl can take. But falsely to accuse, is as spiteful as hell, and deadly as the blood of dragons.

Stoicos occidit Baream, delator amicum [m].

This is the direct murder of the tongue, for 'Life and death are in the hand of the tongue,' said the Hebrew proverb: and it was esteemed so vile a thing, that when Jezebel commanded the elders of Israel to suborn false witnesses against Naboth, she gave them instructions to ' take two men, the sons of Belial;' none else were fit for the employment.

---

[1] Pro Qu. 8.   [m] Juv. 3. 116.

Quid non audebis, perfida lingua, loqui*?

This was it that broke Ephraim in judgment, and executed
the fierce anger of the Lord upon him; God gave him over
to be oppressed by a false witness, " quoniam cœpit abire
post sordes," therefore he suffered calumny, and was overthrown in judgment. This was it that humbled Joseph in
fetters, and " the iron entered into his soul;" but it crushed
him not so much as the false tongue of his revengeful mistress, " until his cause was known, and the word of the Lord
tried him." This was it that slew Abimelech, and endangered David; it was a sword ' in manu linguæ Doeg,' ' in
the hand of Doeg's tongue.' By this, Ziba cut off the legs
of Mephibosheth, and made his reputation lame for ever; it
thrust Jeremy into the dungeon, and carried Susanna to her
stake, and our Lord to his cross; and therefore, against the
dangers of a slandering tongue, all laws have so cautiously
armed themselves, that, besides the severest prohibitions of
God, often recorded in both Testaments, God hath chosen it
to be one of his appellatives to be the defender of them, a
party for those, whose innocency and defenceless state
make them most apt to be undone by this evil spirit; I
mean pupils, and widows, the poor, and the oppressed°. And
in pursuance of this charity, the imperial laws have invented
a ' juramentum de calumnia,' an oath to be exhibited to the
actor or plaintiff, that he believes himself to have a just
cause, and that he does not implead his adversary ' calum-
niandi animo,' ' with false instances,' and indefensible alle-
gations; and the defendant is to swear, that he thinks himself to use only just defences, and perfect instances of resisting; and both of them obliged themselves, that they
would exact no proof but what was necessary to the truth
of the cause. ' And all· this defence was nothing but necessary guards. For, ' a spear, and a sword, and an arrow,
is a man that speaketh false witness against his neighbour.'
And therefore, the laws of God added yet another bar against
this evil, and the false accuser was to suffer the punishment
of the objected crime : and, as if this were not sufficient, God
hath in several ages wrought miracles, and raised the dead to
life, that, by such strange appearances, they might relieve the
oppressed innocent, and load the false accusing tongue with

* Mart. 7. 24.   ° Levit. vi. Zech. vii. Luke, iii.

shame and horrible confusion. So it happened in the case
of Susanna, the spirit of a man was put into the heart of a
child to acquit the virtuous woman; and so it was in the case
of Gregory, bishop of Agrigentum, falsely accused by Sabinus and Crescentius; God's power cast the devil out of
Eudocia, the devil, or spirit of slander, and compelled her to
speak the truth. St. Austin, in his book ' De Cura pro Mor-
tuis,' tells of a dead father that appeared to his oppressed
son, and, in a great matter of law, delivered him from the
teeth of false accusation [p]. So was the church of Monts
rescued by the appearance of Aia, the deceased wife of Hi-
dulphus, their earl, as it appears in the Hanovian story; and
the Polonian Chronicles tell the like of Stanislaus, bishop of
Cracovia, almost oppressed by the anger and calumny of
Boleslaus their king; God relieved him by the testimony of
St. Peter, their bishop, or a phantasm like him. But, whether
these records may be credited or no, I contend not; yet, it
is very material which Eusebius relates of the three false
witnesses accusing Narcissus, bishop of Jerusalem, of an in-
famous crime, which they did, affirming it under several
curses [q]: the first wishing, that, if he said false, God would
destroy him with fire; the second, that he might die of the
king's-evil; the third, that he might be blind; and so it came
to pass; the first, being surprised with fire in his own roof,
amazed and intricated, confounded and despairing, paid the
price of his slander with the pains of most fearful flames:
and the second perished by pieces, and chirurgeons, and torment: which when the third saw, he repented of his fault,
cried mightily for pardon, but wept so bitterly, and found at
the same time the reward of his calumny, and the acceptation of his repentance: κακουργότερον οὐδὲν διαβολῆς ἐστί
τῳ, said Cleanthes; ' Nothing is more operative of spiteful
and malicious purposes, than the calumniating tongue.' In
the temple at Smyrna, there were looking-glasses which represented the best face as crooked, ugly, and deformed; the
Greeks call these ἑτερόσχημα and παράχροα: and so is every
false tongue; it lies in the face of heaven, and abuses the
ears of justice; it oppresses the innocent, and is secretly revenged of virtue; it defeats all the charity of laws, and arms
the supreme power, and makes it strike the innocent; it

makes frequent appeals to be made to heaven, and causes an oath, instead of being the end of strife, to be the beginning of mischief; it calls the name and testimony of God to seal an injury; it feeds and nourishes cruel anger, but mocks justice, and makes mercy weep herself into pity, and mourn because she cannot help the innocent.

5. The last instance of this evil I shall now represent, is *cursing*, concerning which I have this only to say; that although the causeless curse shall return upon the tongue that spake it, yet, because very often there is a fault on both sides, when there is reviling or cursing on either, the danger of a cursing tongue is highly to be declined, as the biting of a mad dog, or the tongue of a smitten serpent. For, as envy is in the evil eye, so is cursing in the reproachful tongue; it is a kind of venom and witchcraft, an instrument by which God oftentimes punishes anger and uncharitableness; and by which the devil gets power over the bodies and interests of men: for he that works by Thessalic ceremonies, by charms, and nonsense words, by figures and insignificant characterisms, by images and by rags, by circles and imperfect noises, hath more advantage and real title to the opportunities of mischief, by the cursing tongue; and though God is infinitely more ready to do acts of kindness than of punishment, yet God is not so careless a regarder of the violent and passionate wishes of men, but he gives some over to punishment, and chastises the follies of rage, and the madness of the tongue, by suffering it to pass into a farther mischief than the harsh sound and horrible accents of the evil language. " By the tongue we bless God and curse men," saith St. James; λοιδορία is κατάρα, ' reproaching is cursing, ' and both of them opposed to εὐλογία, to ' blessing;' and there are many times and seasons in which both of them pass into real effect These are the particulars of the second.

3. I am now to instance in the third sort of filthy communication, that in which the devil does the most mischief; by which he undoes souls; by which he is worse than Διάβολος, ' an accuser :' for though he accuses maliciously, and instances spitefully, and heaps objections diligently, and aggravates bitterly, and, with all his power endeavours to represent the separate souls to God as polluted and unfit to come into his presence, yet this malice is ineffective, because

the scenes are acted before the wise Judge of men and angels, who cannot be abused; before our Father, and our Lord, who knows whereof we be made, and remembereth that we are but dust; before our Saviour, and our elder brother, who hath felt our infirmities, and knows how to pity, to excuse, and to answer for us: but though this accusation of us cannot hurt them who will not hurt themselves, yet this malice is prevailing when the spirit of *flattery* is let forth upon us. This is the Ἀπολλύων, 'the destroyer,' and is the most contrary thing to charity in the whole world: and St. Paul noted it in his character of charity, Ἡ ἀγάπη οὐ περπερεύεται, "Charity vaunteth not itself;" so we translate it, but certainly not exactly, for it signifieth 'easiness,' complying foolishly, and flattering; "charity *flattereth* not;" Τί ἐστι τὸ περπερεύεσθαι; πᾶν ὃ μὴ διὰ χρείαν, ἀλλὰ διὰ καλλωπισμὸν παραλαμβάνεται, saith Suidas, out of St. Basil; "It signifies any thing that serves rather for ornament than for use," for pleasure than for profit.

> Et eu plectuntur poetæ quàm suo vitio sæpiùs,
> Ductabilitate nimiâ vestrâ ant perperitudine;

saith the comedy; "The poets suffer more by your easiness and flattery, than by their own fault."—And this is it which St. Paul says is against charity. For if to call a man 'fool and vicious,' be so high an injury, we may thence esteem what a great calamity it is to be so; and therefore, he that makes him so, or takes a course he shall not become other, is the vilest enemy to his person and his felicity: and this is the mischief that is done by flattery; it is a design against the wisdom, against the repentance, against the growth and promotion of a man's soul. He that persuades an ugly, deformed man, that he is handsome,—a short man that he is tall,—a bald man that he hath a good head of hair,—makes him to become ridiculous and a fool, but does no other mischief. But he that persuades his friend, that is a goat in his manners, that he is a holy and a chaste person,—or that his looseness is a sign of a quick spirit, —or that it is not dangerous, but easily pardonable,—a trick of youth, a habit that old age will lay aside as a man pares his nails,—this man hath given great advantage to his friend's mischief; he hath made it grow in all the dimensions of the sin, till it grows in-

ᶠ 1 Cor. xiii. 5.

tolerable, and perhaps unpardonable. And let it be considered ; what a fearful destruction and contradiction of friendship or service it is, so to love myself and my little interest, as to prefer it before the soul of him whom I ought to love ! By my flattery I lay a snare to get twenty pounds, and rather than lose this contemptible sum of money, I will throw him that shall give it me (as far as I can) into hell, there to roar beyond all the measures of time or patience. Can any hatred be more, or love be less, can any expression of spite be greater, than that it be said, 'You will not part with twenty pounds to save your friend's, or your patron's, or your brother's, soul ?' and so it is with him that invites him to, or confirms him in, his folly, in hopes of getting something from him ; he will see him die, and die eternally, and help forward that damnation, so he may get that little by it. Every state is set in the midst of danger, as all trees are set in the wind, but the tallest endure the greatest violence of tempest : no man flatters a beggar ; if he does a slovenly and a rude crime, it is entertained with ruder language, and the mean man may possibly be affrighted from his fault, while it is made so uneasy to him by the scorn and harsh reproaches of the mighty. But princes and nobles often die with this disease : and when the courtiers of Alexander counterfeited his wry neck, and the servants of the Sicilian tyrant pretended themselves dimsighted, and on purpose rushed one against another, and overthrew the meat as it was served to his table, only because the prince was shortsighted, they gave them sufficient instances in what state of affairs they stood with them that waited ; it was certain they would commend every foolish answer, and pretend subtilty in every absurd question, and make a petition that their base actions might pass into a law, and be made to be the honour and sanctity of all the people : and what proportions or ways can such great personages have towards felicity, when their vice shall be allowed and praised, every action that is but tolerable shall be accounted heroical, and if it be intolerable among the wise, it shall be called virtuous among the flatterers ? Carneades said bitterly, but it had in it too many degrees of truth ; That princes and great personages never learn to do any thing perfectly well, but to ride the great horse ; " quia scilicet ferociens bestia adulari non didicit,"

" because the proud beast knows not how to flatter," but will as soon throw him off from his back, as he will shake off the son of a porter.—But a flatterer is like a neighing horse, that neigheth under every rider, and is pleased with every thing, and commends all that he sees, and tempts to mischief, and cares not, so his friend may but perish pleasantly. And, indeed, that is a calamity that undoes many a soul; we so love our peace, and sit so easily upon own good opinions, and are so apt to flatter ourselves, and lean upon our own false supports, that we cannot endure to be disturbed or awakened from our pleasing lethargy. For we care not to be safe, but to be secure, not to escape hell, but to live pleasantly; we are not solicitous of the event, but of the way thither, and it is sufficient, if we be persuaded all is well; in the mean time, we are careless whether indeed it be so or no, and therefore we give pensions to fools and vile persons to abuse us, and cozen us of felicity. But this evil puts on several shapes, which we must discover, that they may not cozen us without our observation. For all men are not capable of an open flattery. And therefore, some will dress their hypocrisy and illusion so, that you may feel the pleasure, and but secretly the compliance and tenderness to serve the ends of your folly. " Perit procari, si latet," said Plancus; 'If you be not perceived, you lose your reward; if you be too open, you lose it worse.'

1. Some flatter by giving great names, and propounding great examples; and thus the Egyptian villains hung a tumbler's rope upon their prince, and a piper's whistle; because they called their Ptolemy by the name of Apollo, their god of music. This put buskins upon Nero, and made him fiddle in all the great towns of Greece. When their lords were drunkards, they called them Bacchus; when they were wrestlers, they saluted them by the name of Hercules; and some were so vain, as to think themselves commended, when their flatterers told aloud, that they had drunk more than Alexander the conqueror. And indeed nothing more abuses easy fools, that only seek for an excuse for their wickedness, a patron for their vice, a warrant for their sleepy peace,—than to tell stories of great examples remarked for the instances of their temptation. When old Cato commended meretricious mixtures, and, to prevent adulteries, permitted fornica-

tion, the youth of the succeeding ages had warrant enough
to go 'ad olentes fornices,' into their chambers of filthy
pleasure;

Quidam notus homo cum exiret fornice; Macte
Virtute esto, inquit sententia dia Catonis[a]:

And it would pass the goblets in a freer circle, if a flattering
man shall but say, " Narratur et prisci Catonis Sæpe mero
caluisse virtus," " That old Cato would drink hard at sunset[b]." When Varro had noted, that wise and severe Sallust,
who, by excellent sententious words, had reproved the follies
of lust, was himself taken in adultery; the Roman youth
did hug their vice, and thought it grew upon their nature
like a man's beard, and that the wisest men would lay their
heads upon that threshold; and Seneca tells, that the women
of that age despised adultery of one man only; and hated it
like marriage, and despised that as want of breeding, and
grandeur of spirit; because the braver Spartans did use to
breed their children promiscuously, as the herdsmen do
cattle from the fairest bulls. And Arrianus tells that the
women would defend their baseness by the doctrine of Plato,
who maintained the community of women. This sort of
flattery is therefore more dangerous, because it makes the
temptation ready for mischief, apted and dressed with proper material, and imitable circumstances. The way of discourse is far about, but evil examples kill quickly.

2. Others flatter by imitation : for when a crime is rare
and insolent, singular and out of fashion, it must be a great
strength of malice and impudence that must entertain it; but
the flattering man doing the vice of his lord takes off the
wonder, and the fear of being stared at; and so encourages
it by making it popular and common. Plutarch tells of one
that divorced himself from his wife, because his friend did
so, that the other might be hardened in the mischief; and
when Plato saw his scholars stoop in the shoulders, and
Aristotle observed his to stammer, they began to be less troubled with those imperfections, which they thought common
to themselves and others.

3. Some pretend rusticity and downright plainness, and
upon the confidence of that, humour their friend's vice, and
flatter his ruin. Seneca observed it of some of his time;

* Hor. S. 1. 2. 31.   † Hor. Od. 3. 21. 11.

" Alius quâdam adulatione clam utebàtur parce, alius ex
aperto palam, rusticitate simulatâ, quasi simplicitas illa ars
non sit;" They pretend they love not to dissemble, and
therefore they cannot hide their thoughts ; let their friend
take it how he will, they must commend that which is commendable ; and so, man, that is willing to die quietly, is content with the honest-heartiness and downright simplicity of
him, that with an artificial rudeness dressed the flattery.

4. Some will dispraise themselves, that their friend may
think better of himself, or less severely of his fault.

5. Others will reprove their friend for a trifle, but with
a purpose to let him understand, that this is all; for the honest man would have told his friend if it had been worse.

6. Some will laugh and make a sport of a vice, and can
hear their friend tell the cursed narrative of his adultery, of
his drunkenness, of his craft and unjust purchases; and all
this shall prove but a merry scene; as if damnation were a
thing to be laughed at, and the everlasting ruin of his friend
were a very good jest.   But thus the poor sinner shall not be
affrighted from his danger, nor chastised by severe language ;
but the villain that eats his meat, shall take him by the hand,
and dance about the pit till he falls in, and dies with shame
and folly. Thus the evil spirit puts on shapes enough ; none
to affright the man, but all to destroy him; and yet it is
filthy enough, when it is invested with its own character.

Γαστὴρ ὅλον τὸ σῶμα, πανταχῆ βλέπων
Ὀφθαλμὸς, ἕρπων τοῖς ὀδοῦσι θηρίον.

" The parasite or flatterer is a beast that is all belly, looking
round with his eye, watchful, ugly, and deceitful, and creeping on his teeth;" they feed him, and he kills them that reach
him bread ; for that is the nature of all vipers.

I have this one thing only to insert, and then the caution
will be sufficient, viz. that we do not think all praise given
to our friend to be flattery, though it be in his presence. For
sometimes praise is the best conveyance for a precept, and
it may nourish up an infant-virtue, and make it grow up
towards perfection, and its proper measures and rewards.
Friendship does better please our friend than flattery, and
though it was made also for virtue, yet it mingles pleasures
in the chalice: Εἰς ὕμματ' εὔνου φωτὸς ἐσβλέψαι γλυκύ· " It is

delicious to behold the face of a friendly and a sweet person ":" and it is not the office of a friend always to be sour, or at any time morose; but free, open, and ingenuous, candid and humane, not denying to please, but ever refusing to abuse or corrupt. For as adulterine metals retain the lustre and colour of gold, but not the value; so flattery, in imitation of friendship, takes the face and outside of it, the delicious part; but the flatterer uses it to the interests of vice, and a friend by it serves virtue; and therefore, Plutarch well compared friendship to medicinal ointments, which however delicious they be, yet they are also useful, and minister to healing : but flattery is sweet and adulterate, pleasant, but without health. He, therefore, that justly commends his friend to promote and encourage his virtue, reconciles virtue with his friend's affection, and makes it pleasant to be good ; and he that does so, shall also better be suffered when he reproves, because the needing person shall find, that then is the opportunity and season of it, since he denied not to please so long as he could also profit. I only add this advice ; that since self-love is the serpent's milk that feeds this viper, flattery,—we should do well to choke it with its mother's milk; I mean, learn to love ourselves more, for then we should never endure to be flattered. For he that, because he loves himself, loves to be flattered, does, because he loves himself, love to entertain a man to abuse him, to mock him, and to destroy him finally. But he that loves himself truly, will suffer fire, will endure to be burnt, so he may be purified ; put to pain, so he may be restored to health ; for, ' of all sauces' (said Evenus), sharpness, severity, and ' fire, are the best.'

^a Eurip. Ion. 7.32. Halseman. p. 107.

SERMON XXV.

THE DUTIES OF THE TONGUE.

——

PART IV.

—————— *But that which is good to the use of edifying, that it may minister grace unto the hearers.*—Ephes. iv. latter part of ver. 29.

" LOQUENDI magistros habemus homines, tacendi Deos," said one ; " Men teach us to speak, and God teaches us to hold our tongue." The first we are taught by the lectures of our schools ; the latter, by the mysteries of the temple. But now, in the new institution, we have also a great master of speaking ; and though silence is one of the great paths of innocence, yet holy speaking is the instrument of spiritual charity, and is a glorification of God; and therefore, this kind of speaking is a degree of perfection beyond the wisdom and severity of silence. For, although garrulity and foolish inordinate talking are a conjunction of folly and sin, and the prating man, while he desires to get the love of them he converses with, incurs their hatred ; while he would be admired, is laughed at; he spends much and gets nothing; he wrongs his friends, and makes sport to his enemies, and injures himself; he is derided when he tells what others know, he is endangered if he tells a secret and what they know not ; he is not believed when he tells good news, and when he tells ill news he is odious; and therefore, that silence, which is a cure of all this evil, is an excellent portion of safety and religion :—yet it is with holy speaking and innocent silence as it is with a hermit and a bishop; the first goes to a good school, but the second is proceeded towards greater perfection ; and therefore, the practical life of ecclesiastical governors, being found in the way of holiness and zeal, is called 'status perfectionis:' a more excellent and perfect condition of life, and far beyond the retirements and inoffensive life of those innocent persons, which do so much less of profit, by how much charity is better than meditation, and going to heaven by religion and charity, by serving God and con-

verting souls, is better than going to heaven by prayers and
secret thoughts: so it is with silence and religious communication. That does not offend God, this glorifies him:
that prevents sin, this sets forward the interests of religion.
And therefore Plutarch said well, " Qui generosè et regio
more instituuntur, primum tacere, deinde loqui discunt :"
" To be taught first to be silent, then to speak well and
handsomely, is education fit for a prince ;" and that is St.
Paul's method here : first we are taught how to restrain our
tongues, in the foregoing instances,—and now we are called to
employ them in religion.

1. We must speak " that which is good," ἀγαθόν τι, any
thing that may serve the ends of our God and of our neighbour, in the measures of religion and usefulness. But it is
here as in all other propositions of religion. To us,—who
are in the body, and conducted by material phantasms, and
understanding nothing but what we feel, or is conveyed to us
by the proportions of what we do or have,—God hath given a
religion that is fitted to our condition and constitution. And
therefore, when we are commanded to love God, by this love
Christ understands obedience ; when we are commanded to
honour God, it is by singing and reciting his praises, and
doing things which cause reputation and honour : and even
here, when we are commanded to speak that which is good,
it is instanced in such good things which are really profitable,
practically useful ; and here the measures of God are especially by the proportions of our neighbour : and therefore,
though speaking honourable things of God be an employment
that does honour to our tongues and voices, yet we must
tune and compose even these notes so, as may best profit
our neighbour; for so it must be λόγος ἀγαθὸς, ' good speech,'
such as is εἰς οἰκοδομὴν τῆς χρείας, ' for the edification of necessity :' the phrase is a Hebraism, where the genitive case
of a substantive is put for the adjective; and means, that
our speech be apted to necessary edification, or such edification as is needful to every man's particular case ; that is,
that we so order our communication, that it be apt to instruct the ignorant, to strengthen the weak, to recall the
wanderer, to restrain the vicious, to comfort the disconsolate,
to speak a word in season to every man's necessity, ἵνα δῷ
χάριν, ' that it may minister grace ;' something that may

2 B 2

please and profit them, according as they shall need; all which I shall reduce to these three heads :

1. To instruct.
2. To comfort.
3. To reprove.

1. Our conversation must be διδακτικὸς, 'apt to teach.' For since all our hopes on our part depend upon our obedience to God, and conformity to our Lord Jesus, by whom our endeavours are sanctified and accepted, and our weaknesses are pardoned, and all our obedience relies upon, and is encouraged and grounded in, faith, and faith is founded naturally and primarily in the understanding,—we may observe, that it is not only reasonably to be expected, but experimentally felt, that, in weak and ignorant understandings, there are no sufficient supports for the vigorousness of a holy life ; there being nothing, or not enough, to warrant and strengthen great resolutions, to reconcile our affections to difficulties, to make us patient of affronts, to receive deeper mortifications, and ruder usages, unless where an extraordinary grace supplies the want of ordinary notices, as the Apostles were enabled to their preaching; but he, therefore, that carries and imports into the understanding of his brother, notices of faith, and incomes of spiritual propositions, and arguments of the Spirit, enables his brother towards the work and practices of a holy life : and though every argument, which the Spirit of God hath made and recorded in Holy Scripture, is of itself inducement great enough to endear obedience ; yet it is not so in the event of things to every man's infirmity and need; but in the treasures of the Spirit, in the heaps and variety of institution, and wise discourses, there will not only be enough to make a man without excuse, but sufficient to do his work, and to cure his evil, and to fortify his weaker parts, and to comply with his necessities : for although God's sufficient grace is present to all that can use it, yet, if there be no more than that, it is a sad consideration to remember, that there are but few that will be saved, if they be helped but with just so much as can possibly do the work : and this we may well be assured of, if we consider that God is never wanting to any man in what is simply necessary : but then, if we add this also, that of the vast numbers of men, who might possibly be saved, so

few really are so, we shall perceive, that that grace which only is sufficient, is not sufficient; sufficient to the *thing*, is not sufficient for the *person;* and therefore, that God does usually give us more, and we need more yet; and unless God "works in us to will and to do," we shall neither ' will' nor ' do;' though to will be in the power of our hand, yet we will not will; it follows from hence, that all they, who will comply with God's method of graciousness, and the necessities of their brethren, must endeavour, by all means, and in all their own measures and capacities, to lay up treasures of notices and instructions in their brother's soul, that, by some argument or other, they may be met withal, and taken in every corner of their conversation. Add to this, that the duty of a man hath great variety, and the souls of men are infinitely abused, and the persuasions of men are strangely divided, and the interests of men are a violent and preternatural declination from the strictnesses of virtue, and the resolutions of men are quickly altered, and very hardly to be secured, and the cases of conscience are numerous and intricate, and every state of life hath its proper prejudice, and our notices are abused by our affections, and we shall perceive that men generally need knowledge enough to overpower all their passions, to root out their vicious inclinations, to master their prejudice, to answer objections, to resist temptations, to refresh their weariness, to fix their resolutions, and to determine their doubts; and therefore, to see your brother in a state of ignorance, is to see him unfurnished and unprepared to all good works; a person safe no longer than till a temptation comes, and one that cannot be saved but by an absolute, unlimited predestination, a favour of which he hath no promise, no security, no revelation; and although, to do this, God hath appointed a special order of men, the whole ecclesiastical order, whom he feeds at his own charges, and whom men rob at their own peril, yet this doth not disoblige others: for every master of a family is to instruct, or cause his family to be instructed, and catechised; every governor is to instruct his charge, every man his brother, not always in person, but ever by all possible and just provisions. For if the people die for want of knowledge, they who are set over them, shall also die for want of charity. Here, therefore, we must remember, that it is the duty of us all, in our several measures and proportions, to instruct those that need it, and whose necessity is made ready for our ministration; and let us tremble to think, what will be the sad account which we shall make, when even our families are not taught in the fundamentals of religion; for how can it be possible for those, who could not account concerning the stories of Christ's life and death, the ministries of their redemption, the foundation of all their hopes, the great argument of all their obediences; how can it be expected, that they should ride in triumph over all the evils, which the devil, and the world, and their own follies, daily present to them, in the course of every day's conversation? And it will be an ill return to say, that God will require no more of them than he hath given them; for suppose that be true in your own sense, yet he will require it of thee, because thou gavest them no more; and, however, it is a formidable danger, and a trifling hope, for any man to put all the hopes of his being saved upon the only stock of ignorance; for if his ignorance should never be accounted for, yet it may leave him in that state, in which his evils shall grow great, and his sins may be irremediable.

2. Our conversation must be παράκλητος, 'apt to comfort' the disconsolate; and than this, men in present can feel no greater charity: for, since half the duty of a Christian in this life consists in the exercise of passive graces, and the infinite variety of Providence, and the perpetual adversity of chances, and the dissatisfaction and emptiness that are in things themselves, and the weariness and anguish of our spirit, do call us to the trial and exercise of patience, even in the days of sunshine, and much more in the violent storms that shake our dwellings, and make our hearts tremble; God hath sent some angels into the world, whose office is to refresh the sorrows of the poor, and to lighten the eyes of the disconsolate; he hath made some creatures whose powers are chiefly ordained to comfort; wine, and oil, and society, cordials, and variety; and time itself is checkered with black and white; stay but till to-morrow, and your present sorrow will be weary, and will lie down to rest. But this is not all. The third person of the holy Trinity is known to us by the name and dignity of the "Holy Ghost, the Comforter," and God glories in the appellative, that he is "the Father of mer-

cies, and the God of all comfort;" and therefore, to minister in the office, is to become like God, and to imitate the charities of heaven; and God hath fitted mankind for it: he most needs it, and he feels his brother's wants, by his own experience; and God hath given us speech, and the endearments of society, and pleasantness of conversation, and powers of seasonable discourse, arguments to allay the sorrow, by abating our apprehensions and taking out the sting, or telling the periods of comfort, or exciting hope, or urging a precept, and reconciling our affections, and reciting promises, or telling stories of the divine mercy, or changing it into duty, or making the burden less by comparing it with greater, or by proving it to be less than we deserve, and that it is so intended, and may become the instrument of virtue. And, certain it is, that as nothing can better do it, so there is nothing greater, for which God made our tongues, next to reciting his praises, than to minister comfort to a weary soul. And what greater measure can we have, than that we should bring joy to our brother, who, with his dreary eyes, looks to heaven and round about, and cannot find so much rest as to lay his eyelids close together; than that thy tongue should be tuned with heavenly accents, and make the weary soul to listen for light and ease, and when he perceives that there is such a thing in the world, and in the order of things, as comfort and joy, to begin to break out from the prison of his sorrows, at the door of sighs and tears, and, by little and little, melt into showers and refreshment? This is glory to thy voice, and employment fit for the brightest angel. But so have I seen the sun kiss the frozen earth, which was bound up with the images of death, and the colder breath of the north; and then the waters break from their enclosures, and melt with joy, and run in useful channels; and the flies do rise again from their little graves in walls, and dance awhile in the air, to tell that there is joy within, and that the great mother of creatures will open the stock of her new refreshment, become useful to mankind, and sing praises to her Redeemer: so is the heart of a sorrowful man under the discourses of a wise comforter; he breaks from the despairs of the grave, and the fetters and chains of sorrow; he blesses God, and he blesses thee, and he feels his life returning; for to be miserable is death, but nothing is life but to be comforted; and God is pleased with no music from below so much as in the thanksgiving-songs of relieved widows, of supported orphans, of rejoicing, and comforted, and thankful persons. This part of communication does the work of God and of our neighbours, and bears us to heaven in streams of joy made by the overflowings of our brother's comfort. It is a fearful thing to see a man despairing. None knows the sorrow and the intolerable anguish but themselves, and they that are damned; and so are all the loads of a wounded spirit, when the staff of a man's broken fortune bows his head to the ground, and sinks like an osier under the violence of a mighty tempest. But therefore, in proportion to this, I may tell the excellency of the employment, and the duty of that charity, which bears the dying and languishing soul from the fringes of hell, to the seat of the brightest stars, where God's face shines, and reflects comforts, for ever and ever. And though God hath, for this, especially entrusted his ministers and servants of the church, and hath put into their hearts and notices great magazines of promises, and arguments of hope, and arts of the Spirit, yet God does not always send angels on these embassies, but sends a man, " ut sit homo homini Deus," " that every good man in his season, may be to his brother in the place of God," to comfort and restore him; and that it may appear, how much it is the duty of us all to minister comfort to our brother, we may remember, that the same words and the same arguments do oftentimes more prevail upon our spirits, when they are applied by the hand of another, than when they dwell in us, and come from our own discoursings. This is indeed λόγος χρηστὸς and ἀγαθὸς, it is, εἰς οἰκοδομὴν τῆς χρείας, ' to the edification of our needs,' and the greatest and most holy charity.

3. Our communication must in its just season be ἐλεγκτικός, 'we must reprove' our sinning brother; " for the wounds of a friend are better than the kisses of an enemy," saith Solomon[x]: we imitate the office of ' the great Shepherd and Bishop of souls,' if we go "to seek and save that which was lost;" and it is a fearful thing to see a friend go to hell undisturbed, when the arresting him in his horrid progress may possibly make him to return; this is a course that will change

our vile itch of judging and censuring others, into an act of charity ; it will alter slander into piety, detraction into counsel, revenge into friendly and most useful offices, that the viper's flesh may become Mithridate, and the devil be defeated in his malicious employment of our language. He is a miserable man, whom none dares tell of his faults so plainly, that he may understand his danger ; and he that is incapable and impatient of reproof, can never become a good friend to any man. For, besides that himself would never admonish his friend when he sins, (and if he would, why should not himself be glad of the same charity ?) he is also "proud, and scorner is his name ;" he thinks himself exempt from the condition and failings of men ; or, if he does not, be had rather go to hell than be called to his way by an angry sermon, or driven back by the sword of an angel, or endure one blushing, for all his hopes and interests of heaven. It is no shame to be reproved, but to deserve it ; but he that deserves it, and will do so still, shall increase his shame into confusion, and bring upon himself a sorrow bigger than the calamities of war, and plagues, and hospitals, and poverty. He only is truly wise, and will be certainly happy, that so understands himself and hates his sin, that he will not nurse it, but get to himself a reprover on purpose, whose warrant shall be liberty, whose thanks shall be amendment, whose entertainment shall be obedience ; for a flattering word is like a bright sunshine to a sore eye, it increases the trouble, and lessens the sight ;

Hæc demum sapiet dictio quæ feriet;

'The severe word of the reproving man is wise and healthful :' but because all times, and all circumstances, and all persons, are not fit for this employment:

Plurima sunt, quæ
Non audent homines pertusâ dicere lænâ ? ;

'Some will not endure that a poor man, or an obliged person, should reprove them,' and themselves are often so unprofitable servants, that they will rather venture their friend's damnation, than hazard their own interest ; therefore, in the performance of this duty of useful communication, the following measures are fit to be observed.

1. Let not your reproof be public and personal:—if it be
public, it must be in general; if it be personal, it must be
in private; and this is expressly commanded by our blessed
Saviour: "If thy brother offends, tell it him between him
and thee;" for if it comes afterward, in case of contumacy,
to be declared in public, it passes from fraternal correction
to ecclesiastical discipline.   When Socrates reproved Plato
at a feast, Plato told him, 'it had been better he had told him
his fault in private; for to speak it publicly is indecency:'
Socrates replied; ' And so it is for you, publicly to condemn
that indecency.'   For it is the nature of man to be spiteful
when he is shamed, and to esteem that the worst of evils,
and therefore, to take impudence and perseverance for its cover, when his shame is naked: and for this indiscretion,
Aristomenes, the tutor of Ptolemy, who, before the Corinthian ambassadors reproved the king for sleeping at the solemn audience, profited nothing, but enraged the prince, and
was himself forced to drink poison.   But this wariness is
not always necessary.   For, 1. A public and an authorized
person may do it publicly, and may name the person as himself shall judge expedient.

——— secuit Lucilius urbem,—
Te Lupe, te Muci,—et genuinam fregit in illis ª.

Lucilius was a censor of manners, and by his office he had
warrant and authority.   2. There are also some cases in
which a public reproof is prudent; and that is, when the
crime is great, but not understood to be any at all; for then
it is instruction and catechism, and lays aside the affront and
trouble of reproof.   Thus Ignatius the martyr did reprove
Trajan sacrificing at the altar in the sight of all the officers
of the army; and the Jews were commanded to reprove the
Babylonians for idolatry in the land of their captivity*: and
if we see a prince, in the confidence of his pride, and carelessness of spirit, and heat of war, spoil a church, or rob
God, it is then fit to tell him the danger of sacrilege, if
otherwise he cannot well be taught his danger, and his duty.
3. There are some circumstances of person, in which, by interpretation, duty, or custom, a leave is indulged or presumed,
that liberty may be prudently used, publicly to reprove the

ª Persius i. 114.   * Jer. x. 11.

public vices: so it was in the old days of the Romans ; vice had then so little footing and authority, so few friends and advocates, that the prophets and poets used a bolder liberty to disgrace whatsoever was amiss ;

> unde illa priorum
> Scribendi quodcunque animo flagrante liberet
> Simplicitas [b].

And much of the same liberty is still reserved to pulpits, and to the bishop's office, save only, that although they may reprove publicly, yet they may not often do it personally.

2. Use not to reprove thy brother for every thing, but for great things only :—for this is the office of a tutor, not of a friend; and few men will suffer themselves to abide always under pupillage. When the friend of Philotimus, the physician, came to him to be cured of a sore finger, he told him, "Heus tu, non tibi cum reduvia est negotium!" he let his finger alone, and told him, 'that his liver was imposthumate :' and he that tells his friend that his countenance is not grave enough in the church, when it may be the man is an atheist, offers him a cure that will do him no good: and to chastise a trifle is not a worthy price of that noblest liberty and ingenuity, which becomes him that is to heal his brother's soul. But when a vice stains his soul, when he is a fool in his manners, when he is proud, and impatient of contradiction, when he disgraces himself by talking weakly, and yet believes himself wise and above the confidence of a sober person, then it concerns a friend to rescue him from folly. So Solon reproved Crœsus, and Socrates Alcibiades, and Cyrus chid Cyaxares, and Plato told to Dion, that of all things in the world he should beware of that folly "by which men please themselves, and despise a better judgment:" "quia ei vitio adsidet solitudo," " because that folly hath in it singularity," and is directly contrary to all capacities of a friendship, or the entertainments of necessary reproof.

3. Use not liberty of reproof in the days of sorrow and affliction;—for the calamity itself is enough to chastise the gaieties of sinning persons, and to bring them to repentance ; it may be sometimes fit to insinuate the mention of the cause of that sorrow, in order to repentance, and a cure : but severe

[b] Juv. 1. 151.

and biting language is then out of season, and it is like putting vinegar to an inflamed and smarting eye, it increases the anguish, and tempts unto impatience. In the accidents of a sad person, we must do as nurses to their falling children, snatch them up and still their cryings, and entertain their passion with some delightful avocation; but chide not then, when the sorrowful man needs to be refreshed. When Crates, the cynic, met Demetrius Phalereus in his banishment and trouble, he went to him and spoke to him friendly, and used his philosophy in the ministries of comfort, and taught him to bear his trouble nobly, and so wrought upon the criminal and wild Demetrius; and he moved him to repentance, who, if he had been chidden (as he expected), would have scorned the manners of the cynic, and hated his presence and institution; and Perseus killed Euchus and Eulæus, for reproving his rashness, when he was newly defeated by the Romans.

4. Avoid all the evil appendages of this liberty :—for since to reprove a sinning brother is, at the best, but an unwelcome and invidious employment, though it may also be understood to be full of charity; yet, therefore, we must not make it to be hateful by adding reproach, scorn, violent expressions, scurrility, derision, or bitter invectives. Jerome invited Epicharmus to supper; and he, knowing that Jerome had unfortunately killed his friend, replied to his invitation, " Atqui nuper cum amicos immolares, non vorâsti," " I think I may come, for when thou didst sacrifice thy friends, thou didst not devour them." This was a bitter sarcasm, and might, with more prudence and charity, have been avoided. They that intend charitably and conduct wisely, take occasions and proper seasons of reproof, they do it by way of question and similitude, by narrative and apologues, by commending something in him that is good, and discommending the same fault in other persons, by way that may disgrace that vice, and preserve the reputation of the man. Ammonius, observing that his scholars were nice and curious in their diet, and too effeminate for a philosophical life, caused his freed-man to chastise his boy for not dining without vinegar, and all the while looked upon the young gentlemen, and read to them a lecture of severity. Thus our dearest Lord reproved St. Peter; he looked upon him when the sign was

given with the crowing of the cock, and so chid him into a shower of penitential tears. Some use to mingle praises with their reprehensions, and to invite their friend's patience to endure remedy, by ministering some pleasure with their medicine; for as no wise man can well endure to be praised by him that knows not how to dispraise, and to reprove; so neither will they endure to be reproved by him that knows not how to praise; for reproof from such a man betrays too great a love of himself, and an illiberal spirit: he that will reprove wisely, must efform himself into all images of things which innocently and wisely he can put on; not by changing his manners, his principles, and the consequences of his discourse (as Alcibiades was supposed to do), for it is best to keep the severity of our own principles, and the manner of our own living: for so Plato lived at Syracuse, just as he lived in the Academy; he was the same to Dionysius that he was to Dion: but this I mean, that he who means to win souls, and prevail to his brother's institution, must, as St. Paul did, effigiate and conform himself to those circumstances of living and discourse, by which he may prevail upon the persuasions, by complying with the affections and usages of men. · · ·

These are the measures by which we are to communicate our counsels and advices to our erring brethren: to which I add this last advice, that no man should, at that time in which he is reproved, give counsel and reproof to his reprover, for that betrays an angry spirit, and makes discord out of piety, and changes charity into wrangling; and it looking like a revenge, makes it appear that himself took the first reproof for an injury.

That which remains now is, that I persuade men to do it, and that I persuade men to suffer it; it is sometimes hard to do it, but the cause is only, because it is hard to bear it; for if men were but apprehensive of their danger, and were not desirous to die, there were no more to be said in this affair; they would be as glad to entertain a severe reprover as a careful physician; of whom because most men are so willing to make use, so thankful for their care, so great valuers of their skill, such lovers of their persons,—no man is put to it to persuade men to be physicians, because there is no need to persuade men to live, or to be in health: if therefore men would as willingly be virtuous as be healthful, as will-

ingly do no evil as suffer none, be as desirous of heaven as
of a long life on earth, all the difficulties and temptations
against this duty of reproving our sinner-brother would soon
be concealed ; but let it be as it will, we must do it in duty
and piety to him that needs, and if he be impatient of it, he
needs it more : " Et per hujusmodi offensas emetiendum est
confragosum hoc iter :" it is a troublesome employment, but
it is duty and charity; and therefore, when it can, with hope
of success, with prudence and piety, be done, no other consideration ought to interpose. And for the other part, those
I mean who ought to be reproved,—they are to remember,
that themselves give pensions to the preacher on purpose to
be reproved if they shall need it ;—that God hath instituted a
holy order of men to that very purpose, that they should be
severally told of all that is amiss ;—that themselves chide their
children and their servants for their good, and that they may
amend;—and that they endure thirst to cure their dropsies ;—
that they suffer burnings to prevent the gangrenes ;—and endure the cutting off a limh to preserve their lives;—and therefore, that it is a strange witchcraft and a prodigious folly,
that, at so easy a mortification as the suffering of a plain
friendly reproof, they will not set forward their interest of
heaven, and suffer themselves to be set forward in their hopes
of heaven :

————— dura fatemur
Esse ; sed, ut valeas, multa dolenda feras.

And when all remember, that flattery and importune silence
suffer the mighty to perish like fools and inconsiderate persons, it ought to awake our spirits, and make us to attend to
the admonition of a friend, with a silence great as midnight,
and watchful as a widow's eyes. It was a strange thing, that
Valentinian should, in the midst of so many Christian pre-
lates, make a law to establish polygamy, and that no bishop
should dare to reprehend him. The effect of it was this, that
he had a son by a second wife, the first heing alive and not
divorced, and he left him heir of a great part of the empire ;
and what the effect of that was to his soul, God, who is his
judge, best knows.

If now at last it be inquired,—whether every man is
bound to reprove every man, if he sins, and if he converse
with him,—I answer, that if it should be so, it were to no

purpose, and therefore for it there is no commandment; every man that can, may instruct him that wants it; but every man may not reprove him that is already instructed. That is an act of charity, for which there are no measures, but the other's necessity, and his own opportunity; but this is also an act of discipline, and must, in many cases, suppose an authority; and in all cases such a liberty as is not fit to be permitted to mean, and ignorant, and inferior persons. I end this with the saying of a wise person, advising to every one concerning the use of the tongue, "Aut lucrentur vitam loquendo, aut tacendo abscondant scientiam;' if they speak, let them minister to the good of souls; if they speak not, let them minister to sobriety; in the first, they serve the end of charity; in the other, of humility.

TWENTY-SEVEN SERMONS

PREACHED AT

GOLDEN GROVE;

BEING FOR THE

SUMMER HALF-YEAR,

BEGINNING ON WHITSUNDAY, AND ENDING ON THE
TWENTY-FIFTH SUNDAY AFTER TRINITY.

THE RIGHT HONOURABLE

AND TRULY NOBLE

RICHARD LORD VAUGHAN,

EARL OF CARBERY, BARON OF EMLIN AND MOLINGAR, KNIGHT OF THE HONOURABLE ORDER OF THE BATH.

MY LORD,

I now present to your Lordship a copy of those Sermons, the publication of which was first designed by the appetites of that hunger and thirst of righteousness, which made your dear Lady (that rare soul) so dear to God, that he was pleased speedily to satisfy her, by carrying her from our shallow and impure cisterns, to drink out of the fountains of our Saviour. My Lord, I shall but prick your tender eye, if I shall remind your Lordship how diligent a hearer, how careful a recorder, how prudent an observer, how sedulous a practiser, of holy discourses she was; and that therefore it was, that what did slide through her ear, she was desirous to place before her eye, that by those windows they might enter in, and dwell in her heart: but because, by this truth, I shall do advantage to the following discourses, give me leave (my Lord) to fancy, that this book is derived upon your Lordship almost in the nature of a legacy from her, whose every thing was dearer to your Lordship than your own eyes ; and that what she was pleased to believe apt to minister to her devotions, and the religions of her pious and discerning soul,—may also be allowed a place in your closet, and a portion of your retirement, and a lodging in your thoughts, that they may encourage and instruct your practice, and promote that interest which is, and ought to be, dearer to you, than all those blessings and separations, with which God hath remarked your family and person.

My Lord, I confess the publication of these Sermons can so little serve the ends of my reputation, that I am therefore pleased the rather to do it, because I cannot at all be tempted, in so doing, to minister to any thing of vanity. Sermons may please when they first strike the ear, and yet appear flat and ignorant, when they are offered to the eye, and to an understanding that can consider at leisure. I remember, that a young gentleman of Athens, being to answer for his life, hired an orator to make his defence, and it pleased him well at his first reading; but when the young man, by often reading it that he might recite it publicly by heart, began to grow weary and displeased with it, the orator bade him

consider, that the judges and the people were to hear
it but once, and then it was likely they, at that first
instant, might be as well pleased as he.   This hath
often represented to my mind the condition and fortune of sermons, and that I now part with the advantage they had in their delivery; but I have sufficiently answered myself in that, and am at rest perfectly in my thoughts as to that particular, if I can
in any degree serve the interest of souls, and (which
is next to that) obey the piety, and record the memory, of that dear saint, whose name and whose soul
is blessed : for in both these ministries I doubt not
but your Lordship will be pleased, and account as if
I had done also some service to yourself: your religion makes me sure of the first, and your piety
puts the latter past my fears.   However, I suppose,
in the whole account of this affair, this publication
may be esteemed but like preaching to a numerous
auditory; which if I had done, it would have been
called either duty or charity ; and therefore, will not
now so readily be censured for vanity, if I make use
of all the ways I can, to minister to the good of souls.
But because my intentions are fair in themselves,
and I hope, are acceptable to God, and will be fairly
expounded by your Lordship (whom for so great
reason I so much value),—I shall not trouble you or
the world with an apology for this so free publishing
my weaknesses : I can better secure my reputation,
by telling men how they ought to entertain sermons ;

for if they that read or hear, do their duty aright, the preacher shall soon be secured of his fame, and untouched by censure.

1. For it were well if men would not inquire after the learning of the sermon, or its deliciousness to the ear or fancy, but observe its usefulness; not what concerns the preacher, but what concerns themselves; not what may take a vain reflection upon him, but what may substantially serve their own needs; that the attending to his discourses may not be spent in vain talk concerning him or his disparagements, but may be used as a duty and a part of religion, to minister to edification and instruction. When St. John reckoned the principles of evil actions, he told but of three,—the lust of the flesh, the lust of the eyes, and the pride of life. But there was then also in the world (and now it is grown into age, and strength, and faction) another lust, the lust of the ear,—and a fifth also, the lust of the tongue. Some people have an insatiable appetite in hearing; and hear only that they may hear, and talk, and make a party: they enter into their neighbour's house to kindle their candle, and espying there a glaring fire, sit down upon the hearth, and warm themselves all day, and forget their errand; and, in the meantime, their own fires are not lighted, nor their families instructed or provided for, nor any need served, but a lazy pleasure, which is useless and impudent. Hearing or reading sermons, is, or ought to be, in

order to practise; for so God intended it, that faith should come by hearing, and that charity should come by faith, and by both together we may be saved. For a man's ears (as Plutarch calls them) are ' virtutum ansæ,' by them we are to hold and apprehend virtue; and unless we use them as men do vessels of dishonour, filling them with things fit to be thrown away, with any thing that is not necessary, we are by them more nearly brought to God than by all the senses beside. For although things placed before the eye, affect the mind more readily than the things we usually hear; yet the reason of that is, because we hear carelessly, and we hear variety : the same species dwells upon the eye, and represents the same object in union and single representment; but the objects of the ear are broken into fragments of periods, and words, and syllables, and must be attended with a careful understanding : and because every thing diverts the sound, and every thing calls off the understanding, and the spirit of a man is truantly and trifling; therefore it is, that what men hear does so little affect them, and so weakly work towards the purposes of virtue : and yet nothing does so affect the mind of man as those voices, to which we cannot choose but attend ; and thunder and all loud voices from heaven rend the most stormy heart, and make the most obstinate pay to God the homage of trembling and fear; and the still voice

of God usually takes the tribute of love, and choice,
and obedience.   Now since hearing is so effective an
instrument of conveying impresses and images of
things, and exciting purposes, and fixing resolutions,
unless we hear weakly and imperfectly ; it will be
of the greater concernment that we be curious to
hear in order to such purposes, which are perfective
of the soul and of the Spirit, and not to dwell in fancy and speculation, in pleasures and trifling arrests,
which continue the soul in its infancy and childhood,
never letting it go forth into the wisdom and virtues
of a man.   I have read concerning Dionysius of Sici-
ly, that, being delighted extremely with a minstrel
that sung well, and struck his harp dexterously, he
promised to give him a great reward; and that raised
the fancy of the man, and made him play better.
But when the music was done, and the man waited
for his great hope, the king dismissed him empty,
telling him, that he should carry away as much of
the promised reward as himself did of the music,
and that he had paid him sufficiently with the pleasure of the promise for the pleasure of the song :
both their ears had been equally delighted, and the
profit just none at all.   So it is in many men's hearing sermons: they admire the preacher, and he
pleases their ears, and neither of them both bear along
with them any good ; and the hearer hath as little
good by the sermon, as the preacher by the air of

the people's breath, when they make a noise, and admire, and understand not. And that also is a second caution I desire all men would take.

2. That they may never trouble the affairs of preaching and hearing respectively, with admiring the person of any man. To admire a preacher is such a reward of his pains and worth, as if you should crown a conqueror with a garland of roses, or a bride with laurel; it is an indecency, it is no part of the reward, which could be intended for him. For though it be a good-natured folly, yet it hath in it much danger: for by that means the preacher may lead his hearers captive, and make them servants of a faction, or of a lust; it makes them so much the less to be servants of Christ, by how much they call any man 'master upon earth;' it weakens the heart and hands of others: it places themselves in a rank much below their proper station, changing from hearing the word of God, to admiration of the persons and faces of men; and it being a fault that falls upon the more easy natures and softer understandings, does more easily abuse a man. And though such a person may have the good fortune to admire a good man and a wise; yet it is an ill disposition, and makes him liable to every man's abuse. "Stupidum hominem quavis oratione percelli," said Heraclitus; "An undiscerning person is apt to be cozened by every oration." And, besides this, that preacher, whom some do admire, others will most

certainly envy; and that also is to be provided against with diligence : and you must not admire too forwardly, for your own sake, lest you fall into the hands of a worse preacher; and for his sake, whom, when you admire, you also love, for others will be apt to envy him.

3. But that must by all men be avoided; for envy is the worst counsellor in the world, and the worst hearer of a wise discourse. I pity those men who live upon flattery and wonder, and while they sit at the foot of the doctor's chair, stare in his face, and cry, Ἀκριβῶς, ὦ μεγάλου φιλοσόφου! "Rarely spoken, admirably done!" They are like callow and unfeathered birds, gaping perpetually to be fed from another's mouth, and they never come to the knowledge of the truth; such a knowledge as is effective, and expressed in a prudent and holy life. But those men that envy the preacher, besides that they are great enemies of the Holy Ghost, and are spitefully evil, because God is good to him, they are also enemies to themselves. He that envies the honours or the riches of another, envies for his own sake, and he would fain be rich with that wealth, which sweats in his neighbour's coffers : but he that envies him that makes good sermons, envies himself, and is angry because himself may receive the benefit, and be improved, or delighted, or instructed, by another. He that is apt fondly to admire any man's person, must cure himself by considering, that the preacher

is God's minister and servant; that he speaks God's word, and does it by the divine assistance; that he hath nothing of his own but sin and imperfection; that he does but his duty, and that also hardly enough; that he is highly answerable for his talent, and stands deeply charged with the cure of souls; and therefore, that he is to be highly esteemed for the work's sake, not for the person: his industry and his charity are to be beloved, his ability is to be accounted upon another stock, and for it the preacher and the hearer are both to give God thanks; but nothing is due to the man for that, save only that it is the rather to be employed, because by it we may better be instructed: but if any other reflection be made upon his person, it is next to the sin and danger of Herod and the people, when the fine oration was made μετὰ πολλῆς φαντασίας, "with huge fancy;" the people were pleased, and Herod was admired, and God was angry, and an angel was sent to strike him with death and with dishonour. But the envy against a preacher is to be cured by a contrary discourse; and we must remember, that he is in the place of God, and hath received the gift of God, and the aids of the Holy Ghost; that by his abilities God is glorified, and we are instructed, and the interests of virtue and holy religion are promoted; that by this means God, who deserves that all souls should serve him for ever, is likely to have a fairer harvest of glory and service; and therefore, that envy is against him; that if we envy because *we* are not the instrument of this good to others, we must consider, that we desire the praise to ourselves, not to God. Admiration of a man supposes him to be inferior to the person so admired, but then he is pleased so to be; but envy supposes him as low, and he is displeased at it; and the envious man is not only less than the other man's virtue, but also contrary: the former is a vanity, but this is a vice; that wants wisdom, but this wants wisdom and charity too; that supposes an absence of some good, but this is a direct affliction and calamity.

4. And, after all this, if the preacher be not despised, he may proceed cheerfully in doing his duty, and the hearer may have some advantages by every sermon. I remember that Homer says, the woers of Penelope laughed at Ulysses, because at his return he called for a loaf, and did not, to shew his gallantry, call for swords and spears. Ulysses was so wise as to call for that he needed, and had it, and it did him more good than a whole armory would in his case. So is the plainest part of an easy and honest sermon; it is the sincere milk of the word, and nourishes a man's soul, though represented in its own natural simplicity; and there is hardly any orator but you may find occasion to praise something of him. When Plato misliked the order and disposition of the oration of Lysias, yet he praised the good words and the elocution of the man. Euripides was commended

for his fulness, Parmenides for his composition, Phocylides for his easiness, Archilochus for his argument, Sophocles for the unequalness of his style; so may men praise their preacher : he speaks pertinently, or he contrives wittily, or he speaks comely, or the man is pious, or charitable, or he hath a good text, or he speaks plainly, or he is not tedious, or, if he be, he is at least industrious, or he is the messenger of God ; and that will not fail us, and let us love him for that. And we know those that love, can easily commend any thing, because they like every thing : and they say, fair men are like angels,—and the black are manly,— and the pale look like honey and the stars,—and the crook-nosed are like the sons of kings,—and if they be flat, they are gentle and easy,—and if they be deformed, they are humble, and not to be despised, because they have upon them the impresses of divinity, and they are the sons of God. He that despises his preacher, is a hearer of arts and learning, not of the word of God ; and though, when the word of God is set off with advantages and entertainments of the better faculties of our humility, it is more useful and of more effect ; yet, when the word of God is spoken truly, though but read in plain language, it will become the disciple of Jesus to love that man whom God sends, and the public order and the laws have employed,—rather than to despise the weakness of him who delivers a mighty word.

Thus it is fit that men should be affected and employed when they hear and read sermons ; coming hither not as into a theatre, where men observe the gestures or noises of the people, the brow and eyes of the most busy censurers, and make parties, and go aside with them that dislike every thing, or else admire not the things, but the persons ; but as to a sacrifice, and as to a school where virtue is taught and exercised, and none come but such as put themselves under discipline, and intend to grow wiser, and more virtuous to appease their passion, from violent to become smooth and even, to have their faith established, and their hope confirmed, and their charity enlarged. They that are otherwise affected, do not do their duty : but if they be so minded as they ought, I and all men in my employment shall be secured against the tongues and faces of men, who are ' ingeniosi in alieno libro,' ' witty to abuse and undervalue another man's book.' And yet, besides these spiritual arts already reckoned, I have one security more : for (unless I deceive myself) I intend the glory of God sincerely, and the service of Jesus, in this publication : and therefore, being I do not seek myself or my own reputation, I shall not be troubled if they be lost in the voices of busy people, so that I be accepted of God, and found of him in the day of the Lord's visitation.

My Lord, it was your charity and nobleness that gave me opportunity to do this service (little or great) unto religion ; and whoever shall find any ad-

vantage to their soul by reading the following discourses, if they know how to bless God, and to bless
all them that are God's instruments in doing them
benefit, will (I hope) help to procure blessings to
your person and family, and say a holy prayer, and
name your Lordship in their litanies, and remember,
that at your own charges you have digged a well,
and placed cisterns in the highways, that they may
drink and be refreshed, and their souls may bless
you. My Lord, I hope this, even because I very
much desire it, and because you exceedingly deserve
it; and, above all, because God is good and gracious,
and loves to reward such a charity, and such a religion, as is yours, by which you have employed me in
the service of God, and in the ministries to your family. My Lord, I am, most heartily, and for very
many dear obligations,

Your Lordship's most obliged,

Most humble,

And most affectionate servant,

TAYLOR.

SERMONS.

OF THE SPIRIT OF GRACE.

*But ye are not in the flesh, but in the Spirit, if so be that the
Spirit of God dwell in you. Now if any man have not the
Spirit of Christ, he is none of his. And if Christ be in you,
the body is dead, because of sin ; but the Spirit is life, because
of righteousness.*—Rom. viii. 9, 10.

Tʜɪs day, in which the church commemorates the descent of
the Holy Ghost upon the Apostles, was the first beginning
of the Gospel of Jesus Christ. This was the first day that
the religion was professed: now the Apostles first opened
their commission, and read it to all the people. "The Lord
gave *his Spirit* (or, the Lord gave his Word), and great was the
company of the preachers." For so I make bold to render
that prophecy of David. Christ was 'the Word' of God,
'Verbum æternum;' but the Spirit was the Word of God,
'Verbum patefactum:' Christ was the Word manifested *in*
the flesh ; the Spirit was the Word manifested *to* flesh, and
set in dominion over, and in hostility against, the flesh. The
Gospel and the Spirit are the same thing ; not in substance ;
but 'the manifestation of the Spirit is the Gospel of Jesus
Christ:' and because he was this day manifested, the Gospel
was this day first preached, and it became a law to us, called
"the law of the Spirit of life *;" that is, a law taught us by the
Spirit, leading us to life eternal. But the Gospel is called
'the Spirit ;' 1. Because it contains in it such glorious mysteries, which were revealed by the immediate inspirations of
the Spirit, not only in the matter itself, but also in the man‑

* Rom. viii. 2.

ner and powers to apprehend them.   For what power of human understanding could have found out the incarnation of
a God ; that two natures [a finite, and an infinite] could have
been concentred into one hypostasis (or person) ; that a virgin should be a mother; that dead men should live again ;
that the κόνις ὀστέων λυθέντων, ' the ashes of dissolved bones'
should become bright as the sun, blessed as the angels, swift
in motion as thought, clear as the purest noon ; that God
should so love us, as to be willing to be reconciled to us, and
yet that himself must die that he might pardon us ; that
God's most holy Son should give us his body to eat, and his
blood to crown our chalices, and his Spirit to sanctify our
souls, to turn our bodies into temperance, our souls into
minds, our minds into spirit, our spirit into glory ; that he,
who can give us all things, who is Lord of men and angels,
and King of all the creatures, should pray to God for us without intermission ; that he, who reigns over all the world,
should, at the day of judgment, ' give up the kingdom to God
the Father,' and yet, after this resignation, himself and we
with him should for ever reign the more gloriously ; that we
should be justified by faith in Christ, and that charity should
be a part of faith, and that both should work as acts of duty,
and as acts of relation ; that God should crown the imperfect endeavours of his saints with glory, and that a human
act should be rewarded with an eternal inheritance ; that the
wicked, for the transient pleasure of a few minutes, should
be tormented with an absolute eternity of pains ; that the
waters of baptism, when they are hallowed by the Spirit, shall
purge the soul from sin ; and that the spirit of man should be
nourished with the consecrated and mysterious elements, and
that any such nourishment should bring a man up to heaven :
and, after all this, that all Christian people, all that will be
saved, must be partakers of the divine nature, of the nature, the
infinite nature, of God, and must dwell in Christ, and Christ
must dwell in them, and they must be in the Spirit, and the
Spirit must be for ever in them ? These are articles of so mysterious a philosophy, that we could have inferred them from
no premises, discoursed them upon the stock of no natural
or scientifical principles ; nothing but God and God's Spirit
could have taught them to us : and therefore the Gospel is
' Spiritus patefactus,' ' the manifestation of the Spirit,' ' ad

ædificationem [b] (as the Apostle calls it), 'for edification,' and building us up to be a holy temple to the Lord.

2. But when we had been taught all these mysterious articles, we could not, by any human power, have understood them, unless the Spirit of God had given us a new light, and created in us a new capacity, and made us to be a new creature, of another definition. 'Animalis homo,' ψυχικὸς, that is, as St. Jude expounds the word, πνεῦμα μὴ ἔχων, "The animal, or the natural man, the man that hath not the Spirit, cannot discern the things of God, for they are spiritually discerned [c];" that is, not to be understood but by the light proceeding from the Sun of Righteousness, and by that eye whose bird is the holy Dove, whose candle is the Gospel.

> Scio incapacem te sacramenti, impie,
> Non posse cœcis mentibus mysterium
> Haurire nostrum : nil diurnum nox capit [d].

He that shall discourse Euclid's elements to a swine, or preach (as venerable Bede's story reports of him) to a rock, or talk metaphysics to a boar, will as much prevail upon his assembly, as St. Peter and St. Paul could do upon uncircumcised hearts and ears, upon the indisposed Greeks, and prejudicate Jews. An ox will relish the tender flesh of kids with as much gust and appetite, as an unspiritual and unsanctified man will do the discourses of angels or of an Apostle, if he should come to preach the secrets of the Gospel. And we find it true by a sad experience. How many times doth God speak to us by his servants the prophets, by his Son, by his Apostles, by sermons, by spiritual books, by thousands of homilies, and arts of counsel and insinuation; and we sit as unconcerned as the pillars of a church, and hear the sermons as the Athenians did a story, or as we read a gazette? And if ever it come to pass, that we tremble, as Felix did, when we hear a sad story of death, of ' righteousness and judgment to come,' then we put it off to another time, or we forget it, and think we had nothing to do but to give the good man a hearing; and as Anacharsis said of the Greeks, they used money for nothing but to cast account withal; so our hearers make use of sermons and discourses evangelical, but to fill up void spaces of their time, to help to tell an hour with, or pass it without tediousness. The reason of this is,

[b] 1 Cor. xii. 7.   [c] 1 Cor. ii. 14.   [d] Prudent.

a sad condemnation to such persons; they have not yet entertained the Spirit of God, they are in darkness: they were washed in water, but never baptized with the Spirit; 'for these things are spiritually discerned.' They would think the preacher rude, if he should say,—they are not Christians, they are not within the covenant of the Gospel:—but it is certain, that ' the Spirit of manifestation' is not yet upon them; and that is the first effect of the Spirit, whereby we can be called sons of God, or relatives of Christ. If we do not apprehend, and greedily suck in, the precepts of this holy discipline, as aptly as merchants do discourse of gain, or farmers of fair harvests, we have nothing but the name of Christians; but we are no more such really, than mandrakes are men, or sponges are living creatures.

3. The Gospel is called ' Spirit,' because it consists of spiritual promises and spiritual precepts, and makes all men that embrace it truly, to he spiritual men; and therefore St. Paul adds an epithet beyond this, calling it "a quickening Spirit[e]," that is, it puts life into spirits, which the law could not. The law bound us to punishment, but did not help us to obedience, because it gave not the promise of eternal life to its disciples. ' The Spirit,' that is, ' the Gospel,' only does this: and this alone is it which comforts afflicted minds, which puts activeness into wearied spirit, which inflames our cold desires, and does ἀναζωπυρεῖ, ' blows up sparks' into live coals, and coals up to flames, and flames into perpetual burnings. And it is impossible that any man,—who believes and considers the great, the infinite, the unspeakable, the un-imaginable, and never-ceasing joys, that are prepared for all the sons and daughters of the Gospel,—should not desire them: and, unless he be a fool, he cannot but use means to obtain them, effective, hearty pursuances. For it is not directly in the nature of a man to neglect so great a good; there must be something in his manners, some obliquity in his will, or madness in his intellectuals, or incapacity in his naturals, that must make him sleep such a reward away, or change it for the pleasure of a drunken fever, or the vanity of a mistress, or the rage of a passion, or the unreasonableness of any sin. However, this promise is the life of all our actions, and the Spirit that first taught it, is the life of our souls.

e 1 Cor. xv. 45.

4. But, beyond this, is the reason which is the consummation of all the faithful. The ' Gospel' is called the ' Spirit,' because by and in the Gospel, God hath given to us not only ' the Spirit of manifestation,' that is, of instruction and of catechism, of faith and confident assent; but the ' Spirit of confirmation, or obsignation' to all them that believe and obey the Gospel of Christ: that is, the power of God is come upon our hearts, by which, in an admirable manner, we are made sure of a glorious inheritance; made sure (I say) in the nature of the thing; and our own persuasions also are confirmed with an excellent, a comfortable, a discerning, and a reasonable hope : in the strength of which, and by whose aid, as we do not doubt of the performance of the promise, so we vigorously pursne all the parts of the condition, and are enabled to work all the work of God, so as not to be affrighted with fear, or seduced by vanity, or oppressed by lust, or drawn off by evil example, or abused by riches, or imprisoned by ambition and secular designs. This the Spirit of God does work in all his servants ; and is called, ' the Spirit of obsignation, or the confirming Spirit,' because it confirms our hope, and assures our title to life eternal; and by means of it, and other its collateral assistances, it also confirms us in our duty, that we may not only profess in word, but live lives according to the Gospel. And this is the sense of " the Spirit" mentioned in the text; " Ye are not in the flesh, but in the Spirit, if so he that the Spirit of God dwell in you :" that is, if ye be made partakers of the Gospel, or of ' the Spirit of manifestation;' if ye be truly entitled to God, and have received the promise of the Father, then are ye not carnal men ; ye are ' spiritual,' ye are ' in the Spirit :' if ye have the Spirit in one sense to any purpose, ye have it also in another : if the Spirit be in you, you are in it ; if it hath given you hope, it hath also enabled and ascertained your duty. For ' the Spirit of manifestation' will but upbraid you in the shame and horrors of a sad eternity, if you have not ' the Spirit of obsignation :' if the Holy Ghost be not come upon you to great purposes of holiness, all other pretences are vain,—ye are still in the flesh, which shall never inherit the kingdom of God.

" In the Spirit :" that is, in the power of the Spirit. So the Greeks call him ἔνθεον, ' who is possessed by a spirit,' whom God hath filled with a celestial immission ; he is said

to be in God, when God is in him. And it is a similitude
taken from persons encompassed with guards ; they are ' in
custodia,' that is ' in their power,' under their command,
moved at their dispose ; they rest in their time, and receive
laws from their authority, and admit visitors whom they appoint, and must be employed as they shall suffer: so are
men who are in the Spirit ; that is, they believe as he teaches,
they work as he enables, they choose what he calls good,
they are friends of his friends, and they hate with his hatred :
with this only difference, that persons in custody are forced
to do what their keepers please, and nothing is free but
their wills ; but they that are under the command of the Spirit, do all things which the Spirit commands, but they do them
cheerfully ; and their will is now the prisoner, but it is ' in
libera custodia,' the will is where it ought to be, and where it
desires to be, and it cannot easily choose any thing else, because it is extremely in love with this, as the saints and angels in their state of beatific vision cannot choose but love
God ; and yet the liberty of their choice is not lessened, because the object fills all the capacities of the will and the
understanding. Indifferency to an object is the lowest degree of liberty, and supposes unworthiness or defect in the
object, or the apprehension : but the will is then the freest
and most perfect in its operation, when it entirely pursues
a good with so certain determination and clear election, that
the contrary evil cannot come into dispute or pretence.
Such in our proportions is the liberty of the sons of God ;
it is a holy and amiable captivity to the Spirit : the will of
man is in love with those chains, which draw us to God, and
loves the fetters that confine us to the pleasures and religion
of the kingdom. And as no man will complain that his
temples are restrained, and his head is prisoner, when it is
encircled with a crown ; so when the Son of God hath made
us free, and hath only subjected us to the service and dominion of the Spirit, we are free as princes within the circle of
their diadem, and our chains are bracelets, and the law is a law
of liberty, and ' his service is perfect freedom ;' and the more
we are subjects, the more ' we shall reign as kings ;' and the
faster we run, the easier is our burden ; and Christ's yoke is
like feathers to a bird, not loads, but helps to motion, without them the body falls ; and we do not pity birds, when in
summer we wish them unfeathered and callow, or bald as

eggs, that they might be cooler and lighter. Such is the load and captivity of the soul, when we do the work of God, and are his servants, and under the government of the Spirit. They that strive to be quit of this subjection, love the liberty of outlaws, and the licentiousness of anarchy, and the freedom of sad widows and distressed orphans : for so rebels, and fools, and children, long to be rid of their princes, and their guardians, and their tutors, that they may be accursed without law, and be undone without control, and be ignorant and miserable without a teacher, and without discipline. He that is in the Spirit, is under tutors and governors, until the time appointed of the Father, just as all great heirs are ; only, the first seizure the Spirit makes is upon the will. He that loves the yoke of Christ, and the discipline of the Gospel, he is in the Spirit, that is, in the Spirit's power.

Upon this foundation the Apostle hath built these two propositions. 1. Whosoever hath not the Spirit of Christ, he is none of his : he does not belong to Christ at all : he is not partaker of his Spirit, and therefore shall never be partaker of his glory. 2. Whosoever is in Christ is dead to sin, and lives to the Spirit of Christ : that is, lives a spiritual, a holy, and a sanctified life. These are to be considered distinctly.

1. All that belong to Christ have the Spirit of Christ. Immediately before the ascension, our blessed Saviour bid his disciples "tarry in Jerusalem, till they should receive the promise of the Father." Whosoever stay at Jerusalem, and are in the actual communion of the church of God, shall certainly receive this promise. "For it is made to you and to your children" (saith St. Peter), "and to as many as the Lord our God shall call."—All shall receive the Spirit of Christ, the promise of the Father, because this was the great instrument of distinction between the law and the Gospel. In the law, God gave his Spirit, 1. to some ; to them, 2. extra-regularly ; 3. without solemnity, 4. in small proportions, like the dew upon Gideon's fleece ; a little portion was wet sometimes with the dew of heaven, when all the earth besides was dry. And the Jews called it ' filiam vocis,' ' the daughter of a voice," still, and small, and seldom, and that by secret whispers, and sometimes inarticulate, by way of enthusiasm, rather than of instruction ; and God spake by

the prophets, transmitting the sound as through an organ-pipe, things which themselves oftentimes understood not. But in the Gospel, the Spirit is given without measure: first poured forth upon our head Christ Jesus; then descending upon the beard of Aaron, the fathers of the church, and thence falling, like the tears of the balsam of Judea, upon the foot of the plant, upon the lowest of the people. And this is given regularly to all that ask it, to all that can receive it, and, by a solemn ceremony, and conveyed by a sacrament: and is now, not the daughter of a voice, but the mother of many voices, of divided tongues, and united hearts; of the tongues of prophets, and the duty of saints; of the sermons of apostles, and the wisdom of governors: it is the parent of boldness and fortitude to martyrs, the fountain of learning to doctors, an ocean of all things excellent to all who are within the ship and bounds of the catholic church: so that old men, and young men, maidens, and boys, the scribe and the unlearned, the judge and the advocate, the priest and the people, are full of the Spirit, if they belong to God. Moses's wish is fulfilled, and all the Lord's people are prophets in some sense or other.

In the wisdom of the ancients it was observed, that there are four great cords, which tie the heart of man to inconvenience, and a prison, make it a servant of vanity, and an heir of corruption; 1. pleasure, and, 2. pain; 3. fear, and, 4. desire.

Πρὸς τὰ τετράχορδα δ' ὅλον,
τὴν ἡδονὴν, ἐπιθυμίαν, λύπην, φόβον,
ἀσπλετός γε καὶ πολλῆς μάχης ἥσα.

These are they that exercise all the wisdom and resolutions of man, and all the powers that God hath given him.

οὗτοι γὰρ, οὗτοι καὶ διὰ σπλάγχνων ἀεὶ
χωροῦσι καὶ κινοῦσιν ἀνθρώπων κέας, said Agathon.

These are those evil spirits that possess the heart of man, and mingle with all his actions; so that either men are tempted to, 1. 'lust by pleasure,' or, 2. to 'baser arts by covetousness,' or, 3. to 'impatience by sorrow,' or, 4. to 'dishonourable actions by fear:' and this is the state of man by nature, and under the law, and for ever, till the Spirit of God came, and by four special operations cured these four in-

conveniences, and restrained or sweetened these unwholesome waters.

· 1. God gave us his Spirit that we might be insensible of
worldly pleasures, having our souls wholly filled with spiritual and heavenly relishes. For when God's Spirit hath entered us, and possessed us as his temple, or as his dwelling,
instantly we begin to taste manna, and to loathe the diet of
Egypt; we begin to consider concerning heaven, and to prefer eternity before moments, and to love the pleasures of the
soul above the sottish and beastly pleasures of the body.
Then we can consider that the pleasures of a drunken meeting cannot make recompense for the pains of a surfeit, and
that night's intemperance; much less for the torments of
eternity: then we are quick to discern that the itch and scab
of lustful appetites is not worth the charges of a chirurgeon ;
much less can it pay for the disgrace, the danger, the sickness, the death, and the hell, of lustful persons. Then we
wonder that any man should venture his head to get a crown
unjustly; or that, for the hazard of a victory, he should throw
away all his hopes of heaven certainly.

A man that hath tasted of God's Spirit, can instantly discern the madness that is in rage, the folly and the disease that
are in envy, the anguish and tediousness that are in lust, the
dishonour that is in breaking our faith and telling a lie;
and understands things truly as they are; that is, that charity is the greatest nobleness in the world; that religion
hath in it the greatest pleasures; that temperance is the best
security of health ; that humility is the surest way to honour. And all these relishes are nothing but antepasts of
heaven, where the quintessence of all these pleasures shall
be swallowed for ever; where the chaste shall follow the·
Lamb, and the virgins sing there where the mother of God
shall reign; and the zealous converters of souls, and labourers in God's vineyard, shall worship eternally; where
St. Peter and St. Paul do wear their crowns of righteousness; and the patient persons shall be rewarded with Job,
and the meek persons with Christ and Moses, and all with
God: the very expectation of which,—proceeded from a hope
begotten in us by ' the Spirit of manifestation,' and bred up
and strengthened by 'the Spirit of obsignation,'—is so delicious an entertainment of all our reasonable appetites, that a
spiritual man can no more be removed or enticed from the love

of God and of religion, than the moon from her orb, or a mother from loving the son of her joys and of her sorrows.

This was observed by St. Peter; "As new-born babes, desire the sincere milk of the word, that ye may grow thereby ; if so be that ye have tasted that the Lord is gracious[f]." When once we have tasted the grace of God, the sweetnesses of his Spirit; then no food but ' the food of angels,' no cup but ' the cup of salvation,' the ' divining cup,' in which we drink salvation to our God, and call upon the name of the Lord with ravishment and thanksgiving. And there is no greater external testimony that we are in the Spirit, and that the Spirit dwells in us, than if we find joy and delight and spiritual pleasure in the greatest mysteries of our religion ; if we communicate often, and that with appetite, and a forward choice, and an unwearied devotion, and a heart truly fixed upon God, and upon the offices of a holy worship. He that loathes good meat, is sick at heart, or near it; and he that despises, or hath not an holy appetite to, the food of angels, the wine of elect souls, is fit to succeed the prodigal at his banquet of sin and husks, and to be partaker of the table of devils : but all they who have God's Spirit, love to feast at the supper of the Lamb, and have no appetites but what are of the Spirit, or servants to the Spirit. I have read of a spiritual person who saw heaven but in a dream, but such as made great impression upon him, and was represented with vigorous and pertinacious phantasms, not easily disbanding; and when he awaked he knew not his cell, he remembered not him that slept in the same dorter, nor could tell how night and day were distinguished, nor could discern oil from wine ; but called out for his vision again : "Redde mihi campos meos floridos, columnam auream, comitem Hieronymum, assistentes angelos;" "Give me my fields again, my most delicious fields, my pillar of a glorious light, my companion St. Jerome, my assistant angels."— And this lasted till he was told of his duty, and matter of obedience, and the fear of a sin had disenchanted him, and caused him to take care, lest he lose the substance out of greediness to possess the shadow.

And if it were given to any of us to see paradise, or the third heaven (as it was to St. Paul), could it be that ever we should love any thing but Christ, or follow any guide but

[f] 1 Pet. ii. 2.

the Spirit, or desire any thing but heaven, or understand any thing to be pleasant but what shall lead thither? Now what a vision can do, that the Spirit doth certainly to them that entertain him. They that have him really, and not in pretence only, are certainly great despisers of the things of the world. The Spirit doth not create or enlarge our appetites of things below: spiritual men are not designed to reign upon earth, but to reign over their lusts and sottish appetites. The Spirit doth not inflame our thirst of wealth, but extinguishes it, and makes us to ' esteem all things as loss, and as dung, so that we may gain Christ.' No gain then is pleasant but godliness, no ambition but longings after heaven, no revenge but against ourselves for sinning; nothing but God and Christ: "Deus meus, et omnia:" and " date nobis animas, cætera vobis tollite," as the king of Sodom said to Abraham; " Secure but the souls to us, and take our goods." Indeed, this is a good sign that we have the Spirit.

St. John spake a hard saying, but by the Spirit of manifestation we are all taught to understand it: " Whosoever is born of God, doth not commit sin, for his seed remaineth in him; and he cannot sin, because he is born of God[f]." The seed of God is the Spirit, which hath a plastic power to efform us ' in similitudinem filiorum Dei,' ' into the image of the sons of God;' and as long as this remains in us, while the Spirit dwells in us, we cannot sin; that is, it is against our natures, our reformed natures, to sin. And as we say, we cannot endure such a potion, we cannot suffer such a pain; that is, we cannot without great trouble, we cannot without doing violence to our nature; so all spiritual men, all that are born of God, and the seed of God remains in them, ' they cannot sin;' cannot *without trouble*, and doing against their natures, and their most passionate inclinations. A man, if you speak naturally, can masticate gums, and he can break his own legs, and he can sip up, by little draughts, mixtures of aloes, and rhubarb, of henbane, or the deadly nightshade; but he cannot do this naturally, or willingly, or cheerfully, or with delight. Every sin is against a good man's nature; he is ill at ease when he hath missed his usual prayers, he is amazed if he have fallen into an error, he is infinitely ashamed of his imprudence; he remembers a sin as he thinks of an enemy, or the horrors of a midnight apparition: for all his capacities, his understanding, and his choosing faculties, are filled up with the opinion and persuasions, with the love and with the desires, of God. And this, I say, is the great benefit of the Spirit, which God hath given to us as an antidote against worldly pleasures. And, therefore, St. Paul joins them as consequent to each other: "For it is impossible for those who were once enlightened, and have tasted of the heavenly gift, and were made partakers of the Holy Ghost, and have tasted the good word of God, and the powers of the world to come, &c.[b]" First, we are enlightened in baptism, and by 'the Spirit of manifestation,' the revelations of the Gospel:—then we relish and taste interior excellences, and we receive the Holy Ghost, ' the Spirit of confirmation,' and he gives us a taste of the powers of the world to come ; that is, of the great efficacy that is in the article of eternal life, to persuade us to religion and holy living :—then we feel that as the belief of that article dwells upon our understanding, and is incorporated into our wills and choice, so we grow powerful to resist sin by the strengths of the Spirit, to defy all carnal pleasure, and to suppress and mortify it by the powers of this article: those are ' the powers of the world to come.'

2. The Spirit of God is given to all who truly belong to Christ, as an antidote against sorrows, against impatience, against the evil accidents of the world, and against the oppression and sinking of our spirits under the cross. There are in Scripture noted two births besides the natural ; to which also by analogy we may add a third. The first is, to be born of water and the Spirit. It is ἓν διὰ δυοῖν, one thing signified by a divided appellative, by two substantives, "water and the Spirit," that is, ' Spiritus aqueus,' the 'Spirit moving upon the waters of baptism.' The second is, to be born of ' Spirit and fire ;' for so Christ was promised to "baptize us with the Holy Ghost and with fire;" that is, ' cum Spiritu igneo,' 'with a fiery Spirit,' the Spirit as it descended in Pentecost in the shape of fiery tongues. And as the watery Spirit washed away the sins of the church, so the Spirit of fire enkindles charity and the love of God. Τὸ πῦρ καθαίρει, τὸ ὕδωρ ἁγνίζει (says Plutarch), the Spirit is the same

under both the titles, and it enables the church with gifts and graces. And from these there is another operation of the new birth, but the same Spirit, the Spirit of rejoicing, or ' spiritus exultans, spiritus lætitiæ.' " Now the God of hope fill you with all *joy* and peace in believing, that ye may abound in hope through the power of the Holy Ghost[i]." There is a certain joy and spiritual rejoicing, that accompanies them in whom the Holy Ghost doth dwell; a joy in the midst of sorrow : a joy given to allay the sorrows of secular troubles, and to alleviate the burden of persecution. This St. Paul notes to this purpose : "And ye became followers of us, and of the Lord, having received the word in much affliction, with joy of the Holy Ghost[k]." Worldly afflictions and spiritual joys may very well dwell together; and if God did not supply us out of his storehouses, the sorrow of this world would be more and unmixed, and the troubles of persecution would be too great for natural confidences. For who shall make him recompense that lost his life in a duel, fought about a draught of wine, or a cheaper woman? What arguments shall invite a man to suffer torments in testimony of a proposition of natural philosophy? And by what instruments shall we comfort a man who is sick, and poor, and disgraced, and vicious, and lies cursing, and despairs of any thing hereafter? That man's condition proclaims what it is to want the Spirit of God, ' the Spirit of comfort.' Now this Spirit of comfort is the hope and confidence, the certain expectation of partaking, in the inheritance of Jesus; this is the faith and patience of the saints; this is the refreshment of all wearied travellers, the cordial of all languishing sinners, the support of the scrupulous, the guide of the doubtful, the anchor of timorous and fluctuating souls, the confidence and the staff of the penitent. He that is deprived of his whole estate for a good conscience, by the Spirit he meets this comfort, that he shall find it again with advantage in the day of restitution : and this comfort was so manifest in the first days of Christianity, that it was no unfrequent thing to see holy persons court a martyrdom, with a fondness as great as is our impatience and timorousness in every persecution. Till the Spirit of God comes upon us, we are ὀλιγόψυχοι. " Inopis nos atque pusilli finxerunt animi;" ' we have little souls,' little

---

[i] Rom. xv. 13.   [k] 1 Thes. i. 6.

faith, and as little patience; we fall at every stumbling-block, and sink under every temptation; and our hearts fail us, and we die for fear of death, and lose our souls to preserve our estates or our persons, till the Spirit of God 'fills us with joy in believing:' and the man that is in a great joy, cares not for any trouble that is less than his joy; and God hath taken so great care to secure this to us, that he hath turned it into a precept, 'Rejoice evermore;' and, " Rejoice in the Lord always, and again I say rejoice[l]." But this rejoicing must be only in the hope that is laid up for us, ἐν ἐλπίδι χαίροντες· so the Apostle, 'rejoicing in hope[m].' For although God sometimes makes a cup of sensible comfort to overflow the spirit of a man, and thereby loves to refresh his sorrows; yet this is from a secret principle not regularly given, not to be waited for, not to be prayed for, and it may fail us if we think upon it : but the hope of life eternal can never fail us, and the joy of that is great enough to make us suffer any thing, or to do any thing.

> ———— Ibimus, ibimus,
> Ut cunque praecedes, supremum
> Carpere iter comites parati[a].

To death, to bands, to poverty, to banishment, to tribunals, any whither in hope of life eternal: as long as this anchor holds, we may suffer a storm, but cannot suffer shipwreck. And I desire you, by the way, to observe how good a God we serve, and how excellent a religion Christ taught, when one of his great precepts is, that we should " rejoice and be exceeding glad :" and God hath given us the spirit of rejoicing, not a sullen melancholy spirit, not the spirit of bondage or of a slave, but the Spirit of his Son, consigning us by a holy conscience to 'joys unspeakable and full of glory.' And from hence you may also infer, that those who sink under a persecution, or are impatient in a sad accident, they put out their own fires which the Spirit of the Lord hath kindled, and lose those glories which stand behind the cloud.

[l] 1 Thes. v. 16.   [m] Rom. xii. 12.   [a] Hor. Od. 2. 17.

SERMON II.

PART II.

3. The Spirit of God is given us as an antidote against evil concuspiscences and sinful desires, and is then called ' the Spirit of prayer and supplication.' For, ever since the affections of the outward man prevailed upon the ruins of the soul, all our desires were sensual, and therefore hurtful : for, ever after, our body grew to be our enemy. In the loosenesses of nature, and amongst the ignorance or imperfection of Gentile philosophy, men used to pray with their hands full of rapine, and their mouths full of blood ; and their hearts full of malice ; and they prayed accordingly, for an opportunity to steal, for a fair body, for a prosperous revenge, for a prevailing malice, for the satisfaction of whatsoever they could be tempted to by any object, by any lust, by any devil, whatsoever.

The Jews were better taught; for God was their teacher, and he gave the Spirit to them in single rays. But as the ' Spirit of obsignation' was given to them under a seal, and within a veil so the ' Spirit of manifestation,' or ' patefaction,' was like the gem of a vine, or the bud of a rose, plain ' indices' and significations of life, and principles of juice and sweetness ; but yet scarce out of the doors of their causes : they had the infancy of knowledge, and revelations to them were given as catechism is taught to our children : which they read with the eye of a bird, and speak with the tongue of a bee, and understand with the heart of a child ; that is, weakly and imperfectly. And they understand so little, that, 1. they thought God heard them not, unless they spake their prayers, at least, efforming their words within their lips; and, 2. their forms of prayer were so few and seldom, that to teach a form of prayer, or to compose a collect, was thought a work fit for a prophet, or the founder of an institution. 3. Add to this, that, as their promises were temporal, so were their hopes; as were their hopes, so were their desires : and, according to their desires, so were their prayers. And although the Psalms of David was their great office, and the treasury of devotion to their nation,—and very worthily ; yet it was full of wishes, for temporals, invocations of God the avenger, on God the

Lord of hosts, on God the enemy of their enemies : and they desired their nation to be prospered, and themselves blessed, and distinguished from all the world by the effects of such desires. This was the state of prayer in their synagogues ; save only that it had also this allay ; 4. that their addresses to God were crass, material, typical, and full of shadows and imaginary, and patterns of things to come ; and so in its very being and constitution was relative and imperfect. But that we may see how great things the Lord hath done for us, God hath poured his Spirit into our hearts, ' the Spirit of prayer and supplication.'

And now, 1. Christians ' pray in their spirit,' with sighs and groans, and know that God, who dwells within them, can as clearly distinguish those secret accents, and read their meaning in the Spirit, as plainly as he knows the voice of his own thunder, or could discern the letter of the law written in the tables of stone by the finger of God.

2. Likewise, " the Spirit helpeth our infirmities ; for we know not what we should pray for, as we ought." That is, when God sends an affliction or persecution upon us, we are indeed extreme apt to lay our hand upon the wound, and never take it off, but when we lift it up in prayer to be delivered from that sadness ; and then we pray fervently to be cured of a sickness, to be delivered from a tyrant, to be snatched from the grave, not to perish in the danger. But the Spirit of God hath, from all sad accidents, drawn the veil of error and the cloud of intolerableness, and taught us that our happiness cannot consist in freedom or deliverances from persecutions, but in patience, resignation, and noble sufferance ; and that we are not then so blessed when God hath turned our scourges into ease and delicacy, as when we convert our very scorpions into the exercise of virtues : so that now the Spirit having helped our infirmities, that is, comforted our weaknesses and afflictions, our sorrows and impatience, by this proposition, that " All things work together for the good of them that fear God," he taught us to pray for grace, for patience under the cross, for charity to our persecutors, for rejoicing in tribulation, for perseverance and holdness in the faith, and for whatsoever will bring us safely to heaven.

3. Whereas only a Moses or a Samuel, a David or a Daniel, a John the Baptist or the Messias himself, could de-

scribe and indite forms of prayer and thanksgiving to the tune and accent of heaven ; now every wise and good man is instructed perfectly in the Scriptures, —which are the writings of the Spirit,—what things he may, and what things he must ask for.

4. The Spirit of God hath made our services to be spiritual, intellectual, holy, and effects of choice and religion, the consequence of a spiritual sacrifice, and of a holy union with God. The prayer of a Christian is with the effects of the ' Spirit of sanctification ;' and then we pray with the Spirit, when we pray with holiness, which is the great fruit, the principal gift, of the Spirit. And this is by St. James called "the prayer of faith," and is said to be certain that it shall prevail. Such a praying with the Spirit when our prayers are the voices of our spirits, and our spirits are first taught, then sanctified by God's Spirit, shall never fail of its effect ; because then it is that ' the Spirit himself maketh intercession for us;' that is, hath enabled us to do it upon his strengths; we speak his sense, we live his life, we breathe his accents, we desire in order to his purposes, and our persons are gracious by his holiness, and are accepted by his interpellation and intercession in the act and offices of Christ. This is ' praying with the Spirit.'—To which, by way of explication, I add these two annexes of holy prayer, in respect of which also every good man prays with the Spirit.

5. The Spirit gives us great relish and appetite to our prayers ; and this St. Paul calls " serving of God in his Spirit," ἐν πνεύματί μου; that is, with a willing mind : not as Jonas did his errand, but as Christ did die for us; he was straitened till he had accomplished it. And they—that say their prayers out of custom only, or to comply with external circumstances, or collateral advantages, or pray with trouble and unwillingness,—give a very great testimony that they have not the Spirit of Christ within them, that Spirit which maketh intercession for the saints : but he that delighteth in his prayers, not by a sensible or fantastic pleasure, but whose choice dwells in his prayers, and whose conversation is with God in holy living, and praying accordingly, that man hath the Spirit of Christ, and therefore belongs to Christ; for by this Spirit it is that Christ prays in heaven for us: and if we

* Rom. i. 9.

do not pray on earth in the same manner according to our measures, we had as good hold our peace; our prayers are an abominable sacrifice, and send up to God no better a perfume, than if we burned ' assa foetida,' or the raw flesh of a murdered man upon the altar of incense.

6. The Spirit of Christ and of prayer helps our infirmities, by giving us confidence and importunity. I put them together : for as our faith is, and our trust in God, so is our hope, and so is our prayer ; weary or lasting, long or short, not in words, but in works and in desires : for the words of prayer are no part of the Spirit of prayer. Words may be the body of it, but the Spirit of prayer always consists in holiness, that is, in holy desires and holy actions. Words are not properly capable of being holy; all words are in themselves servants of things ; and the holiness of a prayer is not at all concerned in the manner of its expression, but in the spirit of it, that is, in the violence of its desires, and the innocence of its ends, and the continuance of its employment. This is the verification of that great prophecy which Christ made, that " in all the world the true worshippers should worship in spirit and in truth ;" that is, with a pure mind, with holy desires, for spiritual things, according to the mind of the Spirit, in the imitation of Christ's intercession, with perseverance, with charity or love. That is the Spirit of God, and these are the spiritualities of the Gospel, and the formalities of prayers as they are Christian and evangelical.

7. Some men have thought of a seventh way, and explicate our praying in the Spirit by a mere volubility of language : which indeed is a direct undervaluing the Spirit of God and of Christ, ' the Spirit of manifestation and intercession :' it is to return to the materiality and imperfection of the law ; it is to worship God in outward forms, and to think that God's service consists in shells and rinds, in lips and voices, in shadows and images of things ; it is to retire from Christ to Moses, and, at the best, it is going from real graces to imaginary gifts. And when praying with the Spirit hath in it so many excellences, and consists of so many parts of holiness and sanctification, and is an act of the inner man ; we shall be infinitely mistaken, if we let go this substance, and catch at the shadow, and sit down and rest in the imagination of an improbable, unnecessary, use-

less gift of speaking, to which the nature of many men, and the art of all learned men, and the very use and confidence of ignorant men, is too abundantly sufficient. Let us not so despise the Spirit of Christ, as to make it no other than the breath of our lungs. For though it might be possible, that at the first, and when forms of prayer were few and seldom, the Spirit of God might dictate the very words to the Apostles, and first Christians; yet, it follows not, that therefore he does so still, to all that pretend praying with the Spirit. For if he did not then, at the first, dictate words (as we know not whether he did or. no), why shall he be supposed to do so now? If he did then, it follows that he does not now: because his doing it then, was sufficient for all men since: for so the forms taught by the Spirit, were patterns for others to imitate, in all the descending ages of the church. There was once an occasion so great, that the Spirit of God did think it a work fit for him, to teach a man to weave silk, or embroider gold, or work in brass (as it happened to Bezaleel and Aholiah): but then, every weaver or worker in brass may, by the same reason, pretend that he works by the Spirit, as that he prays by the Spirit, if by prayer he means forming the words. For although in the case of working, it was certain that the Spirit did teach,—in the case of inditing or forming the words, it is not certain whether he did or no: yet because in both it was extraordinary (if it was at all), and ever since in both it is infinitely needless; to pretend the Spirit, in forms of every man's making (even though they be of contrary religions, and pray one against the other), it may serve an end of a fantastic and hypochondriacal religion, or a secret ambition, but not the ends of God, or the honour of the Spirit.

The Jews in their declensions to folly and idolatry did worship the stone of imagination, that is, certain smooth images, in which, by art-magic, pictures and little faces were represented, declaring hidden things and stolen goods; and God severely forbade this baseness[p]. But we also have taken up this folly, and worship the stone of imagination: we beget imperfect phantasms and speculative images in our fancy, and we fall down and worship them; never considering, that the Spirit of God never appears through such spectres. Prayer is one of the noblest exercises of Christian religion; or rather, it is that duty in which all graces are concentred. Prayer is charity, it is faith, it is a conformity to God's will, a desiring according to the desires of heaven, an imitation of Christ's intercession, and prayer must suppose all holiness, or else it is nothing: and therefore, all that in which men need God's Spirit, all that is in order to prayer. Baptism is but a prayer, and the holy sacrament of the Lord's supper is but a prayer; a prayer of sacrifice representative, and a prayer of oblation, and a prayer of intercession, and a prayer of thanksgiving. And obedience is a prayer, and begs and procures blessings: and if the Holy Ghost hath sanctified the whole man, then he hath sanctified the prayer of the man, and not till then. And if ever there was, or could be, any other praying with the Spirit, it was such a one as a wicked man might have; and therefore, it cannot be a note of distinction between the good and bad, between the saints and men of the world. But this only, which I have described from the fountains of Scripture, is that which a good man can have, and therefore, this is it in which we ought to rejoice; ' that he that glories, may glory in the Lord.'

Thus, I have (as I could) described the effluxes of the Holy Spirit upon us in his great channels. But the great effect of them is this: that as by the arts of the spirits of darkness and our own malice, our souls are turned into flesh (not in the natural sense, but in the moral and theological), and ' *animalis* homo' is the same with ' *carnalis*,' that is, his soul is a servant of the passions and desires of the flesh, and is flesh in its operations and ends, in its principles and actions: so, on the other side, by the grace of God, and " the promise of the Father," and the influences of the Holy Ghost, our souls are not only recovered from the state of flesh, and reduced back to the entireness of animal operations, but they are heightened into spirit, and transformed into a new nature. And this is a new article, and now to be considered.

St. Jerome tells of the custom of the empire: when a tyrant was overcome, they used to break the head of his statues, and upon the same trunk to set the head of the conqueror, and so it passed wholly for the new prince. So it is

in the kingdom of grace. As soon as the tyrant sin is overcome, and a new heart is put into us, or that we serve under
a new head, instantly we have a new name given us, and we
are esteemed a new creation; and not only changed in
manners, but we have a new nature within us, even a third
part of an essential constitution. This may seem strange;
and indeed it is so: and it is one of the great mysterious-
nesses of the Gospel. Every man naturally consists of soul
and body; but every Christian man that belongs to Christ,
hath more: for he hath body, and soul, and spirit. My text
is plain for it: "If any man have not the Spirit of Christ,
he is none of his." And by *Spirit* is not meant only the
graces of God, and his gifts enabling us to do holy things:
there is more belongs to a good man than so. But as when God
made man, he made him after his own image, and breathed
into him the spirit of life, and he was made 'in animam vi-
ventem,' 'into a living soul;' then he was made a man:
so in the new creation, Christ, 'by whom God made the
worlds,' intends to conform us to his image, and he hath
given us 'the Spirit of adoption,' by which we are made sons
of God; and by the spirit of a new life we are made new
creatures, capable of a new state, entitled to another manner of duration, enabled to do new and greater actions in
order to higher ends; we have new affections, new understandings, new wills: "vetera transierunt, et ecce omnia no-
va facta sunt;" "all things are become new." And this
is called 'the seed of God,' when it relates to the principle and cause of this production; but the thing that is produced, is a spirit, and that is as much in nature beyond a
soul, as a soul is beyond a body. This great mystery I
should not utter but upon the greatest authority in the world,
and from an infallible doctor; I mean St. Paul, who from
Christ taught the church more secrets than all the whole
college besides; "And the very God of peace sanctify you
wholly: and I pray God that your whole spirit, and soul, and
body, be preserved blameless unto the coming of our Lord
Jesus Christ[q]." We are not sanctified wholly, nor preserved
in safety, unless, besides our souls and bodies, our spirit
also be kept blameless. This distinction is nice, and infinitely above human reason: but "The word of God" (saith

the same Apostle) " is sharper than a two-edged sword,
piercing even to the dividing asunder the soul and the spirit[r]:" and that hath taught us to distinguish the principle
of a new life from the principle of the old, the celestial and
the natural; and thus it is.

The Spirit (as I now discourse of it) is a principle infused
into us by God, when we become his children, whereby
we live the life of grace, and understand the secrets of
the kingdom, and have passions and desires of things
beyond and contrary to our natural appetites, enabling
us not only to sobriety, which is the duty of the body,—
not only to justice, which is the rectitude of the soul,—but
to such a sanctity as makes us like to God; for so saith
the Spirit of God, " Be ye holy, as I am: be pure, be
perfect, as your heavenly Father is pure, as he is perfect:"
which because it cannot be a perfection of degrees, it must
be ' in similitudine naturæ,' ' in the likeness of that nature'
which God hath given us in the new birth, that by it we
might resemble his excellency and holiness. And this I conceive to be the meaning of St. Peter, " According as his
Divine power hath given unto us all things that pertain to
life and godliness" (that is, to this new life of godliness),
" through the knowledge of him, that hath called us to glory
and virtue : whereby are given unto us exceeding great
and precious promises, that by these you might be partakers
of the divine nature[s]:" so we read it; but it is something
mistaken : it is not the τῆς θείας φύσεως, ' the divine nature ;'
for God's nature is indivisible, and incommunicable ; but it
is spoken ' participative,' or ' per analogiam,' "partakers of
a divine nature," that is, of this new and godlike nature
given to every person that serves God, whereby he is sanctified, and made the child of God, and framed into the likeness
of Christ. The Greeks generally call this χάρισμα, 'a gracious
gift,' an extraordinary super-addition to nature ; not a single
gift in order to single purposes, but a universal principle;
and it remains upon all good men during their lives, and
after their death, and is that ' white stone' spoken of in the
Revelation, " and in it a new name written, which no man
knoweth but he that hath it[t]:" and by this, God's sheep, at the
day of judgment, shall be discerned from goats. If their spi-

[r] Heb. iv. 12.   [s] 2 Epist. i. 3, 4.   [t] Apoc. ii. 17.

rits be presented to God pure and unblamable, this great χάρισμα, this talent, which God hath given to all Christians to improve in the banks of grace and religion, if they bring this to God increased and grown up to the fulness of the measure of Christ (for it is Christ's Spirit; and as it is in us, it is called "the supply of the Spirit of Jesus Christ " "), then we shall be acknowledged for sons, and our adoption shall pass into an eternal inheritance in the portion of our elder brother.

I need not to apply this discourse : the very mystery itself is in the whole world the greatest engagement of our duty that is imaginable, by the way of instrument, and by the way of thankfulness.

Quisquis magna dedit, voluit sibi magna rependi ;

" He that gives great things to us, ought to have great acknowledgments :"—and Seneca said concerning wise men, "That he that doth benefits to others, hides those benefits ; as a man lays up great treasures in the earth, which he must never see with his eyes, unless a great occasion forces him to dig the graves, and produce that which he buried; but all the while the man was hugely rich, and he had the wealth of a great relation." So it is with God and us : for this huge benefit of the Spirit, which God gives us, is for our good deposited into our souls; not made for forms and ostentation, not to be looked upon, or serve little ends; but growing in the secret of our souls, and swelling up to a treasure, making us in this world rich by title and relation ; but it shall be produced in the great necessities of doomsday. In the mean time, if the fire be quenched, the fire of God's Spirit, God will kindle another in his anger that shall never be quenched: but if we entertain God's Spirit with our own purities, and employ it diligently, and serve it willingly (for God's Spirit is a loving Spirit), then we shall really be turned into spirits. Irenæus had a proverbial saying, " Perfecti sunt, qui tria sine querela Deo exhibent ;" "They that present three things right to God, they are perfect ;"—that is, a chaste body, a righteous soul, and a holy spirit. And the event shall be this, which Maimonides expressed not amiss,—though he did not at all understand the secret of this mystery ; the soul of man in this life is "in potentia ad esse spiritum,"

* Phil. i. 19.

" it is designed to be a spirit," but in the world to come it
shall be actually as very a spirit as an angel is.   And this
state is expressed by the apostle, calling it " the earnest of
the Spirit :" that is, here it is begun, and given as an antepast
of glory, and a principle of grace ; but then we shall have it
" in plenitudine.'

———— regit idem spiritus artus
Orbe alio ————

Here and there it is the same ; but here we have the earnest,
there the riches and the inheritance.

But then, if this be a new principle, and be given us in
order to the actions of a holy life, we must take care that we
receive not ' the Spirit of God in vain,' but remember that it
is a new life: and as no man can pretend that a person is
alive, that doth not always do the works of life ; so it is certain no man hath the Spirit of God, but he that lives the life
of grace, and doth the works of the Spirit, that is, ' in all holiness, and justice, and sobriety."

"Spiritus qui accedit animo, vel Dei est, vel dæmonis," said
Tertullian : " Every man bath within him the Spirit of God
or the spirit of the devil."—The spirit of fornication is an
unclean devil, and extremely contrary to the Spirit of God ;
and so is the spirit of malice or uncharitableness ; for the
Spirit of God is the Spirit of love : for as by purities God's
Spirit sanctifies the body, so by love he purifies the soul, and
makes the soul grow into a spirit, into a divine nature.   But
God knows that even in Christian societies, we see the devils
walk up and down every day and every hour; the devil of
uncleanness, and the devil of drunkenness ; the devil of malice, and the devil of rage ; the spirit of filthy speaking, and
the spirit of detraction ; a proud spirit, and the spirit of rebellion : and yet all call ' Christian.'   It is generally supposed,
that unclean spirits walk in the night, and so it used to be ;
" for they that are drunk are drunk in the night," said the
Apostle.   But Suidas tells of certain 'empusæ' that used to
appear at noon, at such times as the Greeks did celebrate the
funerals of the dead ; and at this day some of the Russians
fear the noon-day devil, which appeareth like a mourning widow to reapers of hay and corn, and uses to break their arms
and legs, unless they worship her. The prophet David speaketh of both kinds : " Thou shalt not be afraid for the terror

by night; and, 'à ruina et dæmonio meridiano,' from the devil at noon thou shalt be free[x]." It were happy if we were so: but besides the solemn followers of the works of darkness, in the times and proper seasons of darkness, there are very many who act their scenes of darkness in the face of the sun, in open defiance of God, and all laws, and all modesty. There is in such men the spirit of impudence, as well as of impiety. And yet I might have expressed it higher; for every habitual sin doth not only put us into the power of the devil, but turns us into his very nature: just as the Holy Ghost transforms us into the image of God.

Here, therefore, I have a greater argument to persuade you to holy living than Moses had to the sons of Israel. "Behold, I have set before you life and death, blessing and cursing;" so said Moses: but I add, that I have, upon the stock of this scripture, set before you the good Spirit and the bad, God and the devil: choose unto whose nature you will be likened, and into whose inheritance you will be adopted, and into whose possession you will enter. If you commit sin, 'you are of your father the devil,' ye are begot of his principles, and follow his pattern, and shall pass into his portion, when ye are led captive by him at his will; and remember what a sad thing it is to go into the portion of evil and accursed spirits, the sad and eternal portion of devils. But he that hath the Spirit of God, doth acknowledge God for his Father and his Lord, he despises the world, and hath no violent appetites for secular pleasures, and is dead to the desires of this life, and his hopes are spiritual, and God is his joy, and Christ is his pattern and support, and religion is his employment, and 'godliness is his gain:' and this man understands the things of God, and is ready to die for Christ, and fears nothing but to sin against God; and his will is filled with love, and it springs out in obedience to God, and in charity to his brother. And of such a man we cannot make judgment by his fortune, or by his acquaintance; by his circumstances, or by his adherences; for they are the appendages of a natural man: but 'the spiritual is judged of no man;' that is, the rare excellences, that make him happy, do not yet make him illustrious, unless he will reckon virtue to be a great fortune, and holiness to be great wisdom, and

God to be the best friend, and Christ the best relative, and
the Spirit the hugest advantage, and heaven the greatest reward. He that knows how to value these things, may sit
down and reckon the felicities of him, that hath the Spirit of
God.

The purpose of this discourse is this: that since the Spirit of God is a new nature, and a new life put into us, we
are thereby taught and enabled to serve God by a constant
course of holy living, without the frequent returns and intervening of such actions, which men are pleased to call ' sins of
infirmity.' Whosoever hath the Spirit of God, lives the life
of grace. The Spirit of God rules in him,. and is strong according to its age and abode, and allows not of those often
sins, which we think unavoidable, because we call them ' natural infirmities.'

" But if Christ be in you, the body is dead because of
sin ; but the Spirit is life because of righteousness." The
state of sin is a state of death. The state of a man under the
law was a state of bondage and infirmity, as St. Paul largely
describes him in the seventh chapter to the Romans : but
he that hath the Spirit, is made alive, and free and strong,
and a conqueror over all the powers and violences of sin.
Such a man resists temptations, falls not under the assault
of sin, returns not to the sin which he last repented of, acts
no more that error which brought him to shame and sorrow :
but he that falls under a crime, to which he still hath a strong
and vigorous inclination, he that acts his sin, and then curses
it, and then is tempted, and then sins again, and then weeps
again, and calls himself miserable, but still the enchantment
hath confined him to that circle; this man hath not the Spirit : " for where the Spirit of God is, there is liberty ;" there
is no such bondage, and a returning folly to the commands
of sin. But, because men deceive themselves with calling
this bondage a pitiable and excusable infirmity, it will not
be useless to consider the state of this question more particularly, lest men, from the state of a pretended infirmity, fall
into a real death.

1. No great sin is a sin of infirmity, or excusable upon that
stock. But that I may be understood, we must know that every
sin is, in some sense or other, a sin of infirmity. When a man
is in the state of spiritual sickness or death, he is in a state of

infirmity ; for he is a wounded man, a prisoner, a slave, a sick man, weak in his judgment, and weak in his reasonings, impotent in his passions, of childish resolutions, great inconstancy, and his purposes untwist as easily as the rude conjecture of uncombining cables in the violence of a northern tempest: and he that is thus in infirmity cannot be excused ; for it is the aggravation of the state of his sin ; he is so infirm that he is in a state unable to do his duty. Such a man is a ' servant of sin,' a slave of the devil, an heir of corruption, absolutely under command : and every man is so, who resolves for ever to avoid such a sin, and yet for ever falls under it. For what can he be but a servant of sin, who fain would avoid it, but cannot ? that is, he hath not the Spirit of God within him ; Christ dwells not in his soul; for ' where the Son is, there is liberty :' and all that are in the Spirit, are the sons of God, and servants of righteousness, and therefore freed from sin.—But there are also sins of infirmity which are single actions, intervening seldom, in little instances unavoidable, or through a faultless ignorance : such as these are always the allays of the life of the best men ; and for these Christ hath paid, and they are never to be accounted to good men, save only to make them more wary and more humble. Now concerning these it is that I say, No great sin is a sin of excusable or unavoidable infirmity : because, whosoever hath received the Spirit of God, hath sufficient knowledge of his duty, and sufficient strengths of grace, and sufficient advertency of mind, to avoid such things as do great and apparent violence to piety and religion. No man can justly say, that it is a sin of infirmity that he was drunk : for there are but three causes of every sin ; a fourth is not imaginable. 1. If ignorance cause it, the sin is as full of excuse as the ignorance was innocent. But no Christian can pretend this to drunkenness, to murder, to rebellion, to uncleanness : for what Christian is so uninstructed but that he knows adultery is a sin ? 2. Want of observation is the cause of many indiscreet and foolish actions. Now at this gap many irregularities do enter and escape ; because in the whole it is impossible for a man to be of so present a spirit, as to consider and reflect upon every word and every thought. But it is, in this case, in God's laws otherwise than in man's : the great flies cannot pass through without observation, little ones do ; and a man cannot be drunk, and never take notice of it; or tempt his neighbour's wife before he be aware: therefore, the less the instance is, the more likely is it to be a sin of infirmity: and yet, if it be never so little, if it be observed, then it ceases to be a sin of infirmity. 3. But, because great crimes cannot pretend to pass undiscernibly, it follows that they must come in at the door of malice, that is, of want of grace, in the absence of the Spirit; they destroy wherever they come, and the man dies if they pass upon him.

It is true, there is flesh and blood in every regenerate man, but they do not both rule: the flesh is left to tempt, but not to prevail. And it were a strange condition, if both the godly and the ungodly were captives to sin, and infallibly should fall into temptation and death, without all difference, save only that the godly sins unwillingly, and the ungodly sins willingly. But if the same things be done by both, and God in both be dishonoured, and their duty prevaricated, the pretended unwillingness is the sign of a greater and a baser slavery, and of a condition less to be endured: for the servitude which is against me, is intolerable: but if I choose the state of a servant, I am free in my mind.

> ———— Libertatis servaveris umbram,
> Si, quidquid jubearo, velis.   Tot rebus iniquis
> Parnimus victi : venia est bæc sola pudoris,
> Degenerisque metûs, nil jam potuisse negari [a].

Certain it is, that such a person who fain would, but cannot, choose but commit adultery or drunkenness, is the veriest slave to sin that can be imagined, and not at all freed by the Spirit, and by the liberty of the sons of God; and there is no other difference, but that the mistaken good man feels his slavery, and sees his chains and his fetters; but therefore, it is certain that he is, because he sees himself to be, a slave. No man can be a servant of sin and a servant of righteousness, at the same time; but every man that hath the Spirit of God, is a servant of righteousness: and therefore, whosoever find great sins to be unavoidable, are in a state of death and reprobation, as to the present, because they willingly or unwillingly (it matters not much whether of the two) are servants of sin.

2. Sins of infirmity, as they are small in their instance,

so they put on their degree of excusableness only according
to the weakness or infirmity of a man's understanding. So
far as men (without their own fault) understand not their
duty, or are possessed with weakness of principles, or are
destitute and void of discourse, or discerning powers and
acts,—so far, if a sin creeps upon them, it is as natural, and as
free from a law, as is the action of a child; but if any thing
else be mingled with it, if it proceed from any other principle, it is criminal, and not excused by our infirmity, because
it is chosen; and a man's will hath no infirmity, but when
it wants the grace of God, or is mastered with passions and
sinful appetites: and that infirmity is the state of unregene-
ration.

3. The violence or strength of a temptation is not sufficient to excuse an action, or to make it accountable upon
the stock of a pitiable and innocent infirmity, if it leaves the
understanding still able to judge; because a temptation cannot have any proper strengths but from ourselves; and because we have in us a principle of baseness, which this temptation meets, and only persuades me to act, because I love it.
Joseph met with a temptation as violent and as strong as any
man; and it is certain there are not many Christians but
would fall under it, and call it a sin of infirmity, since they
have been taught so to abuse themselves, by sewing fig-leaves
before their nakedness: but because Joseph had a strength
of God within him, the strength of chastity, therefore it
could not at all prevail upon him. Some men cannot by any
art of hell be tempted to be drunk; others can no more resist an invitation to such a meeting, than they can refuse to
die if a dagger were drunk with their heart-blood, because
their evil habits made them weak on that part. And some
man, that is fortified against revenge, it may be, will certainly
fall under a temptation to uncleanness: for every temptation is great or small according as the man is; and a good
word will certainly lead some men to an action of folly,
while another will not think ten thousand pounds a considerable argument to make him tell one single lie against his
duty or his conscience.

4. No habitual sin, that is, no sin that returns constantly
or frequently; that is repented of and committed again, and
still repented of, and then again committed; no such sin is

excusable with a pretence of infirmity: because that sin is
certainly noted, and certainly condemned, and therefore returns, not because of the weakness of nature, but the weakness of grace: the principle of this is an evil spirit, an habitual aversation from God, a dominion and empire of sin.
And, as no man, for his inclinations and aptness to the sins
of the flesh, is to be called carnal, if he corrects his inclinations, and turns them into virtues: so no man can be called
spiritual for his good wishes and apt inclinations to goodness, if these inclinations pass not into acts, and these acts
into habits and holy customs, and walkings and conversation with God.   But as natural concupiscence corrected becomes the matter of virtue, so these good inclinations and
condemnings of our sin, if they be ineffective and end in sinful actions, are the perfect signs of a reprobate and unrege-
nerated state.

The sum is this: an animal man, a man under the law,
a carnal man (for as to this they are all one), is sold under
sin, he is a servant of corruption, he falls frequently into the
same sin to which he is tempted, he commends the law, he
consents to it that it is good, he does not commend sin, he
does some little things against it; but they are weak and
imperfect, his lust is stronger, his passions violent and unmortified, his habits vicious, his customs sinful, and he lives
in the regions of sin, and dies and enters into its portion.
But a spiritual man, a man that is in a state of grace, who
is born anew of the Spirit, that is regenerate by the Spirit of
Christ, he is led by the Spirit, he lives in the Spirit, he does
the works of God cheerfully, habitually, vigorously; and although he sometimes slips, yet it is but seldom, it is in small
instances; his life is such, as he cannot pretend to he justified by works and merit, but by mercy and the faith of Jesus
Christ; yet he never sins great sins: if he does, he is for
that present fallen from God's favour. and though possibly
he may recover (and the smaller or seldomer the sin is, the
sooner may be his restitution); yet, for the present (I say), he
is out of God's favour.   But he that remains in the grace of
God, sins not by any deliberate, consultive, knowing act:
he is incident to such a surprise as may consist with the
weakness and judgment of a good man; but whatsoever is,
or must be considered, if it cannot pass without considera-

tion, it cannot pass without sin, and therefore cannot enter upon him while he remains in that state. For ' he that is in Christ, in him the body is dead by reason of sin.' And the Gospel did not differ from the law, but that the Gospel gives grace and strength to do whatsoever it commands; which the law did not: and the greatness of the promise of eternal life is such an argument to them that consider it, that it must needs be of force sufficient to persuade a man to use all his faculties and all his strength, that he may obtain it. God exacted all upon this stock; God knew this could do every thing: " Nihil non in hoc præsumpsit Deus," said one. This will make a satyr chaste, and Silenus to be sober, and Dives to be charitable, and Simon Magus himself to despise reputation, and Saul to turn from a persecutor to an apostle. For since God hath given us reason to choose, and a promise to exchange for our temperance and faith, and charity and justice; for these (I say), happiness, exceeding great happiness, that we shall be kings, that we shall reign with God, with Christ, with all the holy angels for ever, in felicity so great, that we have not now capacities to understand it, our heart is not big enough to think it; there cannot in the world be a greater inducement to engage us, a greater argument to oblige us, to do our duty. God hath not in heaven a bigger argument; it is not possible any thing in the world should be bigger; which because the Spirit of God hath revealed to us, if by this strength of his we walk in his ways, and be ingrafted into his stock, and bring forth his fruits, ' the fruits of the Spirit,'—then ' we are in Christ,' and ' Christ in us,'—then we walk in the Spirit,—and ' the Spirit dwells in us,'—and our portion shall be there, where 'Christ by the Spirit maketh intercession for us'—that is, at the right hand of his Father, for ever and ever. Amen.

SERMON III.

THE DESCENDING AND ENTAILED CURSE CUT OFF.

PART I.

*I the Lord thy God am a jealous God, visiting the iniquity of
the fathers upon the children unto the third and fourth generation of them that hate me :*
*And shewing mercy unto thousands of them that love me, and
keep my commandments.*—Exod. xx. 5, 6.

It is not necessary that a commonwealth should give pensions to orators, to dissuade men from running into houses
infected with the plague, or to entreat them to be out of love
with violent torments, or to create in men evil opinions concerning famine or painful deaths : every man hath a sufficient
stock of self-love, upon the strength of which he hath entertained principles strong enough to secure himself against
voluntary mischiefs, and from running into states of death
and violence. A man would think that this I have now said,
were in all cases certainly true ; and I would to God it were:
for that which is the greatest evil, that which makes all
evils, that which turns good into evil, and every natural evil
into a greater sorrow, and makes that sorrow lasting and
perpetual ; that which sharpens the edge of swords, and
makes agues to be fevers, and fevers to turn into plagues ;
that which puts stings into every fly, and uneasiness to every
trifling accident, and strings every whip with scorpions,—you
know I must needs mean sin ; that evil men suffer patiently,
and choose willingly, and run after it greedily, and will not
suffer themselves to be divorced from it : and therefore, God
hath hired servants to fight against this evil ; he hath set
angels with fiery swords to drive us from it, he hath employed
advocates to plead against it, he hath made laws and decrees
against it, he hath dispatched prophets to warn us of it, and
hath established an order of men, men of his own family,
and who are fed at his own charges,—I mean the whole order
of the clergy, whose office is like watchmen, to give an alarm

at every approach of sin, with as much affrightment as if an
enemy were near, or the sea broke in upon the flat country;
and all this only to persuade men not to be extremely miserable, for nothing, for vanity, for a trouble, for a disease:
for some sins naturally are diseases, and all others are natural nothings, mere privations or imperfections, contrary to
goodness, to felicity, to God himself. And yet God hath
hedged sin round about with thorns, and sin of itself too
brings thorns; and it abuses a man in all his capacities, and
it places poison in all those seats and receptions, where he
could possibly entertain happiness : for if sin pretend to
please the sense, it doth first abuse it shamefully, and then
humours it : it can only feed an imposture ; no natural, reasonable, and perfective appetite: and besides its own essential
appendages and proprieties, things are so ordered, that a fire
is kindled round about us, and every thing within us, above,
below us, and on every side of us, is an argument against,
and an enemy to sin ; and, for its single pretence, that it
comes to please one of the senses, one of those faculties
which are in us, the same they are in a cow, it hath an evil
so communicative, that it doth not only work like poison,
to the dissolution of soul and body, but it is a sickness
like the plague, it infects all our houses, and corrupts the air
and the very breath of heaven : for it moves God first to
jealousy, and that takes off his friendship and kindness towards us; and then to anger, and that makes him a resolved enemy ; and it brings evil, not only upon ourselves,
but upon all our relatives, upon ourselves and our children,
even the children of our nephews, ' ad natos natorum, et qui
nascentur ab illis[a],' to the third and fourth generation. And
therefore, if a man should despise the eye or sword of man,
if he sins, he is to contest with the jealousy of a provoked
God : if he doth not regard himself, let him pity his pretty
children : if he he angry, and hates all that he sees, and is
not solicitous for his children, yet let him pity the generations which are yet unborn ; let him not bring a curse upon
his whole family, and suffer his name to rot in curses and
dishonours; let not his memory remain polluted with an
eternal stain. If all this will not deter a man from sin, there
is no instrument left for that man's virtue, no hopes of his feli-

[a] Virg. Æn. 3. 98.

city, no recovery of his sorrows and sicknesses; but he must sink under the strokes of a jealous God into the dishonour of eternal ages, and the groanings of a never-ceasing sorrow.

"God is a jealous God"—That is the first and great stroke he strikes against sin; he speaks after the manner of men; and, in so speaking, we know that he is jealous,—is suspicious,—he is inquisitive,—he is implacable. 1. God is pleased to represent himself a person very ' suspicious,' both in respect of persons and things. For our persons we give him cause enough: for we are sinners from our mother's womb: we make solemn vows, and break them instantly; we cry for pardon, and still renew the sin; we desire God to try us once more, and we provoke him ten times farther; we use the means of grace to cure us, and we turn them into vices and opportunities of sin; we curse our sins, and yet long for them extremely; we renounce them publicly, and yet send for them in private, and shew them kindness; we leave little offences,but our faith and our charity are not strong enough to master great ones; and sometimes we are shamed out of great ones, but yet entertain little ones; or if we disclaim both, yet we love to remember them, and delight in their past actions, and bring them home to us, at least by fiction of imagination, and we love to be betrayed into them: we would fain have things so ordered by chance or power, that it may seem necessary to sin, or that it may become excusable, and dressed fitly for our own circumstances; and for ever we long after the flesh-pots of Egypt, the garlic and the onions: and we do so little esteem manna, the food of angels, we so loathe the bread of heaven, that any temptation will make us return to our fetters and our bondage. And if we do not tempt ourselves, yet we do not resist a temptation; or if we pray against it, we desire not to be heard; and if we be assisted, yet we will not work together with those assistances: so that unless we be forced, nothing will be done. We are so willing to perish, and so unwilling to be saved, that we minister to God reason enough to suspect us, and therefore it is no wonder that God is jealous of us. We keep company with harlots and polluted persons; we are kind to all God's enemies, and love that which he hates: how can it be otherwise but that we should be suspected? Let us make our best of it, and see if we can recover the good opinion of God ; for as yet we are but suspected persons. 2. And therefore God is 'inquisitive;' he looks for that which he fain would never find : God sets spies upon us ; he looks upon us himself through the curtains of a cloud, and he sends angels to espy us in all our ways, and permits the devil to winnow us and to accuse us, and erects a tribunal and witnesses in our own consciences, and he cannot want information concerning our smallest irregularities. Sometimes the devil accuses : but he sometimes accuses us falsely, either maliciously or ignorantly, and we stand upright in that particular by innocence ; and sometimes by penitence; and all this while our conscience is our friend. Sometimes our conscience does accuse us unto God ; and then we stand convicted by our own judgment. Sometimes, if our conscience acquit us, yet we are not thereby justified : for, as Moses accused the Jews, so do Christ and his apostles acouse us, not in their persons, but by their works and by their words, by the thing itself, by confronting the laws of Christ, and our practices. Sometimes the angels, who are the observers of all our works, carry up sad tidings to the court of heaven against us. Thus two angels were the informers against Sodom : but yet these were the last ; for before that time the cry of their iniquity had sounded loud and sadly in heaven. And all this is the direct and proper effect of his jealousy, which sets spies upon all the actions, and watches the circumstances, and tells the steps, and attends the business, the recreations, the publications, and retirements, of every man, and will not suffer a thought to wander, but he uses means to correct its error, and to reduce it to himself. For he that created us, and daily feeds us, he that entreats us to be happy with an importunity so passionate as if not we, but himself were to receive the favour ; he that would part with his only Son from his bosom and the embraces of eternity, and give him over to a shameful and cursed death for us, cannot but be supposed to love us with a great love, and to own us with an entire title, and therefore, that he would fain secure us to himself with an undivided passion. And it cannot but be infinitely reasonable : for to whom else should any of us belong but to God ? Did the world create us ? or did lust ever do us any good ? Did Satan ever suffer one stripe for our advantage? Does not he study all the ways

to ruin us? Do the sun or the stars preserve us alive? or do
we get understanding from the angels? Did ever any joint
of our body knit, or our heart ever keep one true minute of
a pulse, without God? Had not we been either nothing, or
worse, that is, infinitely, eternally miserable, but that God
made us capable, and then pursued us with arts and devices
of great mercy to force us to be happy? Great reason therefore there is, that God should he jealous lest we take any of
our duty from him, who hath so strangely deserved it all,
and give it to a creature, or to our enemy, who cannot be
capable of any. But, however, it will concern us with much
caution to observe our own ways, since 'we are made a spec-
tacle to God, to angels, and to men.' God hath set so many
spies upon us, the blessed angels and the accursed devils,
good men and had men, the eye of heaven, and eye of that
eye, God himself,—all watching lest we rob God of his honour,
and ourselves of our hopes. For by this prime intention he
hath chosen so to get his own glory, as may best consist
with our felicity: his great design is to be glorified in our
being saved. 3. God's jealousy hath a sadder effect than
all this. For all this is for mercy; but if we provoke this
jealousy, if he finds us in our spiritual whoredoms, he is implacable, that is, he is angry with us to eternity, unless we
return in time; and if we do, it may he, he will not be appeased in all instances; and when he forgives us, he will
make some reserves of his wrath; he will punish our persons
or our estate, he will chastise us at home or abroad, in our bodies or in our children; for he will visit our sins upon our
children from generation to generation: and if they be made
miserable for our sins, they are unhappy in such parents;
but we bear the curse and the anger of God, even while they
hear his rod. "God visits the sins of the fathers upon the
children." That's the second great stroke he strikes against
sin, and is now to be considered.

That God doth so is certain, because he saith he doth:
and that this is just in him so to do, is also as certain therefore, because he doth it. For as his laws are our measures,
so his actions and his own will are his own measures. He
that hath right over all things and all persons, cannot do
wrong to any thing. He that is essentially just (and there
could be no such thing as justice, or justice itself could not

be good, if it did not derive from him), it is impossible for him to be unjust. But since God is pleased to speak after the manner of men, it may well consist with our duty to inquire into those manners of consideration, whereby we may understand the equity of God in this proceeding, and to be instructed also in our own danger if we persevere in sin.

1. No man is made a sinner by the fault of another man without his own consent: for to every one God gives his choice, and sets life and death before every of the sons of Adam; and therefore, this death is not a consequent to any sin but our own. In this sense it is true, that if ' the fathers eat sour grapes, the children's teeth shall not be set on edge :' and therefore the sin of Adam, which was derived to all the world, did not bring the world to any other death but temporal, by the intermedial stages of sickness and temporal infelicities. And it is not said that ' *sin* passed upon all men,' but ' *death;*' and that also no otherwise but ἐφ' ᾧ πάντες ἡμαρτον, "inasmuch as all men have sinned ;" as they have followed the steps of their father, so they are partakers of this death. And therefore, it is very remarkable, that death brought in by sin was nothing superinduced to man; man only was reduced to his own natural condition, from which before Adam's fall he stood exempted by supernatural favour : and therefore, although the taking away that extraordinary grace or privilege was a punishment ; yet the suffering the natural death was directly none, but a condition of his creation, natural, and therefore not primarily evil ; but, if not good, yet at least indifferent. And the truth and purpose of this observation will extend itself, if we observe, that before any man died, Christ was promised, by whom death was to lose its sting, by whom death did cease to be an evil, and was, or might be, if we do belong to Christ, a state of advantage. So that we, by occasion of Adam's sin, being returned to our natural certainty of dying, do still, even in this very particular, stand between the blessing and the cursing. If we follow Christ, death is our friend : if we imitate the prevarication of Adam, then death becomes an evil ; the condition of our nature becomes the punishment of our own sin, not of Adam's. For although his sin brought death in, yet it is only our sin that makes death to be evil. And I desire this to be observed, because it is of great use in vindicating

the divine justice in the matter of this question. The material part of the evil came from our father upon us : but the formality of it, the sting and the curse, is only by ourselves.

2. For the fault of others many may become miserable, even all or any of those whose relation is such to the sinner, that he in any sense may, by such inflictions, be punished, execrable or oppressed.   Indeed it were strange, if, when a plague were in Ethiopia, the Athenians should be infected ; or if the house of Pericles were visited, Thucydides should die for it. For although there are some evils which (as Plutarch saith) are " ansis et propagationibus prædita, incredibili celeritate in longinquum penetrantia," such which can dart evil influences, as porcupines do their quills ; yet as at so great distances the knowledge of any confederate events must needs be uncertain ; so it is also useless, because we neither can join their causes, nor their circumstances, nor their accidents, into any neighbourhood of conjunction. Relations are seldom noted at such distances ; and if they were, it is certain so many accidents will intervene, that will outweigh the efficacy of such relations, that by any so far distant events we cannot be instructed in any duty, nor understand ourselves reproved for any fault. But when the relation is nearer, and is joined under such a head and common cause, that the influence is perceived, and the parts of it do usually communicate in benefit, notice, or infelicity,—especially if they relate to each other as superior and inferior,— then it is certain the sin is infectious ; I mean, not only in example, but also in punishment.

And of this I shall shew, 1. In what instances it is so. 2. For what reasons it is so, and justly so. 3. In what degree, and in what cases, it is so. 4. What remedies there are for this evil.

1. It is so in kingdoms, in churches, in families, in political, artificial, and even in accidental societies.

When David numbered the people, God was angry with him ; but he punished the people for the crime ; seventy thousand men died of the plague. And when God gave to David the choice of three plagues, he chose that of the pestilence, in which the meanest of the people, and such which have the least society with the acts and crimes of kings, are most commonly devoured ; whilst the powerful and sinning persons, by arts of physic, and flight, by provisions of nature, and accidents, are more commonly secured. But the story of the kings of Israel hath·furnished us with an example fitted with all the stranger circumstances in this question. Joshua had sworn to the Gibeonites, who had craftily secured their lives by exchanging it for their liberties: almost five hundred years after, Saul, in zeal to the men of Israel and Judah, slew many of them. After this Saul dies, and no question was made of it: but, in the days of David, there was a famine in the land three years together; and God, being inquired of, said, it was because of Saul's killing the Gibeonites^a. What had the people to do with their king's fault? Or, at least, the people of David with the fault of Saul? That we shall see anon. But see the way that was appointed to expiate the crime and the calamity. David took seven of Saul's sons, and hung them up against the sun; and after that, God was entreated for the land. The story observes one circumstance more; that, for the kindness of Jonathan, David spared Mephibosheth. Now this story doth not only instance in kingdoms, but in families too. The father's fault is punished upon the sons of the family, and the king's fault upon the people of his land; even after the death of the king, after the death of the father. Thus God visited the sin of Ahab partly upon himself, partly upon his sons: "I will not bring the evil in his days, but in his son's days will I bring the evil upon his house^b." Thus did God slay the child of Bathsheba for the sin of his father David: and the whole family of Eli, all his kindred of the nearer lines, were thrust from the priesthood, and a curse made to descend upon his children for many ages, 'that all the males should die young, and in the flower of their youth.' The boldness and impiety of Cham made his posterity to be accursed, and brought slavery into the world. Because Amalek fought with the sons of Israel at Rephidim, God took up a quarrel against the nation for ever. And, above all examples, is that of the Jews, who put to death the Lord of life, and made their nation to be an anathema for ever, until the day of restitution: "His blood be upon us, and upon our children." If we shed innocent blood, if we provoke God to wrath, if we oppress the poor, if we 'crucify the Lord of life again,

and put him to an open shame,' the wrath of God will be
upon us and upon our children, to make us a cursed family;
and we are the sinners, to be the stock and original of the
curse; the pedigree of the misery shall derive from us.

This last instance went farther than the other of families
and kingdoms. For not only the single families of the Jews
were made miserable for their fathers' murdering the Lord of
life, nor also was the nation alone extinguished for the sins
of their rulers, but the religion was removed; it ceased to be
God's people; the synagogue was rejected, and her veil rent,
and her privacies dismantled; and the Gentiles were made to
be God's people, when the Jews' enclosure was disparked. I
need not farther to instance this proposition in the case of na-
tional churches; though it is a sad calamity that is fallen
upon all the seven churches of Asia, to whom the Spirit of
God wrote seven epistles by St. John; and almost all the
churches of Africa, where Christ was worshipped, and now
Mahomet is thrust in substitution, and the people are servants,
and the religion is extinguished; or, where it remains, it
shines like the moon in an eclipse, or like the least spark of
the Pleiades, seen but seldom, and that rather shining like a
glow-worm than a taper enkindled with a beam of the Sun of
Righteousness. I shall add no more instances to verify the
truth of this, save only I shall observe to you, that even there
is danger in being in evil company, in suspected places, in
the civil societies and fellowship of wicked men.

> ———— Vetabo, qui Cereris sacrum
> Volgarit arcanæ, sub isdem
>   Sit trabibus, fragilemque mecum
> Solvat phaselum. Sæpe Diespiter
> Neglectus, incesto addidit integrum [c].

And it happened to the mariners who carried Jonah, to be in
danger with a horrid storm, because Jonah was there, who
had sinned against the Lord. Many times the sin of one man
is punished by the falling of a house or a wall upon him, and
then all the family are like to be crushed with the same ruin:
so dangerous, so pestilential, so infectious a thing is sin, that
it scatters the poison of its breath to all the neighbourhood,
and makes that the man ought to be avoided like a person
infected with a plague.

Next I am to consider, why this is so, and why it is just-

[c] Hor. Od. 3. 2.

ly so. To this I answer, 1. Between kings and their people, parents and their children, there is so great a necessitude, propriety, and intercourse of nature, dominion, right, and possession,—that they are by God and the laws of nations reckoned as their goods and their blessings. " The honour of a king is in the multitude of his people ;—and, Children are a gift that cometh of the Lord,—and, Happy is that man that hath his quiver full of them:—and, Lo thus shall the man be blessed that feareth the Lord ; his wife shall be like the fruitful vine by the walls of his house, his children like olive-branches round about his table."—Now if children he a blessing, then to take them away in anger is a curse : and if the loss of flocks and herds, the burning of houses, the blasting of fields, be a curse ; how much greater is it to lose our children, and to see God slay them before our eyes, in hatred to our persons, and detestation and loathing of our baseness ? When Job's messengers told him the sad stories of fire from heaven, the burning his sheep, and that the Sabeans had driven his oxen away, and the Chaldeans had stolen his camels ; these were said arrests to his troubled spirit : but it was reserved as the last blow of that sad execution, that the ruins of a house had crushed his sons and daughters to their graves.   Sons and daughters are greater blessings than sheep and oxen : they are not servants of profit, as sheep are, but they secure greater ends of blessing ; they preserve your names ; they are so many titles of provision and providence ; every new child is a new title of God's care of that family : they serve the ends of honour, of commonwealths and kingdoms ; they are images of our souls, and images of God, and therefore are great blessings; and, by consequence, they are great riches, though they are not to be sold for money : and surely he that hath a cabinet of invaluable jewels, will think himself rich, though he never sells them. " Does God take care for oxen ?" said our blessed Saviour: much more for you: yea, all and every one of your children are of more value than many oxen. When therefore God, for your sins, strikes them with crookedness, with deformity, with foolishness, with impertinent and caitiff spirits, with hasty or sudden deaths ; it is a greater curse to you than to lose whole herds of cattle, of which, it is certain, most men would be very sensible. They are our goods; they are our blessings from God; therefore we are stricken when for our sakes they die. Therefore, we may properly be punished by evils happening to our relatives.

2. But as this is a punishment to us, so it is not unjust as to them, though they be innocent. For all the calamities of this life are incident to the most godly persons in the world: and since the King of heaven and earth was made a man of sorrows, it cannot be called unjust or intolerable, that innocent persons should be pressed with temporal infelicities; only in such cases we must distinguish the misery from the punishment: for that all the world dies is a punishment of Adam's sin; but it is no evil to those single persons that ' die in the Lord,' for they are blessed in their death. Jonathan was killed the same day with his father the king; and this was a punishment to Saul indeed, but to Jonathan it was a blessing: for since God had appointed the kingdom to his neighbour, it was more honourable for him to die fighting the Lord's battle, than to live and see himself the lasting testimony of God's curse upon his father, who lost the kingdom from his family by his obedience. That death is a blessing, which ends an honourable and prevents an inglorious life. And our children, it may be, shall be sanctified by a sorrow, and purified by the fire of affliction, and they shall receive the blessing of it; but it is to the fathers a curse, who shall wound their own hearts with sorrow, and cover their heads with a robe of shame, for bringing so great evil upon their house.

3. God hath many ends of providence to serve in this dispensation of his judgments. 1. He expresses the highest indignation against sin, and makes his examples lasting, communicative, and of great effect; it is a little image of hell; and we shall the less wonder that God with the pains of eternity punishes the sins of a time, when with our eyes we see him punish a transient action with a lasting judgment. 2. It arrests the spirits of men, and surprises their loosenesses, and restrains their gaiety, when we observe that the judgments of God find us out in all relations, and turn our comforts into sadness, and make our families the scene of sorrows, and we can escape him no where: and by sin are made obnoxious not alone to personal judgments, but are made like the fountains of the Dead Sea, springs of the lake of Sodom; instead of refreshing our families with

blessings, we leave them brimstone and drought, and poison, and an evil name, and the wrath of God, and a treasure of wrath, and their fathers' sins, for their portion and inheritance. Naturalists say, that when the leading goats in the Greek islands have taken an 'eryngus,' or sea holly, into their mouths, all the herd will stand still, till the herdsman comes and forces it out, as apprehending the evil that will come to them all, if any of them, especially their principals, taste an unwholesome plant. And, indeed, it is of a general concernment, that the master of a family, or the prince of a people, from whom, as from a fountain, many issues do derive upon their relatives, should be springs of health, and sanctity, and blessing. It is a great right and propriety that a king hath in his people, or a father in his children, that even their sins can do these a mischief, not only by a direct violence, but by the execution of God's wrath. God hath made strange bands and vessels, or channels of communication between them, when even the anger of God shall be conveyed by the conduits of such relations. That would be considered. It binds them nearer than our new doctrine will endure. But it also binds us to pray for them, and for their holiness, and good government, as earnestly as he would to be delivered from death, or sickness, or poverty, or war, or the wrath of God in any instance. 3. This also will satisfy the fearfulness of such persons, who think the evil prosperous, and call the proud happy. No man can be called happy till he be dead; nor then neither, if he lived viciously. Look how God bandles him in his children, in his family, in his grand-children: and as it tells that generation, which sees the judgment, that God was all the while angry with him; so it supports the spirits of men in the interval, and entertains them with the expectation of a certain hope: for if I do not live to see his sin punished, yet his posterity may find themselves accursed, and feel their fathers' sins in their own calamity; and the expectation or belief of that may relieve my oppression, and ease my sorrows, while I know that God will bear my injury in a lasting record, and, when I have forgot it, will bring it forth to judgment. The Athenians were highly pleased when they saw honours done to the posterity of Cimon, a good man and a rare citizen, but murdered for being wise and virtuous: and when at the same time they saw a decree of banishment pass against the children of Lacharis and Aristo, they laid their hands upon their mouths, and with silence did admire the justice of the Power above.

The sum of this is ; that, in sending evils upon the posterity of evil men, God serves many ends of providence, some of wisdom, some of mercy, some of justice, and contradicts none. For the evil of the innocent son is the father's punishment upon the stock of his sin, and his relation; but the sad accident happens to the son, upon the score of nature, and many ends of providence and mercy. To which I add, that if any, even the greatest temporal evil, may fall upon a man, as blindness did upon the blind man in the Gospel, when "neither he nor his parents have sinned;" much more may it do so, when his parents have, though he have not. For there is a nearer or more visible commensuration of justice between the parent's sin and the son's sickness, than between the evil of the son and the innocence of the father and son together. The dispensation therefore is righteous and severe.

3. I am now to consider in what degree and in what cases this is usual, or to be expected. It is in the text instanced in the matter of worshipping images. God is so jealous of his honour, that he will not suffer an image of himself to be made, lest the image dishonour the substance; nor any image of a creature to be worshipped, though with a less honour, lest that less swell up into a greater. And he that is thus jealous of his honour, and therefore so instances it, is also very curious of it in all other particulars : and though to punish the sins of fathers upon the children be more solemnly threatened in this sin only, yet we find it inflicted indifferently in any other great sin, as appears in the former precedents.

This one thing I desire to be strictly observed ; that it is with much error and great indiligence usually taught in this question, that the wrath of God descends from fathers to children, only in case the children imitate and write after their fathers' copy ; supposing these words—" of them that hate me"—to relate to the children. But this is expressly against the words of the text, and the examples of the thing. God afflicts good children of evil parents for their fathers' sins ; and the words are plain and determinate, God visits the sins of the fathers "in tertiam et quartam generationem eorum qui oderunt me," "to the third generation of them, of those fathers that hate me;" that is, upon the great grand-children of such parents. So that if the great-grandfathers be haters of God and lovers of iniquity, it may entail a curse upon so many generations, though the children be haters of their fathers' hatred, and lovers of God. And this hath been observed even by wise men among the heathens, whose sto-ries tell, that Antigonus was punished for the tyranny of his father Demetrius, Phyleus for his father Augeas, pious and wise Nestor for his father Neleus : and it was so in the case of Jonathan, who lost the kingdom and his life upon the stock of his father's sins ; and the innocent child of David was slain by the anger of God, not against the child, who never had deserved it, but the father's adultery. I need not here repeat what I said in vindication of the divine justice; but I observed this, to represent the danger of a sinning fa-ther or mother, when it shall so infect the family with curses, that it shall ruin a wise and innocent son ; and that virtue and innocence, which shall by God be accepted as sufficient through divine mercy to bring the son to heaven, yet, it may be, shall not be accepted to quit him from feeling the curse of his father's crime in a load of temporal infelicities : and who but a villain would ruin and undo a wise, a virtuous, and his own son ? But so it is in all the world. A traitor is condemned to suffer death himself, and his posterity are made beggars and dishonourable : his escutcheon is reversed, his arms of honour are extinguished, the nobleness of his an-cestors is forgotten : but his own sin is not, while men, by the characters of infamy, are taught to call that family ac-cursed which had so base a father. Tiresias was esteemed unfortunate, because he could not see his friends and child-ren : the poor man was blind with age. But Athamas and Agave were more miserable, who did see their children, but took them for lions and stags : the parents were miserably frantic. But of all, they deplored the misery of Hercules, who, when he saw his children, took them for enemies, and endeavoured to destroy them. And this is the case of all vicious parents. That 'a man's enemies were they of his own house,' was accounted a great calamity : but it is worse when we love them tenderly and fondly, and yet do them all the despite we wish to enemies. But so it is, that in many cases we do more mischief to our children, than if we should strangle them when they are newly taken from their mother's knees, or tear them in pieces as Medea did her brother Absyrtus. For to leave them to inherit a curse, to leave them to an entailed calamity, a misery, a disease, the wrath of God for an inheritance, that it may descend upon them, and remark the family like their coat of arms; is to be the parent of evil, the ruin of our family, the causes of mischief to them who ought to be dearer to us than our own eyes. And let us remember this when we are tempted to provoke the jealous God; let us consider, that his anger hath a progeny, and a descending line, and it may break out in the days of our nephews. A Greek woman was accused of adultery, because she brought forth a blackamoor; and could not acquit herself, till she had proved that she had descended in the fourth degree from an Ethiopian: her great-grandfather was a moor. And, if naturalists say true, that nephews are very often liker to their grandfathers than to their fathers; we see that the semblance of our souls, and the character of the person, is conveyed by secret and undiscernible conveyances. Natural production conveys original sin; and therefore, by the channels of the body, it is not strange that men convey an hereditary sin. And lustful sons are usually born to satyrs; and monsters of intemperance to drunkards: and there are also hereditary diseases; which if in the fathers they were effects of their sin, as it is in many cases, it is notorious that the father's sin is punished, and the punishment conveyed by natural instruments. So that it cannot be a wonder, but it ought to be a huge affrightment from a state of sin; if a man can be capable of so much charity as to love himself in his own person, or in the images of his nature, and heirs of his fortunes, and the supports of his family, in the children that God hath given him. Consider therefore that you do not only act your own tragedies when you sin, but you represent and effect the fortune of your children; you slay them with your own barbarous and inhuman hands. Only be pleased to compare the variety of estates, of your own and your children. If they on earth be miserable many times for their fathers' sins, how great a state of misery is that in hell which they suffer for their own? And how vile a person is that father or mother, who for a little money, or to please a lust, will be a parricide, and imbrue his hands in the blood of his own children.

SERMON IV.

PART II.

4. I AM to consider what remedies there are for sons to cut off this entail of curses; and whether, and by what means, it is possible for sons to prevent the being punished for their fathers' sins. And since this thing is so perplexed and intricate, hath so easy an objection, and so hard an answer, looks so like a cruelty, and so unlike a justice (though it be infinitely just, and very severe, and a huge enemy to sin); it cannot be thought but that there are not only ways left to reconcile God's proceeding to the strict rules of justice, but also the condition of man to the possibilities of God's usual mercies. One said of old, "Ex tarditate si Dii sontes prætereant, et insontes plectant, justitiam suam non sic rectè resarciunt:" "If God be so slow to punish the guilty, that the punishment be deferred till the death of the guilty person; and that God shall be forced to punish the innocent, or to let the sin quite escape unpunished; it will be something hard to join that justice with mercy, or to join that action with justice." Indeed, it will seem strange, but the reason of its justice I have already discoursed: if now we can find how to reconcile this to God's mercy too, or can learn how it may be turned into a mercy, we need to take no other care, but that, for our own particular, we take heed we never tempt God's anger upon our families, and that by competent and apt instruments we endeavour to cancel the decree, if it be gone out against our families; for then we make use of that severity which God intended; and ourselves shall be refreshed in the shades, and by the cooling brooks of the divine mercy, even then when we see the wrath of God breaking out upon the families round about us.

First; the first means to cut off the entail of wrath and cursings from a family, is, for the sons to disavow those sig-

nal actions of impiety, in which their fathers were deeply
guilty, and by which they stained great parts of their life,
or have done something of very great unworthiness and disreputation. "Si quis paterni vitii nascitur hæres, nascitur
et pœnæ;" "The heir of his father's wickedness, is the heir
of his father's curse." And a son comes to inherit a wickedness from his father, three ways.

1. By approving, or any ways consenting to his father's
sin: as by speaking of it without regret or shame; by pleasing himself in the story; or by having an evil mind, apt to
counsel or do the like, if the same circumstances should occur. For a son may contract a sin, not only by derivation
and the contagion of example, but by approbation; not only
by a corporal, but by a virtual contact; not only by transcrib-
ing an evil copy, but by commending it: and a man may
have "animum leprosum in cute munda," 'a leprous and a
polluted mind' even for nothing, even for an empty and ineffective lust. An evil mind may contract the curse of an
evil action. And though the son of a covetous father prove
a prodigal; yet, if he loves his father's vice, for ministering
to his vanity, he is disposed not only to a judgment for his
own prodigality, but also to the curse of his father's avarice.

2. The son may inherit the father's wickedness by imitation and direct practice; and then the curse is like to come
to purpose; a curse by accumulation, a treasure of wrath:
and then the children, as they arrive to the height of wickedness by a speedy passage, as being thrust forward by an
active example, by countenance, by education, by a seldom
restraint, by a remiss discipline; so they ascertain a curse
to the family, by being a perverse generation, a family set
up in opposition against God, by continuing and increasing
the provocation.

3. Sons inherit their fathers' crimes by receiving and enjoying the purchases of their rapine, injustice and oppression, by rising upon the ruin of their father's souls, by sitting
warm in the furs which their fathers stole, and walking in
the grounds which are watered with the tears of oppressed
orphans and widows. Now, in all these cases, the rule holds.
If the son inherits the sin, he cannot call it unjust, if he
inherits also his father's punishment. But, to rescind the
fatal chain, and break in sunder the line of God's anger, a

son is tied in all these cases to disavow his father's crime. But because the cases are several, he must also in several manners do it.

1. Every man is bound not to glory in, or speak honour of, the powerful and unjust actions of his ancestors: but as all the sons of Adam are bound to be ashamed of that original stain, which they derived from the loins of their abused father, they must be humbled in it, they must deplore it as an evil mother, and a troublesome daughter; so must children account it amongst the crosses of their family, and the stains of their honour, that they passed through so impure channels, that in the sense of morality as well as nature they can " say to corruption, Thou art my father, and to rottenness, Thou art my mother." I do not say, that sons are bound to publish or declaim against their fathers' crimes, and to speak of their shame in piazzas and before tribunals; that indeed were a sure way to bring their fathers' sins upon their own heads, by their own faults. No: like Shem and Japhet, they must go backward, and cast a veil upon their nakedness and shame, lest they bring the curse of their fathers' angry dishonour upon their own impious and unrelenting heads. Noah's drunkenness fell upon Ham's head, because he did not hide the openness of his father's follies: he made his father ridiculous; but did not endeavour either to amend the sin, or to wrap the dishonour in a pious covering. He that goes to disavow his father's sin by publishing his shame, hides an ill-face with a more ugly vizor, and endeavours by torches and fantastic lights to quench the burning of that house which his father set on fire: these fires are to be smothered, and so extinguished. I deny not, but it may become the piety of a child to tell a sad story, to mourn, and represent a real grief for so great a misery, as is a wicked father or mother: but this is to be done with a tenderness as nice as we would dress an eye withal: it must be only with designs of charity, of counsel, of ease, and with much prudence, and a sad spirit. These things being secured, that which in this case remains, is, that in all intercourses between God and ourselves we disavow the crime.

Children are bound to pray to God to sanctify, to cure, to forgive, their parents: and even, concerning the sins of our forefathers, the church hath taught us in her litanies, to pray

that God would be pleased to forgive them, so that neither
we, nor they, may sink under the wrath of God for them :
" Remember not, Lord, our offences, nor the offences of
our forefathers, neither take thou vengeance of our sins:"
Ours, in common and conjunction. And David confessed to
God, and humbled himself for the sins of his ancestors and
decessors : " Our fathers have done amiss, and dealt wickedly, neither kept they thy great goodness in remembrance,
but were disobedient at the sea, even at the Red Sea." So
did good King Josiah; " Great is the wrath of the Lord, which
is kindled against us, because our fathers have not hearkened
unto the words of this book[d]." But this is to be done between God and ourselves : or, if in public, then to be done
by general accusation; that God only may read our particular sorrows in the single shame of our families, registered in
our hearts, and represented to him with humiliation, shame,
and a hearty prayer.

2. Those curses, which descend from the fathers to the
children by imitation of the crimes of their progenitors, are to
be cut off by special and personal repentance and prayer, as
being a state directly opposite to that which procured the
curse: and if the sons be pious, or return to an early and
severe course of holy living, they are to be remedied as other
innocent and pious persons are, who are sufferers under
the burdens of their relatives, whom I shall consider by and
by. Only observe this; that no public or imaginative dis-
avowings, no ceremonial and pompous rescission of our fathers' crimes, can be sufficient to interrupt the succession of
the curse, if the children do secretly practise or approve what
they in pretence or ceremony disavow. And this is clearly
proved; and it will help to explicate that difficult saying of
our blessed Saviour, " Wo unto you, for ye build the sepulchres of the prophets, and your fathers killed them. Truly
ye bear witness that ye allow the deeds of your fathers :
for they killed them, and ye build their sepulchres[e]:" that
is, the Pharisees were huge hypocrites, and adorned the
monuments of the martyr-prophets, and in words disclaimed
their fathers' sin, but in deeds and design they approved
it ; 1. Because they secretly wished all such persons dead ;
" colebant mortuos, quos nollent superstites :" In charity

---

to themselves some men wish their enemies in heaven, and
would be at charges for a monument for them, that their
malice, and their power, and their bones, might rest in the
same grave; and yet that wish and that expense is no testimony of their charity, but of their anger. 2. These men
were willing that the monuments of those prophets should
remain, and be a visible affrightment to all such bold persons
and severe reprehenders as they were; and, therefore, they
builded their sepulchres to be as beacons and publications of
danger to all honest preachers. And this was the account
St. Chrysostom gave of the place. 3. To which also the
circumstances of the place concur. For they only said, " If
they had lived in their fathers' days, they would not have
done as they did^f;" but it is certain they approved it, because
they pursued the same courses: and, therefore, our blessed
Saviour calls them γενεὰν ἀποκτίνουσαν, not only the children of them that did kill the prophets, but ' a killing generation;' the sin also descends upon you, for ye have the same
killing mind : and although you honour them that are dead,
and cannot shame you; yet you design the same usages
against them that are alive, even against the Lord of the prophets, against Christ himself, whom ye will kill. And as
Dion said of Caracalla, Πᾶσι τοῖς ἀγαθοῖς ἀνδράσιν ἀχθόμενος,
τιμᾷν τινὰς αὐτῶν ἀποθανόντας ἐπλάττετο, " The man was troublesome to all good men when they were alive, but did them
honour when they were dead^g ;" and when Herod had killed
Aristobulus, yet he made him a most magnificent funeral : so,
because the Pharisees were of the same humour, therefore our
blessed Saviour bids them " to fill up the measure of their fathers' iniquity ^h;" for they still continued the malice, only they
painted it over with a pretence of piety, and of disavowing their
fathers' sin ; which if they had done really, their being children of persecutors, much less the ' adorning of the prophets'
sepulchres,' could not have been just cause of a woe from
Christ; this being an act of piety, and the other of nature,
inevitable and not chosen by them, and therefore not chargeable upon them. He therefore that will to real purposes
disavow his father's crimes, must do it heartily, and humbly,
and charitably, and throw off all affections to the like actions. For he that finds fault with his father for killing

^f Matt. xxiii. 30.   ^g Reimar. t. 2. p. 1302.   ^h Matt. xxiii. 32.

Isaiah or Jeremy, and himself shall kill Aristobulus and John the Baptist; he that is angry because the old prophets were murdered, and shall imprison and beggar and destroy the new ones; he that disavows the persecution in the primitive times, and honours the memory of the dead martyrs, and yet every day makes new ones; he that blames the oppres- sion of the country by any of his predecessors, and yet shall continue to oppress his tenants, and all that are within his gripe; that man cannot hope to be eased from the curse of his father's sins: he goes on to imitate them, and, there- fore, to fill up their measure, and to reap a full treasure of wrath.

3. But concerning the third, there is yet more difficulty. Those persons that inherit their fathers' sins by possessing the price of their fathers' souls, that is, by enjoying the goods gotten by their fathers' rapine, may certainly quit the inherit- ance of the curse, if they quit the purchase of the sin, that is, if they pay their fathers' debts; his debts of contract, and his debts of justice; his debts of intercourse, and his debts of oppression. I do not say that every man is bound to re- store all the land, which his ancestors have unjustly snatch- ed: for when by law the possession is established, though the grandfather entered like a thief, yet the grandchild is 'bonæ fidei' possessor, and may enjoy it justly. And the rea- sons of this are great and necessary; for the avoiding eter- nal suits, and perpetual diseases of the rest and conscience; because there is no estate in the world that could be enjoy- ed: by any man honestly, if posterity were bound to make restitution of all the wrongs done by their progenitors. But although the children of the far-removed lines are not obliged to restitution, yet others are: and some for the same, some for other reasons.

1. Sons are tied to restore what their fathers did usurp, or to make agreement and an acceptable recompense for it, if the case be visible, evident, and notorious, and the op- pressed party demands it: because in this case the law hath not settled the possession in the new tenant; or if a judge hath, it is by injury; and there is yet no collateral accident- al title transferred by long possession, as it is in other cases: and therefore, if the son continues to oppress the same per- son whom his father first injured, he may well expect to be

the heir of his father's curse, as well as of his cursed purchase.

2. Whether by law and justice, or not, the person be obliged, nay, although by all the solemnities of law the unjust purchase be established, and that in conscience the grandchildren be not obliged to restitution in their own particulars, but may continue to enjoy it without a new sin; yet if we see a curse descending upon the family for the old oppression done in the days of our grandfathers, or if we probably suspect that to be the cause; then, if we make restitution, we also most certainly remove the curse, because we take away the matter upon which the curse is grounded. I do not say, we sin, if we do not restore: but that, if we do not, we may still be punished. The reason of this is clear and visible: for as without our faults, in many cases, we may enjoy those lands which our forefathers got unjustly; so without our faults we may be punished for them. For as they have transmitted the benefit to us, it is but reasonable we should suffer the appendant calamity. If we receive good, we must also venture the evil that comes along with it. " Res transit cum suo onere:" " All lands and possessions pass with their proper burdens."—And if any of my ancestors was a tenant, and a servant, and held his lands as a villain to his lord ; his posterity also must do so, though accidentally they become noble. The case is the same. If my ancestors entered unjustly, there is a curse and a plague that is due to that oppression and injustice ; and that is ' the burden of the land,' and it descends all along with it. And although I, by the consent of laws, am a just possessor, yet I am obliged to the burden that comes with the land : I am indeed another kind of person than my grandfather; he was a usurper, but I am a just possessor ; but, because in respect of the land this was but an accidental change, therefore I still am liable to the burden, and the curse that descends with it. But the way to take off the curse is to quit the title ; and yet a man may choose. It may be, to lose the land would be the bigger curse : but, if it be not, the way is certain how you may be rid of it. There was a custom among the Greeks, that the children of them, that died of consumptions or dropsies, all the while their fathers' bodies were burning on their funeral piles, did sit with their feet in cold water, hoping

that such a lustration and ceremony would take off the
lineal and descending contagion from the children.   I know
not what cure they found by their superstition : but we may
be sure, that if we wash (not our feet, but) our hands of all
the unjust purchases which our fathers have transmitted to us,
their hydropic thirst of wealth shall not transmit to us a consumption of estate, or any other curse.   But this remedy is
only in the matter of injury or oppression, not in the case of
other sins ; because other sins were transient ; and, as the
guilt did not pass upon the children, so neither did the exterior and permanent effect : and, therefore, in other sins (in
case they do derive a curse) it cannot be removed, as in the
matter of unjust possession it may be ; whose effect (we may
so order it) shall no more stick to us, than the guilt of our fathers' personal actions.

The sum is this : as kingdoms use to expiate the faults
of others by acts of justice ; and as churches use to 'remove
the accursed thing' from sticking to the communities of the
faithful, and the sins of Christians from being required of
the whole congregation, by excommunicating and censuring
the delinquent persons ; so the heirs and sons of families are
to remove from their house the curse descending from their
fathers' loins—1. by acts of disavowing the sins of their
ancestors ; 2. by praying for pardon ; 3. by being humbled
for them ; 4. by renouncing the example ; and, 5. quitting
the affection to the crimes : 6. by not imitating the actions
in kind, or in semblance and similitude : and, lastly, 7. by
refusing to rejoice in the ungodly purchases, in which their
fathers did amiss, and dealt wickedly.

Secondly ; but, after all this, many cases do occur, in
which we find that innocent sons are punished. The remedies I have already discoursed of, are for such children, who
have, in some manner or other, contracted and derived the
sin upon themselves : but if we inquire how those sons,—who
have no intercourse or affinity with their fathers' sins, or
whose fathers' sins were so transient that no benefit or effect
did pass upon their posterity,—how they may prevent, or take
off, the curse that lies upon the family for their fathers'
faults ; this will have some distant considerations.

1. The pious children of evil parents are to stand firm
upon the confidence of the divine grace and mercy, and

upon that persuasion to begin to work upon a new stock. For it is as certain, that he may derive a blessing upon his posterity, as that his parents could transmit a curse : and if any man by piety shall procure God's favour to his relatives and children, it is certain that he hath done more than to escape the punishment of his father's follies. ' If sin doth abound,' and evils by sin are derived from his parents; ' much more shall grace super-abound,' and mercy by grace. If he was in danger from the crimes of others, much rather shall he be secured by his own piety. For if God punishes the sins of the fathers to four generations; yet he rewards the piety of fathers to ten, to hundreds, and to thousands. Many of the ancestors of Abraham were persons not noted for religion, but suffered in the public impiety and almost universal idolatry of their ages : and yet all the evils that could thence descend upon the family, were wiped off; and God began to reckon with Abraham upon a new stock of blessings and piety; and he was, under God, the original of so great a blessing, that his family, for fifteen hundred years together, had from him a title to many favours ; and whatever evils did chance to them in the descending ages, were but single evils in respect of that treasure of mercies, which the father's piety had obtained to the whole nation. And it is remarkable to observe, how blessings did stick to them for their father's sakes, even whether they would or no. For, first, his grandchild Esau proved a naughty man, and he lost the great blessing which was entailed upon the family ; but he got, not a curse, but a less blessing : and yet, because he lost the greater blessing, God excluded him from being reckoned in the elder line : for God, foreseeing the event, so ordered it, that he should first lose his birthright, and then lose the blessing ; for it was to be certain, the family must be reckoned for prosperous in the proper line ; and yet God blessed Esau into a great nation, and made him the father of many princes. Now the line of blessing being reckoned in Jacob, God blessed his family strangely, and by miracle, for almost five generations. He brought them from Egypt by mighty signs and wonders : and when for sin they all died in their way to Canaan, two only excepted, God so ordered it, that they were all reckoned as single deaths ; the nation still descended, like a river, whose waters were drunk up for the beverage of an army, but still it keeps its name and current, and the waters are supplied by showers, and springs, and providence. After this, iniquity still increased, and then God struck deeper, and spread curses upon whole families; he translated the priesthood from line to line, he removed the kingdom from one family to another: and still they sinned worse; and then we read that God smote almost a whole tribe; the tribe of Benjamin was almost extinguished about the matter of the Levite's concubine: but still God remembered his promise, which he made with their forefathers, and that breach was made up. After this we find a great rupture made, and ten tribes fell into idolatry, and ten tribes were carried captives into Assyria, and never came again: but still God remembered his covenant with Abraham, and left two tribes. But they were restless in their provocation of the God of Abraham; and they also were carried captive: but still God was the God of their fathers, and brought them back, and placed them safe, and they grew again into a kingdom, and should have remained for ever, but that they killed one that was greater than Abraham, even the Messias; and then they were rooted out, and the old covenant cast off, and God delighted no more to be called 'the God of Abraham,' but the 'Father of our Lord Jesus Christ.' As long as God kept that relation, so long for the fathers' sakes they had a title and an inheritance to a blessing: for so saith St. Paul, "As touching the election, they are beloved, for the fathers' sakes [b]."

I insist the longer upon this instance, that I may remonstrate how great, and how sure, and how preserving mercies a pious father of a family may derive upon his succeeding generations: and if we do but tread in the footsteps of our father Abraham, we shall inherit as certain blessings. But then, I pray, add these considerations.

2. If a great impiety and a clamorous wickedness hath stained the honour of a family, and discomposed its title to the divine mercies and protection, it is not an ordinary piety that can restore this family. An ordinary even course of life, full of sweetness and innocence, will secure every single person in his own eternal interest: but that piety, which must be a spring of blessings, and communicative to others,

[b] Rom. xi. 28.

that must plead against the sins of their ancestors, and begin a new bank of mercies for the relatives; that must be a great and excellent, a very religious state of life. A small pension will maintain a single person : but he that hath a numerous family, and many to provide for, needs a greater providence of God, and a bigger provision for their maintenance : and a small revenue will not keep up the dignity of a great house; especially if it be charged with a great debt. And this is the very state of the present question. That piety that must be instrumental to take off the curse imminent upon a family, to bless a numerous posterity, to secure a fair condition to many ages, and to pay the debts of their fathers' sins, must be so large, as that, all necessary expenses and duties for his own soul being first discharged, it may be remarkable in great expressions, it may be exemplar to all the family, it may be of universal efficacy, large in the extension of parts, deep in the intention of degrees : and then, as the root of a tree receives nourishment not only sufficient to preserve its own life, but to transmit a plastic juice to the trunk of the tree, and from thence to the utmost branch and smallest germ that knots in the most distant part; so shall the great and exemplar piety of the father of a family not only preserve to the interest of his own soul the life of grace and hopes of glory, but shall be a quickening spirit, active and communicative of a blessing, not only to the trunk of the tree, to the body and rightly-descending line, but even to the collateral branches, to the most distant relatives, and all that shall claim a kindred, shall have a title to a blessing. And this was the way that was prescribed to the family of Eli, upon whom a sad curse was entailed, that there should not be an old man of the family for ever, and that they should be beggars, and lose the office of priesthood : by the counsel of R. Johanan, the son of Zaccheus, all the family betook themselves to a great, a strict, and a severe religion ; and God was entreated to revoke his decree, to be reconciled to the family, to restore them to the common condition of men, from whence they stood separate by the displeasure of God against the crime of Eli, and his sons Hophni and Phineas. This course is sure either to take off the judgment, or to change it into a blessing; to take away the rod, or the smart and evil of it ; to convert the punishment into a mere natural or human chance, and that chance to the opportunity of a virtue, and that virtue to the occasion of a crown.

3. It is of great use for the securing of families, that every master of a family order his life so, that his piety and virtue be as communicative as is possible; that is, that he secure the religion of his whole family by a severe supravision and animadversion, and by cutting off all those unprofitable and hurtful branches which load the tree, and hinder the growth, and stock and disimprove the fruit, and revert evil juice to the very root itself. Calvisius Sabinus laid out vast sums of money upon his servants to stock his house with learned men; and brought one that could recite all Homer by heart, a second that was ready at Hesiod,—a third, at Pindar,—and for every of the lyrics, one; having this fancy, that all that learning was his own, and whatsoever his servants knew, made him so much the more skilful. It was noted in the man for a rich and prodigal folly: but if he had changed his instance, and brought none but virtuous servants into his house, he might better have reckoned his wealth upon their stock, and the piety of his family might have helped to bless him, and to have increased the treasure of his master's virtue. Every man that would either cut off the title of an old curse, or secure a blessing upon a new stock, must make virtue as large in the fountain as he can, that it may the sooner water all his relatives with fruitfulness and blessings. And this was one of the things that God noted in Abraham, and blessed his family for it, and his posterity: 'I know that Abraham will teach his sons to fear me.' When a man teaches his family to know and fear God, then he scatters a blessing round about his habitation. And this helps to illustrate the reason of the thing, as well as to prove its certainty. We hear it spoken in our books of religion, that the faith of the parents is imputed to their children to good purposes, and that a good husband sanctifies an ill wife, and ' a believing wife, an unbelieving husband;' and either of them makes the children to be sanctified, ' else they were unclean and unholy;' that is, the very designing children to the service of God is a sanctification of them; and therefore St. Jerome calls Christian children " candidatos fidei Christianæ.' And if this very designation of them makes them holy, that

is, acceptable to God, entitled to the promises, partakers of
the covenant, within the condition of sons; much more shall
it be effectual to greater blessings, when the parents take
care that the children shall be actually pious, full of sobriety,
full of religion; then it becomes a holy house, a chosen generation, and an elect family; and then there can no evil happen
to them, but such which will bring them nearer to God: that
is, no cross, but the cross of Christ; no misfortune, but that
which shall lead them to felicity; and if any semblance of a
curse happens in the generations, it is but like the anathema
of a sacrifice; not an accursed, but a devoted thing: for so
the sacrifice, upon whose neck the priest's knife doth fall, is so
far from being accursed, that it helps to get a blessing to all
that join in the oblation. So every misfortune, that shall discompose the ease of a pious and religious family, shall but
make them fit to be presented unto God; and the rod of
God shall be like the branches of fig-trees, bitter and sharp
in themselves, but productive of most delicious fruit. No
evil can curse the family whose stock is pious, and whose
'branches are holiness to the Lord.' If any leaf or any
boughs shall fall untimely, God shall gather them up, and
place them in his temple, or at the foot of his throne; and
that family must needs be blessed, whom infelicity itself
cannot make accursed.

4. If a curse be feared to descend upon a family for the
fault of their ancestors, pious sons have yet another way to
secure themselves, and to withdraw the curse from the family, or themselves from the curse; and that is, by doing some
very great and illustrious act of piety, an action 'in gradu
heroico,' as Aristotle calls it, 'an heroical action.' If there
should happen to be one martyr in a family, it would reconcile the whole kindred to God, and make him, who is more
inclined to mercy than to severity, rather to be pleased with
the relatives of the martyr, than to continue to be angry with
the nephews of a deceased sinner. I cannot insist long upon
this: but you may see it proved by one great instance in the
case of Phineas, who killed an unclean prince, and turned
the wrath of God from his people. He was zealous for God
and for his countrymen, and did a heroical action of zeal:
"Wherefore" (saith God), "Behold I give unto him my covenant
of peace, and he shall have it, and his seed after him; even

the covenant of an everlasting priesthood; because he was zealous for his God, and made an atonement for the children of Israel." Thus the sons of Rechab obtained the blessing of an enduring and blessed family, because they were most strict and religious observers of their father's precepts, and kept them after his death, and abstained from wine for ever; and no temptation could invite them to taste it; for they had as great reverence to their father's ashes, as, being children, they had to his rod and to his eyes. Thus a man may turn the wrath of God from his family, and secure a blessing for posterity, by doing some great noble acts of charity; or a remarkable chastity like that of Joseph; or an expensive, an affectionate religion and love to Christ and his servants, as Mary Magdalen did. Such things as these which are extraordinary egressions and transvolations beyond the ordinary course of an even piety, God loves to reward with an extraordinary favour; and gives them testimony by an extraregular blessing.

One thing more I have to add by way of advice; and that is, that all parents and fathers of families, from whose loins a blessing or a curse usually does descend, be very careful, not only generally in all the actions of our lives (for that I have already pressed), but particularly in the matter of repentance; that they be curious that they finish it, and do it thoroughly: for there are certain ὑστερήματα μετανοίας, 'leavings of repentance,' which make that God's anger is taken from us so imperfectly: and although God, for his sake who died for us, will pardon a returning sinner, and bring him to heaven through tribulation and a fiery trial; yet,—when a man is weary of his sorrow, and his fastings are a load to him, and his sins are not so perfectly renounced, or hated as they ought,—the parts of repentance, which are left unfinished, do sometimes fall upon the heads or upon the fortunes of the children. I do not say, this is regular and certain; but sometimes God deals thus: for this thing hath been so, and therefore it may be so again. We see it was done in the case of Ahab; he " humbled himself, and went softly, and lay in sackcloth," and called for pardon, and God took from him a judgment which was falling heavily upon him : but we all know his repentance was imperfect and lame : the same evil fell upon his sons ; for so said God: " I will bring the evil upon his house in his son's days." Leave no arrears for thy posterity to pay; but repent with an integral, a holy and excellent repentance, that God being reconciled to thee thoroughly, for thy sake also he may bless thy seed after thee.

And, after all this, add a continual, a fervent, a hearty, a never-ceasing prayer for thy children, ever remembering, when they beg a blessing, that God hath put much of their fortune into your hands; and a transient formal ' God bless thee,' will not outweigh the load of a great vice, and the curse which scatters from thee by virtual contact, and by the channels of relation, if thou heest a vicious person : nothing can issue from thy fountain but bitter waters. And, as it were a great impudence for a condemned traitor to beg of his injured prince a province for his son for his sake: so it is an ineffective blessing we give our children, when we beg for them what we have no title to for ourselves ; nay, when we convey to them nothing but a curse. The prayer of a sinner, the unhallowed wish of a vicious parent, is but a poor donative to give to a child who sucked poison from his nurse, and derives cursing from his parents. They are punished with a doubled torture in the shame and pain of the damned, who, dying enemies to God, have left an inventory of sins and wrath to be divided amongst their children. But they that can truly give a blessing to their children, are such as live a blessed life, and pray holy prayers, and perform an integral repentance, and do separate from the sins of their progenitors, and do illustrious actions, and begin the blessing of their family upon a new stock. For as from the eyes of some persons there shoots forth an evil influence, and some have an evil eye, and are infectious, some look healthfully as a friendly planet, and innocent as flowers ; and as some fancies convey private effects to confederate and allied bodies ; and between the very vital spirits of friends and relatives there is a cognation, and they refresh each other like social plants; and a good man is a[i] friend to every good man : and (they say) that a usurer knows a usurer, and one rich man another, there being by the very manners of men contracted a similitude of nature, and a communication of effects : so in parents and their children there is so great a society of nature and of manners, of blessing and

[i] Διαμένει ἀν τούτων φιλία, ἕως ἂν ἀγαθοὶ ὦσιν ἡ δ' ἀρετὴ μόνιμον. *Arist.*

cursing, that an evil parent cannot perish in a single death; and holy parents never eat their meal of blessing alone, but they make the room shine like the fire of a holy sacrifice; and a father's or a mother's piety makes all the house festival and full of joy from generation to generation. Amen.

SERMON V.

THE INVALIDITY OF A LATE OR DEATH-BED REPENTANCE.

PART I.

Give glory to the Lord your God, before he cause darkness, and before your feet stumble upon the dark mountains, and while ye look for light (or, lest while ye look for light), he shall turn it into the shadow of death, and make it gross darkness.—
Jeremiah, xiii. 16.

GOD is the eternal fountain of honour and the spring of glory; in him it dwells essentially, from him it derives originally; and when an action is glorious, or a man is honourable, it is because the action is pleasing to God, in the relation of obedience or imitation, and because the man is honoured by God, and by God's vicegerent: and therefore, God cannot be dishonoured, because all honour comes from himself; he cannot but be glorified, because to be himself is to be infinitely glorious. And yet he is pleased to say, that our sins dishonour him, and our obedience does glorify him. But as the sun, the great eye of the world, prying into the recesses of rocks and the hollowness of valleys, receives species or visible forms from these objects, but he beholds them only by that light which proceeds from himself: so does God, who is the light of that eye; he receives reflexes and returns from us, and these he calls 'glorifications' of himself, but they are such which are made so by his own gracious acceptation. For God cannot be glorified by any thing but by himself, and by his own instruments, which he makes as mirrors to reflect his own excellency; that by seeing the glory of

such emanations, he may rejoice in his own works, because
they are images of his infinity. Thus when he made the
beauteous frame of heaven and earth, he rejoiced in it, and
glorified himself; because it was the glass in which he beheld his wisdom and almighty power. And when God destroyed the old world, in that also he glorified himself; for
in those waters he saw the image of his justice,—they were
the looking-glass for that attribute; and God is said 'to
laugh at' and ' rejoice in the destruction of a sinner,' because
he is pleased with the economy of his own laws, and the excellent proportions he hath made of his judgments consequent to our sins. But, above all, God rejoiced in his holy
Son; for he was the image of the Divinity, ' the character
and express image of his person;' in him he beheld his own
essence, his wisdom, his power, his justice, and his person;
and he was that excellent instrument designed from eternal
ages to represent, as in a double mirror, not only the glories
of God to himself, but also to all the world; and he glorified
God by the instrument of obedience, in which God beheld
his own dominion and the sanctity of his laws clearly represented ; and he saw his justice glorified, when it was fully
satisfied by the passion of his Son: and so he hath transmitted to us a great manner of the divine glorification, being
become to us the author and example of giving glory to God
after the manner of men, that is, by well-doing and patient
suffering, by obeying his laws and submitting to his power,
by imitating his holiness and confessing his goodness, by
remaining innocent or becoming penitent; for this also is
called in the text " giving glory to the Lord our God."

For he that hath dishonoured God by sins, that is, hath
denied, by a moral instrument of duty and subordination, to
confess the glories of his power, and the goodness of his
laws, and hath dishonoured and despised his mercy, which
God intended as an instrument of our piety, hath no better
way to glorify God, than by returning to his duty, to advance
the honour of the divine attributes, in which he is pleased
to communicate himself, and to have intercourse with man.
He that repents, confesses his own error, and the righteousness of God's laws,—and by judging himself confesses
that he deserves punishment,—and therefore, that God is
righteous if he punishes him: and, by returning, con-

fesses God to be the fountain of felicity, and the foundation of true, solid, and permanent joys, saying in the sense and passion of the disciples, "Whither shall we go? for thou hast the words of eternal life :" and, by humbling himself, exalts God, by making the proportions of distance more immense and vast. And as repentance does contain in it all the parts of holy life, which can be performed by a returning sinner (all the acts and habits of virtue being but parts, or instances, or effects of repentance): so all the actions of a holy life do constitute the mass and body of all those instruments, whereby God is pleased to glorify himself. For if God is glorified in the sun and moon, in the rare fabric of the honeycombs, in the discipline of bees, in the economy of pismires, in the little houses of birds, in the curiosity of an eye, God being pleased to delight in those little images and reflexes of himself from those pretty mirrors, which, like a crevice in the wall, through a narrow perspective, transmit the species of a vast excellency: much rather shall God be pleased to behold himself in the glasses of our obedience, in the emissions of our will and understanding; these being rational and apt instruments to express him, far better than the natural, as being nearer communications of himself.

But I shall no longer discourse of the philosophy of this expression: certain it is, that in the style of Scripture, repentance is the great ' glorification of God ;' and the prophet, by calling the people to ' give God glory,' calls upon them ' to repent,' and so expresses both the duty and the event of it; the event being "glory to God on high, peace on earth, and good-will towards men" by the sole instrument of repentance. And this was it which Joshua said to Achan, " Give, I pray thee, glory to the Lord God of Israel, and make confession unto him[k] :" that one act of repentance is one act of glorifying God. And this David acknowledged ; " Against thee only have I sinned : ' ut tu justificeris,' that thou mightest be justified or cleared[l] :" that is, that God may have the honour of being righteous, and we the shame of receding from so excellent a perfection ; or, as St. Paul quotes and explicates the place, " Let God be true, and every man a liar; as it is written, that thou mightest be justified in thy sayings, and mightest overcome when thou art judged[m]."

[k] Joshua, vii. 19.   [l] Psal. li. 4.   [m] Rom. iii. 4.

But to clear the sense of this expression of the prophet, observe the words of St. John; "And men were scorched with great heat, and blasphemed the name of God, who hath power over those plagues: and they repented not to give him glory[a]."

So that having strength and reason from these so many authorities, I may be free to read the words of my text thus; "Repent of all your sins, before God cause darkness, and before your feet stumble upon the dark mountains." And then we have here the duty of repentance, and the time of its performance. It must be μετάνοια εὔκαιρος, 'a seasonable and timely repentance,' a repentance which must begin before our darkness begin, a repentance in the day-time; "ut dum dies est, operemini," "that ye may work while it is to-day:" lest, if we 'stumble upon the dark mountains,' that is, fall into the ruins of old age, which makes a broad way narrow, and a plain way to be a craggy mountain; or if we stumble and fall into our last sickness, instead of health God send us to our grave,—and instead of light and salvation, which we then confidently look for, he make our state to be outer darkness, that is, misery irremediable, misery eternal.

This exhortation of the prophet was always full of caution and prudence, but now it is highly necessary; since men, who are so clamorously called to repentance, that they cannot avoid the necessity of it, yet, that they may reconcile an evil life with the hopes of heaven, have crowded this duty into so little room, that it is almost strangled and extinct; and they have lopped off so many members, that they have reduced the whole body of it to the dimensions of a little finger, sacrificing their childhood to vanity, their youth to lust and to intemperance, their manhood to ambition and rage, pride and revenge, secular desires, and unholy actions; and yet still farther, giving their old age to covetousness and oppression, to the world and the devil: and, after all this, what remains for God and for religion? Oh, for that they will do well enough: upon their death-bed they will think a few godly thoughts, they will send for a priest to minister comfort to them, they will pray and ask God forgiveness, and receive the holy sacrament, and leave their goods behind them, disposing them to their friends and relatives, and some

[a] Rev. xvi. 9.

dole and issues of the alms-basket to the poor; and if after all this they die quietly, and like a lamb, and be canonized by a bribed flatterer in a funeral sermon, they make no doubt but they are children of the kingdom, and perceive not their folly, till without hope of remedy, they roar in their expectations of a certain, but a horrid eternity of pains. Certainly nothing hath made more ample harvests for the devil, than the deferring of repentance upon vain confidences, and lessening it in the extension of parts as well as intention of degrees, while we imagine that a few tears and scatterings of devotion, are enough to expiate the baseness of a fifty or a threescore years' impiety. This I shall endeavour to cure, by shewing what it is to repent, and that repentance implies in it the duty of a life, or of many and great, of long and lasting parts of it; and then, by direct arguments, shewing that repentance put off to our death-bed, is invalid and ineffectual, sick, languid, and impotent, like our dying bodies and disabled faculties.

1. First, therefore, repentance implies a deep sorrow, as the beginning and introduction of this duty: not a superficial sigh or tear, not a calling ourselves sinners and miserable persons; this is far from that 'godly sorrow that worketh repentance:' and yet I wish there were none in the world, or none amongst us, who cannot remember that ever they have done this little towards the abolition of their multitudes of sins: but yet, if it were not a hearty, pungent sorrow, a sorrow that shall break the heart in pieces, a sorrow that shall so irreconcile us to sin, as to make us rather choose to die than to sin, it is not so much as the beginning of repentance. But in Holy Scripture, when the people are called to repentance, and sorrow (which is ever the prologue to it) marches sadly, and first opens the scene, it is ever expressed to be great, clamorous, and sad: it is called 'a weeping sorely' in the next verse after my text; 'a weeping with the bitterness of heart;' 'a turning to the Lord with weeping, fasting, and mourning°;' 'a weeping day and night;' the 'sorrow of heart;' the 'breaking of the spirit;' the 'mourning like a dove,' and 'chattering like a swallowᴾ.' And if we observe the threnes and sad accents of the Prophet Jeremy, when he wept for the sins of his nation; the

° Ezek. xxvii. 31.   ᴾ Joel, ii. 13.

heart-breakings of David, when he mourned for his adultery and murder; and the bitter tears of St. Peter, when he washed off the guilt and baseness of his fall, and the denying his Master; we shall be sufficiently instructed in this ' præludium' or ' introduction' to repentance; and that it is not every breath of a sigh, or moisture of a tender eye, not every crying " Lord have mercy upon me," that is such a sorrow, as begins our restitution to the state of grace and divine favour; but such a sorrow, that really condemns ourselves, and by an active, effectual sentence, declares us worthy of stripes and death, of sorrow and eternal pains, and willingly endures the first to prevent the second; and weeps, and mourns, and fasts, to obtain of God but to admit us to a possibility of restitution. And although all sorrow for sins hath not the same expression, nor the same degree of pungency and sensitive trouble, which differs according to the temper of the body, custom, the sex, and accidental tenderness [q]; yet it is not a godly sorrow, unless it really produce those effects: that is, 1. that it makes us really to hate, and 2. actually to decline sin; and 3. produce in us a fear of God's anger, a sense of the guilt of his displeasure; and 4. then such consequent trouble as can consist with such apprehension of the divine displeasure: which, if it express not in tears and hearty complaints, must be expressed in watchings and strivings against sin; in confessing the goodness and justice of God threatening or punishing us; in patiently bearing the rod of God; in confession of our sins; in accusation of ourselves; in perpetual begging of pardon, and mean and base opinions of ourselves; and in all the natural productions from these, according to our temper and constitution: it must be a sorrow of the reasonable faculty, the greatest in its kind: and if it be less in kind, or not productive of these effects, it is not a godly sorrow, not the ' exordium' of repentance.

But I desire that it be observed, that sorrow for sins is not repentance; not that duty which gives glory to God, so as to obtain of him that he will glorify us. Repentance is a great volume of duty; and godly sorrow is but the frontispiece or title-page; it is the harbinger or first introduction to it: or, if you will consider it in the words of St. Paul,

[q] See Rule of H. Living. D. of Repentance, vol. iv. p. 257.

" Godly sorrow worketh repentance¹ :" sorrow is the parent, and repentance is the product. And, therefore, it is a high piece of ignorance to suppose, that a crying out and roaring for our sins upon our death-bed can reconcile us to God : our crying to God must be so early and so lasting, as to be able to teem and produce such a daughter, which must live long, and grow from an embryo to an infant, from infancy to childhood, from thence to the fulness of the stature of Christ; and then it is a holy and a happy sorrow. But if it be a sorrow only of a death-bed, it is a fruitless shower; or like the rain of Sodom, not the beginning of repentance, but the kindling of a flame, the commencement of an eternal sorrow. For Ahab had a great sorrow, but it wrought nothing upon his spirit; it did not reconcile his affections to his duty, and his duty to God. Judas had so great a sorrow for betraying the innocent blood of his Lord, that it was intolerable to his spirit, and he ' burst in the middle.' And if mere sorrow be repentance, then hell is full of penitents; for 'there is weeping, and wailing, and gnashing of teeth, for evermore.'

Let us, therefore, beg of God, as Caleb's daughter did of her father ; " Dedisti mihi terram aridam, da etiam et irriguam," "Thou hast given me a dry land, give me also a land of waters, a dwelling-place in tears, rivers of tears :" " Ut, quoniam non sumus digni oculos orando ad cœlum levare, at simus digni oculos plorando cæcare," as St. Austin's expression is; " That because we are not worthy to lift up our eyes to heaven in prayer, yet we may be worthy to weep ourselves blind for sin."—The meaning is, that we beg sorrow of God, such a sorrow as may be sufficient to quench the flames of lust, and surmount the hills of our pride, and may extinguish our thirst of covetousness ; that is a sorrow that shall be an effective principle of arming all our faculties against sin, and heartily setting upon the work of grace, and the persevering labours of a holy life. I shall only add one word to this : that our sorrow for sin is not to be estimated by our tears and our sensible expressions, but by our active hatred and dereliction of sin ; and is many times unperceived in outward demonstration. It is reported of the mother of Peter Lombard, Gratian, and Comestor, that she

¹ 2 Cor. vii. 10.

having bad three sons begotten in unhallowed embraces, upon her death-bed did omit the recitation of those crimes to her confessor; adding this for apology, that her three sons proved persons so eminent in the church, that their excellence was abundant recompense for her demerit; and therefore, she could not grieve, because God had glorified himself so much by three instruments so excellent; and that although her sin had abounded, yet God's grace did superabound. Her confessor replied, " At dole saltem, quod dolere non possis," " Grieve that thou canst not grieve." And so must we always fear, that our trouble for sin is not great enough, that our sorrow is too remiss, that our affections are indifferent: but we can only be sure that our sorrow is a godly sorrow, when it worketh repentance; that is, when it makes us bate and leave all our sin, and take up the cross of patience or penance; that is, confess our sin, accuse ourselves, condemn the action by hearty sentence: and then, if it bath no other emanation but fasting and prayer for its pardon, and hearty industry towards its abolition, our sorrow is not reprovable.

2. For sorrow alone will not do it; there must follow a total dereliction of our sin; and this is the first part of repentance. Concerning which I consider, that it is a sad mistake amongst many that do some things towards repentance, that they mistake the first addresses and instruments of this part of repentance for the whole duty itself. Confession of sins is in order to the dereliction of them: but then confession must not be like the unlading of a ship to take in new stowage; or the vomits of intemperance, which ease the stomach that they may continue the merry meeting. But such a confession is too frequent, in which men either comply with custom, or seek to ease a present load or gripe of conscience, or are willing to dress up their souls against a festival, or hope for pardon upon so easy terms: these are but retirings back to leap the farther into mischief; or but approaches to God with the lips. No confession can be of any use, but as it is an instrument of shame to the person, of humiliation to the man, and dereliction of the sin: and receives its recompense but as it adds to these purposes: all other is like ' the bleating of the calves and the lowing of the oxen,' which Saul reserved after the spoil of Agag; they

proclaim the sin, but do nothing towards its cure; they serve God's end to make us justly to be condemned out of our own mouths, but nothing at all towards our absolution. Nay, if we proceed farther to the greatest expressions of humiliation (parts of which, I reckon fasting, praying for pardon, judging and condemning of ourselves by instances of a present indignation against a crime); yet unless this proceed so far as to a total deletion of the sin, to the extirpation of every vicious habit, God is not glorified by our repentance, nor we secured in our eternal interest. Our sin must be brought to judgment, and, like Antinous in Homer, laid in the midst, as the sacrifice and the cause of all the mischief.

Ἀλλ' ὁ μὲν ἤδη κεῖται, ὃς αἴτιος ἔπλετο πάντων.   Od. χ. 48.

This is the murderer, this is the 'Achan,' this is ' he that troubles Israel:' let the sin be confessed and carried with the pomps and solemnities of sorrow to its funeral, and so let the murderer be slain. But if after all the forms of confession and sorrow, fasting and humiliation, and pretence of doing the will of God, we ' spare Agag and the fattest of the cattle,' our delicious sins,—and still leave an unlawful king, and a tyrant-sin to reign in our mortal bodies, we may pretend what we will towards repentance, but we are no better penitents than Ahab; no nearer to the obtaining of our hopes than Esau was to his birthright, ' for whose repentance there was no place left, though he sought it carefully with tears.'

3. Well, let us suppose our penitent advanced thus far, as that he decrees against all sin, and in his hearty purposes resolves to decline it, as in a severe sentence he hath condemned it as his betrayer and his murderer; yet we must be curious (for now only the repentance properly begins) that it be not only like the springings of the thorny or the high-way ground, soon up and soon down: for some men, when a sadness or an unhandsome accident surprises them, then they resolve against their sin; but like the goats in Aristotle, they give their milk no longer than they are stung; as soon as the thorns are removed, these men return to their first hardness, and resolve then to act their first temptation. Others there are who never resolve against a sin, but either when they have no temptation to it, or when their

appetites are newly satisfied with it; like those who immediately after a full dinner resolve to fast at supper, and they keep it till their appetite returns, and then their resolution unties like the cords of vanity, or the gossamer against the violence of the northern wind. Thus a lustful person fills all the capacity of his lust; and when he is wearied, and the sin goes off with unquietness and regret, and the appetite falls down like a horseleech, when it is ready to burst with putrefaction and an unwholesome plethory, then he resolves to be a good man, and could almost vow to be a hermit; and hates his lust, as Amnon hated his sister Tamar, just when he had newly acted his unworthy rape: but the next spring-tide that comes, every wave of the temptation makes an inroad upon the resolution, and gets ground, and prevails against it, more than his resolution prevailed against his sin. How many drunken persons, how many swearers, resolve daily and hourly against their sin, and yet act them not once the less for all their infinite heap of shamefully-retreating purposes! That resolution that begins upon just grounds of sorrow and severe judgment, upon fear and love, that is made in the midst of a temptation, that is inquisitive into all the means and instruments of the cure, that prays perpetually against a sin, that watches continually against a surprise, and never sinks into it by deliberation; that fights earnestly, and carries on the war prudently, and prevails, by a never-ceasing diligence against the temptation; that only is a pious and well-begun repentance. They that have their fits of a quartan, well and ill for ever, and think themselves in perfect health when the ague is retired, till its period returns, are dangerously mistaken. Those intervals of imperfect and fallacious resolution are nothing but states of death: and if a man should depart this world in one of those godly fits, as he thinks them, he is no nearer to obtain his blessed hope, than a man in the stone-cholic is to health when his pain is eased for the present, his disease still remaining, and threatening an unwelcome return. That resolution only is the beginning of a holy repentance, which goes forth into act, and whose acts enlarge into habits, and whose habits are productive of the fruits of a holy life.

From hence we are to take our estimate, whence our resolutions of piety must commence. He that resolves

not to live well, till the time comes that he must die, is
ridiculous in his great design, as he is impertinent in his
intermedial purposes, and vain in his hope. Can a dying
man to any real effect resolve to be chaste? For virtue
must be an act of election, and chastity is the contesting
against a proud and an imperious lust, active flesh, and
insinuating temptation. And what doth he resolve against,
who can no more be tempted to the sin of unchastity,
than he can return back again to his youth and vigour?
And it is considerable, that since all the purposes of a
holy life which a dying man can make, cannot be reduced
to act; by what law, or reason, or covenant, or revelation,
are we taught, to distinguish the resolution of a dying man
from the purposes of a living and vigorous person? Suppose
a man in his youth and health, moved by consideration of the
irregularity and deformity of sin, the danger of its productions, the wrath and displeasure of Almighty God, should resolve to leave the puddles of impurity, and walk in the paths of
righteousness; can this resolution alone put him into the state
of grace? Is he admitted to pardon and the favour of God, before he hath in some measure performed actually, what he so
reasonably hath resolved? by no means. For resolution and
purpose is, in its own nature and constitution, an imperfect act,
and therefore can signify nothing without its performance and
consummation. It is as a faculty is to the act, as spring is to
the harvest, as seed-time is to the autumn, as eggs are to
birds, or as a relative to its correspondent: nothing without
it. And can it be imagined, that a resolution in our health
and life shall be effectual without performance? And shall
a resolution, barely such, do any good upon our death-bed?
Can such purposes prevail against a long impiety rather
than against a young and a newly-begun state of sin? Will
God at an easier rate pardon the sins of fifty or sixty years,
than the sins of our youth only, or the iniquity of five years,
or ten? If a holy life be not necessary to be lived, why shall
it be necessary to resolve to live it? But if a holy life be necessary, then it cannot be sufficient merely to resolve it, unless this resolution go forth in an actual and real service.
Vain therefore is the hope of those persons, who either go
on in their sins before their last sickness, never thinking
to return into the ways of God, from whence they have wan-

dered all their life, never renewing their resolutions and vows of holy living : or if they have, yet their purposes are for ever blasted with the next violent temptation. More prudent was the prayer of David; "Oh spare me a little, that I may recover my strength, before I go hence and be no more seen." And something like it was the saying of the emperor Charles the Fifth ; "Inter vitæ negotia et mortis diem oportet spatium intercedere." Whenever our holy purposes are renewed, unless God gives us time to act them, to mortify and subdue our lusts, to conquer and subdue the whole kingdom of sin, to rise from our grave, and be clothed with nerves and flesh and a new skin, to overcome our deadly sicknesses, and by little and little to return to health and strength; unless we have grace and time to do all this, our sins will lie down with us in our graves. For when a man hath contracted a long habit of sin, and it hath been growing upon him ten or twenty, forty or fifty years, whose acts he hath daily or hourly repeated, and they are grown to a second nature to him,—and have so prevailed upon the ruins of his spirit, that the man is taken captive by the devil at his will, he is fast bound, as a slave tugging at the oar; that he is grown in love with his fetters, and longs to be doing the work of sin :—is it likely that after all this progress and growth in sin (in the ways of which he runs fast without any impediment); is it, I say, likely, that a few days or weeks of sickness can recover him ? The special hinderances of that state I shall afterward consider. But, can a man supposed so prompt to piety and holy living, a man, I mean, that hath lived wickedly a long time together, can he be of so ready and active a virtue upon the sudden, as to recover, in a month or a week, what he hath been undoing in twenty or thirty years ? Is it so easy to build, that a weak and infirm person, bound hand and foot, shall be able to build more in three days than was a-building above forty years ? Christ did it in a figurative sense ; but in this, it is not in the power of any man so suddenly to be recovered from so long a sickness. Necessary therefore it is that all these instruments of our conversion, confession of sins,—praying for their pardon,—and resolution to lead a new life,—should begin "before our feet stumble upon the dark mountains ;" lest we leave the work only resolved upon to be begun, which it is necessary we should in many degrees finish, if ever we mean to escape the eternal darkness. " For that we should actually abolish the whole body of sin and death,—that we should crucify the old man with his lusts,—that we should lay aside every weight, and the sin that doth so easily beset us,—that we should cast away the works of darkness,—that we should awake from sleep, and arise from death,—that we should redeem the time,—that we should cleanse our hands and purify our hearts,—that we should have escaped the corruption (all the corruption) that is in the whole world through lust,—that nothing of the old leaven should remain in us,—but that we be wholly a new lump, thoroughly transformed and changed in the image of our mind;"—these are the perpetual precepts of the Spirit, and the certain duty of man : and that to have all these in purpose only, is merely to no purpose, without the actual eradication of every vicious habit ; and the certain abolition of every criminal adherence, is clearly and dogmatically decreed every where in the Scripture. " For" (they are the words of St. Paul) " they that are Christ's, have crucified the flesh, with the affections and lusts*:" the work is actually done, and sin is dead or wounded mortally, before they can in any sense belong to Christ, to be a portion of his inheritance : and, " He that is in Christ, is a new creature†." For " in Christ Jesus nothing can avail but a new creature*;" nothing but a "keeping the commandments of God*." Not all tears, though we should weep like David and his men at Ziklag, 'till they could weep no more,' or the women of ' Ramah,' or like ' the weeping in the valley of Hinnom,' could suffice, if we retain the affection to any one sin, or have any unrepented of, or unmortified. It is true, that ' a contrite and a broken heart God will not despise :' no, he will not. For if it be a hearty and permanent sorrow, it is an excellent beginning of repentance ; and God will to a timely sorrow give the grace of repentance : he will not give pardon to sorrow alone ; but that which ought to be the proper effect of sorrow, that God shall give. He shall then open the gates of mercy, and admit you to a possibility of restitution : so that you may be within the covenant of repentance, which if you actually perform, you may expect God's promise. And in this sense confession will obtain our pardon, and hu-

* Gal. v. 24.　† Gal. vi. 15.　* Gal. v. 6.　* 1 Cor. vii. 19.

miliation will be accepted, and our holy purposes and pious resolutions shall be accounted for; that is, these being the first steps and addresses to that part of repentance which consists in the abolition of sins, shall be accepted so far as to procure so much of the pardon, to do so much of the work of restitution, that God will admit the returning man to a farther degree of emendation, to a nearer possibility of working out his salvation. But then, if this sorrow, and confession, and these strong purposes, begin then when our life is declined towards the west, and is now ready to set in darkness and a dismal night; because of themselves they could but procure an admission to repentance, not at all to pardon and plenary absolution, by shewing that on our death-bed these are too late and ineffectual, they call upon us to begin betimes, when these imperfect acts may be consummate and perfect, in the actual performing those parts of holy life, to which they were ordained in the nature of the thing, and the purposes of God.

4. Lastly, suppose all this be done, and that by a long course of strictness and severity, mortification and circumspection, we have overcome all our vicious and baser habits, contracted and grown upon us like the ulcers and evils of a long surfeit, and that we are clean and swept; suppose that he hath wept and fasted, prayed and vowed to excellent purposes; yet all this is but the one half of repentance (so infinitely mistaken is the world, to think any thing to be enough to make up repentance): but to renew us, and restore us to the favour of God, there is required far more than what hath been yet accounted for. See it in the Second of St. Peter, chap. i. vers. 4, 5. "Having escaped the corruption that is in the world through lust: and besides this, giving all diligence, add to your faith virtue, to virtue knowledge, to knowledge temperance, to temperance patience, and so on, to godliness, to brotherly kindness, and to charity: these things must be in you and abound." This is the sum total of repentance: we must not only have overcome sin, but we must after great diligence have acquired the habits of all those Christian graces, which are necessary in the transaction of our affairs, in all relations to God and our neighbour, and our own persons. It is not enough to say, "Lord, I thank thee, I am no extortioner, no

adulterer, not as this publican;" all the reward of such a penitent is, that when he hath escaped the corruption of the world, he hath also escaped those heavy judgments which threatened his ruin.

> ' Nec furtum feci, nec fugi,' si mihi dicat
> Servus : ' Habes pretium ; loris non ureris,' aio ;
> ' Non hominem occidi :'—' Non pasces in cruce corvos y.'

" If a servant have not robbed his master, nor offered to fly from his bondage, he shall escape the ' furca,' his flesh shall not be exposed to birds or fishes;" but this is but the reward of innocent slaves. It may be, we have escaped the rod of the exterminating angel, when onr sins are crucified ; but we shall never ' enter into the joy of the Lord,' unless after we have ' put off the old man with his affections and lusts,' we also ' put on the new man in righteousness and holiness of life.'[z] And this we are taught in most plain doctrine by St. Paul; " Let us lay aside the weight that doth so easily beset us;" that is the one half: and then it follows, " Let us run with patience the race tbat is set before us." These are the ' fruits meet for repentance,' spoken of by St. John Baptist; that is, when we renew our first undertaking in baptism, and return to our courses of innocence.

> Parcus Deorum cultor et infrequens,
> Insanientis dum sapientiæ
>   Consultus erro, nunc retrorsum
>   Vela dare, atque iterare cursos
> Cogor relictos[a] .

The sense of which words is well given us hy St. John ; " Remember whence thou art fallen ; repent, and do thy first works[b]." For all our hopes of heaven rely upon that covenant, which God made with us in baptism ; which is, " That being redeemed from our vain conversation, we should serve him in holiness and righteousness all our days." Now when any of us hath prevaricated our part of the covenant, we must return to that state, and redeem the intermedial time spent in sin, by our doubled industry in the ways of grace : we must he reduced to our first estate, and make some proportionable returns of duty for our sad omissions, and great violations of our baptismal vow. For God having made no covenant with us but that which is consigned in baptism ; in the same pro-

---

y Hor. ep. 1. 16. 46.　　ᶻ Heb. xii. 1.　　ᵃ Hor. Od. 1. 34. 2.　　ᵇ Revel. 2.

portion in which we retain or return to that, in the same we are to expect the pardon of our sins, and all the other promises evangelical; but no otherwise, unless we can shew a new gospel, or be baptized again by God's appointment. He, therefore, that by a long habit, by a state and continued course of sin, hath gone so far from his baptismal purity, as that he hath nothing of the Christian left upon him but his name; that man hath much to do to make his garments clean, to purify his soul, to take off all the stains of sin, that his spirit may be presented pure to the eyes of God, who beholds no impurity. It is not an easy thing to cure a long-contracted habit of sin. Let any intemperate person but try in his own instance of drunkenness; or the swearer, in the sweetening his unwholesome language: but then so to command his tongue that he never swear, but that his speech be prudent, pious, and apt to edify the hearer, or in some sense to glorify God; or to become temperate, to have got a habit of sobriety, or chastity, or humility, is the work of a life. And if we do but consider that he that lives well from his younger years, or takes up at the end of his youthful heats, and enters into the courses of a sober life early, diligently, and vigorously, shall find himself, after the studies and labours of twenty or thirty years' piety, but a very imperfect person, many degrees of pride left unrooted up, many inroads of intemperance or beginnings of excess, much indevotion and backwardness in religion, many temptations to contest against, and some infirmities which he shall never say he hath mastered; we shall find the work of a holy life is not to be deferred till our days are almost done, till our strengths are decayed, our spirits are weak, and our lust strong, our habits confirmed, and our longings after sin many and impotent: for what is very hard to be done, and is always done imperfectly, when there is length of time, and a less work to do, and more abilities to do it withal; when the time is short, and almost expired, and the work made difficult and vast, and the strengths weaker, and the faculties are disabled, will seem little less than absolutely impossible. I shall end this general consideration with the question of the Apostle; " If the righteous scarcely be saved," if it be so difficult to overcome our sins, and obtain virtuous habits; difficult, I say, to a righteous, a sober, and well-living person,—" where shall

the ungodly and the sinner appear?" what shall become of
him, who, by his evil life, hath not only removed himself from
the affections, but even from the possibilities of virtue?—
He that hath lived in sin, will die in sorrow.

SERMON VI.

PART II.

But I shall pursue this great and necessary truth, First, by
shewing what parts and ingredients of repentance are assigned, when it is described in Holy Scripture: Secondly,
by shewing the necessities, the absolute necessities, of a holy
life, and what it means in Scripture to 'live holily:' Thirdly,
by considering what directions or intimations we have concerning the last time of beginning to repent; and what is
the longest period that any man may venture with safety.
And in the prosecution of these particulars, we shall remove
the objections, those aprons of fig-leaves, which men use for
their shelter to palliate their sin, and to hide themselves from
that from which no rocks or mountains shall protect them,
though they fall upon them; that is, the wrath of God.

First, That repentance is not only an abolition and extinction of the body of sin, a bringing it to the altar, and
slaying it before God and all the people; but that we must
also χρυσὸν κέρασι περιχεύειν, 'mingle gold and rich presents,'
the oblation of good works and holy habits with the sacrifice,
I have already proved: but now if we will see repentance in
its stature and integrity of constitution described, we shall
find it to be the one-half of all that which God requires of
Christians. Faith and repentance are the whole duty of a
Christian. Faith is a sacrifice of the understanding to God ;
repentance sacrifices the whole will : that gives the knowing ;
this gives up all the desiring faculties : that makes us disciples; this makes us servants of the holy Jesus. Nothing
else was preached by the Apostles, nothing was enjoined as
the duty of man, nothing else did build up the body of
Christian religion. So that as faith contains all that knowledge, which is necessary to salvation ; so repentance com-
prehends in it all the whole practice and working duty of a

returning Christian. And this was the sum total of all that
St. Paul preached to the Gentiles, when, in his farewell-ser-
mon to the bishops and priests of Ephesus, he professed that
he " kept back nothing that was profitable" to them[c]; and
yet it was all nothing but this, 'repentance towards God,
and faith in our Lord Jesus Christ.' So that whosoever believes in Jesus Christ and repents towards God, must make
his accounts according to this standard, that is, to believe
all that Christ taught him, and to do all that Christ commanded. And this is remarked in St. Paul's catechism[d],
where he gives a more particular catalogue of fundamentals:
he reckons nothing but sacraments and faith; of which he
enumerates two principal articles, "resurrection of the dead,
and eternal judgment." Whatsoever is practical, all the
whole duty of man, the practice of all obedience, is called
'repentance from dead works:' which, if we observe the
singularity of the phrase, does not mean 'sorrow;' for sorrow from dead works, is not sense; but it must mean 'mu-
tationem status,' a conversion from dead works, which (as
in all motions) supposes two terms; from dead works to living
works; from ' the death of sin,' to ' the life of righteousness.'
I will add but two places more, out of each Testament
one; in which, I suppose, you may see every lineament of
this great duty described, that you may no longer mistake
a grasshopper for an eagle; sorrow and holy purposes, for
the entire duty of repentance. In Ezekiel, xviii. 21. you
shall find it thus described: "But if the wicked will turn
from all his sins that he hath committed, and keep all my
statutes, and do that which is lawful and right, he shall surely live, he shall not die." Or, as it is more fully described in
Ezekiel, xxxiii. 14. "When I say unto the wicked, Thou
shalt surely die: if he turn from his sin, and do that which
is lawful and right; if the wicked restore the pledge, give
again that he hath robbed, walk in the statutes of life without committing iniquity; he shall surely live, he shall not
die." Here only is the condition of pardon; to leave all
your sins, to keep all God's statutes, to walk in them, to
abide, to proceed, and make progress in them; and this,
without the interruption by a deadly sin,—' without committing iniquity,—to make restitution of all the wrongs he hath

done, all the unjust money he hath taken, all the oppressions he hath committed, all that must be satisfied for, and repaid according to our ability : we must make satisfaction for all injury to our neighbour's fame, all wrongs done to his soul ; he must be restored to that condition of good things thou didst in any sense remove him from : when this is done according to thy utmost power, then thou hast repented truly, then thou hast a title to the promise ; " Thou shalt surely live, thou shalt not die," for thy old sins thou hast formerly committed. Only be pleased to observe this one thing ; that this place of Ezekiel is it, which is so often mistaken for that common saying, " At what time soever a sinner repents him of his sins from the bottom of his heart, I will put all his wickedness out of my remembrance, saith the Lord." For although ' at what time soever a sinner does repent,' as repentance is now explained, God will forgive him,—and that repentance, as it is now stated, cannot be done ' at what time soever,' not upon a man's death-bed ; yet there are no such words in the whole Bible, nor any nearer to the sense of them, than the words I have now read to you out of the Prophet Ezekiel. Let that, therefore, no more deceive you, or be made a colour to countenance a persevering sinner, or a death-bed penitent.

Neither is the duty of repentance to be bought at an easier rate in the New Testament. You may see it described in 2 Cor. vii. 10, 11. " Godly sorrow worketh repentance." Well ! but what is that repentance which is so wrought? This it is : " Behold this selfsame thing that ye sorrowed after a godly sort, what carefulness it wrought in you, yea, what clearing of yourselves, yea, what indignation, yea, what fear, yea, what vehement desire, yea, what zeal, yea, what revenge !" These are the fruits of that sorrow that is effectual ; these are the parts of repentance : ' clearing ourselves' of all that is past, and great ' carefulness' for the future ; ' anger' at ourselves for our old sins, and ' fear' lest we commit the like again ; ' vehement desires' of pleasing God, and 'zeal' of holy actions, and ' a revenge' upon ourselves for our sins, called by St. Paul, in another place, " a judging ourselves, lest we be judged of the Lord[a]." And in pursuance of this truth, the primitive church did not admit

[a] 1 Cor. xi. 31.

a sinning person to the public communions with the faithful, till, besides their sorrow, they had spent some years in an ἀγαθοεργία, in 'doing good works,' and holy living; and especially in such actions which did contradict that wicked inclination, which led them into those sins, whereof they were now admitted to repent. And therefore, we find that they stood in the station of penitents seven years, thirteen years, and sometimes till their death, before they could be reconciled to the peace of God, and his holy church.

> ———— Scelerum si bene pœnitet,
> Eradenda cupidinis
> Pravi sunt elementa; et tenerœ nimis
> Mentes asperioribus
> Formandœ studiis[f].

Repentance is the institution of a philosophical and severe life, an utter extirpation of all unreasonableness and impiety, and an address to, and a final passing through, all the parts of holy living.

Now consider, whether this be imaginable or possible to be done upon our death-bed, when a man is frighted into an involuntary, a sudden, and unchosen piety. Ὁ μετανοῶν οὐ φόβῳ τῶν ἐναντίων τὴν τοῦ κακοῦ πρᾶξιν αἱρήσεται, saith Hierocles[g]. He that never repents till a violent fear be upon him, till he apprehend himself to be in the jaws of death, ready to give up his unready and unprepared accounts, till he sees the Judge sitting in all the addresses of dreadfulness and majesty, just now, as he believes, ready to pronounce that fearful and intolerable sentence of, " Go, ye cursed, into everlasting fire ;" this man does nothing for the love of God, nothing for the love of virtue : it is just as a condemned man repents that he was a traitor; but repented not till he was arrested, and sure to die : such a repentance as this, may still consist with as great an affection to sin as ever he had[h]; and, it is no thanks to him, if, when the knife is at his throat, then he gives good words and flatters. But, suppose this man in his health, and in the midst of all his lust, it is evident that there are some circumstances of action, in which the man would have refused to commit his most pleasing sin. Would not the son of

---

[f] Hor. Od. 3. 24.

[g] ἡ δὲ μετάνοια αὕτη φιλοσοφίας ἀρχὴ γίνεται, καὶ τῶν ἀνοήτων ἔργων τε καὶ λόγων φυγὴ, καὶ τῆς ἀμεταμελήτου ζωῆς ἡ πρώτη παρασκευή. Hierocles, Needham, p. 126.

[h] See Life of Jesus, Disc. of Repentance, part 2.

Tarquin have refused to ravish Lucretia, if Junius Brutus had
been by him? Would the impurest person in the world act his
lust in the market-place? or drink off an intemperate goblet, if
a dagger were placed at his throat? In these circumstances
their fear would make them declare against the present acting their impurities.   But does this cure the intemperance
of their affections? Let the impure person retire to his closet, and Junius Brutus be engaged in a far-distant war, and
the dagger be taken from the drunkard's throat, and the fear
of shame, or death, or judgment, be taken from them all; and
they shall no more resist their temptation, than they could
before remove their fear: and you may as well judge the
other persons holy, and haters of their sin, as the man upon
his death-bed to be penitent; and rather they than he, by
how much this man's fear, the fear of death, and of the infinite pains of hell, the fear of a provoked God, and an angry eternal Judge, are far greater than the apprehensions of
a public shame, or an abused husband, or the poniard of an
angry person.   These men then sin not, because they dare
not; they are frighted from the act, but not from the affection; which is not to be cured but by discourse, and reasonable acts, and human considerations; of which that man is
not naturally capable, who is possessed with the greatest
fear, the fear of death and damnation.   If there had been
time to curse his sin, and to live the life of grace, I deny not
but God might have begun his conversion with so great a
fear, that he should never have wiped off its impression[i]:
but if the man dies then, dies when he only declaims against,
and curses his sin, as being the author of his present fear
and apprehended calamity; it is very far from reconciling
him to God or hopes of pardon, because it proceeds from a
violent[k], unnatural, and intolerable cause; no act of choice,
or virtue, but of sorrow, a deserved sorrow, and a miserable,
unchosen, unavoidable fear;

> —— moriensque recepit
> Quas nollet victurus aquas——

He curses sin upon his death-bed, and makes a panegyric of

---

[i] Cogimur à suetis animum suspendere rebus;
   Atque ut vivamus, vivere desinimus.   Cornel. Gal.
[k] Nec ad rem pertinet ubi inciperet, quod placuerat ut fieret.

virtue, which, in his life-time, he accounted folly, and trouble, and needless vexation.

Quæ mens est hodie, cur eadem non puero fuit?
Vel cur his animis incolumen non redeant genæ[1]?

I shall end this first consideration with a plain exhortation; that since repentance is a duty of so great and giant-like bulk, let no man crowd it up into so narrow room, as that it be strangled in its birth for want of time, and air to breathe in: let it not be put off to that time when a man hath scarce time enough to reckon all those particular duties, which make up the integrity of its constitution. Will any man hunt the wild boar in his garden, or bait a bull in his closet? Will a woman wrap her child in her handkerchief, or a father send his son to school when he is fifty years old? These are indecencies of providence, and the instrument contradicts the end: and this is our case. There is no room for the repentance, no time to act all its essential parts: and a child, who hath a great way to go before he be wise, may defer his studies, and hope to become learned in his old age, and upon his death-bed; as well as a vicious person may think to recover from all his ignorances and prejudicate opinions, from all his false principles and evil customs, from his wicked inclinations and ungodly habits, from his fondnesses of vice, and detestations of virtue, from his promptness to sin, and unwillingness to grace, from his spiritual deadness and strong sensuality, upon his death-bed (I say), when he hath no natural strength, and as little spiritual; when he is criminal and impotent, hardened in his vice and soft in his fears, full of passion and empty of wisdom; when he is sick and amazed, and timorous and confounded, and impatient, and extremely miserable.

And now when any of you is tempted to commit a sin, remember that sin will ruin you, unless you repent of it. But this, you say, is no news, and so far from affrighting you from sin, that (God knows) it makes men sin the rather. For, therefore, they venture to act the present temptation, because they know, if they repent, God will forgive them; and therefore, they resolve upon both, to sin now, and repent hereafter.

Against this folly I shall not oppose the consideration

[1] Hor. Od. 4. 10.

of their danger, and that they neither know how long they shall live, nor whether they shall die or no in this very act of sin; though this consideration is very material, and if they should die in it, or before it is washed off, they perish: but I consider these things. 1. That he that resolves to sin upon a resolution to repent, by every act of sin makes himself more incapable of repenting, by growing more in love with sin, by remembering its pleasures, by serving it once more, and losing one degree more of the liberty of our spirit. And if you resolve to sin now, because it is pleasant, how do you know that your appetite will alter? Will it not appear pleasant to you next week, and the next week after that, and so for ever? And still you sin, and still you will repent; that is, you will repent when the sin can please you no longer: for so long as it can please you, so long you are tempted not to repent, as well as now to act the sin: and the longer you lie in it, the more you will love it. So that it is in effect to say, I love my sin now, but I will hereafter hate it; only I will act it awhile* longer, and grow more in love with it, and then I will repent; that is, then I will be sure to hate it, when I shall most love it. 2. To repent, signifies to be sorrowful, to be ashamed, and to wish it had never been done. And then see the folly of this temptation; I would not sin, but that I hope to repent of it; that is, I would not do this thing, but that I hope to be sorrowful for doing it, and I hope to come to shame for it, heartily to be ashamed of my doings, and I hope to be in that condition, that I would give all the world I had never done it; that is, I hope to feel and apprehend an evil infinitely greater than the pleasures of my sin. And are these arguments fit to move a man to sin? What can affright a man from it, if these invite him to it? It is as if a man should invite one to be a partner of his treason, by telling him, If you will join with me, you shall have all these effects by it; you shall be hanged, drawn and quartered, and your blood shall be corrupted, and your estate forfeited, and you shall have many other reasons to wish you had never done it. He that should use this rhetoric, in earnest, might well be accounted a madman; this is to scare a man, not to allure him: and so is the other when we understand it truly. 3. For I consider, he that repents, wishes he had never done that sin. Now I ask, does he wish so upon reason, or without reason? Surely, if he may, when he hath satisfied his lust, ask God pardon, and be admitted upon as easy terms for the time to come, as if he had not done the sin, he hath no reason to be sorrowful, or wish he had not done it. For though he hath done it, and pleased himself by 'enjoying the pleasure of sin for that season,' yet all is well again; and let him only be careful now, and there is no hurt done, his pardon is certain. How can any man, that understands the reason of his actions and passions, wish that he had never done that sin in which then he had pleasure, and now he feels no worse inconvenience. But he that truly repents, wishes and would give all the world, he had never done it: surely then his present condition in respect of his past sin hath some very great evil in it, why else should he be so much troubled? True, and this it is. He that hath committed sins after baptism, is fallen out of the favour of God, is tied to hard duty for the time to come, to cry vehemently unto God, to call night and day for pardon, to be in great fear and tremblings of heart, lest God should never forgive him, lest God will never take off his sentence of eternal pains; and in this fear, and in some degrees of it, he will remain all the days of his life: and if he hopes to be quit of that, yet he knows not how many degrees of God's anger still hang over his head; how many sad miseries shall afflict, and burn, and purify him in this world, with a sharpness so poignant as to divide the marrow from the bones; and for these reasons, as a considering man that knows what it is to repent, wishes with his soul he had never sinned, and, therefore, grieves in proportion to his former crimes, and present misery, and future danger.

And now suppose that you can repent when you will, that is, that you can grieve when you will;—though no man can do it, no man can grieve when he please, though he could shed tears when he list, he cannot grieve without a real or apprehended felicity; but, suppose it;—and that he can fear when he please, and that he can love when he please, or what he please; that is, suppose a man be able to say to his palate, Though I love sweetmeats, yet to-morrow will I hate and loathe them, and believe them bitter and distasteful things; suppose, I say, all these impossibilities: yet since repentance does suppose a man to be in a state of such real misery, that he hath reason to curse the day in which he sinned, is this a fit argument to invite a man that is in his wits, to sin? to sin in hope of repentance? as if danger of falling into hell, and fear of the divine anger, and many degrees of the divine judgments, and a lasting sorrow, and a perpetual labour, and a never-ceasing trembling, and a troubled conscience, and a sorrowful spirit, were fit things to be desired or hoped for.

The sum is this: he that commits sins shall perish eternally, if he never does repent. And, if he does repent, and yet untimely, he is not the better; and if he does not repent with an entire, a perfect, and complete repentance, he is not the better. But if he does, yet repentance is a duty full of fears, and sorrow, and labour; a vexation to the spirit; an afflictive, penal, or punitive duty; a duty which suffers for sin, and labours for grace, which abides and suffers little images of hell in the way to heaven: and though it be the only way to felicity, yet it is beset with thorns and daggers of sufferance, and with rocks and mountains of duty. Let no man therefore dare to sin upon the hopes of repentance: for he is a fool and a hypocrite, that now chooses and approves what he knows hereafter he must condemn.

2. The second general consideration is, the necessity, the absolute necessity, of holy living. God hath made a covenant with us, that we must give up ourselves, 'bodies' and souls, not a dying, but 'a living' and healthful 'sacrifice[1].' He hath forgiven all our old sins, and we have bargained to quit them, from the time that we first come to Christ, and give our names to him, and to keep all his commandments. We have taken the sacramental oath, like that of the old Roman militia, πειθαρχήσειν, καὶ ποιήσειν τὸ προσταττόμενον ὑπὸ τῶν ἀρχόντων κατὰ δύναμιν, we must 'believe,' and 'obey,' and 'do all that is commanded us,' and keep our station, and fight against the flesh, the world, and the devil, not to throw away our military girdle; and we are to do what is bidden us, or to die for it, even all that is bidden us, 'according to our power.' For, pretend not that God's commandments are impossible. It is dishonourable to think God enjoins us to do more than he enables us to do; and it is a contradiction to say we cannot do all that we can; and

[1] Rom. xii. 1.

"through Christ which strengthens me, I can do all things," saith St. Paul. However, we can do to the utmost of our strength, and beyond that we cannot take thought; impossibilities enter not into deliberation; but, according to our abilities and natural powers, assisted by God's grace, so God hath covenanted with us to live a holy life. " For in Christ Jesus, nothing availeth but a new creature, nothing but faith working by charity, nothing but keeping the commandments of God." They are all the words of St. Paul before quoted; to which he adds, " and as many as walk according to this rule, peace be on them and mercy." This is the covenant, ' they are the Israel of God ;' upon those ' peace and mercy' shall abide. If they become a new creature, wholly ' transformed in the image of their mind ;' if they have faith, and this faith be an operative working faith, a faith that produces a holy life, ' a faith that works by charity ;' if they ' keep the commandments of God,' then they are within the covenant of mercy, but not else : for ' in Christ Jesus nothing else availeth.' To the same purpose are those words, (Heb. xii. 14.) "Follow peace with all men, and holiness, without which no man shall see the Lord." ' Peace with all men' implies both justice and charity, without which it is impossible to preserve peace : ' holiness' implies all our duty towards God, universal diligence : and this must be ' followed,' that is, pursued with diligence, in a lasting course of life and exercise : and without this we shall never see the face of God. I need urge no more authorities to this purpose ; these two are as certain and convincing as two thousand : and since thus much is actually required, and is the condition of the covenant ; it is certain that sorrow for not having done what is commanded to be done, and a purpose to do what is necessary to be actually performed, will not acquit us before the righteous judgment of God. " For the grace of God hath appeared to all men, teaching us, that denying ungodliness and worldly lusts, we should live godly, justly, and soberly, in this present world." For upon these terms alone, we must "look for the blessed hope, the glorious appearing of the great God, and our Saviour Jesus Christ ᵃ." I shall no longer insist upon this particular, but only propound it to your consideration. To what purpose

ᵃ Tit. ii. 11, 12.

are all those commandments in Scripture, of every page almost in it, of living holily, and according to the commandments of God,—of adorning the gospel of God,—of walking as in the day,—of walking in light,—of pure and undefiled religion,—of being holy as God is holy,—of being humble and meek, as Christ is humble,—of putting on the Lord Jesus,—of living a spiritual life,—but that it is the purpose of God, and the intention and design of Christ dying for us, and the covenant made with man, that we should expect heaven upon no other terms in the world, but of a holy life, in the faith and obedience of the Lord Jesus?

Now if a vicious person, when he comes to the latter end of his days, one that hath lived a wicked, ungodly life, can, for any thing he can do upon his death-bed, be said to live a holy life; then his hopes are not desperate: but he that hopes upon this only, for which God hath made him no promise, I must say of him as Galen said of consumptive persons, Ἡι πλέον ἐλπίζουσιν, ταύτῃ μᾶλλον κακῶς ἔχουσι, " The more they hope, the worse they are:" and the relying upon such hopes is an approach to the grave and a sad eternity.

> Peleos et Priami transit, vel Nestoris ætas,
> Et fuerat serum jam tibi desinere.
> Eja age, rumpe moras; quò te sperabimus usque?
> Dum, quid sis dubitas, jam potes esse nihil *.

And now it will be a vain question to ask, whether or no God cannot save a dying man that repents after a vicious life. For it is true, God can do it if he please, and he 'can raise children to Abraham out of the stones,' and he can make ten thousand worlds, if he sees good; and he can do what he list, and he can save an ill-living man though he never repent at all, so much as upon his death-bed: all this can he do. But God's power is no ingredient into this question: we are never the better that God can do it, unless he also will: and whether he will or no, we are to learn from himself, and what he hath declared to be his will in Holy Scripture. Nay, since God hath said, that ' without actual holiness no man shall see God,' God by his own will hath restrained his power; and though absolutely he can do all things, yet he cannot do against his own word. And, indeed, the rewards of heaven are so great and glorious, and Christ's

* Martial. 2. 64.

' burden is so light, his yoke is so easy,' that it is a shameless impudence to expect so great glories at a less rate than so little a service, at a lower rate than a holy life. It cost the eternal Son of God his life's blood to obtain heaven for us upon that condition : and who then shall die again for us, to get heaven for us upon easier conditions ? What would you do, if God should command you to kill your eldest son, or to work in the mines for a thousand years together, or to fast all thy life-time with bread and water ? were not heaven a great bargain even after all this ? And when God requires nothing of us but to live soberly, justly, and godly,—which very things of themselves to men are a very great felicity, and necessary to his present well-being,—shall we think this to be a load, and an insufferable burden ? And that heaven is so little a purchase at that price, that God in mere justice will take a death-bed sigh or groan, and a few unprofitable tears and promises, in exchange for all our duty ? Strange it should be so : but stranger, that any man should rely upon such a vanity, when from God's word he hath nothing to warrant such a confidence. But these men do like the tyrant Dionysius, who stole from Apollo his golden cloak, and gave him a cloak of Arcadian homespun, saying, that this was lighter in summer, and warmer in winter. These men sacrilegiously rob God of the service of all their golden days, and serve him in their hoary head, in their furs and grave-clothes, and pretend that this late service is more agreeable to the divine mercy on one side, and human infirmity on the other, and so dispute themselves into an irrecoverable condition ; having no other ground to rely upon a death-bed or late-begun repentance, but because, they resolve to enjoy the pleasures of sin : and for heaven they will put that to the venture of an after-game.   These men sow in the flesh, and would reap in the Spirit ; live to the devil, and die to God : and therefore, it is but just in God that their hopes should he desperate, and their craft be folly, and their condition be the unexpected, unfeared inheritance of an eternal sorrow.

3. Lastly ; our last inquiry is into the time, the last or latest time of beginning our repentance. Must a man repent a year or two, or seven years, or ten, or twenty, before his death ? or what is the last period, after which all repentance

will be untimely and ineffectual? To this captious question I have many things to oppose. 1. We have entered into covenant with God, to serve him from the day of our baptism to the day of our death. He hath "sworn this oath to us, that he would grant unto us, that we, being delivered from fear of our enemies, might serve him without fear, in holiness and righteousness before him, all the days of our life*." Now although God will not τῆς ἀνθρωπίνης καὶ κοινῆς ἀσθενείας ἐπιλανθάνεσθαι, 'forget our infirmities,' but pass by the nakednesses of an honest, a watchful, and industrious person ; yet the covenant he makes with us, is from the day of our first voluntary profession to our grave; and according as we by sins retire from our first undertaking, so our condition is insecure : there is no other covenant made with us, no new beginnings of another period; but if we be returned, and sin be cancelled, and grace be actually obtained, then we are in the first condition of pardon : but because it is uncertain when a man can have mastered his vices, and obtained the graces, therefore no man can tell any set time when he must begin. 2. Scripture, describing the duty of repenting sinners, names no other time but ' to-day:' "*to-day* if ye will hear his voice, harden not your hearts." 3. The duty of a Christian is described in Scripture to be such as requires length of time, and a continual industry. "Let us run with patience the race, that is set before us?:" and "consider him that endured such contradiction of sinners against himself, lest ye be wearied and faint in your minds." So great a preparation is not for the agony and contention of an hour, or a day, or a week, but for the whole life of a Christian, or for great parts of its abode. 4. There is a certain period and time set for our repentance, and beyond that all our industry is ineffectual. There is ' a day of visitation, our own day ;' and there is ' a day of visitation,' that is ' God's day.' This appeared in the case of Jerusalem : " O Jerusalem, Jerusalem, if thou hadst known the time of thy visitation, at least in this thy day." Well, they neglected it; and then there was a time of God's visitation, which was 'his day,' called in Scripture "the day of the Lord ;" and because they had neglected their own day, they fell into inevitable ruin : no repentance could have prevented their final ruin. And

* Luke i. 73, 74.   P Heb. xii. 1. 3.

this, which was true in a nation, is also clearly affirmed true in the case of single persons. "Look diligently, lest any fail of the grace of God; lest there be any person among you as Esau, who sold his birth-right, and afterward, when he would have inherited the blessing, he was rejected; for he found no place for his repentance, though he sought it carefully with tears[q]." Esau had time enough to repent his bargain as long as he lived ; he wept sorely for his folly, and carefulness sat heavy upon his soul; and yet he was not heard, nor his repentance accepted; for the time was past. And ' take heed,' saith the Apostle, lest it come to pass to any of you to be in the same case. Now if ever there be a time, in which repentance is too late, it must be the time of our death-bed, and the last time of our life. And after a man is fallen into the displeasure of Almighty God, the longer he lies in his sin without repentance and emendation, the greater is his danger, and the more of his allowed time is spent; and no man can antecedently, or beforehand, be sure that the time of his repentance is not past ; and those who neglect the call of God, and refuse to hear him call in the day of grace, "God will laugh at them when their calamity comes : they shall call, and the Lord shall not hear them." And this was the case of the five foolish virgins, when the arrest of death surprised them : they discovered their want of oil, they were troubled at it ; they begged oil, they were refused ; they did something towards the procuring of the oil of grace, for they went out to buy oil : and, after all this stir, the Bridegroom came before they had finished their journey, and they were shut out from the communion of the Bridegroom's joys.

Therefore, concerning the time of beginning to repent, no man is certain but he that hath done his work. "Mortem venientem nemo hilaris excipit, nisi qui se ad eam din composuerat," said Seneca[r]: "He only dies cheerfully, who stood waiting for death in a ready dress of a long preceding preparation." He that repents to-day, repents late enough that he did not begin yesterday : but he that puts it off till to-morrow, is vain and miserable.

> ———— hodie jam vivere, Postume, serum est :
> Ille sapit, quisquis, Postume, vixit heri[s].

[q] Heb. xii. 15, &c.   [r] Epist. 30.   [s] Mart. 5. 58.

Well ; but what will you have a man do that hath lived wickedly, and is now cast upon his death-bed? shall this man despair, and neglect all the actions of piety, and the instrument of restitution in his sickness? No, God forbid. Let him do what he can then ; it is certain it will be little enough ; for all those short gleams of piety and flashes of lightning will help towards alleviating some degrees of misery ; and if the man recover, they are good beginnings of a renewed piety : and Ahab's tears and humiliation, though it went no-farther, had a proportion of a reward, though nothing to the proportions of eternity. So that he that says, it is every day necessary to repent, cannot be supposed to discourage the piety of any day : a death-bed piety, when things are come to that sad condition, may have many good purposes : therefore, even then neglect nothing that can be done.—Well ; but shall such persons despair of salvation? To them I shall only return this : that they are to consider the conditions, which, on one side, God requires of us ; and, on the other side, whether they have done accordingly. Let them consider upon what terms God hath promised salvation, and whether they have made themselves capable, by performing their part of the obligation. If they have not, I must tell them, that, not to hope where God hath made no promise, is not the sin of despair, but the misery of despair. A man hath no ground to hope, that ever he shall be made an angel, and yet that not hoping is not to be called despair : and no man can hope for heaven without repentance ; and for such a man to despair, is not the sin, but the misery. If such persons have a promise of heaven, let them shew it, and hope it, and enjoy it : if they have no promise, they must thank themselves, for bringing themselves into a condition without the covenant, without a promise hopeless and miserable.

But will not trusting in the merits of Jesus Christ save such a man? For that, we must be tried by the word of God, in which there is no contract at all made with a dying person, that lived in name a Christian, in practice a heathen : and we shall dishonour the sufferings and redemption of our blessed Saviour, if we think them to be an umbrella to shelter impious and ungodly living. But that no such person may, after a wicked life, repose himself on his death-bed upon Christ's merits, observe but these two places of Scripture :

" Our Saviour Jesus Christ, who gave himself for us"—what to do? that we might live as we list, and hope to be saved by his merits? no:—but "that he might redeem us from all iniquity, and purify to himself a peculiar people, zealous of good works. These things speak and exhort," saith St. Paul.—But, more plainly yet in St. Peter; " Christ bare our sins in his own body on the tree,"—to what end? " that we, being dead unto sin, should live unto righteousness[u]." Since therefore our living a holy life is the end of Christ's dying that sad and holy death for us, he that trusts on it to evil purposes, and to excuse his vicious life, does, as much as lies in him, make void the very purpose and design of Christ's passion, and dishonours the blood of the everlasting covenant; which covenant was confirmed by the blood of Christ; but, as it brought peace from God, so it requires a holy life from us[x].

But why may not we be saved, as well as the thief upon the cross? even because our case is nothing alike. When Christ dies once more for us, we may look for such another instance; not till then. But this thief did but then come to Christ, he knew him not before; and his case was, as if a Turk, or heathen, should be converted to Christianity, and be baptized, and enter newly into the covenant upon his death-bed: then God pardons all his sins. And so God does to Christians when they are baptized, or first give up their names to Christ by a voluntary confirmation of their baptismal vow: but when they have once entered into the covenant, they must perform what they promise, and do what they are obliged. The thief had made no contract with God in Jesus Christ, and therefore failed of none; only the defailances of the state of ignorance Christ paid for at the thief's admission: but we, that have made a covenant with God in baptism, and failed of it all our days, and then return at ' night, when we cannot work,' have nothing to plead for ourselves; because we have made all that to be useless to us, which God, with so much mercy and miraculous wisdom, gave us to secure our interest and hopes of heaven.

And therefore, let no Christian man, who hath covenanted with God to give him the service of his life, think that God

---

[u] Titus, ii. 14.   [x] 1 Pet. ii. 24.
[x] See Life of Jesus, Disc. of Repentance, part 2.

will be answered with the sighs and prayers of a dying man: for all that great obligation, which lies upon us, cannot be transacted in an instant, when we have loaded our soul with sin, and made them empty of virtue ; we cannot so soon grow up to ' a perfect man in Christ Jesus :' οὐδὲν τῶν μεγάλων ἄφνω γίνεται'. You cannot have an apple or a cherry, but you must stay its proper periods, and let it blossom and knot, and grow and ripen; " and in due season we shall reap, if we faint not," saith the Apostle : far much less may we expect that the fruits of repentance, and the issues and degrees of holiness, shall be gathered in a few days or hours. Γνώμης δ' ἀνθρώπου καρπὸν θέλεις οὕτω δι' ὀλίγου καὶ εὐκόλως κτήσασθαι. You must not expect such fruits in a little time, nor with little labour.

Suffer not therefore yourselves to be deceived by false principles and vain confidences : for no man can in a moment root out the long-contracted habits of vice, nor upon his death-bed make use of all that variety of preventing, accompanying, and persevering grace, which God gave to man in mercy, because man would need it all, because without it he could not be saved; nor, upon his death-bed, can he exercise the duty of mortification, nor cure his drunkenness then, nor his lust, by any act of Christian discipline, nor run with patience nor ' resist unto blood,' nor ' endure with long-sufferrance ;' but he can pray, and groan, and call to God, and resolve to live well when he is dying.   But this is but just as the nobles of Xerxes, when in a storm they were to lighten the ship, to preserve their king's life ; they did προσκυνέοντας ἐπιπηδᾶν εἰς τὴν θάλασσαν, they " did their obeisance, and leaped into the sea :" so, I fear, do these men pray, and mourn, and worship, and so leap overboard into an ocean of eternal and intolerable calamity : from which God deliver us, and all faithful people.

> Hunc volo laudari qui sine morte potest '.
>
> Vivere quòd propero pauper, nec inutilis annis,
>   Da veniam ; properat vivere nemo satis.
> Differat hoc, patrios optat qui vincere census,
>   Atriaque immodicis arctat imaginibus '.

' *Arrian. Epictet. l. 1. c. 15.*   ' Martial. 1. 9. 6.   ' Ib. 2. 90. 3.

SERMON VII.

THE DECEITFULNESS OF THE HEART.

———

PART I.

The heart is deceitful above all things, and desperately wicked;
who can know it?—Jeremiah, xvii. 9.

Folly and subtilty divide the greatest part of mankind;
and there is no other difference but this; that some are crafty
enough to deceive, others foolish enough to be cozened and
abused : and yet the scales also turn; for they that are the
most crafty to cozen others, are the veriest fools, and most of
all abused themselves. They rob their neighbour of his
money, and lose their own innocency; they disturb his rest,
and vex their own conscience; they throw him into prison,
and themselves into hell; they make poverty to be their
brother's portion, and damnation to be their own. Man
entered into the world first alone; but as soon as he met with
one companion, he met with three to cozen him: the serpent,
and Eve, and himself, all joined,—first to make him a fool,
and to deceive him, and then to make him miserable. But
he first cozened himself, 'giving himself up to believe a lie;'
and, being desirous to listen to the whispers of a tempting
spirit, he sinned before he fell; that is, he had within him a
false understanding, and a depraved will : and these were the
parents of his disobedience, and this was the parent of his infelicity, and a great occasion of ours. And then it was that
he entered, for himself and his posterity, into the condition
of an ignorant, credulous, easy, wilful, passionate, and impotent person; apt to be abused, and so loving to have it so,
that if nobody else will abuse him, he will be sure to abuse
himself; by ignorance and evil principles being open to an
enemy, and by wilfulness and sensuality doing to himself the
most unpardonable injuries in the whole world. So that the
condition of man, in the rudeness and first lines of its visage,
seems very miserable, deformed, and accursed.

For a man is helpless and vain; of a condition so exposed
to calamity, that a raisin is able to kill him; any trooper out

of the Egyptian army, a fly can do it, when it goes on God's
errand; the most contemptible accident can destroy him, the
smallest chance affright him, every future contingency, when
but considered as possible, can amaze him; and he is encompassed with potent and malicious enemies, subtle and implacable: what shall this poor helpless thing do? Trust in
God? him he hath offended, and he fears him as an enemy;
and, God knows, if we look only on ourselves, and on our
own demerits, we have too much reason so to do. Shall he
rely upon princes? God help poor kings; they rely upon their
subjects, they fight with their swords, levy force with their
money, consult with their counsels, hear with their ears, and
are strong only in their union, and many times they use all
these things against them; but, however, they can do nothing
without them while they live, and yet if ever they can die,
they are not to be trusted to. Now kings and princes die so
sadly and notoriously, that it was used for a proverb in holy
Scripture, " Ye shall die like men, and fall like one of the
princes." Whom then shall we trust in? In our friend? Poor
man! he may help thee in one thing, and need thee in ten:
he may pull thee out of the ditch, and his foot may slip and
fall into it himself: he gives thee counsel to choose a wife,
and himself is to seek how prudently to choose his religion:
he counsels thee to abstain from a duel, and yet slays his
own soul with drinking: like a person void of all understanding, he is willing enough to preserve thy interest, and is very
careless of his own; for he does highly despise to betray or
to be false to thee, and in the mean time is not his own friend,
and is false to God; and then his friendship may be useful to
thee in some circumstances of fortune, but no security to thy
condition.   But what then? shall we rely upon our patron,
like the Roman clients, who waited hourly upon their persons,
and daily upon their baskets, and nightly upon their lusts,
and married their friendships, and contracted also their hatred
and quarrels? this is a confidence will deceive us. For they
may lay us by, justly or unjustly; they may grow weary of
doing benefits, or their fortunes may change; or they may be
charitable in their gifts, and burdensome in their offices; able
to feed you, but unable to counsel you; or your need may be
longer than their kindnesses, or such in which they can give
you no assistance : and, indeed, generally it is so, in all the

instances of men. We have a friend that is wise; but I need not his counsel, but his meat: or my patron is bounti-ful in his largesses; but I am troubled with a sad spirit; and money and presents do me no more ease than perfumes do to a broken arm. We seek life of a physician that dies, and go to him for health, who cannot cure his own breath or gout; and so become vain in our imaginations, abused in our hopes, restless in our passions, impatient in our calamity, unsupported in our need, exposed to enemies, wandering and wild, without counsel, and without remedy. At last, after the infatuating and deceiving all our confidences without, we have nothing left us but to return home, and dwell within ourselves: for we have a sufficient stock of self-love, that we may be confident of our own affections, we may trust ourselves surely; for what we want in skill we shall make up in diligence, and our industry shall supply the want of other circumstances: and no man understands my own case so well as I do myself, and no man will judge so faithfully as I shall do for myself; for I am most concerned not to abuse myself; and if I do, I shall be the loser, and therefore may best rely upon myself. Alas! and God help us! we shall find it to be no such matter: for we neither love ourselves well, nor understand our own case; we are partial in our own questions, deceived in our sentences, careless of our interests, and the most false, perfidious creatures to ourselves in the whole world: even the " heart of a man," a man's own heart, " is deceitful above all things, and desperately wicked; who can know it?" and who can choose but know it?

And there is no greater argument of the deceitfulness of our hearts than this, that no man can know it all; it cozens us in the very number of its cozenage. But yet we can reduce it all to two heads. We say, concerning a false man, Trust him not, for he will deceive you; and we say concerning a weak and broken staff, Lean not upon it, for that will also deceive you. The man deceives because he is false, and the staff because it is weak; and the heart, because it is both. So that it is "deceitful above all things;" that is, failing and disabled to support us in many things, but in other things, where it can, it is false and " desperately wicked." The first sort of deceitfulness is its calamity, and the second is its iniquity; and that is the worse calamity of the two.

1. The heart is deceitful in its strength; and when we
have the growth of a man, we have the weaknesses of a child :
nay, more yet, and it is a sad consideration, the more we are
in age, the weaker in our courage. It appears in the heats
and forwardnesses of new converts, which are like to the
great emissions of lightning, or like huge fires, which flame
and burn without measure, even all that they can ; till from
flames they descend to still fires, from thence to smoke, from
smoke to embers, and from thence to ashes ; cold and pale,
like ghosts, or the fantastic images of death. And the primitive church were zealous in their religion up to the degree
of cherubims, and would run as greedily to the sword of the
hangman, to die for the cause of God, as we do now to the
greatest joy and entertainment of a Christian spirit,—even to
the receiving of the holy sacrament. A man would think it
reasonable, that the first infancy of Christianity should, according to the nature of first beginnings, have been remiss,
gentle, and inactive ; and that, according as the object or
evidence of faith grew, which in every age hath a great degree of argument superadded to its confirmation, so should
the habit also and the grace ; the longer it lasts, and the
more objections it runs through, it still should shew a
brighter and more certain light to discover the divinity of
its principle; and that after the more examples, and new accidents and strangenesses of providence, and daily experience, and the multitude of miracles, still the Christian should
grow more certain in his faith, more refreshed in his hope,
and warm in his charity ; the very nature of these graces increasing and swelling upon the very nourishment of experience, and the multiplication of their own acts. And yet,
because the heart of man is false, it suffers the fires of the
altar to go out, and the flames lessen by the multitude of
fuel. But, indeed, it is because we put on strange fire, and
put out the fire upon our hearths by letting in a glaring sunbeam, the fire of lust, or the heats of an angry spirit, to
quench the fire of God, and suppress the sweet cloud of incense. The heart of man hath not strength enough to think
one good thought of itself; it cannot command its own attentions to a prayer of ten lines long, but, before its end, it
shall wander after something that is to no purpose ; and no
wonder, then, that it grows weary of a holy religion, which

consists of so many parts as make the business of a whole
life. And there is no greater argument in the world of our
spiritual weakness, and the falseness of our hearts in the
matters of religion, than the backwardness which most men
have always, and all men have sometimes, to say their
prayers; so weary of their length, so glad when they are
done, so witty to excuse and frustrate an opportunity: and
yet there is no manner of trouble in the duty, no weariness
of bones, no violent labours; nothing but begging a blessing, and receiving it; nothing but doing ourselves the greatest honour of speaking to the greatest person, and greatest
King of the world: and, that we should be unwilling to do
this, so unable to continue in it, so backward to return to it,
so without gust and relish in the doing it, can have no visible
reason in the nature of the thing, but something within us,
a strange sickness in the heart, a spiritual nauseating or
loathing of manna, something that hath no name; but we
are sure it comes from a weak, a faint, and false heart.

And yet this weak heart is strong in passions, violent in
desires, irresistible in its appetites, impatient in its lust,
furious in anger: here are strengths enough, one should
think. But so have I seen a man in a fever, sick and distempered, unable to walk, less able to speak sense, or to do an
act of counsel; and yet, when his fever had boiled up to a
delirium, he was strong enough to beat his nursekeeper and
his doctor too, and to resist the loving violence of all his
friends, who would fain bind him down to reason and his
bed: and yet we still say, he is weak, and sick to death.
Θέλω γὰρ εἶναι τόνους ἐν σώματι, ἀλλ' ὡς ὑγιαίνοντι, ὡς
ἀθλοῦντι. For these strengths of madness are not health,
but furiousness and disease. Οὐκ εἰσὶ τόνοι, ἀλλὰ ἀτονία
ἕτερον τρόπον, " It is weakness another way[b]." And so are
the strengths of a man's heart: they are fetters and manacles;
strong, but they are the cordage of imprisonment; so strong,
that the heart is not able to stir. And yet it cannot but be
a huge sadness, that the heart shall pursue a temporal interest with wit and diligence, and an unwearied industry;
and shall not have strength enough, in a matter that concerns
its eternal interest, to answer one objection, to resist one

[b] Arrian.

assault, to defeat one art of the devil; but shall certainly and infallibly fall, whenever it is tempted to a pleasure.

This, if it be examined, will prove to be a deceit, indeed, a pretence, rather than true upon a just cause; that is, it is not a natural, but a moral and a vicious, weakness : and we may try it in one or two familiar instances. One of the great *strengths*, shall I call it ? or weaknesses of the heart, is,—that it is strong, violent and passionate in its lusts, and weak and deceitful to resist any.   Tell the tempted person, that if he act his lust, he dishonours his body, makes himself a servant to folly, and one flesh with a harlot; be ' defiles the temples of God,' and him that defiles a temple, ' will God destroy :' tell him, that the angels, who love to be present in the nasti- ness and filth of prisons, that they may comfort and assist chaste souls and holy persons there abiding, yet they are im- patient to behold or come near the filthiness of a lustful person : tell him, that this sin is so ugly, that the devils, who are spirits, yet they delight to counterfeit the acting of this crime, and descend unto the daughters or sons of men, that they may rather lose their natures, than not to help to set a lust forward : tell them these and ten thousand things more; you move them no more, than if you should read one of Tully's orations to a mule : for the truth is, they have no power to resist it, much less to master it; their heart fails them when they meet their mistress; and they are driven like a fool to the stocks, or a bull to the slaughter-house. And yet their heart deceives them; not because it cannot re- sist the temptation, but because it will not go about it : for it is certain, the heart can, if it list.   For let a boy enter into your chamber of pleasure, and discover your folly, either your lust disbands, or your shame hides it; you will not, you dare not, do it before a stranger-boy : and yet, that you dare do it before the eyes of the all-seeing God, is impudence and folly, and a great conviction of the vanity of your pretence, and the falseness of your heart.   If thou beest a man given to thy appetite, and thou lovest a pleasant morsel as thy life, do not declaim against the precepts of temperance as impossible : try this once; abstain from that draught, or that dish.   I cannot.   No?   Give this man a great blow on the face, or tempt him with twenty pounds, and he shall fast from morning till night, and then feast himself with your money, and plain wholesome meat. And if chastity and temperance be so easy, that a man may be brought to either of them with so ready and easy instruments; let us not suffer our heart to deceive us by the weakness of its pretences, and the strength of its desires : for we do more for a boy than for God, and for twenty pounds than heaven itself.

But thus it is in every thing else : take a heretic, a rebel, a person that hath an ill cause to manage; what he wants in the strength of his reason, he shall make it up with diligence ; and a person that hath right on his side, is cold, indiligent, lazy, and inactive, trusting that the goodness of his cause will do it alone. But, so wrong prevails, while evil persons are zealous in a bad matter, and others are remiss in a good ; and the same person shall be very industrious always, when he hath least reason so to be. That is the first particular, the heart is deceitful in the managing of its natural strengths ; it is naturally and physically strong, but morally weak and impotent.

2. The heart of man is deceitful in making judgment concerning its own acts. It does not know when it is pleased or displeased; it is peevish and trifling; it would, and it would not; and it is in many cases impossible to know whether a man's heart desires such a thing or not. St. Ambrose hath an odd saying, " Facilius inveneris innocentem, quàm qui pœnitentiam dignè egerit;" "It is easier to find a man that lived innocently, than one that hath truly repented him," with a grief and care great according to the merit of his sins. Now suppose, a man that hath spent his younger years in vanity and folly, and is by the grace of God apprehensive of it, and thinks of returning to sober counsels ; this man will find his heart so false, so subtle and fugitive, so secret and undiscernible, that it will be very hard to discern whether he repents or no. For if he considers that he hates sin, and therefore repents ; alas ! he so hates it, that he dares not, if he be wise, tempt himself with an opportunity to act it : for in the midst of that which he calls hatred, he hath so much love left for it, that if the sin comes again and speaks him fair, he is lost again, he kisses the fire, and dies in its embraces. And why else should it be necessary for us to pray, that ' we be not led into temptation,' but because we

hate the sin, and yet love it too well; we curse it, and yet
follow it; we are angry at ourselves, and yet cannot be without it; we know it undoes us, but we think it pleasant. And
when we are to execute the fierce anger of the Lord upon
our sins, yet we are kind-hearted, and spare the Agag, the
reigning sin, the splendid temptation; we have some kindnesses left towards it.

These are but ill signs. How then shall I know, by some infallible token, that I am a true penitent? What and if I weep
for my sins? will you not then give me leave to conclude
my heart right with God, and at enmity with sin? It may
be so. But there are some friends that weep at parting; and,
is not thy weeping a sorrow of affection? It is a sad thing to
part with our long companion. Or, it may be thou weepest,
because thou wouldest have a sign to cozen thyself withal:
for some men are more desirous to have a sign, than the thing
signified; they would do something to shew their repentance,
that themselves may believe themselves to be penitents, having no reason from within to believe so. And I have seen
some persons weep heartily for the loss of sixpence, or for
the breaking of a glass, or at some trifling accident; and
they that do so, cannot pretend to have their tears valued at
a bigger rate than they will confess their passion to be, when
they weep; they are vexed for the dirtying of their linen, or
some such trifle, for which, the least passion is too big an
expense. So that a man cannot tell his own heart by his
tears, or the truth of his repentance by those short gusts of
sorrow. How then? Shall we suppose a man to pray against
his sin? So did St. Austin; when, in his youth, he was
tempted to lust and uncleanness, he prayed against it, and
secretly desired that God would not hear him: for here the
heart is cunning to deceive itself. For, no man did ever heartily pray against his sin in the midst of a temptation to it,
if he did in any sense or degree listen to the temptation: for
to pray against a sin, is to have desires contrary to it, and
that cannot consist with any love or any kindness to it. We
pray against it, and yet do it; and then pray again, and do
it again: and we desire it, and yet pray against the desires;
and that is almost a contradiction. Now, because no man
can be supposed to will against his own will, or choose
against his own desires; it is plain, that we cannot know

whether we mean what we say when we pray against sin, but by the event: if we never act it, never entertain it, always resist it, ever fight against it, and finally do prevail; then, at length, we may judge our own heart to have meant honestly in that one particular.

Nay, our heart is so deceitful in this matter of repentance, that the masters of spiritual life are fain to invent suppletory arts and stratagems to secure the duty. And we are advised to mourn, because we do not mourn; to be sorrowful, because we are not sorrowful. Now, if we be sorrowful in the first stage, how happens it that we know it not? Is our heart so secret to ourselves? But if we be not sorrowful in the first period, how shall we be so, or know it, in the second period? For we may as well doubt concerning the sincerity of the second, or reflex act of sorrow, as of the first and direct action. And, therefore, we may also as well be sorrowful the third time, for want of the just measure or hearty meaning of the second sorrow, as be sorrowful the second time, for want of true sorrow at the first; and so on to infinite. And we shall never be secure in this artifice, if we be not certain of our natural and hearty passion in our direct and first apprehensions.

Thus many persons think themselves in a good estate, and make no question of their salvation, being 'confident only because they are confident; and they are so, because they are bidden to be so; and yet they are not confident at all, but extremely timorous and fearful. How many persons are there in the world, that say they are sure of their salvation, and yet they dare not die? And, if any man pretends that he is now sure he shall be saved, and that he cannot fall away from grace; there is no better way to confute him, than by advising him to send for the surgeon, and bleed to death. For what would hinder him? not the sin; for it cannot take him from God's favour: not the change of his condition; for he says, he is sure to go to a better: why does he not then say, κέκρικα, like the Roman gallants when they 'decreed' to die. The reason is plainly this, they say they are confident, and yet are extremely timorous; they profess to believe that doctrine, and yet dare not trust it; nay, they think they believe, but they do not: so false is a man's heart, so deceived in its own acts, so great a stranger to its own sentence and opinions.

3. The heart is deceitful in its own resolutions and purposes : for many times men make their resolutions only in their understanding, not in their will; they resolve it fitting to be done, not decree that they will do it; and instead of beginning to be reconciled to God by the renewed and hearty purposes of holy living, they are advanced so far only as to be convinced, and apt to be condemned by their own sentence.

But suppose our resolutions advanced farther, and that our will and choices also are determined; see how our hearts deceive us.

1. We resolve against those sins that please us not, or where temptation is not present, and think, by an over-acted zeal against some sins, to give an indulgence for some others. There are some persons who will be drunk; the company, or the discourse, or the pleasure of madness, or an easy nature and a thirsty soul, something is amiss, that cannot be helped: but they will make amends, and the next day pray twice as much. Or, it may be, they must satisfy a beastly lust; but they will not be drunk for all the world; and hope, by their temperance, to commute for their want of chastity. But they attend not the craft of their secret enemy, their heart: for it is not love of the virtue; if it were, they would love virtue in all its instances[c]; for chastity is as much a virtue as temperance, and God hates lust as much as he hates drunkenness. But this sin is against my health, or, it may be, it is against my lust; it makes me impotent, and yet impatient; full of desire, and empty of strength. Or else I do an act of prayer, lest my conscience become unquiet, while it is not satisfied, or cozened with some intervals of religion : I shall think myself a damned wretch if I do nothing for my soul; but if I do, I shall call the one sin that remains, nothing but my infirmity; and therefore it is my excuse: and my prayer is not my religion, but my peace, and my pretence, and my fallacy.

2. We resolve against our sin, that is, we will not act it in those circumstances as formerly. I will not be drunk in

---

[c] Virtutem si unam amiseris (etsi amitti Virtus non potest), sed si unam confessus fueris te non habere, nullam te esse habiturum? *Cicer.* T. Q. 2. 13. Davis.

the streets; but I may sleep till I be recovered, and then come forth sober: or, if I be overtaken, it shall be in civil and genteel company. Or it may be not so much; I will leave my intemperance and my lust too, but I will remember it with pleasure; I will revolve the past action in my mind, and entertain my fancy with a morose delectation in it, and, by a fiction of imagination, will represent it present, and so be satisfied with a little effeminacy or fantastic pleasure. Beloved, suffer not your hearts so to cozen you; as if any man can be faithful in much, that is faithless in a little. He certainly is very much in love with sin, and parts with it very unwillingly, that keeps its picture, and wears its favour, and delights in the fancy of it, even with the same desire as a most passionate widow parts with her dearest husband, even when she can no longer enjoy him: but certainly her staring all day upon his picture, and weeping over his robe, and wringing her hands over his children, are no great signs that she hated him. And just so do most men hate, and accordingly part with, their sins.

3. We resolve against it when the opportunity is slipped, and lay it aside as long as the temptation please, even till it come again, and no longer. How many men are there in the world, that against every communion renew their vows of holy living? men that for twenty, for thirty, years together, have been perpetually resolving against what they daily act; and sure enough they did believe themselves. And yet if a man had daily promised us a courtesy, and failed us but ten times, when it was in his power to have done it,—we should think we had reason never to believe him more. And can we then reasonably believe the resolutions of our hearts, which they have falsified so many hundred times? We resolve against a religious time, because then it is the custom of men, and the guise of the religion: or we resolve when we are in a great danger; and then we promise any thing, possible or impossible, likely or unlikely, all is one to us; we only care to remove the present pressure; and when that is over, and our fear is gone, and no love remaining, our condition being returned to our first securities, our resolutions also revert to their first indifferences: or else we cannot look a temptation in the face, and we resolve against it, hoping never to be troubled with its arguments and importunity. Epictetus

tells us of a gentleman returning from banishment, who, in his journey towards home, called at his house, told a sad story of an imprudent life, the greatest part of which being now spent, he was resolved for the future to live philosophically, and entertain no business, to be candidate for no employment, not to go to the court, not to salute Cæsar with ambitious attendances, but to study, and worship the gods, and die willingly, when nature or necessity called him. It may be, this man believed himself, but Epictetus did not. And he had reason: for ἀπήντησαν αὐτῷ παρὰ Καίσαρος πινακίδες, "letters from Cæsar met him" at the doors, and invited him to court; and he forgot all his promises, which were warm upon his lips; and grew pompous, secular, and ambitious, and gave the gods thanks for his preferment [a]. Thus many men leave the world, when their fortune hath left them; and they are severe and philosophical, and retired for ever, if for ever it be impossible to return: but let a prosperous sunshine warm and refresh their sadnesses, and make it but possible to break their purposes, and there needs no more temptation; their own false heart is enough; they are like 'Ephraim in the day of battle, starting aside like a broken bow.'

4. The heart is false, deceiving and deceived, in its intentions and designs. A man hears the precepts of God enjoining us to give alms of all we possess; he readily obeys with much cheerfulness and alacrity, and his charity, like a fair-spreading tree, looks beauteously: but there is a canker at the heart; the man blows a trumpet to call the poor together, and hopes the neighbourhood will take notice of his bounty. Nay, he gives alms privately, and charges no man to speak of it, and yet hopes by some accident or other to be praised both for his charity and humility. And if, by chance, the fame of his alms come abroad, it is but his duty to 'let his light so shine before men,' that God may be 'glorified,' and some of our neighbours be relieved, and others edified. But then, to distinguish the intention of our heart in this instance, and to seek God's glory in a particular, which will also conduce much to our reputation, and to have no filthy adherence to stick to the heart, no reflection upon ourselves, or no complacency and delight in popular noises,—is the nicety of abstraction, and requires an angel to do it. Some men

are so kind-hearted, so true to their friend, that they will watch his very dying groans, and receive his last breath, and close his eyes. And if this be done with honest intention, it is well: but there are some that do so, and yet are vultures and harpies; they watch for the carcass, and prey upon a legacy. A man with a true story may be malicious to his enemy, and by doing himself right may also do him wrong: and so false is the heart of man, so clancular and contradictory are its actions and intentions, that some men pursue virtue with great earnestness, and yet cannot with patience look upon it in another: it is beauty in themselves, and deformity in the other. Is it not plain, that not the virtue, but its reputation, is the thing that is pursued? And yet, if you tell the man so, he thinks he hath reason to complain of your malice or detraction. Who is able to distinguish his fear of God, from fear of punishment, when, from fear of punishment, we are brought to fear God? And yet the difference must be distinguishable in new converts and old disciples; and our fear of punishment must so often change its circumstances, that it must be at last a fear to offend out of pure love, and must have no formality left to distinguish it from charity. It is easy to distinguish these things in precepts, and to make the separation in the schools; the head can do it easily, and the tongue can do it: but when the heart comes to separate alms from charity, God's glory from human praise, fear from fear, and sincerity from hypocrisy; it does so intricate the questions, and confound the ends, and blind and entangle circumstances, that a man hath reason to doubt that his very best actions are sullied with some unhandsome excrescency, something to make them very often to be criminal, but always to be imperfect.

Here, a man would think, were enough to abate our confidence, and the spirit of pride, and to make a man eternally to stand upon his guard, and to keep a strict watch upon his own heart, as upon his greatest enemy from without. "Custodi, libera me de meipso, Deus;" it was St. Austin's prayer; "Lord, keep me, Lord, deliver me from myself." If God will keep a man that he be not 'felo de se,' that 'he lay no violent bands upon himself,' it is certain nothing else can do him mischief. Οὔτε Ζεὺς, οὔτε μοῖρα, οὔτε Ἐριννὺς, as Agamemnon said; "Neither Jupiter, nor destinies, nor the

furies," but it is a man's self, that does him the mischief. The
devil can but tempt, and offer a dagger at the heart; unless
our hands thrust it home, the devil can do nothing, but what
may turn to our advantage. And in this sense we are to
understand the two seeming contradictories in Scripture:
" Pray that ye enter not into temptation," said our blessed
Saviour; and, " Count it all joy when you enter into divers
temptations," said one of Christ's disciples. The case is
easy. When God suffers us to be tempted, he means it but
as a trial of our faith, as the exercise of our virtues, as the
opportunity of reward; and in such cases we have reason to
count it all joy; since the " trial of our faith worketh patience, and patience experience, and experience causeth hope,
and hope maketh not ashamed:" but yet, for all this, ' pray
against temptations:' for when we get them into our hands, we
use them as blind men do their clubs, neither distinguish person nor part; they strike the face of their friends as soon as
the back of the enemy; our hearts betray us to the enemy, we
fall in love with our mischief, we contrive how to let the lust
in, and leave a port open on purpose, and use arts to forget
our duty, and give advantages to the devil. He that uses a
temptation thus, hath reason to pray against it; and yet our
hearts do all this and a thousand times more; so that we
may engrave upon our hearts the epitaph, which was digged
into Thyestes' grave-stone;

> Nolite, hospites, ad me adire ; illico isthic ;
> Ne contagio mea bonis umbrave obsit :
> Meo tanta vis sceleris io corpore hærat [d].

There is so much falseness and iniquity in man's heart,
that it defiles all the members : it makes the eyes lustful,
and the tongue slanderous; it fills the head with mischief, and
the feet with blood, and the hands with injury, and the present condition of man with folly, and makes his future state
apt to inherit eternal misery. But this is but the beginning
of those throes and damnable impieties which proceed out
of the heart of man, and defile the whole constitution. I
have yet told but the *weaknesses* of the heart; I shall the
next time tell you the *iniquities*, those inherent devils which
pollute and defile it to the ground, and make it " desperately
wicked," that is, wicked beyond all expression.

[d] Cicero de Orat. III. c. 41. Harles. p. 567.

SERMON VIII.

PART II.

Ἀρχὴ φιλοσοφίας συναίσθησις τῆς αὐτοῦ ἀσθενίας, καὶ ἀδυναμίας περὶ τὰ ἀναγκαῖα, "It is the beginning of wisdom to know a man's own weaknesses and failings, in things of greatest necessity*:" and we have here so many objects to furnish out this knowledge, that we find it with the longest and latest, before it be obtained. A man does not begin to know himself till he be old, and then he is well stricken in death. A man's heart at first being like a plain table; unspotted, indeed, but then there is nothing legible in it: as soon as ever we ripen towards the imperfect uses of our reason, we write upon this table such crooked characters, such imperfect configurations, so many fooleries, and stain it with so many blots and vicious inspersions, that there is nothing worth the reading in our hearts for a great while: and when education and ripeness, reason and experience, Christian philosophy and the grace of God, have made fair impressions, and written the law in our hearts with the finger of God's Holy Spirit, we blot out this hand-writing of God's ordinances, or mingle it with false principles and interlinings of our own; we disorder the method of God, or deface the truth of God; either we make the rule uneven, we bribe or abuse our guide, that we may wander with an excuse; or if nothing else will do it, we turn head and profess to go against the laws of God. Our hearts are blind, or our hearts are hardened; for, these are two great arguments of the wickedness of our hearts; they do not see, or they will not see, the ways of God; or, if they do, they make use of their seeing, that they may avoid them.

1. Our hearts are blind, wilfully blind. I need not instance in the ignorance and involuntary nescience of men; though if we speak of the necessary parts of religion, no man is ignorant of them without his own fault: such ignorance is always a direct sin, or the direct punishment of a sin: a sin is either in its bosom, or in its retinue. But the ignorance that I now intend, is a voluntary, chosen, delightful ig-

* Epict. Arrian.

norance, taken in upon design, even for no other end, but
that we may perish quietly and infallibly. God hath opened
all the windows of heaven, and sent the Sun of Righteousness
with glorious apparition, and hath discovered the abysses of
his own wisdom, made the second person in the Trinity to
be the doctor and preacher of his sentences and secrets, and
the third person to be his amanuensis or scribe, and our
hearts to be the book in which the doctrine is written, and
miracles and prophecies to be its arguments, and all the
world to be the verification of it : and those leaves contain
within their folds all that excellent morality, which right reason picked up after the shipwreck of nature, and all those
wise sayings which singly made so many men famous for
preaching some one of them ; all them Christ gathered, and
added some more out of the immediate book of revelation.
So that now the wisdom of God hath made every man's heart
to be the true vetonica, in which he hath imprinted his own
lineaments so perfectly, that we may dress ourselves like
God, and have the air and features of Christ our elder brother ;
that we may be pure as God is, perfect as our Father, meek
and humble as the Son, and may have the Holy Ghost within
us, in gifts and graces, in wisdom and holiness. This hath
God done for us; and see what we do for him. We stand
in our own light, and quench God's : we love darkness more
than light, and entertain ourselves accordingly. For how
many of us are there, that understand nothing of the ways of
God; that know no more of the laws of Jesus Christ than
is remaining upon them since they learned the children's
catechism ? But, amongst a thousand, how many can explicate and unfold for his own practice the ten commandments,
and how many sorts of sins are there forbidden ? which therefore pass into action, and never pass under the scrutinies of
repentance, because they know not that they are sins ? Are
there not very many, who know not the particular duties of
' meekness,' and never consider concerning ' long-suffering ?'.
and if you talk to them of growth in grace, or the Spirit of
obsignation, or the melancholic lectures of the cross, and
imitation of, and conformity to, Christ's sufferings, or adherences to God, or rejoicing in him, or not quenching the
Spirit; you are too deep-learned for them. And yet these
are duties set down plainly for our practice, necessary to be

acted in order to our salvation. We brag of light, and reformation, and fulness of the Spirit: in the meantime we understand not many parts of our duty. We inquire into something that they make us talk, or be talked of, or that we may trouble a church, or disturb the peace of minds: but in things that concern holy living, and that wisdom of God whereby we are wise unto salvation, never was any age of Christendom more ignorant than we. For, if we did not wink hard, we must needs see, that obedience to supreme powers, denying of ourselves, humility, peacefulness, and charity, are written in such capital text letters, that it is impossible to be ignorant of them. And if the heart of man had not rare arts to abuse the understanding, it were not to be imagined that any man should bring the thirteenth chapter to the Romans, to prove the lawfulness of taking up arms against our rulers: but so we may abuse ourselves at noon, and go to bed, if we please to call it midnight. And there have been a sort of witty men, that maintained that snow was hot. I wonder not at the problem: but that a man should believe his paradox, and should let eternity go away with the fallacy, and rather lose heaven than leave his foolish argument; is a sign that wilfulness and the deceiving heart is the sophister, and the great ingredient into our deception.

But, that I may be more particular; the heart of man uses devices that it may be ignorant.

1. We are impatient of honest and severe reproof; and order the circumstances of our persons and addresses, that we shall never come to the true knowledge of our condition. Who will endure to bear his curate tell him, that he is covetous, or that he is proud? Λέγει, ὦ δεινῆς ὕβρεως. It is calumny and reviling, if he speak it to his head, and relates to his person: and yet if he speak only in general, every man neglects what is not recommended to his particular. But yet, if our physician tell us, You look well, sir, but a fever lurks in your spirits; Ἀσίτησον, σήμερον ὕδωρ πίε, "Drink juleps, and abstain from flesh;"—no man thinks it shame or calumny to be told so: but when we are told that our lives is inflamed with lust or anger, that our heart is vexed with envy, that our eyes roll with wantonness; and, though we think all is well, yet we are sick, sick unto death, and near to a sad and fatal sentence; we shall think that man that

tells us so, is impudent or uncharitable ; and yet he hath
done him no more injury than a deformed man receives
daily from his looking-glass, which if he shall dash against
the wall, because it shews him his face just as it is, his face
is not so ugly as his manners.   And yet our heart is so impatient of seeing its own stains, that, like the elephant, it
tramples in the pure streams, and first troubles them, then
stoops and drinks, when he can least see his huge deformity.

2. In order to this, we heap up teachers of our own, and
they guide us, not whither, but which way, they please : for
we are curious to go our own way, and careless of our hospital or inn at night.   A fair way, and a merry company,
and a pleasant easy guide, will entice us into the enemy's
quarters ; and such guides we cannot want : " Improbitati
occasio nunquam defuit ;" " If we have a mind to be wicked,
we shall want no prompters ;" and false teachers, at first
creeping in unawares, have now so filled the pavement of
the church, that you can scarce set your foot on the ground
but you tread upon a snake.   Cicero (l. 7. ad Atticum) un-
dertakes to bargain with them that kept the Sibyls' books,
that for a sum of money they should expound to him what
he please ; and, to be sure, " ut quidvis potius quàm regem
proferrent ;" " They shall declare against the government of
kings, and say, that the gods will endure any thing rather
than monarchy in their beloved republic."   And the same
mischief God complains of to be among the Jews : " The
prophets prophesy lies, and my people love to have it so :
and what will the end of these things be ?"—even the same
that Cicero complained of, " Ad opinionem imperatorum
fictas esse religiones[f];" men shall have what religion they
please, and God shall be entitled to all the quarrels of covetous and ambitious persons ; καὶ Πυθίαν φιλιππίζειν, as Demos-
thenes wittily complained of the oracle ; an answer shall be
drawn out of Scripture to countenance the design, and God
made the rebel against his own ordinances.   And then we
are zealous for the Lord God of hosts, and will live and die
in that quarrel.   But is it not a strange cozenage, that our
hearts shall be the main wheel in the engine, and shall set
all the rest on working ?   The heart shall first put his own
candle out, then put out the eye of reason, then remove the

[f] De Divinat. l. 2.

land-mark, and dig down the causeways, and then either hire a blind guide, or make him so : and all these arts to get ignorance, that they may secure impiety.   At first, man lost his innocence only in hope to get a little knowledge : and ever since then, lest knowledge should discover his error, and make him return to innocence, we are content to part with that now, and to know nothing that may discover or discountenance our sins, or discompose our secular designs. And, as God made great revelations, and furnished out a wise religion, and sent his Spirit to give the gift of faith to his church, that, upon the foundation of faith, he might build a holy life : now our hearts love to retire into blindness, and sneak under covert of false principles, and run to a cheap religion, and an inactive discipline, and make a faith of our own, that we may build upon it ease, and ambition, and a tall fortune, and the pleasures of revenge, and do what we have a mind to ; scarce once in seven years denying a strong and an unruly appetite upon the interest of a just conscience and holy religion.   This is such a desperate method of impiety, so certain arts and apt instruments for the devil, that it does his work entirely, and produces an infallible damnation.

3. But the heart of man hath yet another stratagem to secure its iniquity by the means of ignorance ; and that is, incogitancy or inconsideration.   For there is wrought upon the spirits of many men great impressions by education, by a modest and temperate nature, by human laws, and the customs and severities of sober persons, and the fears of religion, and the awfulness of a reverend man, and the several arguments and endearments of virtue : and it is not in the nature of some men to do an act in despite of reason, and religion, and arguments, and reverence, and modesty, and fear ; but men are forced from their sin by the violence of the grace of God, when they hear it speak.   But so a Roman gentleman kept off a whole band of soldiers, who were sent to murder him, and his eloquence was stronger than their anger and design : but, suddenly, a rude trooper rushed upon him, who neither had nor would hear him speak ; and he thrust his spear into that throat, whose music had charmed all his fellows into peace and gentleness. So do we. The grace of God is armour and defence enough, against the most violent incursion of the spirits and the works of dark-

ness; but then we must hear its excellent charm s, and con‑
sider its reasons, and remember its precepts, and dwell with
its discourses. But this the heart of man loves not. If I
be tempted to uncleanness, or to an act of oppression, in‑
stantly the grace of God represents to me, that the pleasure
of the sin is transient and vain, unsatisfying and empty ; that
I shall die, and then I shall wish too late that I had never
done it. It tells me, that I displease God who made me,
who feeds me, who blesses me, who fain would save me. It
represents to me all the joys of heaven, and the horrors and
amazements of a sad eternity; and, if I will stay and hear
them, ten thousand excellent things besides, fit to be twist‑
ed about my understanding for ever. But here the heart of
man shuffles all these discourses into disorder, and will not
be put to the trouble of answering the objections; but, by a
mere wildness of purpose, and rudeness of resolution, ven‑
tures ' super totam materiam,' at all, and does the thing,
not because it thinks it fit to do so, but because it will not
consider whether it be or no ; it is enough, that it pleases a
pleasant appetite. And if such incogitancy comes to be ha‑
bitual, as it is in very many men,—first by resisting the mo‑
tions of the Holy Spirit, then by quenching him,—we shall
find the consequence to be, first an indifferency,—then a
dulness,—then a lethargy,—then a direct hating the ways of
God ;—and it commonly ends in a wretchlessness of spirit, to
be manifested on our death-bed ; when the man shall pass
hence, not like the shadow, but like the dog, that departeth
without sense, or interest, or apprehension, or real concern‑
ment, in the considerations of eternity : and it is but just,
when we will not hear our King speak and plead, not to
save himself, but us, to speak for our peace, and innocency,
and salvation, to prevent our ruin, and our intolerable cala‑
mity. Certainly, we are much in love with the wages of
death, when we cannot endure to hear God call us back, and
' stop our ears against the voice of the charmer, charm he
ever so wisely.'

Nay, farther yet, we suffer the arguments of religion to
have so little impression upon our spirits, that they operate
but like the discourses of childhood, or the problems of un‑
certain philosophy. A man talks of religion but as of a
dream, and from thence he awakens into the businesses of

the world, and acts them deliberately, with perfect action
and full resolution, and contrives, and considers, and lives
in them: but when he falls asleep again, or is taken from
the scene of his own employment and choice, then he dreams
again, and religion makes such impressions as is the conversation of a dreamer, and he acts accordingly. Theocritus
tells of a fisherman, that dreamed he had taken χρύσιον
ἰχθὺν, 'a fish of gold'; upon which being overjoyed, he
made a vow, that he would never fish more: but when he
waked, he soon declared his vow to be null, because he
found his golden fish was escaped away through the holes
of his eyes, when he first opened them. Just so we do in
the purposes of religion; sometimes, in a good mood, we seem
to see heaven opened, and all the streets of the heavenly Jerusalem paved with gold and precious stones, and we are ravished with spiritual apprehensions, and resolve never to return to the low affections of the world, and the impure adherences of sin: but when this flash of lightning is gone,
and we converse again with the inclinations and habitual desires of our false hearts, those other desires and fine considerations disband, and the resolutions, taken in that pious
fit, melt into indifference and old customs. He was prettily
and fantastically troubled, who, having used to put his trust
in dreams, one night dreamed that all dreams were vain ;
for he considered, if so, then this was vain, and the dreams
might be true for all this: but if they might be true, then
this dream might be so upon equal reason: and then dreams
were vain, because this dream, which told him so, was true ;
and so round again. In the same circle runs the heart of
man: all his cogitations are vain, and yet he makes especial
use of this, that that thought which thinks so, that is vain ;
and if that be vain, then his other thoughts, which are vainly
declared so, may be real, and relied upon. And so do we:
those religious thoughts which are sent into us to condemn
and disrepute the thoughts of sin and vanity, are esteemed
the only dreams: and so all those instruments which the
grace of God hath invented for the destruction of impiety,
are rendered ineffectual, either by our direct opposing them,
or (which happens most commonly) by our want of considering them.

The effect of all is this, that we are ignorant of the things of God. We make religion to be the work of a few hours in the whole year; we are without fancy or affection to the severities of holy living; we reduce religion to the believing of a few articles, and doing nothing that is considerable; we pray seldom, and then but very coldly and indifferently; we communicate not so often as the sun salutes both the tropics; we profess Christ, but dare not die for him; we are factious for a religion, and will not live according to its precepts; we call ourselves Christians, and love to be ignorant of many of the laws of Christ, lest our knowledge should force us into shame, or into the troubles of a holy life. All the mischiefs that you can suppose to happen to a furious inconsiderate person, running after the wildfires of the night, over rivers, and rocks, and precipices, without sun or star, or angel or man, to guide him; all that, and ten thousand times worse, may you suppose to be the certain lot of him, who gives himself up to the conduct of a passionate, blind heart, whom no fire can warm, and no sun can enlighten; who hates light, and loves to dwell in the regions of darkness. That is the first general mischief of the heart, it is possessed with blindness, wilful and voluntary.

2. But the heart is hard too. Not only folly, but mischief also, is bound up in the heart of man. If God strives to soften it with sorrow and sad accidents, it is like an ox, it grows callous and hard. Such a heart was Pharaoh's. When God makes the clouds to gather round about us, we wrap our heads in the clouds, and, like the malecontents in Galba's time, "tristitiam simulamus, contumaciæ propiores," "we seem sad and troubled, but it is doggedness and murmur."—Or else, if our fears be pregnant, and the heart yielding, it sinks low into pusillanimity and superstition; and our hearts are so childish, so timorous, or so impatient, in a sadness, that God is weary of striking us, and we are glad of it. And yet, when the sun shines upon us, our hearts are hardened with that too; and God seems to be at a loss, as if he knew not what to do to us. War undoes us, and makes us violent; peace undoes us, and makes us wanton; prosperity makes us proud; adversity renders us impatient; plenty dissolves us, and makes us tyrants; want makes us greedy, liars, and rapacious.

Πᾶς οὖν τις ἂν σώσειε ταιαύτην πόλιν,
Ἡ μήτε χλαῖνα, μήτε συρύρα ξυμφέρει[a] ;

' No fortune can save that city, to whom neither peace nor war can do advantage.' And what is there left for God to mollify our hearts, whose temper is like both to wax and dirt; whom fire hardens, and cold hardens; and contradictory accidents produce no change, save that the heart grows worse and more obdurate for every change of Providence? But here also I must descend to particulars.

1. The heart of man is strangely proud. If men commend us, we think we have reason to distinguish ourselves from others, since the voice of discerning men hath already made the separation. If men do not commend us, we think they are stupid, and understand us not; or envious, and hold their tongues in spite. If we are praised by many, then "Vox populi, vox Dei," "Fame is the voice of God." If we be praised but by few, then "Satis unus, satis nullus;" we cry, ' These are wise, and one wise man is worth a whole herd of the people.' But if we be praised by none at all, we resolve to be even with all the world, and speak well of nobody, and think well only of ourselves. And then we have such beggarly arts, such tricks, to cheat for praise. We inquire after our faults and failings, only to be told we have none, but did excellently; and then we are pleased: we rail upon our actions, only to be chidden for so doing; and then he is our friend who chides us into a good opinion of ourselves, which however all the world cannot make us part with. Nay, humility itself makes us proud; so false, so base, is the heart of man. For humility is so noble a virtue, that even pride itself puts on its upper garment: and we do like those who cannot endure to look upon an ugly or a deformed person, and yet will give a great price for a picture extremely like him. Humility is despised in substance, but courted and admired in effigy. And Æsop's picture was sold for two talents, when himself was made a slave at the price of two philippics. And because humility makes a man to be honoured, therefore we imitate all its garbs and postures, its civilities and silence, its modesties and condescensions. And, to prove that we are extremely proud, in the midst of all this pageantry, we should be extremely angry at any man that should say we are proud;

* Aristoph. Ran. 1459. Brunck.

and, that is a sure sign we are so. And in the midst of all our arts to seem humble, we use devices to bring ourselves into talk ; we thrust ourselves into company, we listen at doors, and, like the greatbeards in Rome that pretended philosophy and strict life, ὀβιλίσκον κατεπιόντες περιπατοῦμεν, "we walk by the obelisk[*]," and meditate in piazzas, that they that meet us may talk of us, and they that follow may cry out,῾Ω μεγάλου φιλοσόφου! Behold! there goes an excellent man! He is very prudent, or very learned, or a charitable person, or a good housekeeper, or at least very humble.

2. The heart of man is deeply in love with wickedness, and with nothing else; against not only the laws of God, but against his own reason, its own interest, and its own securities. For is it imaginable, that a man, who knows the laws of God, the rewards of virtue, the cursed and horrid effects of sin ; that knows, and considers, and deeply sighs at, the thought of the intolerable pains of hell ; that knows the joys of heaven to be unspeakable, and that concerning them there is no temptation, but that they are too big for man to hope for, and yet he certainly believes, that a holy life shall infallibly attain thither : is it, I say, imaginable, that this man should, for a transient action, forfeit all this hope, and certainly and knowingly incur all that calamity ? Yea, but the sin is pleasant, and the man is clothed with flesh and blood, and their appetites are material, and importunate, and present ; and the discourses of religion are concerning things spiritual, separate and apt for spirits, angels, and souls departed. To take off this also, we will suppose the man to consider, and really to believe, that the pleasure of the sin is sudden, vain, empty, and transient ; that it leaves bitterness upon the tongue, before it is descended into the bowels ; that there it is poison, and " makes the belly to swell, and the thigh to rot ;" that be remembers, and actually considers, that as soon as the moment of sin is past, he shall have an intolerable conscience, and does, at the instant, compare moments with eternity, and with horror remembers, that the very next minute he is as miserable a man as is in the world : yet that this man should sin ? Nay, suppose the sin to have no pleasure at all, such as is the sin of swearing ; nay, sup-

[*] Arrian, Upton, t. 1. p. 60.

·pose it to have pain in it, such as is the sin of envy, which never can have pleasure in its actions, but much torment and consumption of the very heart: what should make this man sin so for nothing, so against himself, so against all reason and religion, and interest, without pleasure, for no reward? Here the ¡heart betrays itself to be "desperately wicked." What man can give a reasonable account of such a man, who, to prosecute his revenge, will do himself an injury, that he may do a less to him that troubles him. Such a man hath given me ill language: Οὔτε τὴν κεφαλὴν ἀλγεῖ, οὔτετὸν ὀφθαλμον, οὔτε τὸν ἰσχίον, οὔτε τὸν ἀγρὸν ἀπολλύει, "My head aches not for his language, nor hath he broken my thigh, nor carried away my land:" but yet this man must be requited; well, suppose that. But then let it be proportionably; you are not undone, let not him be so.—Oh, yes; for else my revenge triumphs not;—well, if you do, yet remember, he will defend himself, or the law will right him; at least, do not do wrong to yourself by doing him wrong: this were but prudence, and self-interest. And yet we see, that the heart of some men hath betrayed them to such furiousness of appetite, as to make them willing to die, that their enemy may be buried in the same ruins. Jovius Pontanus tells of an Italian slave, I think, who, being enraged against his lord, watched his absence from home, and the employment and inadvertency of his fellow-servants: he locked the doors, and secured himself for awhile, and ravished his lady; then took her three sons up to the battlements of the house, and, at the return of his lord, threw one down to him upon the pavement, and then a second, to rend the heart of their sad father, seeing them weltering in their blood and brains. The lord begged for his third, and now his only son, promising pardon and liberty if he would spare his life. The slave seemed to bend a little, and, on condition his lord would cut off his own nose, he would spare his son. The sad father did so, being willing to suffer any thing rather than the loss of that child. But as soon as he saw his lord all bloody with his wound, he threw the third son and himself down together upon the pavement. The story is sad enough, and needs no lustre and advantages of sorrow to represent it: but if a man sets himself down, and considers sadly, he cannot easily tell, upon what sufficient inducement, or what principle, the slave should so certainly, so horridly, so presently, and then so eternally, ruin himself. What could he propound to himself as a recompense to his own so-immediate tragedy? There is not in the pleasure of the revenge, nor in the nature of the thing, any thing to tempt him; we must confess our ignorance, and say, that "The heart of man is desperately wicked;" and that is the truth in general, but we cannot fathom it by particular comprehension.

For when the heart of man is bound up by the grace of God, and tied in golden bands, and watched by angels, tended by those nursekeepers of the soul, it is not easy for a man to wander; and the evil of his heart is but like the ferity and wildness of lions' whelps: but when once we have broken the edge, and got into the strengths of youth, and the licentiousness of an ungoverned age, it is wonderful to observe, what a great inundation of mischief, in a very short time, will overflow all the banks of reason and religion. Vice first is pleasing,—then it grows easy,—then delightful,—then frequent,—then habitual,—then confirmed;—then the man is impenitent,—then he is obstinate,—then he resolves never to repent,—and then he is damned.—And by that time he is come half-way in this progress, he confutes the philosophy of the old moralists: for they, not knowing the vileness of man's heart, not considering its desperate, amazing impiety, knew no other degree of wickedness but this, that men preferred sense before reason, and their understandings were abused in the choice of a temporal before an intellectual and eternal good: but they always concluded, that the will of man must of necessity follow the last dictate of the understanding, declaring an object to be good, in one sense or other. Happy men they were that were so innocent, that knew no pure and perfect malice, and lived in an age in which it was not easy to confute them. But, besides that now the wells of a deeper iniquity are discovered, we see, by too sad experience, that there are some sins proceeding from the heart of a man, which have nothing but simple and unmingled malice: actions of mere spite, doing evil because it is evil, sinning without sensual pleasures, sinning with sensual pain, with hazard of our lives, with actual torment, and sudden deaths, and certain and present damnation; sins against the Holy Ghost, open hostilities, and professed enmities, against God and all virtue. I can go no farther, because there is not in the world, or in the nature of things, a greater evil. And that is the nature and folly of the devil; he tempts men to ruin, and hates God, and only hurts himself and those he tempts, and does himself no pleasure, and some say he increases his own accidental torment.

Although I can say nothing greater, yet I had many more things to say, if the time would have permitted me to represent the falseness and baseness of the heart. 1. We are false ourselves, and dare not trust God. 2. We love to be deceived, and are angry if we be told so. 3. We love to seem virtuous, and yet hate to be so. 4. We are melancholic and impatient, and we know not why. 5. We are troubled at little things, and are careless of greater. 6. We are overjoyed at a petty accident, and despise great and eternal pleasures. 7. We believe things, not for their reasons and proper arguments, but as they serve our turns, be they true or false. 8. We long extremely for things that are forbidden us; and what we despise when it is permitted us, we snatch at greedily, when it is taken from us. 9. We love ourselves more than we love God; and yet we eat poisons daily, and feed upon toads and vipers, and nourish our deadly enemies in our bosom, and will not be brought to quit them; but brag of our shame, and are ashamed of nothing but virtue, which is most honourable. 10. We fear to die, and yet use all means we can to make death terrible and dangerous. 11. We are busy in the faults of others, and negligent of our own. 12. We live the life of spies, striving to know others, and to be unknown ourselves. 13. We worship and flatter some men and some things, because we fear them, not because we love them. 14. We are ambitious of greatness, and covetous of wealth, and all that we get by it is, that we are more beautifully tempted; and a troop of clients run to us as to a pool, which first they trouble, and then draw dry. 15. We make ourselves unsafe by committing wickedness, and then we add more wickedness, to make us safe and beyond punishment. 16. We are more servile for one courtesy that we hope for, than for twenty that we have received. 17. We entertain slanderers, and, without choice, spread their calumnies; and we hug flatterers, and know they abuse us. And if I should gather the abuses, and impieties, and deceptions, of the heart, as Chrysippus did the oracular lies of Apollo into a table, I fear they would seem remediless, and beyond the cure of watchfulness and religion.   Indeed, they are great and many; but the grace of God is greater; and 'if iniquity abounds,' then 'doth grace superabound:' and that is our comfort and our medicine, which we must thus use.

1. Let us watch our heart at every turn.

2. Deny it all its desires that do not directly, or by consequence, end in godliness : at no hand be indulgent to its fondnesses and peevish appetites.

3. Let us suspect it as an enemy.

4. Trust not to it in any thing.

5. But beg the grace of God with perpetual and importunate prayer, that he would be pleased to bring good out of these evils ; and that he would throw the salutary wood of the cross, the merits of Christ's death and passion, into these salt waters, and make them healthful and pleasant.

And in order to the managing these advices, and acting the purposes of this prayer, let us strictly follow a rule, and choose a prudent and faithful guide, who may attend our motions, and watch our counsels, and direct our steps, and 'prepare the way of the Lord, and make his paths straight,' apt, and imitable.   For without great watchfulness, and earnest devotion, and a prudent guide, we shall find that true in a spiritual sense, which Plutarch affirmed of a man's body in the natural : that of dead bulls arise bees; from the carcasses of horses, hornets are produced : but the body of man brings forth serpents.   Our hearts, wallowing in their own natural and acquired corruptions, will produce nothing but issues of hell, and images of the old serpent the devil, for whom is provided the everlasting burning.

SERMON IX.

THE FAITH AND PATIENCE OF THE SAINTS; OR, THE RIGHTEOUS CAUSE OPPRESSED.

PART I.

For the time is come that judgment must begin at the house of
God: and if it first begin at us, what shall the end be of them
that obey not the Gospel of God?
And if the righteous scarcely be saved, where shall the ungodly
and the sinner appear?—1 Peter, iv. 17, 18.

So long as the world lived by sense, and discourses of natural reason, as they were abated with human infirmities,
and not at all heightened by the Spirit and divine revelations; so long men took their accounts of good and bad
by their being prosperous or unfortunate: and amongst the
basest and most ignorant of men, that only was accounted
honest which was profitable; and he only wise, that was
rich; and those men beloved of God, who received from
him all that might satisfy their lust, their ambition, or their
revenge.

——— Fatis accede, Deisque,
Et cole felices, miseros fuge: sidera terrâ
Ut distant, ut flamma mari, sic utile recto [x].

But because God sent wise men into the world, and they
were treated rudely by the world, 'and exercised with evil
accidents, and this seemed so great a discouragement to
virtue, that even these wise men were more troubled to reconcile virtue and misery, than to reconcile their affections
to the suffering; God was pleased to enlighten their reason
with a little beam of faith, or else heightened their reason
by wiser principles than those of vulgar understandings, and
taught them in the clear glass of faith, or the dim perspective of philosophy, to look beyond the cloud, and there to
spy that there stood glories behind their curtain, to which
they could not come but by passing through the cloud, and
being wet with the dew of heaven and the waters of afflic-

tion. And according as the world grew more enlightened
by faith, so it grew more dark with mourning and sorrows.
God sometimes sent a light of fire, and a pillar of a cloud,
and the brightness of an angel, and the lustre of a star, and
the sacrament of a rainbow, to guide his people through their
portion of sorrows, and to lead them through troubles to
rest: but as the Sun of Righteousness approached towards
the chambers of the east, and sent the harbingers of light
peeping through the curtains of the night, and leading on
the day of faith and brightest revelation; so God sent degrees of trouble upon wise and good men, that now, in the
same degree in the which the world lives by faith, and not by
sense, in the same degree they might be able to live in virtue
even while she lived in trouble, and not reject so great a
beauty, because she goes in mourning, and hath a black
cloud of cyprus drawn before her face. Literally thus: God
first entertained their services, and allured and prompted on
the infirmities of the infant-world by temporal prosperity;
but by degrees changed his method; and, as men grew
stronger in the knowledge of God, and the expectations of
heaven, so they grew weaker in their fortunes, more afflicted
in their bodies, more abated in their expectations, more subject to their enemies, and were to endure the contradiction
of sinners, and the immission of the sharpnesses of Providence and divine economy.

First, Adam was placed in a garden of health and pleasure, from which when he fell, he was only tied to enter into
the covenant of natural sorrows, which he and all his posterity till the flood ran through: but in all that period they
had the whole wealth of the earth before them; they needed
not fight for empires, or places for their cattle to graze in;
they lived long, and felt no want, no slavery, no tyranny,
no war; and the evils that happened, were single, personal,
and natural; and no violences were then done, but they
were like those things which the law calls 'rare contingencies;' for which as the law can now take no care and make
no provisions, so then there was no law, but men lived free,
and rich, and long, and they exercised no virtues but natural, and knew no felicity but natural: and so long their
prosperity was just as was their virtue, because it was a natural instrument towards all that which they knew of happi-

ness. But this public easiness and quiet, the world turned
into sin ; and unless God did compel men to do themselves
good, they would undo themselves: and then God broke in
upon them with a flood, and destroyed that generation, that
he might begin the government of the world upon a new
stock, and bind virtue upon men's spirits by new bands, endeared to them by new hopes and fears.

Then God made new laws, and gave to princes the power
of the sword, and men might be punished to death in certain
cases, and man's life was shortened, and slavery was brought
into the world and the state of servants : and then war began,
and evils multiplied upon the face of the earth ; in which it
is naturally certain that they that are most violent and injurious, prevailed upon the weaker and more innocent ; and
every tyranny that began from Nimrod to this day, and
every usurper, was a peculiar argument to shew that God began to teach the world virtue by suffering ; and that therefore
he suffered tyrannies and usurpations to be in the world, and
to be prosperous, and the rights of men to be snatched away
from the owners, that the world might be established in potent and settled governments, and the sufferers be taught all
the passive virtues of the soul. For so God brings good out of
evil, turning tyranny into the benefits of government, and violence into virtue, and sufferings into rewards. And this was
the second change of the world : personal miseries were
brought in upon Adam and his posterity, as a punishment of
sin in the first period ; and in the second, public evils were
brought in by tyrants and usurpers, and God suffered them
as the first elements of virtue, men being just newly put to
school to infant sufferings. But all this was not much.

Christ's line was not yet drawn forth ; it began not to appear in what family the King of sufferings should descend,
till Abraham's time ; and therefore, till then there were no
greater sufferings than what I have now reckoned. But when
Abraham's family was chosen from among the many nations,
and began to belong to God by a special right, and he was
designed to be the father of the Messias ; then God found
out a new way to try him, even with a sound affliction, commanding him to offer his beloved Isaac : but this was accepted, and being intended by Abraham, was not intended
by God : for this was a type of Christ, and therefore was also

but a type of sufferings. And excepting the sufferings of
the old periods, and the sufferings of nature, and accident,
we see no change made for a long time after; hut God having
established a law in Abraham's family, did build it upon promises of health, and peace, and victory, and plenty, and
riches; and so long as they did not prevaricate the law of
their God, so long they were prosperous: but God kept a
remnant of Canaanites in the land, like a rod held over them,
to vex or to chastise them into obedience, in which while
they persevered, nothing could hurt them; and that saying
of David needs no other sense but the letter of its own expression, "I have been young, and now am old; and yet I
never saw the righteous forsaken, nor his seed begging their
bread." The godly generally were prosperous, and a good
cause seldom had an ill end, and a good man never died an
ill death,—till the law had spent a great part of its time, and
it descended towards its declension and period. But, that
the great Prince of sufferings might not appear upon his
stage of tragedies without some forerunners of sorrow, God
was pleased to choose out some good men, and honour them,
by making them to become little images of suffering. Isaiah,
Jeremiah, and Zechariah, were martyrs of the law; but these
were single deaths: Shadrach, Meshech, and Abednego, were
thrown into a burning furnace, and Daniel into a den of lions,
and Susanna was accused for adultery; but these were but
little arrests of the prosperity of the godly. As the time
drew nearer that Christ should be manifest, so the sufferings
grew bigger and more numerous: and Antiochus raised up
a sharp persecution in the time of the Maccabees, in which,
many passed through the red sea of blood into the bosom of
Abraham; and then Christ came. And that was the third
period in which the changed method of God's providence
was perfected: for Christ was to do his great work by sufferings, and by sufferings was to enter into blessedness; and
by his passion he was made Prince of the catholic church,
and as our head was, so must the members be. God made
the same covenant with us that he did with his most holy
Son, and Christ obtained no better conditions for us than for
himself; that was not to be looked for; "The servant must
not be above his master; it is well if he be as his master: if
the world persecuted him, they will also persecute us:" and

"from the days of John the Baptist, the kingdom of heaven suffers violence, and the violent take it by force;" not 'the violent doers,' but 'the sufferers of violence :' for though the old law was established in the promises of temporal prosperity; yet the Gospel is founded in temporal adversity; it is directly a covenant of sufferings and sorrows; for now "the time is come that judgment must begin at the house of God." That is the sense and design of the text; and I intend it as a direct antimony to the common persuasions of tyrannous, carnal, and vicious men, who reckon nothing good but what is prosperous: for though that proposition had many degrees of truth in the beginning of the law, yet the case is now altered, God hath established its contradictory; and now every good man must look for persecution, and every good cause must expect to thrive by the sufferings and patience of holy persons: and, as men do well, and suffer evil, so they are dear to God; and whom he loves most, he afflicts most, and does this with a design of the greatest mercy in the world.

1. Then, the state of the Gospel is a state of sufferings, not of temporal prosperities. This was foretold by the prophets: "A fountain shall go out of the house of the Lord, 'et irrigabit torrentem spinarum' (so it is in the Vulgar Latin), and it shall water the torrent of thorns[y]," that is, the state or time of the Gospel, which, like a torrent, shall carry all the world before it, and, like a torrent, shall be fullest in ill weather; and by its banks shall grow nothing but thorns and briers, sharp afflictions, temporal infelicities, and persecution. This sense of the words is more fully explained in the book of the prophet Isaiah. "Upon the ground of my people shall thorns and briers come up; how much more in all the houses of the city of rejoicing[z]? Which prophecy is the same in the style of the prophets, that my text is in the style of the Apostles. The house of God shall be watered with the dew of heaven, and there shall spring up briers in it: 'Judgment must begin there;' but how much more 'in the houses of the city of rejoicing;' how much more amongst 'them that are at ease in Sion,' that serve their desires, that satisfy their appetites, that are given over to their own heart's lust, that so serve themselves, that they never serve God, that 'dwell in the city of rejoicing?' They are like Dives, whose portion was

in this life, 'who went in fine linen, and fared deliciously
every day :' they, indeed, trample upon their briers and thorns,
and suffer them not to grow in their houses; but the roots
are in the ground, and they are reserved for fuel of wrath in
the day of everlasting burning. Thus, you see, it was prophesied, now see how it was performed ; Christ was the captain of our sufferings, and he began.

He entered into the world with all the circumstances of
poverty. He had a star to illustrate his birth; but a stable
for his bedchamber, and a manger for his cradle. The angels
sang hymns when he was born ; but he was cold and cried,
uneasy and unprovided. He lived long in the trade of a
carpenter; he, by whom God made the world, had, in his first
years, the business of a mean and ignoble trade. He did good
wherever he went; and almost wherever he went, was abused.
He deserved heaven for his obedience, but found a cross in
his way thither: and if ever any man had reason to expect
fair usages from God, and to be dandled in the lap of ease,
softness, and a prosperous fortune, he it was only that could
deserve that, or any thing that can be good. But, after he
had chosen to live a life of virtue, of poverty, and labour, he
entered into a state of death ; whose shame and trouble were
great enough to pay for the sins of the whole world. And
I shall choose to express this mystery in the words of Scripture. He died not by a single or a sudden death, but he was
the 'Lamb slain from the beginning of the world:' for he
was massacred in Abel, saith St. Paulinus; he was tossed
upon the waves of the sea in the person of Noah; it was he
that went out of his country, when Abraham was called from
Charran, and wandered from his native soil ; he was offered
up in Isaac, persecuted in Jacob, betrayed in Joseph, blinded
in Samson, affronted in Moses, sawed in Isaiah, cast into
the dungeon with Jeremiah: for all these were types of
Christ suffering. And then his passion continued even after
his resurrection. For it is he that suffers in all his members; it is he that 'endures the contradiction of all sinners;'
it is he that is 'the Lord of life, and is crucified again, and
put to open shame'. in all the sufferings of his servants, and
sins of rebels, and defiances of apostates and renegadoes,
and violence of tyrants, and injustice of usurpers, and the
persecutions of his church. It is he. that is stoned in St.

Stephen, flayed in the person of St. Bartholomew: he was roasted upon St. Laurence's gridiron, exposed to lions in St. Ignatius, burnt in St. Polycarp, frozen in the lake where stood forty martyrs of Cappadocia. "Unigenitus enim Dei ad peragendum mortis suæ sacramentum consummavit omne genus humanarum passionum," said St. Hilary; "The sacrament of Christ's death is not to be accomplished but by suffering all the sorrows of humanity."

All that Christ came for, was, or was mingled with, sufferings: for all those little joys which God sent, either to recreate his person, or to illustrate his office, were abated, or attended with afflictions; God being more careful to establish in him the covenant of sufferings, than to refresh his sorrows. Presently after the angels had finished their ballelujahs, he was forced to fly to save his life; and the air became full of shrieks of the desolate mothers of Bethlehem for their dying babes. God had no sooner made him illustrious with a voice from heaven, and the descent of the Holy Ghost upon him in the waters of baptism, but he was delivered over to be tempted and assaulted by the devil in the wilderness. His transfiguration was a bright ray of glory; but then also he entered into a cloud, and was told a sad story what he was to suffer at Jerusalem. And upon Palm Sunday, when he rode triumphantly into Jerusalem, and was adorned with the acclamations of a King and a God, he wet the palms with his tears, sweeter than the drops of manna, or the little pearls of heaven, that descended upon Mount Hermon; weeping, in the midst of this triumph, over obstinate, perishing, and malicious Jerusalem. For this Jesus was like the rainbow, which God set in the clouds as a sacrament to confirm a promise, and establish a grace; he was half made of the glories of the light, and half of the moisture of a cloud; in his best days he was but half triumph and half sorrow: he was sent to tell of his Father's mercies, and that God intended to spare us; but appeared not but in the company or in the retinue of a shower, and of foul weather. But I need not tell that Jesus, beloved of God, was a suffering person: that which concerns this question most, is, that he made for us a covenant of sufferings: his doctrines were such as expressly and by consequent enjoin and suppose sufferings, and a state of affliction; his very promises were sufferings; his beatitudes were sufferings; his rewards, and his arguments to invite men to follow him, were only taken from sufferings in this life, and the reward of sufferings hereafter.

For if we sum up the commandments of Christ, we shall find humility,—mortification,—self-denial,—repentance,— renouncing the world,—mourning,—taking up the cross,— dying for him,—patience and poverty,—to stand in the chiefest rank of Christian precepts, and in the direct order to heaven: "He that will be my disciple, must deny himself, and take up his cross, and follow me." We must follow him that was crowned with thorns and sorrows, him that was drenched in Cedron, nailed upon the cross, that deserved all good, and suffered all evil: that is the sum of Christian religion, as it distinguishes from all religions in the world. To which we may add the express precept recorded by St. James; " Be afflicted, and mourn, and weep; let your laughter be turned into mourning, and your joy into weeping[a]." You see the commandments: will you also see the promises? These they are. " In the world ye shall have tribulation; in me, ye shall have peace:—Through many tribulations ye shall enter into heaven:—He that loseth father and mother, wives and children, houses and lands, for my name's sake and the Gospel, shall receive a hundred fold in this life, with persecution;" that is part of his reward: and, " He chastiseth every son that he receiveth;—if ye be exempt from sufferings, ye are bastards, and not sons." These are some of Christ's promises: will you see some of Christ's blessings that he gives his church? " Blessed are the poor: blessed are the hungry and thirsty: blessed are they that mourn: blessed are the humble: blessed are the persecuted[b]." Of the eight beatitudes, five of them have temporal misery and meanness, or an afflicted condition, for their subject. Will you at last see some of the rewards which Christ hath propounded to his servants, to invite them to follow him? " When I am lifted up, I will draw all men after me:" when Christ is "lifted up, as Moses lift up the serpent in the wilderness," that is, lifted upon the cross, then " he will draw us after him."—" To you it is given for Christ," saith St. Paul, when he went to sweeten and to flatter the Philippians[c]: well, what is given to them? some great favours surely; true; " It is not only

a James, iv. 9.   b Matt. v.   c Phil. i. 29.

given that you believe in Christ,"—though that be a great matter—" but also that you suffer for him," that is the highest of your honour. And therefore St. James, " My brethren, count it all joy when ye enter into divers temptations [d]:" and St. Peter; "Communicating with the sufferings of Christ, rejoice [e]." And St. James again; " We count them blessed that have suffered [f]:" and St. Paul, when he gives his blessing to the Thessalonians, useth this form of prayer ; " Our Lord direct your hearts in the charity of God, and in the patience and sufferings of Christ [g]." So that if we will serve the King of sufferings, whose crown was of thorns, whose sceptre was a reed of scorn, whose imperial robe was a scarlet of mockery, whose throne was the cross ; we must serve him in sufferings, in poverty of spirit, in humility and mortification ; and for our reward we shall have persecution, and all its blessed consequents.   " Atque hoc est esse Christianum."

Since this was done in the green tree, what might we expect should be done in the dry ? Let us, in the next place, consider how God hath treated his saints and servants in the descending ages of the Gospel : that if the best of God's servants were followers of Jesus in this covenant of sufferings, we may not think it strange concerning the fiery trial, as if some new thing had happened to us [h]. For as the Gospel was founded in sufferings, we shall also see it grow in persecutions : and as Christ's blood did cement the cornerstones, and the first foundations ; so the blood and sweat, the groans and sighings, the afflictions and mortifications, of saints and martyrs, did make the superstructures, and must at last finish the building.

If we begin with the Apostles, who were to persuade the world to become Christian, and to use proper arguments of invitations, we shall find that they never offered an argument of temporal prosperity ; they never promised empires and thrones on earth, nor riches, nor temporal power : and it would have been soon confuted, if they who were whipt and imprisoned, banished and scattered, persecuted and tormented, should have promised sunshine days to others, which they could not to themselves. Of all the Apostles there was not one, that died a natural death but only St. John [i]; and

---

[d] James, i. 2.   [e] 1 Pet. iv. 13.   [f] James, v. 11.
[g] 2 Thes. iii. 5.   Heb. ii. 10.   [h] 1 Pet. iv. 12.   [i] Tertul. S. Hieron.

did he escape? Yes: but he was put into a cauldron of scalding lead and oil before the Porta Latina in Rome, and escaped death by miracle, though no miracle was wrought to make him escape the torture. And, besides this, he lived long in banishment, and that was worse than St. Peter's chains. "Sanctus Petrus in vinculis, et Johannes ante Portam Latinam," were both days of martyrdom, and church-festivals. And after a long and laborious life, and the affliction of being detained from his crown, and his sorrows for the death of his fellow-disciples, he died full of days and sufferings. And when St. Paul was taken into the apostolate, his commissions were signed in these words; "I will shew unto him how great things he must suffer for my name[k]:" And his whole life was a continual suffering. "Quotidie morior" was his motto, "I die daily;" and his lesson that he daily learned was, to 'know Christ Jesus, and him crucified;' and all his joy was 'to rejoice in the cross of Christ;' and the changes of his life were nothing but the changes of his sufferings, and the variety of his labours. For though Christ hath finished his own sufferings for expiation of the world; yet there are ὑστερήματα θλίψεων, 'portions that are behind of the sufferings' of Christ, which must be filled up by his body, the church; and happy are they that put in the greatest symbol: for 'in the same measure you are partakers of the sufferings of Christ, in the same shall ye be also of the consolation.' And therefore, concerning St. Paul, as it was also concerning Christ, there is nothing, or but very little, in Scripture, relating to his person and chances of his private life, but his labours and persecutions; as if the Holy Ghost did think nothing fit to stand upon record for Christ but sufferings.

And now began to work the greatest glory of the divine providence: here was the case of Christianity at stake. The world was rich and prosperous, learned and full of wise men; the Gospel was preached with poverty and persecution, in simplicity of discourse, and in demonstration of the Spirit: God was on one side, and the devil on the other; they each of them dressed up their city; Babylon upon earth, Jerusalem from above. The devil's city was full of pleasure, triumphs, victories, and cruelty; good news, and great wealth;

[k] Acts, ix. 16.

conquest over kings, and making nations tributary : they
' bound kings in chains, and the nobles with links of iron ;'
and the inheritance of the earth was theirs: the Romans
were lords over the greatest part of the world ; and God permitted to the devil the firmament and increase, the wars and
the success of that people giving to him an entire power of
disposing the great change of the world, so as might best increase their greatness and power : and he therefore did it,
because all the power of the Roman greatness was a professed
enemy to Christianity.   And on the other side, God was to
build up Jerusalem, and the kingdom of the Gospel ; and
he chose to build it of hewn stone, cut and broken : the
Apostles he chose for preachers, and they had no learning ;
women and mean people were the first disciples, and they
had no power ; the devil was to lose his kingdom, he wanted no malice : and therefore he stirred up, and, as well as
he could, he made active all the power of Rome, and all
the learning of the Greeks, and all the malice of barbarous
people, and all the prejudice and the obstinacy of the Jews,
against this doctrine and institution, which preached, and
promised, and brought, persecution along with it.   On the
one side, there was ' scandalum crucis ;' on the other, 'patien-
tia sanctorum :' and what was the event ? They that had overcome the world, could not strangle Christianity. But so have
I seen the sun with a little ray of distant light challenge all
the power of darkness, and, without violence and noise, climbing up the hill, hath made night so to retire, that its memory
was lost in the joys and spritefulness of the morning : and
Christianity without violence or armies, without resistance
and self-preservation, without strength or human eloquence,
without challenging of privileges or fighting against tyranny,
without alteration of government and scandal of princes, with
its humility and meekness, with toleration and patience, with
obedience and charity, with praying and dying, did insensibly
turn the world into Christian, and persecution into victory.
    For Christ too began, and lived, and died in sorrows,
perceiving his own sufferings to succeed so well, and that
' for suffering death, he was crowned with immortality,' resolved to take all his disciples and servants to the fellowship
of the same suffering, that they might have a participation
of his glory ; knowing, God had opened no gate of heaven

but ' the narrow gate,' to which the cross was the key. And
since Christ now being our high-priest in heaven, intercedes
for us by representing his passion, and the dolours of the
cross, that even in glory he might still preserve the mercies
of his past sufferings, for which the Father did so delight in
him; he also designs to present us to God dressed in the
same robe, and treated in the same manner, and honoured
with ' the marks of the Lord Jesus;' " He hath predestinated
us to be conformable to the image of his Son." And if under
a head crowned with thorns, we bring to God members cir-
cled with roses, and softness, and delicacy, triumphant members in the militant church, God will reject us, he will not
know us who are so unlike our elder brother: for we are
members of the Lamb, not of the lion; and of Christ's suffering part, not of the triumphant part: and for three hundred
years together the church lived upon blood, and was nourished with blood; the blood of her own children. Thirty-three
bishops of Rome in immediate succession were put to violent and unnatural deaths; and so were all the churches of
the east and west built; the cause of Christ and of religion
was advanced by the sword, but it was the sword of the persecutors, not of resisters or warriors: they were ' all baptized
into the death of Christ;' their very profession and institution is to live like him, and, when he requires it, to die for
him; that is the very formality, the life and essence, of Christianity. This, I say, lasted for three hundred years, that the
prayers, and the backs, and the necks of Christians fought
against the rods and axes of the persecutors, and prevailed,
till the country, and the cities, and the court itself, was filled
with Christians. And by this time the army of martyrs was
vast and numerous, and the number of sufferers blunted the
hangman's sword. For Christ had triumphed over the princes
and powers of the world, before he would admit them to
serve him; he first felt their malice, before he would make
use of their defence; to shew, that it was not his necessity
that required it, but his grace that admitted kings and queens
to be nurses of the church.

And now the church was at ease, and she that sucked the
blood of the martyrs so long, began now to suck the milk of
queens. Indeed it was a great mercy in appearance, and
was so intended, but it proved not so. But then the Holy

Ghost, in pursuance of the design of Christ, who meant by suffering to perfect his church, as himself was by the same instrument,—was pleased, now that persecution did cease, to inspire the church with the Spirit of mortification and austerity; and then they made colleges of sufferers, persons who, to secure their inheritance in the world to come, did cut off all their portion in this, excepting so much of it as was necessary to their present being ; and by instruments of humility, by patience under, and a voluntary undertaking of, the cross, the burden of the Lord,—by self-denial, by fastings and sackcloth, and pernoctations in prayer, they chose then to exercise the active part of the religion, mingling it as much as they could with the suffering.

And indeed it is so glorious a thing to be like Christ, to be dressed like the Prince of the catholic church, who was 'a man of sufferings,' and to whom a prosperous and unafflicted person is very unlike, that in all ages the servants of God have ' put on the armour of righteousness, on the right hand and on the left :' that is, in the sufferings of persecution, or the labours of mortification ; in patience under the rod of God, or by election of our own ; by toleration, or self-denial ; by actual martyrdom, or by aptness or disposition towards it ; by dying for Christ, or suffering for him ; by being willing to part with all when he calls for it, and by parting with what we can for the relief of his poor members. For, know this, there is no state in the church so serene, no days so prosperous, in which God does not give to his servants the powers and opportunities of suffering for him ; not only they that die for Christ, but they that live according to his laws, shall find some lives to part with, and many ways to suffer for Christ. To kill and crucify the old man and all his lusts, to mortify a beloved sin, to fight against temptations, to do violence to our bodies, to live chastely, to suffer affronts patiently, to forgive injuries and debts, to renounce all prejudice and interest in religion, and to choose our side for truth's sake (not because it is prosperous, but because it pleases God), to be charitable beyond our power, to reprove our betters with modesty and openness, to displease men rather than God, to be at enmity with the world, that you may preserve friendship with God, to deny the importunity and troublesome kindness of a drinking friend, to own truth in despite of danger or scorn, to despise shame, to refuse worldly pleasures when they tempt your soul beyond duty or safety, to take pains in the cause of religion, the ' labour of love,' and the crossing of your anger, peevishness and morosity : these are the daily sufferings of a Christian ; and, if we perform them well, will have the same reward, and an equal smart, and greater labour, than the plain suffering the hangman's sword. This I have discoursed, to represent unto you, that you cannot be exempted from the similitude of Christ's sufferings : that God will shut no age nor no man from his portion of the cross; that we cannot fail of the result of this predestination, nor without our own fault be excluded from the covenant of sufferings. ' Judgment must begin at God's house,' and enters first upon the sons and heirs of the kingdom; and if it be not by the direct per- secution of tyrants, it will be by the direct persecution of the devil, or infirmities of our own flesh. But because this was but the secondary meaning of the text, I return to make use of all the former discourse.

Let no Christian man make any judgment concerning his condition or his cause, by the external event of things. For although in the law of Moses, God made with his people a covenant of temporal prosperity, and " his saints did bind the kings of the Amorites, and the Philistines, in chains, and their nobles with links of iron, and then, that was the honour which all his saints had :" yet, in Christ Jesus, he made a covenant of sufferings. Most of the graces of Christ- ianity are suffering graces, and God hath predestinated us to sufferings, and we are baptized into suffering, and our very communions are symbols of our duty, by being the sa- crament of Christ's death and passion ; and Christ foretold to us tribulation, and promised only that he would be with us in tribulation, that he would give us his Spirit to assist us at tribunals, and his grace to despise the world, and to con- temn riches, and boldness to confess every article of the Christian faith, in the face of armies and armed tyrants. And he also promised that ' all things should work together for the best to his servants,' that is, he would ' out of the eater bring meat, and out of the strong issue sweetness,' and crowns and sceptres should spring from crosses, and that the cross itself should stand upon the globes and sceptres of princes ; but he never promised to his servants, that they should pursue kings and destroy armies, that they should reign over nations, and promote the cause of Jesus Christ, by breaking his commandment. ' The shield of faith, and the sword of the Spirit, the armour of righteousness, and the weapons of spiritual warfare ;' these are they by which Christianity swelled from a small company, and a less reputation, to possess the chairs of doctors, and the thrones of princes, and the hearts of all men. But men, in all ages, will be tampering with shadows and toys. The Apostles at no hand could endure to hear that Christ's ' kingdom was not of this world,' and that their Master should die a sad and shameful death; though, that way, he was to receive his crown, and ' enter into glory.' And, after Christ's time, when his disciples had taken up the cross, and were marching the King's highway of sorrows, there were a very great many, even the generality of Christians, for two or three ages together, who fell a dreaming, that Christ should come and reign upon earth again for a thousand years, and then the saints should reign in all abundance of temporal power and fortunes : but these men were content to stay for it till after the resurrection ; in the meantime, took up their cross, and followed after their Lord, the King of sufferings. But now-a-days, we find a generation of men who have changed the covenant of sufferings into victories and triumphs, riches and prosperous chances, and reckon their Christianity by their good fortunes ; as if Christ had promised to his servants no heaven hereafter, no Spirit in the meantime to refresh their sorrows ; as if he had enjoined them no passive graces ; but, as if to be a Christian, and to be a Turk, were the same thing. Mahomet entered and possessed by the sword : Christ came by the cross, entered by humility ; and his saints ' possess their souls in patience.'

God was fain to multiply miracles to make Christ capable of being a ' man of sorrows :' and shall we think he will work miracles to make us delicate ? He promised us a glorious portion hereafter, to which if all the sufferings of the world were put together, they are not worthy to he compared ; and shall we, with Dives, choose our portion of ' good things in this life ?' If Christ suffered so many things only that he might give us glory, shall it be strange that we shall suffer who are to receive his glory ? It is in vain to think we shall obtain glories at an easier rate, than to drink of the brook in the way in which Christ was drenched.   When the devil appeared to St. Martin, in a bright splendid shape, and said he was Christ; he answered, " Christus non nisi in Cruce apparet suis, in hac vita."   And when St. Ignatius was newly tied in a chain to be led to his martyrdom, he cried out, " Nunc incipio esse Christianus."   And it was ob-served by Minutius Felix, and was indeed a great and excel-lent truth, " Omnes viri fortes, quos Gentiles prædicabant in exemplum, ærumnis suis inclyti floruerunt;" ' the Gentiles in their whole religion never propounded any man imitable, un-less the man were poor or persecuted.'   Brutus stood for his country's liberty, but lost his army and his life; Socrates was put to death for speaking a religious truth; Cato chose to be on the right side, but happened to fall upon the op-pressed and the injured; he died together with his party.

Victrix causa Deis placuit, sed victa Catoni[1].

And if God thus dealt with the best of heathens, to whom he had made no clear revelation of immortal recompenses ; how little is the faith, and how much less is the patience of Christians, if they shall think much to suffer sorrow, since they so clearly see with the eye of faith the great things which are laid up for them, that are ' faithful unto the death ?' Faith is useless, if now in the midst of so great pretended lights, we shall not dare to trust God, unless we have all in hand that we desire; and suffer nothing, for all we can hope for.   They that live by sense, have no use of faith: yet, our Lord Jesus, concerning whose passions the Gospel speaks much, but little of his glorifications; whose shame was pub-lic, whose pains were notorious, but his joys and transfigu-rations were secret, and kept private; he who would not suffer his holy mother, whom in great degrees he exempted from sin,—to be exempted from many and great sorrows, cer-tainly intends to admit none to his resurrection but by the doors of his grave, none to glory but by the way of the cross. " If we be planted into the likeness of his death, we shall be also of his resurrection ;" else on no terms.   Christ took away sin from us, but he left us our share of sufferings; and the cross, which was first printed upon us, in the waters of baptism, must for ever be born by us in penance, in mortification, in self-denial, and in martyrdom, and toleration, according as God shall require of us by the changes of the world, and the condition of the church.

For Christ considers nothing but souls, he values not their estates or bodies, supplying our want by his providence; and we are secured that our bodies may be killed, but cannot perish, so long as we preserve our duty and our consciences. Christ, our captain, hangs naked upon the cross: our fellow-soldiers are cast into prison, torn with lions, rent in sunder with trees returning from their violent bendings, broken upon wheels, roasted upon gridirons, and have had the honour not only to have a good cause, but also to suffer for it; and by faith, not by armies,—by patience, not by fighting, have overcome the world. " Et sit anima mea cum Christianis;" " I pray God my soul may he among the Christians." And yet the Turks have prevailed upon a great part of the Christian world, and have made them slaves and tributaries, and do them all spite, and are hugely prosperous: but when Christians are so, then they are tempted and put in danger, and never have their duty and their interest so well secured, as when they lose all for Christ, and are adorned with wounds or poverty, change or scorn, affronts or revilings, which are the obelisks and triumphs of a holy cause. Evil men and evil causes had need have good fortune and great success to support their persons and their pretences; for nothing but innocence and Christianity can flourish in a persecution. I sum up this first discourse in a word: in all the Scripture, and in all the authentic stories of the church, we find it often that the devil appeared in the shape of an ' angel of light,' but was never suffered so much as to counterfeit a persecuted sufferer. Say no more, therefore, as the murmuring Israelites said, ' If the Lord he with us, why have these evils apprehended us ?' for if to be afflicted be a sign that God hath forsaken a man, and refuses to own his religion or his question, then he that oppresses the widow, and murders the innocent, and puts the fatherless to death, and follows Providence by doing all the evils that he can, that is, all that God suffers him,—he, I say, is the only saint and servant of God: and upon the same ground the wolf and the fox may boast, when they scatter and devour a flock of lambs and harmless sheep.

SERMON X.

PART II.

2. It follows now that we inquire concerning the reasons of the divine Providence in this administration of affairs, so far as he hath been pleased to draw aside the curtain, and to unfold the leaves of his counsels and predestination. And for such an inquiry we have the precedent of the Prophet Jeremy; "righteous art thou, O Lord, when I plead with thee; yet let us talk to thee of thy judgments. Wherefore doth the way of the wicked prosper? wherefore are all they happy, that deal very treacherously? thou hast planted them, yea they have taken root: they grow, yea they bring forth fruit[m]." Concerning which in general the Prophet Malachi gives this account after the same complaint made: "and now we call the proud happy; and they that work wickedness are set up; yea they that tempt God are even delivered. They that feared the Lord, spake often one to another; and the Lord hearkened and heard, and a book of remembrance was written before him, for them that feared the Lord and thought upon his name. And they shall be mine (saith the Lord of hosts) in that day when I bind up my jewels; and I will spare them, as a man spareth his own son that serveth him. Then shall ye return, and discern between the righteous and the wicked; between him that serveth God, and him that serveth him not[n]." In this interval, which is a valley of tears, it is no wonder if they rejoice who shall weep for ever; and 'they that sow in tears' shall have no cause to complain, when God gathers all the mourners into his kingdom, 'they shall reap with joy.'

For innocence and joy were appointed to dwell together for ever. And joy went not first; but when innocence went away, sorrow and sickness dispossessed joy of its habitation; and now this world must be always a scene of sorrows, and no joy can grow here but that which is imaginary and fantastic. There is no worldly joy, no joy proper for this world, but that which wicked persons fancy to themselves in the hopes and designs of iniquity. He that covets

his neighbour's wife or land, dreams of fine things, and
thinks it a fair condition to be rich and cursed, to be a beast
and die, or to lie wallowing in his filthiness : but those holy
souls who are not in love with the leprosy and the itch for
the pleasure of scratching, they know no pleasure can grow
from the thorns which Adam planted in the hedges of paradise; and that sorrow, which was brought in by sin, must
not go away till it hath returned us into the first condition
of innocence : the same instant that quits us from sin and
the failings of mortality, the same instant wipes all tears
from our eyes ; but that is not in this world.   In the mean
time,

God afflicts the godly, that he might manifest many of his
attributes, and his servants exercise many of their virtues.

> Nec fortuna probat causas, sequiturque merentes,
> Sed vaga per cunctos nullo discrimine fertur :
> Scilicet est aliud, quod nos coguique regatque,
> Majus, et in proprias ducat mortalia leges.

For, without the sufferings of saints, God should lose
the glories, 1. Of bringing good out of evil : 2. Of being
with us in tribulation : 3. Of sustaining our infirmities : 4.
Of triumphing over the malice of his enemies.   5. Without
the suffering of saints, where were the exaltation of the cross,
the conformity of the members to Christ their head, the coronets of martyrs ? 6. Where the trial of our faith ? 7. Or the
exercise of long-suffering ? 8. Where were the opportunities
to give God the greatest love ? which cannot be but by dying
and suffering for him.   9. How should that which the world
calls folly, prove the greatest wisdom ? 10. And God be glorified by events contrary to the probability and expectation of
their causes? 11. By the suffering of saints, Christian religion
is proved to be most excellent; whilst the iniquity and cruelty
of the adversaries prove the ' Illecebra sectæ,' as Tertullian's
phrase is ; it invites men to consider the secret excellences
of that religion, for which and in which men are so willing to
die : for that religion must needs be worth looking into,
which so many wise and excellent men do so much value
above their lives and fortune.   12. That a man's nature is
passible, is its best advantage ; for by it we are all redeemed :
by the passiveness and sufferings of our Lord and brother
we were all rescued from the portion of devils ; and by our

suffering we have a capacity of serving God beyond that of angels; who indeed can sing God's praise with a sweeter note, and obey him with a more unabated will, and execute his commands with a swifter wing and a greater power; but they cannot die for God, they can lose no lands for him; and he that did so for all us, and commanded us to do so for him, is ascended far above all angels, and his heir of a greater glory. 13. ' *Do* this, and live,' was the covenant of the law; but in the Gospel it is, ' *Suffer* this, and live:'—" He that forsaketh house and land, friends and life, for my sake, is my disciple." 14. By the sufferings of saints God chastises their follies and levities, and suffers not their errors to climb up into heresies, nor their infirmities into crimes.

——————παθὼν δί τι νήπιος ἔγνω.

' Affliction makes a fool leave his folly.'—If David numbers the people of Judea, God punishes him sharply and loudly: but if Augustus Cæsar numbers all the world, he is let alone and prospers.

Ille crucem sceleris pretium tulit, hic diadema[o].

And in giving physic, we always call that just and fitting that is useful and profitable: no man complains of his physician's iniquity, if he burns one part to cure all the body; if the belly be punished to chastise the floods of humour, and the evils of a surfeit. Punishments can no other way turn into a mercy, but when they are designed for medicine; and God is then very careful of thy soul, when he will suppress every of its evils, when it first discomposes the order of things and spirits. And what hurt is it to thee, if a persecution draws thee from the vanities of a former prosperity, and forces thee into the sobrieties of a holy life? What loss is it? what misery? Is not the least sin a greater evil than the greatest of sufferings? God smites some at the beginning of their sin; others, not till a long while after it is done. The first cannot say that God is slack in punishing, and have no need to complain that the wicked are prosperous; for they find that God is apt enough to strike: and therefore, that he strikes them, and strikes not the other, is no defect of justice, but because there is not mercy in store for them that sin, and suffer not.

[o] Juv. 13. 105.

15. For if God strikes the godly that they may repent, it is no wonder that God is so good to his servants; but then we must not call that a misery, which God intends to make an instrument of saving them. And if God forbears to strike the wicked out of anger, and because he hath decreed death and hell against them, we have no reason to envy that they ride in a gilded chariot to the gallows: but if God forbear the wicked, that by his long-sufferance they may be invited to repentance, then we may cease to wonder at the dispensation, and argue comforts to the afflicted saints, thus: for if God be so gracious to the wicked, how much more is he to the godly? And if sparing the wicked be a mercy; then, smiting the godly, being the expression of his greater kindness, affliction is of itself the more eligible condition. If God hath some degrees of kindness for the persecutors, so much as to invite them by kindness; how much greater is his love to them that are persecuted? And therefore, his intercourse with them is also a greater favour; and, indeed, it is the surer way of securing the duty: fair means may do it, but severity will fix and secure it. Fair means are more apt to be abused than harsh physic; that may be turned into wantonness, but none but the impudent and grown sinners despise all God's judgments; and therefore, God chooses this way to deal with his erring servants, that they may obtain an infallible and a great salvation. And yet if God spares not his children, how much less the reprobates? and therefore, as sparing the latter commonly is a sad curse, so the smiting the former is a very great mercy. 16. For by this economy God gives us a great argument to prove the resurrection, since to his saints and servants he assigns sorrow for their present portion. Sorrow cannot be the reward of virtue; it may be its instrument and handmaid, but not its reward; and therefore, it may be intermedial to some great purposes, but they must look for their portion in the other life: "For if in this life only we had hope, then we were of all men the most miserable:" It is St. Paul's argument to prove a beatifical resurrection. And we therefore may learn to estimate the state of the afflicted godly to be a mercy great, in proportion to the greatness of that reward, which these afflictions come to secure and to prove.

Nunc et damna juvant; sunt ipsa pericula tanti:
Stantia non poterant tecta probare deos P.

It is a great matter, and infinite blessing, to escape the pains
of hell; and therefore, that condition is also very blessed
which God sends us, to create and to confirm our hopes of
that excellent mercy. 17. The sufferings of the saints are
the sum of Christian philosophy: they are sent to wean us
from the vanities and affections of this world, and to create
in us strong desires of heaven; whiles God causes us to be here
treated rudely, that we may long to be in our country, where
God shall be our portion, and angels our companions, and
Christ our perpetual feast, and never-ceasing joy shall be our
conditions and entertainment. "O death, how bitter art thou
to a man that is at ease and rest in his possessions!"[q] But he
that is uneasy in his body, and unquiet in his possessions,
vexed in his person, discomposed in his designs, who finds
no pleasure, no rest here, will be glad to fix his heart where
only he shall have what he can desire, and what can make
him happy. As long as the waters of persecutions are
upon the earth, so long we dwell in the ark: but where
the land is dry, the dove itself will be tempted to a wandering course of life, and never to return to the house of
her safety. What shall I say more? 18. Christ nourisheth
his church by sufferings. 19. He hath given a single
blessing to all other graces; but to them that are ' persecuted,' he hath promised a double one:[r] it being a double
favour, first to be innocent like Christ, and then to be afflicted
like him. 20. Without this, the miracles of patience, which
God hath given to fortify the spirits of the saints, would signify nothing. "Nemo enim tolerare tanta velit sine causa,
nec potuit sine Deo:" "As no man would bear evils without
a cause, so no man could bear so much without the support-
ing hand of God;" and we need not the Holy Ghost to so
great purposes, if our lot were not sorrow and persecution.
And therefore, without this condition of suffering, the Spirit
of God shall lose that glorious attribute of the Holy Ghost,
' the Comforter.' 21. Is there any thing more yet? Yes.
They that have suffered or forsaken any lands for Christ,
"shall sit upon the thrones, and judge the twelve tribes of
Israel;" so said Christ to his disciples. Nay, "the saints

P Martial. 1. 13. 11.   q Eccles. iv. 11.   r Matt. v. 12.

shall judge angels," saith St. Paul: well therefore might St. Paul say, " I rejoice exceedingly in tribulation." It must be some great thing that must make an afflicted man to rejoice exceedingly; and so it was. For since patience is necessary that we receive the promise, and tribulation does work this; " for a short time it worketh the consummation of our hope, even an exceeding weight of glory;" we have no reason to " think it strange concerning the fiery trial, as if it were a strange thing." It can be no hurt. The church is like Moses's bush, when it is all on fire, it is not at all consumed, but made full of miracle, full of splendour, full of God : and unless we can find something that God cannot turn into joy, we have reason not only to be patient, but rejoice, when we are persecuted in a righteous cause: for love is the soul of Christianity, and suffering is the soul of love. To be innocent, and to be persecuted, are the body and soul of Christianity. " I, John, your brother, and partaker in tribulation, and in the kingdom and patience of Jesus," said St. John :* those were the titles and ornaments of his profession : that is, " I, John, your fellow-Christian;" that is the plain song of the former descant. He, therefore, that is troubled when he is afflicted in his outward man, that his inward man may grow strong, like the birds upon the ruin of the shell, and wonders that a good man should be a beggar, and a sinner be rich with oppression; that Lazarus should die at the gate of Dives, hungry and sick, unpitied and unrelieved; may as well wonder that carrion-crows should feed themselves fat upon a fair horse, far better than themselves ; or that his own excellent body should be devoured by worms and the most contemptible creatures, though it lies there to be converted into glory. That man knows nothing of nature, or Providence, or Christianity, or the rewards of virtue, or the nature of its constitution, or the infirmities of man, or the mercies of God, or the arts and prudence of his loving-kindness, or the rewards of heaven, or the glorifications of Christ's exalted humanity, or the precepts of the Gospel, who is offended at the sufferings of God's dearest servants, or declines the honour and the mercy of sufferings in the cause of righteousness, for the securing of a virtue, for the imitation of Christ, and for the love of God, or the glories of immortality. It cannot, it

* Rev. i. 9.

ought not, it never will be otherwise; the world may as well cease to be measured by time, as good men to suffer affliction. I end this point with the words of St. Paul; " Let as many as are perfect be thus minded: and if any man be otherwise minded, God also will reveal this unto you[t];" *this,* of the covenant of sufferings, concerning which the old prophets and holy men of the temple had many thoughts of heart: but in the full sufferings of the Gospel there hath been a full revelation of the excellency of the sufferings. I have now given you an account of some of those reasons, why God hath so disposed that at this time, that is, under the period of the Gospel, " Judgment must begin at the house of God :" and they are either τιμώριαι, or δοκιμάσιαι, or μαρτύριον, or imitation of Christ's λύτρον, ' chastisements,' or ' trials,' or ' martyrdom,' or ' a conformity to the sufferings of the holy Jesus.'

But now besides all the premises, we have another account to make concerning the prosperity of the wicked: " For if judgment first begin at us, what shall the end be of them that obey not the Gospel of God ?" that is the question of the Apostle, and is the great instrument of comfort to persons ill-treated in the actions of the world. The first ages of the church lived upon promises and prophecies; and because some of them are already fulfilled for ever, and the others are of a continual and a successive nature, and are verified by the actions of every day, therefore we and all the following ages live upon promises and experience. And although the servants of God have suffered many calamities from the tyranny and prevalency of evil men their enemies, yet still it is preserved as one of the fundamental truths of Christianity, that all the fair fortunes of the wicked are not enough to make them happy, nor the persecutions of the godly able to make a good man miserable, nor yet their sadnesses arguments of God's displeasure against them. For when a godly man is afflicted and dies, it is his work and his business; and if the wicked prevail, that is, if they persecute the godly, it is but that which was to be expected from them: for who are fit to be hangmen and executioners of public wrath, but evil and ungodly persons ? And can it be a wonder, that they whose cause wants reason, should betake themselves to the

[t] Phil. iii. 15.

sword? that what he cannot persuade, he may wrest? Only we must not judge of the things of God by the measures of men. Tὰ ἀνθρώπινα, ‘ the things of men’ have this world for their stage and their reward; but the ‘things of God’ relate to the world to come: and for our own particulars we are to be guided by rule, and by the end of all; not by events intermedial, which are varied by a thousand irregular causes. For if all the evil men in the world were unprosperous,—as most certain they are, —and if all good persons were temporally blessed,—as most certainly they are not; yet this would not move us to become virtuous. ‘ If an angel should come from heaven, or one arise from the dead’ and preach repentance, or justice, and temperance, all this would be ineffectual to those, to whom the plain doctrines of God delivered in the law and the prophets, will not suffice.

For why should God work a sign to make us to believe that we ought to do justice; if we already believe he hath commanded it? No man can need a miracle for the confirmation of that which he already believes to be the command of God: and when God hath expressly bidden us to ‘ obey every ordinance of man for the Lord’s sake, the king as supreme, and his deputies as sent by him;’ it is a strange infidelity to think, that a rebellion against the ordinance of God can be sanctified by the success and prevalency of them, that destroy the authority, and the person, and the law, and the religion. The sin cannot grow to its height, if it be crushed at the beginning ; unless it prosper in its progress, a man cannot easily fill up the measure of his iniquity: but then that sin swells to its fulness by prosperity, and grows too big to be suppressed without a miracle; it is so far from excusing or lessening the sin, that nothing doth so nurse the sin as it. It is not virtue, because it is prosperous; but if it had not been prosperous, the sin could never be so great.

> Facere omnia sævè
> Non impune licet, nisi cum facis ————— ˢ

A little crime is sure to smart; but when the sinner is grown rich, and prosperous, and powerful, he gets impunity,

> Jusque datum sceleri ————— ˣ

But that is not innocence: and if prosperity were the voice

ˢ Lucan. 8. 492.   ˣ Id. 1. 2.

of God to approve an action, then no man were vicious but
he that is punished, and nothing were rebellion but that
which cannot be easily suppressed ; and no man were a
pirate but he that robs with a little vessel; and no man could
be a tyrant but he that is no prince; and no man an unjust
invader of his neighbour's rights, but he that is beaten and
overthrown. Then the crime grows big and loud, then it
calls to heaven for vengeance, when it hath been long a
growing, when it hath thriven under the devil's managing ;
when God hath long suffered it, and with patience, in vain
expecting the repentance of a sinner. ' He that treasures up
wrath against the day of wrath,' that man hath been a prosperous, that is, an unpunished, and a thriving sinner: but
then it is the sin that thrives, not the man : and that is the
mistake upon this whole question; for the sin cannot thrive,
unless the man goes on without apparent punishment and
restraint. And all that the man gets by it is, that by a continual course of sin he is prepared for an intolerable ruin.
The Spirit of God bids us look upon the end of these men ;
not the way they walk, or the instrument of that pompous
death. When Epaminondas was asked which of the three
was happiest, himself, Chabrias or Iphicrates, he bid the
man stay till they were all dead; for till then that question
could not be answered. He that had seen the Vandals be-
siege the city of Hippo, and had known the barbarousness
of that unchristened people, and had observed that St. Austin with all his prayers and vows could not obtain peace
in his own days, not so much as a reprieve for the persecution, and then had observed St. Austin die with grief
that very night, would have perceived his calamity more visible than the reward of his piety and holy religion. When
Lewis, surnamed Pius, went his voyage to Palestine upon a
holy end, and for the glory of God, to fight against the Sa-
racens and Turks and Mamelukes, the world did promise to
themselves that a good cause should thrive in the hands of
so holy a man; but the event was far otherwise : his brother
Robert was killed, and his army destroyed, and himself
taken prisoner, and the money which by his mother was
sent for his redemption, was cast away in a storm, and he
was exchanged for the last town the Christians had in Egypt,
and brought home the cross of Christ upon his shoulder in

a real pressure and participation of his Master's sufferings. When Charles the Fifth went to Algiers to suppress pirates and unchristened villains, the cause was more confident than the event was prosperous: and when he was almost ruined in a prodigious storm, he told the minutes of the clock, expecting that at midnight, when religious persons rose to matins, he should be eased by the benefit of their prayers: but the providence of God trod upon those waters, and left no footsteps for discovery: his navy was beat in pieces, and his design ended in dishonour, and his life almost lost by the bargain. Was ever cause more baffled than the Christian cause by the Turks in all Asia and Africa, and some parts of Europe, if to be persecuted and afflicted be reckoned a calamity? What prince was ever more unfortunate than Henry the Sixth of England? and yet that age saw none more pious and devout. And the title of the house of Lancaster was advanced against the right of York for three descents. But then what was the end of these things? The persecuted men were made saints, and their memories are preserved in honour, and their souls shall reign for ever. And some good men were engaged in a wrong cause, and the good cause was sometimes managed by evil men; till that the suppressed cause was lifted up by God in the hands of a young and prosperous prince, and at last both interests were satisfied in the conjunction of two roses, which was brought to issue by a wonderful chain of causes managed by the divine Providence. And there is no age, no history, no state, no great change in the world, but hath ministered an example of an afflicted truth, and a prevailing sin: for I will never more call that sinner prosperous, who, after he hath been permitted to finish his business, shall die and perish miserably; for at the same rate we may envy the happiness of a poor fisherman, who, while his nets were drying, slept upon the rock, and dreamt that he was made a king; on a sudden starts up, and leaping for joy, falls down from the rock, and in the place of his imaginary felicities, loses his little portion of pleasure and innocent solaces he had from the sound sleep and little cares of his humble cottage.

And what is the prosperity of the wicked? To dwell in fine houses, or to command armies, or to be able to oppress

their brethren, or to have much wealth to look on, or many
servants to feed, or much business to dispatch, and great
cares to master ; these things are of themselves neither good
nor bad. But consider, would any man amongst us, looking
and considering beforehand, kill his lawful king, to be heir
of all that which I have named ? Would any of you choose
to have God angry with you upon these terms? Would any
of you be a perjured man for it all? A wise man or a good
would not choose it. Would any of you die an atheist, that
you might live in plenty and power? I believe you tremble
to think of it. It cannot therefore be a happiness to thrive
upon the stock of a great sin. For if any man should contract with an impure spirit, to give his soul up at a certain
day, it may be twenty years hence, upon the condition he
might, for twenty years, have his vain desires; should we not
think that person infinitely miserable? Every prosperous
thriving sinner is in the same condition : within these
twenty years he shall be thrown into the portion of devils,
but shall never come out thence in twenty millions of years.
His wealth must needs sit uneasy upon him, that remembers
that within a short space he shall be extremely miserable ;
and if he does not remember it, he does but secure it the
more. Add that God defers the punishment, and suffers
evil men to thrive in the opportunities of their sin, it may
and does serve many ends of providence and mercy, but
serves no end that any evil man can reasonably wish or propound to themselves eligible.

Bias said well to a vicious person, " Non metuo ne non
sis daturus pœnas, sed metuo ne id non sim visurus;" 'He
was sure the man should be punished, he was not sure he
should live to see it.' And though the Nessinians that were
betrayed and slain by Aristocrates in the battle of Cyprus,
were not made alive again; yet the justice of God was admired, and treason infinitely disgraced, when, twenty years
after, the treason was discovered, and the traitor punished with
a horrid death. Lyciscus gave up the Orchomenians to their
enemies, having first wished his feet, which he then dipped
in water, might rot off, if he were not true to them ; and yet
his feet did not rot till those men were destroyed, and of a
long time after; and yet at last they did. " Slay them not
O Lord, lest my people forget it," saith David. If punish-

ment were instantly and totally inflicted, it would be but a sudden and single document: but a slow and lingering judgment, and a wrath breaking out in the next age, is like an universal proposition, teaching our posterity that God was angry all the while, that he had a long indignation in his breast, that he would not forget to take vengeance. And it is a demonstration, that even the prosperous sins of the present age will find the same period in the Divine revenge, when men see a judgment upon the nephews for the sins of their grandfathers, though in other instances, and for sins acted in the days of their ancestors.

We know that when, in Henry the Eighth or Edward the Sixth's days, some great men pulled down churches and built palaces, and robbed religion of its just encouragements and advantages; the men that did it were sacrilegious : and we find also, that God hath been punishing that great sin ever since ; and bath displayed to so many generations of men, to three or four descents of children, that those men could not be esteemed happy in their great fortunes, against whom God was so angry, that he would shew his displeasure for a hundred years together. When Herod had killed the babes of Bethlehem, it was seven years before God called him to an account: but he that looks upon the end of that man, would rather choose the fate of the oppressed babes, than of the prevailing and triumphing tyrant. It was forty years before God punished the Jews, for the execrable murder committed upon the person of their King, the holy Jesus; and it was so long, that when it did happen, many men attributed it to their killing of St. James their bishop, and seemed to forget the greater crime. But " Non eventu rerum, sed fide verborum stamus ;" " We are to stand to the truth of God's word, not to the event of things :"—because God hath given us a rule, but hath left the judgment to himself; and we die so quickly (and God measures all things by his standard of eternity, and 'one thousand years to God is as but one day'), that we are not competent persons to measure the times of God's account, and the returns of judgment. We are dead before the arrow comes; but the man escapes not, unless his soul can die, or that God cannot punish him. " Ducunt in bonis dies suos, et in momento descendunt ad infernum," that 's their fate : " They spend their days in plenty, and in a moment descend into hell [1]." In the mean time they drink, and forget their sorrow; but they are condemned: they have drunk their hemlock; but the poison does not work yet: the bait is in their mouths, and they are sportive; but the hook hath struck their nostrils, and they shall never escape the ruin. And let no man call the man fortunate, because his execution is deferred for a few days, when the very deferring shall increase and ascertain the condemnation.

But if we should look under the skirt of the prosperous and prevailing tyrant, we should find, even in the days of his joys, such allays and abatements of his pleasure, as may serve to represent him presently miserable, besides his final infelicities. For I have seen a young and healthful person warm and ruddy under a poor and a thin garment, when at the same time an old rich person hath been cold and paralytic under a load of sables, and the skins of foxes. It is the body that makes the clothes warm, not the clothes the body: and the spirit of a man makes felicity and content, not any spoils of a rich fortune wrapt about a sickly and an uneasy soul. Apollodorus was a traitor and a tyrant, and the world wondered to see a bad man have so good a fortune; but knew not that he nourished scorpions in his breast, and that his liver and his heart were eaten up with spectres and images of death: his thoughts were full of interruptions, his dreams of illusions; his fancy was abused with real troubles and fantastic images, imagining that he saw the Scythians flaying him alive, his daughters like pillars of fire dancing round about a cauldron, in which himself was boiling, and that his heart accused itself to be the cause of all these evils. And although all tyrants have not imaginative and fantastic consciences, yet all tyrants shall die and come to judgment; and such a man is not to be feared, not at all to be envied. And, in the mean time, can he be said to escape who hath an unquiet conscience, who is already designed for hell, he whom God hates, and the people curse, and who hath an evil name, and against whom all good men pray, and many desire to fight, and all wish him destroyed, and some contrive to do it? Is this man a blessed man? Is that man prosperous who hath stolen a rich robe, and is in fear to have his throat cut for it, and is fain to defend it with the greatest difficulty and the greatest danger? Does not he drink more sweetly that takes his beverage in an earthen vessel, than he that looks and searches into his golden chalices for fear of poison, and looks pale at every sudden noise, and sleeps in armour, and trusts nobody, and does not trust God for his safety, but does greater wickedness only to escape awhile unpunished for his former crimes? 'Auro bibitur venenum.' No man goes about to poison a poor man's pitcher, nor lays plots to forage his little garden made for the hospital of two bee-hives, and the feasting of a few Pythagorean herb-eaters.

—— οὐδ' ἴσασιν ὅσῳ πλέον ἥμισυ παντὸς,
Οὐδ' ὅσον ἐν μαλάχῃ τι καὶ ἀσφοδέλῳ μέγ' ὄνειαρ [1].

They that admire the happiness of a prosperous, prevailing tyrant, know not the felicities that dwell in innocent hearts, and poor cottagers, and small fortunes.

A Christian, so long as he preserves his integrity to God and to religion, is bold in all accidents, he dares die, and he dares be poor; but if the persecutor dies, he is undone. Riches are beholden to our fancies for their value; and yet the more we value the riches, the less good they are, and by an overvaluing affection they become our danger and our sin: but, on the other side, death and persecution lose all the ill that they can have, if we do not set an edge upon them by our fears and by our vices. From ourselves riches take their wealth, and death sharpens his arrows at our forges, and we may set their prices as we please: and if we judge by the Spirit of God, we must account them happy that suffer; and, therefore, that the prevailing oppressor, tyrant, or persecutor, is infinitely miserable. Only let God choose by what instruments he will govern the world, by what instance himself would be served, by what ways he will chastise the failings, and exercise the duties, and reward the virtues, of his servants. God sometimes punishes one sin with another; pride with adultery, drunkenness with murder, carelessness with irreligion, idleness with vanity, penury with oppression, irreligion with blasphemy, and that with atheism: and therefore it is no wonder, if he punishes a sinner by a sinner. And if David made use of villains and pro-

[1] Hesiod. Ἔργ. 40. Gaisford. p. 6.

fligate persons to frame an army; and Timoleon destroyed the Carthaginians by the help of soldiers, who themselves were sacrilegious; and physicians use poison to expel poisons; and all commonwealths take the basest of men to be their instruments of justice and executions: we shall have no farther cause to wonder, if God raises up the Assyrian to punish the Israelites, and the Egyptians to destroy the Assyrians, and the Æthiopians to scourge the Egyptians; and at last his own hand shall separate the good from the bad in the day of separation, in the day when he makes up his jewels.

Πᾶ ποτε κιραυνὰ Διὸς, ὁ
Πᾶ φαίθων
"Αλιος, εἰ ταῦτ' ἐφορῶντι;
Κρύπτουσι ἕκαλα [a];

God hath many ends of providence to serve by the hands of violent and vicious men. By them he not only checks the beginning-errors and approaching-sins of his predestinate; but by them he changes governments, and alters kingdoms, and is terrible among the sons of men. For since it is one of his glories to convert evil into good, and that good into his own glory, and by little and little to open and to turn the leaves and various folds of providence: it becomes us only to dwell in duty, and to be silent in our thoughts, and wary in our discourses of God; and let him choose the time when he will prune his vine, and when he will burn his thorns; how long he will smite his servants, and when he will destroy his enemies. In the days of the primitive persecutions, what prayers, how many sighings, how deep groans, how many bottles of tears, did God gather into his repository, all praying for ease and deliverances, for halcyon days and fine sunshine, 'for nursing fathers and nursing mothers,' for public assemblies and open and solemn sacraments: and it was three hundred years before God would hear their prayers: and all that while the persecuted people were in a cloud, but they were safe, and knew it not; and God 'kept for them the best wine until the last:' they ventured for a crown, and fought valiantly; they were 'faithful to the death, and they received a crown of life;'

[a] Soph. Electr. 823. Schell.

and they are honoured by God, by angels, and by men.
Whereas in all the prosperous ages of the church, we hear
no stories of such multitudes of saints, no record of them,
no honour to their memorial, no accident extraordinary;
scarce any made illustrious with a miracle, which in the
days of suffering were frequent and popular. And after all
our fears of sequestration and poverty, of death or banishment, our prayers against the persecution and troubles under
it, we may please to remember, that twenty years hence (it
may be sooner, it will not be much longer), all our cares and
our troubles shall be dead; and then it shall be inquired
how we did bear our sorrows, and who inflicted them, and
in what cause: and then he shall be happy that keeps company with the persecuted; and the ' persecutor shall be shut
out amongst dogs and unbelievers.'

He that shrinks from the yoke of Christ, from the burden
of the Lord, upon his death-bed will have cause to remember,
that by that time all his persecutions would have been past, and
that then there would remain nothing for him but rest, and
crowns, and sceptres. When Lysimachus, impatient and overcome with thirst, gave up his kingdom to the Getæ, being a captive, and having drank a lusty draught of wine, and his thirst
now gone, he fetched a deep sigh, and said, " Miserable
man that I am, who for so little pleasure, the pleasure of one
draught, lost so great a kingdom!" Such will be their case,
who, being impatient of suffering, change their persecution
into wealth and an easy fortune : they shall find themselves
miserable in the separations of eternity, losing the glories of
heaven for so little a pleasure, " illiberalis et ingratæ voluptatis causa," as Plutarch calls it, " for illiberal and ungrateful pleasure ;" in which when a man hath entered, he loses the
rights and privileges and honours of a good man, and gets
nothing that is profitable and useful to holy purposes, or necessary to any; but is already in a state so hateful and miserable, that he needs neither God nor man to be revenger,
having already under his splendid robe miseries enough to
punish and betray this hypocrisy of his condition; being
troubled with the memory of what is past, distrustful of the
present, suspicious of the future, vicious in their lives, and
full of pageantry and outsides, but in their death, miserable
with calamities real, eternal, and insupportable. And if it

could be otherwise, virtue itself would be reproached with
the calamity.

Εἰ γὰρ ὁ μὲν θανὼν
Γᾶ τε καὶ οὐδὶν ὢν
Κεῖνται τάλας·
Οἱ δὲ μὴ πάλιν
Δώσουσιν ἀντιφόνους δίκας,
Ἔῤῥοι τ᾿ ἂν αἰδὼς, ἁπάντων
τ᾿ εὐσέβεια θνατῶν [b]

I end with the advice of St. Paul ; " In nothing be terrified
of your adversaries ; which to them is an evident token of
perdition, but to you of salvation, and that of God."

SERMON XI.

PART III.

BUT now, that the persecuted may at least be pitied, and assisted in that of which they are capable, I shall propound
some rules by which they may learn to gather grapes from
their thorns, and figs from their thistles : crowns from the
cross, glory from dishonour. As long as they belong to God,
it is necessary that they suffer persecution or sorrow ; no
rules can teach them to avoid that : but the evil of the suffering and the danger must be declined, and we must use some
such spiritual arts as are apt to turn them into health and
medicine. For it were a hard thing, first to be scourged, and
then to be crucified ; to suffer here, and to perish hereafter :
through the fiery trial and purging fire of afflictions to pass
into hell, that is intolerable, and to be prevented with the
following cautions ; lest a man suffer like a fool and a male-
factor, or inherit damnation for the reward of his imprudent
suffering.

1. They that suffer any thing for Christ, and are ready to
die for him, let them do nothing against him. For certainly
they think too highly of martyrdom, who believe it able to
excuse all the evils of a wicked life. A man may ' give his
body to be burned, and yet have no charity :' and he that
dies without charity, dies without God ; " for God is love."

[b] Soph. Elect. 243. Scheffler.   [c] Phil. i. 28.

And when those who fought in the days of the Maccabees for the defence of true religion, and were killed in those holy wars, yet being dead, were found having about their necks ἱερώματα, or 'pendants consecrated' to idols of the Jamnenses; it much allayed the hope, which, by their dying in so good a cause, was entertained concerning their beatifical resurrection. He that overcomes his fear of death, does well; but if he hath not also overcome his lust, or his anger, his baptism of blood will not wash him clean. Many things may make a man willing to die in a good cause; public reputation, hope of reward, gallantry of spirit, a confident resolution, and a masculine courage; or a man may be vexed into a stubborn and unrelenting suffering: but nothing can make a man live well, but the grace and the love of God. But those persons are infinitely condemned by their last act, who profess their religion to be worth dying for, and yet are so unworthy as not to live according to its institution. It were a rare felicity, if every good cause could be managed by good men only; but we have found that evil men have spoiled a good cause, but never that a good cause made those evil men good and holy. If the governor of Samaria had crucified Simon Magus for receiving Christian baptism, he had no more died a martyr, than he lived a saint. For dying is not enough, and dying in a good cause is not enough; but then only we receive the crown of martyrdom, when our death is the seal of our life, and our life is a continual testimony of our duty, and both give testimony to the excellences of the religion, and glorify the grace of God. If a man be gold, the fire purges him; but it burns him if he be, like stubble, cheap, light, and useless: for martyrdom is the consummation of love. But then it must be supposed, that this grace must have had its beginning, and its several stages and periods, and must have passed through labour to zeal, through all the regions of duty to the perfections of sufferings. And therefore, it is a sad thing to observe, how some empty souls will please themselves with being of such a religion, or such a cause; and though they dishonour their religion, or weigh down the cause with the prejudice of sin, believe all is swallowed up by one honourable name, or the appellative of one virtue. If God had forbid nothing but heresy and treason, then to have been a loyal

man, or of a good belief, had been enough : but he that forbade rebellion, forbids also swearing and covetousness, rapine and oppression, lying and cruelty. And it is a sad thing
to see a man not only to spend his time, and his wealth, and
his money, and his friends, upon his lust, but to spend his
sufferings too, to let the canker-worm of a deadly sin devour
his martyrdom. He, therefore, that suffers in a good cause,
let him be sure to walk worthy of that honour, to which God
hath called him; let him first deny his sins, and then ' deny
himself,' and then he may ' take up his cross and follow
Christ ;' ever remembering, that no man pleases God in his
death, who hath walked perversely in his life.

2. He that suffers in a cause of God, must be indifferent
what the instance be, so that he may serve God. I say, he
must be indifferent in the cause, so it be a cause of God ; and
indifferent in the suffering, so it be of God's appointment.
For some men have a natural aversation to some vices or
virtues, and a natural affection to others. One man will die
for his friend, and another will die for his money : some men
hate to be a rebel, and will die for their prince; but tempt
them to suffer for the cause of the church, in which they
were baptized, and in whose communion they look for heaven, and then they are tempted, and fall away. Or if God
hath chosen the cause for them, and they have accepted it,
yet themselves will choose the suffering. Right or wrong,
some men will not endure a prison ; and some that can yet
choose the heaviest part of the burden, the pollution and
stain of a sin, rather than lose their money; and some had
rather die twice than lose their estates once. In this, our
rule is easy. Let us choose God, and let God choose all the
rest for us ; it being indifferent to us, whether by poverty or
shame, by a lingering or a sudden death, by the hands of a
tyrant-prince, or the despised hands of a base usurper or a
rebel, we receive the crown, and do honour to God and to
religion.

3. Whoever suffer in a cause of God, from the hands of
cruel and unreasonable men, let them not be too forward to
prognosticate evil and death to their enemies ; but let them
solace themselves in the assurance of the divine justice, by
general consideration, and, in particular, pray for them that
are our persecutors. Nebuchadnezzar was the rod in the

hand of God against the Tyrians, and because he destroyed
that city, God rewarded him with the spoil of Egypt : and it
is not always certain that God will be angry with every man,
by whose hand affliction comes upon us. And sometimes
two armies have met, and fought, and the wisest man
amongst them could not say, that either of the princes had
prevaricated either the laws of God, or of nations; and yet,
it may be, some superstitious, easy, and half-witted people
of either side wonder that their enemies live so long. And
there are very many cases of war, concerning which God
hath declared nothing : and although in such cases, he that
yields and quits his title, rather than his charity, and the
care of so many lives, is the wisest and the best man ; yet, if
neither of them will do so, let us not decree judgments from
heaven, in cases where we have no word from heaven, and
thunder from our tribunals, where no voice of God hath declared the sentence. But in such cases, where there is an
evident tyranny or injustice, let us do like the good Samaritan, who dressed the wounded man, but never pursued the
thief; let us do charity to the afflicted, and bear the cross
with nobleness, and ' look up to Jesus, who endured the
cross, and despised the shame:' but let us not take upon us
the office of God, who will judge the nations righteously, and
when he hath delivered up our bodies, will rescue our souls
from the hands of unrighteous judges. I remember in the
story that Plutarch tells, concerning the soul of Thespesius,
that it met with a prophetic genius, who told him many
things that should happen afterward in the world; and the
strangest of all was this ; That there should be a king, " qui
bonus cum sit, tyrannide vitam finiet ;" " an excellent prince
and a good man, should be put to death by a rebel and
usurping power:"—and yet, that prophetic soul could not
tell, that those rebels should, within three years, die miserable and accursed deaths. And in that great prophecy, recorded by St. Paul, " That in the last days, perilous times
should come, and men should be traitors and selfish, having
forms of godliness, and creeping into houses[d] ;" yet he could
not tell us, when these men should come to final shame and
ruin : only by a general signification, he gave this sign of
comfort to God's persecuted servants; " but they shall pro-

ceed no farther, for their folly shall be manifest to all men *;" that is, at long running, they shall shame themselves, and, " for the elects' sake, those days of evil shall be shortened." But you and I may be dead first : and therefore, only remember, that they, that, with a credulous heart and a loose tongue, are too decretory and enunciative of speedy judgments to their enemies, turn their religion into revenge, and therefore, do believe it will be so, because they vehemently desire it should be so ; which all wise and good men ought to suspect, as less agreeing with that charity, which overcomes all the sins and all the evils of the world, and sits down and rests in glory.

4. Do not trouble yourself by thinking how much you are afflicted, but consider how much you make of it : for reflex-acts upon the suffering itself can lead to nothing but to pride, or to impatience, to temptation, or apostasy. He that measures the grains and scruples of his persecution, will soon sit down and call for ease, or for a reward ; will think the time long, or his burden great ; will be apt to complain of his condition, or set a greater value upon his person. Look not back upon him that strikes thee, but upward to God that supports thee, and forward to the crown that is set before thee : and then consider, if the loss of thy estate hath taught thee to despise the world, whether thy poor fortune hath made thee poor in spirit ; and if thy uneasy prison sets thy soul at liberty, and knocks off the fetters of a worse captivity. For then the rod of suffering turns into crowns and sceptres, when every suffering is a precept, and every change of condition produces a holy resolution, and the state of sorrows makes the resolution actual and habitual, permanent and persevering. For as the silk-worm eateth itself out of a seed to become a little worm ; and there feeding on the leaves of mulberries, it grows till its coat be off, and then works itself into a house of silk ; then casting its pearly seeds for the young to breed, it leaveth its silk for man, and dieth all white and winged in the shape of a flying creature : so is the progress of souls. When they are regenerate by baptism, and have cast off their first stains and the skin of worldly vanities, by feeding on the leaves of Scriptures, and the fruits of the vine, and the joys of the

* 2 Tim. iii. 9.

sacrament, they encircle themselves in the rich garments of holy and virtuous habits; then, by leaving their blood, which is the church's seed, to raise up a new generation to God, they leave a blessed memory, and fair example, and are themselves turned into angels, whose felicity is to do the will of God, as their employment was in this world to suffer it. 'Fiat voluntas tua' is our daily prayer, and that is of a passive signification; 'Thy will be done' upon us: and if from thence also we translate it into an active sense, and by suffering evils increase in our aptnesses to do well, we have done the work of Christians, and shall receive the rewards of martyrs.

5. Let our suffering be entertained by a direct election, not by collateral aids and fantastic assistances. It is a good refreshment to a weak spirit to suffer in good company: and so Phocion encouraged a timorous Greek, condemned to die; and he bid him be confident, because that he was to die with Phocion: and when forty martyrs in Cappadocia suffered, and that a soldier, standing by, came and supplied the place of the one apostate, who fell from his crown, being overcome with pain, it added warmth to the frozen confessors, and turned them into consummate martyrs. But if martyrdom were but a fantastic thing, or relied upon vain accidents and irregular chances, it were then very necessary to be assisted by images of things, and any thing less than the proper instruments of religion: but since it is the greatest action of the religion, and relies upon the most excellent promises, and its formality is to be an action of love, and nothing is more firmly chosen (by an after-election at least) than an act of love; to support martyrdom, or the duty of sufferings, by false arches and exterior circumstances, is to build a tower upon the beams of the sun, or to set up a wooden ladder to climb up to heaven; the soul cannot attain so huge and unimaginable felicities by chance and instruments of fancy. And let no man hope to glorify God and go to heaven by a life of sufferings, unless he first begin in the love of God, and from thence derive his choice, his patience, and confidence, in the causes of virtue and religion, like beams, and warmth, and influence, from the body of the sun. Some there are that fall under the burden, when they are pressed hard, because they use not the proper instruments in fortifying the will in patience and resignation, but

endeavour to lighten the burden in imagination ; and when
these temporary supporters fail, the building that relies upon
them, rushes into coldness, recidivation, and lukewarmness :
and, among all instances, that of the main question of the
text is of greatest power to abuse imprudent and less severe
persons.

> Nullos esse Deos, inane cœlum,
> Affirmat Selius ; probátque, quòd se
> Factum, dum negat hoc, videt beatum[f].

When men choose a good cause upon confidence that an
ill one cannot thrive, that is, not for the love of virtue or
duty to God, but for profit and secular interests, they are
easily lost, when they see the wickedness of the enemy to
swell up by impunity and success to a greater evil : for they
have not learned to distinguish a great growing sin from a
thriving and prosperous fortune.

> Ulla si juris tibi pejerati
> Pœna, Barine, nocuisset unquam ;
> Dente si nigro fieres, vel uno
>   Turpior ungui ;
> Crederem [g]:

They that believe and choose because of idle fears and
unreasonable fancies, or by mistaking the accounts of a man
for the measures of God, or dare not commit treason for fear
of being blasted ; may come to be tempted when they see
a sinner thrive, and are scandalized all the way if they die
before him ; or they may come to receive some accidental
hardnesses ; and every thing in the world may spoil such persons, and blast their resolutions. Take in all the aids you
can, and, if the fancy of the standers-by, or the hearing of a
cock crow, can add any collateral aids to thy weakness, refuse it not : but let thy state of sufferings begin with choice,
and be confirmed with knowledge, and rely upon love, and
the aids of God, and the expectations of heaven, and the
present sense of duty ; and then the action will be as glorious in the event, as it is prudent in the enterprise, and religious in the prosecution.

6. Lastly, when God hath brought thee into Christ's
school, and entered thee into a state of sufferings, remember
the advantages of that state : consider, how unsavoury the
things of the world appear to thee, when thou art under the
arrest of death ; remember, with what comforts the Spirit of

God assists thy spirit; set down in thy heart all those intercourses, which happen between God and thy own soul, the
sweetnesses of religion, the vanity of sin's appearances, thy
newly-entertained resolutions, thy longings after heaven, and
all the things of God. ..And if God finishes thy persecution
with death, proceed in them : if he restores thee to the light
of the world, and a temporal refreshment, change but the
scene of sufferings in an active life, and converse with God
upon the same principles, on which, in thy state of sufferings,
thou didst build all the parts of duty. If God restores
thee to thy estate, be not less in love with heaven, nor more
in love with the world; let thy spirit be now as humble, as
before it was broken : and, to whatsoever degree of sobriety
or austerity thy suffering condition did enforce thee, if it
may be turned into virtue, when God restores thee (because
then it was necessary thou shouldest entertain it by an
after-choice), do it now also by a pre-election; that thou
mayest say with David, " It is good for me that I have been
afflicted, for thereby I have learned thy commandments."
And Paphnutius did not do his soul more advantage, when
he lost his right eye, and suffered his left knee to be cut off
for Christianity and the cause of God, than that, in the days
of Constantine and the church's peace, he lived not in the
toleration, but in the active piety of a martyr's condition;
not now a confessor of the faith only, but of the charity of
a Christian.   We may every one live to have need of these
rules; and I do not at all think it safe to pray against it,
but to be armed for it: and to whatsoever degree of sufferings God shall call us, we see what advantages God intends
for us, and what advantages we ourselves may make of it.
I now proceed to make use of all the former discourse, by
removing it a little farther even into its utmost spiritual
sense; which the Apostle does in the last words of the text;
" If the righteous scarcely be saved, where shall the wicked
and the sinner appear ?"

These words are taken out of the Proverbs[b], according to
the translation of the LXX. "If the righteous scarcely be
safe." Where the word μόλις implies that he is safe; but by
'intermedial difficulties:' and σώζεται, he is safe in the midst
of his persecutions; they may disturb his rest, and discompose his fancy, but they are like the fiery chariot to Elias;

[b] Chap. xi. 31.

he is encircled with fire, and rare circumstances, and strange
usages, but is carried up to heaven in a robe of flames. And
so was Noah safe when the flood came; and was the great
type and instance too of the verification of this proposition;
he was ὁ δίκαιος and δικαιοσύνης κῆρυξ, he was put into a
strange condition, perpetually wandering, shut up in a prison
of wood, living upon faith, having never had the experience
of being safe in floods. And so have I often seen young
and unskilful persons sitting in a little boat, when every little
wave sporting about the sides of the vessel, and every motion and dancing of the barge, seemed a danger, and made
them cling fast upon their fellows; and yet all the while they
were as safe as if they sat under a tree, while a gentle wind
shook the leaves into a refreshment and a cooling shade:
and the unskilful, inexperienced Christian shrieks out, whenever his vessel shakes, thinking it always a danger, that the
watery pavement is not stable and resident, like a rock; and
yet all his danger is in himself, none at all from without: for
he is indeed moving upon the waters, but fastened to a rock;
faith is his foundation, and hope is his anchor, and death is
his harbour, and Christ is his pilot, and heaven is his country; and all the evils of poverty, or affronts of tribunals and
evil judges, of fears and sadder apprehensions, are but like
the loud wind blowing from the right point, they make a
noise, and drive faster to the harbour; and if we do not leave
the ship, and leap into the sea; quit the interests of religion,
and run to the securities of the world; cut our cables, and
dissolve our hopes; grow impatient, and hug a wave, and
die in its embraces; we are as safe at sea, safer in the storm
which God sends us, than in a calm when we are befriended
with the world.

2. But μόλις may also signify 'rare;' "If the righteous
is *seldom* safe:" which implies that sometimes he is, even
in a temporal sense. God sometimes sends halcyon days to
his church, and when he promised 'kings and queens to be
their nurses,' he intended it for a blessing; and yet this blessing does oftentimes so ill succeed, that it is the greater blessing of the two, not to give us that blessing too freely. But
μόλις, this is '*scarcely*' done; and yet sometimes it is, and
God sometimes refreshes languishing piety with such arguments as comply with our infirmities: and though it be a
shame to us to need such allectives and infant-gaudes, such

which the heathen world and the first rudiments of the Israelites did need; God, who pities us, and will be wanting in
nothing to us, as he corroborates our willing spirits with
proper entertainments, so also he supports our weak flesh,
and not only cheers an afflicted soul with beams of light,
and antepasts and earnests of glory, but is kind also to our
man of flesh and weakness; and to this purpose he sends
thunderbolts from heaven upon evil men, dividing their
tongues, infatuating their counsels, cursing their posterity,
and ruining their families,

————— ἄλλοτι δ' αὖτι
Ἡ τῶν γε στρατὸν εὐρὺν ἀπώλεσω, ἢ ὅγε τεῖχος,
Ἡ νέας ἐν πόντῳ Κρονίδης ἀποτίνυται αὐτῶν [1].

'Sometimes God destroys their armies, or their strong holds,
sometimes breaks their ships.' But this happens either for
the weakness of some of his servants, and their too great aptness to be offended at a prosperous iniquity, or when he will
not suffer the evil to grow too great, or for some end of
his providence; and yet, if this should be very often, or last
long, God knows the danger, and we should feel the inconvenience. Of all the types of Christ, only Joshua and Solomon were noted to be generally prosperous: and yet the
fortune of the first was to be in perpetual war and danger;
but the other was as himself could wish it, rich, and peaceful, and powerful, and healthful, and learned, and beloved, and
strong, and amorous, and voluptuous, and so he fell; and
though his fall was, yet his recovery was not, upon record.

And yet the worst of evils that happen to the godly, is
better, temporally better, than the greatest external felicity
of the wicked: that in all senses the question may be considerable and argumentative, "If the righteous scarcely be
saved, where shall the ungodly appear?" If it be hard with
good men, with the evil it shall be far worse. But see the difference. The godly man is timorous, and yet safe; tossed
by the seas, and yet safe at anchor; impaired by evil accidents, and righted by divine comforts; made sad with a
black cloud, and refreshed with a more gentle influence;
abused by the world, and yet an heir of heaven; hated by
men, and beloved by God; loses one house, and gets a hundred;-he quits a convenient lodging-room, and purchases a
glorious country; is forsaken by his friends, but never by a

[1] Hesiod. Εργ. 245. Gaisford.

good conscience; he fares hardly, and sleeps sweetly; he
flies from his enemies, but hath no distracting fears; he is
full of thought, but of no amazement; it is his business to
be troubled, and his portion to be comforted; he hath nothing to afflict him, but the loss of that which might be his
danger, but can never be his good; and in the recompense
of this he hath God for his father, Christ for his captain, the
Holy Ghost for his supporter; so that he shall have all the
good which God can give him, and of all that good he hath
the holy Trinity for an earnest and a gage for his maintenance at the present, and his portion to all eternity. But,
though Paul and Silas sang psalms in prison, and under the
hangman's whips, and in an earthquake; yet, neither the
jailor, nor the persecuting magistrates, could do so. For the
prosperity of the wicked, is like a winter's sun, or the joy of
a condemned drunkard; it is a forgetfulness of his present
danger, and his future sorrows, nothing but imaginary arts
of inadvertency: he sits in the gates of the city, and judges
others, and is condemned himself; he is honoured by the
passers-by, and is thought happy, but he sighs deeply; ' he
heapeth up riches, and cannot tell who shall gather them;'
he commands an army, and is himself a slave to his passions;
he sleeps because he needs it, and starts from his uneasy pil-
lows which his thoughtful head hath discomposed; when he
is waking, he dreams of greatness; when he sleeps, he dreams
of spectres and illusions: he spoils a poor man of his lamb,
and himself of his innocence and peace: and in every unjust
purchase, himself is the greatest loser.

Ὃς δὲ κεν αὐτὸς ἕληται, ἀναιδείῃσι πιθήσας,
καί τε σμικρὸν ἐὸν, τό γ' ἐνάχνωσεν φίλον ἦτορ [k].

For, just upon his oppression or injustice, he is turned a devil, and God's enemy, a wolf to his brother, a greedy admirer
of the baits of fishes, and the bread of dogs; he is unsafe
by reason of his sin: for he hath against him the displeasure
of God, the justice of the laws, the shame of the sin, the revenge of the injured person; and God and men, the laws of
nations and private societies, stand upon their defence against
this man: he is unsafe in his rest, amazed in his danger,
troubled in his labours, weary in his change, esteemed a base
man, disgraced and scorned, feared and hated, flattered and
derided, watched and suspected, and, it may be, dies in the

[k] Hesiod. Ἔργ. 357.

middle of his purchase, and at the end is a fool, and leaves
a curse to his posterity.

Τοῦτί τ' ἀμαυρτίφι γαοὶ μετόπισθι λλιωστα ¹.

" He leaves a generation of blacker children behind him ;"
so the poet describes the cursedness of their posterity : and
their memory sits down to eternal ages in dishonour.   And
by this time let them cast up their accounts, and see if, of all
their violent purchases, they carry any thing with them to the
grave but sin, and a guilty conscience, and a polluted soul ;
the anger of God, and the shame of men.   And what help
shall all those persons give to thee in thy flames, who divided and scattered that estate, for which thou diedst for
ever ?

> Audire est operæ pretium, procedere recte
> Qui mœchis non vultis, ut omni parte laborent ;
> Utque illis multo corrupta dolore voluptas,
> Atque hæc rara cadat dura inter sæpe pericla ᵐ.

And let but a sober answerer tell me, if any thing in the
world be more distant either from goodness or happiness,
than to scatter the plague of an accursed soul upon our dearest children ; to make a universal curse ; to be the fountain of a mischief ; to be such a person whom our children
and nephews shall hate, and despise, and curse, when they
groan under the burden of that plague, which their fathers'
sins brought upon the family.   If there were no other account to be given, it were highly enough to verify the intent
of my text ; ' If the righteous scarcely be saved,' or escape
God's angry stroke, the wicked must needs be infinitely
more miserable.

> Νῦν δὲ ἐγὼ μήτ' αὐτὸς ἐν ἀνθρώποισι δίκαιος
> Εἴην, μήτ' ἐμὸς υἱὸς, ἐπεὶ κακὸν ἀνδρα δίκαιον
> Ἔμμεναι ⁿ——

" Neither I nor my son" (said the oldest of the Greek poets)
" would he virtuous, if to be a just person were all one as
to be miserable."   No, not only in the end of affairs, and at
sunset, but all the day long, the godly man is happy, and
the ungodly and the sinner are very miserable.

> Pellitur a populo victus Cato ; tristior ille est
> Qui vicit, fascesque pudet rapuisse Catoni :
> Namque hoc dedecus est populi, morumque ruina.
> Non homo pulsus erat ; sed in uno victa potestas
> Romanumque decus——·—

¹ Hes. Ἔργ. **282**.   ᵐ Hor. S. 1. 2. 37.   ⁿ Hes. Ἔργ. **269**. Gaisf. p. 22.

And there needs no other argument to be added but this
one great testimony ; that though the godly are afflicted and
persecuted, yet even they are blessed, and the persecutors
are the most unsafe.   They are essentially happy whom
affliction cannot make miserable, but turns unto their advantages[o] : and that is the state of the godly.   And they
are most intolerably accursed, who have no portions in
the blessings of eternity, and yet cannot have comfort in
the present purchases of their sin, to whom even their sunshine brings a drought, and their fairest is their foulest
weather : and that is the portion of the sinner and the ungodly.   The godly are not made unhappy by their sorrows : and the wicked are such, whom prosperity itself cannot make fortunate.

3. And yet after all this, it is but μόλις σώζεται, not μόλις
σωθήσεται, he ' escapes but hardly' here: it will be well enough
with him hereafter.   Isaac digged three wells.   The first
was called ' Contention ;' for he drank the waters of strife,
and digged the well with his sword.   The second well was
not altogether so hard a purchase, he got it with some trouble ; but that being over, he had some room, and his fortune
swelled, and he called his well ' Enlargement.'   But his third
he called 'Abundance ;' and then he dipped his foot in oil, and
drank freely as out of a river.   Every good man first ' sows
in tears ;' he first drinks of the bottle of his own tears, sorrow
and trouble, labour and disquiet, strivings and temptations :
but if they pass through a torrent, and virtue becomes easy
and habitual, they find their hearts enlarged and made sprightly by the visitations of God, and refreshment of his Spirit ;
and then their hearts are enlarged, they know how to gather the down and softnesses from the sharpest thistles.

> Τῆς δ' ἀρετῆς ἱδρῶτα θεοὶ προπάροιθεν ἔθηκαν
> 'Αθάνατοι· μακρὸς δὲ καὶ ὄρθιος οἶμος ἐπ' αὐτὴν,
> Καὶ τρηχὺς τὸ πρῶτον· ἐπὴν δ' εἰς ἄκρον ἵκηαι,
> Ρηιδίη δ' ἤπειτα πέλει, χαλεπή περ ἐοῦσα [p].

At first we cannot serve God but by passions and doing
violence to all our wilder inclinations, and suffering the
violence of tyrants and unjust persons : the second days of
virtue are pleasant and easy in the midst of all the appen-

---

[o] Quis curam neget esse te Deorum,
  Propter quem fuit innocens ruina?   *Mart.* 1. 83.
[p] Hesiod. *Ergy.* 287. Gaisford. p. 23.

dant labours. But when the Christian's last pit is digged,
when he is descended to his grave, and hath finished his
state of sorrows and suffering ; then God opens the river
of abundance, the rivers of life and never-ceasing felicities. And this is that which God promised to his people:
" I hid my face from thee for a moment, but with everlasting
kindness will I have mercy on thee, saith the Lord thy redeemer q." So much as moments are exceeded by eternity, and
the sighing of a man by the joys of an angel, and a salutary
frown by the light of God's countenance, a few groans by the
infinite and eternal hallelujahs ; so much are the sorrows of the
godly to be undervalued in respect of what is deposited for
them in the treasures of eternity. Their sorrows can die, but so
cannot their joys. And if the blessed martyrs and confessors
were asked concerning their past sufferings and their present
rest, and the joys of their certain expectation, you should
hear them glory in nothing but in the mercies of God, and
' in the cross of the Lord Jesus.' Every chain is a ray of
light, and every prison is a palace, and every loss is the purchase of a kingdom, and every affront in the cause of God is
an eternal honour, and every day of sorrow is a thousand
years of comfort, multiplied with a never-ceasing numeration ;
days without night, joys without sorrow, sanctity without
sin, charity without stain, possession without fear, society
without envying, communication of joys without lessening :
and they shall dwell in a blessed country, where an enemy
never entered, and from whence a friend never went away.
Well might David say, " Funes ceciderunt mihi in præclaris,"
" The cords" of my tent, my ropes, and the sorrow of my
pilgrimage, " fell to me in a good ground, and I have a
goodly heritage."—And when persecution hews a man down
from a high fortune to an even one, or from thence to the
face of the earth, or from thence to the grave ; a good man
is but preparing for a crown, and the tyrant does but first
knock off the fetters of the soul, the manacles of passion and
desire, sensual loves and lower appetites: and if God suffers
him to finish the persecution, then he can but dismantle the
soul's prison, and let the soul forth to fly to the mountains of
rest: and all the intermedial evils are but like the Persian
punishments ; the executioner tore off their hairs, and rent
their silken mantles, and discomposed their curious dressings,

q Isa. liv. 8.

and lightly touched the skin; yet the offender cried out with most bitter exclamations, while his fault was expiated with a ceremony and without blood. So does God to his servants; he rends their upper garments, and strips them of their unnecessary wealth, and ties them to physic and salutary discipline; and they cry out under usages, which have nothing but the outward sense and opinion of evil, not the real substance. But if we would take the measures of images, we must not take the height of the base, but the proportion of the members; nor yet measure the estates of men by their big-looking supporter, or the circumstance of an exterior advantage, but by its proper commensuration in itself; as it stands in its order to eternity: and then the godly man that suffers sorrow and persecution, ought to be relieved by us, but needs not be pitied in the sum of affairs. But since the two estates of the world are measured by time and by eternity, and divided by joy and sorrow, and no man shall have his portion of joys in both durations; the state of those men is insupportably miserable, who are fatted for slaughter, and are crowned like beasts for sacrifice; who are feared and fear, who cannot enjoy their purchases but by communications with others, and themselves have the least share, but themselves are alone in the misery and the saddest dangers, and they possess the whole portion of sorrows; to whom their prosperity gives but occasions to evil counsels, and strength to do mischief, or to nourish a serpent, or oppress a neighbour, or to nurse a lust, to increase folly, and treasure up calamity. And did ever any man see, or story tell, that any tyrant-prince kissed his rods and axes, his sword of justice, and his imperial ensigns of power ? they shine like a taper, to all things but itself. But we read of many martyrs who kissed their chains, and hugged their stakes, and saluted their hangman with great endearments; and yet, abating the incursions of their seldom sins, these are their greatest evils; and such they are, with which a wise and a good man may be in love. And till the sinners and ungodly men can be so with their deep groans and broken sleeps, with the wrath of God and their portions of eternity; till they can rejoice in death and long for a resurrection, and with delight and a greedy hope can think of the day of judgment; we must conclude that their glass-gems and finest pageantry, their splendid outsides and great powers of evil, cannot make amends for that estate of misery, which is their portion with a certainty as great as is the truth of God, and all the articles of the Christian creed. Miserable men are they, who cannot be blessed, unless there be no day of judgment; who must perish, unless the word of God should fail. If that be all their hopes, then we may with a sad spirit and a soul of pity inquire into the question of the text, " Where shall the ungodly and sinner appear ?" Even there where God's face shall never shine, where there shall be fire and no light, where there shall be no angels, but what are many thousand years turned into devils, where no good man shall ever dwell, and from whence the evil and the accursed shall never be dismissed. ' O my God, let my soul never come into their counsels, nor lie down in their sorrows.'

SERMON XII.

THE MERCY OF THE DIVINE JUDGMENTS; OR, GOD'S METHOD IN CURING SINNERS.

PART I.

Despisest thou the riches of his goodness, and forbearance, and long-suffering, not knowing that the goodness of God leadeth thee to repentance?—Rom. ii. 4.

FROM the beginning of time till now, all effluxes which have come from God, have been nothing but emanations of his goodness, clothed in variety of circumstances. He made man with no other design than that man should be happy, and by receiving derivations from his fountain of mercy, might reflect glory to him. And therefore, God making man for his own glory, made also a paradise for man's use ; and did him good, to invite him to do himself a greater: for God gave forth demonstrations of his power by instances of mercy, and he who might have made ten thousand worlds of wonder and prodigy, and created man with faculties able only to stare upon, and admire, those miracles of mightiness, did choose to instance his power in the effusions of mercy, that, at the same instant, he might represent himself desirable and adorable, in all the capacities of amiability ; viz. as excellent in himself, and profitable to us. For as the sun

sends forth a benign and gentle influence on the seed of
plants, that it may invite forth the active and plastic power
from its recess and secrecy, that by rising into the tallness
and dimensions of a tree, it may still receive a greater and
more refreshing influence from its foster-father, the prince
of all the bodies of light; and in all these emanations, the
sun itself receives no advantage, but the honour of doing benefits: so doth the Almighty Father of all the creatures; he
at first sends forth his blessings upon us, that we, by using
them aright, should make ourselves capable of greater; while
the giving glory to God, and doing homage to him, are
nothing for his advantage, but only for ours; our duties
towards him being like vapours ascending from the earth,
not at all to refresh the region of the clouds, but to return
back in a fruitful and refreshing shower; and God created
us, not that we can increase his felicity, but that he might
have a subject receptive of felicity from him. Thus he
causes us to be born, that we may be capable of his blessings; he causes us to be baptized, that we may have a title
to the glorious promises evangelical; he gives us his Son,
that we may be rescued from hell. And when we constrain
him to use harsh courses towards us, it is also in mercy: he
smites us to cure a disease; he sends us sickness, to procure
our health. And as if God were all mercy, he is merciful in
his first design, in all his instruments, in the way, and in the
end of the journey; and does not only shew the riches of his
goodness to them that do well, but to all men that they may
do well: he is good, to make us good; he does us benefits,
to make us happy. And if we, by despising such gracious
rays of light and heat, stop their progress, and interrupt
their design, the loss is not God's, but ours; we shall be the
miserable and accursed people. This is the sense and pa-
raphrase of my text; " Despisest thou the riches of his
goodness, &c. ?" " Thou dost not know," that is, thou consi-
derest not, that it is for farther benefit that God does thee
this: the ' goodness of God' is not a design to serve his own
ends upon thee, but thine upon him: " the goodness of God
leadeth thee to repentance."

Here then is God's method of curing mankind, χρηστότης, ἀνοχή, μακροθυμία. First, " goodness," or inviting us to
him by sugared words, by the placid arguments of temporal
favour, and the propositions of excellent promises. Secondly,

ἀνοχὴ, at the same time. Although God is provoked every day, yet he does ἀνέχειν, he " tolerates" our stubbornness, he forbears to punish; and when he does begin to strike, takes his hand off, and gives us truce and respite. For so ἀνοχὴ signifies ' laxamentum,' and ' inducias' too. Thirdly, μακροθυμία,˙ still "a long putting off" and deferring his final destroying anger, by using all means to force us to repentance; and this especially by the way of judgments; these being the last reserves of the divine mercy, and however we esteem it, is the greatest instance of the divine long-suffering that is in the world. After these instruments, we may consider the end, the strand upon which these land us, the purpose of this variety, of these labours and admirable arts, with which God so studies and contrives the happiness and salvation of man: it is only that man may be brought by these means unto repentance, and by repentance may be brought to eternal life. This is " the treasure of the divine goodness," the great and admirable efflux of the eternal beneficence, the πλοῦτος χρηστότητος, " the riches of his goodness," which whosoever despises, despises himself and the great interest of his own felicity; he shall die in his impenitence, and perish in his folly.

1. The first great instrument that God chooses to bring us to him, is χρηστότης, ' profit,' or benefit; and this must needs be first, for those instruments whereby we have a being, are so great mercies, that besides that they are such which give us the capacities of all other mercies, they are the advances of us in the greatest instances of promotion in the world. For from nothing to something is an infinite space; and a man must have a measure of infinite passed upon him, before he can perceive himself to be either happy or miserable: he is not able to give God thanks for one blessing, until he hath received many. But then God intends we should enter upon his service at the beginning of our days, because even then he is before-hand with us, and hath already given us great instances of his goodness. What a prodigy of favour is it to us, that he hath passed by so many forms of his creatures, and hath not set us down in the rank of any of them, till we came to be ' paulo minores angelis,' ' a little lower than the angels!' and yet from the meanest of them God can perfect his own praise. The deeps and the snows, the hail and the rain, the birds of the air and the

fishes of the sea, they can and do glorify God, and give him
praise in their capacity; and yet he gave them no speech,
no reason, no immortal spirit, or capacity of eternal blessedness: but he hath distinguished us from them by the absolute issues of his predestination, and hath given us a lasting
and eternal spirit, excellent organs of perception, and wonderful instruments of expression, that we may join in con-
cert with the morning-star, and bear a part in the chorus
with the angels of light, to sing hallelujah to the great Father of men and angels.

But was it not a huge chain of mercies, that we were not
strangled in the regions of our own natural impurities, but
were sustained by the breath of God from perishing in the
womb, where God formed us 'in secreto terræ,' told our
bones, and kept the order of nature, and the miracles of creation; and we lived upon that which, in the next minute after
we were born, would strangle us if it were not removed? but
then God took care of us, and his hands of providence clothed
us and fed us. But why do I reckon the mercies of production, which in every minute of our being are alike and continued, and are miracles in all senses, but that they are common and usual? I only desire you to remember, that God
made all the works of his hands to serve him. And, indeed,
this mercy of creating us such as we are, was not "to lead
us to repentance," but was a design of innocence: he intended
we should serve him as the sun and the moon do, as fire and
water do; never to prevaricate the laws he fixed to us, that
we might have needed no repentance. But since we did
degenerate, and being by God made better and more noble
creatures than all the inhabitants of the air, the water and
the earth besides,—we made ourselves baser and more ignoble
than any: for no dog, crocodile, or swine, was ever God's
enemy, as we made ourselves. Yet then from thenceforward
God began his work of "leading us to repentance" by the
"riches of his goodness." He causeth us to be born of
Christian parents, under whom we were taught the mysteriousness of its goodness and designs for the redemption of man;
and by the design of which religion, repentance was taught
to mankind, and an excellent law given for distinction of
good and evil. And this is a blessing, which though possibly we do not often put into our eucharistical litanies to give
God thanks for; yet if we sadly consider what had become

of us, if we had been born under the dominion of a Turkish
lord, or in America, where no Christians do inhabit, where
they worship the devil, where witches are their priests, their
prophets, their physicians, and their oracles; can we choose
but apprehend a visible notorious necessity of perishing in
those sins, which we then should not have understood by
the glass of a divine law to have declined, nor by a revelation
have been taught to repent of? But since the best of men
does, in the midst of all the great advantages of laws, and
examples, and promises, and threatenings, do many things
he ought to be ashamed of, and needs to repent of; we can
understand the riches of the divine goodness best, by considering, that the very design of our birth and education in the
Christian religion is, that we may recover of and cure our
follies by the antidote of repentance, which is preached to
us as a doctrine, and propounded as a favour; which was
put into a law, and purchased for us by a great expense;
which God does not more command to us as a duty, than he
gives us as a blessing. For now that we shall not perish for
our first follies, but be admitted to new conditions, to be re-
paired by second thoughts, to have our infirmities excused,
and our sins forgiven, our habits lessened, and our malice
cured, after we were wounded, and sick, and dead, and buried, and in the possession of the devil; this was such a blessing, so great riches of the divine goodness, that it was taught
to no religion but the Christian, revealed by no lawgiver but
Christ, so it was a favour greater than ever God gave to the
angels and devils: for although God was rich in the effusion
of his goodness towards them, yet they were not admitted
to the condition of second thoughts; Christ never shed one
drop of blood for them, "his goodness did not lead them to
repentance:" but to us it was, that he made this largess of
his goodness; to us, to whom he made himself a brother,
and sucked the paps of our mother; he paid the scores of
our sin, and shame, and death, only that we might be admitted to repent, and that this repentance might be effectual to
the great purposes of felicity and salvation. And if we could
consider this sadly, it might make us better to understand
our madness and folly in refusing to repent; that is, to be
sorrowful,—and to leave all our sins,—and to make amends
by a holy life.—For that we might be admitted and suffered
to do so, God was fain to pour forth all the riches of his

goodness : it cost our dearest Lord the price of his dearest blood, many a thousand groans, millions of prayers and sighs, and at this instant he is praying for our repentance; nay, he hath prayed for our repentance these sixteen hundred years incessantly, night and day, and shall do so till dooms-day ; " He sits at the right hand of God making intercession for us." And that we may know what he prays for, he hath sent us ambassadors to declare the purpose of all his design; for St. Paul saith, "We are ambassadors for Christ, as though he did beseech you by us ; we pray you in Christ's stead to be reconciled to God." The purpose of our embassy and ministry is a prosecution of the mercies of God, and the work of redemption, and the intercession and mediation of Christ : it is the work of atonement and reconciliation that God designed, and Christ died for, and still prays for, and we preach for, and you all must labour for.

And therefore here consider, if it be not infinite impiety to " despise the riches of such a goodness," which at so great a charge, with such infinite labour and deep mysterious arts, invites us to repentance ; that is, to such a thing as could not be granted to us unless Christ should die to purchase it; such a glorious favour, that is the issue of Christ's prayers in heaven, and of all his labours, his sorrows and his sufferings on earth. If we refuse to repent now, we do not so much refuse to do our own duty, as to accept of a reward. It is the greatest and the dearest blessing that ever God gave to men, that they may repent : and therefore, to deny it or delay it, is to refuse health, brought us by the skill and industry of the physician ; it is to refuse liberty indulged to us by our gracious Lord. And certainly we had reason to take it very ill, if, at a great expense, we should purchase a pardon for a servant, and he, out of a peevish pride or negligence, shall refuse it ; the scorn pays itself, the folly is its own scourge, and sits down in an inglorious ruin.

After the enumeration of these glories, these prodigies of mercies and loving-kindnesses, of Christ's dying for us, and interceding for us, and merely that we may repent and be saved ; I shall less need to instance those other particularities whereby God continues, as by so many arguments of kindness, to sweeten our natures, and make them malleable to the precepts of love and obedience, the twin-daughters of holy repentance : but the poorest person amongst us, be-

sides the blessing and graces already reckoned, hath enough
about him, and the accidents of every day, to shame him into
repentance. Does not God send his 'angels to keep thee in all thy
ways?' are not they ministering spirits sent forth to wait upon
thee as thy guard? art not thou kept from drowning, from frac-
ture of bones, from madness, from deformities, by the riches
of the divine goodness? Tell the joints of thy body; dost
thou want a finger? and if thou dost not understand how
great a blessing that is, do but remember, how ill thou canst
spare the use of it when thou hast but a thorn in it. The
very privative blessings, the blessings of immunity, safe-
guard, and integrity, which we all enjoy, deserve a thanksgiving of a whole life. If God should send a cancer upon
thy face, or a wolf into thy breast, if he should spread a
crust of leprosy upon thy skin, what wouldest thou give to
be but as now thou art? Wouldest not thou repent of thy
sins upon that condition? Which is the greater blessing?
To be kept from them, or to be cured of them? And why
therefore shall not this greater blessing lead thee to repentance? Why do we, not so aptly, promise repentance
when we are sick, upon the condition to be made well, and
yet perpetually forget it when we are well? As if health never
were a blessing, but when we have it not. Rather I fear the
reason is, when we are sick we promise to repent, because
then we cannot sin the sins of our former life; but in health
our appetites return to their capacity, and in all the way
" we despise the riches of the divine goodness," which preserves us from such evils, which would be full of horror and
amazement, if they should happen to us.

Hath God made any of you all chapfallen? Are you affrighted with spectres and illusions of the spirits of darkness? How many earthquakes have you been in? How many
days have any of you wanted bread? How many nights have
you been without sleep? Are any of you distracted of your
senses? And if God gives you meat and drink, health and
sleep, proper seasons of the year, entire senses and a useful
understanding; what a great unworthiness is it to be unthankful to so good a God, so benign a Father, so gracious
a Lord? All the evils and baseness of the world can shew
nothing baser and more unworthy than ingratitude : and
therefore it was not unreasonably said of Aristotle, Εὐτυχία
φιλόθεος, " Prosperity makes a man love God," supposing

men to have so much humanity left in them, as to love him
from whom they have received so many favours.   And Hippocrates said, that although poor men use to murmur against
God, yet rich men will be offering sacrifice to their Deity,
whose beneficiaries they are.   Now, since the riches of
the divine goodness are so poured out upon the meanest of
us all, if we shall refuse to repent (which is a condition so
reasonable, that God requires it only for our sake, and that it
may end in our felicity), we do ourselves despite, to be unthankful to God; that is, we become miserable, by making
ourselves basely criminal.   And if any man, whom God
hath used to no other method but of his sweetness and the
effusion of mercies, brings no other fruits but the apples of
Sodom in return of all his culture and labours ;   God will cut
off that unprofitable branch, that with Sodom it may suffer
the flames of everlasting burning.

> Οἷα σὺ τοὺς Σωτῆρας, ὦ Φιλήρατε,
> Τρυφῆς ἀπάσης μεταλαβόντας ἐν βίῳ,
> Πεφυγέναι τὸ Θεῖον ὡς λεληθότας [r] ;

If here we have good things, and a continual shower of
blessings, to soften our stony hearts, and we shall remain obdurate against those sermons of mercy which God makes us
every day, there will come a time when this shall be upbraided to us, that we had not νοῦν ἀντίτυπον, a thankful
mind, but made God to sow his seed upon the sand, or upon
the stones, without increase or restitution.   It was a sad
alarm which God sent to David by Nathan, to upbraid his
ingratitude : "I anointed thee king over Israel, I delivered
thee out of the hand of Saul, I gave thee thy master's house
and wives into thy bosom, and the house of Israel and Judah ; and if this had been too little, I would have given thee
such and such things: wherefore hast thou despised the
name of the Lord ?"   But how infinitely more can God say
to all of us than all this came to; he hath anointed us kings
and priests in the royal priesthood of Christianity; he hath
given us his Holy Spirit to be our guide, his angels to be our
protectors, his creatures for our food and raiment; he hath
delivered us from the hands of Satan, hath conquered death
for us, hath taken the sting out, and made it harmless and
medicinal, and proclaimed us heirs of heaven, coheirs with
the eternal Jesus : and if, after all this, we despise the com-

[r] Philemon. Clerici. p. 360.

mandment of the Lord, and defer and neglect our repentance, what shame is great enough, what miseries are sharp enough, what hell painful enough, for such horrid ingratitude? St. Lewis the king having sent Ivo, bishop of Chartres, on an embassy, the bishop met a woman on the way, grave, sad, fantastic, and melancholic, with fire in one hand, and water in the other. He asked, what those symbols meant. She answered, My purpose is with fire to burn Paradise, and with my water to quench the flames of hell, that men may serve God without the incentives of hope and fear, and purely for the love of God. But this woman began at the wrong end: the love of God is not produced in us, after we have contracted evil habits, till God, with 'his fan in his hand, hath thoroughly purged the floor,' till he hath cast out all the devils, and swept the house with the instrument of hope and fear, and with the achievements and efficacy of mercies and judgments. But then, since God may truly say to us, as of old to his rebellious people, 'Am I a dry tree to the house of Israel?' that is, Do I bring them no fruit? Do they ' serve me for nought?' and he expects not our duty till first we feel his goodness ; we are now infinitely inexcusable to throw away so great riches, to "despise such a goodness."

However, that we may see the greatness of this treasure of goodness, God seldom leaves us thus : for he sees (be it spoken to the shame of our natures, and the dishonour of our manners), he sees that his mercies do not allure us, do not make us thankful, but (as the Roman said), " Felicitate corrumpimur," 'We become worse for God's mercy,' and think it will be always holiday ; and are like the crystal of Arabia, hardened not by cold, but made crusty and stubborn by the warmth of the divine fire, by its refreshments and mercies : therefore, to demonstrate that God is good indeed, he con] tinues his mercies still to us, but in another instance ; he is merciful to us in punishing us, that we may be led to repentance by such instruments which will scare us from sin ; he delivers us up to the pædagogy of the divine judgments : and there begins the second part of God's method, intimated in the word ἀνοχή, or " forbearance." God begins his cure by caustics, by incisions and instruments of vexation, to try if the disease that will not yield to the allectives of cordials and perfumes, frictions and baths, may be forced out by deleteries, scarifications, and more salutary, but less pleasing, physic.

2. 'Aνοχὴ, "Forbearance," it is called in the text; which signifies 'laxamentum' or 'inducias:' that is, when the decrees of the divine judgments temporal are gone out, either wholly to suspend the execution of them, which is 'induciæ,' or 'a reprieve;' or else, when God hath struck once or twice, he takes off his hand, that is 'laxamentum,' an 'ease or remission' of his judgment. In both these, although 'in judgment God remembers mercy,' yet we are under discipline, we are brought into the penitential chamber; at least we are shewed the rod of God: and if, like Moses's rod, it turns us into serpents, and that we repent not, but grow more devils; yet then it turns into a rod again, and finishes up the smiting, or the first-designed affliction.

But I consider it first in general. The riches of the divine goodness are manifest in beginning this new method of curing us, by severity and by a rod. And, that you may not wonder that I expound this 'forbearance' to be an act of mercy punishing, I observe, that, besides that the word supposes the method changed, and it is a mercy about judgments, and their manner of execution; it is also, in the nature of the things, in the conjunction of circumstances, and the designs of God, a mercy when he threatens us or strikes us into repentance.

We think that the way of blessings and prosperous accidents, is the finer way of securing our duty; and that when our heads are anointed, our cups crowned, and our tables full, the very caresses of our spirits will best of all dance before the ark, and sing perpetual anthems to the honour of our benefactor and patron, God: and we are apt to dream that God will make his saints reign here as kings in a millenary kingdom, and give them the riches and fortunes of this world, that they may rule over men, and sing psalms to God for ever. But I remember what Xenophanes says of God,

Οὔτι δέμας θνητοῖσιν ὁμοίιος, οὔτι νόημα.

" God is like to men neither in shape nor in counsel ;" he knows that his mercies confirm some, and encourage more, but they convert but few: alone they lead men to dissolution of manners, and forgetfulness of God, rather than repentance : not but that mercies are competent and apt instruments of grace, if we would; but because we are more dispersed in our spirits, and, by a prosperous accident, are melted into joy and garishness, and drawn off from the sobriety of recollection. 'Jeshurun waxed fat and kicked.' Many are not able to suffer and endure prosperity; it is like the light of the sun to a weak eye; glorious indeed in itself, but not proportioned to such an instrument. Adam himself (as the rabbins say) did not dwell one night in Paradise, but was poisoned with prosperity, with the beauty of his fair wife, and a beauteous tree: and Noah and Lot were both righteous and exemplary, the one to Sodom, the other to the old world, so long as they lived in a place in which they were obnoxious to the common suffering; but as soon as the one of them had escaped from drowning, and the other from burning, and were put into security, they fell into crimes which have dishonoured their memories for above thirty generations together, the crimes of drunkenness and incest. Wealth and a full fortune make men licentiously vicious, tempting a man with power to act all that he can desire or design viciously.

> Inde iræ faciles ————
> Namque ut opes nimias mundo fortuna subacto
> Intulit, et rebus mores cessere secundis,
> ———— Cultus, gestare decoros
> Vix auribus, rapuere mares ;—totoque accenuitur orbe
> Quo gens quæque perit ————. *

And let me observe to you, that though there are in the New Testament many promises and provisions made for the poor in that very capacity, they having a title to some certain circumstances and additionals of grace and blessing; yet to rich men our blessed Saviour was pleased to make none at all, but to leave them involved in general comprehensions, and to have a title to the special promises only, by becoming poor in spirit, and in preparation of mind, though not in fortune and possession. However, it is hard for God to persuade us to this, till we are taught it by a sad experience, that those prosperities which we think will make us serve God cheerfully, make us to serve the world and secular ends diligently, and God not at all.

Repentance is a duty that best complies with affliction; it is a symbolical estate, of the same complexion and constitution; half the work of repentance is done by a sad accident, our spirits are made sad, our gaieties mortified, our wildness corrected, the water-springs are ready to run over: but if God should grant our desires, and give to most men

* Lucan. 1. 160.

prosperity, with a design to lead them to repentance, all his
pomp, and all his employment, and all his affections and passions, and all his circumstances, are so many degrees of distance from the conditions and nature of repentance.   It was
reported by Dio concerning Nero's mother, that she often
wished that her son might be emperor, and wished it with so
great passion, that, upon that condition, she cared not though
her son might kill her.   Her first wish and her second
fear were both granted :   but when she began to fear that her
son did really design to murder her, she used all the art
and instruments of diversion that a witty and a powerful, a
timorous person and a woman, could invent or apply.   Just
so it is with us :   so we might have our wishes of prosperity,
we promise to undergo all the severities of repentance ;   but
when we are landed upon our desire, then every degree of
satisfaction of those sensualities is a temptation against repentance ;   for a man must have his affections weaned from
those possessions, before he can be reconciled to the possibilities of repentance.

And because God knows this well, and loves us better
than we do ourselves, therefore he sends upon us the scrolls
of vengeance, ' the hand-writing upon the wall,' to denounce
judgment against us :   for God is so highly resolved to bring
us to repentance some way or other, that if, by his goodness,
he cannot shame us into it, he will try if, by his judgments,
he can scare us into it :   not that he strikes always as soon as
he hath sent his warrants out ;   οὐδὲ τοῖς ἁμαρτάνουσιν εὐθὺς
ἐπέξεισιν ὁ Θεός· ἀλλὰ δίδωσι χρόνον εἰς μετάνοιαν, καὶ τὴν τοῦ
ὀφειλήματος ἴασιν, said Philo.   Thus God sent Jonas, and denounced judgments against Nineveh;   but with the ἀνοχὴ,
with the ' forbearance' of forty days for the time of their escape, if they would repent.   When Noah, the great preacher
of righteousness, denounced the flood to all the world, it was
with the ἀνοχὴ, with the ' forbearance' of a hundred and
twenty years.   And when the great extermination of the
Jewish nation, and their total deletion from being God's
people, was foretold by Christ, and decreed by God ; 'yet they
had the ἀνοχὴ, of forty years, in which they were perpetually called to repentance.   These were reprieves and deferrings
of the stroke.

But sometimes God strikes once, and then forbears.   And
such are all those sadnesses, which are less than death :   every

sickness, every loss, every disgrace, the death of friends and nearest relatives, sudden discontents ; these are all of them the louder calls of God to repentance ; but still, instances of forbearance.

Indeed, many times this forbearance makes men impudent. It was so in the case of Pharaoh ; when God smote him, and then forbore, Pharaoh's heart grew callous and insensible, till God struck again : and this was the meaning of these words of God, " I will harden the heart of Pharaoh," that is, I will forbear him ; smite him, and then take the blow off: "Sic enim Deus induravit Pharaonis cor," said St. Basil. For as water taken off from fire will sooner congeal and become icy, than if it had not been attenuated by the heat; so is the heart of some men ; when smitten by God, it seems soft and pliable, but taken off from the fire of affliction, it presently becomes horrid, then stiff, and then hard as a rock of adamant, or as the gates of death and hell. But this is beside the purpose and intention of the divine mercy; this is an ἀντιπερίστασις, a plain ' contradiction' to the riches of God's goodness ; this is to be evil, because God is good; to burn with flames, because we are cooled with water; this is to put out the lamps of heaven, or (if we cannot do it) to put our own eyes out, lest we should behold the fair beauty of the Lord, and he enamoured of his goodness, and repent, and live. O take heed of despising this goodness ; for this is one of God's latest arts to save us ; he hath no way left beyond this, but to punish us with a lasting judgment and a poignant affliction. In the tomb of Terentia, certain lamps burned under ground many ages together; but as soon as ever they were brought into the air, and saw a bigger light, they went out, never to be re-enkindled. So long as we are in the retirements of sorrow, of want, of fear, of sickness, or of any sad accident, we are burning and shining lamps ; but when God comes with his ἀνοχὴ, with his ' forbearance,' and lifts us up from the gates of death, and carries us abroad into the open air, that we converse with prosperity and temptation, we go out in darkness ; and we cannot be preserved in heat and light, but by still dwelling in the regions of sorrow. And if such be our weaknesses or our folly, it concerns us to pray against such deliverances, to be afraid of health, to beg of God to continue a persecution, and not to deny us the mercy of an affliction.

And do not we find all this to be a great truth in ourselves? Are we so great strangers to our own weaknesses
and unworthiness, as not to remember when God scared us
with judgments in the neighbourhood, where we lived in a
great plague, or if we were ever in a storm, or God had sent
a sickness upon us? Then we may please to remember, that
repentance was our business, that we designed mountains of
piety, renewed our holy purposes, made vows and solemn
sacraments to God to become penitent and obedient persons:
and we may also remember, without much considering, that
as soon as God began to forbear us, we would no longer forbear to sin, but add flame to flame, a heap of sins to a treasure of wrath, already too big; being like Pharaoh or Herod,
or like the ox and mule, more hardy and callous for our
stripes; and melted in the fire, and frozen harder in the cold;
worse for all our afflictions, and the worse for all God's judgments; not bettered by his goodness, nor mollified by his
threatenings: and what is there more left for God to do
unto us? He that is not won by the sense of God's mercy,
can never find any thing in God that shall convert him; and
he whom fear and sense of pain cannot mend, can never find
any argument from himself that shall make him wise. This
is sad, that nothing from without, and nothing from within,
shall move us: nothing in heaven, and nothing in hell; neither love, nor fear; gratitude to God, nor preservation of ourselves, shall make us to repent.　Θεοῦ δὲ πληγὴν οὐχ ὑπερ-
πηδᾷ βροτός· That shall be his final sentence: he shall never
escape that ruin from which the greatest art of God could
not entice, nor his terror scare him: "he loved cursing,
therefore shall it happen to him; he loved not blessing, therefore shall it be far from him."

Let, therefore, every one of us take the account of our
lives, and read over the sermons that God hath made us:
besides that sweet language of his mercy, and his ' still voice'
from heaven, consider what voices of thunder you heard, and
presently that noise ceased, and God was heard in the ' still
voice' again. What dangers have any of you escaped? were
you ever assaulted by the rudeness of an ill-natured man?
Have you never had a dangerous fall, and escaped it? Did
none of you ever escape drowning, and in a great danger saw
the forbearance of God? Have you never been sick (as you
feared) unto death? Or, suppose none of these things have

happened, hath not God threatened you all, and forborne to smite you? or smitten you, and forborne to kill you? That is evident.   But if you had been a privado, and of the cabinet-council with your guardian angel, that from him you might have known how many dangers you have escaped, how often you have been near a ruin, so near, that if you had seen your danger with a sober spirit, the fear of it would have half killed you; if he had but told you how often God had sent out his warrants to the exterminating angel, and our blessed Saviour by his intercession hath obtained a reprieve, that he might have the content of rejoicing at thy conversion and repentance; if you had known from him the secrets of that providence which governs us in secret, and how many thousand times the devil would have done thee hurt, and how often himself, as a ministering spirit of God's "goodness and forbearance," did interpose and abate, or divert a mischief which was falling on thy head: it must needs cover thy head with a cloud of shame and blushing at that ingratitude and that folly, that neither will give God thanks, nor secure thy own well-being.

Hadst thou never any dangerous fall in thy intemperance? Then God shewed thee thy danger, and that he was angry at thy sin; but yet did so pity thy person, that he would forbear thee a little longer, else that fall had been into thy grave.   When thy gluttony gave thee a surfeit, and God gave thee a remedy, his meaning then was, that thy gluttony rather should be cured than thy surfeit; that repentance should have been thy remedy, and abstinence and fasting should be thy cure.   Did ever thy proud or revengeful spirit engage thee upon a duel, or a vexatious lawsuit, and God brought thee off with life or peace? His purpose then was, that his mercy should teach thee charity.   And he that cannot read the purposes of God written with the finger of judgment (for as yet his whole hand is not laid on), either is consigned to eternal ruin, because God will no more endeavour his cure; or, if his mercy still continues and goes on in long-suffering, it shall be by such vexatious instruments, such caustics and corrosives, such tormenting and desperate medicaments, such which, in the very cure, will soundly punish thy folly and ingratitude.   For, deceive not yourselves, God's mercy cannot be made a patron for any man's impiety; the purpose of it is to bring us to repentance: and God will do it by the mercies of his mercies, or by mercies of his judgments; he either will break our hearts into a thousand fragments of contrition, or break our bones in the ruins of the grave and hell. And since God rejoices in his mercy above all his works, he will be most impatient that we shall despise that in which he most delights, and in which we have the greatest reason to delight; the riches of that goodness which is essential, and part of his glory, and is communicated to us, to bring us to repentance, that we may partake of that goodness, and behold that glory.

SERMON XIII.

PART II.

3. Μακροθυμία, 'Long-suffering.'—In this one word are contained all the treasures of the divine goodness: here is the length and extension of his mercy: "Pertrahit spiritum super nos Dominus," so the Syrian interpreter reads, Luke, xviii. 7. "God holds his breath:" he retains his anger within him, lest it should come forth and blast us. And here is also much of the divine justice: for although God suffers long, yet he does not let us alone; he forbears to destroy us, but not to punish us: and in both he, by many accidents, gives probation of his power; according to the prayer of the wise man, Ἐλεεῖς δὲ πάντας, ὅτι πάντα δύνασαι· καὶ παρορᾷς ἁμαρτήματα ἀνθρώπων εἰς μετάνοιαν· "Thou art merciful towards us all, because thou canst do all things; and thou passest by the sins of men, that they may repent." And, that God shall support our spirit, and preserve our patience, and nourish our hope, and correct our stubbornness, and mortify our pride, and bring us to him, whether we will or no, by such gracious violences and merciful judgments, which he uses towards us as his last remedies, is not only the demonstration of a mighty mercy, but of an almighty power. So hard a thing it is to make us leave our follies and become wise, that, were not the mercies of God an effective pity, and clothed in all the way of its progress with mightiness and power, every sinner should perish irrevocably. But this is the fiery trial, the last purgatory fire which God uses, to burn the

<hr/>

' Wisd. xi. 24.

thistles, and purify the dross. When the gentle influence of a sunbeam will not wither them, nor the weeding hook of a short affliction cut them out; then God comes with fire to burn us, with the axe laid to the root of the tree.   But then observe, that when we are under this state of cure, we are so near destruction, that the same instrument that God uses for remedy to us, is also prepared to destroy us; the fire is as apt to burn us to ashes, as to cleanse us when we are so overgrown; and the axe as instrumental to cut us down for fuel, as to square us for building in God's temple: and therefore when it comes thus far, it will be hard discerning what the purpose of the axe is; and, whether the fire means to burn, we shall know it by the change wrought upon ourselves. For what Plato said concerning his dream of purgatory, is true here: "Quicunque non purgatus migrat ad inferos, jacebit in luto; quicunque vero mitratus illuc accesserit, habitabit cum Deis:" " He that dies in his impurity, shall lie in it for ever; but he that descends to his grave purged and mitred,— that is,—having quitted his vices, ' et superinduens justitiam,' ' being clothed with righteousness,' shall dwell in light and immortality."   It is sad that we put God to such extremities: and, as it happens in long diseases, those which physicians use for the last remedies, seldom prevail; and when consumptive persons come to have their heads shaven, they do not often escape: so it is when we put God to his last remedies: God indeed hath the glory of his patience and his long-suffering, but we seldom have the benefit and the use of it.   For if when our sin was young, and our strength more active, and our habits less, and virtue not so much a stranger to us,—we suffered sin to prevail upon us, to grow stronger than the ruins of our spirit, and to lessen us into the state of sickness and disability, in the midst of all those remedies which God used to our beginning-diseases: much more desperate is our recovery, when our disease is stronger, and our faculties weaker; when our sins reign in us, and our thoughts of virtue are not alive.

However, although I say this, and it is highly considerable to the purpose that we never suffer things to come to this extremity, yet, if it be upon us, we must do as well as we can: but then we are to look upon it as a design of God's last mercy, beyond which, if we protract our repentance, our condition is desperately miserable. The whole state of which

mercy we understand by the parable of the king reckoning
with his servants, that were in arrears to him : " One was
brought to him which owed him ten thousand talents : but
forasmuch as he had not to pay, his Lord commanded him
to be sold, and his wife and children, and all that he had, and
payment to be made." The man, you see, was under the arrest ; the sentence was passed upon him, he was a condemned
man : but, before the execution of it, he fell down and worshipped, and said, Κύριε, μακροθύμησον ; " Lord, ' suffer me
longer awhile ;' have patience with me, and I will pay thee
all." This tells its meaning : this is ' a long-sufferance,' by
being ' a forbearance' only of execution of the last sentence,
a putting off damnation upon a longer trial of our emendation ; but in the meantime it implies no other case, but that,
together with his long-sufferance, God may use all other severities and scourges to break our untamed spirits, and to
soften them with hammers ; so death be put off, no matter
else what hardships and loads of sufferance we have. " Hic
ure, hic seca, ut in æternum parcas ;" so St. Austin prayed :
" Here, O Lord, cut me, here burn me ; spare me not now,
that thou mayest spare me for ever." And it is just like the
mercy used to a madman, when he is kept in a dark room,
and tamed with whips ; it is a cruel mercy, but such as his
condition requires ; he can receive no other mercy, all things
else were cruelly unmerciful.

I remember what Bion observed wittily of the punishment
inflicted upon the daughters of Danaus, whom the old poets
feigned to be condemned in hell to fill a bottomless tub with
water, and, to increase the pain (as they fancied), this water
they were to carry in sieves, and never to leave work till the
tub were full ; it is well (says he), since their labour must be
eternal, that it is so gentle ; for it were more pains to carry
their water in whole vessels, and a sad burden to go loaden
to a leaking tub with unfruitful labours.—Just so is the condition of those persons, upon whom a wrath is gone out : it
is a sad sentence, but acted with a gentle instrument ; and
since they are condemned to pay the scores of their sins with
the sufferance of a load of judgments, it is well they are such
as will run quite through them, and not stick upon them to
eternity. "Omnes enim pœnæ non exterminantes, sunt me-
dicinales ;" " All punishments whatsoever, which do not destroy us, are intended to save us ;" they are lancets which

make a wound, but to let forth the venom of our ulcers. When God slew twenty-three thousand of the Assyrians for their fornication, that was a final justice upon their persons, and consigned them to a sad eternity: for beyond such an infliction there was no remedy. But when God sent lions to the Assyrian inhabitants of Samaria, and the judgment drove them to inquire after the manner of the God of the land, and they sent for priests from Jerusalem to teach them how to worship the God of Israel; that was a mercy and a judgment too : 'the long forbearance of God,' who destroyed not all the inhabitants, 'led' the rest 'unto repentance.'

1. And I must make this observation to you ; that when things come to this pass, that God is forced to the last remedies of judgments, this long-sufferance will little or nothing concern particular persons, but nations and communities of men: for those who are smitten with judgment, if God takes his hands off again, and so opens a way for their repentance by prolonging their time; that comes under the second part of God's method, the ἀνοχὴ, or ' forbearance:' but if he smites a single person with a final judgment, that is ' a long-suffering,' not of him, but towards others ; and God hath destroyed my neighbour, to make me repent, my neighbour's time being expired, and the date of his possibility determined. For a man's death-bed is but an ill station for a penitent; and a final judgment is no good monitor to him, to whom it is a severe executioner. They that perished in the gainsaying of Korah, were out of the conditions of repentance. But the people that were affrighted with the neighbourhood of the judgment, and the expresses of God's anger manifested in such visible remonstrances, they were the men called unto repentance. But concerning the whole nations or communities of men, this long-sufferance is a sermon of repentance; loud, clamorous, and highly argumentative. When God suffered the mutinies, the affronts, the baseness and ingratitude, the follies and relapses, of the children of Israel, who murmured against God ten times in the wilderness ; God sent evil angels among them, and fiery serpents, and pestilence, and fire from heaven, and prodigies from the earth, and a prevailing sword of the enemies : and in all these accidents, although some innocent persons felt the contingencies and variety of mortality, yet those wicked persons who fell by the design of God's anger, were made ex-

amples unto others, and instances of God's forbearance to
the nation: and yét this forbearance was such, that although
God preserved the nation in being, and in title to the first
promises, yet all the particular persons that came from
Egypt, died in the wilderness, two only excepted.

2. And I desire you to observe this, that you may truly
estimate the arts of the divine justice and mercy. For all
the world being one continual and entire argument of the
divine mercy, we are apt to abuse that mercy to vain confidences and presumption; first mistaking the end, as if God's
mercy would be indulgent to our sin, to which it is the
greatest enemy in the world: for it is a certain truth, that
the mercy of God is as great an enemy to sin as his justice
is; and as God's justice is made the handmaid of his mercy
to cure sin, so it is the servant also and the instrument to
avenge our despite and contempt of mercy; and in all the
way, where a difference can be, there justice is the less principal. And it were a great sign of folly, and a huge mistake,
to think our Lord and our friends do us offices of kindness,
to make themselves more capable of affronts; and that our
fathers' care over us, and provision for us, can tempt us to
disobey them: the very purpose of all those emanations is,
that their love may return in duty, and their providence be
the parent of our prudence, and their care be crowned with
our piety; and then we shall all be crowned, and shall return
like the year, that ends into its own circle; and the fathers
and the children, the benefactors and the beneficiary, shall
knit the wreath, and bind each other in the eternal enclosures
and circlings of immortality. But besides, as the men who
presume to sin because of God's mercy, do mistake the very
end and design of God's mercy, so they also mistake the
economy of it, and the manner of its ministration.

3. For if God suffers men to go on in sins, and punishes
them not, it is not a mercy, it is not a forbearance; it is a
hardening them, a consigning them to ruin and reprobation:
and themselves give the best argument to prove it; for they
continue in their sin, they multiply their iniquity, and every
day grow more enemy to God; and that is no mercy,
that increases their hostility and enmity with God. A prosperous iniquity is the most unprosperous condition in the
whole world. ' When he slew them, they sought him, and
turned them early, and inquired after God:' but as long as

they prevailed upon their enemies, ' they forgot that God was their strength, and the high God was their redeemer.' It was well observed by the Persian ambassador of old; when he was telling the king a sad story of the overthrow of all his army by the Athenians, he adds this of his own; that the day before the fight, the young Persian gallants, being confident they should destroy their enemies, were drinking drunk, and railing at the timorousness and fears of religion, and against all their gods, saying, there were no such things, and that all things came by chance and industry, nothing by the providence of the Supreme Power. But the next day, when they had fought unprosperously, and, flying from their enemies, who were eager in their pursuit, they came to the river Strymon, which was so frozen that their boats could not launch, and yet it began to thaw, so that they feared the ice would not bear them; then you should see the bold gallants, that the day before said there was no God, most timorously and superstitiously fall upon their faces, and beg of God, that the river Strymon might bear them over from their enemies. What wisdom, and philosophy, and perpetual experience, and revelation, and promises, and blessings, cannot do, a mighty fear can; it can allay the confidences of bold lust and imperious sin, and soften our spirit into the lowness of a child, our revenge into the charity of prayers, our impudence into the blushings of a chidden girl; and therefore, God hath taken a course proportionable: for he is not so unmercifully merciful, as to give milk to an infirm lust, and hatch the egg to the bigness of a cockatrice. And, therefore, observe how it is that God's mercy prevails over all his works; it is even then when nothing can be discerned but his judgments: for as when a famine had been in Israel in the days of Ahab for three years and a half, when the angry prophet Elijah met the king, and presently a great wind arose, and the dust blew into the eyes of them that walked abroad, and the face of the heavens was black and all tempest, yet then the prophet was the most gentle, and God began to forgive, and the heavens were more beautiful than when the sun puts on the brightest ornaments of a bridegroom, going from his chambers of the east: so it is in the economy of the divine mercy; when God makes our faces black, and the winds blow so loud till the cordage cracks, and our gay fortunes split, and our houses are dressed with cypress and yew, ' and the mourners go about the streets,' this is nothing but the ' pompa misericordiæ,' this is the funeral of our sins, dressed indeed with emblems of mourning, and proclaimed with sad accents of death; but the sight is refreshing, as the beauties of the field which God had blessed, and the sounds are healthful as the noise of a physician.

This is that riddle spoken of in the Psalm, "Calix in manu Domini vini meri plenus misto;" " The pure impure, the mingled unmingled cup[a]:" for it is a cup in which God hath poured much of his severity and anger, and yet it is pure unmingled; for it is all mercy. And so the riddle is resolved, and our cup is full and made more wholesome; " Lymphatum crescit, dulcescit, lædere nescit:" it is some justice, and yet it is all mercy; the very justice of God being an act of mercy; a forbearance of the man or the nation, and the punishing the sin. Thus it was in the case of the children of Israel; when they ran after the bleating of the idolatrous calves, Moses prayed passionately, and God heard his prayer, and forgave their sin unto them. And this was David's observation of the manner of God's mercy to them; " Thou wast a God and forgavest them, though thou tookest vengeance of their inventions[a]." For God's mercy is given to us by parts, and to certain purposes. Sometimes God only so forgives us, that he does not cut us off in the sin, but yet lays on a heavy load of judgments: so he did to his people, when he sent them to school under the discipline of seventy years' captivity. Sometimes he makes a judgment less, and forgives in respect of the degree of the infliction, he strikes more gently; and whereas God had designed, it may be, the death of thyself, or thy nearest relative, be is content to take the life of a child. And so he did to David, when he forbore him; " The Lord hath taken away thy sin, thou shalt not die; nevertheless, the child that is born unto thee, *that* shall die[b]." Sometimes he puts the evil off to a farther day; as he did in the case of Ahab and Hezekiah: to the first he brought the evil upon his house, and to the second he brought the evil upon his kingdom in his Son's days, God forgiving only so as to respite the evil, that they should have peace in their own days. And thus when we have committed a sin against God, which hath highly provoked him to anger, even upon our repentance we are not sure to be forgiven, so as we

   [a] Psal. lxxv. 8.   [a] Psal. xcix. 8.   [b] 2 Sam. xii. 13, 14.

understand forgiveness, that is, to hear no more of it, never to be called to an account : but we are happy if God so forgive us, as not to throw us into the insufferable flames of hell, though he smite us till we groan for our misery, till we 'chatter like a swallow,' as David's expression is.   And though David was an excellent penitent ; yet after he had lost the child begotten of Bathsheba, and God had told him he had forgiven him, yet he raised up his darling son against him, and forced him to an inglorious flight, and his son lay with his father's concubines in the face of all Israel. So that when we are forgiven, yet it is ten to one but God will make us to smart and roar for our sins, for the very disquietness of our souls.

For if we sin and ask God forgiveness, and then are quiet, we feel so little inconvenience in the trade, that we may more easily be tempted to make a trade of it indeed. I wish to God that for every sin we have committed, we could heartily cry ' God mercy' and leave it, and judge ourselves for it, to prevent God's anger : but when we have done all that we commonly call repentance, and when possibly God hath forgiven us to some purposes, yet, it may be, he punishes our sin when we least think of it ; that sin which we have long since forgotten.   It may be, for the lust of thy youth thou hast a healthless old age.   An old religious person long ago complained it was his case.

> Quos nimis effrænes habui, nunc vapulo renes :
> Sic Ioitur javenis culpa, dolore senis.

It may be, thy sore eyes are the punishment of intemperance seven years ago ; or God cuts thy days shorter, and thou shalt die in a florid age ; or he raises up afflictions to thee in thine own house, in thine own bowels ; or hath sent a gangrene into thy estate ; or with an arrow out of his quiver he can wound thee, and the arrow shall stick fast in thy flesh, although God hath forgiven thy sin to many purposes.   Our blessed Saviour ' was heard in all that he prayed' (said the Apostle): and he prayed for the Jews that crucified him, "Father forgive them, for they know not what they do :" and God did forgive that great sin, but how far ? whereas it was just in God to deprive them of all possibility of receiving benefit from the death of Christ, yet God admitted them to it ; he gave them time, and possibilities, and helps, and great advantages to bring them to repentance; he did not presently shut them up in his final and eternal anger; and yet he had finally resolved to destroy their city and nation, and did so, but forbore them forty years, and gave them all the helps of miracles and sermons apostolical to shame them, and force them into sorrow for their fault. And before any man can repent, God hath forgiven the man in one degree of forgiveness; for he hath given him grace of repentance, and taken from him that final anger of the spirit of reprobation: and when a man hath repented, no man can say that God hath forgiven him to all purposes, but hath reserves of anger to punish the sin, to make the man afraid to sin any more; and to represent, that when any man hath sinned, whatever he does afterward, he shall be miserable as long as he lives, vexed with its adherences and its neighbourhood and evil consequence. For as no man that hath sinned, can, during his life, ever return to an integral and perfect innocence: so neither shall he be restored to a perfect peace, but must always watch and strive against his sin, and always mourn and pray for its pardon, and always find cause to hate it, by knowing himself to be for ever in danger of enduring some grievous calamity, even for those sins for which he hath truly repented him, for which God hath, in many gracious degrees, passed his pardon: this is the manner of dispensation of the divine mercy, in respect of particular persons and nations too.

But sometimes we find a severer judgment happening upon a people; and yet in that sad story God's mercy sings the triumph, which although it be much to God's glory, yet it is a sad story to sinning people. Six hundred thousand fighting men, besides women and children and decrepit persons, came out of Egypt; and God destroyed them all in the wilderness, except Caleb and Joshua: and there it was that God's mercy prevailed over his justice, that he did not destroy the nation, but still preserved a succession to Jacob, to possess the promise. God drowned all the world except eight persons; his mercy there also prevailed over his justice, that he preserved a remnant to mankind; his justice devoured all the world, and his mercy, which preserved but eight, had the honour of the prevailing attribute. God destroyed Sodom and the five cities of the plain, and rescued but four from the flames of that sad burning, and of the four lost one in the flight; and yet his mercy prevailed over his justice, because he did not destroy all.

And in these senses we are to understand the excellency of the divine mercy: even when he smites, when 'he rebukes us for sin,' when he makes 'our beauty to fail, and our flesh to consume away like a moth fretting a garment,' yet then his mercy is the prevailing ingredient. If his judgments be but fines set upon our heads, according to the mercy of our old laws, 'salvo contenemento,' 'so as to preserve our estates,' to continue our hopes and possibilities of heaven: all the other judgments can be nothing but mercies, excellent instruments of grace, arts to make us sober and wise, to take us off from our vanity, to restrain our wildnesses, which, if they were left unbridled, would set all the world on fire. God's judgments are like the censures of the church, in which a sinner is 'delivered over to Satan to be buffeted; that the spirit may be saved.' The result of all this is, that God's mercies are not, ought not, cannot be instruments of confidence to sin, because the very purpose of his mercy is to the contrary; and the very manner of his economy and dispensation is such, that God's mercy goes along in complexion and conjunction with his judgments: the riches of his forbearance is this, that he forbears to throw us into hell, and sends the mercies of his rod to chide us unto repentance, and the mercies of his rod to punish us for having sinned, and that when we have sinned we may never think ourselves secured, nor ever be reconciled to such dangers and deadly poisons. This, this is the manner of the divine mercy. Go now, fond man, and, because God is merciful, presume to sin, as having grounds to hope that thou mayest sin, and be safe all the way! If this—hope, shall I call it, or sordid flattery, could be reasonable, then the mercies of God would not lead us to repentance; so unworthy are we in the sense and largeness of a wide fortune and pleasant accident. For impunity was never a good argument to make men to obey laws. "Quotusquisque reperitur, qui impunitate proposita abstinere possit injuriis? Impunitas est maxima peccandi illecebra," said Cicero.[c] And therefore, the wisdom of God hath so ordered the actions of the world, that the most fruitful showers shall be wrapped up in a cover of black clouds, that health shall be conveyed by bitter and ill-tasted drugs;

[c] Cicer. pro Mil. 44.

that the temples of our bodies shall be purged by whips, and that the cords of the whip shall be the cords of love, to draw us from the entanglings of vanity and folly. This is the long-suffering of God, the last remedy to our diseased souls, ἀναίσθητος, ὅστις πολλὰ παθὼν οὐ σωφρονίζεται, said Phalaris ; unless we be senseless, we shall be brought to sober courses by all those sad accidents and wholesome, but ill-tasted mercies, which we feel in all the course and succession of the divine long-sufferance.

The use of all the premises is that, which St. Paul expresses in the text, that " we do not despise all this :" and he only despises not, who serves the ends of God in all these designs of mercy, that is, he that repents him of his sins. But there are a great many despisers ; all they that live in their sins, they that have more blessings than they can reckon hours in their lives, that are courted by the divine favour and wooed to salvation, as if mankind were to give, not to receive, so great a blessing, all they that answer not to so friendly summons,—they are despisers of God's mercies : and although God overflows with mercies, and does not often leave us to the only hopes of being cured by unctions and gentle cataplasms, but proceeds farther, and gives us ' stribium,' or prepared steel, sharp arrows of his anger, and the sword, and the hand of sickness ; yet we are not sure of so much favour as to be entertained longer in God's hospital, but may be thrust forth among the ' incurabili.' Plutarch reports concerning swine, that their optic nerves are so disposed to turn their eyes downward, that they cannot look upwards, nor behold the face of heaven, unless they be thrown upon their backs. Such swine are we : we seldom can look up to heaven, till God by his judgments throws us upon our backs ; till he humbles us and softens us with showers of our own blood, and tears of sorrow ; and yet God hath not promised that he will do so much for us ; but for aught we know, as soon as ever the devil enters into our swinish and brutish hearts, we shall run down the hill, and perish in the floods and seas of intolerable misery. And therefore, besides that it is a huge folly in us, that we will not be cured with pleasant medicines, but must be longing for coloquintida, and for vomits, for knives and poniards instead of the gentle showers of the divine refreshments, besides that this is an imprudence and sottishness ; we do infinitely put it to the venture, whether we shall be in a saveable condition or no, after the rejection of the first state of mercies. But, however, then begins the first step of the judgment and pungent misery, we are perishing people; or, if not, yet at the least not to be cured without the abscission of a member, without the cutting off a hand or a leg, or the putting out of an eye: we must be cut, to take the stone out of our hearts, and that is the state of a very great infelicity; and if we escape the stone, we cannot escape the surgeon's knife; if we escape death, yet we have a sickness; and though that be a great mercy in respect of death, yet it is as great a misery in respect of health. And that is the first punishment for the despite done to the first and most sensible mercies; we are fallen into a sickness, that cannot be cured but by disease and hardship.

But if this despite runs farther, and when the mercies look on us with an angry countenance, and that God gives us only the mercy of a punishment, if we despise this too, we increase but our misery, as we increase our sin. The sum of which is this: that if Pharaoh will not be cured by one plague, he shall have ten; and if ten will not do it, the great and tenth wave, which is far bigger than all the rest, the severest and the last arrow of the quiver, then we shall perish in the Red Sea, the sea of flames and blood, in which the ungodly shall roll eternally.

But some of these despisers are such as are unmoved when God smites others; like Gallio, when the Jews took Sosthenes, and beat him in the pleading-place, he "cared for none of these things;" he was not concerned in that interest: and many Gallios there are among us, that understand it not to be a part of the divine method of God's 'long-sufferance,' to strike others to make us afraid. But however we sleep in the midst of such alarms, yet know, that there is not one death in all the neighbourhood but is intended to thee; every crowing of the cock is to awake thee to repentance: and, if thou sleepest still, the next turn may be thine; God will send his angel, as he did to Peter, and smite thee on thy side, and wake thee from thy dead sleep of sin and sottishness. But beyond this some are despisers still, and hope to drown the noises of Mount Sinai, the sound of cannons, of thunders and lightnings, with a counter-noise of revelling and clamorous roarings, with merry meetings; like the sacrifices to Moloch, they sound drums and trumpets, that they might not hear the sad shriekings of their children, as they were dying in the cavity of the brazen idol: and when their conscience shrieks out or murmurs in a sad melancholy, or something that is dear to them is smitten, they attempt to drown it in a sea of drink, in the heathenish noises of idle and drunken company; and that which God sends to lead them to repentance, leads them to a tavern, not to refresh their needs of nature, or for ends of a tolerable civility, or innocent purposes; but, like the condemned persons among the Levantines, they tasted wine freely, that they might die and be insensible.   I could easily reprove such persons with an old Greek proverb mentioned by Plutarch, Περὶ τῆς Εὐθυμίας, οὔτε ποδάγρας ἀπαλλάττει κάλκιος, 'You shall ill be cured of the knotted gout, if you have nothing else but a wide shoe.' But this reproof is too gentle for so great a madness : it is not only an incompetent cure, to apply the plaister of a sin or vanity to cure the smart of a divine judgment ; but it is a great increaser of the misery, by swelling the cause to bigger and monstrous proportions.   It is just as if an impatient fool, feeling the smart of his medicine, shall tear his wounds open, and throw away the instruments of his cure, because they bring him health at the charge of a little pain, Ἐγγὺς Κυρίου πλήρης μαστίγων, "He that is full of stripes" and troubles, and decked round about with thorns, he "is near to God :" but he that, because he sits uneasily when he sits near the King that was crowned with thorns, shall remove thence, or strew flowers, roses and jessamine, the down of thistles and the softest gossamer, that he may die without pain, die quietly and like a lamb, sink to the bottom of hell without noise ; this man is a fool, because he accepts death if it arrest him in civil language, is content to die by the sentence of an eloquent judge, and prefers a quiet passage to hell before going to heaven in a storm.

That Italian gentleman was certainly a great lover of his sleep, who was angry with the lizard that waked him, when a viper was creeping into his mouth : when the devil is entering into us to poison our spirits, and steal our souls away while we are sleeping in the lethargy of sin, God sends his sharp messages to awaken us ; and we call that the enemy, and use arts to cure the remedy, not to cure the disease. There are some persons that will never be cured, not because the sickness is incurable, but because they have ill stomachs, and cannot keep the medicine. Just so is his case that so despises God's method of curing him by these instances of long-sufferance, that he uses all the arts he can to be quit of his physician, and to spill his physic, and to take cordials as soon as his vomit begins to work. There is no more to be said in this affair, but to read the poor wretch's sentence, and to declare his condition. As at first, when he despised the first great mercies, God sent him sharpness and sad acci-dents to ensober his spirits: so now that he despises his mercy also, the mercy of the rod, God will take it away from him, and then I hope all is well. Miserable man that thou art! this is thy undoing; if God ceases to strike thee, be-canse thou wilt not mend, thou art sealed up to ruin and reprobation for ever; the physician hath given thee over, he hath no kindness for thee. This was the desperate estate of Judah, " Ah, sinful nation! a people laden with iniquity : they have forsaken the Lord, they have provoked the Holy One of Israel. Why should ye be stricken any more [d]?" This is the ἀνάθεμα μαρὰν ἀθὰ, the most bitter curse, the greatest excommunication, when the delinquent is become a heathen and a publican without the covenant, out of the pale of the church; the church hath nothing to do with them: " for what have I to do with them that are without?" said St. Paul. It was not lawful for the church any more to punish them. And this court Christian is an imitation and parallel of the justice of the court of heaven : when a sinner is not mended by judgments at long-running, God cuts him off from his inheritance, and the lot of sons; he will chastise him no more, but let him take his course, and spend his por-tion of prosperity, such as shall be allowed him in the great economy of the world. Thus God did to his vineyard which he took such pains to fence, to plant, to manure, to dig, to cut, and to prune : and when, after all, it brought forth wild grapes, the last and worst of God's anger was this; " Auferam sepem ejus [e];" God had fenced it with a hedge of thorns, and ' God would take away all that hedge,' he would not leave a thorn standing, not one judgment to reprove or admonish them, but all the wild beasts, and wilder and more beastly lusts, may come and devour it, and trample it down in scorn.

And now what shall I say, but those words quoted by St.

Paul in his sermon, " Behold ye despisers, and wonder, and perish ';" perish in your own folly by stubbornness and ingratitude.   For it is a huge contradiction to the nature and designs of God : God calls us, we refuse to hear ; he invites us with fair promises, we hear and consider not ; he gives us blessings, we take them and understand not his meaning ; we take out the token, but read not the letter : then he threatens us, and we regard not ; he strikes our neighbours, and we are not concerned : then he strikes us gently, but we feel it not : then he does like the physician in the Greek epigram, who being to cure a man of lethargy, locked him into the same room with a madman, that he by dry-beating him might make him at least sensible of blows ; but this makes us instead of running to God, to trust in unskilful physicians, or, like Saul, to run to a Pythonisse ; we run for cure to a crime, we take sanctuary in a pleasant sin ; just as if a man, to cure his melancholy, should desire to be stung with a tarantula, that at least he may die merrily.   What is there more to be done that God hath not yet done ? He is forced at last to break off with a " Curavimus Babylonem, et non est sanata," " We dressed and tended Babylon," but she was incurable : there is no help but such persons must die in their sins, and lie down in eternal sorrow.

' Acts, xiii. 41.

END OF THE FIFTH VOLUME.

Printed by J. F. Dove, St. John's Square.

Made in United States
North Haven, CT
26 January 2024

47895193R00369